The Musnad *of* Ahl al-Bayt

The Musnad *of* Ahl al-Bayt

Forty *full-chained Hadiths* on the Family of the Prophet

صلى الله عليه وعلى آله وصحبه وسلم

Narrated from forty of his descendants out of forty books

by

Gibril Fouad Haddad

First Arabic edition 2016 at Dar al-Futuhat, Jakarta
Second Arabic edition 2019 at Dar Tayba, Beirut
(مُسنَد أهل البيت المُسمَّى حُسْنُ المَآل والمَآرِب في فضل الآل والأقارب
بأربعين حديثاً مسنَداً عن أربعين شريفاً من أربعين كتاباً)
Third Arabic edition and first English translation 2022 at
Institute for Spiritual & Cultural Advancement, Fenton, MI (USA)

Published in the US by Institute for Spiritual & Cultural Advancement
17195 Silver Parkway #401, Fenton, MI 48430 USA
Tel: (888) 278-6624 Fax:(810) 815-0518
Email: info@sufilive.com
Web: http://www.sufilive.com
Purchase online at: http://www.isn1.net

Book covers and inside text designed and typeset by Qaf Qasyoun.

ISBN: 978-1-938058-63-9

Cataloging-in-Publication Data

Haddad, Gibril Fouad, 1960-

The *Musnad* of *Ahl al-Bayt*. Forty full-chained Hadiths on the Family of the Prophet narrated from forty of his descendants out of forty books. صلى الله عليه وعلى آله وصحبه وسلم. Third revised Arabic edition and first English translation and commentary by the author.
502 p. (239 p. English + 263 p. Arabic) 23 cm. Index.
1. Muḥammad, Prophet, -632 -- Family. 2. Muḥammad, Prophet -- Companions. 3. Hadith -- texts. 4. Hadith -- Authorities -- Early works to 1800. 5. Hadith -- Criticism, interpretation, etc. 6. Hadith -- Teachers. I. Author. II. Title. III. Title: مُسنَد أهل البيت المُسمَّى حُسْنُ المَآل والمَآرِب في فضل الآل والأقارِب بأربعين حديثاً مسنَداً عن أربعين شريفاً من أربعين كتاباً.

بِسۡمِ ٱللَّهِ ٱلرَّحۡمَٰنِ ٱلرَّحِيمِ

﴿ذَٰلِكَ ٱلَّذِي يُبَشِّرُ ٱللَّهُ عِبَادَهُ ٱلَّذِينَ ءَامَنُواْ وَعَمِلُواْ ٱلصَّٰلِحَٰتِۗ
قُل لَّآ أَسۡـَٔلُكُمۡ عَلَيۡهِ أَجۡرًا إِلَّا ٱلۡمَوَدَّةَ فِي ٱلۡقُرۡبَىٰۗ وَمَن يَقۡتَرِفۡ
حَسَنَةً نَّزِدۡ لَهُۥ فِيهَا حُسۡنًاۚ إِنَّ ٱللَّهَ غَفُورٌ شَكُورٌ ٢٣﴾

الشورى

اللهم صل على محمد وآل محمد

﴿ وَءَايَةٌ لَّهُمۡ أَنَّا حَمَلۡنَا ذُرِّيَّتَهُمۡ فِي ٱلۡفُلۡكِ ٱلۡمَشۡحُونِ ﴿٤١﴾ ﴾ يس

And a sign for them is that We carried their dhurriyya *in the laden ship* (36:41), “that is, their ancestors on the ship of Nūḥ ﷺ, as the term *dhurriyya* is used for forefathers just as it is used for descendants” (al-Wāḥidī).

To

Fouad Hammad

Taher Nazim

Abdulghani

Alauddin

Muhammad Karim

عَنْ عُتْبَةَ بْنِ عَبْدٍ السُّلَمِيِّ: قَالَ رَسُولُ اللهِ ﷺ: إِنَّ رَبِّي وَعَدَنِي أَنْ يُدْخِلَ مِنْ أُمَّتِي الجَنَّةَ سَبْعِينَ أَلْفاً بِغَيْرِ حِسَابٍ ثُمَّ يُتْبِعَ كُلَّ أَلْفٍ بِسَبْعِينَ أَلْفاً ثُمَّ يَحْثِي بِكَفِّهِ ثَلَاثَ حَثَيَاتٍ فَكَبَّرَ عُمَرُ، فَقَالَ النَّبِيُّ ﷺ: إِنَّ السَّبْعِينَ أَلْفَ الأَوَّلَ يُشَفِّعُهُمْ فِي آبَائِهِمْ وَأُمَّهَاتِهِمْ، وَأَرْجُو أَنْ يَجْعَلَ اللهُ أُمَّتِي أَدْنَى الحَثَوَاتِ الأَوَاخِرَ. الفسوي في المعرفة والتاريخ والطبراني وابن حبان واللفظ له والبيهقي.

ʿUtba b. ʿAbd al-Sulamī said the Messenger of Allah said: “Truly my Lord has promised me to bring into Paradise, of my Umma, 70,000 without account, then to let 70,000 more follow each thousand, and then to scoop up with His hand three scoops.” ʿUmar said: *Allāhu akbar!* The Prophet continued: “He will let the first 70,000 intercede for their fathers and mothers, and I hope that Allah will put my Umma in the first of the latter scoops.”
Ṣaḥīḥ Ibn Ḥibbān.

Contents

Epigraphs: *Basmala*; al-Shūrā 42:23; *Ṣalawāt* 5
Dedication 7
Preface to the English translation and third Arabic edition 13
Table of contents by compilation, contemporary shaykh, place of the shaykh or narration, and narrator 19

Exordium 23

1. The Quraysh 27
2. The *Ṣalāt Ibrāhīmiyya* 29
3. The Prophet, Fāṭima, al-Ḥasan, al-Ḥusayn and ʿAlī 35
   Shaykh ʿĪsā al-Fādānī's inspiration of the present work 36
4. The Banū Hāshim and the Banū al-Muṭṭalib 37
   al-Zubayr's nursery rhyme for the Prophet 41
   al-Shāfiʿī's poetry for *Ahl al-Bayt* 42
5. The *Ahl al-Bayt* and the *Anṣār* 43
6. The Prophet, Fāṭima, ʿAlī, Ḥasan, Ḥusayn, Umm Salama 45
7. "The Book of Allah and the people of my House" 49
8. The Quraysh 53
   Versions of the *Ṣalāt Ibrāhīmiyya* 55
9. al-Ḥasan b. ʿAlī 57
10. Muḥammad al-Mahdī 61
11. al-ʿAbbās b. ʿAbd al-Muṭṭalib 65
12. The Banū ʿAbd al-Muṭṭalib 69
13. al-Ḥasan, al-Ḥusayn, ʿAlī and Fāṭima 73
14. The Prophet's marriage relatives 77
15. The Banū Hāshim 81
16. Durra bint Abī Lahab 85
17. "My family are a security for my Community" 89
   They are the *awliyā* and the *abdāl* per Ḥakīm Tirmidhī 91
18. "The people of my House compare to the ark of Nūḥ" 93

19. ʿAlī b. Abī Ṭālib 97
20. *Ahl al-Bayt* and ʿAlī b. Abī Ṭālib 101
21. al-Ḥasan and al-Ḥusayn 105
22. al-Ḥasan, al-Ḥusayn and Fāṭima 107
23. Fāṭima's children 109
24. Maryam bint ʿImrān and Khadīja bint Khuwaylid 115
25. ʿAlī b. Abī Ṭālib 117
Ibn Ḥajar's poetry on the Prophet's miracles and *nūr* 119
26. Fāṭima and Usāma b. Zayd 121
27. The Prophet, Fāṭima, al-Ḥasan, al-Ḥusayn, Umm Salama 125
Wāthila b. al-Asqaʿ 129
28. The Prophet and *Ahl al-Bayt* 131
29. Umm Hāniʾ bint Abī Ṭālib and *Ahl al-Bayt* 135
None of *Ahl al-Bayt* will enter Hellfire 137
30. "Allah has preferred the Quraysh in seven attributes" 139
31. Fāṭima and Maryam bint ʿImrān 141
32. *Ahl al-Bayt* and Thawbān the Prophet's *mawlā* 143
33. "My blood ties are firmly kept here and hereafter" 147
34. The Banū Hāshim, the Quraysh, Muḍar and the Arabs 149
35. "Whoever harms ʿAlī has certainly harmed me" 155
36. al-ʿAbbās b. ʿAbd al-Muṭṭalib and his sons 159
37. The Prophet's near family and his wives 163
Love of the Prophet's *Ṣaḥāba* (Companions) 165
38. al-ʿAbbās and the House of ʿAbd al-Muṭṭalib 167
Shaykh Hisham's *khilāfa* and his patient endurance 169
The author's link to Shaykh Hisham before Islam 170
39. Salmān al-Fārisī 171
Mawlana Shaykh Nazim's phrase about the author 173
Three dreams about Mawlana Shaykh Nazim 174
40. "Make the provision of Muḥammad's family sustenance" 175
41. al-ʿAbbās b. ʿAbd al-Muṭṭalib 179
42. The Prophet and *Ahl al-Bayt* 181
43. The children of ʿAbd al-Muṭṭalib 185

Continuation of the Exordium and conclusion on the meaning of the *Āl* with an overview of works and statements on their special features in the sacred Law and wisdom 189
Divine justice in the equality of lineages under the Law 189
Divine bounty in the superiority of *Ahl al-Bayt* in *Ākhira* 192
Ahl al-Sunna venerate *Ahl al-Bayt* and all the Companions 194
ʿAbd al-Nabī Aḥmadnagrī on the hierarchies of the *Āl* 195
al-Subkī, Ibn Ḥajar and others on the hierarchies of the *Āl* 198
al-Qārī's non-committal 199
al-Mallawī on the *Samarqandiyya* on figures of speech 199
Suyūṭī's *al-ʿAjājat al-zarnabiyya fil-sulālat al-Zaynabiyya* 200
Ibn ʿĀbidīn on *kafāʾa* (marriage suitability) in Ḥanafī *fiqh* 202
Saqqāf b. ʿAlī al-Kāf al-Saqqāf on al-Shāfiʿī's view 205
Ibn Ḥajar on al-Bukhārī's and al-Shāfī's views of *kafāʾa* 206
Ibn ʿArabī on the duty and benefit of loving the *Ahl al-Bayt* 209
The secret of Salmān al-Fārisī 209
The *mawlā* of a people and the true slave of Allah 210
Meaning of uncleanness in al-Aḥzāb 33:33 210
Ahl al-Bayt are under the Law but they are forgiven 211
Divine care reaches ʿAlī and Salmān's descendants 212
The supreme station of *quṭb* behind Salmān's level 213
Treat their punishable wrongdoing as an act of God 214
Give up your rights for them; love what they love 215
To forgive their wronging of us is a cleansing for us 215
Affectionate love for the near relatives (Shūrā 42:23) 216
The divine beguilement of whoever ignores such love 217
Conclusion: gratitude to Allah and service of *Ahl al-Bayt* 219

A descriptive bibliography of books written on this subject 221

Colophon and dating of this book 235
Hadith Index 237
About the author 239

Preface to the English translation and the third Arabic edition

"The term *musnad* refers, among Hadith scholars, to a report that has an uninterrupted chain back to its origin, and is used mostly for Prophetic reports."
(al-Khaṭīb al-Baghdādī)

To the One God belong all glory, praise and thanks for His guidance, whereto we would never be guided had He not guided us. May He lavish His blessings and greetings of peace and safety upon our liegelord and mainstay, our beloved Master Muḥammad, and upon his Family, his Companions, and their followers in excellence to the Day of mutual cries and great dispersal.

Musnad Ahl al-Bayt—unbroken-chained hadiths from and about the people of the Prophet's House—is a reference-work that combines several aspects which make it unique of its kind. It offers an authentic corpus of Prophetic hadiths that are relied upon in the correct understanding of an important aspect of the faith and practice of Islam; it is conveyed with well-documented chains of transmission spanning fifteen centuries of historic narrators down to the contemporary masters from whom the author received those hadiths; it applies the criteria of fully-sourced hadith narration in bilingual format within the anthological *arbaʿīn* genre in threefold fashion: forty-odd hadiths out of forty-odd books from forty-odd teachers; it treats a topic that forms the core of a Muslim's requisite knowledge of the obligation of love for *Ahl al-Bayt*, the House of the Prophet Muḥammad—upon him and them blessings and peace. Finally, it does so in the inclusive perspective of the *sawād al-aʿẓam*, the "overwhelming majority" understanding of the Muslims that are known as *Ahl al-Sunna wal-Jamāʿa*, the Followers of the Prophet's Way and of the Congregation of the Companions.

The subject is of tremendous import to every believer in the Prophet, who is the paradigm and the objective of such love. Anyone's claim of love for the Creator begins with love of those He sent, without exception: *We do not discriminate between any of His Messengers* (Baqara 2:285). It also extends, in proportion with what we know of their great mercy, to love of all those they loved. It is only natural that the historical culmination of those blessed beings with Muḥammad, the Seal of Prophets and Messengers–upon him and them blessings and peace–has made the last Umma the most assiduous in the love of their Prophet and of his family near and at large. Imam al-Shāfiʿī defined the latter as the entirety of the believers until the end of time.

A picture of coherence and consistency emerges from the collective weight of these contents, centered as they are on belief, trust in the guidance that nurtures the relationship between human beings and the divine, knowledge, practice and the benefits of lives inspired by virtue and love of what counts. The latter is, moreover, understood in the holistic manner which the Prophet embodied and taught. Muslims are thus enjoined to speak highly of all persons and groups linked back to him with the possessive adjective *his* such as blood relatives, wives, in-laws (fathers, brothers, sons, cousins), associates (all the Companions), clan (the Banū Hāshim), tribe (the Quraysh), panethnicity (the Arabs) and offspring to the end of time (Hasanis and Husaynis). The fact that this type of treatment of the subject is nearly impossible to find is a poignant illustration of Abū Bakr b. ʿAyyāsh's (d. 193/809) famous saying that "The Sunna (Prophet's Way) in Islam is more rare and precious yet than Islam is rare and precious among the rest of the creeds."

This book is also a testimony to methodology. It serves to show that hadith transmission combines critical sourcing, historiography, sacred Law, biography and lexicography in the service of the Prophetic heritage. It brings to life synchronic and diachronic layers of scholars who strove to convey what they had, as faithfully as they had received it, constantly shining meaning upon it as the cornerstone of its practice. This inter-generational documented connection of the Umma with its sources—the link-by-link, spoken-and-written transfer of revealed knowledge, rigor, truth in reporting, and the orthodox understanding and practice of what is conveyed—were and continue to be the mission of Hadith scholarship. All the above demonstrates the care brought by scrupulous pious ulema to the preservation of Hadith, second only to that of the Qur'ān as the foundation of the Faith-system and of the lofty character of its Umma.

Sadly, many an industrious collector of *ijāza* (certificate of Hadith transmission) nowadays, due to lack of training, is unaware of the function of their *isnād* and clueless of who narrates what from whom, the status of narrators and texts, or the roles of their contents in doctrine, law and the fields they cover. Among the knowledgeable, some take the road of vanity and view *ijāza*s as trophies for name-dropping; others bear antipathy for their own *mujīz* (*ijāza* grantor) due to some perceived unorthodoxy, like the one who travelled from Riyadh to Damascus, got *ijāza* and then, before walking out the door of his new shaykh said, "Tsk! He's a Sufi." Others ask blessing from that tree–which reaches them *in shā Allāh*–but superficially, with no intention of cultivating, partaking in, or sharing its fruit with others. All the above have traded away the substance of *isnād* and Hadith learning for the veneer, and are meddlers rather than genuine scholars and seekers of this particular art. Let students and the lay public know from which type they take it.

A greater factor yet in the Umma's alienation from its own heritage is the absorption and regurgitation by ever more of its secularized "Islamic Studies" pundits, of Orientalist misrepresentations of Hadith–graduates of the persuasion of our former teachers at Columbia–perpetuating their distortion of *isnād* chains as a manufactured, retroactive, anti-chronological artefact of authority put up long after the times they claim to reflect. Such revisionism flows from the more strident anti-spiritual view of revealed Scriptures, last or exclusively—in any case foremost on the block—the Qur'ān itself, as mere literature. The latter agenda drones on about the Qur'ān's "collective authorship," the former about *muḥaddithūn* as fictioneers. In this respect the responsibility of academia looms large, and one cannot help but ponder the quip (by one of our teachers in this volume, Shaykh Abū Sa'īd al-Majd) that "the university was instituted in Muslim countries to fight the mosque."

Special thanks go to my *isnād* teacher Shaykh Muḥammad Abū al-Hudā al-Ya'qūbī, who is also mentioned herein, for elevating the *adab* and vetting the chains of transmission, names, and dates among other details for the second Arabic edition of this book, with the same insights he had shown in his critiques of the narration-centered works of three other teachers of mine–the late Shaykh Ḥusayn ʿUsayrān's *thabat* entitled *Minnat al-Raḥmān*, Shaykh Muḥammad Āl Rashīd's *thabat* of Shaykh ʿAbd al-Fattāḥ Abū Ghudda, *Imdād al-Fattāḥ*, and Shaykh Muḥammad Muṭīʿ al-Ḥāfiẓ's full-chained forty-Hadith *shamāʾīl* compilation, *al-Anwār al-Nabawiyya*, which I was honored to teach in England. I have added corrections and refinements to this third Arabic edition and used authorial license to further improve on the latter, here and there in the English translation, especially in the descriptive bibliographical section.

Last but not least among the special aspects of the present work is its doubling as a *thabat* and a *riḥla*—a précis of Hadith teachers and travelogue of 25 locales: Aleppo, Bāb Tūmā (Damascus), Batu Pahat (Malaysia), Beirut, Brunei, Cairo, Damascus, Fez, Jakarta, Jeddah, Kafarsūsa (Damascus), Kayfūn (Lebanon), Kuala Lumpur, Lefke (Cyprus), Mecca, Medina, Mīdān (Damascus), Mizza (Damascus), Qasyūn (Damascus), Ṣabbūra (Syria), Singapore, Taʿizz, Tampin (Malaysia), Tangiers and Tarim—which I hope to complement, if Allah grants life, with two sister tomes, the *Musalsalāt al-masmūʿa* (Pattern-chained hadiths narrated through audition) and the *Mashyakha* (Catalogue of teachers) which have both been completed in Arabic and await translation. The three works are meant to repay more formally, *in shāʾ Allāh*, some of the debt I owe to the more than two hundred luminaries I was priviledged to reach and learn from by bringing something of what I have witnessed of their lives and their lights to the attention of the public.

It should be noted that the second Arabic edition published by Dar Tayba in Beirut almost three years ago as of writing this has not yet been brought out on the Arabic book market because of the renewed intensity of the trials and hard times which the people of my native country have endured again in recent years. Such is the divine custom with the blessed land and its people. When the Prophet Ibrāhīm–upon him peace–went up Mount Lebanon and reached the top, the One God said to him, "Look all around you, Ibrāhīm! Everywhere your gaze reaches is pure and holy land" (al-Rāzī, *al-Tafsīr al-kabīr*). The Prophet said–upon him the blessings and peace of Allah–"Whoever takes up residence in one of the cities of Shām is a mujahid" [Ibn ʿAsākir, *Taʿziyat al-Muslim*]. "When the One God puts you in dire straits, closes up the avenues of sustenance in your face, and hardens the hearts of His slaves towards you, then know that He wants to bring you near Him; so stand firm and do not despair" (Abū al-Ḥasan al-Shādhilī). This work is also dedicated to them in the humble hope that its blessing may benefit them and lighten their burden.

Allah alone is the Grantor of success. May readers benefit from these pages a quarter century in the making and say a prayer for all those named herein, in firm expectation of the blessed Day He promises, when *We have stripped away all ill-feeling from their breasts; rivers flow underneath them and they say, "Praise be to the One God who has guided us to this! Had the One God not guided us we should never have been guided. The Messengers of our nurturing Lord verily brought the truth!" Then it is proclaimed to them, "That is Paradise; you have been given it as your inheritance for what you have done"* (Aʿrāf 7:43).

Contents by compilation, contemporary shaykh, place of the shaykh or the narration, and narrator from the Prophet ﷺ

Hadith Book	Shaykh	Location	Narrator	Page
1 Maʿmar b. Rāshid, *Jāmiʿ*	Ṣalāḥ Fakhrī	Beirut	Ibn Abī Ḥathma	27
2 *Muwaṭṭaʾ* of Mālik b. Anas	Muḥammad al-Yaʿqūbī	Damascus	Abū Ḥumayd al-Sāʿidī	29
3 *Musnad* of al-Ṭayālisī	Ibrāhīm b. ʿAqīl	Taʿizz	ʿAlī b. Abī Ṭālib	35
4 *Musnad* of al-Shāfiʿī	ʿIṣām ʿArār ʿAbd Allāh al-Ghumāri	Mīdān Tangiers	Jubayr b. Muṭʿim	37
5 *Muṣannaf* of Ibn Abī Shayba	ʿAbbās al-Saqqāf	Singapore	Abū Saʿīd al-Khudrī	43
6 Aḥmad, *Musnad*	Yūsuf al-Rifāʿī	Mizza Damascus	Umm Salama	45
7 al-Dārimī, *Sunan*	Muḥammad b. ʿAlawī	Mecca	Zayd b. Arqam	49
8 *Ṣaḥīḥ* of al-Bukhārī	Bassām al-Ḥamzāwī Abūl-Layth Khayrābādī	Kafarsūsa Damascus Kuala Lumpur	Abū Hurayra	53
9 *Ṣaḥīḥ* of Muslim	Aḥmad al-Ḥaddād Sājid al-Raḥmān al-Ṣiddīqī	Jeddah Brunei	al-Barāʾ b. ʿĀzib	57
10 Abū Dāwūd, *Sunan*	ʿUmar & ʿAṭṭās b. Ḥafīẓ	Tarim	Ibn Masʿūd	61
11 Ibn Mājah, *Sunan*	Ḥasan ʿAṭṭās Zakariyyā Bā Gharīb	Singapore	al-ʿAbbās b. ʿAbd al-Muṭṭalib	65
12 al-Fākihī, *Akhbār Makka*	ʿAbd Allāh al-Kattānī	Damascus	Ibn ʿAbbās	69
13 al-Tirmidhī, *Jāmiʿ*	Tāj Kattānī Sāmir Naṣṣ	Damascus Tampin Malaysia	ʿAlī b. Abī Ṭālib	73

14 *Musnad* of al-Ḥārith b. Abī Usāma	Salīm al-Ḥammāmī / Yūsuf al-Mar'ashlī	Mīdān, Damascus / Beirut	Ibn 'Amr or Ibn 'Umar	p. 77
15 *al-Sunna* of Ibn Abī 'Āṣim	Darwīsh al-Khatīb	Aleppo	'Ā'isha	81
16 His *al-Āḥād wal-Mathānī*	'Alī al-Jafrī	Kayfūn Lebanon	'Ammār b. Yāsir et al.	85
17 *Nawādir al-Uṣūl*, al-Ḥakīm	Sālim al-Shāṭirī	Brunei	Salama b. al-Akwa'	89
18 *Musnad* of al-Bazzār	'Adnān al-Majd	Bāb Tūmā, Damascus	'Abd Allāh b. Zubayr	93
19 al-Nasā'ī, *Sunan*	Muḥd. Zakī Ibrāhīm / Sāmir al-Naṣṣ	Cairo / Tampin Malaysia	'Alī b. Abī Ṭālib	97
20 al-Nasā'ī, *Khaṣā'iṣ 'Alī*	'Aqīl al-Mahdalī	Brunei	Zayd b. Arqam	101
21 Nasā'ī, *al-Sunan al-Kubrā*	Zayn b. Sumayṭ	Jakarta	Usāma b. Zayd	105
22 *Faḍā'il al-Ṣaḥāba*, Nasā'ī	'Abd Allāh al-Junayd	Singapore	Ḥudhayfa b. Yamān	107
23 Abū Ya'lā, *Musnad*	Abū Sa'īd & Abū Ṭayyib Quwaydir	Mizza Mīdān	Fāṭima bint Rasūl Allāh	109
24 al-Ṭabarī, *Tafsīr*	'Abd Allāh al-Talīdī	Tangiers	'Abd Allāh b. Ja'far	115
25 al-Dūlābī, *al-Dhurriyyat al-Ṭāhira*	Murshid 'Ābidīn / Muṭī' Ḥāfiẓ	Damascus	Umm Salama	117
26 al-Baghawī, *Musnad Usāma*	Nūr & Ṣāliḥ al-Khaṭīb	Damascus	Usāma b. Zayd	121
27 al-Ṭaḥāwī, *Mushkil al-Āthār*	'Alī 'Aydrūs / Sa'īd Kaḥīl	Batu Pahat Malaysia / Homs	Umm Salama	125
28 Ibn Ḥibbān, *Ṣaḥīḥ*	Muḥ. 'Ajāj & Ṣāliḥ al-Khaṭīb	Damascus	Abū Sa'īd al-Khudrī	131

29 al-Ṭabarānī, *Muʿjam Kabīr*	ʿAlī al-Ḥaddād	Jakarta	*mursal* Ibn Abī Rāfiʿ	p. 135
30 al-Ṭabarānī, *Muʿjam Awsaṭ*	ʿAbd al-Qādir al-Ḥaddād	Jakarta	al-Zubayr b. ʿAwwām	139
31 al-Ājurrī, *al-Sharīʿa*	Mālik al-Sanūsī	Medina	Abū Saʿīd al-Khudrī	141
32 *Faḍāʾil al-Ṣaḥāba*, Qaṭīʿī	ʿĪsā b. Sumayṭ	Singapore	Thawbān	143
33 al-Ḥākim, *Mustadrak*	Fātiḥ al-Kattānī	Ṣabbūra Damascus	Abū Saʿīd al-Khudrī	147
34 His *Maʿrifat ʿUlūm al-Ḥadīth*	Nūr al-Dīn ʿItr	Qasyūn Damascus	Ibn ʿUmar	149
35 Abū Nuʿaym *Maʿrifat al-Ṣaḥāba*	ʿAbd al-ʿAzīz al-Ghumārī	Tangiers	ʿAmr b. Sha's	155
36 His *Dalāʾil al-Nubuwwa*	Aḥmad b. Idrīs Sūdānī	Kuala Lumpur	Ibn Abī Usayd	159
37 al-Bayhaqī, *Shuʿab al-Īmān*	ʿUmar Sālim al- Miḥḍār	Batu Pahat Malaysia	Abū Laylā al-Anṣārī	163
38 His *Dalāʾil al-Nubuwwa*	Hisham Kabbani Ḥusayn ʿUsayrān	Kuala Lumpur Beirut	al-Muṭṭalib b. Abī Wadāʿa	167
39 al-Baghawī, *Tafsīr*	Nāẓim ʿĀdil al-Ḥaqqānī	Lefke Cyprus	ʿAmr b. ʿAwf	171
40 His *Anwār al-Shamāʾil*	ʿAbd al-Maqṣūd Fāris	Singapore	Abū Hurayra	175
41 Ibn ʿAsākir, *Arbaʿīn ʿAwālī*	ʿAbd al-Razzāq al-Ḥalabī	Damascus	Saʿd b. Abī Waqqāṣ	179
42 His *Arbaʿīn al-Buldāniyya*	ʿAbd al-Raḥmān al-Kattānī Muḥ. Muṭīʿ al-Ḥāfiẓ	Fez Damascus	Ibn ʿAbbās	181
43 al-Maqdisī, *al-Aḥādīth al-Mukhtāra*	ʿAlī al-Saqqāf Āl Ṣāfī	Jakarta	ʿUthmān b. ʿAffān	185

In the Name of Allah, all-Beneficent, most Merciful
The blessings and greetings of the One God be on our liegelord Muḥammad and his Family and Companions

Glory to the One God Who chose the believers out of the family of our liegelord Ibrāhīm and the family of our liegelord ʿImrān and the family of our liegelord Yāsīn and the family of our liegelord Muḥammad over the worlds! He commanded, in His immutable revelation, to love the relatives of His Prophet Muḥammad–upon him and them blessings and peace–and He addressed men and women among them so that the worlds would know how much He had honored them and to what great ranks He had raised them, saying, *Allah only desires to remove uncleanness from you, People of the House, and to cleanse you with a thorough cleansing!* (Aḥzāb 33:33). He thus honored and purified every believer that affirms that station for them as an act of worship and submission to the Divine wish pleasing to His Prophet. Blessings and peace on the best of those who trod the earth, our liegelord, beloved and patron Muḥammad, who expounded the meanings of universal justice in the obtainment of the ranks of honor for the near and the far–all being equally apt to reach them–then gave priority to the meanings of lavish virtue specific to the people of election; namely, to the most virtuous people of his House. May Allah bless him and his pure and fair family and greet them all with fond salutations of peace!

To proceed: countless explicit noble Hadith texts have come to us on the virtues of the Prophetic relatives, such as their being at the summits of the high levels of Paradise; the fact that whoever holds fast to the Qur'ān and to them will never go astray; that they are like the Ark of Nūḥ: whoever boards it is safe, whoever declines drowns; that they are a protection from dissent for the Community; that they are the leaders of the people of Paradise; that Allah has promised He will never punish them; that Allah will cause whoever angers them to enter the Fire; that faith does not enter one's heart until one loves them for the sake of Allah and for the sake of their relationship to the Prophet; that whoever fights against them is as one fighting on the side of the Great Liar of the end of times; that whoever lends one of them a hand, the Prophet himself shall recompense him on the Day of resurrection; that there is not one of them but will have a chance to intercede on that Day; that every man may vacate his seat for his brother except the Banū Hāshim: they should rise for no one. Shaykh ʿAbd al-Hādī al-Ḥāyik said in his quintupling of Imam al-Suhaylī's prayer–may Allah have mercy on both of them:

Refuge of those in need, I come running to You,
observing the duty owed to the noble House.
Let Your Beloved water me the day that I am raised!
Never does Your bounty let the hopeful despair.
Kindness is more ample, gifts are vaster than that!

Another quintupling of some verses of Shaykh Muḥyī al-Dīn Ibn ʿArabī by the erudite Sharif scholar Ḥāmid b. Aḥmad b. ʿUbayd Allāh al-ʿAṭṭār states:

Cling to their sanctuary; endear yourself to them;
for on the Day of Resurrection they're overlords.
Do not care for naysayers—people of perdition.
For the Envoy never demanded wages for guidance
When he conveyed; only affectionate love for the near kin.

These, then, are forty-three full-chained hadiths on the excellence of the Prophetic House, their high rank and the importance of advocating, loving and defending them. They were all narrated to this writer by Sharifs, whether by them verbatim or through my own reading before them, or through the reading of someone else while I listened, or by virtue of my personal permission or a universal permission to narrate from them. I gathered and verified the wordings, then I documented and commented the hadiths, aiming to cite only authentic reports in this volume. At times I paired two of my Sharif shaykhs, or one Sharif with a non-Sharif among those I narrate from, for some subtle reason, or to adduce an audition, or to make up for some weakness in one of the two chains so as to meet the book's standard, or in pursuit of a briefer chain—even though the more trustworthy the additional links are, the shorter the chain is in reality. I sourced each full-chained report to a different Hadith book according to its original reporters and gave it its own chapter. In each chapter I may follow up with additional germane reports without their chains–either from the same book or from other works–that are for the most part sound or fair, together with benefits related to transmission, history, spiritual meanings or language in order to enhance understanding of the chapter and familiarity with the reporters. I conclude in the best way with philological and juridical excerpts bearing on some aspects of wisdom and secrets related to *Ahl al-Bayt* advocacy.

* * *

In all, these are 43 fully-chained hadiths sourced to 43 hadith books through 49 Sharif shaykhs, by which I dearly hope to obtain the intercession of their grandfather the Prophet—upon him and his Family blessings and peace — and their own intercession. May this work help repay the thanks owed for the Godly, Prophetic and saintly favors lavished on this helpless pauper, in the tradition of the imams of this art who compiled books of *Arbaʿīn* in the past. I have entitled the Arabic version of this book **"The Fair Outcome and Best Goals consisting in 40 Hadiths**

Fully-Chained through 40 Sharifs from 40 Books,
on the Excellence of the Prophetic House and
Relatives." Allah is the Grantor of success
towards what He prizes and loves!
May Allah bless our liegelord
Muḥammad, his Family
and Companions,
and grant all
abundant
peace!
Am-
in.

1 The *Jāmiʿ* of Maʿmar b. Rāshid (95-153/714-770)

THE SHARIF OF BEIRUT Shaykh Ṣalāḥ al-Dīn b. Khiḍr b. Maḥmūd Fakhrī al-Ḥusaynī (b. 1367/1948)–may Allah save him–the director of Dār al-Fatwā in Lebanon and author of *Maḥāsin al-āthār fī sīrat al-Shaykh Mukhtār* (a life of his teacher the Mufti of Lebanon Mukhtār al-ʿAlaylī), informed me in Beirut, from the scrupulous Hadith scholar Maḥmūd b. Qāsim Baʿuyūn al-Rankūsī al-Dimashqī (d. 1405/1985), from Shaykh Badr al-Dīn al-Ḥasanī (1267-1354/1851-1935), from Shaykh ʿAbd al-Qādir b. Ṣāliḥ al-Khaṭīb (1221-1288/1806-1871), from al-Wajīh ʿAbd al-Raḥmān al-Kuzbarī (1184-1262/1770-1846) the grandson, from Shaykh Muṣṭafā al-Raḥmatī al-Ayyūbī, from the saintly knower Shaykh ʿAbd al-Ghanī al-Nābulusī, from al-Najm al-Ghazzī, from his father Badr al-Dīn al-Ghazzī al-ʿĀmirī, from Shaykh al-Islām Zakariyyā al-Anṣārī, from the hadith master Ibn Ḥajar who said: ʿAbd Allāh b. ʿUmar b. ʿAlī al-Azharī related to me as I read it before him, from Abū al-Ḥasan ʿAlī b. al-ʿIzz ʿUmar al-Maqdisī and Zaynab bint al-Kamāl, the first by hearing it from Abū al-ʿAbbās Aḥmad b. Abū al-Khayr, and Zaynab by license from Yūsuf b. Khalīl. Both (Aḥmad and Yūsuf) said, Masʿūd al-Jammāl informed us—Yūsuf said "through audition" and the other said "by license"—Abū ʿAlī al-Ḥaddād informed us, Abū Nuʿaym informed us, Sulaymān b. Aḥmad al-Ṭabarānī narrated to us, Isḥāq b. Ibrāhīm al-Dabirī informed us, ʿAbd al-Razzāq informed us, saying: **Maʿmar b. Rāshid** related to us, from al-Zuhrī, from Sahl b. Abī

Ḥathma, that the Messenger of Allah–upon him blessings and peace of Allah–said: "**Do not teach the Quraysh. Learn from them. Do not put yourself ahead of the Quraysh and do not keep aloof from them either. Verily a Qurayshī possesses the same as the strength of two men other than themselves.**"

Al-Zuhrī said, meaning in acumen. This is a sound dispatched (*mursal*) hadith. Ibn Abī Shayba and Bayhaqī (in the *Sunan*) narrated it and it has witness-chains. ʿAbd al-Razzāq, al-Shāfiʿī and Aḥmad narrated from ʿAbd Allāh b. Ḥanṭab: the Messenger of Allah–upon him blessings and peace–addressed us on the day of Jumuʿa saying, "**People! Put the Quraysh first and do not put yourselves ahead of them. Learn from them and do not teach them or lord it over them.**" This is al-Shāfiʿī's wording. Ibn Abī ʿĀṣim also narrates from Jubayr b. Muṭʿim, from the Prophet: "**For they know more than you.**" Al-Ṭabarānī in *al-Kabīr* and al-Bazzār have this addition from ʿAbd Allāh b. al-Sā'ib, the second also from ʿAlī: "**Were it not that Quraysh might gloat I would tell them what Allah has in store for the best of them.**" See also the main hadith in chapter §8 below on al-Bukhārī's *Ṣaḥīḥ*.

(Benefit) Ibn Ḥajar said that al-Bukhārī in his *Ṣaḥīḥ* narrated from al-Ḥumaydī first because he is the most learned Qurayshī he took from. See more on his words on these hadiths in the second part of this book.

(Note) Whoever tried to restrict the meanings and applications of this hadith to the first generation(s) exclusively, has committed an innovation of misguidance and has strayed from the truth.

2 The *Muwaṭṭa'* of Mālik b. Anas (93-179/712-795)

THE METICULOUS sober savant, oft-visited globe-trotter, inheritor of 40 Islamic sciences unique to him of all the scholars of Syro-Palestine, the renewer of the sciences of narration in our time, the summoner to Allah and transmissologist, the scrupulous Sufi, hadith scholar and philologist, the brave *mujāhid*, polyglot preacher and vocalist, dear, generous and of the best counsel, our teacher and pillar in formal Hadith transmission and narration Sayyid Muḥammad Abū al-Hudā al-Ya'qūbī al-Ḥasanī (b. 1963)–Allah save him–son of the erudite imam of Syro-Palestine Sayyid Ibrāhīm al-Ya'qūbī (1363-1406/1944-1986) who was mufti of the Malikis then the Hanafis in the Umawī Mosque, related to us—in his house in the Jisr al-Abyaḍ quarter of Damascus in 1998, as I attended the complete reading of the *Muwaṭṭa'* before him in four sittings: my father narrated to me—as most of the *Muwaṭṭa'* was read before him in my presence, and by permission for all of it—al-Sayyid Muḥammad Makkī al-Kattānī (1312-1393/1895-1973) informed us, Shaykh 'Umar Ḥamdān al-Mahrasī informed us, the *muḥaddith* of Ḥijāz Shaykh Fāliḥ al-Ẓāhirī al-Mālikī (d. 1328/1910) informed us—Sayyid Makkī also relates from him directly—I heard the *Muwaṭṭa'* in the relation of Yaḥyā b. Yaḥyā al-Laythī from Shaykh al-Islām Muḥammad b. 'Alī al-Sanūsī (1202-1276/1788-1860), Abū Ḥafṣ 'Umar b. 'Abd al-Karīm al-'Aṭṭār al-Makkī informed us, Shaykh Ṣāliḥ b. Muḥammad al-Fullānī informed us, our aged teacher Muḥammad b. Sinna al-

Fullānī informed us, the aged Sharif Muḥammad b. ʿAbd Allāh al-Wullātī informed us (the latter two are controverted), Abū ʿUthmān Saʿīd Qaddūra (d. 1066/1656) informed us, Shaykh Abū ʿUthmān Saʿīd b. Aḥmad al-Maqqarī al-Tilimsānī (d. 1010/ 1602) the mufti of Tlemcen for 60 years informed us, Abū ʿAbd Allāh Muḥammad b. al-Ḥāfiẓ Muḥammad b. ʿAbd al-Jalīl al-Tannasī informed us, my father informed us, Imām Ibn Marzūq the grandson informed us, from his father, from his grandfather Ibn Marzūq senior, Abū ʿAbd Allāh Muḥammad b. Jābir b. Muḥammad al-Qaysī al-Wādī Āshī informed us, the jurist Abū Muḥammad ʿAbd Allāh b. Muḥammad b. Hārūn al-Qurṭubī and the qadi of the *Jamāʿa* Abū al-ʿAbbās Aḥmad b. Muḥammad b. al-Ghammāz both informed us, the first saying, the qadi Abū al-Qāsim Aḥmad b. Yazīd b. Aḥmad b. Baqīy al-Qurṭubī informed us—and he is the last to narrate from him—Muḥammad b. ʿAbd al-Raḥmān b. ʿAbd al-Ḥaqq al-Khazrajī informed us–he is the last to narrate from him–Muḥammad b. Faraḥ the *mawlā* of Ibn al-Ṭallāʿ al-Qurṭubī informed us—he is the last to narrate from him—the qadi Abū al-Walīd Yūnus b. ʿAbd Allāh b. Mughīth al-Qurṭubī informed us–and he is the last to narrate from him–Abū ʿĪsā Yaḥyā b. ʿAbd Allāh b. Yaḥyā al-Qurṭubī informed us—he is the last to narrate from him. (Another route) The *ḥāfiẓ* al-Sanūsī from the supercentenarian Abū Ṭālib Muḥammad b. ʿAlī b. al-Shārif al-Māzūnī (1100-1233/1689-1818), from the aged erudite transmissologist and one of the seven renewers of the science of *isnād* in the Hijaz: the Sharifa and jurist Quraysh bint ʿAbd al-Qādir al-Ṭabariyya, from her father's teacher the aged *musnid* ʿAbd al-Wāḥid b. Ibrāhīm b. Aḥmad al-Ḥaṣṣārī

(910-after 1011/1504-after 1602), from Sharaf al-Dīn ʿAbd al-Ḥaqq al-Sinbāṭi, Jalāl al-Dīn al-Suyūṭī, Shaykh al-Islām Zakariyyā al-Anṣārī and al-Shams Muḥammad b. Ibrāhīm al-Ghamrī (786-849/ 1384-1445) the last living student of Ibn Ḥajar in the world—and this is a very high chain. Sinbāṭī said: the Imām Badr al-Dīn al-Nassāba related it to us in its entirety through the *ḥāfiẓ* Shams al-Dīn al-Sakhāwī's reading of it in five sittings, saying: Imām Muḥammad b. Jābir al-Qaysī al-Wādī Āshī informed us of it with a higher chain by one link. Al-Suyūṭī said: the *ḥāfiẓ* al-Taqī b. Fahd related it to me, al-Burhān al-Abināsī related it to us, al-Wādī Āshī informed us of it. Shaykh al-Islām said: Abū Isḥāq Ibn Ṣadaqa al-Ḥanbalī, the *ḥāfiẓ* Ibn Ḥajar and al-ʿIzz Ibn Furāt all related it to me, the first saying: Abū al-ʿAbbās Aḥmad b. al-Ḥasan al-Suwaydāwī informed us of it, al-Taqī al-Akhnā'ī al-Mālikī informed us of it among others, the *ḥāfiẓ* al-Sharaf al-Dimyāṭī informed us of it, Abū al-Faḍl ʿAbd al-ʿAzīz b. ʿAbd al-Wahhāb b. Ismāʿīl b. al-Ṭāhir al-Zuhrī al-Mālikī informed us of it, my grandfather Abū Ṭāhir Ismāʿīl informed us of it, the jurist Abū Bakr Muḥammad b. al-Walīd al-Ṭurṭūshī informed us of it, the jurist Abū al-Walīd Sulaymān b. Khalaf al-Bājī informed us of it, Abū al-Walīd al-Ṣaffār informed us of it. The *ḥāfiẓ* Ibn Ḥajar said: from Najm al-Dīn Muḥammad b. ʿAlī al-Bālisī, from Muḥammad b. ʿAlī al-Makfī, from Muḥammad b. al-Dīlāṣī, from ʿAbd al-ʿAzīz b. ʿAbd al-Wahhāb al-Mālikī. (Another route) Ibn Ḥajar also from the aged transmissologist ʿUmar b. Ḥasan b. Amīla al-Marāghī, from ʿIzz al-Dīn Aḥmad b. Ibrāhīm al-Fārūthī, from Abū Isḥāq Ibrāhīm b. Yaḥyā b. Abī Ḥuffāẓ al-Maknāsī, from Abū al-Ḥusayn Muḥammad b. Muḥammad b. Zarqūn, from Abū ʿAbd Allāh Aḥmad b. Muḥammad b. Ghalbūn, from Abū ʿUmar ʿUthmān b. Aḥmad al-Qayjāṭī, from the abovementioned Abū ʿĪsā Yaḥyā al-Qurṭubī. Al-ʿIzz Ibn al-Furāt said: from al-ʿIzz Ibn Jamāʿa, from the *musnid* Abū Jaʿfar Aḥmad b. Ibrāhīm b. al-Zubayr al-Thaqafī al-Gharnāṭī, from Ibn Khalīl, from Ibn Zarqūn, from al-Khawlānī, from al-Ṭalmankī, from Abū ʿĪsā al-Qurṭubī, my paternal great-uncle Abū Marwān ʿUbayd Allāh b. Yaḥyā b. Yaḥyā the jurist of Cordoba and *musnid* of Andalusia narrated to me, my father Yaḥyā b. Yaḥyā al-Laythī al-Maṣmūdī narrated to me, the Imam of the Abode of Emigration **Mālik b. Anas** informed us by audition for it all but three chapters at the end of *iʿtikāf* which are from Ziyād b. ʿAbd al-Raḥmān b. Shabṭūn, from Mālik, from ʿAbd Allāh b. Abī Bakr b. Muḥammad b. ʿAmr b. Ḥazm, from his father, from ʿAmr b. Sulaym al-Zuraqī who said, Abū Ḥumayd [ʿAbd al-Raḥmān b. ʿAmr] al-Sāʿidī related to me that they said: "Messenger of Allah, how do we invoke blessing on you?" The Messenger of Allah–upon him blessings and peace–said: "**Say: 'O Allah, bless Muḥammad, his wives and his offspring, as You blessed the family of Ibrāhīm; and grace Muḥammad, his wives and his offspring, as You graced the family of Ibrāhīm. Truly You are most glorious and sublime!'**"

This hadith is agreed upon. The two arch-masters, *Sunan* authors and Aḥmad in his *Musnad* narrated it through Mālik. In al-Bukhārī's *al-Adab al-mufrad* from Abū Hurayra: "**Whoever says, 'O Allah, bless Muḥammad and the family of Muḥammad as You blessed Ibrāhīm and the family of Ibrāhīm; grace Muḥammad and the family of Muḥammad as You graced Ibrāhīm and the family of Ibrāhīm; and grant mercy to Muḥammad and the family of Muḥammad as You granted mercy to Ibrāhīm and the family of Ibrāhīm!' I will witness for that one with a great witnessing on**

the Day of resurrection and intercede for him." The *ḥāfiẓ* al-Sakhāwī declared it fair in *al-Qawl al-badī'*. Also from Abū Hurayra, the Prophet said: **"Whoever is happy to collect for himself an ample measure when invoking blessings on us–the people of the House–let him say: 'O Allah, bless Muḥammad, his wives the mothers of the believers, his offspring and the people of his House, as You blessed the family of Ibrāhīm. Truly You are most glorious and sublime!'"** Abū Dāwūd, al-Bukhārī in *al-Tārīkh al-Kabīr*, and al-Bayhaqī in the *Kubrā*, *al-I'tiqād* and *al-Shu'ab* narrated it. The latter then said: "It is as if the Prophet–upon him blessings and peace–singled out the mention of his wives and offspring to signify emphasis, then resumed generalizing, so that he would include the wives and offspring as being part of the people of his House. May Allah bless and greet him and them and his wives one and all!" Its wording is near that of Abū Ḥumayd al-Sā'idī.

(A note of benefit.) It is sunna to (also) invoke blessings on the Prophetic Family upon entering and exiting the mosque. Qadi Ismā'īl al-Mālikī said in *Faḍl al-ṣalāt 'ala al-Nabī*: Yaḥyā b. 'Abd al-Ḥamīd narrated to us, 'Abd al-'Azīz b. Muḥammad b. 'Abd Allāh b. al-Ḥasan narrated to us, from his mother Fāṭima bint al-Ḥusayn, from Fāṭima the daughter of the Prophet–upon him and them blessings and peace–who said: "The Messenger of Allah said to me: **'When you enter the mosque, say: "In the Name of Allah, salam upon the Messenger of Allah! O Allah, bless Muḥammad and the family of Muḥammad, forgive us and yield for us the gates of Your mercy!" When you finish, say the same but with the words, "and yield for us the gates of Your mercy**."'"" Ibn al-Qayyim brought it up in *Jalā' al-khāṭir* as the narrative of Abū al-'Abbās al-Thaqafī. Aḥmad, Tirmidhī and Ibn Mājah narrated something identical. Tirmidhī said: "Fāṭima's hadith is fair even if its chain is disconnected as Fāṭima bint al-Ḥusayn did not make contact with [her grandmother] Fāṭima senior, who only lived for a few months after the Prophet." Its completion is in the chapter on al-Bukhārī.

(Beneficial minutiae.) Ibn Ḥajar related from al-Wādī Āshī in *al-Mu'jam al-mufahras* that Ibn Hārūn's chain is remarkable for two things: its men are all Cordobans up to Yaḥyā b. Yaḥyā, and it contains no *ijāza* [i.e. it is all from live reading]. Abū Sālim al-'Ayyāshī said in his *Fihris* that two people named "Yaḥyā b. Yāḥyā" narrated the *Muwaṭṭa'* from Mālik: Abū Muḥammad Yaḥyā b. Yaḥyā b. Kathīr b. Waslās al-Laythī al-Andalusī (d. 234/849), and Abū Zakariyyā' Yaḥyā b. Yaḥyā b. Bukayr b. 'Abd al-Raḥmān al-Tamīmī al-Ḥanẓalī al-Naysābūrī (d. 226/841), from the latter of whom al-Bukhārī and Muslim narrated in their respective *Ṣaḥīḥ*s.

(Two warnings.) An error crept into some of the transmission catalogues such as al-Fādānī's *Itḥāf al-mustafīd bi-ghurar al-asānīd* and our teacher al-Mālikī's *al-'Uqūd al-Lu'lu'iyya* where they said, "the qadi Abū al-ʿAbbās Aḥmad b. Yazīd" instead of "the qadi Abū al-Qāsim Aḥmad b. Yazīd," substituting Aḥmad b. Yazīd's teknonym with that of Ibn al-Ghammāz. Ours is the correct version as taken from al-Kattānī's *Fihris al-fahāris*, al-Fādānī's *Asānīd al-faqīh Ibn Ḥajar al-Haytamī*, Abū Sālim al-ʿAyyāshī's *Iqtifāʾ al-athar baʿda dhahābi ahl al-athar*; and Allah knows best. Second, the name "Muḥammad b. Sinna" was omitted in al-Fādānī's *Itḥāf al-mustafīd bi-ghurar al-asānīd* while al-Sayyid Fāliḥ al-Ẓāhirī (from the Arab tribe of al-Ẓawāhir) did assert it in his 1323/1905 *Ḥusn al-wafā li-ikhwān al-ṣafā*, published in his lifetime. He also has another large *thabat* entitled *al-Shaym al-bāriq min ḍaym al-marāhiq*.

(Important warning.) Imam al-Kawtharī said in his catalogue of teachers: "The veracity of Ṣāliḥ al-Fullānī's narration from other than the Hijazis needs to be reconsidered." Shaykh Aḥmad al-Ghumārī wrote a tract denouncing Ṣāliḥ al-Fullānī as weak to the point that he positively declared that al-Fullānī's teacher Ibn Sinna and the latter's teacher al-Wāwulātī (the correct spelling is Wullātī as we gave it) do not exist in reality. Allah Most High knows best.

(Benefits) The Pakistani encyclopedist, Qādirī-Akbarī Shaykh of Hadith and *tafsīr* in al-Jāmiʿa al-Ashrafiyya University in Lahore, and author of books on Quranic commentary and its sciences including a 40-volume marginalia on Bayḍāwī's *Anwār al-tanzīl* entitled *Azhār al-tas-hīl*; ḥadīth and its sciences, Arabic and its disciplines including poetry and prosody, history, logic and astronomy, Muḥammad Mūsā b. Shīr Muḥammad b. Aḥmad al-Rūḥānī al-Bāzī (1356-1419/1937-1998), authored a hefty 450-page Arabic treatise in minuscule letters in which he left no stone unturned in examining every facet of the grammar, rhetoric, parsing, style, *fiqh*, Quranic and Hadith commentaries and other aspects of the words and meanings of the *Ṣalāt Ibrāhīmiyya* described in this chapter entitled *Fatḥ al-ʿAlīm bi-ḥall ishkāl al-tashbīh al-ʿaẓīm fī ḥadīth "Ka-mā ṣallayta ʿalā Ibrāhīm"* (The disclosure of the All-Knowing in solving the complexity of the magnificent comparison in the hadith **"as You blessed Ibrāhīm"**). He also wrote a same-sized treatise entitled *al-Nahj al-sahl ilā mabāḥith al-āl wal-ahl* (The easy access to the enquiries about the *āl* and the *ahl*). See on the latter difference the second part of this book.

3 The *Musnad* of Abū Dāwūd al-Ṭayālisī (133-204/751-819)

THE JURIST mufti of Taʿizz (Yemen), transmissologist and litterateur, al-Ḥabīb Ibrāhīm b. ʿUmar b. ʿAqīl b. ʿAbd Allāh Āl Yaḥyā al-Ḥusaynī al-Shāfiʿī (1327-1415/1909-1994) informed us, from the mufti of Ḥaḍramawt al-Ḥabīb ʿAbd al-Raḥmān b. ʿUbayd Allāh al-Saqqāf (1300-1375/1883-1956), from the mufti of Mecca al-Sayyid Abū al-ʿAbbās Aḥmad b. Zaynī Daḥlān al-Makkī al-Shāfiʿī (1232-1304/1817-1886)—a high chain—from ʿUthmān b. Ḥasan al-Dimyāṭī (1197-1265/1783-1849), from the savant Muḥammad b. ʿAlī al-Shinwānī al-Azharī (d. 1235/1820), from the Sharif hadith master Abū al-Fayḍ Muḥammad Murtaḍā al-Zabīdī (1145-1205/1732-1791), Muḥammad b. Muḥammad al-Qirmī al-Maqdisī narrated to us, Muḥammad b. Aḥmad al-Khalīlī narrated to us, the transmissologist qadi Burhān al-Dīn Ibrāhīm b. Abī Sharīf al-Maqdisī al-Miṣrī narrated to us, Muḥammad b. ʿAbd al-Hādī al-Ḥaṣṣārī narrated to us, al-Jalāl ʿAbd al-Raḥmān b. Abī Bakr al-Suyūṭī narrated to us, the transmissologist of the world Muḥammad b. Muqbil al-Ḥalabī narrated to us through permission, Muḥammad b. Ibrāhīm al-Ṣāliḥī narrated to us, Abū ʿAbd Allāh al-Dhahabī narrated to us, Aḥmad b. Salāma narrated to us in writing, Masʿūd al-Jammāl and Abū al-Makārim Aḥmad b. Jaʿfar al-Labbān al-Taymī informed us, Abū ʿAlī al-Ḥasan b. Aḥmad b. al-Ḥasan al-Ḥaddād the Qur'ān master narrated to us, Abū Nuʿaym the Hadith master narrated to us, ʿAbd Allāh b. Jaʿfar b. Aḥmad al-Aṣbahānī narrated to us, Yūnus b.

Ḥabīb b. ʿAbd al-Qāhir al-ʿIjlī narrated to us, **Abū Dāwūd Sulaymān b. Dāwūd b. al-Jārūd al-Ṭayālisī** narrated to us, ʿAmr b. Thābit narrated to us, from his father, from Abū Fākhita: ʿAlī said: "The Messenger of Allah–upon him blessings and peace–visited us and stayed the night. **Al-Ḥasan and al-Ḥusayn were sleeping then al-Ḥasan asked for water. The Messenger of Allah rose to fetch our girba and squeezed water into a cup to give it to him. Al-Ḥusayn tried to take it to drink, but he prevented him and started with al-Ḥasan. Fāṭima said: 'Messenger of Allah, it seems you love him more?' He said, 'No, but he was the first to ask for water.' Then he said: 'I, you, and these two**—I believe he also said: **and this sleeper, meaning ʿAlī—on the Day of resurrection will all be in one same place.'"**

Ṭabarānī in *al-Kabīr*, Abū Nuʿaym in the *Maʿrifa* and Ibn ʿAsākir all narrated it through Ṭāyālisī. Aḥmad in the *Musnad* and *Faḍā'il* narrated it through other chains in the wording **"the Messenger of Allah rose to an ewe lamb we had and milked it, and behold, she gave milk"**; also Bazzār in the wording **"the Messenger of Allah rose to fetch a vessel we had and poured [water] in a cup."** Ibn Abī ʿĀṣim and Abū Yaʿlā also narrated it in short form. The hadith is sound overall. The *qirba* or girba [*OED*] is a waterskin for storing water or milk.

(Benefit and subtle point) The shaykh of our teachers, Shāfiʿī jurist of Indonesian origin, *muḥaddith* and transmissologist of the world Abū al-Fayḍ ʿAlam al-Dīn Muḥammad Yāsīn b. Muḥammad ʿĪsā al-Fādānī al-Makkī (1335-1410/1916-1990) narrated it full-chained in *al-Arbaʿūn min arbaʿīna kitāban ʿan arbaʿīna shaykhan* (Forty hadiths out of 40 books from 40 shaykhs) where he said: "It conveys the merit of the Prophetic Family and their state of nearness to him on the Day of resurrection." He also narrated in *al-Arbaʿūn ʿan arbaʿīna shaykhan min arbaʿīna baladan* (Forty hadiths from 40 shaykhs from 40 regions) with his full chain from ʿAbd Allāh b. ʿUkaym, **"Verily Allah revealed to me three things about ʿAlī b. Abī Ṭālib the night I was taken on a journey…"** They are among the hadith works that inspired the framework of the present book, as are Ibn ʿAsākir's *Buldāniyya* (see §42), itself patterned after Abū Ṭāhir al-Silafī's *Arbaʿīn*. May Allah raise their station and reward them on behalf of the Umma!

4 The *Musnad* of al-Shāfiʿī (150-204/767-820) which consists of hadiths heard by Abū al-ʿAbbās al-Aṣamm from al-Rabīʿ b. Sulaymān out of *Kitāb al-umm* and *al-Mabsūṭ* which a Naysābūrī scholar rearranged under chapter-headings

THE LEARNED SUFI SAYYID ʿIṣām ʿArār of Damascus, son of the savant Yūsuf ʿArār al-Ḥasanī, narrated to us in his house in Maydān, from al-Sayyid Muḥammad al-Muntaṣir b. Muḥammad al-Zamzamī al-Kattānī and from al-Zamzamī directly, both from the latter's father, the Hadith master Muḥammad b. Jaʿfar al-Kattānī and Shaykh ʿUmar al-Maḥrasī.

(Another route) THE HADITH SCHOLAR of the world *al-ḥāfiẓ* Abū al-Faḍl ʿAbd Allāh b. Muḥammad b. al-Ṣiddīq al-Ghumārī al-Maghribī al-Tānjī al-Ḥasanī (1327-1413/1909-1993) also informed us with a high chain, from both Muḥammad b. Jaʿfar and al-Maḥrasī, the first from his father Shaykh Jaʿfar b. Idrīs b. al-Ṭāʾiʿ al-Kattānī al-Fāsī al-Ḥasanī al-Idrīsī, from Shaykh Minnat Allāh al-Azharī, from al-Kuzbarī with his above-mentioned chain to the Hadith master Ibn Ḥajar, the second from Sayyid Aḥmad b. Ismāʿīl al-Barzanjī, from al-Sayyid Aḥmad b. Zaynī Daḥlān, from Shaykh ʿUthmān al-Dimyāṭī, from al-Amīr al-Kabīr (see Nasāʾī's *Sunan* below), from Abū al-Ḥasan ʿAlī b. Aḥmad al-Ṣaʿīdī, from Shams al-Dīn Muḥammad b. Aḥmad b. Muḥammad b. Saʿīd—known as Ibn ʿAqīla al-Makkī.

(Another route) Higher by two links: al-Ghumārī, from the transmissologist of his time Aḥmad b. Muḥammad b. ʿAbd al-ʿAzīz b. Rāfiʿ al-Ḥusaynī al-Ṭahṭāwī (1275-1355/1859-1936), from the savant Shams al-Dīn Abū ʿAbd al-Wahhāb Muḥammad b. Muṣṭafā al-Khuḍarī al-Dimyāṭī al-Kabīr al-Azharī (d. 1287/1870), from al-Amīr al-Kabīr with a short chain—al-Ṭahṭāwī affirmed this narrative route in *al-Masʿā al-ḥamīd fī bayān wa-taḥrīr al-asānīd* as did al-Kattānī in *Fihris al-fahāris*—from al-Ṣaʿīdī, from Ibn ʿAqīla, from Abū al-Asrār Ḥasan b. ʿAlī al-ʿUjaymī, from al-Shams Mūḥammad b. ʿAlāʾ al-Dīn al-Bābilī, from Sālim al-Sanhūrī, from al-Shihāb al-Ramlī, from the *ḥāfiẓ* Shams al-Dīn Abū al-Khayr al-Sakhāwī, from Ibn Ḥajar.

(Another route) Al-ʿUjaymī, from al-Qushāshī, from al-Shams al-Ramlī, from Shaykh al-Islām, from the *ḥāfiẓ* Ibn Ḥajar, Abū ʿAlī Muḥammad b. Muḥammad b. ʿAlī al-Zaftāwī *thumma* al-Ḥīrī and Abū al-Ḥasan ʿAlī b. Muḥammad b. Muḥammad b. Abī al-Majd al-Dimashqī, with the *ijāza* of both shaykhs—if not their audition for at least part of it—from Sitt al-Wuzarāʾ Wazīra bint ʿUmar b. Asʿad b. al-Munajjā al-Tanūkhiyya, Abū ʿAbd Allāh al-Ḥusayn b. Abī Bakr al-Mubārak b. Muḥammad b. Yaḥyā al-Zabīdī informed us, Abū Zurʿa Ṭāhir b. Muḥammad b. Ṭāhir informed us, Abū al-Ḥasan Makkī b. Muḥammad b. Manṣūr b. ʿIllān al-Sallār informed us, the qadi Abū Bakr Aḥmad b. al-Ḥasan al-Ḥīrī informed us, Abū al-ʿAbbās Muḥammad b. Yaʿqūb b. Yūsuf al-Aṣamm narrated to us, al-Rabīʿ b. Sulaymān al-Murādī informed us, **Imam Abū ʿAbd Allāh Muḥammad b. Idrīs al-Shāfiʿī** informed us, Muṭarrif b. Māzin related to us, from Maʿmar b. Rāshid, from Ibn Shihāb, Muḥammad b. Jubayr b. Muṭʿim related to me, from his father: "When the Messenger of Allah–upon him blessings and peace–distributed the shares of relatives among the Banū Hāshim and Banū al-Muṭṭalib, I went to see him together with ʿUthmān b. ʿAffān and we said: 'Messenger of Allah, these brothers of ours from the Banū Hāshim, we do not deny their merit, in light of your position which Allah gave you with regard to them; but what about our brothers from the Banū al-Muṭṭalib? You gave to them and left us out, when our kinship and their kinship [to you] are one and the same!' The Messenger of Allah–upon him blessings and peace–said: **'The Banū Hāshim and the Banū al-Muṭṭalib are but one and the same thing, like this'—and he interlaced his fingers.**'" With the same chain to al-Shāfiʿī he said: my paternal uncle Muḥammad b. ʿAlī b. Shāfiʿ related to me, from ʿAlī b. al-Ḥusayn, from the Messenger of Allah–upon him blessings and peace–the same, with the addition: **"may Allah curse whoever differentiates between the Banū Hāshim and Banū al-Muṭṭalib!"**

Al-Bukhārī, Aḥmad and the *Sunan* authors narrated it except al-Tirmidhī. Al-Bukhārī said: ʿAbd Allāh b. Yūsuf narrated to us, al-Layth narrated to us from ʿAqīl, from Ibn Shihāb, from Ibn al-Musayyib, from Jubayr b. Muṭʿim: "I went to see the Messenger of Allah–upon him blessings and peace–with ʿUthmān b. ʿAffān and we said: 'Messenger of Allah, you gave to Banū al-Muṭṭalib and left us out, when we and they are at the same level of kinship with regard to you.' He said: **'The Banū al-Muṭṭalib and Banū Hāshim are but one and the same thing.**'" Al-Layth said: Yūnus narrated to me adding that Jubayr said: "And the Prophet did not distribute anything to Banū ʿAbd Shams nor to Banū Nawfal." Ibn Isḥāq said: "'ʿAbd Shams, Hāshim and al-Muṭṭalib are all brothers from the same mother–ʿĀtika bint Murra–and Nawfal was their brother from a different mother." Bayhaqī said in *Manāqib al-Shāfiʿī*: "The reason he said this–Allah knows best–is that Hāshim b. ʿAbd Manāf the great-grandfather of the Prophet married a woman of the Banū al-Najjār in Medina who bore him Shaybat al-Ḥamd the grandfather of the Prophet; then Hāshim died as Shayba was with his mother. After he grew up his paternal uncle al-Muṭṭalib b. ʿAbd Manāf took him from his mother and brought him to Mecca which they entered with the nephew riding behind his uncle on the same mount, so people said, 'A slave al-Muṭṭalib owns.' The name stuck and they called him ʿAbd al-Muṭṭalib. When the Messenger of Allah was sent on his mission his people harmed him and tried to kill him, so Banū Hāshim and Banū al-Muṭṭalib—Muslims and pagans—all rose to his defense and refused to surrender him. When the rest of Quraysh realized they could not lay hold of him with them in the way they decided to write among themselves a writ against Banū Hāshim and Banū al-Muṭṭalib in which they stipulated they would neither marry nor trade with them. Abū Ṭālib led them into the moutain gorges bordering Mecca in which they all suffered greatly for two or three years. Allah then sent them deliverance in the form of earthworms unleashed on their document until they devoured all it contained of [or: except] the Names of Allah Most High. The Messenger of Allah–upon him blessings and peace–was told of it and he then told Abū Ṭālib who used it to win the argument over his people until they anulled the writ. There is also another great merit to the Prophet's singling out Banū Hāshim and Banū al-Muṭṭalib with the share of the relatives and his statement '**The Banū al-Muṭṭalib and Banū Hāshim are but one and the same thing;**' namely, that Allah has forbidden them to be recipients of (obligatory) charity and He compensated them with that share of the fifth of the spoils. He said: '**(Receiving) charity is illicit for Muḥammad and for the family of Muḥammad**' [al-Khaṭīb; its origin is in the *Sunan*], indicating thereby that his family over whom he ordered us to invoke blessings alongside him, are the very same for whom Allah declared charity illicit and whom He compensated with that share of the fifth. So the Muslims among Banū Hāshim and Banū al-Muṭṭalib are part of our *ṣalawāt* on the family of our Prophet in our obligatory and voluntary prayers, and al-Shāfiʿī, who is a Muṭṭalibī, is part of them and part of those of the Prophet's House whom he commanded us to love for his sake."

Al-Fasawī in *al-Maʿrifa wal-tārīkh* said that ʿUbayd Allāh b. Mawhib said: "The first to differentiate between the Banū Hāshim and the Muṭṭalib in designation was ʿAbd al-Malik."

Among the Muṭṭalibī intimates was ʿAbd Allāh b. al-Zubayr b. ʿAbd al-Muṭṭalib the paternal cousin of the Prophet and son of ʿĀtika bint Abī Wahb al-Makhzūmiyya. He became Muslim, emigrated and died a martyr at the battle of Ajnādayn in the caliphate of Abū Bakr – Allah be well-pleased with all of them. It is cited in *Dhakhā'ir al-ʿuqbā* without chain that the Prophet used to call him "**My paternal cousin and beloved.**" Ibn Ḥajar said in *al-Iṣāba* that al-Zubayr narrated through Ḥusayn b. ʿAlī that of those who stood their ground at Ḥunayn were al-ʿAbbās, ʿAlī, ʿAbd Allāh b. al-Zubayr and others. Al-

Wāqidī, Ibn ʿĀʾidh and Abū Ḥudhayfa said the same while al-Mubarrid recounted in *al-Kāmil* that ʿAbd Allāh b. al-Zubayr came to the Prophet, who dressed him with a tunic and sat him next to him, saying, **"He is my mother's son, and his father treated me like a son."** It is said that al-Zubayr b. ʿAbd al-Muṭṭalib would make the Prophet hop as a child while declaiming,

Muḥammad son of ʿAbdam
live blessed a life of charm
in honor most sublime!

Al-Wāqidī and others said he was killed in Ajnādayn in the year 13/634. The first of the fallen was a Byzantine duelling with ʿAbd Allāh, then another who took over. ʿAbd Allāh's body was later found surrounded by ten enemy dead. The day the Prophet died ʿAbd Allāh was around 30. Shaykh Musāʿid Sālim al-ʿAbd al-Jādir cited in his book *Maʿālī al-rutab li-man jamaʿa bayna sharafay al-ṣuḥba wal-nasab* (an encyclopedia of Ahl al-Bayt Companions) from al-Bukhārī's *Ṣaḥīḥ* that ʿUrwa b. al-Zubayr said: "ʿAbd Allāh b. al-Zubayr was the most beloved of people to ʿĀʾisha after the Prophet and Abū Bakr, and he treated her like family. One day he went to see her with a group of Banū Zuhra and she served them like a mother because of their close kinship to the Messenger of Allah–upon him blessings and peace."

Ibn ʿĀdil said in his *Tafsīr al-lubāb fī ʿulūm al-Kitāb* on the verse *And know that whatever you gained of spoils, one fifth of it belongs to Allah, His Prophet and the (Prophet's) kins* (al-Anfāl 8:41): "It means one fifth of the fifth of the spoils goes to the kins, namely the relatives of the Prophet. They differed as to their identity. One party said they are all of Quraysh while another said they are those for whom (obligatory) charity is illicit. Mujāhid and ʿAli b. al-Ḥusayn said they are Banū Hāshim and Banū al-Muṭṭalib. As for Banū ʿAbd Shams and Banū Nawfal they get none of it even if the four are brothers in light of the hadith of Jubayr b. Muṭʿim. The scholars also differed whether the portion of the kins is still in force today; most said yes, and it is the position of al-Shāfiʿī and Mālik, while the speculative jurists (Hanafis) said no, and that the portion of the Prophet and that of the kins are both reabsorbed into the fifth, so that the fifth of the spoils is distributed among three categories: orphans, the poor and travellers. Some said it is given to the poor among the kindred as opposed to the rich; in other words they are given it due to their poverty, not their parentage. In actuality the Book and the Sunna indicate that it is in force just as the caliphs practiced after the time of the Prophet, without preferential treatment for the poor, because the Prophet and the caliphs after him used to give to al-ʿAbbās b. ʿAbd al-Muṭṭalib regardless of his great wealth. Al-Shāfiʿī annexed it to inheritance that is deserved in the name of parentage, with the difference that it is given to near and far relatives equally but, he said, the male is given preference over the female two shares to one."

Al-Bayhaqī narrated in his *Manāqib* with his chains back to Imam al-Shāfiʿī–Allah be well-pleased with him–this poetry:

I call upon my Lord to witness that ʿUthmān is virtuous
and that ʿAlī's virtue is overly special

The above is reminiscent of a similar line in Ibn al-Mubārak's *Dīwān*, but al-Shāfiʿī probably said it better.

Al-Shāfiʿī also declaimed:

The family of the Prophet are my expedient;
they are my intermediary to him.
I hope tomorrow to be given (for it)
with my right hand the record of my deeds.

He also declaimed:

O rider, stop at the Muḥaṣṣab in Minā and
shout to every sitting and standing one in Khayf,
Before the dawn, when the pilgrims surge to Minā,
an outpouring like the swells of mighty Euphrates:
"Truly I love the children of the Elect one,
and I count it among my categorical obligations!
"If loving Muḥammad's family is to be a Rāfiḍī
let human beings and the jinn witness I am a Rāfiḍī!"

He also declaimed:

When we accord superior merit to ʿAlī we become
preferentialist Rāfiḍīs according to ignoramuses;
And the merit of Abū Bakr, whenever I mention it,
I am called a hater of Ahl al-Bayt for mentioning it;
I am forever both a Rāfiḍī and an Ahl al-Bayt hater,
for loving both of them, until I lie down in my grave!

He also declaimed in his *Dīwān*:

O family of the Prophet, your love
is an obligation decreed by Allah in the Qur'ān.
It is enough honor for you that whoever
does not invoke blessing on you, his prayer is nil!

5 The *Muṣannaf* of Ibn Abī Shayba (159-235/776-850)

THE ELDER of Singapore, Ḥabīb ʿAbbās b. Muḥammad b. ʿAlī al-Saqqāf (1342-1439/1923-2018)–may Allah have mercy on him–related to me as I read it before him in his house there, from his teacher the savant Shaykh ʿAbd al-Qādir b. ʿAbd al-Muṭṭalib al-Mandīlī (after the town of Mandīlīn in Sumatra, Indonesia) al-Makkī al-Shāfiʿī (1322 -1385/1904-1965), from Sayyid Ḥasan b. Saʿīd b. Muḥammad Yamānī al-Ḥasanī (1312-1391/1895-1971) and from the Sībawayh of his time the savant Muḥammad ʿAlī b. Ḥusayn b. Ibrāhīm al-Mālikī al-Makkī (1287-1368/ 1870-1949), the first from his father and Sayyid ʿAbd al-Raḥmān b. Aḥmad al-Dahhān, the second from Sayyid Zayn al-ʿĀbidīn Bakrī b. Muḥammad Shaṭṭā al-Dimyāṭī al-Makkī al-Ḥusaynī (1266-1310/1850-1893) the author of *Iʿānat al-ṭālibīn* on Shāfiʿī law, the three of them (Ḥusayn b. Ibrāhīm al-Mālikī, al-Dahhān and Bakrī al-Dimyāṭī) from the mufti of Mecca Sayyid Aḥmad b. Zaynī Daḥlān, from ʿUthmān b. Ḥasan al-Dimyāṭī, from al-Amīr al-Kabīr (see Nasāʾī's *Sunan* below), from *Shaykh al-shuyūkh* Badr al-Dīn Muḥammad b. Sālim al-Ḥafnāwī al-Shāfiʿī al-Khalwatī who died in a gathering reading al-Tirmidhī's *Shamāʾil*, from al-Budayrī, from Mullā Ibrāhīm al-Gūrānī al-Kurdī al-Naqshbandī, from his teacher al-Ṣafī al-Qushāshī al-Madanī, from Shams al-Dīn al-Ramlī, from Shaykh al-Islām Zakariyyā, from the transmissologist of Egypt al-ʿIzz ʿAbd al-Raḥīm b. Muḥammad b. ʿAbd al-Raḥīm b. al-Furāt al-Ḥanafī, from Shaykh al-Islām Tāj al-Dīn al-Subkī, from the Hadith master al-Dhahabī, from the Hadith master Ibn Ṭarkhān, from the transmissologist Ḍiyā' al-Dīn Mūsā b. ʿAbd al-Qādir al-Jīlānī (539-618/ 1144-1221), from the transmissologist of Baghdad Saʿīd b. Aḥmad b. al-Ḥasan al-Ḥanbalī, from the peerless trustworthy Hadith master **Abū Bakr ʿAbd Allāh b. Muḥammad Ibn Abī Shayba** al-ʿAbsī (by alliance) al-Kūfī, Abū Usāma narrated to us, from Zakariyyā, from ʿAṭiyya, from Abū Saʿīd, that the Messenger of Allah–upon him the blessings and peace of Allah–said: "**Behold! My pouch to which I resort is the people of my House, and my guts are the Helpers (*Anṣār*)! Therefore pardon their offenders and accept from their doers of good.**"

Al-Tirmidhī narrated it and he declared it fair. Aḥmad in the *Musnad*, Abū Yaʿlā and Ibn al-Jaʿd also narrated through ʿAṭiyya al-Kūfī that the Prophet said: "**The Helpers are my guts and the people of my House and the pouch to which I resort. Therefore pardon their offender and accept from their doers of good.**" Al-Khaṭṭābī said: "He gave the simile of the guts because the latter are the home of the nutrition of a living being by which it endures." Al-Tūrabashtī said: "The *karish* (guts) stand for the stomach for a human being. The Arabs use that term to mean the belly, which is the place in which secrets are hidden, while the *ʿayba* (pouch) is the place where provisions are hidden. The first is an inward matter and the second an outward one. It is possible he used them as similes to point out their special positions with regard to him in his public and private matters." Qadi ʿIyāḍ said in *al-Ikmāl* that Ibn al-Anbārī said: "It means, 'my guts are my companions and my group on whom I depend.' The literal lexical meaning of *karish* is 'the group'. The fact that he made the *Anṣār* his pouch is a reference to their unique status with regard to him, because he apprises them of his secrets."

(Note of benefit.) The Iraqi historian and philologist Dr. Layth Suʿūd Jāsim, author of a biography of Ibn ʿAbd al-Barr and other books, informed me that the كوراني tribal sub-group originally belong to the Kurds of Iraq and that the initial *kāf* in their name is therefore a hard Persian گ /g/ so that it is pronounced Gūrānī.

6 The *Musnad* of Aḥmad b. Ḥanbal (164-241/781-855)

THE MINISTER OF STATE, globe-trotter Sharif, author, caller to Allah, scholar, high-born and influential Sayyid Abū Yaʿqūb Yūsuf b. al-Sayyid Hāshim al-Rifāʿī al-Kuwaytī (1351-1439/1932-2018)–Allah have mercy on him–narrated to me verbatim in his Mizza house on the outskirts of Damascus, our certifying teacher the Sharif ʿAbd al-Qādir b. Aḥmad b. ʿAbd al-Raḥmān b. ʿUbayd Allāh al-Saqqāf al-Say'ūnī al-Ḥijāzī (1331-1431/1913-2010) related to me, from his father, from his teacher the savant and transmissologist of Yemen Sayyid ʿAydarūs b. ʿUmar b. ʿAydarūs al-Ḥabshī, from his father (d. 1250/1834), from the two Sharifs ʿUmar and ʿAlawī (author of *Sharḥ rātib al-Ḥaddād* and of *Miṣbāḥ al-anām fī radd shubuhāt al-mubtadiʿ al-Najdī al-ladhī aḍalla bihā al-ʿawamm*, one of the early treatises against Muḥammad b. ʿAbd al-Wahhāb and his sect) the two sons of Aḥmad b. Ḥasan al-Ḥaddād, from their grandfather Ḥasan (d. 1188/1774), from his father *al-Quṭb* ʿAbd Allāh b. ʿAlawī b. Muḥammad al-Ḥaddād (d. 1132/1720), Ṣafī al-Dīn Aḥmad b. Muḥammad b. Yūnus al-Qushāshī al-Madanī related to us, Abū al-Mawāhib Aḥmad b. ʿAlī b. ʿAbd al-Quddūs al-ʿAbbāsī al-Khāmī al-Thinnāwī informed us, ʿAlī b. Ḥusām al-Dīn al-Muttaqī al-Hindī informed us, Imam ʿAbd al-Wahhāb b. Aḥmad al-Shaʿrānī informed us, the two Hadith masters Shaykh al-Islām Zakariyyā al-Anṣārī and al-Jalāl ʿAbd al-Raḥmān b. Abī Bakr al-Suyūṭī (who authored *ʿUqūd al-zabarjad ʿalā Musnad al-Imām Aḥmad*) informed us, the

Hadith master Abū al-Faḍl ʿAlī b. Ḥajar al-ʿAsqalānī (who authored *al-Qawl al-musaddad fīl-dhabb ʿan Musnad al-Imām Aḥmad*) informed us, the Hadith master and legend of the Quran experts Abū al-Khayr Muḥammad b. Muḥammad b. ʿAlī b. al-Jazarī (who authored *al-Musnad al-aḥmad fīmā yataʿallaqu bi-Musnad al-Imām Aḥmad*) informed us, Abū Ḥafṣ ʿUmar b. Amīla al-Marāghī informed us, the seal of transmissologists al-Fakhr Abū al-Ḥasan ʿAlī b. Aḥmad b. ʿAbd al-Wāḥid Ibn al-Bukhārī al-Saʿdī al-Anṣārī (596-690/ 1200-1291) narrated to us, Abū ʿAlī Ḥanbal b. ʿAbd Allāh b. al-Fariḥ al-Ruṣāfī narrated to us, Abū al-Qāsim Hibat Allāh b. Muḥammad b. ʿAbd al-Wāḥid b. al-Ḥuṣayn informed us, Abū ʿAlī al-Ḥasan b. ʿAlī al-Tamīmī Ibn al-Mudhhib, Abū Bakr Aḥmad b. Jaʿfar al-Qaṭīʿī narrated to us, Abū Muḥammad ʿAbd Allāh b. Aḥmad b. Muḥammad b. Ḥanbal narrated to us, **my father narrated** to me, ʿAbd Allāh b. Numayr narrated to us, ʿAbd al-Malik—meaning Ibn Abī Sulaymān—narrated to us, from ʿAṭā' b. Abī Rabāḥ, someone narrated to me who had heard Umm Salama say the Prophet–upon him blessings and peace–was in her house when Fatima came in with a cauldron (*burma*) containing meat broth. He said, "**Call your husband and your two sons**." Umm Salama relates, "ʿAlī, al-Ḥasan and al-Ḥusayn came in and sat to eat from the meat broth with him on his bedding, on top of a bench (*dukkān*); under him was his Khaybarī cloak. I was praying in the room. Allah Almighty revealed this verse, *Allah only desires to remove impurity from you, People of the House, and to cleanse you with a thorough cleansing!* (al-Aḥzāb 33:33). At this he took the remaining part of the cloak and covered them with it, then he stretched out his hand and waved (*alwā*) it at the sky, saying: '**O Allah, these are the people of my House and my intimates, so remove impurity from them and cleanse them with a thorough cleansing!**' whereupon I put my head inside the house and said, 'And me with you, Messenger of Allah?' He said '**You will reap goodness! You will reap goodness!**'"

Al-Ṭabarānī narrated it in *al-Muʿjam al-kabīr*. In the *Musnad* also from Umm Salama: "As the Messenger of Allah–upon him blessings and peace–was in my house one day the servant said, ''Alī and Fāṭima are at the door.' Hearing this he said to me, 'Get up and move aside from the people of my House for my sake.' I got up and moved aside in the house a little bit. 'Alī and Fāṭima came in with al-Ḥasan and al-Ḥusayn—they were little boys then—whom they placed in his lap, and he kissed them both. Then he grabbed 'Alī with one hand and Fāṭima with the other, kissed her and him, let down on [all four of] them (*aghdafa ʿalayhim*) a black garment, and said, '**O Allah, unto You, not unto the Fire, me and the people of my House!**' I said, 'And me, Messenger of Allah?' He said, 'And you!'" Al-Dūlābī narrated it in *al-Kunā wal-asmā'* and al-Tirmidhī in his *Sunan* in short form through Sufyān, from Zubayd, from Shahr. He said: "This hadith is fair and sound and is the finest thing narrated to that effect. It is also narrated from 'Umar b. Abī Salama, Anas b. Mālik, Abū al-Ḥamrā', Maʿqil b. Yasār and 'Ā'isha–Allah be well-pleased with all of them."

Sayyid Yūsuf said: "The *burma* is a clay pot where water is made to cool, or honey is kept, or dates and the like; the *dukkān* is an elevated bench; *khaybarī* means made in Khaybar; *alwā* means to point; 'I put my head inside the house' means under the cloak; 'You will reap goodness' means he did not allow her to enter; 'he grabbed 'Alī with one hand and Fāṭima with the other' means he put each of his two noble hands on the neck of each; *fa-aghdafa ʿalayhim* means he threw or cast."

Sayyid Yūsuf's statement that "he did not allow her to enter" applies to one of the narrations and not in absolute terms, and Allah knows best. Their promised lofty destiny is made clear in the narrations of al-Ḥārith b. Abī Usāma in his *Musnad* and Ibn 'Asākir in *al-Arbaʿīn fī manāqib ummahāt al-mu'minīn* (Forty hadiths on the Mothers of the believers) as mentioned in the former's chapter (§14).

(Note of benefit.) Shaykh Muḥammad al-Tāwudī b. Sawda said in his *Fahrasa* that the meaning of *ʿaydarūs* is, "Sultan of the friends of Allah" (*sulṭān al-awliyā'*).

7 The *Sunan* of ʿAbd Allāh b. ʿAbd al-Raḥmān al-Dārimī (181-255/ 797-869)

THE SHAYKH AL-ISLAM of the Sacred Sanctuary, transmissologist, summoner to Allah, educator of *Ahl al-Sunna*, author and mujahid against falsehood and heterodoxy, Sayyid Muḥammad Ḥasan b. ʿAlawī b. ʿAbbās b. ʿAbd al-ʿAzīz al-Mālikī al-Ḥasanī al-Makkī (1367-1425/1948-2004)–may Allah have mercy on him–informed me in his house in the Ruṣayfa district of Mecca the Magnificent the year of the Greater Pilgrimage in 1999 from his father and from Shaykh Ḥasan b. Muḥammad al-Mashshāṭ, both of them from ʿUmar Ḥamdān al-Maḥrasī, from Aḥmad al-Barzanjī, from Aḥmad b. Zaynī Daḥlān; (a shorter route) al-Mālikī also from Ḥasan b. Saʿīd Yamānī (1312-1391/ 1895-1971), from Sayyid ʿAbd al-Raḥmān b. Aḥmad al-Dahhān, from Daḥlān, from ʿUthmān b. Ḥasan al-Dimyāṭī; (a shorter route) al-Mālikī also from al-Ḥabīb Sālim b. Aḥmad b. Jindān the descendant of Shaykh Abū Bakr b. Sālim with a high chain, from the mufti of Batavia Ḥabīb ʿUthmān b. ʿAbd Allāh b. ʿAqīl b. Yaḥyā al-ʿAlawī, from ʿUthmān b. Ḥasan al-Dimyāṭī, from al-Amīr al-Kabīr (see below, chapter on al-Nasāʾī's *Sunan*), from al-Ḥafnāwī, from al-Budayrī, from Mullā Ibrāhīm al-Gūrānī, from Ṣafī al-Dīn Aḥmad al-Qushāshī, from al-Shams al-Ramlī, from Shaykh al-Islām Zakariyyā al-Anṣārī, from the *musnid* of the world Muḥammad b. Muqbil al-Ḥalabī from Juwayriya bint Aḥmad al-Kurdī al-Hakkārī, Abū al-Ḥasan ʿAlī b.

ʿUmar al-Kurdī related to us, the transmissologist of his time Abū al-Munajjā ʿAbd Allāh b. ʿUmar b. ʿAlī b. Zayd al-Ḥarīmī al-Qazzāz al-Baghdādī—famed as Ibn al-Lattī (545-635/1150-1238)—related to us as we attended it in full, Abū al-Waqt ʿAbd al-Awwal al-Sajzī al-Harawī related to us, Abū al-Ḥusayn ʿAbd al-Raḥmān al-Dāwūdī related to us, ʿAbd Allāh b. Aḥmad al-Sarakhsī related to us, Abū ʿImrān ʿĪsā b. ʿUmar al-Samarqandī related to us, **Abū Muḥammad ʿAbd Allāh b. ʿAbd al-Raḥmān b. al-Faḍl al-Tamīmī al-Dārimī** related to us, Jaʿfar b. ʿAwn narrated to us, Abū Ḥayyān narrated to us, from Yazīd b. Ḥayyān, from Zayd b. Arqam–Allah be well-pleased with him–that the Prophet–upon him blessings and peace–one day stood to preach and he glorified and praised Allah, then said: **"O people! I am only human: the messenger of my Lord is about to come to me and I must answer him! Verily I am leaving among you the two weighty things; the first is the Book of Allah, containing guidance and light, so hold to the Book of Allah and do what is says!"** He urged and encouraged then said, **"And the people of my House! I remind you of Allah about the people of my House!"** three times.

Aḥmad and Muslim narrated it. The latter added that Ḥuṣayn b. Sabra asked, "And who are the people of his House, Zayd? Are not his women part of the people of his House?" He replied, "His wives are part of the people of his House, but the people of his House [here] are those who are deprived of the [obligatory] charity after him." "And who are they?" "The house of ʿAlī, the house of ʿAqīl, the house of Jaʿfar and the house of ʿAbbās." "Are all of these deprived of the [obligatory] charity?" Zayd said yes.

Al-Ṭībī said, "Meaning: 'I warn you of Allah regarding them,' so the reminder has the sense of an admonition." Al-Tirmidhī—he said it is fair and single-chained—and al-Ḥākim in the *Mustadrak* also narrated from Zayd that the Messenger of Allah said: **"Verily I am leaving among you that which, if you hold fast to it, you will never go**

astray after me—one is greater than the other: the Book of Allah, a rope extended from heaven to earth; and my *'Itra* (intimate family), the people of my House. The two shall never part ways until they come up to me at the Basin. So be very careful how you treat the two of them after I leave you!" Aḥmad and Abū Yaʿlā also narrated it from Abū Saʿīd al-Khudrī while Tirmidhī and al-Ṭabarānī also narrated it from Jābir. There is another famous version of it which will come up in the chapter of al-Nasāʾī's *Khaṣāʾiṣ amīr al-muʾminīn ʿAlī*, if Allah wills.

(Benefits and explanations.) Wives belong to the *Āl* just as the offspring do, as mentioned in the chapter on the *Muwaṭṭaʾ* and ʿĀʾisha's saying in *Ṣaḥīḥ Muslim* **"Muḥammad's *Āl* never ate to satiety three nights in a row since he came to Medina, not even from barley, and that until he was taken back."** They are also of the *Ahl* as in the saying of Allah citing Ibrāhīm's guests—upon our Prophet and them blessings and peace—*They said, Do you marvel at the decree of Allah? The mercy of Allah and His blessings be upon you, people of the house! Verily He is Praiseworthy, Glorious* (Hūd 11:73). *Ahl al-Bayt* is understood as the wives in the latter verse according to the vast majority of the commentators. Indeed Bukhārī has it from ʿĀʾisha in the context of the Great Lie story that the Prophet–upon him blessings and peace–said: "**Who will exonerate us with regard to a man I was told harmed one of my House?**" Meaning her. It is also related from Anas in the two *Ṣaḥīḥ*s, "the Prophet went to ʿĀʾisha's chamber and said, **'Peace upon you, *Ahl al-Bayt*, and the mercy of Allah!' to which she replied, 'And upon you peace and the mercy of Allah! How do you find your *Ahl*? May Allah bless you.'** He went on to visit the chambers of all of his wives, saying to them what he had said to ʿĀʾisha and they would say to him what ʿĀʾisha had said."

Mullā ʿAlī al-Qārī said in *Mirqāt al-mafātīḥ*: "**I remind you of Allah** means 'I warn you about Him with regard to the people of my house.' He made the manifest meaning implicit to focus attention on their status and to notify [them] of the underlying reason. The meaning is 'I warn you of the right of Allah to their being protected, catered for, respected, honored, loved and cherished.' Al-Ṭībī said, 'That is, I warn you of Allah concerning the people of my House and I say to you, Beware Allah, do not harm them, but rather protect them! So the reminder stands for admonition. This is indicated by the wording in Muslim **Then he admonished and reminded**.' I say (meaning al-Qārī): The distinction between the two has already been discussed and it is preferable to understand each as fundamental expressions (*taʾsīs*). He repeated the phrase **I remind you of Allah about the people of my House!** to impart intensity. It would not be farfetched to say that he meant his *Āl* by one and his spouses by the other in light of what was said before, that both are referred to as *Ahl al-Bayt*."

As for *zakāt* it is not remitted to the Banū Hāshim by consensus, nor to Banū al-Muṭṭalib according to al-Shāfiʿī nor to their clients such as Thawbān the *mawlā* of the Prophet–upon him blessings and peace–(see the chapter on Qaṭīʿī's addenda to *Faḍā'il al-ṣaḥāba*), or such as Salmān al-Fārisī whom the Prophet manumitted, whereupon he became his client (see his hadith in the chapter on al-Baghawī's *Tafsīr*), or his nurse Umm Ayman Baraka al-Ḥabashiyya whom he inherited from his father and manumitted when he married Khadīja. She was one of the first Emigrants and he said of her, "**Whoever is pleased to marry a woman from the people of Paradise, let him marry Umm Ayman!**" Ibn Saʿd narrated it in *mursal* mode. Hearing this, Zayd married her and she bore him Usāma–Allah be well-pleased with them. He narrated with a flimsy chain from a shaykh of the Banū Saʿd b. Bakr that the Prophet would say to Umm Ayman: "**My mother!**" and would say "**This woman is the remnant of the people of my House.**" Ibn ʿAbd al-Barr cited consensus on the prohibition of *zakāt* for his wives as mentioned in Suyūṭī's *Unmūdhaj*.

Some of the scholars deemed it permissible to give the *Ahl al-Bayt* from the monies of *zakāt* in compensation for the Fifth (*khumus*) when the latter is no longer duly paid to them, as related by al-Ṭabarī in *Ikhtilāf al-fuqahā'* and al-Ṭaḥāwī in *Sharḥ maʿānī al-āthār* from Abū Ḥanīfa "when they are deprived of the portion of the kin (*sahm ulī al-qurbā*), because it is a matter of vital need and necessity." Al-Sakhāwī said in *Istijlāb irtiqā' al-ghuraf*: "This is also quoted from al-Abharī—a Mālikī—and is even a 'valid consideration' (*wajh*) according to one of the Shafiʿīs." The editor of that work footnoted, "Abū Saʿīd al-Iṣṭakhrī held it as mentioned in *al-Majmūʿ sharḥ al-Muhadhdhab*." Otherwise, the sacred texts explicitly declare the *zakāt* as prohibited for *Ahl al-Bayt* and the Prophet–upon him blessings and peace–called it "**used hand-wash**" and "**the dregs of people.**" Suyūṭī said in *al-Khaṣā'iṣ al-kubrā*: "The scholars said that since charity is the dregs of people, his lofty position was exempted from it and the exemption took effect for his *Āl* as well. Also, charity is given out of compassion that assumes the lowliness of the taker; so they were given the spoils instead, which are taken through might and honor on the assumption of the taker's might and the lowliness of the one it is taken from. The scholars of the Predecessors differed whether this ruling also applied to other Prophets or whether it was exclusive to him alone; al-Ḥasan al-Baṣrī took the first position and Sufyān b. ʿUyayna the second. Furthermore: both *zakāt* and voluntary charity are one and the same in relation to the Prophet; but **as for his *Āl*, our School holds that only *zakāt* is prohibited for them; as for voluntary charity (*ṣadaqa*), it is licit for them according to the sounder view**." The Hanbalis hold the same view as shown in Ibn Qudāma's *Mughnī* and al-Mardāwī's *Inṣāf*, as do most of the Hanafis as shown in al-Jaṣṣāṣ's *Aḥkām al-Qur'ān*.

8 The *Ṣaḥīḥ* of Muḥammad b. Ismāʿīl al-Bukhārī (194-256/810-870)

THE METICULOUS teacher and scholar Sayyid Bassām b. ʿAbd al-Karīm b. Muḥammad Ḥusayn b. ʿAbd al-Karīm b. Muḥammad Salīm b. Muḥammad Nasīb b. Ḥamza al-Ḥamzāwī al-Shāfiʿī al-Ḥusaynī narrated to me in his residence in Kafarsūsa; also the researcher in the sciences of hadith Dr. Muḥammad Abū al-Layth b. al-Ḥājj Shams al-Dīn al-Khayr Ābādī related to me through my reading to him of part of the book and his reading to me part of it; on the basis of both their auditions of it from Shaykh ʿAbd al-Rashīd al-Nuʿmānī al-Nadwī (1914-1999) and from Sayyid Fakhr al-Dīn b. Aḥmad al-Ḥusaynī al-Ajmīrī al-Murad Ābādī (1307-1392/1890-1972) respectively, both Nuʿmānī and al-Ajmīrī having heard it from the Deobandi *muḥaddith* Shaykh al-Hind Maḥmūd Ḥasan al-ʿUthmānī (1268-1339/1852-1921), from the *muḥaddith* Shaykh ʿAbd al-Ghanī al-Dihlawī, from Muḥammad Isḥāq al-Dihlawī, from Shah ʿAbd al-ʿAzīz b. Aḥmad b. ʿAbd al-Raḥīm al-Dihlawī, my father Shah Walī Allāh al-Dihlawī related to us, Abū Ṭāhir Muḥammad ʿAbd al-Samīʿ b. Ibrāhīm al-Gūrānī related to us, Abū al-Asrār Ḥasan b. ʿAlī al-ʿUjaymī related to us, ʿĪsā b. Muḥammad al-Thaʿālibī Abū Mahdī al-Jaʿfarī (d. 1080/1669) related to us, Abū al-ʿAzaʾim Sulṭān b. Aḥmad b. Salamat al-Mazzāḥī related to us, Aḥmad b. Khalīl b. Ibrāhīm al-Subkī related to us, Najm al-Dīn Muḥammad b. Aḥmad al-Ghayṭī al-Sakandarī related to us, Shaykh al-

Islām al-Qāḍī Zakariyyā b. Muḥammad al-Anṣārī related to us, Ibrāhīm b. Ṣadaqa al-Ḥanbalī related to us, Abū al-Najm ʿAbd al-Raḥīm b. ʿAbd al-Wahhāb b. ʿAbd al-Karīm b. Razīn al-Ḥamawī related to us, the aged *musnid* of the world famously known as Ibn al-Shiḥna Shaykh Aḥmad b. Abī Ṭālib al-Ḥajjār al-Ḥanafī al-Dimashqī related to us, Sirāj al-Dīn Abū ʿAbd Allāh al-Ḥusayn b. al-Mubārak al-Rabaʿī al-Zabīdī al-Baghdādī related to us, Abū al-Waqt ʿAbd al-Awwal b. ʿĪsā al-Sijzī al-Harawī related to us, Shaykh al-Islām Abū al-Ḥasan ʿAbd al-Raḥmān b. Muḥammad b. Muẓaffar al-Dāwūdī al-Būshanjī related to us, Shaykh al-Islām Abū Muḥammad ʿAbd Allāh b. Aḥmad b. Ḥammūyah al-Sarakhsī related to us, Shaykh al-Islām Abū ʿAbd Allāh Muḥammad b. Yūsuf b. Maṭar al-Farabrī/Firabrī related to us, the Commander of the Believers in Hadith, Shaykh al-Islām **Abū ʿAbd Allāh Muḥammad b. Ismāʿīl al-Bukhārī** related to us, Qutayba b. Saʿīd narrated to us, al-Mughīra narrated to us, from Abū al-Zinād, from al-Aʿraj, from Abū Hurayra–Allah be well-pleased with him–that the Prophet–upon him blessings and peace–said: **"People are to follow Quraysh in this great matter: Muslims follow their Muslims and unbelievers follow their unbelievers. People are vessels: the best of them in pagan times are the best of them in Islam once they become learned and understand. You will find that some of the best people are those who hate this great matter the most until they become involved in it.**"

Al-Bukhārī and Muslim narrated it. Sayyid Bassām said Ibn Ḥajar said al-Bukhārī began his *Ṣaḥīḥ* by narrating from al-Ḥumaydī the Hāshimi due to the hadith **Put Quraysh first and do not put yourselves ahead of them** as already discussed, and this is similar. Ibn al-Mulaqqin said in *al-Tawḍīḥ*, his commentary on al-Bukhārī's *Ṣaḥīḥ*, "His saying **those who hate this great matter the most** means rulership: whoever obtains it without asking receives support, and whoever obtains it after pursuing it is left to himself. Hating it is because he knows the difficulty of doing justice in it and he knows of next-worldly accountability. Al-Khaṭṭābī said 'Its meaning is that when they become involved it becomes impermissible to continue to hate it, because if they remain reluctant they will not meet its demands.'" Al-Nawawī cited Qadi 'Iyāḍ as saying, "It is possible it means Islam just as took place with 'Umar b. al-Khaṭṭāb, Khālid b. al-Walīd, 'Amr b. al-'Āṣ, 'Ikrima b. Abī Jahl, Suhayl b. 'Amr and others who became Muslim when Mecca was conquered, and among those who loathed Islam at first, but when they entered it they loved it and strove to the utmost in its behalf."

(Notes of benefit.) Sayyid Bassām said: "The best of the forms of invoking blessings on the Prophet–upon him blessings and peace–are two, the first being the well-known *Ṣalāt Ibrāhīmiyya*, while the second is, **O Allah, bless Muḥammad, his wives, his offspring and his *Āl* just as You blessed Ibrāhīm in all the worlds. Truly You are all-praiseworthy and glorious! And grace Muḥammad, his wives, his offspring and his *Āl* just as You graced Ibrāhīm in all the worlds. Truly You are all-praiseworthy and glorious!**" He said most of the commentators of Hadith and those of the two *Ṣaḥīḥ*s said that the Prophet–upon him blessings and peace–regularly recited the second form in his prayer. Furthermore, Imam al-Nawawī–may Allah have mercy on him–said in *al-Adhkār*: "The best is for one to say, **O Allah, bless Muḥammad Your slave and Messenger the unlettered Prophet, and the *Āl* of Muḥammad, his wives and his offspring, just as You blessed Ibrāhīm and the *Āl* of Ibrāhīm; and grace Muḥammad the unlettered Prophet and the *Āl* of Muḥammad, his wives and his offspring, just as You graced Ibrāhīm and the *Āl* of Ibrāhīm in all the worlds. Truly You are all-praiseworthy and glorious!** For the latter form is the most inclusive of all that the narrations conveyed. We narrated this modality out of the two *Ṣaḥīḥ*s of al-Bukhārī and Muslim from Ka'b b. 'Ujra, from the Messenger of Allah–upon him blessings and peace–except for a small part which is nevertheless sound as narrated from other than Ka'b." He concluded his magnificent book *Riyāḍ al-ṣāliḥīn* with it. Finally, it is mentioned in Qadi 'Iyāḍ's *Shifā* that al-Ḥasan al-Baṣrī used to say, "Whoever wants a quaff from the Basin of the Elect Prophet, let him say: **O Allah, bless Muḥammad, his *Āl*, his Companions, his children, his wives, his offspring, the people of his wives, his in-laws, his helpers, his partisans, his lovers, his Community, and ourselves with all of them, O most merciful of the merciful!**"

9 The *Ṣaḥīḥ* of Muslim b Ḥajjāj al-Naysābūrī (206-261/ 821-875)

THE NOBLE JURIST, *muḥaddith* and author of books, Dr. Sājid al-Raḥmān b. Ishfāq al-Raḥmān al-Bakrī al-Ṣiddīqī al-Kandihlawī al-Sindī al-Ḥanafī (1362-1433/1433-2011) related to me through my reading to him for all of *Ṣaḥīḥ Muslim* in his house in the Sultanate of Brunei Darussalam while al-Ḥabīb Aḥmad Mashhūr b. Ṭaha al-Ḥaddād al-Ḥusaynī (1325-1416/1907-1995) informed me with a short chain, the first one saying, the jurist and *muḥaddith* Shaykh Ẓafar Aḥmad al-ʿUthmānī al-Tahānawī and the erudite *muḥadddith* Muḥammad Yūsuf al-Banūrī related to me through its being read before them, the first one through its being read before Muḥammad Shabbīr al-ʿUthmānī al-Tahānawī, through its being read before the erudite major scholar Anwar Shāh b. Muʿaẓẓam Shāh al-Kashmīrī and the second from Anwar Shāh al-Kashmīrī directly. The latter said: I read before the *muḥaddith* Shaykh Muḥammad Isḥāq al-Kashmīrī al-Madanī, from Khayr al-Dīn Nuʿmān b. Maḥmūd al-Ālūsī (d. 1317/1899), from his father Sayyid Abū al-Thanā' Shihāb al-Dīn Maḥmūd b. ʿAbd Allāh al-Ālūsī al-Ḥusaynī (d. 1270/ 1854) of Iraq, the author of the famous *Tafsīr Rūḥ al-Maʿānī*, from ʿAbd al-Laṭīf b. ʿAlī Fatḥ Allāh al-Bayrūtī (d. 1205?/1791?)—he bestowed universal permission to narrate from him—from the *musnid* of Syro-Palestine, *Shaykh al-Ḥadīth* and imam of Shafiʿis in the Umayyad Mosque Shihāb al-Dīn Aḥmad b. ʿUbayd Allāh b. ʿAskar al-ʿAṭṭār, Shaykh Muḥammad b. Sulaymān al-Kurdī al-Madanī informed me, from the imam and jurist of his time Muḥammad Sa'īd al-Shāfi'ī, famous as Sunbul, from the *muḥaddith* of Mecca Shihāb al-Dīn al-Nakhlī, by virtue of his audition of most of *Ṣaḥīḥ Muslim* from al-Shams al-Bābilī–and the whole through license–from Abū al-Najā Sālim b. Muḥammad al-Sanhūrī, through his reading before Najm al-Dīn Muḥammad al-Ghayṭī through his audition of its entirety before Shaykh al-Islām Zakariyyā al-Anṣārī, the *ḥāfiẓ* and teacher al-Zayn Abū al-Na'īm Riḍwān b. Muḥammad al-'Aqbī (Ibn Ḥajar's dictation assistant) related to me through my reading before him, al-Sharaf Abū Ṭāhir Muḥammad b. Muḥammad b. 'Abd al-Laṭīf al-Kwayk al-Raba'ī al-Takrītī *thumma* al-Iskandarī al-Qāhirī related to us by audition, Abū Muḥammad 'Abd al-Raḥmān b. Muḥammad b. 'Abd al-Ḥamīd b. 'Abd al-Hādī al-Maqdisī *thumma* al-Ṣāliḥī informed us—he had come to Cairo—saying, Abū al-'Abbās Aḥmad b. 'Abd al-Dā'im b. Ni'ma al-Nābulusī informed us by audition before him, Abū 'Abd Allāh Muḥammad b. 'Alī b. Ṣadaqa al-Ḥarrānī informed us by audition before him, the jurist of the holy Sanctuary Abū 'Abd Allāh Muḥammad b. al-Faḍl b. Aḥmad al-Ṣā'idī al-Furāwī informed us; (another route) al-Ḥabīb Aḥmad Mashhūr said, from al-Ḥabīb Aḥmad b. al-Ḥasan al-'Aṭṭās with a high chain, from Muḥammad 'Ābid al-Sindī, from the transmissologist of Yemen the *ḥāfiẓ* Wajīh al-Dīn 'Abd al-Raḥmān b. Sulaymān b. Yaḥyā al-Ahdal, from his father the mufti of Zabid, from his grandfather Imam Yaḥyā b. 'Umar Maqbūl al-Ahdal, from Abū Bakr b. 'Alī al-Ahdal, from his paternal uncle Yūsuf b. Muḥammad al-Baṭṭāḥ al-Ahdal, from the *muḥaddith* of Yemen Sayyid al-Ṭāhir b. Ḥusayn al-Ahdal, from the Hadith master and historian of Yemen and the reviver of the sciences of Hadith in it Muḥammad b. ʿUmar, famous as Ibn al-Dībaʿ—not Daybaʿ but with a long ī, meaning "white" in Nubian—al-Shaybānī al-ʿAbdarī al-Zabīdī al-Shāfiʿī al-Atharī (866-944/1462-1537) the author of the famous *Mawlid*, from the *muḥaddith* of Yemen Zayn al-Dīn Abū al-ʿAbbās Aḥmad b. Aḥmad b. ʿAbd al-Laṭīf al-Sharjī al-Zabīdī al-Taʿizzī (d. 893/1488) the author of *al-Tajrīd al-ṣarīḥ*, from Shams al-Dīn Muḥammad b. Aḥmad b. Muḥammad al-Jazarī al-Dimashqī, Abū al-ʿAbbās Aḥmad b. ʿAbd al-Karīm b. Ḥusayn al-Ṣūfī informed us by audition, the righteous *shaykha* Umm Muḥammad Zaynab bint ʿUmar al-Kindī informed us by audition, the aged *musnid* of Khurāsān Abū al-Ḥasan al-Mu'ayyad b. Muḥammad b. ʿAlī al-Ṭūsī related it to me, from al-Furāwī, Abū al-Ḥusayn ʿAbd al-Ghāfir b. Muḥammad al-Fārisī informed us, Abū Aḥmad Muḥammad b. ʿĪsā b. ʿAmrūyah al-Julūdī, Ibrāhīm b. Muḥammad b. Sufyān informed us, **Muslim b. al-Ḥajjāj b. Muslim al-Qushayrī al-Naysābūrī** informed us by audition before him, Muḥammad b. Bashshār and Abū Bakr b. Nāfiʿ narrated to us, the latter saying, Ghundar narrated to us, Shuʿba narrated to us, from ʿAdī—namely Ibn Thābit—from al-Barā' who said "**I saw the Messenger of Allah–upon him blessings and peace–putting al-Ḥasan b. ʿAlī on his shoulders and saying, 'O Allah, I do love him, so do love him!**'"

Al-Tirmidhī narrated it and said it is "fair and sound;" also Ṭabarānī, with the addition, **and do love whoever loves him!** It is also narrated from ʿĀ'isha by al Ṭabarānī in *al Kabīr* and Ibn ʿAsākir, and from Saʿīd b. Zayd b. ʿAmr b. Nufayl with a sound chain as indicated by al-Haythamī in *Majmaʿ al-zawā'id.*

10 The *Sunan* of Abū Dāwūd (202-275/818-888)

THE TWO BROTHERS al-Ḥabīb ʿUmar and al-Ḥabīb ʿAṭṭās the sons of the erudite scholar Ḥabīb Muḥammad b. Sālim b. Ḥafīẓ b. al-Shaykh Abī Bakr informed us, from their martyred father, from his teacher the erudite *musnid* Shams al-Dīn Abū ʿAbd Allāh Muḥammad b. Sālim b. ʿAlawī al-Sarī Bā Hārūn Jamal al-Layl al-Ḥusaynī al-Tarīmī, from the *musnid* Shams al-Dīn Muḥammad b. Nāṣir al-Ḥāzimī al-Atharī with a high chain, from the *musnid* of Yemen al-Wajīh ʿAbd al-Raḥmān b. Sulaymān b. Yaḥyā b. ʿUmar Maqbūl al-Ahdal with the chain that was just mentioned to Ibn al-Dībaʿ—Sayyid ʿAbd al-Ḥayy al-Kattānī voiced admiration at the beauty of this chain in his *Fihris*—from his teacher the Hadith master Shams al-Dīn Abū al-Khayr Muḥammad b. ʿAbd al-Raḥmān al-Sakhāwī, from his teacher the Hadith master Ibn Ḥajar who said in *al-Muʿjam al-mufahras*: Abū ʿAlī Muḥammad b. Aḥmad b. ʿAlī b. ʿAbd al-ʿAzīz al-Fāḍilī al-Bazzāz al-Mahdawī, known as Ibn al-Muṭarriz, related to me through my reading of its entirety before him, Abū al-Maḥāsin Yūsuf b. ʿUmar b. Ḥusayn al-Khutanī informed us by audition before him in 724/1324, the hadith master Zakī al-Dīn Abū Muḥammad ʿAbd al-ʿAẓīm b. ʿAbd al-Qawī al-Mundhirī and Abū al-Faḍl Muḥammad b. Muḥammad b. Muḥamad al-Bakrī informed us, Abū Ḥafṣ ʿUmar b. Muḥammad b. Maʿmar b. Ṭabarzad al-Baghdādī informed us by audition before him in Damascus, the two masters Abū al-Badr Ibrāhīm b. Muḥammad b. Manṣūr al-Karkhī and Abū al-Fatḥ Mufliḥ

b. Aḥmad al-Dūmī informed us, Abū ʿUmar al-Qāsim b. Jaʿfar b. ʿAbd al-Wāḥid al-Hāshimī informed us, Abū ʿAlī Muḥammad b. Aḥmad b. ʿAmr al-Lu'lu'ī informed us **Abū Dāwūd Sulaymān b. al-Ashʿath b. Isḥāq b. Bishr b. Shaddād b. ʿAmr b. ʿAmir al-Azdī al-Sijistānī** informed us (i) Musaddad narrated to us that ʿUmar b. ʿUbayd narrated to them; (another route) (ii) Muḥammad b. al-ʿAlā' narrated to us, Abū Bakr—i.e. Ibn ʿAyyāsh—narrated to us; (another) (iii) Musaddad narrated to us, Yaḥyā narrated to us, from Sufyān; (another) (iv) Aḥmad b. Ibrāhīm narrated to us, ʿUbayd Allāh b. Mūsā narrated to us, Zā'ida related to us; (another) (v) Aḥmad b. Ibrāhīm narrated to us, ʿUbayd Allāh b. Mūsā narrated to me, from Fiṭr—to the same effect—all of them from ʿĀṣim, from Zirr, from ʿAbd Allāh [b. Masʿūd], from the Prophet–upon him blessings and peace–who said, "**Even if only one day of this world remained**"—Zā'ida said in his version, "**Allah would prolong that day,**" after which they concurred —"**until He sends on that day a man who is of me or of the people of my House, his name matching mine and his father's name matching my father's.**" Fiṭr's version adds, "**He will fill the earth with equity and justice the way it had been filled with injustice and oppression**" while Sufyān's version has, "**the world will not pass or will not finish until the Arabs will be under the sovereignty of a man of my House whose name will match my name.**"

Aḥmad, al-Tirmidhī, Ibn Ḥibbān, al-Ḥākim, al-Ṭabarānī and others narrated it, some of it in short form. Tirmidhī said, "Similar narrations came from ʿAlī, Abū Saʿīd, Umm Salama and Abū Hurayra. This particular one is a fair and sound hadith." The *ḥāfiẓ* Muḥammad b. Jaʿfar al-Kattānī ranked it as mass-transmitted in *Naẓm al-mutanāthir* as there are no less than twenty Companions among those who narrated about the advent of the Mahdī. He said several scholars related from the *ḥāfiẓ* al-Sakhāwī that it is mass-transmitted. The latter said so in *Fatḥ al-Mughīth* and quoted Abū al-Ḥasan al-Āburrī's (d. 363/974) words in *Maghānī al-wafā bi-ma'ānī al-Iktifā*: "The reports are definitely mass-transmitted and widespread due to the abundance of their reporters from the Prophet–upon him peace–about the coming of the Mahdi and the fact he shall reign for seven years and fill the earth with justice." In his incomplete book on the Mahdī kept in the King 'Abd al-'Azīz Āl Sa'ūd Foundation in Casablanca, Abū al-'Alā' Idrīs b. Muḥammad b. Idrīs al-'Irāqī al-Fāsī (1120-1184/1708-1770) said the hadiths are mass-transmitted on the Mahdī or almost so, and several strict scholars are categorical about the first."

Al-Kattānī also said: "Furthermore, in the commentary on doctrine by Shaykh Muḥammad b. Aḥmad al-Saffārīnī al-Ḥanbalī it is said verbatim, 'The narrations on his coming out are many, to the point of reaching mass transmission in meaning, and this has become widely held by the ulema of *Ahl al-Sunna* to the point it is counted among their firm beliefs. It has been related from those already mentioned of the Companions and others who were not mentioned with numerous narrations, and from the Successors after them in a way that imparts categorical knowledge. Thus belief in the coming out of the Mahdī is obligatory, just as it has been resolved among the people of knowledge and recorded among the beliefs of *Ahl al-Sunna wal-Jamā'a*.'"

(Notes) The upshot of what precedes is that the name of the Mahdī is Muḥammad b. 'Abd Allāh and not Muḥammad b. al-Ḥasan 'Askarī as claimed by the Shī'ī sect. Furthermore, al-'Askarī is a descendant of al-Ḥusayn while the Mahdī is a descendant of al-Ḥasan as also narrated by Abū Dāwūd in his *Sunan* from our liegelord 'Alī–Allah be well-pleased with him–who looked at his son al-Ḥasan and said, "**Truly this son of mine is a leader as the Prophet called him, and there shall come out of his loins a man named after your Prophet and resembling him in character rather than physically.**" Then he retold the account of his filling the earth with justice. 'Alī al-Qārī said in *al-Mirqāt*: "This hadith is an explicit proof over what we already said, namely that the Mahdī is of the offspring of al-Ḥasan and will be affiliated to al-Ḥusayn from his mother's side, which reconciles all the evidence. This shows the falsehood of the Shī'ī claim that 'the Mahdī is Muḥammad b. al-Ḥasan 'Askarī who is the Awaited Rightener' for the latter is of the offpsring of al-Ḥusayn without contest."

(Warning) The agreement of mass transmission status among the experts in the transmission of the Sunna and reports constitutes a rebuttal of non-experts who try to disseminate doubt about the veracity of the Mahdī and of his coming out at the end of time, as when they say, "sound reports about it are unexplicit and explicit reports about it are weak," which is untrue, because the actuality of mass transmission makes the examination of chains superfluous as long as they are not forged. Allah is the grantor of success.

11 The *Sunan* of Ibn Mājah (209-273/824-886)

THE IMAM OF THE BĀ ʿALAWĪ Mosque in Singapore Ḥabīb Ḥasan b. Muḥammad b. Sālim b. Aḥmad b. Ḥasan b. ʿAbd Allāh al-ʿAṭṭās (b. 1371/1951) related to me through my reading before him; and (another route) Shaykh Zakariyyā Bā Gharīb b. ʿAbd Allāh b. Aḥmad b. ʿAbd Allāh b. ʿUmar b. Āl al-Shaykh Muḥammad al-Naqīb Bā Gharīb al-Ḥaḍramī al-Tarīmī (1354-1430/ 1936-2009)–Allah have mercy on him–informed me, the first from his father, from his grandfather al-Ḥabīb Sālim, from the shining knower Ḥabīb Aḥmad b. Ḥasan al-ʿAṭṭās, the second from the erudite jurist, *muḥaddith*, man of letters, and descendant of ʿAbbād b. Bishr al-Awsī al-Anṣārī al-Ḥaḍramī–Allah be well-pleased with him–Shaykh ʿUmar b. ʿAbd Allāh b. Aḥmad b. ʿAbd Allāh b. Abī Bakr b. Sālim al-Khaṭīb al-Anṣārī al-Khazrajī al-Ḥaḍramī al-Tarīmī al-Singafūrī al-Shāfiʿī (1326-1418/1908-1997), from his paternal uncle the erudite Shaykh Abū Bakr b. Aḥmad b. ʿAbd Allāh al-Khaṭīb, from al-Ḥabīb Aḥmad b. Ḥasan al-ʿAṭṭās, from Abū Bakr and Ṣāliḥ the two sons of ʿAbd Allāh al-ʿAṭṭās, both of them from al-Wajīh ʿAbd al-Raḥmān al-Ahdal, from the *ḥāfiẓ* Muḥammad Murtaḍā al-Zabīdī, from the *muḥaddith* of Medina Abū al-Ḥasan al-Sindī al-Ṣaghīr—Muḥammad b. Ṣādiq al-Sindī (1125-1187/1713-1771)—from the *muḥaddith* of the Hijaz Muḥammad Ḥayāt al-Sindī and Sālim b. ʿAbd Allāh al-Baṣrī, both of them from the latter's father the *musnid* ʿAbd Allāh b. Sālim al-Baṣrī, from his teacher Muḥammad b. ʿAlā' al-Dīn al-Bābilī, from Burhān al-Dīn Ibrāhīm b. Ibrāhīm b. Ḥasan al-Laqānī and ʿAlī b. Ibrāhīm al-Ḥalabī, both of them from Shams al-Dīn Muḥammad b. Aḥmad al-Ramlī, from Shaykh al-Islām Zakariyyā, from the Hadith master Ibn Ḥajar, through reading before Abū al-ʿAbbās Aḥmad b. ʿUmar b. ʿAlī b. ʿAbd al-Ṣamad b. Abī al-Badr al-Baghdādī al-Lu'lu'ī who resided in Cairo, the Hadith master Abū al-Ḥajjāj Yūsuf b. al-Zakī ʿAbd al-Raḥmān al-Mizzī informed us through an integral reading I attended in his presence, Shaykh al-Islām Shams al-Dīn ʿAbd al-Raḥmān b. Abī ʿUmar b. Qudāma al-Maqdisī informed us of it by audition, Abū Muḥammad Muwaffaq al-Dīn ʿAbd Allāh b. Aḥmad b. Qudāma informed us by audition, Abū Zurʿa Ṭāhir b. Abī al-Faḍl al-Maqdisī informed us by audition for its entirety, Abū Manṣūr Muḥammad b. Ḥusayn b. Aḥmad b. al-Haytham al-Muqawwimī al-Qazwīnī by audition for its entirety, Abū Ṭalḥa al-Qāsim b. Abī al-Mundhir al-Khaṭīb informed us, Abū al-Ḥasan ʿAlī b. Ibrāhīm b. Salama al-Qaṭṭān informed us, **Abū ʿAbd Allāh Muḥammad b. Yazīd al-Qazwīnī, known as Ibn Mājah**, informed us, Muḥammad b. Ṭarīf narrated to us, Muḥammad b. Fuḍayl narrated to us, al-Aʿmash narrated to us, from Abū Sabra al-Nakhaʿī, from Muḥammad b. Kaʿb al-Quraẓī, from al-ʿAbbās b. ʿAbd al-Muṭṭalib who said, "We would chance on a band of the Quraysh chatting, but as soon as they saw us they would stop talking. We mentioned that to the Prophet–upon him blessings and peace–and he said, '**What is the matter with certain people who are chatting then, as soon as they see a man from the people of my House, they stop talking? I swear by Allah that faith does not**

enter any man's heart until he first loves them for the sake of Allah and for the sake of their kinship to me!'"

A fair hadith. Tirmidhī, Aḥmad, al-Nasā'ī in *al-Sunan al-kubrā* and *Faḍā'il al-ṣaḥāba*, al-Baghawī in *Maṣābīḥ al-Sunna* and Ibn Naṣr al-Marwazī in *al-Sunna* all narrated something identical as expounded by al-Sakhāwī in *Istijlāb irtiqā' al-ghuraf bi-ḥubbi aqribā' al-Rasūl wa-dhawī al-sharaf* (Procuring the ascent to the upper rooms through love of the Prophet's relatives and the noble). Also to that effect from Ibn ʿAbbās, from the Prophet: "**People! Who on earth is dearest to Allah?**" We said "You." He said, "**Well, al-ʿAbbās is part of me and I am part of him; do not harm al-ʿAbbās for that would be harming me. Whoever insults al-ʿAbbās has insulted me.**" ʿAbd Allāh b. Aḥmad narrated it in *Zawā'id faḍā'il al-Ṣaḥāba* and Ibn ʿAsākir, also from Ibn Masʿūd.

(Beneficial points.) Shaykh Zakariyyā was born in the Bā Gharīb Mosque which is known today as the Khadīja Mosque in Singapore. His father Shaykh ʿAbd Allāh (1300-1388/1883-1968) was nick-named *al-Muʿallim* (the teacher). He is the one that drew up the supplication entitled *Īṣāl al-ujūr li-ahl al-qubūr* (The conveyance of rewards to the dwellers of graves) which is famous in southeast Asian countries. I was told that Shaykh ʿUmar al-Khaṭīb would humble himself before Shaykh Zakariyyā and kiss his hand out of respect for the latter's father, who used to be Shaykh ʿUmar's teacher–may Allah have mercy on them all. It is related from Shaykh Zakariyyā's grandfather that he performed Hajj on foot 35 times and his fourth-generation grandfather is described as *Ṣāḥib al-kanziyya* (Owner of the treasure-chest) in reference to the abundance of his sciences; he was made a *quṭb* (spiritual Pole) of the highest *ṣiddīq*s and 1,000 memorizers of the Qur'ān graduated at his hand, among them the *Quṭb* ʿAbd Allāh al-Ḥaddād–may Allah be well-pleased with them.

12 *Akhbār Makka fī qadīm al-dahr wa-ḥadīthih* of Abū al-ʿAbbās al-Fākihī (217?-280?/832?-893?)

THE PHYSICIAN AND NOBLE SUFI Sayyid Dr. ʿAbd Allāh b. Muḥammad Makkī al-Kattānī narrated to me in his clinic in Damascus–may Allah guard her–from his father the *musnid* Muḥammad Makkī b. Muḥammad b. Jaʿfar al-Kattānī al-Dimashqī (d. 1393/1973), from the *muḥaddith* of the Hijaz the Sharif Fāliḥ al-Ẓāhirī (d. 1328/1910), from *al-ḥāfiẓ* Muḥammad b. ʿAlī al-Sanūsī al-Khaṭṭābī (1202-1276/1788-1860), with his high chain (mentioned in the chapter on the *Muwaṭṭa'*) to Ibn Ḥajar, Abū ʿAlī al-Fāḍilī related to us by oral permission, from ʿAlī b. ʿUmar al-Khallāṭī, from ʿAbd al-Raḥmān b. Makkī, from his maternal grandfather the *ḥāfiẓ* Abū Ṭāhir al-Silafī, from Abū Yāsir Muḥammad b. ʿAbd al-ʿAzīz al-Baghdādī (d. 495/1102), from the aged transmissologist of Iraq Abū al-Qāsim ʿAbd al-Malik b. Muḥammad b. ʿAbd Allāh Ibn Bishrān al-Umawī–by clientship–al-Qandī al-Baghdādī the admonisher (339-430/950-1039), from Mecca's *musnid* and *muḥaddith* Abū Muḥammad ʿAbd Allāh b. Muḥammad al-Fākihī al-Makkī (d. 353/964) in Mecca, from his father the author of the book **Abū al-ʿAbbās Muḥammad b. Isḥāq b. al-ʿAbbās al-Fākihī al-Makkī** who said, Muḥammad b. Ismāʿīl al-Bukhārī narrated to us, Ismaʿīl b. Abī Uways narrated to us, my father ʿAbd Allāh b. ʿAbd Allāh al-Aṣbaḥī narrated to us, from Ḥumayd b. Qays al-Makkī the client of the Banū Asad b. ʿAbd al-ʿUzzā, from ʿAṭā' b.

Abī Rabāḥ and others of Ibn ʿAbbās's students, from Ibn ʿAbbās, from the Prophet–upon him blessings and peace: **"O Banū ʿAbd al-Muṭṭalib! Truly I have asked Allah three things for you: that He make firm the upright among you; guide those astray among you; and teach the ignorant among you. I also asked Him to make you giving, quick to help and merciful. If a man stood at length between the Corner and the Station, praying and fasting, then met Allah Most High hating the people of the House of Muḥammad, he would enter the Fire!"** The poet said in reference to standing at length: *he kept standing at length like a horse that stands on three legs, lame.*

Al-Ṭabarānī narrated it in his *Muʿjam al-kabīr* as did al-Fasawī in *al-Maʿrifa*, Ibn Abī ʿĀṣim in *al-Sunna*, Ibn Bishrān in *al-Amālī* and al-Ḥākim who said it is sound by Muslim's criterion although al-Bukhārī and Muslim did not narrate it. However, it is among the reports only Ismāʿīl b. Abī Uways narrates, and although the two arch-masters did rely on him, nevertheless it is implausible that only he and his father would have heard this hadith from Ḥumayd b. Qays, from whom took Maʿmar b. Rāshid, Abū Ḥanīfa, Mālik and the two Sufyāns. This is probably why Abū Ḥātim deemed it *munkar* (disclaimed) in the *ʿIlal* and why al-Shāfiʿī did not narrate it, although he was extremely keen on narrating all Prophetic hadiths in praise of the Banū al-Muṭṭalib, even with anonymous or broken chains. Yet, despite all this, Imam al-Bukhārī did not avoid narrating it, and facts support the soundness of its meaning and the realization of the Prophet's supplication, just as the threat of dire punishment is firmly established for whoever hates Fāṭima, ʿAlī and their two sons—as shown in the following chapter and that of *Maʿrifat al-Ṣaḥāba*—or al-ʿAbbās as shown in the chapters of Ibn Mājah's *Sunan* and al-Bayhaqī's *Dalāʾil al-nubuwwa*. It is also related from Abū Saʿīd al-Khudrī that the Prophet said: **"None hates us—the people of the House—but Allah shall make them enter the Fire."** Al-Ḥākim narrated it and declared it sound.

(Difficult words) *Ṣafin* means one who stands and lines up his feet; the second meaning is that *al-ṣāfin* for a horse is when it points up one its hooves and stands on three legs instead of four. The lame beast is the broken-legged one that is unable to walk.

(Commentary) Dr. ʿAbd Allāh b. Makkī al-Kattānī said:

The upright among you, i.e. their flag is high and their houses frequented; **teach the ignorant among you**, i.e. God-given spiritual knowledge; **guide those astray among you** is a reference to the verse of purification; **giving**, i.e. generous, and generosity is innate in them; **quick to help**, *nujud* from *najda*, which is courage and also service. My father was always busy serving people. So they are generous, brave, learned, and these three traits are found in every descendant of *Ahl al-Bayt*, even the uneducated among them. One example is Sayyid ʿAbd al-ʿAzīz al-Dabbāgh. The latter is, with the Kattānīs, the noblest lineage among the Idrīsīs. **Merciful** is from the mercifulness of their grandfather, the 'Gifted Mercy'–upon him blessings and peace–so that their mercifulness is an inheritance, and one of its illustrations is his putting his own shirt on ʿAbd Allāh b. Ubay, and also because divine mercy precedes everything. The first mark of the friend of Allah is his respect for *Ahl al-Bayt* and offspring of the Prophet–upon him blessings and peace–his love for them and his veneration of them, even if he should be one of them: Shaykh ʿAbd al-Qādir al-Saqqāf said, 'Invoking blessings on the *Āl* is a *farḍ* (categorical obligation) for the *Āl*.' They would say of Sayyid Makkī: He kept respect of us without our noticing it. One person told me one day, 'Try to sit behind your father in the gathering.' I did so, after which I saw him inch back his chair little by little until it was flush with mine. At that time I realized the extent of my father's respect for *Ahl al-Bayt*, even those of his own blood. **Hating the people of the House of Muḥammad**–upon him blessings and peace–**he would enter the Fire**, because hatred of *Ahl al-Bayt* is hatred to our liegelord Muḥammad, which constitutes unbelief by consensus. On the other hand, continual love of *Ahl al-Bayt* down the generations is continual love of him–upon him blessings and peace. This is an everlasting staggering miracle for the Prophet Muḥammad that is palpable for all to witness, as distinct from our love for all other Prophets—upon him and them blessings and peace. Finally, the people of the Prophetic House are a big test for human beings today. As it is said, 'violations do not invalidate rights,' by which we mean: whether they are righteous and pious or not; in fact, that is precisely the test.

(Benefit) The Qur'ān memorizer and teacher and noble singer of spiritual poetry Shaykh ʿAbd al-Raḥmān al-Ḥammāmī al-Maydānī declaimed to me from memory out of al-Rawwās's *Dīwān*:

Look well! You will see the honored Purifier is our sire,
and the well-pleasing one—the Lion among men—our father.
Is there, here and now, of Ṭaha's particles in creation,
anything still visible of his human nature but us?

There will come in the Epilogue, *in shāʾ Allāh*, some of the discourse of Shaykh Muḥyī al-Dīn Ibn ʿArabī in support of the meaning of what preceded.

13 The *Jāmiʿ al-Ṣaḥīḥ* of Abū ʿĪsā al-Tirmidhī (209-279/824-892) i.e. his *Sunan*

SAYYIDĪ SHAYKH MUḤAMMAD TĀJ AL-DĪN b. Muḥammad Makkī b. Muḥammad b. Jaʿfar AL-KATTĀNĪ (1345-1433/ 1927-2012)–Allah have mercy on him–related to me through my reading before him in Jāmiʿ al-Dalāmiyya in Damascus after the blessed *ḥaḍra* and before *maghrib* on Tuesday 7 Rabīʿ al-Awwal 1425 which was 27 April 2004, by virtue of his written license from the Greatest *Muḥaddith*, the erudite Shaykh Badr al-Dīn al-Ḥasanī, from his principal teacher Ibrāhīm b. ʿAlī al-Saqqā al-Azharī, from the saintly Shaykh Thuʿaylīb b. Sālim al-Fashnī, from Aḥmad b. ʿAbd al-Fattāḥ al-Mullawī, from the *musnid* ʿAbd Allāh b. Salim al-Baṣrī, from al-Bābilī with his chain—cited in the chapter on *Ṣaḥīḥ Muslim*—to Shaykh al-Islām. (Another route) In addition, the Qur'ān master, Ḥanafī jurist, *muḥaddith*, preacher and physician SHAYKH SĀMIR B. MAMDŪḤ B. SHARĪF AL-NAṢṢ narrated to us the *Jāmiʿ* verbatim in its entirety, from the *musnid* ʿAlam al-Dīn Abū al-Fayḍ Muḥammad Yāsīn b. Muḥammad ʿĪsā al-Fādānī al-Makkī (1335-1412/ 1917-1992), from ʿAbd al-Qādir Shalabī al-Ṭarābulusī, from the transmissologist Muḥammad Abū al-Naṣr al-Khaṭīb, from al-Wajīh ʿAbd al-Raḥmān al-Kuzbarī the younger, from Muṣṭafā b. Muḥammad al-Raḥmatī, from ʿAbd al-Karīm b. Aḥmad al-Sharābātī, from al-Shams Muḥammad b. ʿAqīlā al-Makkī who said he narrated it all-Sufi-chained, from Shaykh

Ḥasan al-ʿUjaymī al-Ṣūfī, from Shaykh Aḥmad b. Muḥammad al-Qushāshī al-Ṣūfī, from his teacher Aḥmad b. ʿAlī al-Shannāwī al-Ṣūfī, from Shaykh ʿAbd al-Wahhāb al-Shaʿrānī al-Ṣūfī, from Zakariyyā b. Muḥammad the Sufi jurist and Shaykh al-Islām, from the knower of Allah Muḥammad b. Zayn al-Dīn al-Marāghī al-ʿUthmānī al-Ṣufī, from the teacher of Sufis Sharaf al-Dīn Ismāʿīl b. Ibrāhīm al-Jabartī al-Ṣūfī, from the teacher of the people of realization Shaykh Muḥyī al-Dīn Muḥammad b. ʿAlī b. ʿArabī al-Ṭā'ī al-Ḥātimī al-Ṣūfī, from the teacher of teachers ʿAbd al-Wahhāb b. ʿAlī b. Sukayna al-Baghdādī al-Ṣūfī, from Abū al-Fatḥ ʿAbd al-Malik b. ʿAbd Allāh al-Karūkhī al-Ṣūfī, from his teacher the verifying Hadith master Abū Ismāʿīl ʿAbd Allāh b. Muḥammad al-Anṣārī al-Harawī the Sufi Shaykh al-Islām, from ʿAbd al-Jabbār al-Jarrāḥī, from Abū al-ʿAbbās Muḥammad b. Aḥmad b. Maḥbūb al-Maḥbūbī, from the author **Abū ʿĪsā Muḥammad b. ʿĪsā b. Sawra b. Mūsā al-Ḍaḥḥāk al-Sulamī al-Būghī**—from Būgh, a village in the vicinity of Tirmidh, an old city in Balkh (north Afghanistan) on the bank of the Jayḥūn, one of the four rivers of Paradise cited in the Hadith—who wept until he became blind, Naṣr b. ʿAlī al-Jahḍamī narrated to us, ʿAlī [al-ʿUrayḍī] b. Jaʿfar b. Muḥammad b. ʿAlī narrated to us, my brother Mūsā [al-Kāẓim] b. Jaʿfar b. Muḥammad related to me, from his father Jaʿfar [al-Ṣādiq] b. Muḥammad, from his father Muḥammad [al-Bāqir] b. ʿAlī, from his father ʿAlī [Zayn al-ʿĀbidīn] b. al-Ḥusayn, from his father, from his grandfather ʿAlī b. Abī Ṭālib, that the Prophet–upon him and them blessings and peace–took Ḥasan and Ḥusayn by the hand and said, **"Whoever loves me and loves these two and their father and mother,**

shall be with me at my level on the Day of resurrection." Abū ʿĪsā said, "This is a fair and single-chained hadith, we do not know it to be narrated from Jaʿfar b. Muḥammad other than thus."

ʿAbd Allāh b. Aḥmad b. Ḥanbal narrated it in the addenda to his father's *Musnad* and Ibn al-Jazarī in *Asnā al-maṭālib fī manāqib Asad Allāh al-ghālib* through al-Qaṭīʿī, from ʿAbd Allāh, from Naṣr b. ʿAlī. Abū Nuʿaym recounted in his *Tārīkh Aṣbahān* that Aḥmad b. Ḥanbal said, "If you were to read this chain of transmission—i.e. the *Ahl al-Bayt* segment—over a madman he would be cured on the spot." Al-Dhahabī, however, said in the *Siyar*:

> This is a very disclaimed hadith. ʿAbd Allāh b. Aḥmad said "When Naṣr narrated this, al-Mutawwakkil ordered he be lashed 100 strokes but Jaʿfar b. ʿAbd al-Wāḥid intervened saying the man was from *Ahl al-Sunna* and he persisted until he left him alone." Al-Khaṭīb said after recounting this: "Al-Mutawakkil only gave the order to lash him because he thought he was a Rāfiḍī." Al-Mutawakkil himself was a Sunni but there was some hatred of *Ahl al-Bayt* in him. As for the narrators of the report they are all trustworthy except for ʿAlī b. Jaʿfar, so it may be the latter did not clinch the exact wording of the hadith. Surely the Prophet–upon him blessings and peace–did not, out of his love and the proclamation of the merit of al-Ḥasan and al-Ḥusayn, place everyone of those who love them on his own level in Paradise! Perhaps what he said was, **"shall be with me in Paradise."**

In the *Mīzān* Dhahabī goes on to deny that Tirmidhī rated it fair or sound, so the grading of *ḥasan* is in some variant manuscript tradition. (E.g. it is not in Mizzī's *Tuḥfat al-ashrāf*.) Then he said, "no one declared ʿAlī b. Jaʿfar malleable," apparently rebutting himself. His grading of "very disclaimed" and the justifications he gives are conjectural at best, if not disparaging.

Al-Tirmidhī narrated other Prophetic hadiths on the same topic besides what we narrate full-chained in this volume. Among them: I. From Ḥudhayfa: "**Verily this is an angel who never came down to earth before tonight. He asked permission of his Lord to greet me and give me the glad tiding that Fāṭima is the leader of the people of Paradise and that al-Ḥasan and al-Ḥusayn are the two leaders of the youth of the people of Paradise.**" II. From Ibn ʿAbbās: "**Love Allah for what He feeds you of His bounties; love me for love of Allah; and love the people of my House for love of me**" (see the chapter of Ibn ʿAsākir's *Buldāniyya*). III. From Zayd b. Arqam, the Prophet–upon him blessings and peace–said to ʿAlī, Fāṭima, al-Ḥasan and al-Ḥusayn, "**I am war for whoever you wage war on and peace**

for whoever you make peace with." He said it was single-chained. It is also related by Ibn Mājah, Bazzār, Ṭabarānī in his three *Mu'jams*, Ibn Abī Shayba, Ibn Ḥibbān, al-Ḥākim and al-Ājurrī in *al-Sharī'a*. It has witness-narrations (i) in Aḥmad's *Musnad* and *Faḍā'il al-Ṣaḥāba*, al-Ḥākim, al-Ṭabarānī in *al-Kabīr* and Ājurrī from Abū Hurayra; (ii) Ibn Shāhīn's *Faḍā'il al-nisā'* from Abū Sa'īd; and (iii) Ibn Jumay''s *Mu'jam al-shuyūkh* and Ibn 'Asākir's *Tārīkh* from Umm Salama. IV. From Ya'lā b. Murra al-'Āmirī: "**Ḥusayn is part of me and I am part of Ḥusayn. Allah love whoever loves Ḥusayn! Ḥusayn is some clan among clans!**" He declared it fair. There are other reports as well. The latter wording is found in Tirmidhī, Aḥmad, Bukhārī in *al-Adab al-mufrad*, Ibn Abī Shayba, al-Ṭabarānī, Ibn Ḥibbān and Abū Nu'aym in *Ma'rifat al-Ṣaḥāba*. Another wording has "**Ḥusayn is part of me and I am part of Ḥusayn. Allah love whoever loves Ḥusayn! Al-Ḥasan and al-Ḥusayn are some two clans among clans!**" in Bukhārī's *Tārīkh*, al-Ṭabarānī's *Mu'jam al-kabīr* and *Musnad al-Shāmiyyīn* and Abū Nu'aym in the *Ma'rifa*. "That is, a nation among nations in goodness. Clans, among Ibrāhīm's children–upon him peace–have the status of tribes among the children of Ismā'īl" (*Nihāya*). It is related from al-Miqdām b. Ma'dīkarb that the Prophet–upon him blessings and peace–said, "**Ḥasan is part of me and al-Ḥusayn is part of 'Alī.**" Narrated by Ṭabarānī and Ibn 'Asākir with a chain graded fair by al-Dhahabī, al-'Irāqī and al-Munāwī despite the fact that its sub-narrator Baqiyya b. al-Walīd used vague transmission terminology. It means "al-Ḥasan resembles me while al-Ḥusayn resembles 'Alī:" al-Ḥasan mostly displayed forbearance and deliberateness like the Prophet–upon him blessings and peace–while al-Ḥusayn showed toughness like 'Alī according to al-Munāwī in *al-Taysīr bi-sharḥ al-Jami' al-ṣaghīr*. Qārī said in the *Mirqāt*: "He meant the division of the two children among the two parents, so the eldest goes to the grandfather and the youngest goes to father as is well-known in custom." A firmly-established report from Abū Bakrat al-Thaqafī in al-Bukhārī's *Ṣaḥīḥ*, the *Musnad* and the *Sunan* has, "As the Prophet–upon him blessings and peace–was giving a sermon al-Ḥasan came, whereupon the Prophet said '**My son right here is a leader. Allah may reconcile, through him, two large factions of the Muslims.**'"

(Subtleties.) Sayyid Tāj told me one time, as we rode together in the same car, that he had seen our liegelord Jibrīl–upon him peace. It is indeed related that on the Night of Worth he greets every single believer; may Allah grant us His greeting and peace! And "the hearts of the knowers have eyes that see what onlookers cannot see" (al-Tustarī). When I returned from pilgrimage he only said: "Did you supplicate for the *Umma*?" I gave him a rare copy of the *Forty Hadiths on the Virtues of Ahl al-Bayt* by his grandfather Muḥammad b. Ja'far. May Allah reunite us with them and our teachers at the feet of their greatest grandfather the greatest Beloved.

14 The *Muntaqā* (Selection) from al-Ḥārith Ibn Abī Usāma's *Musnad* (186-282/802-895)

THE VENERABLE aged Qur'ān master of Damascus and righteous friend of Allah, Shaykh Muḥammad Salīm al-Ḥammāmī al-Maydānī al-Shāfiʿī (1326-1434/1908-2013) –Allah have mercy on him–informed us in his house in the Maydān quarter of Damascus, as did the Hadith teacher in the Faculty of Sharīʿa in the Islamic University of Beirut, the historian and transmissologist Shaykh Yūsuf b. ʿAbd al-Raḥmān b. Fu'ād al-Marʿashlī al-Ḥusaynī (b. 1952) the author of several catalogues of shaykhs, editions and indices; the first one said, Shaykh Badr al-Dīn al-Ḥasanī informed us, from the erudite Sayyid ʿAbd al-Qādir b. Ṣāliḥ al-Khaṭīb, from al-Kuzbarī, with his chain to Shaykh ʿAbd al-Ghanī al-Nābulusī; the second one said, Muḥammad b. ʿAbd al-Razzāq b. Muḥammad al-Khaṭīb al-Ḥasanī informed us, from Abū al-Naṣr Naṣr Allāh b. ʿAbd al-Qādir b. Ṣāliḥ al-Khaṭīb (1253-1325/1837-1907), from ʿAbd Allāh b. Muḥammad al-Tallī al-Shāmī (1115?-1265/1703?-1849), from ʿAbd al-Ghanī al-Nābulusī (1050-1143/1640-1731) if correct, with the chain already mentioned in the chapter on Maʿmar b. Rāshid's *Jāmiʿ* to the *ḥāfiẓ* Ibn Ḥajar, through his reading before the *musnida* Fāṭima bint Muḥammad b. ʿAbd al-Hādī al-Maqdisiyya al-Ṣāliḥiyya, through her license from Ibrāhīm b. Ṣāliḥ b. al-ʿAjmī, through his reading before Yūsuf b. Khalīl the Hadith master who said, Khalīl b. Badr al-Rārānī informed us, Abū

ʿAlī al-Ḥaddād informed us, Abū Nuʿaym informed us, Abū Bakr b. Khallād narrated to us, from **Abū Muḥammad al-Ḥārith b. Muḥammad b. Abī Usāma**, Isḥāq b. Bishr narrated to us, ʿAmmār b. Yūsuf al-Ḍabbī—Sufyān al-Thawrī's legatee—from Hishām b. ʿUrwa, from his father, from ʿAbd Allāh b. ʿUmar or ʿAbd Allāh b. ʿAmr that the Prophet–upon him blessings and peace–said: "**I have asked my nurturing Lord that I not marry into anyone of my Community nor that anyone marry into me except they will be with me in Paradise, and He gave me that.**"

Al-Ṭabarānī and al-Ḥākim narrated it from ʿAbd Allāh b. Abī Awfā. Al-Shirāzī also narrated in *al-Alqāb* from Ibn ʿAbbās that the Messenger of Allah–upon him blessings and peace–said, "**I asked my Lord that I not marry off but to people of Paradise and that I not marry into other than people of Paradise.**" Aḥmad and al-Ḥākim narrated from al-Miswar that the Prophet said: "**Fāṭima is a piece of my flesh, whatever distresses her distresses me and whatever delights her delights me. Verily lineages will all be cut off on the Day of resurrection except my lineage and my line and relationships to me.**" This report is fully documented in the chapter on Abū Yaʿlā's *Musnad*. Munāwī said in *Fayḍ al-Qadīr*: "It appears that this [privilege] includes whoever marries or gets married off among his descendants; this means great tidings for whoever becomes related through marriage to a Sharif or a Sharifa."

The fact that *Ahl al-Bayt* spouses and inlaws are all bound for bliss is clarified by what Ibn ʿAsākir narrated in *al-Arbaʿīn fī manāqib Ummahāt al-muʾminīn*, Hadith 37, from ʿAlī–Allah be well-pleased with him–that the Prophet–upon him blessings and peace–said: "**None that marries into me or that I marry into enters Hellfire.**" He added, "This is a fair hadith from the Commander of the believers Abū al-Ḥasan ʿAlī b. Abī Ṭālib–may Allah ennoble his countenance–and in this hadith there is evidence for the virtue of his brothers and sons-in-law, and this is a testimony that they are in Paradise as long as they are believers, and Allah knows best." Al-Ḥārith also narrated from Muḥammad b. al-Ḥanafiyya—in *mursal* mode—as did Abū Yaʿlā, Ibn Abī al-Dunyā and Ibn ʿAsākir from Abū Hurayra that al-Ḥasan and al-Ḥusayn wrestled in the presence of the Messenger of Allah–upon him blessings and peace–and the latter was saying, "**Go, Ḥasan!**" whereupon Fāṭima said: "Messenger of Allah, it seems he is more beloved to you than al-Ḥusayn?" He replied, "**Jibrīl is helping al-Ḥusayn, and I love to help al-Ḥasan.**"

(Notes of benefit.) Sayyid Muḥammad Abū al-Hudā al-Ya'qūbī said: "We had no doubt that Shaykh Salīm al-Ḥammāmī was one of the Substitutes (*abdāl*)." He also said, "I visited him one time in his house and he went into a room and came out carrying a large sum of money which he gave to me saying: 'I just want you to say, "Salim is from us, the people of the House."'" There are indeed Ḥammāmīs who are Sharifs, namely those that branch off the Ḥusaynī Mūsawīs of Iraq, descendants of Sayyid Hāshim b. Ibrāhīm b. Ja'far b. Mūsā b. Aḥmad al-Madanī who owned a hammam in the Mishrāq district of the city of Najaf in Iraq. Some are 'Umarīs, descendants of the Fārūq 'Umar b. al-Khaṭṭāb–Allah be well-pleased with him–especially in Palestine and Jordan. May Allah shower with abundant blessings and peace the Prophet and his Family!

15 *Al-Sunna* by Ibn Abī ʿĀṣim (206-287/821-900)

THE CENTENARIAN Aleppine specialist of inheritance law Sayyid Muḥammad b. Darwīsh b. Muḥammad al-Khaṭīb b. Muṣṭafā b. Muḥammad ʿArab al-Ḥusaynī al-Shāfiʿī (1322-1432/1904-2011)–Allah have mercy on him–informed us, from his teacher the historian of Aleppo, Shaykh Muḥammad Rāghib al-Ṭabbākh al-Ḥanafī (1293-1370/ 1876-1951), from Sayyid Khālid b. Muḥammad b. ʿAbd al-Sattār al-Atāsī al-Ḥimṣī (1253-1326/1837-1908), from his father Muḥammad, his uncle Saʿīd and Shaykh Muḥammad b. Sulaymān al-Jūkhadār, the first two from ʿAbd al-Sattār al-Atāsī and the third from Sayyid Saʿīd al-Ḥabbāl al-Ḥalabī, both of them from Shams al-Dīn Muḥammad b. ʿAbd al-Raḥmān al-Kuzbarī famed as al-Awsaṭ (1140-1221/1728-1806), from his father ʿAbd al-Raḥmān al-Kuzbarī al-Kabīr, from Abū al-Mawāhib al-Ḥanbalī, from his father ʿAbd al-Bāqī, from Abū Ḥafṣ ʿUmar al-Qārī, from Badr al-Dīn Muḥammad al-Ghazzī, from Shaykh al-Islām al-Qāḍī Zakariyyā, from the *ḥāfiẓ* Ibn Ḥajar, Abū al-ʿAbbās Aḥmad b. Abī Bakr al-Maqdisī and Abū Muḥammad Ibrāhīm b. Muḥammad b. Ṣiddīq both related to us, Isḥāq b. Yaḥyā al-Āmidī informed us, from Yūsuf b. Khalīl the Hadith master, the aged transmissologist Abū Jaʿfar Muḥammad b. Aḥmad b. Naṣr al-Ṣaydalānī informed us (night before ʿEid al-Aḍḥa 509-603/1116-1207) through reading before him, Maḥmūd b. Ismāʿīl al-Ṣayrafī informed us, Abū Bakr Muḥammad b. ʿAbd Allāh b. Shādhān informed us, Abū Bakr ʿAbd Allāh b. Muḥammad al-Qabbāb informed us,

Abū Bakr Aḥmad b. ʿAmr b. al-Ḍaḥḥāk b. Abīʿ Āṣim al-Nabīl al-Shaybānī informed us, Muḥammad b. al-Muthannā b. ʿUbayd narrated to us, Buhlūl b. al-Muwarriq al-Shāmī narrated to us, Mūsā b. ʿUbayda narrated to us, ʿAmr b. ʿAbd Allāh b. Nawfal—a scion of ʿAdī b. Kaʿb — narrated to me, from Muḥammad b. Muslim al-Zuhrī, from Abū Salama b. ʿAbd al-Raḥmān, from ʿĀ'isha–Allah be well-pleased with her–that the Messenger of Allah–upon him blessings and peace–said: **"Jibrīl told me, 'I have turned over the earth, its easts and its wests, and have not found a single man better than Muḥammad, upon him blessings and peace; and I have turned over the earth, its easts and its wests, and have not found any sons of a father better than the Banū Hāshim.'"**

Al-Ṭabarānī narrated it in *al-Awsaṭ*, Abū Nuʿaym in the *Dalā'il* and *Ḥadīth al-Kudaymī*, al-Dūlābī in *al-Dhurriyya al-ṭāhira*, al-Qaṭīʿī in *Zawā'id al-Faḍā'il*, al-Shajarī in his *Amālī al-khamīsiyya* through the latter, al-Ḥākim in *al-Kunā*, Bayhaqī in the *Dalā'il* and Ibn ʿAsākir in his *Tārīkh*. The Hadith master Ibn Ḥajar said in *al-Amālī al-muṭlaqa*: "This is a lone-narrated hadith, Mūsā b. ʿUbayda alone narrates it; and although he is weak and his shaykh is unknown, nevertheless the signs of veracity shine over the pages of this text. Alah knows best." See more on this in the chapter on *Nawādir al-uṣūl*. Bayhaqī said: "These hadiths, although coming through narrators that do not make them sound, nevertheless confirm one another, and their collective meaning all goes back to what we narrated from Wāthila b. al-Asqaʿ and Abū Hurayra, and Allah knows best." By the former he means the hadith, **"I was sent from the best of the generations of the sons of Adam, generation after generation, until I was from the one in which I found myself"** (Bukhārī narrated it) and by the latter the hadith **"Verily Allah Most High selected Kināna out of the children of Ismāʿīl and He selected Quraysh out of Kināna and He selected, out of Quraysh, Banū Hāshim, and he selected me out of Banū Hāshim"** (Muslim narrated it).

Our hadith was also narrated by the Qadi Abū al-Faraj al-Muʿāfā b. Zakariyyā' with his chain in *al-Jalīs al-ṣāliḥ* where he said: "Glory to Allah Who preferred our Prophet Muḥammad over all other Prophets, and He preferred the sons of his ancestor over the sons of all other ancestors, and He made us be part of his Community which is *the best community ever produced for people* (Āl ʿImrān 3:110), and He guided us to declaring him truthful and believing in him, and He granted us the success of following him, and He set us clearly apart from those stubbornly denied him, rebelled against him and envied him, and He protected us from competing with his intimates and his family, relatives and near kin in whatever Allah gave them of His favor and generosity, bringing them near out of His munificence. This is because of His beautiful grant and fair protection. He thereby preferred us to many of his kinsmen, who took up arms against him and did their best to oppose him, many of whom were destroyed in the process: have you not heard what Allah revealed concerning Abū Lahab—yet he was a Hashemite —and the Prophet's saying about Salmān al-Fārisī–Allah be well-pleased with him–who was a foreign non-Arab? Allah also said, *Verily the nearest of people to Ibrāhīm are those who followed him, and this Prophet, and those who believed! Allah is the friend of the believers* (Āl ʿImrān 3:68).

(Note of benefit.) Al-Māwardī said in *al-Ḥāwī al-kabīr*:

> The Baghdad school among our colleagues hold that the Quraysh have different ranks of superiority depending on their nearness to the Prophet and are not, therefore, equally suitable matches to one another, due to (i) this narration from ʿĀ'isha; (ii) and because, as Quraysh was given eminence over the rest of the Arabs through the Messenger of Allah, the nearest in kinship to the Messenger of Allah among them is more eminent than the rest of Quraysh; (iii) and because the fact that they had different ranks on the record by nearness in kinship until they were distributed according to ten different ranks, indicates the same ranking distinction in matching suitability. This being the case, it follows that the Banū Hāshim and the Banū al-Muṭṭalib are all mutually suitable matches, followed next by the rest of the Banū ʿAbd Manāf and the Banū Zuhra. The Banū ʿAbd Shams are not given preference over the Banū Nawfal in marriage matching suitability, nor the Banū ʿAbd al-ʿUzzā over the Banū ʿAbd al-Dār, nor the Banū ʿAbd Manāf over the Banū Zuhra. We join together the latter two in marriage matching suitability—although they do not form one and the same clan—due to al-Awzāʿī's narration from the Prophet–upon him blessings and peace: **"The pure-blooded Quraysh are the two sons of Kilāb"** [Ibn ʿAsākir] meaning the Banū Quṣay and the Banū Zuhra, and because the Prophet goes back to Quṣay through his father and to Zuhra through his mother so they are suitable matches through his two parents. The rest of the Quraysh follow next after the ʿAbd Manāf and the Banū Zuhra, so they are all mutually suitable matches. As for the rest of the Arabs besides the Quraysh they follow the same lines of divergence our colleagues drew for Quraysh. By the Basrians' reasoning they are all suitable marriage matches from ʿAdnān

and Qaḥṭān—the forerunners of the Emigrants and the Helpers respectively; and by the Baghdadis' reasoning, they outrank one another and are not suitable marriage matches: Muḍar above Rabīʿa and ʿAdnān above Qahṭān, in light of the nearness in kinship to the Messenger of Allah–upon him blessings and peace.

16 *Al-Āḥād wal-mathānī* (Single and paired Hadith narrations by Companions) by Ibn Abī ʿĀṣim (206-287/821-900)

THE LEARNED SUFI globe-trotter scholar, eloquent summoner and preacher al-Ḥabīb ʿAlī Zayn al-ʿĀbidīn b. ʿAbd al-Raḥmān al-Jifrī al-Yamanī al-Tarīmī (b. 1971)–Allah guard him–related to me through my reading before him in his father's house in the town of Kayfūn in the southern Metn, Mount Lebanon: Sayyidī al-Ḥabīb Shaykh ʿAbd al-Qādir b. Aḥmad al-Saqqāf–may Allah have mercy on him–related to me, from his father with his chain already mentioned in the chapter of Imam Aḥmad's *Musnad* to the Hadith master Ibn Ḥajar from Abū Hurayra Ibn al-Dhahabī ʿAbd al-Raḥmān b. Muḥammad b. Aḥmad (715-799/1315-1397), from his father the Syro-Turkic Hadith master al-Shams Muḥammad b. Aḥmad b. ʿUthmān b. Qāymāz al-Turkmānī al-Dhahabī (673-748/1275-1347), from his teacher the Hadith master Sharaf al-Dīn al-Dimyāṭī (613-705/1216-1306), from Abū Muḥammad ʿAbd Allāh b. Barakāt b. Ibrāhīm Ibn al-Khushūʿī al-Dimashqī (573-658/1177-1260), from his certifying teacher the expert Hadith master Taqī al-Dīn, Shaykh al-Islam, the liegelord of Hadith masters, Abū Mūsā Muḥammad b. Abī Bakr ʿUmar b. Abī ʿĪsā Aḥmad al-Madīnī (501-581/1108-1185) who said: Abū ʿAlī al-Ḥasan b. Aḥmad b. al-Ḥasan al-Muqri' al-Ḥaddād informed us, Abū al-Qāsim ʿAbd al-Raḥmān b. Muḥammad b. ʿAbd al-Raḥmān narrated to us, Abū Bakr

ʿAbd Allāh b. Muḥammad b. Muḥammad b. Fūrak al-Qabbāb narrated to us, from its author the imam Abū Bakr Aḥmad b. ʿAmr b. Abī ʿĀṣim al-Ḍaḥḥāk b. Mukhallad al-Nabīl al-Qāḍī al-Shaybānī al-Baṣrī al-Ẓāhirī the author of *al-Sunna, Faḍl al-ṣalāt ʿalā al-Nabī*, the *Mawlid, Faḍā'il al-ʿAbbās b. ʿAbd al-Muṭṭalib, Faḍā'il Muʿāwiya b. Abī Sufyān* and *al-Ḥulamā'*, who said in his book *al-Āḥād wal-mathānī*: Abū Saʿīd ʿAbd al-Raḥmān b. Ibrāhīm narrated to us, ʿAbd al-Raḥmān b. Bashīr informed us, from Muḥammad b. Isḥāq, both Nāfiʿ the freedman of Ibn ʿUmar and Zayd b. Aslam narrated to me: (1) from Ibn ʿUmar; (2) from Saʿīd b. Abī Saʿīd al-Maqburī, from Abū Hurayra; (3) from Muḥammad b. al-Munkadir, from Abū Hurayra; and (4) from ʿAmmār b. Yāsir–Allah be well-pleased with them–who [all three] said: "Durra the daughter of Abū Lahab emigrated to Medina and stayed at the house of Rāfiʿ b. al-Muʿallā al-Zuraqī. Some Banū Zurayq women sat next to her and said, 'You are the daughter of Abū Lahab, concerning whom Allah the Almighty said, *Perish the two hands of Abū Lahab and perish he! His wealth and all he acquired availed him nothing* (al-Masad 111:1-2)? Your emigrating avails you nothing!'" Durra went to the Prophet and complained to him about what they had said to her. He calmed her down and said to her: "**Sit.**" Then he led the people in the noon prayer and sat at the pulpit for a time. Then he said, **"O people! Why am I being harmed about my relatives? I swear by Allah that my intercession shall reach [even the remote tribes of] Ḥā, and Ḥakm, and Ṣadā', and Salhab on the Day of resurrection!"**

Ṭaḥāwī narrated it in *Mushkil al-āthār* as **I swear by Allah that my intercession shall be obtained through being related to me, and even Ḥakmā, and Ḥā, and Ṣadā', and Salhab shall obtain it on the**

Day of resurrection through their being related to me! So did al-Ṭabarānī in *al-Kabīr* in the wording **shall certainly reach the clan of Ḥā and Ḥakm** to the end of the report, and Abū Nu'aym in *Ma'rifat al-ṣaḥāba* in the wording **even Arḥā', and Ḥakmā, and Ṣadā', and Salhab through whatever they have on the Day of resurrection through being related to me!** All of them narrate it through the Damascene 'Abd al-Raḥmān b. Bashīr, of whom Abū Ḥātim said he was disclaimed in Hadith. Thus in Ibn Abī Ḥātim's *'Ilal*: "I asked my father about a hadith related by 'Abd al-Raḥmān b. Bashīr"—he mentioned it—"and Ibn Isḥāq's statement, 'This hadith serves to validate the genealogists of Muḍar in deeming these tribes to belong to Ma'add.' My father said, 'I don't consider this hadith sound.'" Ibn Ḥajar graded it weak in the *Iṣāba*. Nonetheless Ibn Bashīr was deemed trustworthy by Duḥaym and Ibn Ḥibbān, and Muḥammad b. 'Ā'idh cited him in good terms as shown in the *Lisān*. It is strengthened by Umm Hāni's similar hadith through trustworthy narrators which is narrated in full in the chapter of the *Mu'jam al-kabīr*. It is authentically related that the Prophet said, "**The best men are the men of Yemen, and belief is Yemeni, and I am Yemeni!** Imam Aḥmad narrated it in his *Musnad* from 'Amr b. 'Abasa. Al-Ḥabīb al-Jifrī said, concerning the meaning of the Prophet's statement **and I am Yemeni**: "The houses of the Banū Hāshim were located in the direction of the Yemeni corner of the Ka'ba." Al-Bayhaqī relates in *Manāqib al-Shāfi'ī* through Yazid b. 'Abd al-Malik al-Nawfalī al-Madanī who is weak, from Sa'īd b. Abī Sa'īd, from Abū Hurayra, that Subay'a the daughter of Abū Lahab came to the Prophet–upon him blessings and peace–and said, "Messenger of Allah, I scandalize people! They are saying I am the daughter of the fuel of hellfire!" The Prophet got up [on the pulpit] in a state of great anger. He said, "**What is wrong with certain people who are hurting me about my relatives? Behold, whoever hurts my relatives hurts me, and whoever hurts me, hurts Allah Most High!**" Al-Dhahabī mentioned it in the *Mīzān* with **my lineage and paternal relatives** instead of **my relatives**. The Hadith Arch-master said in *al-Iṣāba*, "Ibn Mandah documented it through Yazīd b. 'Abd al-Malik al-Nawfalī who is flimsy, from Sa'īd al-Maqburī, from Abū Hurayra." Then he said, "Muḥammad b. Isḥāq and others narrated it from al-Maqburī and they all said, 'Durra the daughter of Abū Lahab came...' and he mentioned something similar. Abū Nu'aym said Durra is the correct version. I say that it is possible she bore two names, one of which was a nickname, or that the story took place with two different women."

17 *Nawādir al-uṣūl* (The Precious Foundations) by al-Ḥakīm al-Tirmidhī (?-?)

SAYYIDĪ al-Ḥabīb Sālim b. ʿAbd Allāh b. ʿUmar al-Shāṭirī (1359-1439/1940-2018)–may Allah have mercy on him–informed us, the erudite al-Ḥabīb Sālim b. Ḥafīẓ b. al-Shaykh Abī Bakr and the grammar and law expert al-Ḥabīb Muḥammad b. Hādī b. Ḥasan al-Saqqāf al-Say'ūnī (1291-1382/1874-1962) informed us, both of them from the transmissologist ʿAydarūs b. ʿUmar al-Ḥabsḥī and the erudite centenarian Shaykh ʿAwaḍ b. Muḥammad al-ʿAfrī al-Zabīdī (1231-1344/1816-1926) and the latter from his father Hādī b. Hasan al-Saqqāf (d. 1336/1918) who is his most important teacher; al-Ḥabshī said in *Minḥat al-Fattāḥ*: from Sayyidī ʿAbd Allāh b. ʿUmar b. Abī Bakr b. Yaḥyā, from Shaykh Yūsuf b. Muḥammad b. ʿAlā' al-Dīn al-Mizjājī, from Sayyid Aḥmad b. Muḥammad Sharīf Maqbūl al-Ahdal, from the transmissologist ʿAbd Allāh b. Sālim al-Baṣrī with a high chain; while al-ʿAfrī and al-Saqqāf said, from Sayyid Ismāʿīl b. Zayn al-ʿĀbidīn al-Barzanjī, from Shaykh Ṣāliḥ al-Fullānī, from Muḥammad b. ʿAbd Allāh al-Maghribī, from the transmissologist of the Hijaz Jamāl al-Dīn ʿAbd Allāh b. Sālim al-Baṣrī with a high chain, who said, I took the *Nawādir* from our teacher Shams al-Dīn Shihab al-Dīn Abū ʿAbd Allāh Muḥammad b. ʿAlā' al-Dīn al-Bābilī al-Shāfiʿī al-Qāhirī, from Zayn al-Dīn ʿAbd Allāh b. Muḥammad al-Niḥrīrī, from Jamāl al-Dīn Yūsuf b. Zakariyyā, from his father Shaykh al-Islām, from Abū al-Faḍl Aḥmad b. Ḥajar who said, Abū al-Ḥasan ʿAlī b. Muḥammad b. Abī al-Majd related to us through his oral permission, from Sulaymān b. Ḥamza al-Ṭayālisī, from ʿĪsā b. ʿAbd al-ʿAzīz—the last of those who narrate from him—from the genealogist Hadith master Abū Saʿd ʿAbd al-Karīm b. Muḥammad al-Samʿānī—the last of those who narrate from him—who said Abū al-Faḍl Muḥammad b. ʿAlī b. Saʿīd b. al-Muṭahhar informed us by permission, the preacher Isḥāq b. Ibrāhīm b. Muḥammad al-Būqī (from Būq in Antioch) informed us, Abū Bakr Muḥammad b. ʿAbd al-Raḥmān al-Muqri' (or al-Maqburī) informed us, Abū Naṣr Aḥmad b. Aḥīd b. Ḥamdān al-Bīkandī informed us, **al-Ḥakīm Muḥammad b. ʿAlī al-Tirmidhī** informed us in the 223rd Foundation: my father narrated to us, al-Ḥimmānī narrated to us, Ibn Numayr narrated to us, from Mūsā b. ʿUbayda, from Iyās b. Salama b. al-Akwaʿ, from his father–may Allah be well-pleased with him: the Messenger of Allah–upon him blessings and peace–said: **"The stars are a security for the dwellers of the sky and my family are a security for my Community."**

Musaddad and Abū Bakr b. Abī Shayba narrated it as well as, from the latter, AbūYaʿlā, al-Ṭabarānī in *al-Kabīr*, Rūyānī in his *Musnad*, Ibn al-Aʿrābī in his *Muʿjam*, al-Fasawī in *al-Maʿrifa wal-tārīkh*, al-Khaṭīb in *al-Muwaḍḍiḥ*, and Ibn ʿAsākir in his *Tārīkh*. Their chains all pivot on Mūsā b. ʿUbayda al-Rabadhī, of whom al-Tirmidhī said, "He is generally considered weak in Hadith in relation to his memorization, though truthful." This is because he was engrossed in worship and is "among the best of people" as stated by al-Bazzār. The Arch-master validated him, as seen in the chapter on Ibn Abī ʿĀṣim's *al-Sunna*. Moreover, the wording **My family are a security for my Community** is also narrated by al-Ḥākim from Ibn ʿAbbās, Jābir, and al-Munkadir b. ʿAbd Allāh b. al-Hudayr al-Tamīmī; by al-Qaṭīʿī in the addenda to Aḥmad b. Ḥanbal's *Faḍā'il al-Ṣaḥāba* from ʿAlī; and by al-Shajarī in his *Amālī* in the wording **My family are a security**

for those on earth through very weak chains, also by al-Daylamī. What is well-preserved is the confinement of that wording to the Companions as in *Ṣaḥīḥ Muslim*. Allah Most High knows best.

Al-Ḥakīm al-Tirmidhī said:

As for his saying **My family are a security for my Community**: his family are those he leaves behind to walk his path after his time, namely the *awliyā* (friends of Allah) and the *abdāl* (substitutes) of whom ʿAlī narrated that the Prophet said "**Verily the substitutes will be in Syro-Palestine and they are forty men; every time one of them dies, Allah replaces him with another. With them rain is watered down; with them victory is won over enemies; with them affliction is deflected from those on earth.**" [Narrated by Aḥmad in the wording **punishment is deflected from the people of Syro-Palestine**, most likely a statement of ʿAlī and it is sound.] Those, then, are the people of the House of the Messenger of Allah and the trust of this Community; when they die, the earth becomes corrupt and the world is ruined. Allah said, *Were it not that Allah repels people from one another, the earth would have been corrupted* (al-Baqara 2:251).

18 The *Musnad* of al-Bazzar (210-292/825-905), 'The Plenteous Sea'

MAWLANA Shaykh Abū Saʿīd Muḥammad ʿAdnān al-Majd al-Ḥasanī (1363-1441/1944-2020)–Allah have mercy on him–the imam and teacher at the Mosque of Shaykh Ruslān at the Bāb Tūmā gate of Damascus—one of its seven gates—narrated to me, my master Shaykh Ibrāhīm al-Yaʿqūbī narrated to me, from his paternal uncle the most learned Shaykh al-Sayyid Muḥammad al-Sharīf al-Yaʿqūbī the imam of the Malikis in the Banū Umayya mosque in Damascus, from the Sharif and *mujāhid* the emir ʿAbd al-Qadir al-Jazāʾirī and the two Sharifs Shaykh Bakrī b. Ḥāmid al-ʿAṭṭār and Shaykh Salīm b. Yāsīn al-ʿAṭṭār (1233-1307/1818-1890), the latter two from the latter's grandfather Ḥāmid b. Aḥmad b. ʿUbayd Allāh, from his father the *mujāhid*, hadith scholar, jurist, exegete, and the imam of the Shafiʿis in the Umawī mosque Shaykh Shihāb al-Dīn Aḥmad al-ʿAṭṭār (1138-1218/1726-1803), from his teacher the Sharif Shams al-Dīn Muḥammad b. ʿAbd al-Raḥmān b. Zayn al-ʿĀbidīn al-Ghazzī (1096-1167/1685-1754), from all of his paternal uncle ʿAbd al-Karīm al-Ghazzī, the Sharif Burhān al-Dīn Ibrāhīm b. Muḥammad b. Kamāl al-Dīn Muḥammad b. Ḥamza al-Naqīb al-Dimashqī, and Shaykh Abu al-Mawāhib Muḥammad b. Taqī al-Dīn ʿAbd al-Bāqī b. ʿAbd al-Bāqī al-Ḥanbalī, the latter from his father, from the Sharif Najm al-Dīn Muḥammad al-Ghazzī, from his father Abū al-Barakāt Badr al-Dīn

Muḥammad b. Radī al-Dīn Muḥammad al-Ghazzī (904-984/1499-1576), from Shaykh al-Islām al-Taqī Abū al-Ṣidq Abū Bakr b. ʿAbd Allāh b. ʿAbd al-Raḥmān—known as Ibn Qāḍī ʿAjlūn (841-928/1438-1522), from his brother Shaykh al-Islām Najm al-Dīn Muḥammad b. ʿAbd Allāh—also known as Ibn Qāḍī ʿAjlūn (831-876/1428-1471)—from the hadith master al-Shams Ibn Nāṣir al-Dīn (777-842/1375-1438), from Sāra bint Shaykh al-Islām al-Taqī al-Subkī (734-805/1334-1403), from her father (683-756/1284-1355), from his teacher, the hadith master of his time, Sharaf al-Dīn al-Dimyāṭī (613-705/1216-1306), from his teacher, the hadith master of his time, Zakī al-Dīn al-Mundhirī (581-656/1185-1258), from his teacher the hadith master ʿAlīb. al-Mufaḍḍal, from his teacher the aged hadith master Abū Ṭāhir al-Silafī (475-576/1082-1180), Abū al-Fatḥ Aḥmad b. Muḥammad b. Aḥmad al-Ḥaddād informed us, ʿAbd al-Ghaffār b. Ibrāhīm al-Mu'addib informed us, the hadith master Abū al-Shaykh ʿAbd al-Allāh b. Muḥammad b. Jaʿfar b. Ḥayyān (d. 369/980) informed us, **Imam Abū Bakr Aḥmad b. ʿAmr b. ʿAbd al-Khāliq al-ʿAtakī al-Bazzār** (after 210-292/after 825-905), Yaḥyā b. Muʿallā b. Manṣūr narrated to us, Saʿīd b. Abī Maryam narrated to us, Ibn Lahīʿa narrated to us, from ʿAbd Allāh b. al-Aswad, from ʿĀmir b. ʿAbd Allāh b. al-Zubayr b. al-ʿAwwām, from his father, that the Prophet–upon him blessings and peace–said: "**The people of my House can be compared to the ark of Nūḥ; whoever boards it is saved and whoever leaves it drowns.**"

This chain of transmission is full of light. Half of it is pattern-chained with Damascene Sharifs and it contains patrilinearity (children from parents), relatives from relatives, star students from their masters and the foremost experts of hadith–may Allah have mercy on them all. Al-

Suyūṭī marked it as fair in *al-Jāmi' al-ṣaghīr* even if it is slightly weak (*layyin*), as the hadith is strengthened by the Prophetic narrations in (1) al-Quḍā'ī's *Musnad al-Shihāb*, Abū Nu'aym's *Ḥilya*, al-Bazzār's *Musnad* and his student Ṭabarānī's *al-Mu'jam al-kabīr* from Ibn 'Abbās; (2) Abū Ya'lā's *Musnad* and, through him, Ibn 'Adī's *Kāmil*, al-Qaṭī'ī's *Faḍā'il al-ṣaḥābā*, al-Ḥākim, al-Quḍā'ī, Ṭabarānī in all three *Mu'jams*, al-Bazzār, al-Fasawī's *al-Ma'rifa wal-tārīkh*, Abū al-Shaykh's *al-Amthāl*, Abū Nu'aym, and al-Ājurrī from Abū Dharr with several chains, some of them with the addition, **"and whoever fights us/them at the end of times is as one who fights on the side of the Arch-liar;"** (3) al-Ṭabārānī in all three *Mu'jams* from Abū Sa'īd al-Khudrī; (4) al-Dūlābī's *al-Asmā' wal-kunā* from Abū al-Ṭufayl; (5) al-Khaṭīb's *Tārīkh* and Ibn 'Asākir's *Tārīkh* from Anas in the wording, **"I and my family can be compared to the ark of Nūḥ: whoever boards it is saved and whoever stays back from it drowns;"** (6) Ibn Abī Shayba's *Muṣannaf* as a saying of 'Alī–Allah honor his face and be well-pleased with all of them–in the wording **"We, in this community, can be compared to the ark of Nūḥ and the writ of reprieve among the Israelites."** Its narrators are those of Muslim except for al-Minhāl b. 'Amr, who is one of al-Bukhārī's.

(Notes of Benefit.) Imam al-Suyūṭī made a valuable summary of the Prophetic family's special merits while citing this hadith in *al-Khaṣā'iṣ al-ṣughrā*—also named *Unmūdhaj al-labīb fī khaṣā'iṣ al-Ḥabīb* (The Sage's Ideal Regarding the Special Characteristics of the Beloved)—in which he said: "It is also mentioned in a report that the Prophet's family are in the highest summit of Paradise; in a hadith, **'the people of my house can be compared to the ark of Nūḥ; whoever boards it is saved and whoever hangs back from it drowns;'** also that whoever holds fast to them and to the Qur'ān will never go astray; and that they are a security (*amān*) for the Community from dissension; and that they are the liegelords of Paradise; and that Allah has promised not to punish them; and that whoever hates them, Allah shall cause him to enter the Fire; and that belief does not enter one's heart until he loves them for the sake of Allah and for the sake of their near relation to the Prophet; and that whoever fights them is as one who fights on the side of the Arch-liar; and that whoever helps them out in any way, the Prophet himself shall recompense him on the Day of resurrection; and that there will not be a single one of them on the Day of resurrection except he will be given the right to intercede; and that a man may give up his seat for his brother except for the Banū Hāshim: they do not have to get up for anyone."

19 al-Nasā'ī's *Sunan* (214-303/ 829-916) known as *al-Mujtabā* (The choice collection)

THE SPIRITUAL guide of the 'Ashīra Muḥammadiyya association in Egypt—one of the Shadhilī Sufi groups there—the jurist, hadith scholar and poet Shaykh Zakī al-Dīn Abū al-Barakāt Muḥammad Zakī Ibrāhīm al-Ḥusaynī al-Azharī (1324 or 1334-1419/1906 or 1916-1998)–Allah have mercy on him–informed us, from the arch-erudite scholar Abū al-Mawāhib Muḥammad Ḥabīb Allāh b. 'Abd Allāh b. Aḥmad Mā Ya'bā al-Shinqīṭī al-Jakanī al-Mālikī (1295-1363/ 1878-1944), from the erudite scholar Shaykh 'Umar b. Barakāt b. Aḥmad al-Shāmī al-Biqā'ī al-Azharī al-Makkī (1245-1313/1830-1895), from Shaykh al-Islām al-Bājūrī (1198-1277/1784-1861); (a shorter route) Shaykh Muḥammad Zakī from the supercentenarian Shaykh Muḥammad al-'Arabī b. 'Abd Allāh b. Ibrāhīm al-'Aqūrī al-Lībī (1240 per al-Mashshāṭ's narration from him-14 Rabi' al-Thānī 1390, aged 150/1825-1970), from al-Bājūrī, from al-Amīr al-Ṣaghīr, from his father al-Amīr al-Kabīr Muḥammad b. Muḥammad b. Aḥmad b. 'Abd al-Qādir b. 'Abd al-'Azīz al-Sinbāwī al-Azharī (1154-1232/1741-1817) from Shihāb al-Dīn al-Mallawī, from al-Mullā Ilyās al-Gūrānī al-Dimashqī, from 'Umar Ibn al-Balawī al-Shāmī, from the centenarian 'Umar al-Zaftāwī, from Shaykh al-Islām Zakariyyā al-Anṣārī; (another route) Shaykh Sāmir al-Naṣṣ also narrated to us verbatim, Shaykh al-Fādānī informed us, from the world transmissologist the erudite Muḥammad

ʿAlī al-Mālikī al-Makkī through audition for much of it and by permission for the rest, from the erudite Shaykh Abū Bakr b. Shaṭṭā al-Makkī known as al-Sayyid al-Bakrī, from al-Sayyid Aḥmad b. Zaynī Daḥlān al-Makkī, from ʿUthmān al-Dimyāṭī, from the erudite ʿAbd Allāh b. Ḥijāzī al-Sharqāwī, from Shams al-Dīn Muḥammad b. Sālim al-Ḥafnāwī; (another route) al-Fādānī from Shaykh ʿUmar b. Ḥamdān al-Maḥrasī by audition for much of it and by permission for the rest, from his Shaykh Fāliḥ b. Muḥammad al-Ẓāhirī, from Muḥammad b. ʿAlī al-Khaṭṭābī al-Sanūsī, from al-Sayyid Muḥammad Murtaḍā al-Zabīdī, from al-Ḥafnāwī, from ʿAbd al-ʿAzīz al-Ziyādī, from al-Shams Muḥammad b. al-ʿAlāʾ al-Bābilī, from Shaykh Sālim b. Muḥammad al-Sanhūrī, from al-Najm Muḥammad b. Aḥmad al-Ghayṭī, from the Qadi Zakariyyā al-Anṣārī, from the Hadith master Aḥmad b. ʿAlī Ibn Ḥajar al-ʿAsqalānī, from Abū Isḥāq Ibrāhīm b. Aḥmad al-Tanūkhī, through his audition from Ayyūb b. Niʿmat Allāh al-Nābulusī, Ismāʿīl b. Aḥmad al-ʿIrāqī informed us, from ʿAbd al-Razzāq b. Ismāʿīl al-Qawmisī, Abū Muḥammad ʿAbd al-Raḥmān b. Aḥmad al-Dūnī informed us by audition, al-Qāḍī Abū Naṣr Aḥmad b. al-Ḥusayn al-Dīnawarī known as al-Kassār reported to us, the Hadith master and qadi Abū Bakr Aḥmad b. Muḥammad b. Isḥāq al-Dīnawarī known as Ibn al-Sunnī reported to us, saying, **the Hadith master Abū ʿAbd al-Raḥmān Aḥmad b. Shuʿayb al-Nasāʾī** reported to us, saying, al-Aʿmash informed us, from ʿAdī, from Zirr, saying, ʿAlī–may Allah be well-pleased with him–said, **"Verily it is indeed the solemn promise of the unlettered Prophet to me: 'Verily none loves you but a believer and none hates you but a hypocrite.'"**

Muslim, al-Tirmidhī, Ibn Mājah and Aḥmad narrated it. Tirmidhī related from Abū Sa'īd al-Khudrī, "Verily we, the assembly of the Helpers, would indeed recognize the hypocrites by their hatred for 'Alī b. Abī Ṭālib." It is also related in Ibn 'Abd al-Barr's *Istī'āb* from Jābir as "We would recognize the hypocrites by nothing else but hatred for 'Alī b. Abī Ṭālib." It is also related in al-Qaṭī'ī's *Zawā'id* to Aḥmad's *Faḍā'il al-Ṣaḥāba*, from Abū Sa'īd al-Khudrī, from the Prophet–upon him the blessings and peace of Allah–**"Whoever hates us, the people of the House, then he is a hypocrite."** A similar report will be mentioned in the chapter of Ibn Ḥibbān's *Ṣaḥīḥ* if Allah wills.

20 al-Nasā'ī's (214-303/829-916) *Khaṣā'iṣ Amīr al-Mu'minīn 'Alī* (The special characteristics of the Commander of the believers 'Alī)

THE FORMER RECTOR of the Jāmi'a Insāniyya University in the Sultanate of Kedah Dār al-Amān, Malaysia, al-Ḥabīb Dr. 'Aqīl b. al-Sayyid 'Alī b. al-Sayyid 'Alawī b. al-Sayyid Ḥasan al-Mahdalī al-Ahdal al-Ḥusaynī al-Indūnīsī al-Azharī the author of many textbooks informed me, from the erudite reformer and litterateur, the qadi and caller unto Allah, Sayyid Abū al-Mawāhib Muḥammad b. 'Abd al-Hādī b. 'Abd al-Raḥmān al-'Ujayl al-Ḥasanī al-Yamānī (1344-1419/1926-1998), author of beneficial works such as *al-Ṣārim al-battār fīl-radd 'alā khuṣūm Āl al-Nabiyyi al-mukhtār* (The cutting saber in answering the adversaries of the family of the elect Prophet), from the erudite poet and pride of the Yemen, the *khaṭīb* of Jāmi' al-'Asqalānī in Aden, Muḥammad b. Sālim b. Ḥusayn al-Kadādī al-Bayḥānī, from the teacher of guides al-Ḥabīb 'Abd Allāh b. 'Umar al-Shāṭirī (1290-1361/1873-1942) from 'Aydarūs al-Ḥabshī, from his father 'Umar b. 'Aydarūs b. 'Abd al-Raḥmān and his uncle Muḥammad b. 'Aydarūs b. 'Abd al-Raḥmān al-Ḥabshī, both of them from al-Imām 'Umar b. 'Abd al-Karīm b. 'Abd al-Rasūl al-'Aṭṭār, from Abū al-Fayḍ Muḥammad b. Muḥammad Murtaḍā al-Zabīdī, from al-Shams Muḥammad b. Sālim al-Ḥifnī (al-Ḥafnāwī) with the chain previously mentioned to Imām al-Nasā'ī who said, Muḥammad b. al-Muthannā reported to us, Yaḥyā b.

Ḥammād narrated to me, Abū ʿAwāna narrated to us, from Sulaymān who said, Ḥabīb b. Abī Thābit narrated to us, from Abū al-Ṭufayl, from Zayd b. Arqam who said, "When the Messenger of Allah–upon him the blessings and peace of Allah–returned from the Farewell Pilgrimage and alighted at the Khumm oasis, he ordered us to set up camp around some big trees, so they were swept (i.e. their area). Then he said, **'I seem to have been called back and I said yes. Verily I have left among you the two weighty matters, one is greater than the other: the Book of Allah and my intimates, the people of my House. So look well how you act after me with regard to the two of them, for verily they shall never part ways until they reach me again at the Basin!'** Then he said, **'Verily Allah is my protecting friend, and I am the protecting friend of every believer.' Then he took ʿAlī by the hand and said, 'Whoever I am the protecting friend of, then this is his protecting friend (*walī*). O Allah, take as Your friend whoever befriends him, and take as Your enemy whoever shows him enmity!'"** Abū al-Ṭufayl said to Zayd, "You heard it from the Messenger of Allah?" He replied, "There was not one person under the tall trees except he saw him with his eyes and heard him with his ears."

Al-Ṭaḥāwī also narrated it in *Sharḥ Mushkil al-Āthār* as did Aḥmad, al-Ḥākim, al-Ṭabarānī in *al-Kabīr* and al-Nasāʾī in the same work in the wording "six rose on the part of Saʿīd [b. Wahb al-Hamdānī] and six on the part of Zayd [b. Yuthayʿ al-Hamdānī], and witnessed they had heard the Messenger of Allah–upon him the blessings and peace of Allah–say about ʿAlī–Allah be well-pleased with him–on the day of the Khumm oasis, **'Is not Allah more deserving of the believers?'** They said yes. He said, **'O Allah! Whoever I am the protecting friend of, then ʿAlī is his protecting friend. O Allah, take as Your friend whoever befriends him, and take as Your enemy whoever shows him enmity!'"** It has a witness-report from Burayda al-Aslamī which they all narrated, as did Ibn Abī Shayba, Ibn Ḥibbān, Abū

Ya'lā, al-Bazzār and al-Dārimī, some of them in short form. It was also narrated from Abū Sarīḥa or Zayd b. Arqam (Shu'ba was unsure), from the Prophet, with the term *mawlā* instead of *walī*. Al-Tirmidhī narrated it—he said it was a fair, lone-narrated hadith—as well as Aḥmad. It was also narrated thus in short form (**O Allah! Whoever I am the protecting friend of, then 'Alī is his protecting friend**) from Sa'd b. Abī Waqqāṣ as narrated by Ibn Mājah and al-Nasā'ī in this book; from Ibn 'Abbās by al-Ḥākim; and from 'Alī and al-Barā'–may Allah be well-pleased with all of them. It is mass-transmitted according to the Hadith masters al-Suyūṭī and al-Kattānī.

Imam al-Shāfi'ī and Imam al-Nawawī explained the *muwālat* (protective friendship) as the *muwālāt* of Islam, support and love in light of the verse *that is because the One God is the protecting friend of those who believe and that the unbelievers have no protecting friend* (Muḥammad 47:11). Al-Dārimī narrated the statement of Ibn Mas'ūd that "***Walā'* is a parentage similar to parental lineage; it cannot be sold and cannot be donated**." Al-Suyūṭī narrated it as a Prophetic hadith in *al-Fānīd fī ḥalāwat al-asānīd* with his chain to al-Rabī' b. Sulaymān, from his Shaykh al-Shāfi'ī, from his Shaykh Muḥammad b. al-Ḥasan, from his Shaykh Abū Yūsuf, from 'Abd Allāh b. Dīnār, from Ibn 'Umar–Allah be well-pleased with him and his father.

There is in his statement–upon him blessings and peace–"**for verily they shall never part ways until they reach me again at the Basin**" evidence that the people of the House are preserved until the Day of Resurrection with divine protection just as Allah preserves His Book, and that they are the guardians of the Sunna and the carriers of its standard for the Muslims. It is narrated from Abū Mijlaz in Ibn Abī Shayba's *Muṣannaf* that he had pelted the stoning-stations [in Hajj] and lost count of how much he had pelted, so he asked Ibn 'Umar who did not reply, then he asked Ibn al-Ḥanafiyya as he was passing by him, so he said, "O servant of Allah, nothing greater than prayer was enjoined upon us as a duty, and when one of us forgets he repeats." Abū Mijlaz said, "I reported his answer to Ibn 'Umar so he said 'Truly they are the people of a House gifted with perspicuity.'" Its gist is in conformity with the sound hadith which Mālik included in the *Muwaṭṭa'* and which al-Ḥākim, al-Bayhaqī and others narrated from Abū Hurayra, Ibn 'Abbās, Anas, and 'Amr b. 'Awf–Allah be well-pleased with them–"**I have left among you two things after which you will never go astray: the Book of Allah and my Sunna; and they will never part ways until they reach me again at the Basin.**" This hadith is "well-preserved, well-recognized, and well-known as coming from the Prophet–upon him the blessings and peace of Allah" as stated by Ibn 'Abd al-Barr, Ibn Ḥazm, the Ghumaris and others. Al-Haythamī said, "The upshot is that the exhortation has been made to hold fast to the Book, the Sunna, and the people of knowledge of the Book and the Sunna that are from *Ahl al-Bayt*, and it is understood from it that all three matters shall endure until the coming of the Hour." Therein is also evidence that the Sunna is protected with the protection of the Book of Allah, just as the early Muslims understood it with respect to the Qur'ān. When Ibn al-Mubārak was asked, "What about these forgeries?" He said, "The giant scholars will live on to face them down!" then he recited the verse *verily We Ourselves have sent down the Remembrance and We are indeed going to preserve it* (al-Ḥijr 15:9). Qadi 'Iyāḍ said in *al-Shifā*: "Blessed is the Umma of Islam for the preservation of its Law, the Qur'ān, by no less than the nurturing Lord of lords, and the pure and purified Sunna of its Prophet–upon him the blessings and peace of Allah–and his pure and excellent Family, may Allah well-pleased with all of them." Then he said, "The exegetes differed as to the meaning of His statement–exalted is He–in the Motherbook, *show us the straight path*, whereby Abū al-'Āliya and al-Ḥasan said *the straight path* is the Messenger of Allah–upon him the blessings and peace of Allah–and the elite of his House and Companions, as cited by al-Māwardī, while Makkī related something similar from both of them and said, "It is the Messenger of Allah–upon him the blessings and peace of Allah–and his two Companions Abū Bakr and 'Umar." Abū al-Layth al-Samarqandī also cited it as Abū al-'Āliya's gloss under His statement–exalted is He–*the path of those whom You have favored* and he said al-Ḥasan confirmed it when news of it reached him. Al-Māwardī also cited it under the same verse as 'Abd al-Raḥmān b. Zayd's gloss.

21 *al-Sunan al-Kubrā* of al-Nasā'ī (214-303/829-916)

THE JURIST of the Bā ʿAlawīs, the paragon of qualities and receptacle of virtues, the leader oft-resorted to, the preserver of the School and the jurist of consensus and divergences, the subduer of innovations and the upholder of the standard of *Ahl al-Sunna*, the Indonesia-born erudite Medinan educator of simple living al-Ḥabīb Abū Muḥammad Zayn b. Ibrāhīm b. Sumayṭ al-Shāfiʿī (b. 1357/1938) informed me in Jakarta, the erudite *muḥaddith* jurist, caller to Allah, qadi of Zanzibar and its hadith teacher, al-Ḥabīb ʿUmar b. Aḥmad b. Abī Bakr b. Sumayṭ Bā ʿAlawī (d. 1387 /1967)—author of *al-Nafḥat al-shadhiyya min al-diyār al-Ḥaḍramiyya* (The fragrant whiff from the abodes of Hadramawt)—informed me, al-Ḥabīb Shaykh b. Muḥammad b. Ḥusayn al-Ḥabshī informed me, from his father the transmissologist knower of Allah and mufti of Mecca, al-Ḥabīb Shams al-Dīn Muḥabbad b. Ḥusayn b. ʿAbd Allāh b. Shaykh al-Ḥabshī who had around 100 shaykhs, Wajīh al-Dīn ʿAbd al-Raḥmān b. Sulaymān b. Yaḥyā b. ʿUmar Maqbūl al-Ahdal informed me, with the chain already mentioned in the chapter of Ibn Mājah's *Sunan* to al-Bābilī, from al-Sanhūrī, from Shihāb al-Dīn Aḥmad Ibn Ḥajar al-Haytamī al-Makkī, from Sharaf al-Dīn ʿAbd al-Ḥaqq al-Sinbāṭī, from the Hadith master Ibn Ḥajar, through reading before Abū Ṭāhir Muḥammad b. Abī al-Yumn al-Rabaʿī, Zaynab bint al-Kamāl Aḥmad b. ʿAbd al-Raḥīm informed us through permission, from Abū al-Qāsim ʿAbd al-Raḥmān b. Makkī the maternal grandson of al-Silafī, from

Abū al-Qāsim Khalaf b. ʿAbd al-Malik b. Bashkuwāl through written permission, Abū Muḥammad ʿAbd al-Raḥmān b. Muḥammad b. ʿAttāb informed us, my father informed us through audition, ʿAbd Allāh b. Rabīʿ informed us, Muḥammad b. Muʿāwiya b. al-Aḥmar informed us, **Abū ʿAbd al-Raḥmān Aḥmad b. Shuʿayb al-Nasāʾī informed us**, saying, Khālid b. Makhlad narrated to me, saying, Mūsā narrated to me (namely b. Yaʿqūb al-Zamʿī) from ʿAbd Allāh b. Abī Bakr b. Zayd b. al-Muhājir, saying, Muslim b. Abī Sahl al-Nabbāl reported to me, saying, al-Ḥasan b. Usāma b. Zayd b. Ḥāritha reported to me, saying, my father (namely Usāma b. Zayd) reported to me, saying, "I knocked at the door of the Messenger of Allah–upon him the blessings and peace of Allah–one night for some need, so he came out carrying something inside his wrap which I could not identify. When I was done with my need I asked 'What is it you are carrying inside your wrap?' He uncovered it and, behold! It was al-Ḥasan and al-Ḥusayn on his haunches. He said, **'These are my sons and my daughter's sons. O Allah! You well know how much I love them, so love them also! O Allah! You well know how much I love them, so love them also!'"**

Al-Tirmidhī narrated it—rating it fair—also Ibn Ḥibbān and Bukhārī in short form. Tirmidhī added **'and love whoever loves them!'** So let one pay attention to the greatness of this supplication and its gravity. Something to this effect is also narrated from Abū Hurayra by Ibn Abī Shayba, and from al-Barāʾ by al-Tirmidhī. There is also in Maʿmar's *Jāmiʿ* a narration from ʿAbd Allāh b. ʿUthmān b. Khutaym in *mursal* mode: the Messenger of Allah–upon him the blessings and peace of Allah–one day put al-Ḥasan and al-Ḥusayn on each of his thighs, then he turned to al-Ḥasan and kissed him, then he turned to al-Ḥusayn and he kissed him, then he said, **"O Allah! Verily I love them, so love them also!"** then he said, **"Verily one's child is cause for cowardice, avarice, ignorance."**

22 al-Nasāʾīʾs (214-303/829-916) *Faḍāʾil al-Ṣaḥāba* (Virtues of the Companions)

THE VENERABLE SHARIF of Singapore, nonagenarian, and valiant defender of its Waqf endowments in the eighties and nineties, al-Ḥabīb ʿAbd Allāh b. Hārūn b. Ḥasan al-Junayd Jamal al-Layl (1349-1439/1930-2018)–Allah have mercy on him–reported to me through my reading before him in his house, from his father, from al-Ḥabīb ʿAbd Allāh b. ʿUmar al-Shāṭirī, from the transmissologist of Yemen al-Ḥabīb ʿAydarūs b. ʿUmar with his chain already cited in the chapter of *The special virtues of ʿAlī* back to the Hadith master Aḥmad b. Shuʿayb al-Nasāʾī, al-Ḥusayn b. Manṣūr reported to us, saying, al-Ḥusayn b. Muḥammad Abū Aḥmad informed us, saying, Isrāʾīl b. Yūnus informed us, from Maysara b. Ḥabīb, from al-Minhāl b. ʿAmr, from Zirr b. Ḥubaysh, from Ḥudhayfa b. al-Yamān who said, "My mother asked me, 'When is the last time you were with the Prophet–upon him the blessings and peace of Allah?' I said since such and such, whereupon she scolded me and insulted me. I said to her, 'Give me a chance and verily I am going to go see the Prophet–upon him the blessings and peace of Allah–and pray the *maghrib* prayer with him, and I will not leave him until he asks forgiveness for the both of us.' I went and prayed the *maghrib* prayer with him, and he kept praying until the *ʿishāʾ*. Then he turned around and I followed him. Someone came across his way to talk to him and took him, so he went and I followed. He heard me

and said, 'Who is this?' I said, 'Ḥudhayfa.' He said, 'What ails you?' I told him what the matter was. He said, 'Allah forgives you and your mother! Did you not see the one who came across my way before?' I said yes. He said, 'It was one of the angels that never ever came down to earth before this night. He asked permission from his nurturing Lord to greet me, and he gave me the glad tidings that al-Ḥasan and al-Ḥusayn are the two liegelords of the young men of Paradise, and that Fāṭima is the liege lady of the women of Paradise.'"

Aḥmad and al-Tirmidhī narrated it—he rated it a fair, lone-narrated report—also Ibn Abī Shayba, Abū Ya'lā, al-Nasā'ī in the *Kubrā*, al-Ṭabarānī in *al-Kabīr* and *al-Awsaṭ*, Ibn Ḥibbān, Abū Nu'aym in the *Ḥilya* and the *Ma'rifa*, al-Bayhaqī in the *Dalā'il* and Ibn 'Asākir through various chains, one or more of them with the addition, **"except for the status of Maryam bint 'Imrān."** It will come up, *in shā' Allāh*, in the chapter of al-Ājurrī's book *al-Sharī'a.*

23 *Musnad Fāṭima bint Rasūl Allāh ṣallā Allāh ʿalayhimā* by Abū Yaʿlā al-Mawṣilī (210-307/ 825-919)

THE LOVER OF *AHL AL-BAYT* my master Shaykh Abū Saʿīd Maḥmūd b. ʿUthmān Quwaydir (1349-1431/1930-2010) reported to me—he would make long emotional supplications and was said to be of the *abdāl* (substitutes) of Syro-Palestine, and his mother was a Ḥusaynī from the Zuʿbī house—through my reading before him in the Jumuʿa mosque of ʿUmar b. ʿAbd al-ʿAzīz in Mizza, Damascus, from his Shaykh Muḥammad Makkī al-Kattānī–Abū Saʿīd and his older brother Abū al-Ṭayyib were of the most assiduous of people in frequenting him–from the *muḥaddith* of the Hijaz Shaykh Fāliḥ al-Ẓāhirī with his five-link chain already cited in the chapter on the *Muwaṭṭaʾ* back to the Hadith master Ibn Ḥajar; (another route) and his brother Shaykh Abū al-Ṭayyib Muḥammad Quwaydir (d. 1427/ 2006)–Allah have mercy on both of them–informed me in his house in al-Maydān, Damascus, from Shaykh Muḥammad Amīn b. Muḥammad Suwayd (1273-1355/1857-1936) from the Sufi transmissologist of Tripoli, Lebanon, Abū al-Maḥāsin Muḥammad b. Khalīl al-Qāwuqjī (1224-1305/ 1809-1888), from al-Amīr al-Kabīr with his six-link chain mentioned in the chapter of Shāfiʿī's *Musnad* back to the Hadith master Ibn Ḥajar, from the world transmissologist Ṣalāḥ al-Dīn Muḥammad b. Aḥmad b. Ibrāhīm b. Abī ʿUmar al-Maqdisī al-Ṣāliḥī, from the transmissologist

Fakhr al-Dīn Ibn al-Bukhārī, from Abū Rawḥ ʿAbd al-Muʿizz b. Muḥammad al-Harawī, Tamīm b. Abī Saʿīd al-Jurjānī narrated to us, Abū Saʿd Muḥammad b. ʿAbd al-Raḥmān al-Kanjarūdhī narrated to us, Mūḥammad b. Aḥmad b. Ḥamdān narrated to us, the Imam Abū Yaʿlā Aḥmad b. ʿAlī b. al-Muthannā al-Mawṣilī narrated to us in Mosul, ʿUthmān b. Abī Shayba narrated to us, Jarīr narrated to us, from Shayba b. Naʿāma, from Fāṭima bint al-Ḥusayn, from Fāṭima al-Kubrā who said that the Messenger of Allah–upon him and his family blessings and peace–said, **"All the children of a mother have a *ʿaṣaba* (agnates) to whom they are affiliated except the children of Fāṭima: for I am their guardian and I am their agnate."**

Ibn ʿAsākir narrated it through Abū Yaʿlā. Al-Ṭabarānī in *al-Kabīr* and al-Khaṭīb in *al-Tārīkh* also narrated it, the first one in the wording **"All the children of a mother are affiliated to agnates"** and the second in the two wordings **"All human children are affiliated to agnates"** or **"to their agnates."** It has a witness-report narrated from Jābir by al-Ṭabarānī and al-Ḥākim. Al-Sakhāwī said in *Istijlāb irtiqāʾ al-ghuraf bi-hubbi aqribāʾi al-Rasūl wa-dhawī al-sharaf* (The propitiation of the ascent to the chambers of Paradise with the love of the relatives of the Prophet and the Sharifs): "It is also narrated from Ibn ʿAbbās by Abū al-Khayr al-Ḥākimī (Aḥmad b. Ismāʿīl b. Yūsuf al-Ṭālqānī (512-590/1118-1194) as 'I and al-ʿAbbās were sitting with the Messenger of Allah–upon him the blessings and peace of Allah–when ʿ**Alī came in and gave the greeting, and the Prophet–upon him the blessings and peace of Allah–greeted him back, got up, hugged him, kissed him between the eyes and sat him to his right. Al-ʿAbbās said, "Messenger of Allah, do you love him?" He said, "Uncle! I swear by Allah that Allah loves him even more than I do. Verily Allah has made the progeny of every Prophet in his own loins, but He made my progeny in the loins of this one."**' Its narrations strengthen one another and Ibn al-Jawzī's statement in *al-ʿIlal al-mutanāhiya* that it is inauthentic is not a good one. Therein is also evidence for his exclusive special attribute of having his daughter's children be affiliated to him. Hence al-Nawawī said in the *Rawḍa* just as found in its *matn* (textus; i.e. al-Rāfiʿī's *Sharḥ al-Wajīz*, itself a commentary on al-Ghazālī's *Wajīz* in Shāfiʿī *fiqh*) with respect to special attributes, "and his children of his daughters are affiliated to him–upon him the blessings and peace of Allah–while the children of the daughters of others are not affiliated to their respective grandfathers in marriage suitability and other than that." Ibn al-Mulaqqin said the same in *Ghāyat al-sūl fī khaṣā'iṣ al-Rasūl* (The ultimate quest regarding the special characteristics of the Messenger) as did al-Suyūṭī in *al-Khaṣā'iṣ al-kubrā* and also *al-Ṣughrā* (i.e. *Unmūdhaj al-labīb* which we read with Shaykh Abū Sa'īd al-Majd and again with Sayyid Yūsuf al-Rifā'ī), and yet another major Shāfi'ī Hadith master, Abū al-Khayr Quṭb al-Dīn Muḥammad b. Muḥammad b. 'Abd Allāh b. Khayḍir al-Khayḍirī al-Dimashqī (821-894/1418-1489) in *al-Lafẓ al-mukarram bi-khaṣā'iṣ al-Nabī* (The honored word on the Prophet's special characteristics); Suyūṭī's student the Hadith master al-Ṣāliḥī in his major *Sīra* entitled *Subul al-hudā wal-rashād* (The paths of guidance and right direction); Qadi 'Iyāḍ in *al-Shifā*.

Al-Sakhāwī also said in *al-Ajwiba al-marḍiyya* (The pleasing answers i.e. Hadith rulings), "I had been asked about this hadith and I spoke about it at length. I drew attention to the fact that it is fit as an evidentiary proof; and from Allah comes all success." Shaykh Aḥmad al-Ghumārī also said in *al-Mudāwī*: "Among its witness-texts is what 'Abd Allāh b. Aḥmad b. Ḥanbal narrated in *Faḍā'il al-Ṣaḥāba* from al-Mustaẓill, that 'Umar b. al-Khaṭṭāb asked Umm Kulthūm's hand in marriage from [her father] 'Alī b. Abī Ṭālib, who declined citing her young age, whereupon he said, "Verily I did not mean for cohabitation, but rather because I heard the Messenger of Allah–upon him the blessings and peace of Allah–say, **'Every line and lineage shall be severed on the Day of Resurrection except my line and my lineage; and all the children of all fathers have agnates only through their father except the children of Fāṭima: verily I myself am their father and their agnates!'**" Also among its witness-texts is what al-Ṭabarānī narrated through Sufyān b. 'Uyayna, from Ja'far b. Muḥammad (b. 'Alī b. al-Ḥusayn b. 'Alī b. Abī Ṭālib) from his father, from Jābir who said, "I heard 'Umar b. al-Khaṭṭāb say to people when he married 'Alī's daughter, 'Congratulate me! I heard the Messenger of Allah–upon him the blessings and peace of Allah–say, **"Severed shall be, on the Day of Resurrection, every line and lineage except my line and lineage."**'" Al-Haythamī said al-Ṭabarānī narrated it in *al-Awsaṭ* and *al-Kabīr*; that the narrators in both cases were all those of the *Ṣaḥīḥ* except al-Ḥasan b. Sahl, and he is trustworthy; and that he also narrated it in *al-Kabīr* from Ibn 'Abbās with this wording, and its narrators are trustworthy. Al-Bayhaqī also narrated it in *Manāqib al-Shāfi'ī* in *mursal* mode from Muḥammad b. 'Alī that 'Umar asked 'Alī for Umm Kulthūm in marriage, until he said, "I heard the Messenger of Allah–upon him the blessings and peace of Allah–say, **'Verily every line and lineage shall be cut off on the Day of Resurrection except whatever is part of my line and my lineage.'**"

The genealogist Ibn Funduq cited a scholar as explaining the *ḥasab* (line) as the *Sharīʿa* (sacred Law) and the *nasab* (lineage) as offspring and the nearest relatives.

(Anecdote) It is mentioned in *Subul al-hudā wal-rashād* that Ibn Abī Ḥātim and Abū al-Shaykh narrated from Abū al-Aswad al-Dīlī; also al-Ḥākim from ʿAbd al-Malik b. ʿUmar and ʿĀṣim b. Bahdala [as did al-Bayhaqī in *al-Kubrā* and Ibn ʿAsākir in *al-Tārīkh*] that they gathered around al-Ḥajjāj and al-Ḥusayn b. ʿAlī was mentioned, so al-Ḥajjāj said "He was not of the Prophet's progeny." Yaḥyā b. Yaʿmur was there, and he said: "You lie, O our Emir!" Ḥajjāj said, "You shall indeed bring me a definite proof for what you said and a confirmation from the Book of Allah, or I will surely kill you with a painful death!" He said, "*And of his* [=Ibrāhīm's] *seed Dāwūd, Sulaymān, Ayyūb, Yūsuf, Mūsā, and Hārūn; and thus We recompense those who do their best; and Zakariyyā, Yaḥyā, ʿĪsā* (al-Anʿām 6:84-85): is not ʿĪsā from the progeny of Ibrāhīm and yet he has no father?" Another wording has "so Allah Most High related that ʿĪsā is from the progeny of Ādam through his mother. Likewise al-Ḥusayn b. ʿAlī is from the progeny of Muḥammad–upon him the blessings and peace of Allah–through al-Ḥusayn's mother."

(The *fiqh* of matrilineal Sharif status) Al-Suyūṭī said in *al-ʿAjājat al-zarnabiyya fil-sulālat al-Zaynabiyya* (The saffroned dust-cloud about the Zaynabī lineage):

> The jurists mentioned that among his exclusive attributes–upon him the blessings and peace of Allah–is the fact that the children of his daughters are affiliated to him by lineage, and they did not mention the same about the children of his daughters' daughters. So the special attribute is only for the highest generation-layer. Thus **the four children of Fāṭima** [i.e. those who went on to have children, namely Ḥasan, Ḥusayn, Umm Kulthūm and Zaynab per Ibn al-Jawzī, *Talqīḥ fuhūm ahl al-athar*, *dhikr al-ināth min awlādihi ṣallā Allahu ʿalayhi wa-sallam* whereas the fifth, al-Muḥassan, did not, per Ibn Isḥāq] are affiliated to him–upon him the blessings and peace of Allah–while the children of Zaynab and those of Umm Kulthūm are affiliated to their respective fathers, ʿAbd Allāh [b. Jaʿfar b. Abī Ṭālib] and ʿUmar [b. al-Khaṭṭāb], and neither to the mother nor to her father–upon him the blessings and peace of Allah–because they are the children of the daughter of his daughter, not the children of his own daughter. So the ruling that applies to them runs per the rule of the sacred Law whereby the child follows the father in lineage, not the mother; but only the children of Fāṭima alone turned out to have this special characteristic and it is limited to the offspring of al-Ḥasan and al-Ḥusayn as indicated by the hadith **"All the children of a mother have a *ʿaṣaba* (agnates)."** Thus lineage and agnation were made specific to them at the exclusion of their two sisters. This is why the later

scholars, just like the earlier scholars, routinely consider that the child of a Sharifa from a non-Sharif father is not a Sharif. If the special characteristic were extended to deem every Sharifa's children as a Sharif, then [obligatory] *ṣadaqa* would be forbidden for them, which is not the case. This scenario is specific to al-Ḥasan and al-Ḥusayn for no other reason than the fact that the issue became limited to them. Otherwise if, hypothetically, Zaynab were also included and she had had a male child, then he would also be exactly like her, even if his father were not a Hāshimī Sharif. For Sharif status did not come to the two of them [=Ḥasan and Ḥusayn] except from him–upon him the blessings and peace of Allah–and from no one else. Know also the name of *al-sharīf* was used, in the first generation, for whoever was from *Ahl al-Bayt* even if he was ʿAbbāsī (a descendant of al-ʿAbbās b. ʿAbd al-Muṭṭalib), ʿAqīlī (a descendant of ʿAqīl b. Abī Ṭālib), hence the historians' phrases "the ʿAbbāsī sharif," "the Zaynabī sharif" etc. When the Fāṭimīs took over Egypt, they restricted sharif status to the offspring of al-Ḥasan and al-Ḥusayn exclusively, and that persisted to this day.

It is narrated from Anas in the two *Ṣaḥīḥ*s that the Prophet–upon him the blessings and peace of Allah–said, **"Verily the sororal nephew of a people is part of them."** Al-Nawawī said, "Those who give uterine descendants a share of inheritance adduced this report as a proof but the vast majority answered that there is nothing in this particular wording that dictates giving them a share of inheritance. Its meaning is only that between such a person and them there is a connection and there are familial ties, without addressing inheritance. The drift of the hadith dictates that what is meant is he is like one of them in the divulging of their secrets in his presence and the like of that."

(Al-Shāfiʿī is a Hāshimī from his mother's side) Al-Bayhaqī said in the *Manāqib*:

Al-Shāfiʿī–Allah have mercy on him–is from the loins of the Banū ʿAbd al-Muṭṭalib b. ʿAbd Manāf on the paternal side, and he is of the Banū Hāshim b. ʿAbd Manāf on the side of his grandmothers that gave birth to his forefathers. We mentioned, regarding his lineage, that the mother of ʿAbd Yazīd—al-Shāfiʿī's grandfather —was al-Shaffāʾ bint Hāshim b. ʿAbd Manāf; that the mother of al-Sāʾib b. ʿUbayd—al-Shāfiʿī's grandfather—was al-Shaffāʾ bint al-Arqam b. Hāshim b. ʿAbd Manāf; and that her mother was Khalda bint Asad b. Hāshim b. ʿAbd Manāf, the sister of Fāṭima bint Asad b. Hāshim who was the mother of ʿAlī b. Abī Ṭālib. So he is a Hāshimī from these aspects which we mentioned, and ʿAlī b. Abī Ṭālib is his grandfather's maternal cousin. Thus he [=al-Shāfiʿī] is a beneficiary of the elect status reported by the Messenger of Allah–upon him the blessings and peace of Allah–and by which the latter clarified their sharif status and pre-eminence over others from two perspectives. May the mercy of Allah and His good pleasure be upon him.

(Subtle point) Abū al-ʿAbbās al-Wansharīsī said in *al-Miʿyār al-muʿrib* (12:385) that the Shaykh and Imam Nāṣir al-Dīn Abū ʿAlī Manṣūr b. Aḥmad al-Mashdālī al-Bijāʾī–Allah have mercy on him–was asked about the question of Sharif status from the maternal side to which he replied, "Whoever only has a Sharif mother may affiliate himself to him–upon him the blessings and peace of Allah–through his mother, and such is supported from various perspectives," which he then mentioned. And Allah is most Knowing and Wise.

24 *Jāmiʿ al-Bayān ʿan Taʾwīl Āy al-Qurʾān* (Encyclopedia of the exposition of the interpretation of the Signs of the Qurʾān) by Abū Jaʿfar Muḥammad b. Jarīr al-Ṭabarī (224-310/839-922)

THE HADITH MASTER OF TANGIERS and its mujtahid, al-Sayyid Abū al-Futūḥ ʿAbd Allāh b. ʿAbd al-Qādir al-Talīdī al-Idrīsī al-Ḥasanī (1347-1438/1928-2017)–Allah have mercy on him–informed me, from Abū al-Hudā Muḥammad al-Bāqir b. Muḥammad b. ʿAbd al-Kabīr al-Kattānī, from his grandfather the mountain of the Sunna and the Faith and the Rabbānī of his time Abū al-Makārim ʿAbd al-Kabīr b. Muḥammad al-Kattānī, from his father Abū ʿAbd Allāh Abū al-Mafākhir Muḥammad b. ʿAbd al-Wāḥid al-Kabīr b. Aḥmad b. ʿAbd al-Wāḥid al-Kattānī (d. 1289/1872), from the two brothers ʿUmar and Abū ʿĪsā al-Mahdī the sons of al-Ṭālib b. Sawda, both from Abū Muḥammad ʿAbd al-Salām al-Azmī, from Shaykh Abū ʿAbd Allāh Muḥammad al-Tāwudī Ibn Sawda (1111-1209/1699-1795)—also spelled Ibn Sūda after one of their fore-mothers or fathers respectively—from the aged Shams al-Dīn Abū ʿAbd Allāh Muḥammad b. ʿAbd al-Salām Bannānī (1083?-1163/1672-1750), from the transmissologist Abū Sālim ʿAbd Allāh b. Muḥammad b. Abī Bakr al-ʿAyyāshī (1037-1090/1628-1679), from Abū al-ʿAbbās Aḥmad b. Muḥammad al-Abbār al-Fāsī (1001-1071/1593-

1661), from al-Khafājī, from al-ʿAlqamī, from al-Suyūṭī, from Shihāb al-Dīn Abū al-Ṭayyib Aḥmad b. Muḥammad b. ʿAlī al-Ḥijāzī (791-875), from Ibrāhīm b. ʿAbd al-Wāḥid al-Tanūkhī, from Aḥmad b. Abī Ṭālib al-Ḥajjār, from Jaʿfar b. ʿAlī al-Hamadhānī, from the Hadith master Abū Ṭāhir al-Silafī, Abū ʿAbd Allāh Muḥammad b. Aḥmad b. Ibrāhīm b. al-Ḥaṭṭāb al-Rāzī informed us, from Abū al-Faḍl Muḥammad b. Aḥmad al-Saʿdī, from al-Khaṣīb b. ʿAbd Allāh b. al-Khaṣīb by audition, from Abū Muḥammad ʿAbd Allāh b. Muḥammad al-Farghānī, **Abū Jaʿfar Muḥammad b. Jarīr al-Ṭabarī informed us,** Yūnus narrated to me, saying, Ibn Wahb reported to us, saying, al-Mundhir b. ʿAbd Allāh al-Ḥizāmī, from Hisham b. ʿUrwa, from his father, from ʿAbd Allāh b. Jaʿfar b. Abī Ṭālib, that the Messenger of Allah–upon him the blessings and peace of Allah–said, **"The best of the women of Paradise is Maryam bint ʿImrān, and the best of the women of Paradise is Khadīja bint Khuwaylid."**

Ṭabarī's chain is sound. Its basis is in the *Musnad*, the two *Ṣaḥīḥ*s and Tirmidhī from ʿAbd Allāh b. Jaʿfar, from ʿAlī, from the Prophet–upon him and them the blessings and peace of Allah. It is also narrated from him, from the Prophet, **"The best of their women is Maryam bint ʿImrān and the best of their women is Khadīja bint Khuwaylid."** I.e. the women of the people of Paradise. (Benefit) Abū al-Makārim al-Kattānī taught Ṭabarī's *Tafsīr* in the Zāwiya Kattāniyya in Fes.

(Benefit) Sayyid Muḥammad Abū al-Huda wrote to me that "the Bannānī house is a famous family in Morocco and one of the historic houses in Fes, which has always had vast renown, social eminence and brilliance in knowledge, politics and trade. They have immense love for the people of the noble Prophetic House and the expression goes in Morocco, 'either a Sharif or a Bannānī,' as a proclamation of the honor of this house, because one of their forefathers ransomed off one of the Sharifs—who was wanted by the sultan of his time—with one of his own sons. He accepted to give up his son but would not give up the Sharif."

25 *al-Dhurriyyat al-Ṭāhira* (The Purest Progeny) by al-Dūlābī (224-310/839-923)

THE NONAGENARIAN QADI Shaykh Muḥammad Murshid b. Muḥammad Abū al-Khayr Ibn ʿĀbidīn al-Dimashqī al-Ṣāliḥī al-Ḥusaynī (1332-1428/1914-2007)–Allah have mercy on him–and Dr. Muḥammad Muṭīʿ al-Ḥāfiẓ reported to us in their Damascus houses, respectively on Barniyya street and the Daḥdāḥ quarter, the first through a reading before him as I listened and the second through my own reading before him; the first said, my father Sayyid Muḥammad Abū al-Khayr ʿĀbidīn (1269-1343/1853-1925) informed us, from his father al-Sayyid Aḥmad b. ʿAbd al-Ghanī b. ʿUmar ʿĀbidīn al-Naqshbandī (1244-1307/1829-1890), from al-Wajīh ʿAbd al-Raḥmān al-Kuzbarī, from Murtaḍā al-Zabīdī; the second said, the qadī of Syro-Palestine and transmissologist, al-Sayyid ʿAbd al-Muḥsin al-Isṭuwānī reported to us, from al-Sayyid Salīm b. Yāsīn b. Ḥāmid al-ʿAṭṭār, from his grandfather al-Sayyid Ḥāmid al-ʿAṭṭār, from the Indo-Yemeni arch-lexicographer and Hadith master al-Sayyid Murtaḍā al-Zabīdī, with the six-link chain already mention in the chapter of al-Nasāʾī's *Mujtabā* to the Hadith arch-master Ibn Ḥajar who said, Abū al-ʿAbbās Aḥmad b. Abī Bakr al-Maqdisī reported it to us in his letter, saying, the qadi Taqī al-Dīn Sulaymān b. Ḥamza b. Abī ʿUmar informed us, saying, al-Ḥasan b. ʿAlī b. al-Sayyid al-Ḥāshimī [thus in the *Muʿjam al-mufahras*], from Abū al-Faḍl Muḥammad b. Nāṣir b. ʿAlī al-Baghdādī

(467-550/1075-1155) by audition before him, Abū al-Ṭāhir Muḥammad b. Aḥmad b. Abī al-Ṣaqr informed us, Abū al-Barakāt Aḥmad b. ʿAbd al-Wāḥid b. Naẓīf informed us, al-Ḥasan b. Rashīq al-ʿAskarī informed us, **Abū Bishr Muḥammad b. Aḥmad b. Ḥammād al-Dūlābī** informed us, Isḥāq b. Yūnus narrated to me, Suwayd b. Saʿīd narrated to us, from al-Muṭṭalib b. Ziyād, from Ibrāhīm b. Ḥayyān, from ʿAbd Allāh b. Ḥasan, from Fāṭima al-Ṣughrā the daughter of Ḥusayn, from al-Ḥusayn b. ʿAlī–Allah be well-pleased with them–who said, **"The Messenger of Allah–upon him the blessings and peace of Allah–was resting with his head on ʿAlī's thigh and was receiving revelation. When it was over he said, 'ʿAlī, did you pray the mid-afternoon prayer?' He said no. The Prophet said, 'O Allah! Verily you know that he was at Your beck and call and at the beck and call of Your Messenger, so bring back the sun for him.' Whereupon He brought it back for him and he prayed. Then the sun set."**

Al-Khaṭīb narrated it in his *Talkhīṣ al-mutashābih* through Suwayd b. Saʿid with the same chain. Ṭabarānī in the *Kabīr*, al-Ṭaḥāwī in *Sharḥ mushkil al-āthār*, Ibn Abī ʿĀṣim in *al-Sunna* and Ibn ʿAsākir all narrated it also but from Asmāʾ bint ʿUmays. Suyūṭī said in the *Laʾāli*ʾ: "I have come upon a stand-alone monograph gathering up all the paths of transmission of this hadith, as documented by Abū al-Ḥasan Shādhān al-Faḍlī," after which he quoted it. Among the major Hadith masters of the early authorities who declared this hadith sound are al-Firyābī in *Dalāʾil al-Nubuwwa*, al-Ṭaḥāwī, and Aḥmad b. Ṣāliḥ while a handful of latter-day hadith Masters rejected it, such as Abū al-Faraj Ibn al-Jawzī, al-Mizzī, Aḥmad Ibn Taymiyya and his three students al-Dhahabī, Ibn al-Qayyim and Ibn Kathīr. Qadi ʿIyāḍ, however, said in *al-Shifā* that al-Ṭaḥāwī in *Mushkil al-āthār* had narrated from Asmāʾ bint ʿUmays through two paths that the Prophet was receiving revelation as he was lying down with his head resting in ʿAli's lap—he mentioned this hadith—and that al-Ṭaḥāwī said, "These two hadiths are firmly established, and their narrators are trustworthy." He said Ṭaḥāwī also related that Aḥmad b. Ṣāliḥ used to say, "One whose way is learning should not fall behind from memorizing the hadith of

Asmā', because it is among the signs of Prophethood." Thus is it cited in *al-Shifā*. Likewise it was declared sound by the Hadith masters Walī al-Dīn al-'Irāqī in *Ṭarḥ al-tathrīb* and Suyūṭī in his monograph *Kashf al-labs fī ḥadīth radd al-shams* (The removal of confusion with regard to the hadith of the bringing back of the sun). Something similar was also related from Jābir with a fair chain as cited in *Majma' al-zawā'id* and *Fatḥ al-Bārī*. Ibn al-Jawzī said, "Ibn Mardūyah narrated it through Dāwūd b. Farāhīj from Abū Hurayra, but Dāwūd is weak according to Shu'ba." Al-Suyūṭī rejected this critique in the *Ta'aqqubāt 'alā al-Mawḍū'āt*, saying "There is a difference of opinion as to Dāwūd. He was never accused of lying. Ibn Ma'īn said, 'There is no harm in him.' Yaḥyā al-Qaṭṭān said, 'He is trustworthy.' Shu'ba narrated from him and said he had grown old. Abu Ḥātim said, 'He changed when he got old, but he is trustworthy and truthful.'"

(Subtle point) The Hadith master Ibn Ḥajar said of the Prophet–upon him blessings and peace–in his poetry album:

and the eye of the sun was brought back after setting
for the father of the Ḥasanayn because of his prayer,
and the eye of Qatāda flowed out but was put back
and was supplied, for his hands' sake, with light!

(Benefit and subtle point) Sayyid Murshid 'Ābidīn kindly gifted me a copy of his 2002 genealogical and bio-historical work *al-Durr al-thamīn fī nasab al-Sādat al-ṭāhirīn* (The costly pearls concerning the lineage of the pure Sharifs)–published at Dār al-Nu'mān in Damascus–with his blessed hand during a visit to his home on 14 Ṣafar 1425 / 4 April 2004. The congruity of its title and contents with the title and contents of this chapter is clear.

26 *Musnad al-ḥibb ibn al-ḥibb* (Full-chained hadiths of the beloved, son of the beloved) by Abū al-Qāsim al-Baghawī (213-317/828-929)

THE SAYYID NŪR AL-DĪN AL-KHAṬĪB informed me in his shop in the Rukn al-Dīn quarter in Damascus, from his father the Sufi transmissologist Muḥammad Ṣāliḥ al-Khaṭīb b. Aḥmad b. ʿAbd al-Raḥmān al-Jīlī al-Ḥasanī al-Dimashqī (1313-1401/1895-1981); (another route) the latter informed me directly through universal *ijāza*, from Shaykh Muḥammad Jamāl al-Dīn al-Qāwuqjī, from Muḥyī al-Sunna Muḥammad ʿĀbid al-Sindī (1190-1257/1776-1841), from his teacher Wajīh al-Dīn ʿAbd al-Raḥmān b. Sulaymān al-Ahdal, from his father, from the transmissologist of Syro-Palestine and redactor of the Ḥanbalī school the Imam Shams al-Dīn Abū al-ʿAwn Muḥammad b. Aḥmad b. Sālim al-Saffārīnī al-Nābulusī al-Dimashqī al-Atharī (1100-1188/1689-1774), from the mufti of the Ḥanbalīs in Damascus Abū al-Mawāhib Muḥammad b. ʿAbd al-Bāqī al-Baʿlī (1044-1126/1634-1714), from his father the teacher of the Qurʾān and *muḥaddith* Taqī al-Dīn ʿAbd al-Bāqī b. ʿAbd al-Bāqī al-Baʿlī al-Atharī (1005-1072/1597-1662) and the *muḥaddith* Imam and jurist of the Four Schools Muḥammad b. Badr al-Dīn b. ʿAbd al-Qādir b. Balbān al-Khazrajī al-Ṣāliḥī (1006-1083/1598-1672) the imam of the Muẓaffarī Mosque (Jāmiʿ al-Ḥanābila), both of them from the mufti of the Ḥanbalīs, the aged *muḥaddith* and qadi

Shihāb al-Dīn Aḥmad b. Abī al-Wafā' ʿAlī b. Mufliḥ al-Wafā'ī (936-1035/1530-1626), the transmissologist of Damascus, the Imam and seal of Hadith masters, Shaykh al-Islām Abū al-Faḍl Shams al-Dīn Muḥammad b. ʿAlī b. Aḥmad b. Ṭūlūn al-Ṣāliḥī (880-953/1475-1546) reported to us, the verifying Hadith master Yūsuf b. Ḥasan b. ʿAbd al-Hādī al-Ḥanbalī al-Dimashqī al-Ṣāliḥī, famously known as Ibn al-Mibrad (841-909/1438-1503) reported to us, from Shihāb al-Dīn Aḥmad b. al-Sharīfa (796-after 871/ 1394-after 1467), the three Shaykhs Ibn al-Ḥarastānī, Ibn al-Bālisī, and al-Mardāwī reported to you by *ijāza*, the Hadith master al-Mizzī informed us likewise, the seal of transmissologists al-Fakhr b. al-Bukhārī informed us, Imam Muwaffaq al-Dīn Ibn Qudāma informed us, from Abū al-Qāsim ʿUbayd Allāh b. ʿAlī b. Muḥammad b. Muḥammad b. al-Ḥusayn b. al-Farrā' (527-580/1133-1184) through his audition from the Hadith master Abū al-Faḍl Muḥammad b. Nāṣir b. Muḥammad al-Salāmī (=from Madīnat al-Salām i.e. Baghdad) (467-550/1075-1155), narrating from the Shaykh of the Ḥanbalīs, Imam Abū al-Wafā' ʿAlī b. ʿAqīl b.Muḥammad al-Baghdādī al-Ẓafarī (431-513/1040-1119), narrating from the qadi Abū Yaʿlā Ibn al-Farrā' al-Ḥanbalī, narrating from Abū al-Ḥasan ʿAlī b. Maʿrūf b. Muḥammad al-Bazzāz al-Ḥanbalī, narrating from the author, the aged transmissologist and proof in himself, **Abū al-Qāsim ʿAbd Allāh b. Muḥammad b. ʿAbd al-ʿAzīz b. al-Marzubān b. Sābūr b. Shāhanshāh al-Baghawī al-Baghdādī** who said, Ibn Manīʿ narrated to us, saying, Hārūn b. ʿAbd Allāh narrated to us, saying, Abū Dāwūd al-Ṭayālisī narrated to us, saying, Abū ʿAwāna [al-Waḍḍāḥ b. ʿAbd Allāh Mawlā Yazīd b. ʿAṭā' al-Yashkurī] narrated to us, saying, ʿUmar

b. Abī Salama narrated to us, from his father ʿAbd al-Raḥmān b. ʿAwf, who said, Usāma b. Zayd–Allah be well-pleased with them–narrated to me, saying, al-ʿAbbās and ʿAlī–upon them peace–said, **"Messenger of Allah! Which one of your closest kin is loveliest to you?" He replied, "The one loveliest to me of my closest kin is Fāṭima the daughter of Muḥammad."** They both said, "Messenger of Allah, we are not asking you about Fāṭima." He said, **"and Usāma b. Zayd, *Allah lavished blessing upon him and you lavished blessing upon him* (al-Aḥzāb 33:37)."**

Al-Tirmidhī narrated it—rating it *ḥasan ṣaḥīḥ*—as well as al-Ṭayālisī, al-Ṭabarānī and al-Ḥākim. Its chain is fair and al-Ḍiyāʾ al-Maqdisī narrated it in *al-Mukhtāra*. Its narrator ʿUmar b. Abī Salama is cited by al-Bukhārī and some of it is found in his *Ṣaḥīḥ* as narrated from Ibn ʿUmar in the wording, **"Word has reached me that you spoke about Usāma—and he is the most beloved of people to me,"** and in Aḥmad, al-Ṭabarānī and al-Ḥākim as **"The most beloved of people to me is Usāma."** It is also in al-Bukhārī in the wording, **"Verily this one is indeed among the most beloved of people to me,"** and in al-Tirmidhī from Anas: the Messenger of Allah–upon him the blessings and peace of Allah–was asked, **"Which of the people of your House is the most beloved to you?" He replied, "al-Ḥasan and al-Ḥusayn." And he would say to Fāṭima, "Call my sons to me," and he would smell them and hug them close to himself."** He rated it *ḥasan gharīb* per al-Mizzī's *Tuḥfat al-Ashrāf.* ʿAbd al-Razzāq also narrated from Fāṭima–Allah be well-pleased with her–that the Prophet–upon him the blessings and peace of Allah–said to her, **"I married you off to the most beloved of my people to me."**

(Benefits) Of the agreed-upon reports are also (1) from ʿAbd Allāh b. ʿAmr b. al-ʿĀṣ, **"I said, 'Which of the people is the most lovely to you?' He said, 'ʿĀʾisha.' I said, 'Among the men.' He said, 'Her father.' I said, 'Then who?' He said, 'ʿUmar b. al-Khaṭṭāb.' And he listed men."** It is also related from Anas and Abū Saʿīd al-Khudrī. (2) From Anas, he–upon him the blessings and peace of Allah–said to the Helpers, **"You are all the most lovely of people to me."** It was also related in the two *Ṣaḥīḥ*s in the wording **"You are all of the most lovely of people to me."** It is possible for "of" to signify emphasis [="indeed"], not partitiveness. The Hadith master Abū Saʿd Ibn al-Sammān (Ismāʿīl b. ʿAlī b. Zanjūyah d. 445/1053) in *al-Muwāfaqa bayna Ahl al-Bayt wal-Ṣaḥāba* (The agreement between the people of the Prophetic House and the Companions of the Prophet) narrated in *mursal* mode from Ja'far b. Muḥammad, from his father that **the Āl (family) of Abū Bakr were called, in the time time of the Messenger of Allah–upon him the blessings and peace of Allah–the Āl (family) of Muḥammad**. Muḥibb al-Dīn al-Ṭabarī mentioned it in *al-Riyāḍ al-naḍira*. It is also narrated in the *Ṣaḥīḥ* of Muslim from Abū Mūsā, "I came from Yemen with my brother and for a long time we did not view Ibn Mas'ūd and his mother other than as members of the household of the Messenger of Allah–upon him the blessings and peace of Allah–due to their frequent entering to see him and adhesion to him." Al-'Azīzī said in his commentary on al-Suyūṭī's *al-Jāmi' al-Ṣaghīr*, "It is well-established that the most lovely of people to him–upon him the blessings and peace of Allah–is Fāṭima, with a number of hadiths whose total imparts virtual mass transmission." He also said in *al-Taysīr*, in explanation of the hadith **"The most beloved of the people of my House to me are al-Ḥasan and al-Ḥusayn,"** "the truth is that Fāṭima has the absolute *aḥabbiyya* (most-beloved status)—that is firmly established through a number of hadiths whose total imparts virtual mass transmission—and other than her is in the [partitive] sense of 'among' or from a different perspective."

27 *Sharḥ mushkil al-āthār* (Exposition of the seemingly contradictory reports) by Abū Jaʿfar al-Ṭaḥāwī (229-321/844-933)

THE VENERABLE ḤABĪB ʿAlī b. Jaʿfar al-ʿAydarūs (d. 1431 /2010) informed us in Batu Pahat, Malaysia across the border with Singapore, and THE ERUDITE SAYYID Muḥammad Saʿīd b. Hāniʾ al-Kaḥīl al-Ḥusaynī al-Ḥimṣī (1353-1433/ 1934-2012) reported to us through my reading before him in his house in Homs–may Allah have mercy on them and protect her, and it may be he descends from the the Sharif Kahīls of the Maghreb who settled in Syro-Palestine–the first from his father, the erudite scholar al-Ḥabīb Jaʿfar b. Aḥmad b. ʿAbd al-Qādir b. Sālim al-ʿAydarūs (1308-1396/ 1891-1976), from Ḥabīb ʿAbd Allāh al-Shāṭirī whose close student he was, from Ḥabīb ʿAydarūs b. ʿUmar al-Ḥabshī, from his paternal uncle Muḥammad b. ʿAydarūs al-Ḥabshī and his father ʿUmar b. ʿAydarūs b. ʿAbd al-Raḥmān al-Ḥabshī, both of them from Shaykh ʿUmar b. ʿAbd al-Karīm al-ʿAṭṭār, from Murtaḍā al-Zabīdī, from al-Ḥafnāwī with the chain already mentioned under al-Nasāʾī's *Mujtabā* to Shaykh al-Islām; (the other chain) al-Kaḥīl said, Shaykh Muḥammad Ibrāhīm al-Khutanī al-Madanī informed me, Shaykh Muḥammad Zāhid b. Ḥasan al-Kawtharī informed me, Shaykh Ḥasan b. ʿAbd Allāh al-Qasṭamūnī informed me, the transmissologist of Tripoli, Lebanon who is buried in Damascus, author of many books and one of the major successors to Mawlanā al-Shaykh Khālid al-Baghdādī in the Naqshbandi path, Sayyid Aḥmad b. Sulaymān al-Arwādī al-Ṭarābulusī (d. 1275/1859) informed me, from the jurist Sayyid Muḥammad Amīn Ibn ʿĀbidīn al-Ḥanafī, from the erudite Abū Zayd ʿAbd al-Raḥmān b. Muḥammad b. Zayn al-Dīn al-Kuzbarī al-Kabīr (1100?-1185/1689?-1771), from the knower of Allah Shaykh ʿAbd al-Ghanī al-Nābulusī, from al-Najm al-Ghazzī, from his father al-Badr al-Ghazzī al-ʿĀmirī, from Shaykh al-Islām Zakariyyā al-Anṣārī, from the Imām and transmissologist of the world ʿIzz al-Dīn Abū Muḥammad ʿAbd al-Raḥīm b. ʿAlī b. al-Ḥusayn b. al-Furāt al-Ḥanafī (759-850/1358-1446), from the *muḥaddith* Abū al-Thanāʾ Shams al-Dīn Maḥmūd b. Khalīfa b. Muḥammad al-Manbijī al-Dimashqī al-Ḥanafī (687-767/1288-1366) from the Hadith master Sharaf al-Dīn ʿAbd al-Muʾmin b. Khalaf b. Abī al-Ḥasan al-Dimyāṭī al-Shāfiʿī (613-705/1216-1306), from the Hadith master and jurist Abū al-Muẓaffar Manṣūr b. Salīm al-Hamdānī al-Iskandarānī al-Shāfiʿī, famously known as Ibn al-ʿImādiyya (607-673/1210-1275)—the author of *Tuḥfat ahl al-Ḥadīth fī īṣāl ijāzat al-qadīm bil-ḥadīth* (The gift to the experts of Hadīth in making the *ijāza* of the old reach the new)—from the transmissologist of Iraq the aged Hadith master Abū al-Ḥasan Muḥammad b. Aḥmad b. ʿUmar al-Baghdādī known as Ibn al-Qaṭīʿī (546-643/1151-1245), from ʿAbd Allāh b. Jarīr al-Kātib (the Scribe)—thus in the *thabat* works, i.e. the copyist Abū Muḥammad ʿAbd Allāh b. Muḥammad b. Jarīr al-Qurashī al-Umawī al-Baghdādī al-Mālikī (510-582/1116-1182), a descendant of Saʿīd b. al-ʿAṣ b. Umayya —from the Hadith master and historian Abū Saʿd Tāj al-Islām ʿAbd al-Karīm b. Muḥammad b. Manṣūr al-Samʿānī al-Marwazī (506-562/1112-1167) the author of *al-Ansāb*

(The genealogies) and grandson of the author of the *Tafsīr*, from Imam Najm al-Dīn Abū Ḥafṣ ʿUmar b. Muḥammad b. Aḥmad al-Nasafī (461-537/1069-1143), from the qadi Abū Manṣūr Aḥmad b. Muḥammad al-Ḥārithī al-Sarakhsī al-Raʾīs (437-512/1046-1118), by permission from the qadi Abū Naṣr Muḥammad b. ʿAlī b. Ḥusayn al-Sarakhsī al-Ḥanafī, from the qadi Abū Muḥammad ʿAbd Allāh b. Muḥammad al-Akfānī—thus in *al-Jawāhir al-muḍīʾa*, but al-Gūrānī has ʿAbd Allāh b. ʿUmar al-Akfānī—from the jurist Abū Bakr Aḥmad b. Muḥammad b. Manṣūr al-Dāmaghānī al-Anṣārī al-Ḥanafī, from Imam **Abū Jaʿfar Aḥmad b. Muḥammad b. Salāma b. Salama al-Azdī al-Miṣrī al-Ṭaḥāwī** in his book *Sharḥ mushkil al-āthār*, "chapter on the exposition of the *mushkil* of what was narrated from him–upon him blessings and peace–as to the meaning of the saying of Allah Most High *Allah only wants to take away from you uncleanness, people of the House, and purify you thoroughly* (Aḥzāb 33:33)—who are they exactly?," whereby he said, Abū Umayya narrated to us, Khālid b. Makhlad al-Qaṭawānī narrated to us, Mūsā b. Yaʿqūb al-Zamʿī narrated to us, Ibn Hāshim b. ʿUtba (i.e. ʿAbd al-Raḥmān b. Hāshim b. ʿUtba b. Abī Waqqāṣ) reported to me, from ʿAbd Allāh b. Wahb, from Umm Salama–Allah be well-pleased with her, that **the Messenger of Allah–upon him the blessings and peace of Allah–gathered together Fāṭima, al-Ḥasan and al-Ḥusayn, and he made them enter under his cloak, then he cried out to Allah Most High, "My nurturing Lord! These are my *Ahl*." Umm Salama said, "I said, 'Messenger of Allah, will you make me enter with them?' He said, 'You are of my *Ahl*.'"**

Al-Ṭabarī narrated it in the *Tafsīr*. The editor of *Mushkil al-āthār* rated its chain as weak, saying, "Khālid b. Makhlad al-Qaṭawānī: Abū Ḥātim said of him, 'His hadith can be written but not be used as proof' while Mūsā b. Ya'qūb has a bad memory." In reality Abū Ḥātim did not add anything after "His hadith can be written" and al-Qaṭawānī is one of the narrators of al-Bukhārī and Muslim in their *Saḥīḥ*s. Al-'Ijlī and Ṣāliḥ Jazara declared him trustworthy and all of Yaḥyā b. Ma'īn, 'Uthmān al-Dārimī and Ibn 'Adī said there is no harm in him. Abū Dāwūd said, "He is truthful but upheld Shī'ism." The latter is the upshot of his status and a more precise statement than just Abū Ḥātim's word concerning him, which is why the Hadith master Ibn Ḥajar used it in *al-Taqrīb*, and the hadith at hand does not support Shī'ism. As for al-Zam'ī, he is also among the narrators of al-Bukhārī and the four *Sunan*. Ibn Ḥajar said in *al-Taqrīb*: "Truthful, with a bad memory." So to merely say that he has a bad memory is inaccurate. Furthermore the hadith is strong in light of what was already mentioned in the chapter on the *Musnad* and what is cited below of witness-texts.

It was also narrated from her–may Allah be well-pleased with her–by al-Ṭabarānī in *al-Kabīr*, **"I said, 'Messenger of Allah, am I of the people of the House?' He said, 'If Allah wills.'"** And in Baghawī's *Sharḥ al-Sunna*, **"I said, 'Messenger of Allah, am I not of the people of the House?' He said, 'Yes you are, if Allah wills.'"** He commented right after it, "This hadith has a sound chain." It is also narrated in *Sharḥ mushkil al-āthār* through Shahr b. Ḥawshab, from her, **"I said, 'Messenger of Allah, am I not of your *ahl*?' He said, 'Yes you are.' He said, 'Enter into the covering.' She said, 'So I entered after he had finished his supplication for his cousin 'Alī, his two sons, and his daughter Fāṭima–upon them peace.'"** Therein is also, through Ibn Lahī'a with a chain to 'Amrat al-Hamdāniyya that the latter asked about 'Alī after he had been killed, so Umm Salama asked her, "Do you love him or do you hate him?" She said, "Neither do I love him nor do I hate him." Umm Salama said, "Allah revealed this verse, *Allah only wants* to the end of it, at a time there was no one else in the house besides Jibrīl, the Messenger of Allah–upon him the blessings and peace of Allah, 'Alī, Fāṭima, al-Ḥasan and al-Ḥusayn, so I said, **'Messenger of Allah, am I from the people of the House?' So he said, 'Verily there is immense goodness in store for you with Allah.'** But I wished he had said, 'Yes you are.' That would have been dearer to me than all whereon the sun rises and sets."

Al-Ṭaḥāwī said–Allah have mercy on him:

> What we narrated of these reports and their contents revealing what the Messenger of Allah–upon him the blessings and peace of Allah–said to Umm Salama indicates that he did not mean that she was among those meant by the verse being recited on this chapter, but that those that were meant were the Messenger of Allah, 'Alī, Fāṭima, al-Ḥasan and al-Ḥusayn–upon them peace–exclusively.

What further indicates what the Messenger of Allah's intent–upon him the blessings and peace of Allah–was when he said to her **"You are of my *ahl*"** in these reports is the hadith of Wāthila b. al-Asqaʿ, **"then he wrapped around them a cloak while I was standing aside, then he said, *Allah only wants* to the end of the verse, then he said, 'O Allah! these are my *ahl*! Verily they are *ahlu ḥaqqin* (people of truth)' whereupon I said, 'Messenger of Allah, and am I of your *ahl*?' He said, 'And you are of my *ahl*.'"** Wāthila said, "So this is the greatest hope of all my hopes."

Al-Haythamī said in *Majmaʿ al-Zawāʾid* of the hadith of Wāthila, "Al-Ṭabarānī narrated it with two chains, one of which through the narrators of the *Ṣaḥīḥ* except Kulthūm b. Ziyād, whom Ibn Ḥibbān declared trustworthy but in whom there is some weakness." It will come up with its full chain in the chapter of the addenda to *Faḍāʾil al-Ṣaḥāba* if Allah wills. Then al-Ṭaḥāwī continued:

> Wāthila is farther away from him–upon him peace–than Umm Salama's remoteness from him, because he is a man from the Banū Layth, not from the Quraysh, while Umm Salama's position in relation to the Quraysh is the same position that she is in relation to him. Thus his statement to Wāthila, **"You are of my *ahl*"** is in the sense of "due to your following me and your believing in me, by virtue of which you are subsumed under my cover." We have found that Allah Most High mentioned in His Book that which indicates this meaning in His statement, *and Nūḥ called out to his nurturing Lord, saying, "My nurturing Lord! Verily my son is from my ahl (family)"* regarding which He answered him by saying to him, *O Nūḥ! Verily he is not from your family; verily he is a deed unrighteous* (Hūd 11:45-46). So, just as it is possible for Him to take him out of his family even though he was his son because he differed with him in the matter of his creed, it is likewise possible for one who conforms with him in the matter of his creed to enter into [the definition of] his *ahl* even if he is not among those who descend from him. An identical example of that is his stating the same to Wāthila. And Allah knows best what is correct.

(Benefit) My beloved friend Dr. Muhammad Munir al-Hayek wrote me that he asked Dr. Samer al-Nass about the report in Ibn Saʿd that "al-Ḥasan and al-Ḥusayn would not see the Mothers of the believers; Ibn ʿAbbās said, 'Their seeing them is halal for them'" and that Dr. Samer replied, "That is sound, due to the[ir] respect of the Houses of the Prophet–upon him the blessings and peace of Allah."

(Benefit) Abū Qurṣāfa Wāthila b. al-Asqaʿ b. Kaʿb b. ʿĀmir of the Banū Layth b. ʿAbd Manāt (7-85/628-704) was of the *Ahl al-Ṣuffa* (people of the Prophet's Mosque-Awning) and he was the last Companion to die in Damascus according to Ibn Ḥajar in *al-Iṣāba*.

28 *Saḥīḥ Ibn Ḥibbān* by Abū Ḥātim Muḥammad b. Ḥibbān al-Bustī (272?-354/885?-965)

THE TEACHER AND AUTHOR Shaykh Muḥammad ʿAjāj al-Khaṭīb b. Muḥammad Tamīm b. Muḥammad Ṣāliḥ Āl al-Shaykh ʿAbd al-Qādir al-Khaṭīb al-Ḥasanī (1932-2021)—Allah have mercy on him—narrated to me verbatim then through my reading before him in his house in Mazza, Damascus, from the transmissologist Muḥammad Ṣāliḥ al-Khaṭīb b. Aḥmad b. ʿAbd al-Raḥmān al-Jīlī al-Ḥasanī al-Dimashqī (1313-1401/1895-1981); (another path) and THE TRANSMISSOLOGIST Muḥammad Ṣāliḥ al-Khaṭīb informed me directly, with his chain already mentioned under al-Baghawī's *Musnad* to al-Sindī, from the jurist and *muḥaddith*, the mufti of the Shāfiʿīs in his time in Mecca the Magnificent, Muḥammad Saʿīd b. Muḥammad Sunbul al-Makkī (d. 1175/1762), from the aged Imam Aḥmad b. Muḥammad al-Nakhlī al-Ṣūfī (1040-1130/1631-1718)–one of the seven renewers of the science of transmission chains in the Hijaz—from the Suyūṭī of his time, the transmissologist of the Two Sanctuaries, the Imam in grammar, Quranic commentary and Hadith, the scholar of the Hijaz in the eleventh Hijri century and the one who taught *Ṣaḥīḥ al-Bukhārī* from beginning to end inside the Kaʿba, Shams al-Dīn Muḥammad ʿAlī b. Muḥammad ʿAllān al-Ṣiddīqī al-ʿAlawī the maternal grandson of the Āl al-Ḥasan, al-Shāfiʿī al-Makkī (996-1057/1588-1647)–author of major commentaries on al-Nawawī's *Adhkār* and *Riyāḍ al-Ṣāliḥīn*, al-

Haytamī's *al-Ta'arruf fīl-aṣlayni wal-taṣawwuf* entitled *al-Talaṭṭuf fīl-wuṣūl ilā al-Ta'arruf*, Muḥammad Birkilī's *al-Ṭarīqat al-Muḥammadiyya* entitled *al-Mawāhib al-fatḥiyya*, a fatwa on the prohibitiveness of smoking, and a refutation of Muḥammad Ibn 'Abd al-Hādī's vicious attack against Shaykh al-Islām al-Taqī al-Subkī's treatise on the hadiths of *ziyāra* entitled *al-Mibrad al-mubkī fī radd al-Ṣārim al-munkī* (The tear-inducing chisel in repelling 'The hurtful sword') among many others—from Shams al-Dīn Muḥammad Ḥijāzī b. Muḥammad al-Sha'rānī al-Wā'iẓ al-Qalqashandī the author of *Fatḥ al-Mawlā al-Naṣīr bi-sharḥ al-Jāmi' al-ṣaghīr*, from the transmissologist Aḥmad b. Sanad, from the Hadith master, transmissologist, Imam and Shaykh al-Islam, Muḥyī al-Sunna Abū 'Amr Fakhr al-Dīn 'Uthmān b. Shams al-Dīn Muḥammad b. Fakhr al-Dīn 'Uthmān b. Nāṣir al-Dīn al-Diyyamī al-Shāfi'ī al-Miṣrī, from his chief teacher the master of Hadith masters Ibn Ḥajar, the Shaykh al-Qurrā' Abū Isḥāq Ibrāhīm b. Aḥmad al-Tanūkhī informed us, from Muḥammad b. Aḥmad b. Abī al-Hayjā' b. al-Zarād, the Hadith master Abū 'Alī al-Ḥasan b. Muḥammad b. Muḥammad al-Bakrī informed us, Abū Rawḥ 'Abd al-'Azīz b. Muḥammad al-Harawī informed us, Tamīm b. Abī Sa'īd al-Jurjānī informed us, Abū al-Ḥasan 'Alī b. Muḥammad al-Baḥḥāthī informed us of it, Abū al-Ḥasan Muḥammad b. Aḥmad b. Hārūn al-Zawzanī informed us, **the Hadith master Abū Ḥātim Muḥammad b. Ḥibbān b. Aḥmad b. Ḥibbān al-Tamīmī al-Bustī** informed us, saying, al-Ḥusayn b. 'Abd Allāh b, Yazīd al-Qaṭṭān reported to us in al-Raqqa, saying, Hishām b. 'Ammār narrated to ut, saying, Asad b. Mūsā narrated to us, saying, Salīm b. Ḥayyān narrated to us, from Abū al-

Mutawakkil al-Nājī, from Abū Saʿīd al-Khudrī–Allah be well-pleased with him–who said, the Messenger of Allah–upon him the blessings and peace of Allah–said, **"By the One in Whose Hand is my soul! No man hates us—the people of the House—except Allah shall cause him to enter Hellfire."**

Al-Ḥākim narrated it and declared it *ṣaḥīḥ* per Muslim's criterion. (Note) This hadith comes in logical sequence with the hadith of the hater of our liegelord ʿAlī–may Allah ennoble his face–which we narrated in the chapter of al-Nasāʾī's *Mujtabā*, and the hadith **"Whoever hates us—the people of the House—then he is a hypocrite"** which also mentioned there. For the final destination of the hypocrite is the Fire. May Allah protect us and you from the punishment of the Fire and from all strifes.

29 *al-Muʿjam al-Kabīr* (The major alphabetical catalogue of transmitters and their reports) by al-Ṭabarānī (260-360/874-971)

THE INDONESIA-BASED ḤABĪB ʿAlī b. Muḥammad al-Ḥaddād al-Tarīmī informed me in Jakarta with a high chain from the supercentenarian al-Ḥabīb Hūd b. Miḥḍār al-Ḥabashī who reached 114 years of age, from the transmissologist of Yemen ʿAydarūs b. ʿUmar b. ʿAydarūs al-Ḥabashī (1237-1314/1822-1896) the author of several published catalogues of teachers– *ʿIqd al-yawāqīt, Simṭ al-ʿayn al-dhahabiyya fī asānīd al-sādat al-ʿAlawiyya, ʿUqūd al-laʾāl fī asānīd al-rijāl,* and *Minḥat al-Fattāḥ al-Fāṭir bi-dhikr asānīd al-sādat al-akābir*–from his paternal uncle Muḥammad b. ʿAydarūs b. ʿAbd al-Raḥmān al-Ḥabashī and his father ʿUmar b. ʿAydarūs b. ʿAbd al-Raḥmān al-Ḥabashī, both of them from the encyclopedic Shaykh ʿUmar b. ʿAbd al-Karīm b. ʿAbd al-Rasūl al-ʿAṭṭār (d. 1249/1833), from the Hadith master Muḥammad b. Muḥammad b. Muḥammad Murtaḍā al-Zabīdī (1145-1205/1732-1791) from al-Shihāb Aḥmad b. ʿAlī b. ʿUmar al-Manīnī, from Abū al-Mawāhib Muḥammad b. ʿAbd al-Bāqī al-Ḥanbalī, from Ayyūb al-Khalwatī al-ʿIdwī, from the aged *muḥaddith* Ibrāhīm al-Aḥdab, al-Shihāb Ibn Ḥajar al-Haytamī, from al-Suyūṭī, Shams al-Dīn Muḥammad b. Muqbil al-Ḥalabī al-Ṣayrafī informed me with a short chain, from Ṣalāḥ al-Dīn Muḥammad b. Ibrāhīm b. Abī ʿUmar al-Maqdisī al-Ṣāliḥī al-Ḥanbalī—the last of Fakhr al-Dīn Ibn al-Bukhārī's companions in the world—from al-Fakhr Ibn al-Bukhārī, from Abū Ja'far al-Ṣaydalānī, Fāṭima bint 'Abd Allāh al-Jūzdāniyya informed us, Abū Bakr Muḥammad b. 'Abd Allāh b. Rīda al-Ḍabbī al-Aṣfahānī informed us, **the Hadith master Abū al-Qāsim Sulaymān b. Aḥmad b. Ayyūb al-Ṭabarānī** reported to us, Zakariyyā b. Yaḥyā al-Sājī narrated to us, Hudba b. Khālid narrated to us, Ḥammād b. Salama narrated to us, from 'Abd al-Raḥmān b. Abī Rāfi', that Umm Hāni' the daughter of Abū Ṭālib came out uncovered with her ear-rings showing, whereupon 'Umar b. al-Khaṭṭāb said to her, "Know that Muḥammad does not suffice you at all!" So she came to the Prophet–upon him the blessings and peace of Allah–and reported it to him. The Messenger of Allah said, **"What ails certain people for them to claim that my intercession does not reach the people of my house? Verily my intercession shall reach even Ḥā and Ḥukm!"** They are two tribes.

It is *mursal* (dispatched with a missing Companion-link). 'Abd al-Razzāq narrated it from Ma'mar, from Khallād b. 'Abd al-Raḥmān, from his father also in *mursal* mode. Al-Haythamī said it is *mursal* and its narrators are trustworthy. 'Abd al-Razzāq also narrated it from Qatāda in *mursal* mode. It is also narrated from Khallād, from his father by 'Abd Allāh the son of Aḥmad b. Ḥanbal in *Faḍā'il al-Ṣaḥāba* (where the spelling is **'Khā' and Ḥukm'**) as well as Ibn 'Adī, al-Sam'ānī in *al-Ansāb*, and al-Bayhaqī in *al-Ba'tah wal-Nushūr* from Abū Hurayra with a full chain, all of them in the wording, **"By the One in Whose Hand is my soul! Verily even Ṣadā' and Salhab shall indeed hope for my intercession."** Al-Ṭabarānī also narrated it in *al-Kabīr* from Ibn 'Umar, Abū Hurayra, and 'Ammār b. Yāsir in the story of Durra bint Abī Lahab and it was mentioned with its chain in the chapter of Ibn Abī 'Āṣim's *al-Āḥād wal-mathānī*. Ḥā and Ḥukm are two remote tribes situated behind the desert of Yabrīn per the *Nihāya*, in the farthest parts of Yemen per al-Sam'ānī but Yāqūt al-Ḥamawī said Yabrīn is a town with abundant date palms and fresh water springs opposite al-Aḥsā' in the area of Banū Sa'd in Baḥrayn. Abū 'Ubayd said Ṣadā and Salhab are two sub-tribes of Yemen.

(The glad tidings of the Prophetic intercession for *Ahl al-Bayt*) The hadith of this chapter is supported by what was also narrated in the *Muʿjam al-kabīr* from Ibn ʿAbbās, who said that the Messenger of Allah–upon him the blessings and peace of Allah–said to Fāṭima–Allah be well-pleased with them–**"Verily Allah is not going to punish you nor your children."** Al-Haythamī said in *Majmaʿ al-zawāʾid* that its narrators were trustworthy. Furthermore al-Ḥākim narrated from Anas–Allah be well-pleased with him–that the Prophet–upon him the blessings and peace of Allah–said, **"My nurturing Lord has made me a promise concerning the people of my House—whoever of them acknowledges Oneness for Allah and conveyance [of the Message] for me—that He will never punish them."** Abū al-Qāsim Ibn Bishrān also narrated in his *Amālī* from ʿImrān b. Ḥuṣayn that the Messenger of Allah–upon him the blessings and peace of Allah–said, **"I asked my nurturing Lord that He not cause anyone of the people of my House to enter the Fire and He gave me that."** The latter noble meaning was affirmed by Ibn ʿAbbās in his commentary on the verse, *and your nurturing Lord shall certainly give you in abundance so that you shall be well-pleased* (al-Ḍuḥā 93:5), whereby he said, "The good pleasure of Muḥammad is that He will not cause anyone of the people of his House to enter Hellfire." Āl-Ṭabarī narrated it and, through him, al-Thaʿlabī. It was also said it consists in intercession for all the believers: al-Thaʿlabī also narrated with his chain to Muḥammad b. ʿAlī (Muḥammad al-Bāqir) that he said, "You Iraqis verily say that the most hope-filled verse in the Qurʾān is, *say, 'O My servants who have been wasteful against their own souls, do not despair of the mercy of the One God'* (al-Zumar 39:53)." They said, "We do say that." He said, "But we—the *Ahl al-Bayt*—say that the most hope-filled verse in the Book of Allah Most High is *and your nurturing Lord shall certainly give you in abundance so that you shall be well-pleased* (al-Ḍuḥā 93:5), namely, intercession." Also narrated in *al-Muʿjam al-kabīr* from Abū Jamīla that al-Ḥasan b. ʿAlī–Allah be well-pleased with him and his father–was made caliph when ʿAlī was killed. One day, as he was leading people in prayer, a man pounced and stabbed him in his hip with a dagger. it took him several months to recover then he stood at the pulpit giving a sermon, in which he said, "O people of Iraq! Beware Allah as to how you treat us! For verily we are your emirs and your guests, and we are the people of the House concerning whom Allah Most High said *Allah only wants to take away from you uncleanness, people of the House, and purify you thoroughly* (al-Aḥzāb 33:33)." And he kept speaking that day until no one caould be seen with dry eyes in the mosque but they were all weeping. Al-Haythamī said in *Majmaʿ al-zawāʾid* that its narrators are trustworthy. Ibn Abī Ḥātim narrated it in the *Tafsīr* as did Ibn ʿAsākir in the *Tārīkh*.

30 *al-Mu'jam al-Awsaṭ* by al-Ṭabarānī (260-360/874-971)

THE ERUDITE EDUCATOR al-Ḥabīb ʿAbd al-Qādir b. Muḥammad b. Aḥmad al-Ḥaddād al-Andūnīsī (d. 1434/ 2012)–Allah have mercy on him–the director of Maʿhad Dār al-Ḥāwī in Jakarta, informed me, from al-Ḥabīb ʿAbd al-Qādir b. Aḥmad Balfaqīh the scholar of eastern Java, from the three erudite knowers of Allah al-Ḥabīb ʿAbd Allāh b. ʿUmar al-Shāṭirī, al-Ḥabīb Aḥmad b. Ḥasan b. ʿAlī al-ʿAṭṭās and al-Ḥabīb ʿAlī b. Muḥammad b. Ḥusayn al-Ḥabshī (1259-1333/1843-1915) the author of *Simṭ al-durar* —all three of them from the transmissologist ʿAydarūs b. ʿUmar, with the chain mentioned in the previous chapter to Abū Jaʿfar al-Ṣaydalānī, Abū ʿAlī al-Ḥaddād informed us, the Hadith master Abū Nuʿaym al-Aṣbahānī informed us, **Abū al-Qāsim Sulaymān b. Aḥmad al-Ṭabarānī** informed us, Muṣʿab narrated to us, my father narrated to me, ʿAbd Allāh b. Muṣʿab b. Thābit b. ʿAbd Allāh b. al-Zubayr informed us, from Hishām b. ʿUrwa, from his father, from al-Zubayr b. al-ʿAwwām, the Messenger of Allah–upon him the blessings and peace of Allah–said, **"Allah has preferred the Quraysh in seven attributes: He preferred them in that they worshipped Allah for ten years while none worshipped Him but the Quraysh; He preferred them in that He granted them victory on the Day of the Elephant while they were still polytheists; He preferred them in that a Sura of the Qurʾān came down about them in which none of the worlds took part other than them, namely *for the pleasant resort of the Quraysh***

(Quraysh 106:1); **and He preferred them in that among them are Prophethood, caliphate, Kaʿba-guardianship, and Hajj water-service."** No one narrated this hadith from Hishām b. ʿUrwa except ʿAbd Allāh b. Muṣʿab, and it is not narrated from al-Zubayr except with this chain.

Al-Bayhaqī narrated it in *Manāqib al-Shāfiʿī* as did Ibn ʿAsākir in the *Tārīkh*, and the Hadith master al-ʿIrāqī rated it *ḥasan* in *Maḥajjat al-qurab fī maḥabbat al-ʿArab*. Al-Bukhārī also narrated it in *al-Tārīkh al-kabīr*, al-Ṭabarānī in *al-Muʿjam al-kabīr*, al-Ḥakim in the *Mustadrak*, and al-Bayhaqī in the *Khilāfiyyāt* from Umm Hāniʾ bint Abī Ṭālib–Allah be well-pleased with her–from the Prophet–upon him the blessings and peace of Allah–pattern-chained with the people of the House at its outset, however, Bukhārī deemed it more likely to be *mursal* through Ibn Shihāb al-Zuhrī.

31 *al-Sharīʿa* by al-Ājurrī (280-360/893-971)

THE LIBYAN TRANSMISSOLOGIST of Medina, al-Sayyid Abū Muḥammad Mālik b. al-ʿArabī b. Aḥmad al-Sharīf b. Muḥammad al-Sharīf b. *al-ḥāfiẓ* Muḥammad b. ʿAlī al-Sanūsī al-Khaṭṭābī (1351-1434/1932-2013)–Allah have mercy on him–informed me, from al-Sayyid Aḥmad b. Muḥammad ʿĀbid b. Muḥammad al-Sharīf known as Ibn Idrīs (d. 1410/1990), also from King Idrīs and from Sayyid Aḥmad Ḥamīda b. Muḥammad b. Aḥmad b. ʿAbd al-Qādir al-Rīfī (d. 1395/1975), all three from the latter's grandfather al-Sayyid Aḥmad al-Rīfī (d. 1329/1911), from the Hadith master Muḥammad b. ʿAlī al-Sanūsī al-Khaṭṭābī (1202-1276/1788-1860), from Abū Ṭālib al-Māzūnī (1100-1233/1689-1818), from Abū Isḥāq Ibrāhīm b. Ḥasan al-Gūrānī al-Kurdī al-Shāfiʿī, from the knower of Allah Most High Ṣafī al-Dīn Aḥmad b. Muḥammad al-Qushāshī al-Madanī al-Anṣārī, from Shams al-Dīn al-Ramlī, from Shaykh al-Islām al-Qāḍī Zakariyyā al-Anṣārī, from Ibn al-Furāt, from ʿIzz al-Dīn Ibn Jamāʿa, from the transmissologist Abal-Zubayr al-Gharnāṭī, from Abū al-Ḥasan Ibn Muḥammad al-Sarrāj, from his maternal uncle the transmissologist Abū Bakr Muḥammad b. Khayr b. ʿUmar b. Khalīfa al-Ishbīlī al-Umawī (d. 575/1179), who said in his catalogue of shaykhs: the book *al-Sharīʿa* by Abū Bakr Muḥammad b. al-Ḥusayn al-Ājurrī–Allah have mercy on him–was narrated to me by the Shaykh and Imam Abū Bakr Muḥammad b. Aḥmad b. Ṭāhir, from Abū ʿAlī al-Ghassānī, from Abū al-ʿĀṣī Ḥakam b. Muḥammad al-

Judhāmī, from Abū ʿAbd Allāh Muḥammad b. Khalīfa al-Balawī, also Abū al-Qāsim ʿUbayd Allāh b. Muḥammad al-Saqaṭī, also Abū al-Faraj ʿAbdūs b. Muḥammad al-Ṭalīlī who all three said, the Shaykh of the Noble Sanctuary, the chronicler, trustworthy *muḥaddith* and Hadith master, the scrupulously pious model of simple living, **Imam Abū Bakr Muḥammad b. al-Ḥusayn b. ʿAbd Allāh al-Ājurrī al-Baghdādī** then al-Makkī informed us, Abū Ḥafṣ ʿUmar b. ʿAbd al-Raḥmān narrated to us, from Yazīd b. Abī Ziyād, from ʿAbd al-Raḥmān b. Abī Nuʿm, from Abū Saʿīd al-Khudrī–Allah be well-pleased with him–who said, ther Messenger of Allah–upon him the blessings and peace of Allah–said, **"Fāṭima is the liege lady of the women of her world but for the status Allah appointed for Maryam bint ʿImrān."**

It is a fair hadith with a good chain and it has a corroborant narrated by al-Ḥākim in the wording, **"Fāṭima is the liege lady of the women of the people of Paradise save for what applies to Maryam bint ʿImrān."** Something similar was narrated among what we cited in the chapter of al-Nasāʾī's *Faḍāʾil al-Ṣaḥāba* (§22).

32 The *Zawā'id* (Addenda) of al-Qaṭī'ī (273-368/886-979) to Aḥmad's *Faḍā'il al-Ṣaḥāba*

THE MUFTI OF SINGAPORE (1972-2010) and noble scholar al-Ḥabīb 'Īsā b. Muḥammad b. Sumayṭ al-Azharī (b. 1358/1939) informed me there, from the Mufti of Johore and erudite scholar of many disciplines al-Ḥabīb 'Alawī b. Ṭāhir al-Ḥaddād (1301-1382/1884-1962) who is buried in the Maḥmūdiyya cemetery in the State of Johore in southern Peninsular Malaysia; and (a higher chain) al-Ḥabīb 'Alawī b. Ṭāhir al-Ḥaddād informed me directly, from his paternal uncle the Imam and Sayyid Ṣāliḥ b. 'Abd Allāh b. Ṭaha al-Ḥaddād and the aged transmissologist 'Umar b. 'Uthmān b. Muḥammad Bā 'Uthmān al-'Amūdī—a student of 'Amūd al-Dīn Sa'īd b. 'Īsā b. Aḥmad—both of them from the Mufti of Yemen and its transmissologist Sayyid Wajīh al-Dīn 'Abd al-Raḥmān b. Sulaymān b. Yaḥyā al-Ahdal with a high chain, from his father, from Imām 'Abd al-Raḥmān b. Aḥmad Bā 'Alawī al-Ḥusaynī, from al-Mullā Ibrāhīm al-Gūrānī, from al-Qushāshī, from Shams al-Dīn Muḥammad al-Ramlī, from Shaykh al-Islām Zakariyyā, from Ibn Ḥajar al-'Asqalānī, Taqī al-Dīn Ibn Fahd and Kamāl al-Dīn Muḥammad b. Muḥammad b. al-Zayn, the first from 'Umar b. Muḥammad b. Aḥmad b. Salmān al-Bālisī and all three from the transmissologist of Syro-Palestine Umm 'Abd Allāh 'Ā'isha bint Muḥammad b. 'Abd al-Hādī al-Maqdisiyya al-Ṣāliḥiyya, both Bālisī and 'Ā'isha from the aged transmissologist and *muḥadditha* of

Syro-Palestine the virgin scholar Umm ʿAbd Allāh Zaynab bint al-Kamāl Aḥmad b. ʿAbd al-Raḥīm b. ʿAbd al-Wāḥid al-Maqdisiyya (646-740/1248-1340), through her *ijāza* from the Hadith master Shams al-Dīn Abū al-Muẓaffar Yūsuf b. Qizughlī b. ʿAbd Allāh Sibṭ (maternal grandson of) Ibn al-Jawzī (581-654/1185-1256) from his grandfather the Hadith master Abū al-Faraj ʿAbd al-Raḥmān b. ʿAlī b. Muḥammad b. al-Jawzī, from his shaykh the Hadith master Abū al-Faḍl Muḥammad b. Nāṣir b. Muḥammad b. ʿAlī al-Baghdādī al-Salāmī, I read before the righteous Shaykh Abū al-Ḥusayn al-Mubārak b. ʿAbd al-Jabbār b. Aḥmad b. al-Qāsim al-Ṣayrafī al-Ṭuyūrī, Abū Ṭāhir Muḥammad b. ʿAlī b. Muḥammad b. Yūsuf al-Muqrī—known as Ibn al-ʿAllāf—informed us through its reading before him, **Abū Bakr Aḥmad b. Jaʿfar b. Ḥamdān b. Mālik al-Qaṭīʿī** informed us through its reading before him, saying, Abū Muslim Ibrāhīm b. ʿAbd Allāh b. Muslim al-Kujjī al-Baṣrī narrated to us, saying, ʿAbd Allāh b. ʿAbd al-Wahhāb al-Ḥajabī informed us, saying, Khālid b. al-Ḥārith narrated to us, saying, Ṭarīf b. ʿĪsā al-ʿAnbarī narrated to me, saying, Yūsuf b. ʿAbd al-Ḥamīd narrated to me, saying, "I met Thawbān and he saw that I was wearing certain [fancy] clothes, so he said 'What are you doing with these clothes?' and he saw a signet-ring on my hand, so he said, 'What are you doing with this signet-ring? Signet-rings are only for kings.' Then Thawbān narrated to us that **the Prophet–upon him the blessings and peace of Allah–summoned the people of his House and he mentioned ʿAlī, Fāṭima and others, so I said, 'Messenger of Allah, am I of the people of the House?' He stayed silent. Then I said, 'Am I of the people of the House?' He stayed silent. Then,**

the third time, he replied, 'Yes, as long as you do not stand at the porches of the rich or go to some emir for a handout.'"

Al-Ṭabarānī narrated it in *al-Awsaṭ*, as did Abū Nuʿaym in the chapter on Thawbān of *Ḥilyat al-awliyāʾ*, al-Bayhaqī in the *Sunan* and *al-Iʿtiqād*, Ibn ʿAsākir in the *Tārīkh*, and al-Shajarī in his *Amālī*, all of them through Khālid b. al-Ḥārith with the above chain. Al-Dhahabī said that Abū Bakr al-Qaṭīʿī was the most proficient-chained of the scholars of his time while al-Dāraquṭnī described him as the trustworthy ascetic and al-Ḥākim said of him, "trustworthy and dependable." As for the narrators of his chain they are solidly established as reliable and trustworthy except Ṭarīf b. ʿĪsā al-ʿAnbarī and his shaykh Yūsuf b. ʿAbd al-Ḥamīd: Bukhārī mentioned them in *al-Tārīkh* and Ibn Abī Ḥātim in *al-Jarḥ wal-taʿdīl*, neither one citing any verdict. Ibn Ḥibbān included Ṭarīf among the trustworthy narrators while al-Dāraquṭnī included him among the weak ones. Mundhirī in *al-Targhīb*, Haythamī in *Majmaʿ al-zawāʾid*, and al-Suyūṭī in *Mā rawāhu al-asāṭīn fī ʿadam al-majīʾ ilā al-salāṭīn* (The pillars' reports on the subject of refraining from visiting sultans) all said its narrators are trustworthy. Ibn Ḥajar in the *Iṣāba* and al-Suyūṭī in *Ḥusn al-muḥāḍara* mentioned that Ibn al-Sakan had narrated it through Yūsuf b. ʿAbd al-Ḥamīd—and Ibn Ḥazm viewed Ibn al-Sakan's *Ṣaḥīḥ* as second to the two *Ṣaḥīḥ*s in reliability according to al-Dhahabī in *Tadhkirat al-ḥuffāẓ*.

(Subtle point) With regard to his remark "What are you doing with this signet-ring? Signet-rings are only for kings," one of my teachers told me that Shaykh Badr al-Dīn al-Ḥasanī–Allah have mercy on him–used to forbid men from wearing rings. However it is a sunna for Shāfiʿīs and Ḥanbalīs as per al-Bayhaqī's *Kitāb al-takhattum* (Book of wearing rings) and Ibn Rajab's identically-titled work.

33 *al-Mustadrak ʿalā al-Ṣaḥīḥayn* (Corrective to the two *Ṣaḥīḥ*s) by al-Hākim al-Naysābūrī (321-405/933-1015)

THE DAMASCUS SUPERCENTENARIAN Sayyid Muḥammad al-Fātiḥ b. Muḥammad al-Makkī b. Muḥammad b. Jaʿfar al-Kattānī (1338-1442/1920-2021) informed us in the house of Sayyidī al-Shaykh Muḥammad Abū al-Hudā al-Yaʿqūbī in al-Ṣabbūra in the Damascus countryside, from al-Sayyid Aḥmad al-Sharīf al-Sanūsī (1290-1351/1873-1932), from his paternal uncle al-Sayyid Muḥammad al-Mahdī al-Sanūsī and from al-Sayyid Aḥmad al-Rīfī, both of them from al-Sayyid Muḥammad b. ʿAlī al-Sanūsī, from Abū Ṭālib Muḥammad b. ʿAlī b. al-Shārif al-Māzūnī, from the Sharifa transmissologist Quraysh bint ʿAbd al-Qādir al-Ṭabariyya, from the transmissologist ʿAbd al-Wāḥid b. Ibrāhīm al-Ḥaṣṣārī, from Shaykh al-Islām Zakariyyā al-Anṣārī, from the Hadith master Ibn Ḥajar who said, Abū Hurayra Ibn al-Dhahabī informed us by *ijāza*, from al-Qāsim b. Muẓaffar Ibn ʿAsākir, from the transmissologist Abū al-Ḥasan Ibn al-Muqayyar, from Abū al-Faḍl al-Mīhanī, from Abū Bakr Aḥmad b. ʿAlī b. Khalaf, from the Hadith master **Abū ʿAbd Allāh Muḥammad b. ʿAbd Allāh b. Ḥamdūn al-Ḍabbī al-Naysābūrī, known as Ibn al-Bayyiʿ**, Abū al-Ḥusayn Aḥmad b. ʿUthmān b. Yaḥyā al-Muqriʾ reported to us in Baghdad, Abū Qilāba al-Riqāshī narrated to us, Abū Ḥudhayfa narrated to us, Zuhayr b. Muḥammad narrated to us, from ʿAbd Allāh b. Muḥammad

b. ʿAqīl, from Ḥamza b. Abī Saʿīd al-Khudrī, from his father–Allah be well-pleased with him–who said, "I heard the Messenger of Allah–upon him the blessings and peace of Allah–say on the pulpit,

> **What ails certain people who say that my blood ties do not benefit? Nay, indeed they do! By Allah! Verily my blood ties are firmly kept in this life and the hereafter and, verily, O people! I am your forerunner at the Basin. And when I come to it, certain men will stand, and this one will say, "Messenger of Allah, I am so and so;" and that one will say, "Messenger of Allah, I am so and so;" and the other one will say, "Messenger of Allah, I am so and so;" but I will say, "I recognize you well, but you have changed things after me and you have gone back to your old ways!"**

Al-Ḥākim said, "This is a sound-chained hadith and the two Masters did not narrate it." It was narrated in various wordings by Abū Dāwūd al-Ṭayālisī, Ibn Abī Shayba, ʿAbd b. Ḥumayd, Aḥmad and Abū Yaʿlā. Al-Haythamī said, "Its narrators are the narrators of the *Ṣaḥīḥ* except ʿAbd Allāh b. Muḥammad b. ʿAqīl, and he was declared trustworthy." Al-Bayhaqī also narrated it in *Manāqib al-Shāfiʿī* with a longer chain, saying, "Abū Muḥammad ʿAbd Allāh b. Yūsuf al-Aṣbahānī narrated to us, Abū Bakr Muḥammad b. al-Ḥusayn al-Qaṭṭān related to us, Ibrāhīm b. al-Ḥārith al-Baghdādī narrated to us, Yaḥyā b. Abī Bukayr narrated to us, Zuhayr b. Muḥammad narrated to us, with the above chain but without the second half, i.e. without the portion starting **'and when I come to it.'**" Ibn ʿAbd al-Barr said in *al-Tamhīd* that Sharīk was asked, "Abū ʿAbd Allāh, in what sense did you construe this hadith?" He replied, "In the sense of the people of the *Ridda*." Al-Ṭabarī narrated it.

34 *Maʿrifat ʿulūm al-Ḥadīth* (Recognition of the categories of the Hadith) by al-Hākim al-Naysābūrī (321-405/933-1015)

THE VENERATED MASTER, directing guide of the imams and producer of the ulema, the author of *Iʿlām al-anām sharḥ Bulūgh al-marām bi-adillat al-aḥkām* (The informing of creatures: commentary on Ibn Ḥajar's 'The attainment of the goal with the proof-texts of legal rulings'), the untiring aged exegete, Hadith arch-master, jurist, legal theorist, lexicographer and peerless educator, the chair of the department of the disciplines of the Qurʾan and the Sunna in the faculty of Sharia in the two universities of Damascus and Aleppo, our teacher Dr. Nūr al-Dīn b. Muḥammad b. Ḥasan al-Ḥalabī al-Dimashqī al-Ḥanafī al-Azharī (1356-1442/1937-2020) al-Ḥasanī al-Ḥusaynī through his father and mother respectively, reported to me through my reading before him in the Ẓabyān mosque near his house in the Muḥajirīn quarter on Mount Qasyūn in Damascus after the Maghrib prayer the night before al-Sabt 17 Rabiʿ al-Ākhar 1425 / 4 June 2004, from his nurturing teacher, maternal uncle and father-in-law, Shaykh al-Islam, the Sharif Hadith master Shaykh Abū al-Najīb ʿAbd Allāh the son of the knower of Allah and erudite scholar Muḥammad Najīb b. al-Ḥājj Muḥammad Sirāj al-Dīn al-Ḥusaynī al-Ḥalabī al-Rifāʿī, from his father Shaykh Muḥammad Najīb, from his teacher or rather his pillar in narration, the Mufti of Aleppo and its region, the erudite scholar Shaykh Bakrī b. Aḥmad al-Zabrī al-Azharī, from his teacher Shaykh Burhān al-Dīn Ibrāhīm b. Muḥammad al-Bājūrī al-Miṣrī, from his teacher al-Amīr al-Ṣaghīr, from his father and teacher Abū ʿAbd Allāh Muḥammad b. Muḥammad al-Amīr al-Kabīr al-Miṣrī al-Mālikī, from his teachers the two Shāfiʿī erudite masters al-Shihāb Aḥmad b. ʿAbd al-Fattāḥ al-Mallawī and al-Shihāb Aḥmad b. al-Ḥasan al-Jawharī, both of them from their teacher the Hadith master and Imam Abū Sālim Jamāl ak-Dīn ʿAbd Allāh b. Sālim al-Baṣrī al-Makkī, from the aged Shaykh ʿAbd al-ʿAzīz b. Muḥammad b. ʿAbd al-ʿAzīz al-Zamzamī al-Makkī, from his father, from his maternal grandfather the arch-jurist Shihāb al-Dīn wal-Dunyā Shaykh Aḥmad b. Muḥammad b. Ḥajar al-Haytamī al-Makkī, from his teacher Shaykh al-Islam Zakariyyāʾ al-Anṣārī, from his teacher the Hadith arch-master Ibn Ḥajar who said in his *Muʿjam al-mufahras* (Alphabetical catalogue of personal readings and teachers) that he had completed the book with two shaykhs with each of whom he read one part: al-Taqī Abū Muḥammad ʿAbd Allāh b. Muḥammad b. Aḥmad b. ʿUbayd Allāh and al-ʿImād Abū Bakr b. Ibrāhīm al-Faraḍī, through their respective *ijāza*s if not their actual audition from Abū ʿAbd Allāh Muḥammad b. Aḥmad b. Abī al-Hayjāʾ b. al-Zarrād, by virtue of his audition of it before the Hadith master Abū ʿAlī al-Ḥasan b. Muḥammad b. Muḥammad al-Bakrī, by virtue of his audition of it before Abū Muḥammad al-Qāsim b. Abī Saʿd ʿAbd Allāh b. ʿUmar al-Ṣaffār, Abū Bakr Wajīh b. Khalaf al-Shīrāzī informed us, **the Hadith master Abū ʿAbd Allāh Muḥammad b. ʿAbd Allāh al-Ḍabbī al-Naysābūrī al-Ḥākim** informed us, Abū al-ʿAbbās Muḥammad b. Yaʿqūb narrated to us, saying, Muḥammad b. Isḥāq al-

Ṣaghānī narrated to us, saying, ʿAbd Allāh b. Bakr al-Sahmī narrated to us, saying, Yazīd b. ʿAwāna narrated to us, from Muḥammad b. Dhakwān al-Ṭāḥī (the Miller) the maternal uncle of Ḥammād b. Zayd's child, from ʿAmr b. Dīnār, from Ibn ʿUmar–Allah be well-pleased with him and his father–who said:

> Behold, we were sitting in the yard outside the door of the Messenger of Allah–upon him the blessings and peace of Allah–when a woman passed by and someone said, "This is the daughter of the Messenger of Allah." Abū Sufyān said, "The similitude of Muḥammad among the Banū Hāshim is that of a fragrant plant in the midst of stench." The woman then went and told the Prophet. The latter came and anger could be seen in his face. He said, **"What is the matter with statements that reach me from certain people? Verily Allah created the heavens as seven heavens, then He chose the highest ones of them and made whomever He wished of His creatures dwell in them. Then He created creatures and He selected, out of creatures, human beings; and He selected, out of human beings, the Arabs; and He selected, out of the Arabs, Muḍar; and He selected, out of Muḍar, the Quraysh; and He selected, out of Quraysh, the Banū Hāshim; and He selected me out of the Banū Hāshim. Thus we come from the best and to the best. So whoever loves the Arabs, then it is for love of me that he loves them; and whoever hates the Arabs, it is for hatred of me that he hates them."**

(Note) Shaykh Nūr al-Dīn ʿItr said, "It is probable that was before Abū Sufyān became Muslim."

Al-Ṭabarānī narrated it in *al-Kabīr* and *al-Awsaṭ* with the wording, **"then He chose the highest one of them and dwelt in it, and He made whomever He wished of His creatures dwell in His heavens."** Al-Haythamī said its chain contains Ḥammād b. Wāqid who is weak but may serve for corroboration, and the rest of its narrators have been declared trustworthy. Al-Ḥākim also narrated it in the *Mustadrak* and al-Bayhaqī in *Dalā'il al-Nubuwwa*, but Ibn Abī Ḥātim mentioned that his father had said it is an unrecognized hadith. I.e. from the aspect of the chain, since the *Mīzān al-i'tidāl* has, "Muḥammad b. Dhakwān: al-Bukhārī said his narrations are disclaimed; al-Nasā'ī said he is not trustworthy; al-Dāraquṭnī said he is weak; but Ibn Ḥibbān strengthened his status." As for the aspect of the text itself, the Hadith master Ibn Ḥajar declared it *ḥasan* (fair) in *al-Amālī al-muṭlaqa* (Free dictations) and its basis is in *Ṣaḥīḥ Muslim*, from Wāthila b. al-Asqa', "I heard the Messenger of Allah–upon him the blessings and peace of Allah–say, **"Verily the One God has purified and elected Kināna out of the children of Ismā'īl; and He purified and elected, Quraysh out of the Kināna; and He purified and elected, out of the Quraysh, the Banū Hāshim; and He purified and elected me out of the Banū Hāshim."** Al-Bayhaqī said of the two hadiths in *Manāqib al-Shāfi'ī*: "Their meaning is one and the same." Thus the meaning of election begins with all human beings and hones in on the Arabs, ultimately leading to the the Prophetic House and the person of the Holy Prophet:

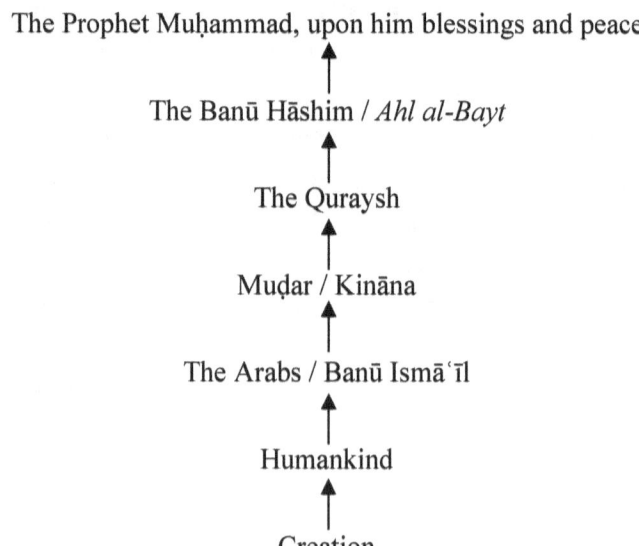

The Prophet Muḥammad, upon him blessings and peace

↑

The Banū Hāshim / *Ahl al-Bayt*

↑

The Quraysh

↑

Muḍar / Kināna

↑

The Arabs / Banū Ismā'īl

↑

Humankind

↑

Creation

Another hadith was narrated by Aḥmad and al-Tirmidhī—he rated it *ḥasan*—from Salmān who said, **"The Messenger of Allah–upon him the blessings and peace of Allah–said to me, 'Salmān, do not hate me lest you part with your faith!' I said, 'Messenger of Allah, how can I hate you when it is with you that Allah has guided us?' He said, 'By hating the Arabs; then you would be hating me.'"** Also among the finest reports in this chapter is the full-chained hadith from Jābir, from the Prophet–upon him blessings and peace of Allah– **"When the Arabs become lowly, Islam becomes lowly"** in the *Musnad* of Abū Yaʿlā. Al-Suyūṭī rated it *ṣaḥīḥ* in *al-Jāmiʿ al-ṣaghīr*.

Then al-Ḥākim continued directly after the hadith:

> Let the student of this science therefore know that every Muḍarī is Arab, for the Muḍar are a branch of the Arabs; every Qurashī is a Muḍarī, for the Quraysh are a branch of the Muḍar; every Hāshimī is a Qurashī, for Hāshim is a branch of the Quraysh, and every ʿAlawī is Hāshimī; but they differed about why the latter were called ʿAlawīs. It was said it is by affiliation to ʿAlī, and it was said, by affiliation to the highest (*aʿlā*) levels in relation to the Messenger of Allah–upon him the blessings and peace of Allah. So whoever recognizes what I alluded to as to the tribe of the Elect one–upon him the blessings and peace of Allah–makes it the model for the rest of the tribes and thus knows that the Muṭṭalibī is Qurashī, the ʿAbshamī is Qurashī—Shaykh Nūr al-Dīn here said "*ʿAbshamī* is a *tarkīb mazjī* (acronymic compound) from ʿAbd Shams"—, the ʿAdawī is Qurashī, and the Umawī is Qurashī, so the origin is Quraysh and all these are offshoots. Likewise, the Nashalīs are Tamīmīs, the Dārimīs are Tamīmīs, the Saʿdīs are Tamīmīs, the Salīṭīs are Tamīmīs, the Qaysīs are Tamīmīs, the Ahtamīs are Tamīmīs. Likewise, the Khazrajīs are Anṣārīs, the Najjārīs are Anṣārīs, the Ḥārithīs are Anṣārīs, the Sāʿidīs are Anṣārīs, the Salimīs are Anṣārīs, and the Awsīs are Anṣārīs. The Messenger of Allah–upon him the blessings and peace of Allah–said, **"In each of the *dūr* (clans, houses) of the Anṣār there is goodness."** (Muslim and Aḥmad.)
>
> This [=the main hadith in this chapter], then, is an archetype for recognition of the offshoots of the main tribes.

35 *Ma'rifat al-Ṣaḥāba* (Recognition of the Companions) by Abū Nu'aym al-Aṣbahānī (336-430/948-1039)

THE *MUḤADDITH* OF TANGIERS al-Sayyid Abū al-Yusr 'Abd al-'Azīz b. Muḥammad b. al-Ṣiddīq al-Ghumārī (1338-1418/1920-1997) informed us, from his father al-Sayyid Muḥammad b. al-Ṣiddīq b. Aḥmad b. 'Abd al-Mu'min al-Ghumārī al-Ḥasanī (d. 1354/1935), from his mother's maternal uncle the aged jurist 'Abd al-Qādir b. Aḥmad b. 'Ajība (d. 1313/1895), from his father the famous wali and author of the Quranic commentary and the marginalia on Ibn 'Aṭā' Allāh's *Ḥikam*, Aḥmad b. 'Ajība (d. 1225/1810), from the Shaykh of the *jamā'a*, al-Tāwudī Ibn Sawda, from al-Shams al-Bannānī, from Abū Sālim al-'Ayyāshī, from al-Shihāb al-Qalyūbī, from al-Shams al-Ramlī, from Shaykh al-Islām Zakariyyā', from the Hadith master Ibn Ḥajar, from Zayn al-Dīn Abū al-Faḍl al-'Irāqī, from Abū al-Faḍl al-'Alā'ī, from al-Mizzī, from al-Dimyāṭī, from al-Mundhirī, from Abū al-Faḍl al-Maqdisī, from the Hadith master 'Abd al-Ghanī b. 'Abd al-Wāḥid b. 'Alī b. Surūr al-Maqdisī, through its reading before Abū Mūsā Muḥammad b. Abī Bakr b. Abī 'Īsā al-Madīnī, al-Ḍiyā' Muḥammad b. Aḥmad b. Abī Bakr al-Jūzadānī, Abū 'Alī Ḥamza b. Abī al-Fatḥ b. 'Abd Allāh 'Atīq Musāfir al-Ṭabarī, all three of them by virtue of their narration from Abū 'Alī al-Ḥaddād, **from the Hadith master Abū Nu'aym Aḥmad b 'Abd Allāh b. Isḥāq al-Aṣbahānī**, 'Abd Allāh b. Ja'far [b.

Aḥmad b. Fāris] narrated to us, Ismāʿīl b. ʿAbd Allāh [b. Masʿūd al-ʿAbdī] narrated to us, Mālik b. Ismāʿīl and Ismāʿīl b. Abān narrated to us, both saying, Masʿūd b. Saʿd al-Juʿfī narrated to us, Muḥammad b. Isḥāq; (another route from Abū Nuʿaym) also, Abū Aḥmad Muḥammad b. Aḥmad b. Isḥāq al-Anmāṭī narrated to us, ʿAbdān b. Aḥmad narrated to us, Zayd b. al-Ḥuraysh narrated to us, Muḥammad b. al-Ṣalt narrated to us, Mindal b. ʿAlī narrated to us, from Muḥammad b. Isḥāq; (another route) also, al-Qāḍī Abū Aḥmad Muḥammad b. Aḥmad b. Ibrāhīm narrated to us, al-Ḥusayn b. ʿAlī b. al-Ḥasan al-Salūlī narrated to us, Muḥammad b. al-Ḥasan al-Salūlī narrated to us, Ṣāliḥ b. Abī al-Aswad narrated to us, from Muḥammad b. Isḥāq; (another route) also, Abū Bakr [Aḥmad b. Jaʿfar b. Ḥamdān] b. Mālik [al-Qaṭīʿī] narrated to us, ʿAbd Allāh b. Aḥmad b. Ḥanbal narrated to us, Yaʿqūb b. Ibrāhīm b. Saʿd narrated to us, my father narrated to me, from Muḥammad b. Isḥāq—the wording is that of Ibrāhīm b. Saʿd—from Abān b. Ṣāliḥ, from al-Faḍl b. Maʿqil b. Sinān, from ʿAbd Allāh b. Niyār al-Aslamī, from ʿAmr b. Shaʾs al-Aslamī—he was among the Companions of Ḥudaybiya—who said, "I went out with ʿAlī–Allah be well-pleased with him–to Yemen and he was rude to me in that trip until I felt aversion in myself towards him, so when I came home I brought my complaint against him out into the open in the mosque until news of that reached the Messenger of Allah–upon him the blessings and peace of Allah. I entered the mosque one early morning as the Messenger of Allah was there with a group of his Companions. When he saw me, he looked at me intently until, when I sat, he said, **"O ʿAmr! By Allah you have harmed me."** I said "I seek refuge in

Allah from ever harming you, Messenger of Allah!" He said, **"Yes you have. Whoever harms ʿAlī has certainly harmed me."** Al-Muḥāribī, Yūnus b. Bukayr, and Abū Zuhayr also narrated it in similar terms from Muḥammad b. Isḥāq.

It is a sound report narrated by Aḥmad in the *Musnad* and the *Faḍāʾil*, al-Bazzār, Ibn Abī Shayba, al-Rūyānī—the latter two in short form—Ibn Ḥibbān, al-Ḥākim, and al-Bayhaqī in the *Dalāʾil*. There is also in al-Nasāʾi's *Khaṣāʾiṣ*, al-Ḥākim and Ibn Abī Shayba from Umm Salama, and in Aḥmad from Saʿd, from the Prophet–upon him the blessings and peace of Allah–the wording, **"Whoever insults ʿAlī has certainly insulted me."** Also in the latter and elsewhere, from ʿAbd al-Muṭṭalib b. Rabīʿa, from the Prophet–upon him the blessings and peace of Allah–**"Whoever harms al-ʿAbbās has certainly harmed me."**

(Subtle lesson) Bayhaqī narrated in the *Manāqib* that ʿAlī b. Abī Ṭālib was mentioned in al-Shāfiʿī's presence, whereupon someone said, "People never deserted ʿAlī b. Abī Ṭālib except for the reason that he did not care about anyone." Whereupon al-Shāfiʿī said, "Not so fast. That is because there were in him four traits, any single one of which would suffice for anyone who possessed it not to have to care about anyone else: ʿAlī b. Abī Ṭālib was a *zāhid* (completely abstemious) and the *zāhid* does not care about the world and its minions; he was a *ʿālim* (knower of Allah) and the *ʿālim* does not care about anyone; he was brave and the brave one does not care about anyone; he was a Sharif and the Sharif does not care about anyone."

36 *Muntakhab dalā'il al-Nubuwwa* (The elite of the signs of Prophethood) by Abū Nuʿaym al-Aṣbahānī (336-430/ 948-1039)

THE SHAYKH OF THE IDRĪSIYYA Aḥmadiyya Shādhiliyya Sufi path, the influential, high-born erudite ascetic and author of books, the globe-trotter knower of Allah and aged caller to Allah, al-Sayyid Aḥmad b. Idrīs b. Muḥammad al-Sharīf al-Sūdānī al-Ummudurmānī al-Azharī (1350-1439/ 1932-2017)–Allah have mercy on him–informed me from his father al-Sayyid Idrīs, from his father al-Sayyid Muḥammad al-Sharīf, from his father al-Sayyid ʿAbd al-ʿĀlī, from his father the knower of Allah al-Sayyid Aḥmad b. Idrīs al-Fāsī the founder of the Aḥmadiyya Sufi path, from Abū al-Mawāhib al-Tāzī, from al-ʿUjaymī, with his three-link chain already mentioned in the chapter of al-Shāfiʿī's *Musnad* to the Hadith master Ibn Ḥajar, with the latter's chain that was just mentioned to the Hadith master ʿAbd al-ʿAẓīm al-Mundhirī (581-656/1185-1258), from the preacher Abū al-Ḥasan Zayn al-Dīn ʿAlī b. Ibrāhīm b. Najā al-Dimashqī al-Miṣrī al-Ḥanbalī al-Anṣārī (508-599/ 1114-1203), the trustworthy Imam and Hadith master Saʿd al-Khayr Muḥammad b. Sahl al-Anṣārī (d. 541/1146)–Allah have mercy on him–reported to us as it was read before him while we listened in the year 539/1145 in the seat of the Caliphate–may Allah restore it–saying, the master jurist Abū Saʿd Muḥammad b. Muḥammad b. Muḥammad al-Muṭarriz–Allah have mercy on him–informed us through as it was read before him in his Ispahan house while I listened, saying, the Imam Abū Nuʿaym Aḥmad b. ʿAbd Allah b. Aḥmad b. Isḥāq informed us as it was read before him, saying, the qadi Abū Aḥmad [Muḥammad b. Aḥmad b. Ibrāhīm] narrated to us, saying, al-Ḥasan b. ʿAlī b. Ziyād narrated to us, saying, ʿAbd al-Raḥmān b. Yaḥyā al-Hāshimī al-Madanī narrated to us, saying, ʿAbd Allāh b. ʿUthmān, from his maternal grandfather Mālik b. Ḥamza b. Abī Usayd al-Sāʿidī who said, I witnessed my grandfather [Abū Usayd Mālik b. Rabīʿa al-Sāʿidī al-Anṣārī] saying, **the Messenger of Allah–upon him the blessings and peace of Allah–said to al-ʿAbbās, "Do not leave early you and yours sons tomorrow, for I have some need of you." Al-ʿAbbās gathered them in a house and the Messenger of Allah came to them and said, "Peace be upon you! How are you this morning?" They said, "We are well and give praise to Allah, may our father and mother be your ransom, Messenger of Allah!" He said, "Come close to one another, come close to one another" which they did. Once they had done his bidding, he covered them all with his mantle and then he said "O Allah, this is al-ʿAbbās, my uncle, and these ones are the people of my House, so cover them against the fire just as I am covering them with my mantle now." Whereupon the threshold and the walls of the house all said, "*Āmīn! Āmīn! Āmīn!*" three times.**

Al-Ṭabarānī narrated it in *al-Kabīr* and *al-Awsaṭ* with a chain al-Haythamī declared fair in *Majmaʿ al-zawāʾid*. It was also narrated by al-Taymī al-Aṣfahānī and al-Bayhaqī, both of them in their books of *Dalāʾil al-Nubuwwa*, and by Ibn Mājah in the *Sunan*, the latter in short form. Ibn Kathīr cited it in *al-Bidāya* in the chapter on the praising of the stones in the section on the signs of Prophethood in the book on the Prophetic *shamāʾil* (personal attributes).

(Benefit) This hadith is among the evidences for collective supplication, as it shows the listeners saying *āmīn* to the supplication of the speaker.

(Historical notes) The nonagenarian Abū al-Ḥasan ʿAlī b. Ibrāhīm b. Najā b. Ghanāʾim al-Nujawī al-Anṣārī al-Dimashqī married Umm ʿAbd al-Karīm Fāṭima the daughter of the Moroccan Hadith master Saʿd al-Khayr al-Anṣārī when she came with her father to Baghdad from Ispahan to attend the audition of hadith. He then took her with him to Egypt where they lived according to al-Dubaythī in his *Tārīkh*. It is also mentioned in the *Sīra Zankiyya* that he kept company with Shaykh ʿAbd al-Qādir al-Jīlānī in Baghdad and said, "I studied hard with him then Allah opened up for me in one year that which He did not open up for others in twenty." He was among the advisors to Salāḥ al-Dīn al-Ayyūbī. Ibn Rajab said in *Dhayl Ṭabaqāt al-Ḥanābila*, "When Salāḥ al-Dīn conquered al-Quds he was with him, and he gave the first Jumuʿa sermon there after that. There was massive attendance on that day." Ibn Nāṣir al-Dīn said in *Tawḍīḥ al-mushtabah*, "He was a highly articulate admonisher who had a following among kings and other than kings, and he possessed wealth and property, including twenty concubines, each of whom was worth a thousand gold dinars."

37 *Shu'ab al-īmān* (The branches of belief) by al-Bayhaqī (384-458/994-1066)

THE NONAGENARIAN ḤABĪB 'Umar b. Sālim al-Miḥḍār (1341-12 Rabī' al-Awwal 1435/1923-14 January 2014)–Allah have mercy on him –informed me in his residence in Batu Pahat, Johore Sultanate, Malaysia, from the Shaykh of the Valley the Imam, educator and knower of Allah al-Ḥabīb 'Alawī b. 'Abd Allāh b. 'Aydarūs b. Shihāb al-Dīn (1303-1386/1886-1966), from the Imam and Mufti of Hadramawt Ḥabīb 'Abd al-Raḥmān b. Muḥammad b. Ḥusayn al-Mashhūr (1250-1320/1834-1902) the author of *Bughyat al-mustarshidīn* (Aim of the seekers of guidance) with a high link, from the erudite Ḥabīb Muḥammad b. Ibrāhīm b. 'Aydarūs b. 'Abd al-Raḥmān b. 'Abd Allāh b. Aḥmad Balfaqīh, from his father Ibrāhīm and his paternal uncle Aḥmad, from their father 'Aydarūs b. 'Abd al-Raḥmān, from his father the arch-erudite scholar 'Abd al-Raḥmān b. 'Abd Allāh b. Aḥmad Balfaqīh (1089-1162/1678-1749), from his father 'Abd Allāh b. Aḥmad Balfaqīh (d. 1112/1700), from al-Ṣafī al-Qushāshī, with his chain already mentioned in the chapter of Ibn Abī Shayba's *Muṣannaf* to the Hadith master Shams al-Dīn al-Dhahabī, Aḥmad b. Salāmat al-Ḥaddād reported to us, the Imam and Hadith master Bahā' al-Dīn Abū Muḥammad al-Qasim–the son of the Hadith master Abū al-Qāsim 'Alī b. al-Ḥusayn b. Hibat Allāh b. 'Abd Allāh al-Shāfi'ī Ibn 'Asākir–(527-600/1133-1204) reported to us as it was read before him, saying, the jurist Abū ʿAbd Allāh Muḥammad b. al-Faḍl al-Ṣāʿidī al-Furāwī (d. 530/1136) and Abū al-Qāsim Zāhir b. Ṭāhir b. Muḥammad al-Shaḥḥāmī (446-533/1054-1139) both reported to us [by *ijāza*], also my father [Abū al-Qāsim Ibn ʿAsākir (499-571/1106-1176) the author of the 70-volume *Tārīkh Dimashq* (History of Damascus)] and Abū al-Ḥasan ʿAlī b. Sulaymān b. Aḥmad al-Murādī al-Shaqūrī (d. 544/1149) both narrated to me from Zāhir who said, the Imam and Hadith master, **the Shaykh of the Sunna, Abū Bakr Aḥmad b. al-Ḥusayn b. ʿAlī b. Mūsā al-Bayhaqī**–Allah have mercy on him–reported to us, saying, Abū ʿAbd Allāh the Hadith master—by whom he means his major teacher al-Ḥākim al-Naysābūrī—reported to us, Abū al-ʿAbbās Muḥammad b. Yaʿqūb reported to us, al-ʿAbbās b. Muḥammad al-Dūrī narrated to us; (another route) also, Aḥmad b. Abī al-ʿAbbās al-Zawzanī reported to us, Abū Bakr b. Khanab narrated to us, Abū Bakr Muḥammad b. Sulaymān al-Bāghandī narrated to us, both [the latter and al-Dūrī] saying, Muḥammad b. ʿImrān b. Abī Laylā narrated to us, Saʿīd b. ʿAmr al-Sakūnī narrated to us, from [Muḥammad b. ʿAbd al-Raḥmān] Ibn Abī Laylā, from al-Ḥakam, from ʿAbd al-Raḥmān b. Abī Laylā, from Abū Laylā who said, the Messenger of Allah–upon him the blessings and peace of Allah–said, **"No servant believes until I become dearer to him than his own life, my near family becomes dearer to him than his near family, my person becomes dearer to him than his own person, and my wives become dearer to him than his own wives."**

Al-Ṭabarānī in the *Kabīr* and the *Awsaṭ*, Abū al-Shaykh in *al-Thawāb*, and al-Shajarī in his *Amālī* all narrated it through Muḥammad b. ʿAbd al-Raḥmān b. Abī Laylā the qadi of Kufa, who is—despite his poor memory in hadith—among the narrators of the *Sunan*, and this hadith is *ṣaḥīḥ* (sound) per the collective weight of its witness-texts. Allah knows best.

Al-Bayhaqī said directly after it:

Part of loving the Prophet–upon him the blessings and peace of Allah–is to love his Companions, because Allah Most High praised them and commended them by saying, *Muḥammad is the Messenger of Allah, and those that are with him are tough against the unbelievers, most merciful with one another* (al-Fatḥ 48:29); *the One God was certainly well-pleased with the believers as they pledged their bond to you under the tree, whereby He knew what was is their hearts, so He sent down tranquility over them and recompensed them with an imminent victory* (al-Fatḥ 48:18); *and the foremost and first of the Emigrants and the Helpers, and those that came after them with what is best, the One God is well-pleased with them, and they are well-pleased with Him* (al-Tawba 9:100) to the end of the verse; *and those that believed, emigrated and struggled in the way of the One God, and those that gave shelter and helped: those ones—they are the believers in truth; theirs is forgiveness and a generous provision* (Anfāl 8:74). Since they hold such a position, they rightly deserve that the entirety of the Muslims must love them and strive to draw near to Allah by loving them, because when Allah Most High is well-pleased with someone He loves that one, and it is obligatory for a slave to love whomever his master loves. It was narrated to us from ʿUmar b. al-Khaṭṭāb, from the Prophet–upon him blessings and peace–that he said **"Keep my Companions in high honor"** [ʿAbd al-Razzāq, al-Ḥumaydī, al-Shāfiʿī in the *Risāla*, al-Ṭayālisī, al-Ṭaḥāwī in *Maʿānī al-āthār*, al-Ṭabarānī in *al-Ṣaghīr*, al-Khaṭīb, and Baghawī in *Sharḥ al-Sunna*] and, in another narration, **"Keep my honor as to my Companions"** [Ibn Mājah and al-Ḥākim, and it has witness-texts, among which **"I instruct you to respect my Companions"** by Tirmidhī and Ḥākim from ʿUmar, also **"Remember you are instructed to show my Companions goodness"** by Aḥmad and al-Ḥākim from Ibn ʿUmar, also **"Treat my Companions excellently"** by Aḥmad, Ibn Abī ʿĀṣim, Abū Yaʿlā, al-Ṭaḥāwī and Ibn Ḥibbān from Jābir, and by Ibn Abī Shayba and Ibn Abī ʿāṣim from ʿUmar]. In the hadith of Abū Saʿīd al-Khudrī, from the Prophet–upon him the blessings and peace of Allah–**"Do not insult my Companions! For if any of you were to spend the same as Uḥud in gold, he would still not amount to the *mudd* (543.4g) of any one of them—nor half of that! And no man hates the Helpers who believes in Allah and the last Day"** [the Six Books and Nasāʾī's *Sunan al-kubrā*; al-Ḥārith and Ṭabarānī also narrate, from Ibn Masʿūd, **"When my Companions are mentioned, hold back!"** Haythamī said its narrators were those of the *Ṣaḥīḥ* except

Mushir b. ʿAbd al-Malik—Ibn Ḥibbān and others rated him trustworthy, and there is disagreement about it].

Among the best compilations in this chapter besides what we have already mentioned: al-Dāraquṭnī's *Faḍāʾil al-Ṣaḥāba*; Abū Nuʿaym's *Faḍāʾil al-Khulafāʾ wa-ghayrihim*; Daḥlān's *al-Fatḥ al-mubīn fī faḍāʾil al-Khulafāʾ al-rāshidīn wa-Ahl al-Bayt al-ṭāhirīn*; al-Talīdī's *Faḍāʾil al-Ṣaḥāba wal-difāʿ ʿan karāmatihim*; ʿAlāʾī's *Taḥqīq munīf al-rutba li-man thabata lahu sharīf al-Ṣuḥba*; Baḥraq's *al-Ḥusām al-maslūl ʿalā muntaqiṣī Aṣḥāb al-Rasūl*; al-Ḍiyāʾ al-Maqdisī's *al-Nahy ʿan sabb al-Aṣḥāb*; and Maḥmūd Shukrī al-Ālūsī's *Ṣabb al-ʿadhāb ʿalā man sabba al-Aṣḥāb*. All of the above are published.

38 *Dalā'il al-Nubuwwa* (The signs of Prophethood) by al-Bayhaqī (384-458/994-1066)

THE GUARDIAN OF MY BLESSING and my spiritual guide, the Quṭb al-Mutaṣarrif (spiritual Pole of complete discretion), the Support from Allah, the Shaykh of the Naqshbandi Sufi path, the Beiruti Sharif Mawlana al-Shaykh Muhammad Hisham b. Hajj Muhammad Salim Kabbani al-Husayni al-Shafi'i (born 1364/1945)–Allah save him–and the Beiruti Naqshbandī Shaykh Ḥusayn b. Aḥmad 'Usayrān al-Shāfi'ī (1329-1426/1911-2005)–Allah have mercy on him–hailing from the Banū Asad b. Khuzayma of Muḍar who were famously devoted to *Ahl al-Bayt*, both informed me from the secretary-general for fatwa in Lebanon the Sharif Muḥammad al-'Arabī al-'Azzūzī al-Zarhūnī al-Fāsī al-Bayrūtī (1308-1382/1891-1962), from his father Abū 'Īsā Muḥammad al-Mahdī, from his father the erudite scholar Muḥammad al-'Arabī b. Muḥammad al-Hāshimī, from Abū Ḥāmid al-'Arabī b. al-Mu'ṭī al-Sharqāwī al-Tādilī, from his teacher Abū al-'Abbās Aḥmad b. Abī al-Qāsim al-Tādilī al-Rubāṭī, from Abū al-'Abbās Muḥammad b. 'Abd al-'Azīz al-Hilālī al-Sijilmāsī, from Abū 'Abd Allāh Muḥammad b. 'Abd al-Jabbār al-'Ayyāshī, from the globe trotter of Morocco Abū Sālim 'Abd Allāh b. Muḥammad b. Abī Bakr al-'Ayyāshī, from the aged Shihāb al-Dīn Aḥmad b. Aḥmad b. Salāmat al-Qalyūbī al-Shāfi'ī, from his teacher al-Shams Muḥammad b. Aḥmad b. Ḥamza al-Ramlī, from Shaykh al-Islām Zakariyyā', Abū Dharr al-Zarkashī reported to me with a high chain, from Abū ʿAbd Allāh al-Bayānī, Abū Ḥafṣ Ibn Ghadīr al-Qawwās reported to us by audition as well as license from the head judge al-Jamāl Abū al-Qāsim al-Ḥarastānī, from Abū ʿAbd Allāh Muḥammad b. al-Faḍl al-Furāwī and ʿAbd al-Jabbār b. Aḥmad al-Khuwārī who both said, its author the Hadith master **Abū Bakr Aḥmad b. al-Ḥusayn al-Bayhaqī**–Allah have mercy on him–reported to us, saying, Abū Manṣūr Muḥammad b. Muḥammad b. ʿAbd Allāh b. Nūḥ–a descendant of Ibrāhīm al-Nakhaʿī in Kufa–reported to us, saying, Abū Jaʿfar Muḥammad b. ʿAlī b. Duḥaym reported to us, saying, Aḥmad b. Ḥāzim b. Abī ʿAzra narrated to us, saying, al-Faḍl b. Dukayn narrated to us, saying, Sufyān narrated to us, from Yazīd b. Abī Ziyād, from ʿAbd Allāh b. al-Ḥārith b. Nawfal, from al-Muṭṭalib b. Abī Wadāʿa who said al-ʿAbbās said, upon hearing what some people were saying about him; (another route) al-Bayhaqī said, and Abū al-Ḥusayn b. al-Faḍl reported to us, ʿAbd Allāh b. Jaʿfar reported to us, Yaʿqūb b. Sufyān narrated to us, Abū Nuʿaym—al-Faḍl b. Dukayn—narrated to us, with its chain to al-Muṭṭalib b. Abī Wadāʿa who said:

> **The Messenger of Allah–upon him the blessings and peace of Allah–when some of what the people were saying** [i.e. about his uncle al-ʿAbbās] **reached him, climbed the pulpit and he praised and glorified Allah then he said, "Who am I?" They said, "You are the Messenger of Allah." He said, "I am Muḥammad the son of ʿAbd Allāh the son of ʿAbd al-Muṭṭalib. Verily Allah created creation and He put me among the best of His creatures; then He divided them into two parts and He put me in the best part; and He made them into tribes, whereupon He put me in the best of them**

as a tribe; and He made them into houses, whereupon He put me in the best of them as a house. Therefore I am the best of you in his House and the best of you in his person."

Aḥmad and Tirmidhī narrated it, the latter rating it fair as did Ibn Ḥajar in *al-Amālī al-muṭlaqa*–and something similar was related from Jābir by Ṭabarānī (*Awsaṭ*) and Ḥākim. Therein is clear evidence his House is the best of all human Houses with an implied specific reference to his parents and agnate uncles and aunts among whom are his maternal cousin and milk-brother, the liegelord of the shahids Ḥamza, ʿAbbās, Arwā, ʿĀtika who said at the time of the Hijra *Brim, eyes, with tears for the acclaimed one, the full moon of Hāshim's House!* and Ṣafiyya who elegized him, saying *my mother be sacrificed for the Messenger, my maternal aunt and paternal uncle, my life first and my dependants!*

(Subtle points) This noble hadith typifies what our beloved teacher and spiritual guide Shaykh Muhammad Hisham Kabbani has endured of harm and hostility for the sake of Allah since before and after the departure of Mawlana Shaykh Muhammad Nazim al-Haqqani–Allah sanctify their secrets–from this world, at which time was contrived a ploy to crowd him out of the Naqshbandi *sajjāda* and cover up the fact he was the rightful true successor to Mawlana Shaykh Nazim and second successor to Mawlana Shaykh ʿAbd Allah Faʾiz al-Daghistani after Mawlana Shaykh Nazim per their own widely-proclaimed final word. This is in addition to his being the eldest spiritual son of these two Shaykhs from the line of the Prophet–upon him peace–who had been the locus of the spiritual gaze of Sultan al-Awliya Shaykh ʿAbd Allah Daghistani (1294-1393/1877-1973) and Shaykh Nazim since youth, and his being raised in a renowned family of scholars between his Ḥasanī maternal uncles Mukhtār (1899-1984) and ʿAbd Allāh al-ʿAlaylī (1333-1417/1914-1996). Shaykh Mukhtār was the general secretary of fatwa in the Republic of Lebanon and head of the Beirut Council of Ulema whom al-ʿAzzūzī described in his *thabat* as "the erudite scholar in the many disciplines, the other half of my soul, my intimate companion in my exile," while his younger brother the arch-scholar and 14th-century renewer of the Arabic language Shaykh ʿAbd Allāh ʿAlaylī, was hailed by ʿAzzūzī as "the wonder of the age, most knowledgeable of them in all the arts especially language and literature, mastering Hadith, *tafsīr* and the two principles with a mastery to which I never saw anyone come near; and as for knowledge of the Arabs' history and their battles then speak of no less than the sea!"

(Benefit) I was introduced to Shaykh ʿUsayrān by my friend the Ḥanafī legal theorist and director of Muḥammad Fātiḥ Institute in Beirut Dr. Basim Itani al-Husayni.

(Subtle benefits) The historic Achrafieh, Beirut building of my teen and pre-teen years stood at 225 Sodeco, off the main artery called Rue de Damas (notorious as the so-called Green Line in the Lebanon war), equidistant to two mosques: Masjid Othman Zu al-Nurayn and Masjid Beydoun. Ours was the only Christian family living therein. The other three families in our building were all Muslims from *Ahl al-Bayt*: the Bayhum on the first floor, our landlords the Ajlani on the second, and the Hedari [=Haydari] on the fourth. We all vacated it when war broke out in 1975. On the next block, as Mawlana Shaykh Hisham Kabbani informed me two decades later, sat the carpet storehouse of his family, on Damascus Road. Thus the outward façade of my pre-Islamic past was unbeknownst neighborhood to the Tree of pure Light while the inward gifts were the outpourings of *jiwār* and *naẓar*. May the fruit of that Tree and the opening of that gift bring the writer and his line under the shade of the noble verse, *Verily those for whom was foreordained the best from Us–those ones are kept far from it* [=the Fire] (al-Anbiyā' 21:101). *Āmīn.*

39 *Ma'ālim al-tanzīl* (The Qur'an commentary entitled The signposts of revelation) by Muḥyī al-Sunna al-Baghawī (433-516/1042-1122)

THE REVIVER OF THE MUḤAMMADAN SUNNA, the Sultan of the Friends of Allah, my nurturing Rabbani Shaykh, Mawlana Shaykh Nāẓim 'Ādil b. Aḥmad b. Ḥasan al-Qubruṣī al-Dimashqī al-Ṣāliḥī al-Naqshbandī al-Ḥaqqānī al-Ḥanafī (1341-1435/1922-2014)–Allah have mercy on him, a descendant of Shaykh 'Abd al-Qādir al-Jīlānī on his father's side and of Mawlāna Jalāl al-Dīn al-Rūmī on his mother's side, narrated to me from his teacher and his teacher's son, the Shaykh of the Qur'ān reciters in Homs, Shaykh 'Abd al-'Azīz b. Muḥammad b. 'Alī 'Uyūn al-Sūd al-Ḥimṣī (1335-1399/1917-1979) who died in prostration, from the transmissologist of the two Sanctuaries Shaykh Abū Ḥafṣ 'Umar b. Ḥamdān al-Maḥrasī al-Tūnisī al-Mālikī al-Makkī, from the blind Shaykh Shams al-Dīn Muḥammad b. Sulaymān Ḥasab Allāh al-Shāfi'ī al-Makkī (1244-1335/1829-1917), from Shaykh 'Abd al-Ghanī al-Dimyāṭī al-Makkī, from Shaykh Aḥmad Zayd 'Alī b. Aḥmad al-Damhūjī al-Azharī (1170-1246/1757-1831), from the erudite Shaykh al-Azhar 'Abd Allāh b. Ḥijāzī b. Ibrāhīm al-Sharqāwī (1150-1227/1737-1812), from his teacher Muḥammad b. Sālim al-Ḥifnī, from Shaykh Muḥammad b. Muḥammad al-Budayrī famed as Ibn al-Mayyit (the dead man's son), from the Sībawayh of his time Shaykh Nūr al-Dīn Abal-Ḍiyā' 'Alī al-Shabrāmallisī, from Burhān al-Dīn Ibrāhīm al-Laqānī al-Mālikī, from Abū al-Najā Sālim al-Sanhūrī, from a-Najm al-Ghayṭī, from Shaykh al-Islām Zakariyyā al-Anṣārī, from al-ʿIzz ʿAbd al-Raḥīm b. al-Furāt, from al-Ṣalāh Ibn Abī ʿUmar, from al-Fakhr Ibn al-Bukhārī, from al-Faḍl Ibn Saʿd al-Nawqānī, from **the Reviver of the Sunna, the Imam, Shāfiʿī jurist and Hadith master Abū Muḥammad al-Ḥusayn b. Masʿūd al-Baghawī** who said in the commentary on Sūrat al-Aḥzab (The confederates), under His statement–exalted is He–*and when We took from the Prophets their covenant* to His statement *and the One God was ever All-Aware of what you all do* (33:7-9), Abū Saʿīd al-Shurayḥī reported to us, Abū Isḥāq al-Thaʿlabī reported to us, ʿAbd Allāh b. Ḥāmid al-Aṣbahānī reported to us, Muḥammad b. Jaʿfar al-Ṭabarī reported to us, Ḥammād b. al-Ḥasan narrated to us, Muḥammad b. Khālid b. ʿAthma narrated to us, Kathīr b. ʿAbd Allāh b. ʿAmr b. ʿAwf narrated to us, my father narrated to me, from his father (ʿAmr b. ʿAwf)–Allah be well-pleased with him–who said:

> **The Messenger of Allah designed the Trench in the year of the Confederates, then he allocated to each ten workers forty cubits (about 24 meters). Then the Emigrants and the Helpers argued about Salmān al-Fārisī, who was a strong man. The Emigrants said, "Salmān is one of us," and the Helpers said, "Salmān is one of us." Whereupon the Prophet–upon him the blessings and peace of Allah–said, "Salmān is one of us, the people of House!"**

This is a famous hadith. Mūsā b. ʿUqba narrated it from al-Zuhrī in *mursal* mode in the *Maghāzī* while Ibn Saʿd in his *Ṭabaqāt*, al-Ṭabarānī in *al-Muʿjam al-kabīr*, Abū al-Shaykh in *Ṭabaqāt al-muḥaddithīn bi-Aṣbahān*, Ṭabarī in the *Tafsīr* and the *Tārīkh*, al-Ḥākim in the *Mustadrak*, al-Bayhaqī in the *Dalāʾil*, Abū Nuʿaym in

Ma'rifat al-Ṣaḥāba and *Akhbār Aṣbahān*, and the *Sīra* authors all narrated it from Ibn Abī Fudayk, from Kathīr b. ʿAbd Allāh al-Muzanī, from his father, from his grandfather ʿAbd al-Raḥmān b. ʿAwf. Ibn Kathīr classed it as single-chained in the *Bidāya* and al-Haythamī said of Kathīr b. ʿAbd Allāh, "The vast majority considered him weak but al-Tirmidhī rated his hadiths as *ḥasan* (fair). The rest of its narrators are trustworthy." It is because of the latter *taḥsīn* that al-Dhahabī said his infamous statement, "This is why the ulema do not depend on al-Tirmidhī's *taḥsīn*." See the effective rebuttal of this statement in the book of our revered teacher Shaykh Nūr al-Dīn ʿItr, *al-Imām al-Tirmidhī wal-muwāzana bayna Jāmi'ihi wa-bayna al-Ṣaḥīḥayn* (Imam al-Tirmidhī and the assessment of his *Jāmi*ʿ in comparison to the two *Ṣaḥīḥ*s)–may Allah reward him for it. It has a witness-report in *Ṭabaqāt al-muḥaddithīn bi-Aṣbahān*, Abū Yaʿlā and al-Bazzār–per Ibn Ḥajar's *Itḥāf al-mahara*–through Naḍr b. Ḥumayd, from Saʿd al-Iskāf, from Abū Jaʿfar Muḥammad b. ʿAlī b. al-Ḥusayn b. ʿAlī b. Abī Ṭālib, from his father, from his father, from his grandfather–may Allah be well-pleased with them. Hence it was said that the sound version is that it is a statement of our liegelord ʿAlī–may Allah be well-pleased with him and make him pleased. It was also narrated by Wāqidī in the *Maghāzī* from Ibn Abī Sabra—i.e. Abū Bakr b. ʿAbd Allāh b. Muḥammad b. Abī Sabra al-Qurashī al-Madanī who is discarded—from Marwān b. Abī Saʿīd b. al-Muʿallā al-Madanī in *mursal* mode. Allah Most High knows best.

(Subtle gifts) I heard Mawlana Shaykh Nazim–may Allah sanctify his soul–in the year 1996 during his second trip to the United States speaking in Turkish to his wife Hajja Amina–Allah have mercy on them–as I was serving them in their hotel room in New York City, and he said to her, "Gibril is one of us." Eight years later, after I finished working on the report **"Salmān is one of us,"** I saw myself in dream on the early morning of the day of Jumuʿa 2 Rabiʿ al-Awwal 1425 (21 April 2004) as if I were Mawlana Shaykh Nazim's actual son and my son Abdulghani was Mawlana's grandson. (Mawlana had given him his name upon birth in reality, just as he had also named my sons Taher and Alauddin–may Allah lavish goodness on them and their older and younger brothers.) In the dream we were in Mawlana's house and I was asking him about the correct spelling of a word I had heard from him, then Abdulghani came in, playing—he was a toddler—so Mawlana said, "Don't let him see us," and he placed his hands before his face like a curtain behind which to hide, but soon I called him over. Then I saw myself carrying Mawlana on my back, and he slept as I carried him from one room to another. When I knelt down he woke up and said to me, "I was travelling as is my habit during sleep, I go here and there." I asked him, "Do you go to those places in reality (at that time), Mawlana?" He said yes. I said, "Like the Prophets?" I.e. your dreams are truth. He said yes. I saw him in dream another time several months after he left this world, on the night before the last Jumuʿa of Ramadan 1435/2014 coming up some stairs towards me as a man at the top of his powers, laughing, and he said to me, "Undo my turban." So I undid it turn by turn while making *dhikr* together with *ḥuḍur* per the rules—a green, heavy turban—then I smelled it, hugged it close and drank it in like Zamzam as I wept. Then I looked at him and saw he had tied on another turban on his head, white and brown. Then he left. After that I saw myself during the days that I was putting the final touches to the first edition of this book in the year 1437/2015 one night before *fajr* as if I was travelling with his most senior caliph without compare, my liegelord Shaykh Muhammad Hisham Kabbani, the Abundant Fruit-brearer from Allah and the Mountain of forbearance and equanimity–may Allah sanctify his secret. There was no one else with the two of us except Allah, and we were as if in a wilderness of mountains crags, valleys and forests. Then I saw two huge palaces close to one another, but they were completely engulfed underwater at the bottom of the sea, as if the valley was now a dark ocean fearful to behold. I said, as if I were a tour guide, "These are palaces belonging to two kings from whom Allah did not accept their acts." Then we headed towards a third palace that was in plain view, which contained the grave of Mawlana Shaykh Nazim–may Allah sanctify his soul. We gave salam and Mawlana Shaykh Hisham raised his hands in supplication. Lo and behold, Mawlana Shaykh Nazim came out and walked over to Shaykh Hisham, hugged him, kissed his face, and said something private to him. Then he wiped my arm and he left. I interpreted it in the same sense as what is mentioned in the previous chapter.

40 *al-Anwār fī shamā'il al-Nabī al-mukhtār* (The lights in the personal attributes of the elect Prophet) by Muḥyī al-Sunna al-Baghawī (433-516/1042-1122)

THE RECTOR OF MADRASAH ALJUNIED AL-ISLAMIAH in Singapore, the educator of simple living and erudite master of Arabic letters and legal theory, my Shaykh the Sayyid ʿAbd al-Maqṣūd ʿAbd al-Muṣawwir b. al-Sayyid Fāris b. al-Sayyid Aḥmad b. al-Sayyid Ismāʿīl al-Ḥasanī al-Qāhirī al-Shāfiʿī (1352?-15 Rabīʿ al-Awwal 1432/1933?-19 February 2011)–Allah have mercy on him–one of the ulema of al-Azhar al-Sharīf, narrated to me, our teacher the erudite Shāfiʿī jurist, *muḥaddith* and man of letters Shaykh ʿUmar b. ʿAbd Allāh b. Aḥmad b. ʿAbd Allāh b. Abī Bakr b. Sālim al-Khaṭīb al-Anṣārī al-Tarīmī al-Singāfūrī (1326-1418/1908-1997) narrated to us from his paternal uncles the erudite peerless scholar Abū Bakr al-Khazrajī al-Tarīmī (d. 1356/1937) and ʿAbd Allāh and Muḥammad the sons of Aḥmad b. Aḥmad b. ʿAbd Allāh b. Abī Bakr b. Sālim al-Khaṭīb, from their father, from al-Sayyid Daḥlān, with his eight-link chain already mentioned in the chapter of al-Shāfiʿī's *Musnad* to Ibn Ḥajar, from al-Ṣalāḥ Ibn Abī ʿUmar, from al-Fakhr Ibn al-Bukhārī, from Abū al-Makārim Faḍl Allāh [ʿUmar?] b. Muḥammad b. Aḥmad b. Muḥammad b. Sulaymān al-Nūqātī al-Shāfiʿī (514-600/1120-1204), by virtue of the *ijāza* obtained for him by his father from the greatest Imam, the leader of simple living,

Shaykh al-Islam, the Reviver of the Sunna, Abū Muḥammad al-Ḥusayn b. Masʿūd al-Farrāʾal-Baghawī —thus named after his father's work as a *farrā'* (skinner) and the town of Bagh, also called Baghshūr, in Khurasan—saying, Ismāʿīl b. ʿAbd al-Qāhir reported to us, ʿAbd al-Ghāfir b. Muḥammad reported to us, Muḥammad b. ʿĪsā reported to us, Ibrāhīm b. Muḥammad b. Sufyān reported to us, Muslim b. al-Ḥajjāj reported to us, Zuhayr b. Ḥarb narrated to me, Muḥammad b. Fuḍayl reported to us, from his father, from ʿUmāra b. al-Qaʿqāʿ, from Abū Zurʿa, from Abū Hurayra–Allah be well-pleased with him–who said, the Messenger of Allah–upon him the blessings and peace of Allah–said, **"O Allah, make the provision of the Family of Muḥammad sustenance!"**

It is in the two *Ṣaḥīḥ*s and the *Sunan*. Ibn al-Athīr said in the *Nihāya* that his expression *qūtan* (sustenance) means "food to the extent of what maintains life and strength." Al-Qurṭubī said, "I.e. give them what suffices of sustenance, whereby they will not be constrained to beg in a humiliating manner, and in which there will not be superfluity that induces luxury and worldly expanse. The meaning of the hadith is that it is a request for sufficiency in food, for sustenance is that which sustains the body and suffices need. In this state there is safety against both the states of wealth and of poverty." Ibn Baṭṭāl said, "Therein is evidence of the viritue of sufficiency in food and the taking of the *bulgha* (sufficient subsistence) from this world and doing without what is beyond that, out of desire for a fuller measure of the bliss of the hereafter and to give preference to that which perdures over that which vanishes. So his Umma ought to follow him as a their model in that." Sayyid ʿAbd al-Maqṣūd Fāris al-Ḥasanī said to me, "It meaning is, 'O Allah, make the provision of the family of Muḥammad *kafāf* (sufficiency in food),' i.e. what consists in independence from people and suffices, as in the *Qāmūs*. The Ḥabīb ʿAlī b. ʿAṭṭās al-Indūnīsī said, 'O my son, never fear, assistance is to the extent of sustenance.'" In this sense the hadith alludes to the reality of dependence on Allah for the people of the House, their endurance of trials, the high honor of their pure souls, and their elect grandfather's preserving and holding in store the highest stations and best homes in the hereafter for them.

(Benefit) Sayyid ʿAbd al-Maqṣūd Fāris said, "Shayh ʿUmar al-Khaṭīb–Allah grant him mercy–had memorized al-Mutanabbī's *Dīwān* and could recite it all to perfection, and we heard before him al-Nawawī's *Minhāj* and other works."

(Special note) Sayyid ʿAbd al-Maqṣūd related to me that he had seen the Prophet–upon him the blessings and peace of Allah–in dream telling him, **"You are ʿAbd al-Muṣawwir (the servant of the Fashioner of forms)."**

41 *al-Arbaʿīn al-abdāl al-ʿawālī al-masmūʿa bil-Jāmiʿ al-Umawī* (The forty convergent-chained hadiths heard in the Umawī Mosque) by Ibn ʿAsākir (499-571/1106-1176)

THE ERUDITE AGED JURIST and teacher in the Great Umawī Mosque in Damascus, Shaykh ʿAbd al-Razzāq b. Muḥammad Ḥasan b. Rashīd b. Ḥasan al-Ḥalabī al-Ḥanafī (1343-1433/1925-2012)–Allah have mercy on him–reported to me through my reading before him in his office in the Umawī Mosque on the third day of the week on 8 Ramadan 1426 (Tuesday 11 October 2005), the erudite Mufti Sayyid Abū al-Yusr ʿĀbidīn informed me, from his grandfather Sayyid Aḥmad b. ʿAbd al-Ghanī ʿĀbidīn, from his paternal uncle the author of the *Ḥāshiya* (Marginalia), Muḥammad Amīn b. ʿUmar b. ʿAbd al-ʿAzīz Ibn ʿĀbidīn (1197-1252/1783-1836) from Hibat Allāh b. Muḥammad al-Baʿlī, from Aḥmad b. ʿAbd al-Fattāḥ al-Mullawī, from the transmissologist ʿAbd Allāh b. Sālim al-Baṣrī, from Muḥammad b. ʿAlāʾ al-Dīn al-Bābilī, from Nūr al-Dīn Sālim b. Muḥammad al-Sanhūrī, from al-Najm al-Ghayṭī and Ibn Ḥajar al-Haytamī, both of them from Shaykh al-Islām Zakariyyā al-Anṣārī, from the Hadith arch-master Ibn Ḥajar, by audition from his teacher the copious transmissologist ʿAlī b. Muḥammad b. Abī al-Majd al-Dimashqī (Ibn al-Ṣāʾigh), from al-Qāsim b. Muẓaffar b. ʿAsākir, Muḥammad b. Naṣr b. Muḥammad reported to us, from **the Hadith master Abū al-Qāsim ʿAlī b. al-Ḥusayn b. Hibat Allāh b. ʿAbd Allāh**

al-Shāfi'ī Ibn 'Asākir (499-571/1106-1176) by audition, Abū al-Qāsim Hibat Allāh b. Muḥammad b. 'Abd al-Wāḥid b. al-Ḥuṣayn reported to us, Abū Ṭālib Muḥammad b. Muḥammad al-Bazzāz reported to us, al-Shāfi'ī reported to us, Mu'ādh b. al-Muthannā reported to us, Ibrāhīm b. Ḥamza and 'Alī b. al-Madīnī reported to us, both of them saying, Muḥammad b. Ṭalḥa reported to us, from Abū Suhayl b. Mālik, from Sa'īd b. al-Musayyib, from Sa'd b. Waqqāṣ who said **the Messenger of Allah–upon him the blessings and peace of Allah–went out to the horse market**–where the sellers of beasts are today–**to equip an expeditionary force, whereupon al-'Abbās b. 'Abd al-Muṭṭalib came forth to the Messenger of Allah by surprise. The latter said, "Here is al-'Abbās, the paternal uncle of your Prophet, the most generous, open-handed man of the Quraysh and the most assiduous in keeping family ties!"** [Ibn 'Asākir:] Nasā'ī narrated it from Ḥumayd b. Makhlad al-Nasā'ī from 'Alī b. 'Abd Allāh b. Ja'far b. al-Madīnī, so it befell me as *muwāfaqa* (concurrent chain to the compiler's teacher through other than the compiler's chain) in his shaykh's shaykh [=Ibn al-Madīnī]. It is counted as a lone-narrated report of Muḥammad b. Ṭalḥa al-Taymī al-Madanī from Abū Suhayl Nāfi' b. Mālik b. Abī 'Āmir al-Aṣbaḥī."

Imam Aḥmad narrated it in the *Musnad* and *Faḍā'il al-Ṣaḥāba* as did al-Nasā'ī in the *Kubrā*, Dawraqī in *Musnad Sa'd b. Abī Waqqāṣ*, al-Ḥākim who rated it *ṣaḥīḥ*, Ibn Ḥibbān in his *Ṣaḥīḥ*, the Hadith master Abū al-Qāsim al-Sahmī in *al-Arba'īn fī faḍā'il al-'Abbās*, al-Ṭabarānī in *al-Awsaṭ*, Ibn 'Asākir in the *Tārīkh*, al-Shāmūkhī in his *Aḥādīth* and al-Mizzī in *Tahdhīb al-Kamāl*. the Hadith master Nūr al-Dīn al-Haythamī rated its chain as strong in *Majma' al-zawā'id* and mentioned it was found in Aḥmad, Abū Ya'lā, al-Bazzār and al-Ṭabarānī in approximately identical wordings.

42 *al-Arbaʿīn al-buldāniyya* (The forty geographical hadiths) by Ibn ʿAsākir (499-571/1106-1176)

THE AGED SAYYID ʿABD AL-RAḤMĀN AL-KATTĀNĪ b. ʿAbd al-Ḥay b. ʿAbd al-Kabīr al-Kattānī al-Fāsī (b. 1338/1920) informed me in his house in Fes on 26 Rajab 1434/June 2013 and my teacher the historian of schools, bibliographer of scholarship and biographer of scholars DR. MUḤAMMAD MUṬĪʿ AL-ḤĀFIẒ b. al-Sayyid Muḥammad Wāṣil al-Ḥanafī al-Naqshbandī (b. 1359/1940)–may Allah guard them both –reported to me through my reading before him in his house in the Daḥdāḥ quarter of Damascus in early Rajab 1427/28 July 2006, the first from his father the transmissologist of the world and author of the most important catalogue of Shuyukh and transmission of the 14th Hijrī century, entitled *Fihris* (or *Fahras*) *al-fahāris*, Abū al-Isʿād ʿAbd al-Ḥay al-Kattānī (1302-1382/1885-1962), from the centenarian Shaykh ʿAbd Allāh b. Darwīsh al-Sukkarī (1227-1329/1812-1911), and the second from his teacher the head of the association of the Ulema of Syro-Palestine, the pillar and erudite aged *muḥaddith* Shaykh Abū al-Khayr Muḥammad Khayr b. Muḥammad b. Ḥusayn b. Bakrī al-Maydānī al-Naqshbandī (1293-1380/1876-1960), from al-Sukkarī, from the jurist of Syro-Palestine Saʿīd b. Ḥasan b. Aḥmad al-Ḥalabī al-Dimashqī (1188-1254/1774-1838), from Ismāʿīl b. Muḥammad al-Mawāhibī, from his father, from his grandfather Ṣāliḥ, from Aḥmad b. Muḥammad al-Nakhlī, from the transmissologist and astronomer Muḥammad b. Muḥammad b. Sulaymān al-Rūdānī al-Maghribī (d. 1094/ 1683); (another route) Saʿīd al-Ḥalabī also from ʿAbd al-Raḥmān and Muḥammad the sons of ʿUthmān al-Ḥalabī, from their father Abū al-Faḍl ʿUthmān al-ʿAqīlī al-Ḥalabī, from Ṭaha b. Muhannā al-Jabartī, from ʿAbd Allāh b. Sālim al-Baṣrī, from al-Rūdānī, from his teacher the Mufti of Algeria Abū ʿUthmān Saʿīd b. Ibrāhīm al-Tunisī al-Jazāʾirī, famed as Qaddūra (d. 1066/1656), from his teacher Abū ʿUthmān Saʿīd b. Aḥmad al-Maqqarī al-Tilimsānī (d. 1010/1602), from Abū Zayd ʿAbd al-Raḥmān b. ʿAlī b. Aḥmad al-ʿĀṣimī al-Sufyānī, famed as Suqqayn (d. 956/1549), from Shaykh al-Islam Zakariyyā al-Anṣārī and al-Burhān al-Qalqashandī, both of them from the Imam of Hadith masters Abū al-Faḍl Aḥmad b. ʿAlī b. Ḥajar (773-852/1372-1448) who said, I read it before Abū al-Ḥasan ʿAlī b. Muḥammad b. Abī al-Majd by virtue of his *ijāza* if not his audition from al-Qāsim b. al-Muẓaffar b. ʿAsākir, and also Abū Hurayra Ibn al-Dhahabī reported to us by *ijāza*, al-Qāsim b. Muẓaffar informed us by audition, my father's paternal uncle ʿIzz al-Dīn Muḥammad b. Aḥmad b. al-Ḥasan the genealogist, also Tāj al-Dīn ʿAbd Allāh b. ʿUmar b. Ḥammūyah, also Naṣr al-Dīn Abū al-Fatḥ Naṣr Allāh b. Makārim al-Anṣārī, also al-ʿIzz Abū Muḥammad ʿAbd al-ʿAzīz b. Muḥammad b. ʿAlī b. Abīh al-Ṣāliḥī informed us as it was read before all of them while I [=al-Qāsim] listened, all four of them saying, Shaykh al-Islam, the Imam and Hadith master **Abū al-Qāsim ʿAlī b. al-Ḥasan b. Hibat Allāh b. ʿAbd Allāh b. al-Ḥusayn al-Shāfiʿī, famed as Ibn ʿAsākir** reported to us as it was read before him while we listened, saying:

The ninth country: Marwu al-Shāhijān (Merv of the Nobles), the fortified interior city of Khurasan built by Dhū al-Qarnayn. The Sufi admonisher Abū Ya'qūb Yūsuf b. Ayyūb b. al-Ḥusayn b. Wahrat al-Hamadhānī reported to us through my reading before him in Merv the month of Rabī' al-Awwal in the year 531/1136, the Sharif qadi Abū al-Ḥusayn Muḥammad b. 'Alī b. Muḥammad b. 'Ubayd Allāh b. 'Abd al-Ṣamad b. al-Muhtadī bil-Lāh informed us verbatim in Baghdad, Abū al-Ḥasan 'Alī b. 'Umar b. Muḥammad b. al-Ḥasan b. Shādhān b. Isḥāq b. Ibrāhīm b. 'Alī b. Isḥāq al-Ḥarbī al-Sukkarī narrated to us by dictation, and I was the *mustamlī* (public crier relaying the dictation to listeners out of range) over it on the day of Jumu'a on the third to last day of Jumādā al-Ākhira in the year 385 (31 July 995) and he said to me, Say, 'I shall indeed connect the juniors with the seniors:" Abū 'Abd Allāh Aḥmad b. al-Ḥasan b. 'Abd al-Jabbār narrated to us, Abū Zakariyyā Yaḥyā b. Ma'īn narrated to us, Hishām b. Yūsuf narrated to us, from 'Abd Allāh b. Sulaymān al-Nawfalī, from Muḥammad b. 'Alī, from his father, from Ibn 'Abbās who said, the Messenger of Allah–upon him the blessings and peace of Allah–said, **"Love Allah for that which He nourishes you of His blessings; and love me with the love of Allah; and love the people of my House for the sake of my love."**

The Hadith master Ibn 'Asākir said, "This is a fair hadith from the hadiths of Abū al-'Abbās 'Abd Allāh b. 'Abbās b. 'Abd al-Muṭṭalib al-Qurashī al-Hāshimī–Allah be well-pleased with him and his father–the paternal cousin of the Messenger of Allah–upon him the blessings and peace of Allah, interpreter of the Qur'ān and arch-scholar of this Umma. It is a *'azīz* ('rare' two-chained) report from his son Abū Muḥammad–it is also said, Abū al-Ḥasan–'Alī b. 'Abd Allāh, which alone his son Abū 'Abd Allāh Muḥammad b. 'Alī Abū al-al-Khalā'if (Father of the caliphs) relates from him, and we did not write it except as the narration of ʿAbd Allāh b. Sulaymān al-Nawfalī from the latter." Tirmidhī narrated it as *bi-ḥubbī*, **"with my love,"** and said it is "fair, single-chained." ʿAbd Allāh b. Aḥmad narrated it in the addenda to the *Faḍāʾil*, Fasawī in *al-Maʿrifa wal-tārīkh*, Ṭabarānī in *al-Kabīr*, Ājurrī in *al-Sharīʿa*, Abū Nuʿaym in the *Ḥilya*, Ḥākim in the *Mustadrak*, rating it sound-chained, Bayhaqī in *al-Shuʿab*, *al-Iʿtiqād*, *al-Manāqib*, *al-Ādāb* and others with the terms *li-ḥubbi-l-Lāh* **"for the sake of the love of Allah"** i.e. "for the sake of Allah's love for me."

(Benefit of the *makhraj* [top] of this chain) The Hadith master al-Dhahabī said in *Siyar aʿlām al-nubalāʾ*: "I read before Abū al-Maʿālī Aḥmad b. Isḥāq b. Muḥammad b. al-Muʾayyad al-Qarāfī in Egypt, Abū al-ʿAbbās Aḥmad b. Abī al-Fatḥ and al-Faraj b. ʿAbd Allāh al-Kātib in Baghdad both reported to us, saying, Muḥammad b. ʿUmar al-Qāḍī reported to us, Abū al-Ḥusayn Aḥmad b. Muḥammad b. al-Naqqūr reported to us, ʿAlī b. ʿUmar al-Ḥarbī reported to us in the year 385/995, Aḥmad b. al-Ḥasan b. ʿAbd al-Jabbār al-Ṣūfī narrated to us, Abū Zakariyyā Yaḥyā b. Maʿīn narrated to us in the year 227/842," etc. the same as above. Dhahabī continued, "This is a single-chained, unique hadith: none narrated it from Ibn ʿAbbās other than his son ʿAlī, and none narrated it from ʿAlī other than his son Muḥammad the Father of the caliphs. The qadi of Sanʿāʾ ʿAbd Allāh b. Sulaymān alone narrated it, and no one narrated it from him other than Hishām. Yaʿqūb al-Fasawī narrated it in his *Tārīkh* from Ziyād b. Ayyūb, from [Yaḥyā] Ibn Maʿīn, and people are indebted for it to Yaḥyā, since al-Nawfalī is not well-known."

(Benefit concerning the locale) Yāqūt al-Ḥamawī said, "Marwu al-Shāhijān is Marw the Magnificent, the most famous of the cities of Khurasan and its *qaṣaba* (inner citadel). As for Shāhijān it is a Persian word that means the sultan's breath, since *jān* is the breath or the spirit and *shāh* is the sultan. It was thus named because of its majestic status among them." The *qaṣaba* is the great city.

(Benefits from our teacher) Dr. Muṭīʿ said "We say 'Hamdān' with *sukūn* of the *mīm* then an undotted *dāl* for the tribe, and 'Hamadhān' with *fatḥ* of the *mīm* followed by a dotted *dhāl* for the country. As for the narrator's statement, 'I shall indeed connect the juniors with the seniors,' it is an allusion to highness in the chain." (Note) Our friend the Sharif genealogist and rector of Abū al-Nūr Institute in Damascus Shaykh Muḥammad Sharīf b. ʿAdnān al-Ṣawwāf said in his *Muʿjam al-usar al-Dimashqiyya* (Dictionary of Damascene families) that the family of al-Ḥāfiẓ (Dibs wa-Zayt) is one of the old families in the ʿUqayba quarter, and it was said they descend from the Quṭb ʿAbd al-Qādir al-Jīlānī al-Ḥasanī al-Ḥusaynī–Allah be well-pleased with him.

(Benefit) The manuscript incipit is "Book of the 40 [hadiths] from 40 [shaykhs] out of 40 [books] to 40 [Companions] in 40 [topics]."

43 *al-Aḥādīth al-mukhtāra* (The selected hadiths) by al-Ḍiyā' al-Maqdisī (569-643/1174-1245)

The educator and caller to Allah al-Ḥabīb ʿAlī b. ʿAbd al-Raḥmān b. Aḥmad b. ʿAbd al-Qādir b. ʿAlī b. ʿUmar b. Saqqāf Āl Ṣāfī al-Indūnīsī (d. Jumuʿa 1 Jumādā al-Ākhira 1442/15 January 2021)–Allah have mercy on him–informed me in his house in Tebet, South Jakarta, from his father, from the centenarian Ḥabīb ʿAlī b. ʿAbd al-Raḥmān b. ʿAbd Allāh al-Ḥabashī al-Batāwī, nicknamed Kwītā (1287-1388/1870-1968), from the knower of Allah, the transmissologist al-Ḥabīb Aḥmad b. Ḥasan al-ʿAṭṭās (1257-1334/1841-1916), from Abū Bakr and Ṣāliḥ the sons of ʿAbd Allāh al-ʿAṭṭās, from Wajīh al-Dīn ʿAbd al-Raḥmān al-Ahdal, from the Hadith master Murtaḍā al-Zabīdī, with the six-link chain cited in the chapter on al-Nasāʾī's *Mujtabā* to the Hadith master Ibn Ḥajar, by virtue of his reading before Umm al-Ḥasan Fāṭima bint Muḥammad b. Aḥmad b. Aḥmad b. Muḥammad b. ʿUthmān b. al-Munajjā al-Tanūkhiyya in Damascus, by virtue of her *ijāza* for the entire work from Abū al-Faḍl Sulaymān b. Ḥamza b. Aḥmad b. ʿUmar b. Abī ʿUmar al-Maqdisī, by virtue of his audition from **the Hadith master Ḍiyāʾ al-Dīn Muḥammad b. ʿAbd al-Wāḥid al-Maqdisī**, and by virtue of her *ijāza* also from ʿĪsā b. ʿAbd al-Raḥmān b. Maʿālī through his audition from al-Ḍiyāʾ, Muḥammad b. Aḥmad b. Naṣr b. Abī al-Fatḥ al-Ṣaydalānī reported to us as it was read before him in Aṣbahān, that Abū ʿAlī al-

Ḥaddād al-Muqri᾽ reported to them as it was read before him while he [=Ibn Abī al-Fatḥ] was present, Aḥmad b. ʿAbd Allāh the Ḥadith master Abū Nuʿaym reported to us, Sulaymān b. Aḥmad al-Ṭabarānī reported to us, Aḥmad b. Muḥammad b. Ṣadaqa narrated to us, Muḥammad b. al-Mu᾽ammal b. al-Ṣabbāḥ narrated to us, Yūsuf b. Nāfiʿ b. ʿAbd Allāh b. Ashras al-Madanī narrated to us, ʿAbd al-Raḥmān b. Abī al-Zinād narrated to us, from his father, from Abān b. ʿUthmān who said, I heard ʿUthmān–Allah be well-pleased with him–say, the Messenger of Allah–upon him the blessings and peace of Allah–said, **"Whoever lends a helping hand to any one of the children of ʿAbd al-Muṭṭalib and then the latter does not pay him back for it in this life, then upon me rests his repayment tomorrow when he meets me."**

ʿAbd Allāh b. Aḥmad narrated it in his addenda to *Faḍā᾽il al-Ṣaḥāba*, al-Ṭabarānī in *al-Awsaṭ*, and al-Khaṭīb in *Tārīkh Baghdād*, all of them through ʿAbd al-Raḥmān b. Abī al-Zinād, from his father, from Abān b. ʿUthmān, I heard ʿUthmān b. ʿAffān say, the Messenger of Allah–upon him the blessings and peace of Allah–said, **"Whoever lends a special helping hand to any of the descendants of ʿAbd al-Muṭṭalib in this world, then upon me rests his recompense when he meets me."** This is al-Khaṭīb's wording. Al-Haythamī said, "It contains ʿAbd al-Raḥmān as mentioned, and he is weak." Ibn al-Jawzī went too far when he included it in the flimsy reports, saying, "This hadith is inauthentic and Aḥmad declared ʿAbd al-Raḥmān b. Abī al-Zinād weak and said he is not used as a proof." Rather, the *Taqrīb* states "he is truthful, his memorization changed when he entered Baghdad, and he was one of the Seven Arch-jurists." He is one of the narrators in the four *Sunan* as well as in al-Bukhārī in the *Ṣaḥīḥ* in *taʿlīq* (chainless) mode, and Muslim in the introduction to his *Ṣaḥīḥ*. Mālik, al-Tirmidhī and al-ʿIjlī all rated him trustworthy while al-Dhahabī said he is fair in narration and the Hadith arch-Master said in the *Fatḥ*, "The upshot of his case is that there is a difference of opinion concerning him, so the ruling that what he alone narrates is sound does not impose itself; rather, at most it is fair." This is why the Hadith master al-Ḍiyā᾽ counted it among the fair reports by narrating it in the *Mukhtāra*. As for al-

Ṭabarānī's statement that Yūsuf b. Nāfiʿ alone narrates from him it is a delusion, since Yūsuf b. Yaʿqūb al-Madīnī (Ibn Salamat al-Mājishūn) followed him up in *Faḍāʾil al-Ṣaḥāba*, as did al-Naḍr b. Ṭāhir in the first of the five *Majalis* of Abū al-Ḥasan al-Azdī. Al-Munāwī's claim that "Abān b. ʿUthmān is controverted"is equally rejected, as the controverted one is a different Abān whereas the son of ʿUthmān b. ʿAffān is a trustworthy Successor and one of Muslim's narrators. ʿAmr b. Shuʿayb said of him, "I never saw more knowledgeable in the Hadith nor more proficient in knowledge of the sacred Law." Ibn ʿAsākir narrated in the *Tārīkh* through Muḥammad b. Yaḥyā b. Ḍurays, ʿĪsā b. ʿAbd Allāh b. Muḥammad b. ʿUmar b. ʿAlī b. Abī Ṭālib narrated to me, my father narrated to me, from his father, from his grandfather, from ʿAlī who said, the Messenger of Allah–upon him the blessings and peace of Allah–said, **"Whoever lends a helping hand to any one of the people of my House, I am recompensing him on the Day of Resurrection."**

(Benefits) It is related from Anas that he said, "They are saying [at the time of the *fitna*] that love for both ʿAlī and ʿUthmān does not unite in a single heart, but Allah has certainly put love of both of them in our hearts." Awzāʿī and Sufyān al-Thawrī said that love of both ʿUthmān and ʿAlī does not unite other than in a believer's heart, as did Ibn al-Mubārak in his *Dīwān* of poetry. The hadith thus covers a shining rule regarding the doing of good deeds for the sake of pleasing Allah by upholding the right of His Messenger–upon him the blessings and peace of Allah–and there is no discussion about the excellence of proving true to love of him by doing good to his offspring and relatives with one's person and one's wealth. Therein also is a notification to keep this-worldly hopes in check and to rest assured of the promptness of reward in the hereafter, as expressed in his statement **"tomorrow,"** as well as the specialness of nearness to him–upon him the blessings and peace of Allah–for whoever rightly deserves it.

Allah Most High is All-Knowing and All-Generous and Wise. Blessings and peace on our liegelord Muḥammad and his Family. Glory, thanks and praise belong to Allah the nurturing Lord of the worlds.

Continuation of the exordium and conclusion on the meaning of the *Āl*

with an overview of works and select statements pertaining to their special features in the sacred Law and wisdom

HAVING CLARIFIED THE MEANINGS OF DIVINE JUSTICE in the superiority of some people over some others, the Messenger of Allah–upon him the blessings and peace of Allah–made right belief the criterion of distinction between the righteous and the unrighteous, not lineage, whereby he said "**Behold! Verily the *Āl* (near relatives) of my father —meaning So and so—are not protecting friends in relation to me. My only protecting friend is Allah and the righteous among the believers.**" He also said "**Verily the nearest of people to me are the Godfearing ones, whoever they may be and wherever they may be.**" He warned the tribespeople most related to him, namely the Quraysh. Abū Hurayra–Allah be well-pleased with him–said, "When the verse *and warn your closest tribal relatives* (al-Shuʿarāʾ 26:214) was revealed, the Prophet–upon him the blessings and peace of Allah–said, "**Assembly of the Quraysh!**" followed by the Banū ʿAbd al-Muṭṭalib, then his paternal uncle al-ʿAbbās, then his paternal aunt Ṣafiyya, then his daughter Fāṭima, saying to them, "**Purchase your lives from Allah! I cannot suffice you in anything apart from Allah!**" And he said, "**If Fāṭima the daughter of Muḥammad were to steal, I swear I would cut off her hand,**" and he said, "**Whoever is slowed down**

by his deeds, his lineage shall not speed him up." One of the commentators—al-Qārī in the *Mirqāt*—said:

> I.e. his lineage shall not advance him, meaning he can never make up for his deficiency by being the possessor of pedigree among his people, as nearness to Allah does not take place through lineage but righteous deeds. Allah Most High said, *verily the most honorable of your in the presence of Allah are the most Godfearing of you* (Ḥujurāt 49:13). The witness to that is that most of the ulema of the early and later scholars have no lineage that they can be proud of; on the contrary, most of the ulema of the early scholars are *mawālī* (clients, manumitted slaves, non-Arabs). Yet, despite that, they are the leaders of the Umma and the wellsprings of mercy, while those who possess high lineages but are not like that, are now consigned by their own ignorance to oblivion. That is why he said–upon him the blessings and peace of Allah–**"Verily Allah elevates many people with this faith-system and he lowers others with it."**

In the same vein al-Tirmidhī related in his *Sunan*–rating it *ḥasan*–from Ibn ʿUmar–may Allah be well-pleased with him and his father–from the Prophet–upon him the blessings and peace of Allah, **"O people! Verily Allah has removed far from you the arrogance of the Time of Ignorance and its self-pride in forefathers. So there are only two types of people: a pious, Godfearing one who is dear to Allah, and a wretched open sinner who is worthless to Allah. Moreover, people are the children of Ādam, and Allah created Ādam from dust. Allah Most High said, *O people! Verily We created you from a male and a female, and We made you nations and tribes so that you might get to know one another. Verily the most honorable of your in the presence of Allah are the most Godfearing of you* (al-Ḥujurāt 49:13)."** And he said, **"My**

***awliyā*ʾ** (relatives, close friends) **on the Day of Resurrection are the Godfearing; so let not people come to me with deeds while you come to me with this world, carrying it on your necks, so that I will say such as this and such as this," to mean no—and he turned aside both ways.** All of the above-cited reports are in the *Ṣaḥīḥ* except the latter, which is in Bukhārī's *al-Adab al-mufrad*, Ibn Abī ʿĀṣim's *al-Sunna* and Abū Dāwūd's *Marāsīl*. The latter also related in his *Sunan* from Ibn ʿUmar, from the Prophet –upon him the blessings and peace of Allah–**"The *fitnat al-sarrā*ʾ (strife of elation)—its smoke seeps from under the feet of a man from the people of my House who claims he is part of me, but he is not part of me. My relatives are only the Godfearing."**

Similarly al-Ṭabarānī narrated it *al-Awsaṭ* and *al-Ṣaghīr* and, through him, Ibn Mardūyah in his *Tafsīr*, al-Bayhaqī in his *Sunan*, Ibn ʿAdī in *al-Kāmil* through Nuʿaym b. Ḥammād: Nūḥ b. Abī Maryam narrated to us, from Yaḥyā b. Saʿīd al-Anṣārī, from Anas who said **the Messenger of Allah–upon him the blessings and peace of Allah–was asked, "Who are your *Āl*?" He replied, "every Godfearing one" and he recited *but its awliyāʾ are only those that are Godfearing, however, most of them do not know* (al-Anfāl 8:34)** i.e. the *awliyā*ʾ of the Kaʿba. Ibn Ḥajar said in the *Fatḥ* that al-Ṭabarānī's chain was terminally flimsy but that al-Bayhaqī narrated something similar from Jābir with a weak chain. The wording of the latter is, **"The *Āl* of Muḥammad are his Umma."** Tammām al-Rāzī also narrated it through Shaybān b. Farrūkh as did al-Bayhaqī in his *Sunan* with a chain containing Nāfiʿ Abū Hurmuz who is also weak, but al-Dhahabī said in the *Mīzān* that it has a follow-up narration from Muslim b. Ibrāhīm. Al-Sakhāwī said in the *Maqāṣid* that it has in fact many witness-reports. Al'Ajlūnī said in *Kashf al-khafā*, "Among them what is found in the two *Ṣaḥīḥs*, spoken by the Prophet–upon him the blessings and peace of Allah–**"Verily the *Āl* of Abū So and so are not *awliyā*'** (relatives, close friends) **of mine. My *walī* is only Allah and the righteous of the believers"** and its conclusion is **"but they have blood ties which I shall refresh with their due refreshment"** (cf. §33 above) meaning "I shall bring them together with their due linkage." The wording **"and the righteous of the believers"** is that of al-Burqānī. The Hadith master al-Zarqānī said in his abridgment of the *Maqāṣid al-ḥasana* that it was overall *ḥasan*. As for **"I am the grandfather of every Godfearing one"** there is no such narration. He also said–upon him the blessings and peace of Allah–**"Behold! there is no superiority to any Arab over any non-Arab nor to any non-Arab over any Arab"**—Aḥmad, al-Ḥārith and Ibn Abī Ḥātim narrated it—so that people would not quit deeds, rest on their laurels and feel pride.

THEN HE INFORMED CREATION OF THE DIVINE BOUNTY lavished upon his near relatives–upon him the blessings and peace of Allah–as being a categorical matter and an everlasting special level, saying, **"Over there a certain lineage has greater proximity some other,"** and, as already narrated, he said that **"every line and lineage shall be severed on the Day of Resurrection except his line and his lineage"** (§23 above). He also said, **"I am Muḥammad b. 'Abd Allāh b. 'Abd al-Muṭṭalib, I am the best of you in his house and the best of you in his person"** (§38 above). He also said, **"He [=Allah] chose,**

from among all human beings, the Arabs" (§34 above). He also said, **"and He elected the Quraysh out of Kināna, and He elected, out of Quraysh, the Banū Hāshim"** (§15, §34 above). He also said, **"If I were to grasp the door-ring of the gate of Paradise, I would never begin to enter except with you, O Banū Hāshim!"** He also said, **"Then, by Allah, I swear that my intercession shall attain my near relatives"** (§16 above). He also said, **"the Book of Allah extended from heaven to earth and my *'Itra* (intimate family), the people of my House. Behold! The two shall never part ways until they come up to me at the Basin,"** whereby the *'Itra* is a subset of the meanings of the divine *ḥifẓ* (protection) for the Glorious Qur'ān (§7, §20 above). He also said about al-Ḥasan, al-Ḥusayn and their parents, **"Whoever loves me and loves these two and their father and mother, shall be with me at my level on the Day of resurrection"** (§13 above). When the lover of the Family of the Prophet–upon him and them the blessings and peace of Allah–is with the Beloved one at that high level, then it is even truer for the beloved ones of his Family themselves to be at a high level, and it is definiteley established without discussion, on the condition spelled out by the Prophet–upon him the blessings and peace of Allah–when he said, **"My nurturing Lord has made me a promise concerning the people of my House, that whoever of them affirms pure monotheism and my Prophetic mission, He will not punish them."** Al-Ḥākim narrated it and rated it *ṣaḥīḥ* but al-Dhahabī rated it *munkar* (disclaimed), while al-Suyūṭī reaffirmed its rating of *ṣaḥīḥ*. Ibn 'Ābidīn adduced it in his treatise *al-'Ilm al-ẓāhir fi naf' al-nasab al-ṭāhir* (The patent knowledge concerning the fact that the pure affiliation is beneficial). [See also above under §29.]

THE SCHOOL OF *AHL AL-SUNNA WAL-JAMĀʿA*, moreover, is to uphold the love and high respect and support of the noble members of the Prophetic House and the totality of the Companions without exception, beginning with the *ʿItra* (intimate relatives), the Mothers of the Believers, and the pure Progeny until the Day of Resurrection. To this effect goes what is narrated from al-Shaʿbī–may Allah have mercy on him–whereby Zayd b. Thābit got ready to ride his mount, whereupon Ibn ʿAbbās took hold of his stirrup (to keep it steady for him), so Zayd said, "Do not do that, cousin of the Messenger of Allah!" But he replied, "Thus were we ordered to treat our people of knowledge." So Zayd b. Thābit kissed Ibn ʿAbbās's hand and said, "Thus were we ordered to treat the people of the House of our Prophet." Yaʿqūb b. Sufyān al-Fasawī narrated it in *al-Maʿrifa wal-Tārīkh* and the Hadith arch-Master declared it sound in *al-Iṣāba*. It was also narrated by Ibn Saʿd in *al-Ṭabaqāt*, al-Ṭabarānī in *al-Kabīr*, al-Ḥākim who declared it *ṣaḥīḥ*, al-Bayhaqī in *al-Madkhal*, al-Khaṭīb in *al-Faqīh wal-mutafaqqih* (The jurist and the student of the Law), and Qadi ʿIyāḍ cited it in *al-Shifā* and said therein, "Know that the *ḥurma* (sacred status) of the Prophet –upon him the blessings and peace of Allah–after his death, his veneration and his magnification are all absolutely required just as they were in the time of his life, including when he is mentioned, when his Hadith and his Sunna are mentioned, and upon hearing his name and his life and deeds, just as they are also when interacting with his *Āl* and his *ʿItra*, and just as the magnification of the people of his House and his

Companions also is." It is mentioned in al-Yāfiʿī's *Mirʾāt al-jinān* (Mirror of the gardens of Paradise), citing *Tārīkh Baghdād*, that Yaḥyā b. Muʿādh al-Rāzī went to see a ʿAlawī in Balkh to visit him and give him salam, whereupon the latter said to him, "May Allah support the *ustadh*! What do you say about us, the *Ahl al-Bayt*?" He said, "What can I say about a clay that was kneaded with the water of revelation, wherein was planted the tree of Prophethood, and which was watered with the water of the Prophetic Message? Does anything other than the musk of guidance and the amber of Godfearingness waft from it?" Hearing this the ʿAlawi stuffed Yaḥyā's mouth with pearls.

(THE *ĀL*: DEFINITION AND HIERARCHIES) I read before my teacher the peerless erudite Sayyid Muḥammad Abū al-Hudā al-Yaʿqūbī–Allah save him–with his chain to the Qadi ʿAbd al-Nabī b. ʿAbd al-Rasūl al-Aḥmadnagrī (1117? -after 1180/1705?-1767) in his four-volume *Jāmiʿ al-ʿulūm fī iṣṭilāḥāt al-funūn* (Encyclopedia of the scholarly sciences on the terminology of the disciplines), known as *Dustūr al-ʿulamāʾ* (Code of the learned ones) published in 1329/1911 at Dāʾirat al-Maʿārif al-Niẓāmiyya, Hyderabad, at the very beginning of the book under the entry *Āl*, that he said:

> ***al-Āl.*** Its original form is *ahl* as indicated by [its diminutive form] *uhayl*, because diminutives are the touchstone of vocables, whereby are known the kernels of their letters and their accidents—i.e. their roots and their additions, whether they are substituted for the original letters or not. So the *hāʾ* was substituted with the *hamza* in light of their [mutual] phonetic nearness, then the second *hamza* was substituted with the *alif*, per the rule in *āmana*.
>
> However, *āl* is used for the highborn, while *ahl* is used both for them and for the lowborn. One says "the cupper's *ahl*,"

not his *āl*, and one says *āl al-Nabī* ﷺ, not his *ahl*. The latter , morever, can be annexed tro place and time as opposed to *āl*, so one says "the *ahl* of Egypt" and "the *ahl* of this time," not *āl Miṣr* and not *āl al-zamān*. Also, *ahl* is put in annexation with Allah Most High but not *āl*: one says *Ahlu-l-Lāh* but not *Ālu-l-Lāh*.

There is a difference of opinion as to who *Āl al-Nabī* ﷺ are. Some said they are the *Āl* of Hāshim and Muṭṭalib [thus defined by al-Shāfiʿī but only, Ibn Hajar said, in the context of zakat and the right to a fifth of the spoils; as for its sense in supplication then it is every Godfearing believer] and some said they are the children of the liegelord of women, Fāṭimāt al-Zahrāʾ–may Allah be well-pleased with her, as al-Nawawī related–Allah have mercy on him. Al-Ṭabarānī narrated with a weak chain, **"Verily the *Āl* of Muḥammad are every Godfearing believer"** and Jalāl al-ʿUlamāʾ [= Jalāl al-Dīn al-Dawwānī] chose it in his commentary on *Hayākil al-nūr* [by Shihāb al-Dīn Yaḥyā al-Suhrawardī al-Maqtūl].

On the immense merits of the *Āl* of the Prophet ﷺ—namely the children of Fāṭima–Allah be well-pleased with her—there are many volumes and tomes. Know that the superiority of the four rightly-guided Caliphs is specific to the exclusion of the children of Fāṭima–Allah be well-pleased with her–as mentioned in *Takmīl al-īmān* [by the *muḥaddith* ʿAbd al-Ḥaqq al-Dihlawī]. Imam Jalāl al-Dīn al-Suyūṭī–Allah have mercy on him–said in *al-Khaṣāʾiṣ al-kubrā* (The major compilation of the exclusive Prophetic qualities) that Ibn ʿAsākir narrated from Anas–Allah be well-pleased with him–that he said, the Messenger of Allah–upon him and his Family the blessings and peace of Allah–said, **"No one is absolutely obligated to get up from where he is sitting except for al-Ḥasan, al-Ḥusayn or their respective progenies."** It is also mentioned in *Shirʿat al-Islām* (The water-channel of Islam) [by Rukn al-Islām Muḥammad b. Abī Bakr al-Ḥanafī, known as Imam Zadah]: "One must give precedence to the descendants of the Messenger–upon him and his Family the blessings and peace of Allah–in walking and in sitting. It is also mentioned in *al-Tashrīḥ* (The exposition) by Imam Fakhr al-Dīn al-Rāzī [cf. *Ḥadiyyat al-ʿārifīn*], "It is impermissible for a learned man to sit above an illiterate ʿAlawī because that would be a faith-related offense." It is also mentioned in *Jāmiʿ al-fatāwā* (Encyclopedia of fatwas) [either by Qaraq Amīr al-Ḥumaydī al-Rūmī (d. 880/1475), or Abū al-Wajāha ʿAbd al-Raḥmān b. ʿĪsā al-Murshidī (d. 1038/1629), or Nāṣir al-Dīn Abū al-Qāsim Muḥammad b. Yūsuf al-Samarqandī (d. 556/1161), all of them Ḥanafī masters]: "The child born of the slave woman of [her] master is free because he is born from his water; likewise, the ʿAlawī's child from a slave woman belonging to someone else is not subsumed under her master's property nor is it permissible to sell it, in keeping the respect and honor due to its grandfather the Messenger of Allah–upon him the blessings and peace of Allah–and no one else shares that ruling in his entire Umma." The same is found in *al-Fatāwā al-Ghiyāthiyya* [by Dāwūd b. Yūsuf al-Khaṭīb al-Ḥanafī]. Likewise Imam ʿAlam al-Dīn al-ʿIrāqī [ʿAbd al-Karīm b. ʿAlī b. ʿUmar al-Anṣārī Ibn Bint al-ʿIrāqī al-Shāfiʿī 623-704/1226-1305]–Allah have mercy on him–said that "Fāṭima and her brother Ibrāhīm are better than the Four Caliphs by general agreement." Imam Mālik said, "I do not view anyone as better than the flesh of the Prophet–upon him the blessings and peace of Allah." Shaykh Ibn Ḥajar al-ʿAsqalānī–Allah have mercy on him–said, "Fāṭima is better than Khadīja and ʿĀʾisha by consensus, then Khadīja, then ʿĀʾisha." Al-Suhaylī used as evidence the hadiths indicating that Fāṭima–Allah be well-pleased with her–is the *baḍʿa* (flesh) / *biḍʿa* (part and parcel) of the Messenger–upon him and his Family the blessings and peace of Allah–to affirm that to insult her incurs unbelief and that, just as the lineage of the Prophet possess pre-eminence over others, likewise his inlaws possess greater honor over others in light of what was narrated in the sound reports from ʿUmar b. al-Khaṭṭāb–Allah be well-pleased with him–that he proposed to marry Umm Kulthūm to ʿAlī. The latter excused himself because of her youg age and the fact he had prepared her to marry his fraternal nephew the son of Ja'far, whereupon 'Umar said, "I did not want cohabitation but I heard the Messenger of Allah–upon him and his family the blessings and peace of Allah–say, **"Every line and lineage shall be severed on the Day of Resurrection except my line and my lineage; and all the children of women have agnates only through their father except the children of Fāṭima: verily I myself am their father and their agnates."**

The soundness of some of his quotations bears revisiting. The Hadith arch-master said in *Fatḥ al-Bārī*:

Al-Subkī the father said, "That which we consider our firm belief in the divine presence is that Fāṭima is superior, then Khadīja, then 'Ā'isha, and the difference of opinion is well-known, but truth is more deserving of being followed." Ibn Taymiyya said, "The preferential factors between Khadīja and 'Ā'isha are approximately identical," as if he adopted non-committal, while Ibn al-Qayyim said, "If by superiority is meant abundance of reward in the divine presence, then such is a matter that cannot be observed because the works of hearts is better than the works of limbs. If what is meant is abundance of knowledge then 'Ā'isha has it without fail; if it is eminence of orginin then Fāṭima has it without fail, and it is a merit in which she has no partner other than her siblings. And if what is meant is the honor of leadership then it was textually established for Fāṭima alone." I say, Fāṭima distinguished herself apart from her sisters in the fact the latter died in the lifetime of the Prophet–upon him and them the blessings and peace of Allah. As for what 'Ā'isha distinguished herself for in merit of knowledge, then Khadīja possessed its equivalent. namely the fact that she was the first one who answered favorably the call to submission, thereafter calling to it and supported its firmness with her life, her wealth, and her complete engagement. Therefore she has a reward identical to that of whoever comes after her, which none can assess but Allah. It was also said that consensus formed as to the superiority of Fāṭima while divergence remained between ʿĀʾisha and Khadīja.

Al-Qārī in the *Mirqāt* cited Suyūṭī in the *Nuqāya* as saying, "We believe that the best of women are Maryam and Fāṭima, while the best of the Mothers of the believers are Khadīja and ʿĀʾisha, concerning whose preferential hierarchy there different positions of which the third one is non-committal." Al-Qārī commented, "Non-committal as to all of them is more appropriate, for there is no categorical evidence in the matter, and conjectural views are mutually opposed and do not impart creeds, which are based on certainties."

* * *

I read in *ʿIqd al-durar al-bahiyya fī sharḥ al-Risālat al-Samarqandiyya* (The necklace of splendid pearls in the explanation of the Samarkand treatise [on figures of speech]) known as *al-Sharḥ al-kabīr* (The major explanation) by al-Shihāb Aḥmad b. ʿAbd al-Fattāḥ al-Mallawī al-Ḥamawī al-Shāfiʿī al-Azharī (1088-1181/1677-1767) in commentary of the statement by the author of the original text, Abū al-Qāsim al-Laythī al-Samarqandī (d. 888/1483), *and blessings be upon the best of creation and his Āl*:

> I.e. his followers. What is meant is his followers in righteous deeds in the way indicated by His statement–exalted is He–*He said, "O Nūḥ! Verily he is not from your family. Verily he is a deed unrighteous; therefore do not request of Me that of which you have no knowledge. I warn you not to be one of the ignorants!"* (Hūd 11:46). And the Companions are the strictest of people in following him–upon him the blessings and peace of Allah–so they are subsumed under the *Āl* and there is no inkling of neglect in the author's expression. As

> for the commentator's statement [='Iṣām al-Dīn al-Isfarāyīnī (d. 945/1538)], "therein is a double-entendre," he meant the stylistic double-entendre—as construed by his grandson 'Alī b. Ismā'īl b. 'Iṣām al-Dīn al-Shāfi'ī al-Makkī famed as al-'Iṣāmī (d. 1007/1599)—which consists in applying a term that has two senses, near and remote, and the latter is the one meant together with its hidden contextual clue. Now he explained the *Āl* as the followers, which is a remote sense because when *al-Āl* is applied in unqualified terms it is usually understood as the believers of Banū Hāshim and Banū al-Muṭṭalib, and in that way is dismissed any would-be objection against the commentator that, "if he meant that the followers is a remote sense in the context of supplication then it is rejected, in light of what will come to the effect that what is meant is not followers in the unqualified sense but followers that have righteous deeds, so we do not concede that the latter is a remote sense, because it is a widespread use that *Āl* is meant in the beautiful sense of followers with righteous deeds, which is the meaning of their statement that the *Āl* of the Prophet–upon him the blessings and peace of Allah–in the context of supplication denotes every Godfearing believer."

Likewise, Imam al-Suyūṭī–Allah have mercy on him–said in *al-'Ajājat al-zarnabiyya fil-sulālat al-Zaynabiyya* (The saffroned dust-cloud about the Zaynabī lineage):

> The name of Sharif applied, in the first generations, to whoever was from the people of the House indifferently, whether they were Ḥasanī; Ḥusaynī; 'Alawī from the seed of Muḥammad b. al-Ḥanafiyya and others of the children of 'Alī b. Abī Ṭālib; Ja'farī; 'Aqīlī; or 'Abbāsī. This is why you will find the *Tārīkh* (Biographical history) of the Hadith master al-Dhahabī crammed with that [terminology] in the entries. He will say "the 'Abbāsī Sharif," "the 'Aqīlī Sharif," "the Ja'farī Sharif," "the Zaynabī Sharif." Then, when the Fatimi caliphs took power in Egypt, they restricted the name of Sharif to the

> progeny of al-Ḥasan and al-Ḥusayn exclusively, and that practice was perpetuated in Egypt to this day. The Hadith master Ibn Ḥajar said in [*Nuzhat al-albāb fī*] *al-Alqāb* (The recreation of hearts concerning monikers), "*the Sharif* in Baghdad is a title for every ʿAbbāsī, and in Egypt for every ʿAlawī." There is no doubt that the old convention is more appropriate, namely the fact that it applies to every ʿAlawī, Jaʿfarī, ʿAqīlī, and ʿAbbāsī as was Dhahabī's practice and as indicated by al-Māwardī among our [Shāfiʿī] colleagues and the qadi Abū Yaʿlā Ibn al-Farrāʾ among the Ḥanbalīs, both of them in *al-Aḥkām al-sulṭāniyya* (The rules of governance). To that effect goes Ibn Mālik's statement in the *Alfiyya* (Thousand-line poem on grammar), *and his perfected Āl the Sharifs*. So there is no doubt that the term Sharifs applies to the above-mentioned progeny of Zaynab. How many times did al-Dhahabī use the term *al-sharīf al-Zaynabī* in his biographical entries! It might also be said that in the usage of the people of Egypt the term *sharaf* might be understood as types: general for all of *Ahl al-Bayt*; specific for the progeny, wherein is subsumed the Zaynabīs, and more specific yet for direct affiliation, which is exclusive to the progeny of Ḥasan and Ḥusayn.

The qadi Shaykh Muḥammad Murshid b. Muḥammad Abū al-Khayr b. Aḥmad b. ʿAbd al-Ghanī b. Muḥammad Amīn ʿĀbidīn–Allah have mercy on all of them–reported to us with his chain as it was read before him while I listened, that his great-granduncle Imam Muḥammad Amīn ʿĀbidīn (1197-1252/1783-1836) said in the chapter on *kafāʾa* (marriage-match suitability) of the book of *nikāḥ* in his famous *Ḥāshiya* (marginalia) on [ʿAlāʾ al-Dīn Muḥammad b. ʿAlī b. Muḥammad al-Ḥaṣkafī's (d. 1088/1595)] *al-Durr al-mukhtār* (The choice pearls) [a commentary on al-Shams Muḥammad b. ʿAbd Allāh b. Aḥmad al-Tumurtāshī's (d.

1004/1595) *Tanwīr al-abṣār*], a latter-day main reference among the Ḥanafī masters:

> [Tumurtāshī:] *A non-Arab is not a suitable marriage match for an Arab woman even if* [Ḥaṣkafī:] the non-Arab were *a learned person* or a sultan, *and this is the sounder position* per the *Fatḥ* [*al-Qadīr* by al-Kamāl Ibn al-Humām] quoting *al-Yanābīʿ* [*fī maʿrifat al-uṣūl wal-tafārīʿ*, a commentary on Qudūrī's *Mukhtaṣar* by al-Rashīd Muḥammad b. Ramaḍān al-Rūmī al-Shiblī (d. 723/1323)], and he [=Zayn al-Dīn b. Ibrāhīm b. Muḥammad Ibn Nujaym (d. 970-1563)] claimed in the *Baḥr* [*al-Rāʾiq*, Ibn Nujaym's commentary on Abū al-Barakāt ʿAbd Allāh b. Aḥmad al-Nasafī's *Kanz al-daqāʾiq*] that it is *ẓāhir al-riwāya* (related from Abū Ḥanīfa and/or his two companions), and the author approved it. However, in the *Nahr* [*al-fāʾiq sharḥ Kanz al-daqāʾiq* by Ibn Nujaym], he explained the *ḥasīb* to mean the possessor of high position and eminence, in which case he is unsuited to marry a ʿAlawiyya—just as in the *Yanābīʿ*—but, if defined as a learned person, then he is suitable, because the honor of knowledge tops the honor of lineage and wealth as decisively affirmed by [Ḥāfiẓ al-Dīn Muḥammad b. Muḥammad b. Shihāb al-Kardarī] al-Bazzāzī (d. 817/1412) [in his *Fatāwā*], which was endorsed by al-Kamāl and others. Its aptness is obvious, hence it was said that ʿĀʾisha is superior to Fāṭima –Allah be well-pleased with both of them–as mentioned by [Shams al-Dīn Muḥammad b. al-Ḥusām al-Khurāsānī] al-Quhustānī (d. 962/1555).
>
> [Commentary by Ibn ʿĀbidīn:] His statement, "however, in the *Nahr*," etc. refers to where he [=Ibn Nujaym] said, "his words [=Ibn al-Humām in the *Fatḥ*] indicate that the non-Arab is not a suitable match for the Arab even if a *ḥasīb*; however, in the *Jāmiʿ* [=*Fatāwā*] of Qāḍīkhān [=Fakhr al-Dīn Ḥasan b. Manṣūr b. Maḥmūd al-Ūzjandī al-Farghānī] (d. 592/1196), 'they said the *ḥasīb* (person of position and power) is a suitable match for the *nasīb* (person of lineage) so the

learned non-Arab is a suitable match for the ignorant Arab and the ʿAlawiyya, because the honor of knowledge tops the honor of lineage.' He [=Ibn al-Humām] endorsed it in *Fatḥ al-Qadīr*. Al-Bazzāzī decisively affirmed it, adding that the poor learned person is a suitable match for the rich ignorant and its aptness is obvious, because the honor of knowledge tops the honor of lineage, so a fortiori that of wealth. Yes, *ḥasab* can also mean high position and eminence as per the *Muḥīṭ* [*al-Burhānī*] by Burhān al-Dīn Maḥmūd b. al-Ṣadr al-Saʿīd Tāj al-Dīn Aḥmad b. al-Ṣadr al-Kabīr ʿAbd al-ʿAzīz al-Bukhārī (551-616/1156-1219)] from Ṣadr al-Islām, and such is not a suitable match for the Arab woman, thus in the *Yanābīʿ*." This is the summary of what is stated in the *Nahr*.

I say, since what the *Yanābīʿ* states validates the unsuitability of the *ḥasīb* as a marriage match for the Arab woman on the basis of the definition of the *ḥasīb* as the possessor of high position and eminence, it follows that what the author [=Tumurtāshī] said about the validation of the unsuitability of the learned person is incorrect, as is the sourcing of that back to the *Yanābīʿ* in its commentary [by Ḥaṣkafī]. Kayr al-Dīn [b. Aḥmad b. ʿAlī b. Zayn al-Dīn] al-Ramlī (993-1081/1585-1670) mentioned [in his *Fatāwā*], citing *Majmaʿ al-fatāwā* [=anonymous compilation, ms. Ẓāhiriyya 6145 dated 866/1462], "the learned person can be a suitable match for the ʿAlawī woman because the honor of *ḥasab* (position and power) is stronger than the honor of lineage, which is the reason it was said that ʿĀʾisha is superior to Fāṭima, because ʿĀʾisha possesses the honor of knowledge—thus in the *Muḥīṭ* [*al-Burhānī*]." He also mentioned that it was definitely affirmed in the *Muḥīṭ*, the *Bazzāziyya*, the *Fayḍ* [*al-Ghaffār fī sharḥ al-Mukhtār* by Muḥammad b. Ibrāhīm b. Aḥmad al-Samwīsī (d. 9th/15th c.)?], *Jāmiʿ al-fatāwā*, the author of the *Durar* [*al-ḥukkām sharḥ Ghurar al-aḥkām* by Mullā Khusrū i.e. Muḥammad b. Farāmūz b. ʿAlī (d. 885/1480)], etc.

The statement of the commentator [=al-Ḥaṣkafī], "and he [=Ibn Nujaym] claimed in the *Baḥr* [*al-Rāʾiq*] etc." conveys that its being *ẓāhir al-riwāya* (related from Abū Ḥanīfa and/or his two companions) is an empty claim devoid of evidence other than their saying in the principal texts and elsewhere that "the Arabs are suitable marriage matches, i.e. therefore other than themselves are not matches for them." But it is no secret that this, even if its outward locution suggests it is meant in unqualified terms, nevertheless the masters restrict it to non-learned people; and how many other such examples there are! For it is the custom of the masters of the School to convey restrictions and conditions for unqualified phrases as an inference from universal rules, or subsidiary questions, or transmitted evidence, and this is the case here. For it was mentioned at the end of the *Fatāwā khayriyya* [by Khayr al-Dīn al-Ramlī], in regard to the ignorant Qurashī who takes precedence over a learned person in a gathering, that this is a prohibited act for him, as the books of the scholars are replete with the precedence of the learned person over the Qurashī, nor did He–exalted is He–differentiate between Qurashīs and others in His statement *or is he who makes long supplications in the watches of the night, prostrating and standing as he fears the hereafter and hopes for the mercy of his Lord—? Say, "Are they equal, those who know and those who do not know?" Only do they heed who possess hearts* (al-Zumar 39:9). And he went on, so look it up.

Since, therefore, the honor of knowledge is stronger than the honor of lineage by virtue of the evidence of the verse, and their explicit statement to that effect dictates that what they said in unqualified terms here is qualified and restricted on the basis of its understanding it as per another passage, it follows that what the masters mentioned does not disagree with the *ẓāhir al-riwāya*. And how can it be correct for anyone to say that such as Abū Ḥanīfa or al-Ḥasan al-Baṣrī and other non-Arabs cannot be a suitable match for the daughter of an ignorant Qurashī, or the daughter of a desert Arab that thinks nothing of splashing his heels with his own urine? So it is no wonder that he [=Ibn Nujaym] categorically affirmed what the masters said—including the author of the *Muḥīṭ* and others, as you already know—and what the verifier Ibn al-Humām endorsed, as did the author of the *Nahr*, and the commentator [=al-Ḥaṣkafī] followed them. Understand this. And Allah–exalted is He–knows best. [End of Ibn ʿĀbidīn's text.]

* * *

My beloved friend the Ḥabīb Dr. Ḥāmid ʿAbd al-Ḥamīd b. ʿAlī al-Mahdalī al-Ahdal al-Azharī–co-founder of Universiti Islam Sultan Sharif Ali in Brunei Darussalam, founder and rector of Jāmiʿat al-Imām al-Ghazālī in Terengganu, Malaysia and younger brother of al-Ḥabīb Dr. ʿAqīl b. ʿAlī b. ʿAlawī b. Ḥasan al-Mahdalī al-Azharī–informed me by *munāwala* (handover), *waṣiyya bil-kitāb* (book bequest) and *ijāza* (permission to narrate), from the jurist, genealogist and historian al-Ḥabīb Saqqāf b. ʿAlī al-Kāf al-Saqqāf al-Tarīmī al-Madanī (b. 1946) who said in his book *Dirāsa fī nasab al-Sāda Banī ʿAlawī dhurriyyat al-Imām al-muhājir Aḥmad b. ʿĪsā* (A study of the lineage of the sons of ʿAlawī masters the descendants of the emigrant Imam Aḥmad b. ʿĪsā [b. Muḥammad al-Naqīb b. ʿAlī al-ʿUrayḍī b. Jaʿfar al-Ṣādiq (273-345/886-956)]):

(Seventh corollary of the ninth inquiry on the rulings specific to *Ahl al-Bayt*: the precondition of matching suitability in the marriage contract.) Arab women specifically, and the women of the Prophetic House among them specifically, require the observance of lineage as a precondition for marriage to them from the perspective that only a Hāshimī man may marry a Hāshimiyya woman. The vast majority said it, including Abu Ḥanīfa, Aḥmad and al-Shāfiʿī–Allah be well-pleased with them. Their authoritative evidence for that is the hadith narrated from the Commander of the Believers our liegelord ʿUmar b. al-Khaṭṭāb–Allah be well-pleased with him–whereby he said, "I will categorically forbid the marrying of the women who possess *aḥsāb* [in the sense of *ansāb* (noble lineages)] except to suitable marriage matches"—al-Dāraquṭnī narrated it [in his *Sunan*; also Ibrāhīm b. Sa'd in his *Juz'*, Muḥammad b. Ḥasan al-Shaybānī in *al-Aṣl*, 'Abd al-Razzāq and Ibn Abī Shayba in their *Muṣannafs*, and al-Bayhaqī in the *Ma'rifa* and the *Sunan*, a *mursal* report strengthened by Imam Aḥmad as narrated by Ibn Rāhūyah in his *Masā'il* and Ibn Rajab in *Sharḥ 'Ilal al-Tirmidhī*]—and the statement of Imam Aḥmad that "other than the Quraysh among the Arabs are not a suitable match for the Quraysh, and other than the Banū Hāshim are not a suitable match for the Banū Hāshim." This is also the position of the Shāfi'īs, and they for this position of theirs they relied on the narration from Wāthila b. al-Asqa' that he heard the Messenger of Allah–upon him and his Family the blessings and peace of Allah–say, **"Verily Allah Most High selected Kināna out of the children of Ismā'īl and He selected Quraysh out of Kināna and He selected, out of Quraysh, Banū Hāshim, and he selected me out of Banū Hāshim."** Muslim, Aḥmad, al-Tirmidhī and al-Sam'ānī narrated it.

* * *

The Hadith arch-master Ibn Ḥajar al-'Asqalānī said in the book of *nikāḥ* (marriage) of his *Fatḥ al-Bārī* (The Disclosure of the Originator):

[Bukhārī's *Ṣaḥīḥ*,] "Chapter of the *akfā' fīl-dīn* (suitable marriage matches in respect to profession of faith) and His statement, *and He is the One Who created, out of water, a human being, then He made him kindred by lineage and by affinity* (نَسَبًا وَصِهْرًا al-Furqān 25:54)."

His statement, "Chapter of the suitable marriage matches in respect to profession of faith:" the plural of *kuf'* with initial *ḍamm* and *sukūn* of the *fā'* followed by a *hamza*, [meaning] the identical specimen and the equivalent. The consideration of *kafāʾa* (matching suitability) in respect to creed is agreed upon; thus the Muslim woman is absolutely illicit for an unbeliever.

His statement, *and He is the One Who created, out of water, a human being, then He made him a* nasab *and a* ṣihr, to the end of the verse: [Yaḥyā b. Ziyād b. ʿAbd Allāh b. Manẓūr] al-Farrāʾ (d. 207/822) said [in *Maʿānī al-Qurʾān*], "the *nasab* is the one to whom marriage is unlawful and the *ṣihr* is the one to whom marriage is lawful." So it is as if, when the author [=al-Bukhārī] saw there was encompassment with the two categories [in the verse], it was apt to hold fast to the universal meaning [i.e. everyone may marry everyone] since there exists applicability to that end except for whatever consideration is indicated by the evidence, namely the exception of the unbeliever[, hence the chapter-title]. Mālik certainly affirmed in definite terms that the consideration of marriage suitability was specific to creed. The same is transmitted from Ibn ʿUmar and Ibn Masʿūd, and, among the Successors, Muḥammad b. Sīrīn and ʿUmar b. ʿAbd al-ʿAzīz.

The vast majority consider marriage suitability to refer to lineage. Abū Ḥanīfa said the Quraysh are suitable matches for one another; the Arabs likewise; but none of the Arabs is a suitable match for the Quraysh, just as none of the non-Arabs is a suitable match for the Arabs. It is a view among the Shāfiʿīs, but the sound view is that the Banū Hāshim and Banū al-Muṭṭalib take precedence over all others, and all other than these are suitable matches for one another. Al-Thawrī took the view that when the *mawlā* (non-Arab) marries the Arab woman, the marriage is annulled, and Aḥmad said the same according to one narration. Al-Shāfiʿī took the middle ground and said "marriage to other than suitable matches is not categorically prohibited so that I should reject the marriage contract; it is only a failing on the part of the woman and the guardians. If they agree to it it is valid, and it is a right of theirs which they have given up. But if they all agreed except one of them, he has the right to annul it." He also mentioned that the significance of making guardianship a precondition in the marriage contract is so that the woman would not irreparably lose herself with an unsuitable match.

There is no firmly-established hadith on the consideration of marriage suitability through lineage. As for what al-Bazzār narrated as a hadith from Muʿādh, from the Prophet–upon him the blessings and peace of Allah–that **"The Arabs are suitable matches for one another, and the *mawālī* (non-Arabs) are suitable matches for one another,"** its chain is weak. Al-Bayhaqī adduced as a proof the hadith of Wāthila, from the Prophet–upon him the blessings and peace of Allah –**"Verily Allah Most High selected Kināna out of the children of Ismāʿīl"** to the end of the hadith–which is sound: Muslim narrated it–but its use as a strong argument in support of that needs reconsideration. However, some added to it the hadith **"Put the Quraysh first and do not put yourselves ahead of them"** [see under the *Jāmiʿ* of Maʿmar b. Rāshid, §1 above]. Ibn al-Mundhir related from al-Buwayṭī, furthermore, that al-Shāfiʿī said that *kafāʾa* (marriage suitability) was in regard to *dīn* (profession of faith). Thus is it found in Buwayṭī's *Mukhtaṣar*. Rāfiʿī said, "And it is a famous disagreement." Al-Abzī related from al-Rabīʿ [b. Abī Sulaymān al-Murādī] that a man asked al-Shāfiʿī about it so he answered, "I am an Arab—do not ask me about this."

* * *

The spiritual understanding of the obligation and benefit of loving the *Ahl al-Bayt*

SHAYKH MUḤYĪ AL-DĪN IBN ʿARABĪ AL-ṬĀʾĪ AL-DIMASHQĪ (558-638/1163-1240)–Allah be well-pleased with him–said in the 29th chapter of the *Futūḥāt al-Makkiyya* (The Meccan Disclosures) which he addressed to the *awliyāʾ* (friends of Allah) and entitled:

On the recognition of the secret of Salmān
that caused him to join the people of the House
and the Aqṭāb (Poles) from whom he inherited it,
and the recognition of their secrets

—it is among the most beneficial teachings I have seen on this subject and Shaykh Muḥammad Abū al-Hudā had me read it before him in Ṣabbūra, after which I read it another time in Singapore with Shaykh ʿAbd al-Maqṣūd al-Sayyid Fāris al-Azharī–Allah have mercy on the latter and preserve the former–as part of my reading before him the treatise by the Baalbek-born historian of Egypt Taqī al-Dīn Aḥmad b. ʿAlī b. ʿAbd al-Qādir al-Maqrīzī (766-845/1365-1442), *Maʿrifat mā yajibu li-Āl al-Bayt al-Nabawī min al-ḥaqqi ʿalā man ʿadāhum* (Recognition of the rights owed to the people of the Prophetic House by all others) in which it is mentioned in full:

> Know–may Allah support you–that it was narrated to us as part of the hadiths from Jaʿfar b. Muḥammad al-Ṣādiq, from his father Muḥammad b. ʿAlī [al-Bāqir], from his father ʿAlī b. al-Ḥusayn [Zayn al-ʿĀbidīn], from his father al-Ḥusayn b. ʿAlī, from his father ʿAlī b. Abī Ṭālib–may Allah be well-pleased with them–from the Messenger of Allah–upon him

the blessings and peace of Allah–that he said, **"The *mawlā* (freedman) of a people is one of them"** [al-Tirmidhī, al-Nasā'ī and al-Ḥākim from Abū Rāfi'; Dārimī from 'Amr b. 'Awf al-Muzanī; Abū Ya'lā and Ṭabarānī from Ibn 'Abbās; Ibn Abī Shayba from Fārisī *mawlā* Banī Mu'āwiya; Aḥmad from Rifā'a and Abī Mūsā; the Two Shaykhs from Anas], and al-Tirmidhī narrated from the Messenger of Allah–upon him the blessings and peace of Allah–that he said, **"The people of the Qur'ān—they indeed are the family of Allah and His intimates!"** and He said–exalted is He–in regard to the special ones among His slaves, *verily My slaves—you* [=the devil] *have no authority over them except whoever follows you of those that are astray* (al-Ḥijr 15:42). So every Godly slave over whom anyone among creatures possesses some right, his servanthood is deficient to the extent of that right. <For that creature pursues him by virtue of its right and wields some authority over him thereby; therefore he is not a purely dedicated slave to Allah.>

But since the Messenger of Allah–upon him the blessings and peace of Allah–is ever a purely dedicated servant whom Allah has certainly purified most thoroughly along with the people of his House, and from whom He has taken away all uncleanness, which is everything that disgraces them—for *rijs* is filth among the Arabs, thus did al-Farrā' convey it—saying *Allah only desires to remove uncleanness from you, People of the House, and to cleanse you with a thorough cleansing!* (Aḥzāb 33:33), it follows that none can be joined to them except one who is purified without fail. For the one who is joined to them is indeed the one who resembles them. So they do not let anyone join them except whoever has the status of purity and holiness. So this is the testimony on the part of the Prophet–upon him the blessings and peace of Allah–on behalf of Salmān al-Fārisī as possessing purity, divine care and protection whereby the Messenger of Allah said of him **"Salmān is one of us, the people of the House!"** [see chapter on Baghawī's *Ma'alim al-tanzīl*, §39 above], and Allah Himself witnessed in their favor as having been purified and having all uncleanness leave them. Since none but the purified and the holy can be joined to them, and since divine tender care befell such a one merely by virtue of being joined to them, then what do you think of the status of the people of the House in themselves? They indeed are the purified ones—or rather they are purity itself.

Thus this verse [=al-Aḥzāb 33:33] indicates that Allah has partnered up the people of the House with the Messenger of Allah–upon him the blessings and peace of Allah–in His statement–may He be exalted–*so that the One God would forgive you what is past of your fault and what is future* (al-Fatḥ 48:2); and what dirt or filth is filthier and dirtier than sins? So Allah purified His Prophet with forgiveness, whereby what constitutes a sin with respect to ourselves, if it were to befall on his part it would be a sin in form, not in meaning, because blame no longer attaches to him for that on the part of Allah, nor on ours per the sacred Law. For if its status were that of a sin, there would accompany whatever accompanies sins of condemnation and His statement would not be true that *Allah only desires to remove uncleanness from you, People of the House, and to cleanse you with a thorough cleansing!* (al-Aḥzāb 33:33).

All the Sharifs–the children of Fāṭima–are thus subsumed until the Day of Resurrection, as is whoever is part of *Ahl al-Bayt* such as Salmān al-Fārisī, under the ruling of this verse with respect to forgiveness. For they are the purified ones as a special exclusive grant from Allah and as tender care for them because of the immense honor of Muḥammad–upon him the blessings and peace of Allah–and the tender care of Allah for him. The full significance and status of this honor for the people of the House will not fully appear other than in the abode of the hereafter, for verily they will be regathered completely forgiven; but as for this world, then whoever among them violates a boundary, the *ḥadd* (statutory penalty) is enforced against them, as for the contrite one whose case reaches the judge that he has committed adultery, theft or imbibing, the *ḥadd* is enforced against him together with the realization of forgiveness, as in the case of Māʿiz [the confessed adulterer who was stoned to death and whom the Prophet declared to be in Paradise] and his likes, whom it is impermissible to blame thereafter.

Furthermore, every Muslim who believes in Allah and in what He sent down must confirm the veracity of Allah–exalted is He–in His statement *to remove uncleanness from you, People of the House, and to cleanse you with a thorough cleansing*, whereby he firmly believes, with regard to everything that issues from the people of the House, that Allah has certainly granted them forgiveness with regard to it. So no Muslim ought to voice condemnation of them, or anything that disgraces the honor of those to whose purification and to the removal of uncleanness from whom Allah has witnessed, neither for any deed they did nor any goodness they achieved in the past, but by virtue of foreordained tender care on the part of Allah to their benefit. *That is the bounty of the One God; He gives it to whomever He wishes. And the One God is the possessor of immense bounty* (al-Jumuʿa 62:4).

And if the report that is reaching us about Salmān al-Fārisī is sound, then he has this level. For if Salmān were to do something that the manifest aspect of the sacred Law considers disgraceful and whose author stands condemned, then someone from whom uncleanness was not removed would be joined with the people of the House, and the latter would have a share of that to the extent of his affiliation to them, yet they are the ones who are purified as textually stipulated. Therefore Salmān is part of them without a doubt, and I hope that that divine tender care reaches down to the descendants of ʿAlī and Salmān just as it has reached the children of al-Ḥasan and al-Ḥusayn, their descendants and the freedmen and women of the people of the House, for verily the mercy of Allah is vast, O wali!

Now, if the level of a creature in the divine presence is such that one who is ascribed to them obtains honor through their honor—while their own honor is not due to their own persons, but only the fact that it is Allah Who elected them and dressed them with the vestment of honor—then what about, O wali!, the one that is ascribed to Him Who possesses praise and glory and honor in Himself and His own Essence? For He is the All-Glorious–glorified and exalted is He–so whoever is annexed to Him among His servants, they are His true slaves, and they are the ones over whom no creature possesses any authority in the hereafter. He–exalted is He–said to Iblīs, *verily My slaves*—whereby He annexed them to Himself—*you have no authority over them* (al-Isrā' 17:65). And you will not find in the Qur'ān slaves being annexed to Him–exalted is He–except the blissful ones in particular, while the wording for other than them comes up as *the slaves* (al-Baqara 2:207, Āl 'Imrān 3:15, 3:20, 3:30, Yāsīn 36:30, Ghāfir 40:31, 40:44, 40:48, Qāf 50:11). What do you think, then, about the protected ones, the preserved ones among them, those who are observant of the boundaries of their Master and are standing by His edicts? Their honor is higher yet and more complete! And these ones—they are the *aqṭāb* (Poles) of this station.

And it is from these *aqṭāb* that Salmān inherited the honor of the station of *Ahl al-Bayt*, so he was–may Allah be well-pleased with him–of the most knowledgeable of people as to what rights Allah owns over His slaves, what the latter possess of superexcellence over creatures; and of the strongest in fulfilling them. It is about him that the Messenger of Allah –upon him the blessings and peace of Allah–said, **"If faith were in the Pleiades, certain men from Persia would have obtained it," and he gestured towards Salmān al-Fārisī** [agreed upon from Abū Hurayra]; and in the Prophet's specification of the Seven Sisters as opposed to other star systems is a wondrous allusion to those who emphatically affirm the

Seven divine Attributes [=the Ashʿarī School], because they are seven chief stars—understand this.

So then the secret of Salmān which caused him to join the people of the House is what the Prophet–upon him the blessings and peace of Allah–gave him of the remittance due for his manumission. And in this there is an astonishing *fiqh*. For he is therefore the freedman of the Prophet–upon him the blessings and peace of Allah–and **"The freedman of a people is one of them"** [see first paragraph above]. And all are the freedmen of the All-True—His mercy encompasses everything, and everything is His slave and His *mawlā*.

Now that the high station of *Ahl al-Bayt* has become clear to you, and that fact that no Muslim ought to condemn them for what might transpire of them at all–for Allah has purified them–then let their condemner know that such goes back to him, even if they have wronged him. For that wronging is a wrong in his own estimation, not in reality—although the letter of the sacred Law does rule that it must be redressed. In fact, the status of their wronging us, in itself, resembles the course of the foreordained decrees in the life of the slave with regard to his property and his life whether through drowning, a fire, or any other such destructive event, or one of those he loves dies or he himself becomes afflicted with something—and all of this fails to concur with his objective. [But] it is not permissible for one to blame the foreordainment of Allah or His decree. Rather, he must face all of that with surrender and acceptance; if he is below this level, then with patient endurance; if he is above that level then [not only surrender and acceptance but] with gratitude. For within the fold of that there are blessings from Allah to this victim.

There is nothing good beyond what we just mentioned. For beyond it there is only despair, anger, lack of acceptance and bad manners with Allah. Thus ought the Muslim to face everything that befalls him on the part of *Ahl al-Bayt* in his wealth, his life, his honor, his family and his kindred, so that he will face all that with acceptance, surrender and patient endurance, and not direct condemnation at them in any way at all. Even if the rulings that are determined by the sacred Law rightly apply to them, it never undermines this [requirement]' on the contrary, it lets it run its course the way he lets the divine decrees run their course. We only declared it forbidden to impute blameworthiness to them as Allah distinguished them from us with something in which we are not on a par with them. As for the fulfillment of rights dictated by the sacred Law, then here is the [example of the] Messenger of Allah–upon him the blessings and peace of Allah–who was taking a loan from the Jews, and when they demanded their rights from him he fulfilled them in the most beautiful way imaginable. If the Jew showed him disrespect he would say, **"Let him be! The one who is owed a right is allowed to speak out"** [agreed upon from Abū Hurayra] and he said on one occasion, **"If Fāṭima the daughter of Muḥammad were to steal, I would cut off her hand."**

Now the putting of laws into place belongs to Allah; He legislates them in any way and manner He wishes. So these rights belong to Allah and despite this He never blamed them. Our discussion, however, only bears upon our own rights and what we have a right to demand of them. In the latter respect we are given a choice: if we wish we exact, and if we wish we give up. The latter is universally preferable to begin with, how then when it comes to *Ahl al-Bayt*? And we have no right to blame anybody to begin with, how then when it comes to *Ahl al-Bayt*? So if we give up demanding our rights and we pardon them in that regard–i.e. what they took from us–then we shall have, in the divine presence, immense credit for **lending a hand** and the position of nearness to Him.

For the Prophet–upon him the blessings and peace of Allah –did not ask of us, upon the prompting of the divine command, *other than affectionate love for the near relatives* (al-Shūrā 42:23), wherein is the secret of keeping family ties. Now who is not going to accept the request of his Prophet in what he asked of him and which he is perfectly capable of doing? In what manner will he face him tomorrow or hope for his intercession, when he did not come to the aid of his Prophet–upon him the blessings and peace of Allah–in what the latter asked of him with respect to love of his near relatives? What to say of the people of his House, who are the most intimate of the near relatives?

Moreover, it is phrased with the term *al-mawadda* which is "to stand firm upon love." For he whose *mawadda* is firm in something will keep company with it in every state, and when *mawadda* accompanies him in every state, he never takes the *Ahl al-Bayt* to task for anything that befalls on their part to his detriment [outwardly], for which it would be his right to make demands of them regarding it. For he gives it up for no other reason than love and out of preference for his own good, not to his own detriment. The truthful lover said,

everything the beloved one does is beloved,

which was phrased as *ḥubb* (love); how then when it comes to *mawadda*? It is truly good news that the name *al-Wadūd* is related among the divine Names. But there is no significance to its standing firm other than for its effect to truly take place in the abode of the hereafter and in Hellfire, for each party according to what the wisdom of Allah dictates concerning them. Another lover said about the same meaning,

I love, because of love of her, black people to the point
I love, because of her love, the black ones among dogs.

And we ourselves have said about this meaning,

I love, for love of you, Abyssinians one and all, and I
fervently crave, for your name, the luminous badr *(full moon)*

It was said that black dogs would snap at him as he endeared himself to her. This is the act of a lover in loving that whose love will not make him one of the blessed in the divine presence, nor will it cause him to inherit nearness to Allah. Can this be for any other reason than truthfulness in love and the firmness of affectionate love in oneself?

So then, if your love were sound for Allah and for His Messenger, you would love the people of the House of the Messenger of Allah–upon him the blessings and peace of Allah–and you would view everything that issues from them towards you which is contrary to your liking and your wishes as an object of beauty in which you bask, as in a blessing, because it came from them, so that you would then come to know that you are the object of special tender care in the presence of Allah, for Whose sake you have loved them, whereby he whom He loves has mentioned you, and you have been on his mind—and they are the people of the House of His Messenger–upon him the blessings and peace of Allah–so that you would give thanks to Allah for this blessing. For they have mentioned you with tongues that are pure through being purified by Allah—a purity beyond your knowledge.

And when we see you in the opposite of this state with the people of the House, you who are in need of them and of the Messenger of Allah–upon him blessings and peace of Allah–since Allah has guided you with him—then how can I myself trust in your affectionate love with which you claim that you dearly love me, and in your keeping of my rights or respect for me, when you are taking such a stance towards the people of your Prophet, mistreating them so? I swear it by Allah! That is for no other reason than a deficiency in your belief, and from the *makr* (scheming) of Allah with you and His gradually leading you on from where you do not know! (Cf. al-Aʿrāf 7:182, al-Qalam 68:44). The concept of *makr* here is for you to say—convinced that you are, in so doing, defending the faith-system of Allah and His sacred Law—in pursuit of your right, that "you ask nothing but what Allah has made permissible for you to ask." But condemnation is latent in that Law-sanctioned demand—hatred, rancor, and your preference of yourself over the people of the House, when you do not even realize it! The effective medicine for such a chronic disease is for you not to deem yourself to possess any right when it comes to them, and to give up your right, lest what I mentioned to you should lurk in its pursuit.

You are not one of the rulers of the Muslims so that you are personally responsible for enforcing some statutory penalty, or redress injustice wrought against someone, or return some right that was usurped from its rightful owners. But if you are a ruler and you must, then do your utmost to convince the rightful owner of the usurped right to give up his right when the one being sued is for it is from the people of the House. If the former refuses, at that time you are personally responsible to let the ruling of the sacred Law come to pass against the latter. But if Allah unveiled for you, O wali! their stations in His presence in the hereafter, you would wish if only you could be some nameless freedman of theirs. May Allah, then, inspire us the uprightness of our lives! See then how high and noble the position of Salmān is! May Allah be well-pleased with all of them.

And now that I have clarified for you the Poles of this station and the fact that they are the elect and choicest slaves of Allah, know then that their secrets—which Allah allowed us to look upon—are completely uknown to the commonality of people or rather, even to most of the special ones who do not have this station. Al-Khaḍir–Allah be well-pleased with him–is among them [=the Poles]. He is one of their major ones, and Allah bore witness on his behalf that He gave him mercy from His presence and taught him, from His side, a certain knowledge (cf. al-Kahf 18:65) wherein he was followed by the Interlocutor of the One God, Mūsā–upon him peace–of whom the Prophet–upon him blessings and peace of Allah–said, **"If Mūsā were alive he would have no other choice but to follow me"** [Aḥmad from Jābir and ʿAbd Allāh b. Thābit; al-Dārimī from Jābir]. So among their secrets is what we have mentioned of the knowledge of the level of *Ahl al-Bayt* and what Allah has said in notification of their lofty station in that. Also among their secrets is the knowledge of the scheming that Allah directs at His slaves in the hatred of them—together with their protesting that they love the Messenger of Allah–upon him the blessings and peace of Allah–and in his asking *affectionate love for the near relatives* (al-Shūrā 42:23)—and he himself is part and parcel of *Ahl al-Bayt*. Thus most people have not implemented what the Messenger of Allah–upon him the blessings and peace of Allah–asked them to implement with regard to him as a divine command, thereby disobeying Allah and His Messenger; and they did not love any of his near relatives except whoever they viewed as showing goodness to them. They loved but their own ulterior motives, and they longed only for their own egos. [End of excerpt from Ibn ʿArabī's *Futūḥāt*, chapter 29, 3:227-240 of the 1405/1985 Osman Yahya edition.]

* * *

In conclusion, the generality of the believers of the people of the House of the Seal of Prophethood–upon him the blessings and peace of Allah–have been granted honor above the generality of the non-affiliated believers. What to say of them if they are also of the Godfearing people of knowledge? Piety towards them, seeking nearness to them and loving them are therefore among the avenues of felicity and salvation from Hellfire, or rather of the highest levels and of the hope of being with the Liegelord of the virtuous–upon him the blessings and peace of Allah. It is therefore obligatory to make them known, make their excellent merits, their high levels and due rights known, to show gratitude over the blessing of their existence in the Umma, and to busy oneself with the obtainment of everything that is pursuant to such excellence of the best ways of keeping the ties of selfless generosity, without excess or laxity and without claiming anyone's holiness before Allah but rather in obedience to the command subauded in His statement–exalted is He–*except affectionate love for the near relatives* (Shūrā 42:23), and by putting into practice uniquely precious aspects that are among the most hope-filled parts of the Sunna of the Elect one–upon him the blessings and peace of Allah–*only in the seeking of the countenance of one's Highest nurturing Lord* (al-Layl 92:20).

Literature on *Ahl al-Bayt* in Arabic: A selected descriptive bibliography

It is in pursuit of the fulfillment of this responsibility that the learned authorities of the past strove in reminding the Umma of the excellent merits and virtues of the people of the House. Among the works to that effect I have seen are the following, listed in chronological order of authors:

- *al-Dhurriyat al-ṭāhirat al-Nabawiyya* (The pure Prophetic progeny) by the Imam and brilliant Hadith master Abū Bishr Muḥammad b. Aḥmad b. Ḥammād b. Sa'īd al-Anṣārī al-Rāzī al-Dūlābī or Dawlābī (224-310/839-923) (§25).
- *Dhakhā'ir al-'uqbā fī faḍā'il dhawī al-qurbā* (Treasures of the hereafter as to the excellences of the Prophetic kin) by the Sharif *muḥaddith* and historian Muḥibb al-Dīn Abū al-'Abbās Aḥmad b. 'Abd Allāh b. Muḥammad al-Ṭabarī al-Makkī (615-694/1218-1295) the grandfather of some of the major transmissologists of the Hijaz. It is an indispensable thorough biographical guide to the Prophetic House although it was flagged by Ibn Ḥajar and Sakhāwī for many weak and forged or chainless reports listed without warning alongside the established ones. He also authored *al-Riyāḍ al-naḍira fī manāqib al-'Ashara* (The radiant groves on the virtues of the Ten [who were promised Paradise]) whose fourth part is a documentation of the merits of our liegelord 'Alī. Both are in print.
- *Ma'rifat mā yajibu li-Āl al-Bayt al-Nabawī min al-ḥaqqi 'alā man 'adāhum* (Recognition of the rights owed to the people of the Prophetic House by all others) by Maqrīzī (see twelve pages up). After reading it

with two of my teachers I taught it in Birmingham in Sha'bān 1429/August 2008 before a group of students among whom were Ustaz Amjad Mahmud b. Ghulam Muhammad, Shaykh Asrar b. Muhammad 'Abd al-Rashid, Dr. Asim b. 'Abid Yusuf al-Habibi and others.

- *al-Nizā' wal-takhāṣum fī-mā bayna Banī Umayya wa-Banī Hāshim* (The antagonism and disagreement between the Banū Umayya and the Banū Hāshim), also by al-Maqrīzī in which he states (p. 88 of the 1937 ed.) that the lineages of all of the sub-tribes of the Quraysh have gone into oblivion except those of al-Ḥasan and al-Ḥusayn. He expands on this also in his massive *Sīra* entitled *Imtā' al-asmā' bi-mā lil-Nabī min al-aḥwāl wal-amwāl wal-ḥafadati wal-matā'* (Delighting the listeners with the Prophet's states, wealth, grandchildren and furnishings).

- *Istijlāb irtiqā' al-ghuraf bi-ḥubbi aqribā' al-Rasūl wa-dhawī al-sharaf* (Procuring the ascent to the upper rooms through love of the Prophet's relatives and the noble) is a hefty tome by the meticulous Hadith master and star student of Ibn Ḥajar, Shams al-Dīn Abū al-Khayr Muḥammad b. 'Abd al-Raḥmān b. Muḥammad al-Sakhāwī (831-902/1428-1497), one of the best Hadith studies on the subject.

- *al-Ishrāf fī bayān faḍl al-ashrāf* (The honorific overview in the exposition of the merit of the Sharifs), an unpublished Azhar manuscript in over 63 folios by the Sharif historian of Medina, *muḥaddith*, jurist and pilgrimologist Nūr al-Dīn Abū al-Ḥasan 'Alī b. 'Afīf al-Dīn 'Abd Allāh b. Aḥmad al-Samhūdī al-Ḥasanī al-Shāfi'ī (844-911/1440-1505).

- *Jawāhir al-ʿiqdayn fī faḍl al-sharafayn al-ʿilm al-jalī wal-nasab al-Nabawī* (The jewels of the two necklaces regarding the excellence of the two honors: shining knowledge and Prophetic lineage), a precious treatise also by al-Samhūdī, which received two editions and of which the second part covers the subject in fifteen chapters and a conclusion as follows:

1. Their superiority due to their origin and purification
2. The Prophet's order to invoke blessings on them
3. The salam of Allah Most High on them in His Book
4. The Prophet's instruction to hold fast to the Book and them
5. Their consisting in safety for the Umma like Nūḥ's Ark
6. The Prophet's family ties are kept whole here and hereafter
7. The divine promise that they will not be punished
8. The Prophet's *duʿā* for their progeny until al-Mahdī
9. The Quranic proofs for the duty of their affectionate love
10. Hadiths showing the same and its being a condition of faith
11. Warnings against hatred or enmity of them as leading to hell
12. The exhortation to keep ties with them & make them happy
13. The early Muslims' practice of venerating *Ahl al-Bayt*
14. Hadiths on their persecution and what ensued to persecutors
15. Pure characters and high energies sought for *Ahl al-Bayt*

Conclusion on their states and high respect of the Companions

- *Iḥyāʾ al-mayt bi-faḍāʾil Āl al-Bayt* (Reviving of the dead through the virtues of the people of the House) by the polymath Shaykh al-Islam and Hadith master, Imam Jalāl al-Dīn Abū al-Faḍl ʿAbd al-Raḥmān b. Kamāl al-Dīn Abī Bakr b. Muḥammad b. Sābiq al-Dīn al-Khuḍayrī al-Shāfiʿī al-Suyūṭī (849-911/1445-1505) who gathered sixty hadiths therein.

- *Musnad Fāṭimat al-Zahrāʾ* by Suyūṭī also, in reality entitled *al-Riwāyāt al-mutaʿalliqa bi-sayyidat nisāʾ al-ʿalamın Fāṭimat al-zahrāʾ khātimat banāt Sayyid al-ʿālamīn–ʿalayh wa-ʿalayhā wa-baʿlihā wa-waladihā wa-sāʾir ahli baytihā ṣalawāt Rabbi al-ʿālamīn* (The reports that pertain to the liege lady of the women of the worlds Fāṭima the Luminous, the seal of the daughters of the Liegelord of the worlds–may the blessing of the Lord of the worlds be upon him and upon her, her husband, her progeny and the rest of the people of her House), a selection of 284 hadiths which is more important and comprensive than *Iḥyā' al-mayt*.

- *Asnā al-maṭālib fī ṣilat al-arḥām wal-aqārib* (The purest quest in keeping ties with kindred and relatives) by the same, a massive encyclopedia on the subject containing abundant *Sīra* illustrations of its ideal as well as violations of it such as the assassinations and attempted assassinations of the Prophet, many prominent Companions, and *Ahl al-Bayt*.

- Forty hadiths on *Ahl al-Bayt* by the arch-jurist Shaykh al-Islam, Shihāb al-Dīn Abū al-ʿAbbās Aḥmad b. Muḥammad b. Muḥammad b. ʿAlī b. Ḥajar al-Haytamī al-Saʿdī al-Anṣārī al-Makkī al-Shāfiʿī (909-974/1503-1567) within his book *al-Ṣawāʿiq al-muḥriqa fīl-raddi ʿalā ahl al-bidaʿ wal-zandaqa* (The scorching thunderbolts in refuting innovators and freethinkers). In the same book Imam al-Haytamī cited the report that whenever a shaykh or a young man from Quraysh or from the Sharifs came to Imam Ahmad, the latter would always give them a position of precedence and walk behind them [al-Khaṭīb, *al-Jāmiʿ fī akhlāq al-rāwī wal-sāmiʿ*; Ibn al-Jawzī, *Manāqib Aḥmad*]. We already mentioned his citation from Aḥmad about the curative virtues of hadith chains containing the names of *Ahl al-Bayt* (see above, §13).

- *al-Itḥāf bi-ḥubb al-Ashrāf* (The gift of love of the Sharifs), a concise and meticulous manual of Hadith, *fiqh*, and history of the subject by the Shaykh al-Azhar Jamāl al-Dīn Abū Muḥammad ʿAbd Allāh b. Muḥammad b. ʿĀmir al-Shāfiʿī al-Shabrāwī (1091-1172/1680-1759) which received several editions. He also wrote poetry, *Manāʾiḥ al-alṭāf fī madāʾiḥ al-ashrāf* (Gifts of subtleties concerning the praises of the Sharifs).

- *Itḥāf Ahl al-Islām bi-mā yataʿallaq bil-Muṣṭafā wa-ahli Baytihi al-kirām* (Gifting the people of submission that which pertains to the Elect one and the noble people of his House) by the Cairene legal theorist, grammarian, *muḥaddith* and student of Shabrāwī, Abū al-ʿIrfān Muḥammad b. ʿAlī al-Ṣabbān (d. 1206/1792).
- *Isʿāf al-rāghibīn fī sīrat al-Muṣṭafā wa-faḍāʾil ahli Baytihi al-ṭāhirīn* (The prompt service to the desirous regarding the biography of the Elect one and the merits of the pure people of his House) also by al-Ṣabbān, who said he finished it in Ramadan 1185 as an expansion and more encyclopedic version of his *Itḥāf*. Both works are *Ahl al-Bayt*-conscious *Sīra*s that compare to Sayyid Aḥmad Daḥlān's two-volume *al-Sīrat al-Nabawiyya wal-āthār al-Muḥammadiyya* totalling 600 pages in minuscule characters published at al-Maṭbaʿa al-Maymaniyya in Cairo in 1310/1893. The *Isʿāf* was published in the margin of the Maymaniyya 1312 edition of Shablanjī's *Nūr al-abṣār*.
- *al-Fatḥ al-mubīn fī faḍāʾil al-Khulafāʾ al-rāshidīn wa-Ahli al-Bayt al-ṭāhirīn* (The manifest victory on the immense merits of the rightly-guided Caliphs and the pure people of the House) by Sayyid Abū al-ʿAbbās Aḥmad b. Zaynī Daḥlān (1232-1304/1817-1886) the Shāfiʿī Mufti of Mecca, published in the margins of the first edition of his *Sīra*. It then received a modern edition at Dār al-Fikr in Beirut at the hand of his great-grandson Dr. Rabīʿ b. Ṣādiq Daḥlān. The

book ends with a large section on al-Ḥasan and *Ahl al-Bayt* then ʿĀʾisha and the Ten promised Paradise.

- *Tārīkh Ashrāf al-Ḥijāz* (History of the Sharifs of the Hihajz), also by Daḥlān and published in Beirut at Dār al-Sāqī in 1993, is actually a study of his *Khulāṣat al-kalām fī bayān umarāʾ al-Balad al-ḥarām* (Epitome of the exposition of the emirs of the Inviolable Country) and of his life and works.

- *Nūr al-abṣār fī manāqib Āl Bayt al-Nabī al-mukhtār* (The light of sights concerning the virtues of the people of the House of the chosen Prophet) by Muʾmin b. Ḥasan Muʾmin al-Shablanjī (1252-after 1322/1836-after 1904) with emphasis on *Ahl al-Bayt* in Egypt.

- *Yanābīʿ al-mawadda li-dhawī al-qurbā* (Wellsprings of affectionate love for the near relatives) by Shaykh Sulaymān b. Ibrāhīm al-Qundūzī al-Ḥanafī (d. 1294/1877) was flagged for its very weak and forged reports on top of its Shīʿism.

- *Manār al-ishrāf ʿalā faḍl ʿuṣāt al-ashrāf wa-mawālīhim min al-aṭrāf* (The lighthouse of vantage over the merit of the sinners among the Sharifs and their clients from the far ends) by the erudite genealogist, jurist, poet and Sufi Abū al-Fayḍ ʿĀshūr b. Muḥammad b. ʿAbīd al-Hilālī al-Khanguī al-Khalwatī al-Masʿūdī (1264-1314/1848-1896), published in 1332/1914 at Algiers' Maṭbaʿa Thaʿālibiyya, which published the first printed *muṣḥaf* in Algeria.

- *Rashfat al-ṣādī min baḥri faḍāʾil banī al-Nabī al-hādī* (A scoop for the parched from the sea of the merits of the sons of the guiding Prophet) by the Shāfiʿī jurist, legal theorist and poet al-Ḥabīb Abū Bakr b. ʿAbd al-

Raḥmān b. Muḥammad b. ʿAlī b. ʿAbd Allāh Āl Shihāb al-Dīn al-Tarīmī (1262-1341/1846-1922) who studied under more than 100 teachers and taught Muḥammad b. ʿAqīl al-ʿAlawī. Like Shabrāwī's *Itḥāf* this is one of the indispensable books of this list from the perspective of thorough integration of Qurʾān and Hadith with *fiqh*, *taṣawwuf*, biographical history and poetry. It was gifted to me by Ḥabīb ʿAbd al-Ḥamīd al-Mahdalī (see 22 pages up). Among its many benefits is the mention of a rare narration with a strong chain to Imam Aḥmad b. Ḥanbal of a thereafter chainless Prophetic hadith stating **"Allah shall appoint at the head of every 100 years a man from the people of my House that shall teach my Umma their *dīn* (faith-system)."** Aḥmad said, "first ʿUmar b. ʿAbd al-ʿAzīz then Muḥammad b. Idrīs al-Shāfiʿī" [Abū Nuʿaym and Ibn ʿAsākir]. This gloss reflects the more general understanding of the term of *Ahl al-Bayt* which the present *Musnad Ahl al-Bayt* strives to include. It also supports Ḥakīm al-Tirmidhī and Ibn ʿArabī's view that *tajdīd* (spiritual renewal), *quṭbiyya* (Polestarhood, the highest spiritual stations) and *Ahl al-Bayt* converge in the Umma, as indicated by Ḥabīb Abū Bakr Āl Shihāb's chapter to that effect, and are in effect identical.

- *al-Sharaf al-muʾabbad li-Āli Muḥammad* (Everlasting honor for the family of Muḥammad) by the prolific Qadi Yūsuf b. Ismāʿīl b. Yūsuf b. Ismāʿīl al-Nabhānī al-Shāfiʿī (1265-1350/1849-1932), published in 1309/1892 and divided into three parts and a conclusion. The first part is a long explanation of the hadith of the *thaqalayn* (weighty matters, see §20 above) which was the impetus for writing the book; the second is on the virtues of the Five (see §3 above); the third discusses the benefits of loving them here and hereafter. The conclusion shows that love of *Ahl al-Bayt* does not benefit if mixed with hatred of the Companions.

- *al-Arbaʿūn al-Kattāniyya fī faḍl Āl Bayt Khayr al-bariyya* (The forty-Hadith Kattānī compilation on the excellence of the people of the House of the Best of creation) by the Hadith master Abū ʿAbd Allāh Muḥammad b. Jaʿfar b. Idrīs b. Muḥammad al-Zamzamī al-Kattānī al-Fāsī (1274-1345/1858-1927). I departed from the style of this work and from that of the Suyūṭī 60 Hadiths, the Haytamī 40 Hadiths, and the *Arbaʿūn al-musnada* of al-Fādānī by pursuing a criterion of authenticity and avoiding repetitiveness.

Some contemporary authors and their works in alphabetical order of titles

- *Ahl al-Bayt fī Miṣr* by ʿAbd al-Ḥafīẓ Faraghlī ʿAlī al-Qarnī focuses on the famous *maqām*s of Sharif ulema and *awliyā* in Egypt and the lives of their dwellers like the earlier works of al-Ṣabbān and al-Shablanjī. Copy gifted from the library of Ḥabīb Ḥāmid al-Mahdalī.
- *al-Aḥādīth al-wārida fīl-sibṭayn al-Ḥasan wal-Ḥusayn* (The hadiths transmitted about the two maternal grandchildren al-Ḥasan and al-Ḥusayn) by ʿUthmān b. Muḥammad al-Khamīs, a technical study of 189 hadiths.
- *Aʿlām al-Shāfiʿiyya min Ahl al-Bayt* by our teacher Shaykh Bassām Ḥamzāwī (see §8) compiling all the Shāfiʿī scholars that belonged to the Prophetic lineage from the fourth to the 14th Hijri century. The book begins with an introduction on the identification, merits, and general history of the *Ahl al-Bayt* followed by an overview of the Shāfiʿī School and its principles.
- *ʿAllimū awlādakum ḥubb Āl al-Nabī* (Teach your children love of the Family of the Prophet) by the late Saudi minister Muḥammad ʿAbduh Yamānī (1359-1431/1940-2010). The title refers to the hadith **"Train your children to acquire three traits: love of your Prophet, love of the people of his House, and reading the Qurʾān; for the carriers of the Qurʾān are in the shade of the One God on the Day there shall be no shade other than His shade, with His Prophets and His chosen ones,"** It is a weak report from ʿAlī b. Abī Ṭālib in al-Daylamī's *Musnad al-Firdaws*, Ibn al-Najjār's *Tārīkh*s and Abū al-Naṣr ʿAbd al-Karīm b. Muḥammad al-Shīrāzī in his *Fawāʾid*.

- *al-Durr al-thamīn fī nasab al-sādat al-ṭāhirīn* (The costly pearls on the lineage of the pure Sharifs) authored and gifted to us by our Shaykh the late qadi Muḥammad Murshid ʿĀbidīn (see §25 above).

- *Ḥiṣn al-salām bayna yaday awlād mawlāy ʿAbd al-Salām* (The fortress of safety in front of the children of my master ʿAbd al-Salām) by the ascetic and erudite Moroccan mujahid and historian al-Ṭāhir b. ʿAbd al-Salām b. ʿAbd al-Wahhāb al-Lahyawī al-ʿAlamī al-Ḥasanī (1917-2013). The title refers to the lineage of the pious Sharif *walī* ʿAbd al-Salām b. Sulaymān b. Abī Bakr b. ʿAlī b. Bū Ḥurma al-ʿAlamī, known as Ibn Mashīsh (559-626/1163-1228), whose grave is in Mount ʿAlam where he lived, near Taṭwān in northern Morocco. The author addresses the issues the Sharifs of his time and area faced such as their Prophetic lineage from al-Ḥasan and al-Ḥusayn through their mother (as shown in Yaḥyā b. Yaʿmur's glosses of al-Anʿām 6:84-85 cited under §23) and their financial rights, both issue as established in the Qurʾān and the Sunna. He also epitomizes al-Ḥasan's importance and legacy to the Sharifs of the Maghrib

- *Ḥiwār ʿilmī ḥawla ʿilm al-ansāb*, a question and answer brief by the genealogist ʿAbd al-Karīm Ḥamzāwī (1933-2019) who pointed out that "categorically genuine lineages are few, conjectural ones many, rejected ones and those exposed as false very many." He also said he appointed his son Shaykh Bassām al-Ḥamzāwī (from whom I received this tract) (see §8) as the *Naqīb al-Ashrāf* of Syria, in the sense of the overseer of the maintenance, education and support of those that are affiliated to the Prophetic lineage in the country.

- *Ma'ālī al-rutab li-man jama'a bayna sharafay al-ṣuḥbati wal-nasab* (The highest ranks for those that possessed the twin honors of Companionship and Lineage) by Musā'id Sālim al-'Abd al-Jādir, published in Kuwait by the author in 2004, a systematic biographical reference-work of 774 pages on the Prophet's offspring, maternal grandchildren, paternal uncles, aunts, and cousins, their children and grandchildren, maternal uncles, cousins, children and grandchildren, totalling 151 Companions that were direct close relatives.
- *Man hum Ahl al-Bayt?* by the Tunisian Dr. al-Ṭāhir b. al-Hādī al-Ḥasanī al-Qarṭājī, a primer that sums up most of the salient points of the Sunni understanding of this subject including the *tafsīr* of the verse of purification as referring first and foremost to the wives of the Prophet but also the Banū Hāshim and most especially the Five (see above, §3). I read this book while on a trip to a Sufi scholars conference in Indonesia, at which time I was honored to meet with the late Shaykh of 'Akkār, North Lebanon and a son of Shaykh 'Abd al-Qādir al-Jīlānī, Shaykh Aḥmad Jalāl b. 'Abd al-Ghanī b. 'Uthmān al-Zu'bī al-Qādirī (d. 1442/2021)–Allah have mercy on him–who penned a *ḍu'ā* on the inside back cover of my copy.
- *al-Mashra' al-rawīy fī manāqib al-Sādat al-kirām Āl Abī 'Alawī* (The quenching channel concerning the virtues of the noble Sayyids the House of Abū 'Alawī) by the astronomer and historian al-Ḥabīb Muḥammad b. Abī Bakr al-Shillī (1030-1093/1621-1682), famous for a two-volume biographical history of the eleventh Hijri century entitled *'Iqd al-jawāhir wal-durar fī akhbar al-qarn al-ḥādī 'ashar* among other works. The *Mashra'* is a similar work specific to the eminent

figures of the Bā ʿAlawīs. It ends with an overview of Sufi authorities and of the principles of the Sufi path.

- *Muntakhabāt min tārīkh naqābat al-ashrāf* (Selections from the history of the overseeship of the Sharifs) by our teacher Shaykh Bassām al-Ḥamzāwī (§8), latest in line in a long series of Ḥamzāwī shaykhs who occupied the historically unremunerated position of overseer in the regions of Syro-Palestine and held the seal of the *Naqīb al-Ashrāf* (Overseer of the Sharifs).

- *Muqtaṭafāt min musnad al-Imām ʿAlī b. Abī Ṭālib wa-ahli Baytihi al-ṭāhirīn* (Anthology of full-chained hadiths of Imam ʿAlī b. Abī Ṭālib and the pure people of his House) by Ḥusayn b. Anīs b. ʿAlawī al-Ḥabshī, gifted to me by Orang Kaya Kaya Imam Paduka Tuan Dato' Dr. Muhammad Afifi al-Akiti (b. 1976) in his Oxford home. The book is a selection of about 200 hadiths narrated from ʿAlī and *Ahl al-Bayt* in the Nine Books (the *Muwaṭṭa'*, *Musnad*, two *Ṣaḥīḥs* and five *Sunan*) which the author–a great-grandson of Ḥabīb ʿAlī b. Muḥammad al-Ḥabshī the author of *Simṭ al-durar*–said was facilitated by the use of three computer software programs: *Mawsūʿat al-ḥadīth* developed by Sakhr in Egypt, *al-Muḥaddith* by Dār al-Ḥadīth in Syria, and *Muṣḥaf al-Dawālij* developed in Riyadh.

- *al-Sādat al-Ashrāf: aʿlām wa-nuqabā' wa-aʿyān* (The leaders and Sharifs: eminent personalities, chiefs, and famous ones) by Dr. ʿAbd Allāh b. Ḥusayn al-Sāda the assistant secretary general of the Union of Arab Historians. This is a massive unfiltered 800-page compilation of biographical entries on Sharifs in no particular order other than that of the successive sources consulted, some of them still in manuscript form, from which the author lifted every relevant entry which he then consigned into his work without any annotation other than the referencing of the sources.

- *Silsilat Āl Bayt al-Nabī ṣallā Allāh ʿalayhi wa-sallam* (Series on the Prophetic House) in three volumes by ʿĀbd al-Ḥafīẓ Fargahlī, ʿAbd al-Ḥamīd Muṣṭafā and Ḥamza al-Nashratī at Cairo's al-Maktabat al-Qayyima (1990?), an encyclopedic work of biographical history that pauses at the texts used by Shīʿīs to demonstrate the aptness of the Sunni understanding. The work includes the wives of the Prophet and the Banū Hāshim at large. It ends with an overview of the *maqām*s of Egypt and a full edition of Suyūṭī's *Iḥyā' al-mayt*. A former loan from Ḥabīb Abū ʿAlī Ḥāmid al-Mahdalī.
- *Silsilat al-uṣūl fī shajarat abnāʾ al-Rasūl* (The genealogy of origins on the tree of the Messenger's sons) by the erudite Algerian qadi and genealogist ʿAbd Allāh b. Muḥammad b. al-Shārif b. ʿAlī Ḥishlāf, written at the request of certain Sharif families of his area.
- *Tuḥfat al-aḥbāb bi-faḍāʾil Āl Sayyidinā Muḥammad ṣāḥib aṭhar wa-ashraf al-ansāb* (The gift to loved ones of the superexcellences of our liegelord Muḥammad the possessor of the purest and noblest of lineages) by Ḥabīb Abū al-Zahrāʾ Lizām b. ʿAydarūs al-Ḥusaynī al-Malāqī of Melaka and Johore, Malaysia, who died in Cairo after a car crash and was known in al-Azhar as Sayyid Niẓām al-Malākī al-Jawharī.

Among the books I have not seen on this noble subject are the *Musnad* of ʿAlī al-Riḍā (148-203/765-818) the son of Mūsā al-Kāẓim (128-183/745-799) on the subject of the excellence of *Ahl al-Bayt*; the monograph on the immense merits of *Ahl al-Bayt* by Abū al-Ḥasan ʿAlī b. Maʿrūf al-Bazzāz (d. after 385/995); *Maʿālim al-ʿItrat al-Nabawiyya wa-maʿārif Ahl al-Bayt al-Fāṭimiyya* (The signposts of the Prophetic intimate relatives and landmarks of the Fātimī people of the House) by the Ḥanbalī Hadith master Abū Muḥammad ʿAbd al-ʿAzīz b. al-Akhḍar al-Junābidhī (d. 611)–from Junābidh near Nishapur; and *Fatḥ al-Wahhāb fī faḍāʾil al-Āl wal-Aṣḥāb* (The disclosure of the All-Giver on the immense merits of the Prophetic House and the Companions) by ʿAbd al-Wahhāb b. Aḥmad al-Shaʿrānī (898-973/1493-1565), all of which are cited in Ḥājjī Khalīfa's descriptive bibliography *Kashf al-ẓunūn* (The removal of conjectures) except Bazzāz's monograph which is cited by Shāh ʿAbd al-ʿAzīz al-Dihlawī in *Bustān al-muḥaddithīn*; *Nashr qalb al-mayt bi-faḍl Ahl al-Bayt* (The resurgence of the dead heart with the excellence of the people of the House) by Jamāl al-Dīn Abū al-Muẓaffar Yūsuf b. Muḥammad b. Masʿūd al-ʿUbādī al-ʿUqaylī al-Surramarrī (696-776/1297-1374); *al-Jāmiʿ li-ṣilat al-arḥām fī nasab al-Sādat al-kirām al-Imāmayn al-Ḥasan wal-Ḥusayn ʿalayhimā al-salām* (The encyclopedia of the keeping of family ties concerning the lineage of the noble Sayyids the two Imams al-Ḥasan and al-Ḥusayn, upon them peace) by the genealogist Sharif Aḥmad Wafqī Muḥammad Yāsīn, a documentation of the family trees of Ḥasanī and Ḥusaynī descendants. Many more are listed in the over 2,000-page *Muʿjam al-mawḍūʿat al-maṭrūqa fil-taʾlīf al-Islāmī* (1:277 -283) and al-Ṭabāṭabāʾī's 1996 *Ahl al-Bayt fil-maktabat al-ʿArabiyya*. Allah guides whomever He will.

A person's but a narrative once gone.
Be a beauteous narrative for mindful ones.

The book ends here. The completion of the first Arabic edition was on the first day of the week the 2nd of Ṣafar 1437, corresponding to the 15th of November 2015; that of the second Arabic edition was on the night before the third day of the week the 6th of Jumādā al-Awwal 1439, corresponding to the 22nd of January 2018; and that of the third Arabic edition and first English translation was on the night before the first day of the week the 17th of Rabiʿ al-Awwal 1443 corresponding to the 23rd of October 2021 at the hand of its soon-gone author, Gibril b. Fouad b. Nasri Haddad al-Salihi. Allah is the Grantor of success. May Allah bless, exalt and greet our Liegelord Muḥammad and all his Family and Companions with most abundant salutations of peace. All glory, praise and thanks belong to the One God the Lord of the worlds.

***

*

Hadith Index

All the children of a mother have a *'aṣaba* (agnates) to whom they are affiliated except the children of Fāṭima: I am their *'aṣaba* 110
Allah created creation and put me among the best of His creatures 168
Allah has preferred the Quraysh in seven attributes 139
Allah is my *walī*, and I am the *walī* of every believer 102
Allah selected, out of human beings, the Arabs 151
Allah selected, out of Quraysh, the Banū Hāshim 151
'Am I [=Thawbān] of the people of the House?' He [=the Prophet] stayed silent. Then, the third time, he replied, 'Yes' 144
Banū Hāshim and the Banū al-Muṭṭalib are one and the same 39
best of the women of Paradise is Maryam and the best of the women of Paradise is Khadīja, The 116
Book of Allah and my intimates, the people of my House: look well how you act after me with regard to the two of them, The 102
Do not teach the Quraysh. Learn from them 28
Even if only one day of this world remained, Allah would prolong it until He sends a man who is of the people of my House 62
Faith does not enter anyone's heart until he first loves *Ahl al-Bayt* 66
Fāṭima is the liege lady of the women of her world 142
Fāṭima is the liege lady of the women of Paradise 108
al-Ḥasan and al-Ḥusayn are the liegelords of the young men of Paradise and Fāṭima is the liege lady of the women of Paradise 108
He gathered Fāṭima, al-Ḥasan and al-Ḥusayn under his cloak 127
Here is al-'Abbās, the paternal uncle of your Prophet, the most generous, open-handed man of the Quraysh 180
I am leaving among you the two weighty things 50, 102
I am the best of you in his House and the best of you in his person 169
I am your forerunner at the Basin. And when I come to it, certain men will stand and say, "Messenger of Allah, I am so and so…" 148
I asked my nurturing Lord that I not marry into anyone of my Community nor that anyone marry into me except they will be with me in Paradise 78
I have not found a single man better than Muḥammad, and I have not found any sons of a father better than the Banū Hāshim 82
I remind you of Allah about the people of my House! 50
I saw the Messenger of Allah putting al-Ḥasan on his shoulders 59
I, you [=Fāṭima], these two and 'Alī on the Day of resurrection will all be in one same place 36
If a man prayed and fasted then met Allah hating *Ahl al-Bayt* he would enter the Fire 70
Love Allah for His blessings, love me with the love of Allah; and love the people of my House 183
Loveliest to me of my closest kin is Fāṭima, The 123
May Allah curse whoever differentiates between the Banū Hāshim and Banū al-Muṭṭalib 39
My intercession shall reach Ḥā, and Ḥakm, and Ṣadā', and Salhab 86

"My nurturing Lord! These are my *Ahl*." "I [=Umm Salama] said, 'will you make me enter with them?' 127
My pouch is the people of my House; my guts are the Helpers 44
No man hates us–*Ahl al-Bayt*–but Allah shall put him in Hellfire 133
None believes until I become dearer to him than his own life 164
None believes until my near family becomes dearer to him than his near family 164
None believes until my wives become dearer to him than his own 164
None loves you [='Alī] but a believer and none hates you but a hypocrite 98
O Allah! Bring back the sun for him [='Alī] 118
O Allah, I do love him [=al-Ḥasan], so do love him! 59
O Allah, make the provision of Muḥammad's Family sustenance 176
O Allah, take as Your friend whoever befriends him [='Alī] 102
O Allah, these [=the Five] are the people of my House and my intimates, so remove impurity from them and cleanse them 47
O Allah, this is al-'Abbās, and these are the people of my House, so cover them against the fire just as I am covering them 160
O Allah! You know how much I love them [=Ḥasan and Ḥusayn] 106
O Banū 'Abd al-Muṭṭalib! I have asked Allah three things for you 70
O people! I am only human: the messenger of my Lord is about to come to me and I must answer him 50
O people! Why am I being harmed about my relatives? 86
Peace be upon you! How are you this morning? 160
People are to follow Quraysh in this great matter 54
People are vessels 54
People of my House can be compared to the ark of Nūḥ; whoever boards it is saved and whoever leaves it drowns, The 94
Qurayshīs possesse the same as the strength of two men, 28
Salmān is one of us, the people of House 172
Say: 'O Allah, bless Muḥammad, his wives and his offspring, as You blessed the family of Ibrāhīm' 32
Stars are a security for the dwellers of the sky and my family are a security for my Community 90
Threshold and the walls of the house all said, "*Āmīn!*", The 160
We [=*Ahl al-Bayt*] come from the best and to the best 151
What ails certain people who say my blood ties do not benefit? 148
What ails certain people who say my intercession does not reach the people of my house? 136
What is the matter with certain people who fall silent as soon as they see a man from the people of my House? 66
Whoever harms 'Alī has certainly harmed me 157
Whoever I am the protecting friend of, this [='Alī] is his *walī* 102
Whoever lends a hand to any of 'Abd al-Muṭṭalib's children 186
Whoever loves the Arabs, it is for love of me that he loves them and whoever hates them, it is for hatred of me that he hates them 151
Whoever loves me and loves these two and their father and mother, shall be with me at my level on the Day of resurrection 74
World will not pass until the Arabs will be under the sovereignty of a man of my House, The 62
You [=Umm Salama] are of my *Ahl* 127

Dr. Gibril Fouad Haddad was born in Beirut, Lebanon and studied in Lebanon, the UK, the US (where he took *shahada* in December 1991), France, and Syria. He holds a doctorate from Kolej Universiti Insaniah, Kedah Darul Aman, Malaysia, and a Ph.D. from Columbia University in New York. He is a *summa cum laude* graduate of the New York University Latin and Greek Institute and was the recipient of several university fellowships including one at the École Normale Supérieure at Rue d'Ulm, Paris, France. He won the State of Qatar's Shaykh Hamad Award for Translation and International Understanding in 2017 for *The Lights of Revelation and the Secrets of Interpretation: Ḥizb One of the Commentary on the Qur'an by al-Bayḍāwī*, which he wrote while a Senior Assistant Professor at Universiti Brunei Darussalam where he currently lives with his family.

He is the author of forty books, most recently an annotated English translation of Nabhani's *The Prophet's Knowledge of the Unseen* صلى الله تعالى عليه وسلم comprising over 700 fully-documented hadiths on the topic; a bio-bibliographical overview of Sunni doctrinal history entitled *The Maturidi School from Abu Hanifa to al-Kawthari*; a study on Hadith, Sīra and ḥudūd entitled *The Incineration of Persons in Jihad, Criminal Penalties and Reprisals: A Critique of ISIS's Argument in Light of the Sources*, whose launch was featured on Malaysia national TV; and a 60-page seminal article, "Tropology and Inimitability: Ibn ʿĀshūr's Theory of Tafsīr in the Ten Prolegomena to al-Taḥrīr wal-Tanwīr" in the first 2019 issue of the *Journal of Qur'anic Studies*. He is presently working on the first-ever complete translation of Imam al-Bayḍāwī's commentary on the Qur'an, *Anwār al-Tanzīl* (The Lights of Revelation).

www.ingramcontent.com/pod-product-compliance
Lightning Source LLC
Chambersburg PA
CBHW030144100526
44592CB00009B/108
* 9 7 8 1 9 3 8 0 5 8 6 3 9 *

مسند أهل البيت

مُسند أهل البيت

المسمّى

حسن المآل والمآرب

في فضل الآل والأقارب

بأربعين حديثاً مُسنداً عن أربعين شريفاً من أربعين كتاباً

رواية وتخريج

د. جبريل بن فؤاد بن نصري حدّاد الصّالحي

بسم الله الرحمن الرحيم

وصلَّى الله على سيِّدنا محمَّد وعلى آله وصحبه وسلَّم

الحمدُ لله الَّذي اصطفى المؤمنين من آل سيِّدنا إبراهيم وآل سيدنا عمران وآل سيدنا ياسين وآل سيدنا محمَّد على العالمين وأمر في محكم التنزيل بالمودّة في قربى نبيّه ﷺ وخاطب الرجال منهم والنساء ليُعلِمَهم تشريفَه لهم ورفعتَه لمقدارهم العظيم ، بقوله تعالى ﴿ إِنَّمَا يُرِيدُ ٱللَّهُ لِيُذْهِبَ عَنكُمُ ٱلرِّجْسَ أَهْلَ ٱلْبَيْتِ وَيُطَهِّرَكُمْ تَطْهِيرًا ﴾ [الأحزاب ٣٣] . فشرَّف وطهَّر كلَّ مؤمنٍ يُقِرُّ لهم بذلك المقام تعبّداً وتسليماً لما يريد اللهُ ويُرضي رسولَه ، والصلاة والسلام على خير من وَطِئَ الثَّرى : سيِّدنا وحبيبنا ومولانا محمَّدٍ الَّذي بين معاني العدل العميم في بلوغ مراتب الشرف للدَّانية والقاصية ، إذ هُم في رجاءِ نيلِها سواسية ، ثم قدَّم عليها معاني الفضل الكريم ، الخاصَّةَ لأهل الاختصاص : آلِ بيتـه الأفضلين ، صلَّى الله عليه وآلـه الطاهرين الطيّبين ، وسلَّم تسليماً .

وبعـد ، فقد ورد في الأحاديث الشريفـة من فضائل أهل البيت ما لا يُحصى من النصوص الصريحـة ، ككونهم في أعلى ذِرْوَةٍ في

الجنّة ، ومَنْ تمسّـك بالقرآن وبهم لن يَضِلَّ ، فهُم في الأمّة مثل سفينة نـوح : مَن رَكِبَها نجا ومن تخلّف عنها غـرِق ، وأنهّم أمانٌ للأمّة من الاختلاف ، وأنهّم سادة الجنة ، وأنّ الله وعد أن لا يعذّبهم ، وأنّ مَن أبغضهـم أدخله الله النار ، ولا يَدْخُـل قلبَ أحدٍ الإيمانُ حتى يحُبَّهم لله ولقرابتهـم منه ﷺ ، وأنّ من قاتلهم كان كمن قاتل مع الدجالّ ، وأنَّ مـن صَنَـع إلى أحدهم يداً كافـأه ﷺ يومَ القيامـة ، وأنهم ما مِن أحد منهم إلا وله شـفاعةٌ يوم القيامـة ، وأن الرجلَ يقوم لأخيه من مجلسـه إلاَّ بَنـي هاشـمٍ ، لا يقومـون لأحـد . وفي تخميس الشيخ عبد الهادي الحايك لأبيات الإمام السُّهَيلي رحمهما الله :

يَـــا مَلْجَـأَ الْقُصَّـادِ جِئْتُكَ سَـاعِيـاً

وَلِذِمَّـةِ الآلِ الْكِـرَامِ مُرَاعِيـــاً

فَاجْعَلْ حَبِيبَكَ يَوْمَ حَشرِْي سَاقِياً

حَاشَـا لجِـودِكَ أَنْ تُقَنِّـطَ رَاجِيـاً

الْفَضْلُ أَجْزَلُ وَالمَوَاهِبُ أَوْسَعُ

وفي تخميس الشريف العلامة الشيخ حامد بن أحمد بن عبيد الله العطّار لأبيات الشيخ محيي الدين الطائي رحمهم الله تعالى :

فَـلازِمْ حِماهُـمْ وَاتخِـذْ عِنْدَهُـمْ يَدَا
فَـإِنَّ لَهُمْ يَوْمَ الْقِيَامَةِ سُــؤْدُدَا
وَلاَ تَعْبَـأَنْ بِالْمُبْطِلِيـنَ أُولِي الـرَّدَى
فَما طَلَـبَ المَبْعُوثُ أَجْراً عَلَى الْهُدَى
بِتَبْلِيغِـهِ إِلَّا الْمَـوَدَّةَ لِلْقُـرْبَى

وهـذه أربعـون حديثاً مسـنَداً في فضل أهـل بيت النبـوّة وعُلُوِّ شـأنهم والحثِّ على ولائهم ومحبّتهـم ونَصرهـم ، كلُّها من رواية مشـايخي الأشراف سـماعاً من ألفاظهم أو عرضـاً عليهم بقراءتي أو قراءةِ غيري وأنا أسـمع أو بحقّ إجازاتهم الخاصّة والعامّة ، جمعتها وخرّجتها وشرحت بعض معانيها وتحرّيت فيها الجِياد ، وربّما قرنت شيخي النسيب بمثله أو بغيره ممّن أروي عنهم لنُكْتة أو لوجود سماع أو جَبرِ سياق على شرط الكتاب أو طلباً للعلوّ - والنزول عن الثقات علـوٌّ . وبَوَّبْتُ لكلّ رواية مُسـنَدَةٍ كتاباً من كتب السُّـنَّة المطهّرة وَفْقَ مخرِّجهـا ، وربّما ذكرت إثْرَها أحاديثَ أخـرى منه أو من غيره جُلُّها صحيحة ، محذوفةَ الأسـانيد ، وما تيسرّ من فوائدَ إسـنادية وتاريخية ولغويّة تكميلاً لمفهوم الباب ومعرفة الرّجال ، وأتبعتها نقولاً لغويّة وفقهيّـة في حِكَمِ وأسرار ولائهم هي مِسـك الختـام . **فجاءت ثلاثةً**

وأربعين حديثاً مسنَداً عن تسعة وأربعين شريفاً من ثلاثة وأربعين كتاباً أرجو بها شفاعة جدّهم المصطفى ﷺ وآله وشفاعتَهم ، وأداءَ واجب الشكر على ما أنعم الله تعالى ثم أنعم رسولُه الكريم ثم أنعموا على هذا المتطفّل الحقير ، وتأسّياً بأئمّة هذا الفنّ الّذين ألّفوا الأربعينات . سمّيت مجموعها (**حُسْنُ المآلِ والمآرِب بالأربعين حديثاً مسنَداً عن أربعين شريفاً من أربعين كتاباً في فضل الآل والأَقَارِب**) .

والله المُوَفِّق لما يحبّ ويرضى ،

وصلّ الله على سيّدنا محمّد

وآله وصحبه وسلّم تسليماً .

❑ ❑ ❑

١

جامع مَعْمَر بن راشد

(٩٥-١٥٣)

لاَ تُعَلِّمُوا قُرَيْشًا ، وَتَعَلَّمُوا مِنْهَا ، وَلاَ تَقَدَّمُوا قُرَيْشًا ، وَلاَ تَأَخَّرُوا عَنْهَا .
فَإِنَّ لِلْقُرَشِيِّ مِثْلَ قُوَّةِ الرَّجُلَيْنِ مِنْ غَيْرِهِمْ

أنبأني السيّد الشيخ صلاح الدين بن خضر بن محمود فَخْرِي الحسيني (ولد ١٣٦٧) ـ حفظه الله ـ ببيروت مدير دار الفتوى بلبنان وصاحب محاسن الآثار في سيرة الشيخ مختار العلايلي ، عن المحدِّث الوَرِع محمود بن قاسم بَعُيُون الرنكوسي الدمشقي (ت ١٤٠٥) ، عن الشيخ بدر الدين الحسني (١٢٦٧-١٣٥٤) ، عن الشيخ عبد القادر الخطيب ، عن الوجيه عبد الرحمن الكزبري الحفيد ، عن الشيخ مصطفى الرحمتي الأيوبي ، عن العارف الشيخ عبد الغني النابلسي ، عن النجم الغزّي ، عن والده البدر الغزّي العامري ، عن شيخ الإسلام زكريا الأنصاري ، عن الحافظ ابن حجر ، قال : أخبرني عبد الله بن عمر بن علي الأزهري فيما قرأت عليه ، عن أبي الحسن

علي بن العز عمر المقدسي وزينب بنت الكمال ، بسماع الأوّل من أبي العبّاس أحمد بن أبي الخير وبإجازة زينب من يوسف بن خليل ، قالا : أنبأنا مسعود الجمّال ، قال يوسف : سماعاً ، والآخر : إجازةً ، أنبأنا أبو علي الحداد ، أنبأنا أبو نعيم ، حدّثنا سليمان بن أحمد الطبراني ، أنبأنا إسحاق بن إبراهيم الدَّبَرِي ، أنبأنا عبد الرزاق ، قال : أخبرنا **معمر بن راشد** ، عن الزهري ، عن سهل بن أبي حَثْمَةَ ، أنَّ رسول الله ﷺ قال : **لَا تُعَلِّمُوا قُرَيْشًا ، وَتَعَلَّمُوا مِنْهَا ، وَلاَ تَقَدَّمُوا قُرَيْشًا ، وَلاَ تَأَخَّرُوا عَنْهَا . فَإِنَّ لِلْقُرَشِيِّ مِثْلَ قُوَّةِ الرَّجُلَيْنِ مِنْ غيرِهِمْ** . [قال الزهري :] يعني في الرأي .

حديث مرسل صحيح ، أخرجه ابن أبي شيبة والبيهقي في السنن وله شواهد ، روى عبد الرزاق والشافعي وأحمد عن عبد الله بن حنطب : خَطَبَنا رسول الله ﷺ يوم الجمعة فقال : **يَا أَيهَا النَّاسُ قَدِّمُوا قُرَيْشًا وَلا تَقَدَّمُوهَا وَتَعَلَّمُوا مِنْهَا وَلا تُعَلِّمُوهَا** ، أَوْ : **تُعَالِمُوهَا** ؛ يَشُكُّ ابْنُ أَبِي فُدَيْكٍ . هذا لفظ الشافعي ، قال : وبلغني عن المزني أنه قال : قوله وَلاَ تُعَالِمُوهَا معناه : لاَ تُفَاخِرُوهَا . وعند ابن أبي عاصم عن جبير بن مطعم مرفوعاً : **فَإِنهُمْ أَعْلَمُ مِنكُمْ** . وعند الطبراني في الكبير عن عبد الله بن السائب والبزار عنه وعن علي زيادة : **وَلَوْلاَ أَنْ تَبطَرَ**

قُرَيْشُ لأَخْبرْتهُا مَا لخِـيَارِهَا عِنْدَ اللهِ تَعَالىَ . قال الحافظ في الفتح : قدّم البخاري الرواية عن الحميدي في صحيحه لكونه أفقه قرشيٍّ أخذ عنه . قلت : قوله **وَلاَ تَأَخَّرُوا عَنْهَا** أي لا تتخلّفوا عنها . ومن قيّده بالصّدر الأوّل فقد ابتدع رأياً وجانب الصواب .

❑ ❑ ❑

٢

موطأ مالك بن أنس

(٩٣-١٧٩)

قُولُوا : اللَّهُمَّ صَلِّ عَلَى مُحَمَّدٍ وَأَزْوَاجِهِ وَذُرِّيَّتِهِ كَمَا صَلَّيْتَ عَلَى آلِ إِبْرَاهِيمَ ، وَبَارِكْ عَلَى مُحَمَّدٍ وَأَزْوَاجِهِ وَذُرِّيَّتِهِ كَمَا بَارَكْتَ عَلَى آلِ إِبْرَاهِيمَ ، إِنَّكَ حَمِيدٌ مَجِيدٌ

أخبرنا في داره بجسر الأبيض في دمشق المحروسة سنة ١٩٩٨م العلاّمة المدقِّق ، الرُّحْلة الرَّحّالة ، الوارث لأربعين علماً من علوم الإسلام ليست عند غيره من أهل الشام ، المجدد لعلوم الرواية في هذا العصر ، المسنِد ، الداعية ، الصوفي الورع ، المحدث اللغوي ، المجاهد الجريء ، الخطيب بلغات العرب والعجم ، المنشد ، العزيز الكريم النصوح الوقور ، أستاذي وعمدتي في علم الرواية والإسناد ، السيد الشريف **محمد أبو الهدى اليعقوبيّ** (ولد ١٩٦٣م) **ابن الإمام علاّمة الشام السيد إبراهيم** (١٣٤٣-١٤٠٦) مفتي المالكية ثم الحنفية في الجامع الأموي ابن القطب السيد إسماعيل بن محمد الصديق بن

محمد الحسن بن محمد العربي الإدريسي الحسني الحنفي المالكي الشاذلي ، قراءةً عليه لجميع الموطّأ بأربعة مجالس وأنا أسمع ، قال : حدثني العلاّمة الوالد رحمه الله تعالى قراءة عليه لأكثر الموطأ وإجازة لجميعه ، أنبأنا الشيخ السيد محمد مكي الكتاني (١٣١٢-١٣٩٣) ، أنا الشيخ عمر حمدان المَحْرَسي ، أنا محدّث الحجاز الشريف الشيخ فالح بن محمد بن عبد الله بن فالح الظاهري المهنّوي المالكي (ت ١٣٢٨) ـ ويروي السيد مكي عنه مباشرة باستجازة والده الحافظ محمد بن جعفر له وبلقائه سماعاً وإجازةً سنة ١٣٢٥ـ قال : سمعت الموطأ رواية يحيى بن يحيى الليثي على شيخ الإسلام محمد بن علي السَّنوسي الخطابي الجَغْبُوبي الشِلَفي ثم المكي (١٢٠٢-١٢٧٦) ، أنا أبو حفص عمر بن عبد الكريم العطار المكي ، أنا الشيخ صالح بن محمد بن نوح الفُلاّني العُمَري (نسبة إلى فُلاّن من قبائل السودان) ، أنا شيخنا المعمّر محمد بن سِنَّة الفُلاّني العمري ، أنا الشريف المعمّر محمد بن عبد الله الوُلاّتي (نسبة إلى وُلاَّتَن من بلاد السودان الغربي) ـ قلت : والكلام فيهما مشهور ـ أنا الشيخ أبو عثمان سعيد بن إبراهيم الجزائري المعروف بقدّورة (ت ١٠٦٦) ، أنا الشيخ أبو عثمان سعيد بن أحمد المَقَّري ـ نسبة لَمقَّرة وهي مدينة بين الزاب والقيروان ـ

التلمساني (ت ١٠١٠) مفتي تلمسان ستين سنة ، أنا أبو عبد الله محمد بن الحافظ محمد بن عبد الجليل التَّنَّسي ، أنا والدي ، أنا الإمام ابن مرزوق الحفيد عن أبيه ، عن جده ابن مرزوق الجد ، أنا أبو عبد الله محمد بن جابر بن محمد القَيسي الوادي آشي ، أنا الفقيه أبو محمد عبد الله بن محمد بن هارون الطائي القرطبي ، وقاضي الجماعة أبو العباس أحمد بن محمد ابن الغَمّاز ، قال الأول : أنا القاضي أبو القاسم أحمد بن يزيد بن أحمد بن بَقِيّ القرطبي وهو آخر من حدّث عنه ، أنا محمد بن عبد الرحمن بن عبد الحق الخزرجي آخر من حدّث عنه ، أنا محمد بن فرح مولى ابن الطَّلاَّع القرطبي آخر من حدّث عنه ، أنا القاضي أبو الوليد يونس بن عبد الله بن مغيث الصفَّار القرطبي آخر من حدّث عنه ، أنا أبو عيسى يحيى بن عبد الله بن يحيى بن يحيى القرطبي آخر من حدّث عنه . (ح) الحافظ السنوسي الخطابي ، عن أبي طالب محمد بن علي بن الشارف المازوني (١١٠٠-١٢٣٣) المعمّر نحو ١٣٣ سنة ، عن المعمّرة العلاّمة المسندة من مسانيد الحجاز السبعة المجددين لعلم الإسناد الشريفة الفقيهة قريش بنت عبد القادر الطبرِيّة ، عن شيخ أبيها المعمّر المسند عبد الواحد بن إبراهيم بن أحمد بن إبراهيم الحصّاري الشافعي

الأثري (٩١٠-بعد ١٠١١) ، عن الشرف عبد الحقّ ابن محمد السنباطي نزيل الحرمين والسيوطي وشيخ الإسلام زكريا الأنصاري والشمس محمد بن إبراهيم الغَمْري (٧٨٦-٨٤٩) ـ وهو آخر أصحاب الحافظ في الدنيا كما في (شرح ألفية السند) للزَّبِيدي ، وهذا الإسناد في غاية العلو ولله الحمد ـ قال السنباطي : أنا به الإمام البدر النسّابة سماعاً لجميعه بقراءة الحافظ الشمس السخاوي في خمسة مجالس ، قال : أنا به بعلوّ درجة الإمام محمد بن جابر القَيسي الوادياشي . وقال السيوطي : أخبرني به الحافظ التقي بن فهد المكي ، أخبرنا به البرهان الأبناسي ، أنا به الوادياشي . وقال شيخ الإسلام : أخبرني به أبو إسحاق بن صدقة الحنبلي والحافظ ابن حجر العسقلاني والعز ابن الفرات ، قال الأول : أنا به أبو العباس أحمد بن الحسن السُّوَيداوي ، أنا به جماعة ، منهم : التقي الأخنائي المالكي ، أنا به الحافظ الشرف الدمياطي ، أنا به أبو الفضل عبد العزيز بن عبد الوهاب بن إسماعيل ابن الطاهر الزهري المالكي ، أنا به جدي أبو طاهر إسماعيل ، أنا به الفقيه أبو بكر محمد بن الوليد الطرطوشي ، أنا به الفقيه أبو الوليد سليمان بن خلف الباجي ، أنا به أبو الوليد الصفّار . وقال الحافظ ابن حجر : عن نجم الدين محمد بن علي بن عقيل البالسي ، عن

محمد بـن علي المكفـي ، عن محمد بن الدِّلاصي ، عـن عبد العزيز بن عبد الوهـاب المالكي (ح) الحافظ أيضاً ، عن المسـنِد المعمّر عمر بن حسـن بن أمِيلَة المراغي ، عن عزّ الدين أحمد بن إبراهيم الفاروثي ، عن أبي إسـحاق إبراهيم بـن يحيى بن أبي حفّـاظ المَكْنَاسي ، عن أبي الحسين محمد بن محمد بن سعيد بن زَرْقون ، عن أبي عبد الله أحمد بن محمد بن عبد الله بن غَلْبون ، عن أبي عمر عثمان بن أحمد الْقَيْجَاطي ، عن أبي عيسـى . وقال العز ابن الفرات : عن ابن جماعة ، عن المسند أبي جعفـر أحمد بـن إبراهيم بن الزبير الثقفـي العاصمي الغرناطي ، عن ابن خليل ، عن ابن زرقون ، عن الخولاني ، عن الطَّلْمَنْكِي ، عن أبي عيسـى يحيى القرطبي ، ثني عـمٌّ والدي : أبو مروان عبيد الله بن يحيى بـن يحيـى فقيه قرطبة ومسـند الأندلس ، ثنـي والدي يحيى بن يحيـى الليثـي المصمودي ، أنا **إمـام دار الهجرة مالك بن أنس** سـماعاً لجميعه إلا أبواباً ثلاثة من آخر الاعتكاف فعن زياد بن عبد الرحمن بن شبطون ، عن **الإمام مالك بن أنس** قال : عَنْ عَبْدِ اللهِ بْنِ أَبِي بَكْرِ بْنِ مُحَمَّدِ بْنِ عَمْرِو بْنِ حَزْمٍ عَنْ أَبِيهِ عَنْ عَمْرِو بْنِ سُـلَيْمٍ الزُّرَقِيِّ أَنَّهُ قَالَ أَخْبَـرَنِي أَبُو حُمَيْدٍ السَّـاعِدِيُّ أَنَّهُمْ قَالُوا : يَا رَسُـولَ اللهِ ، كَيْفَ نُصَلِّي عَلَيْكَ ؟ فَقَالَ رَسُولُ اللهِ ﷺ : **قُولُوا : اللَّهُمَّ صَلِّ عَلَى مُحَمَّدٍ وَأَزْوَاجِهِ**

وَذُرِّيَّتِهِ كَمَا صَلَّيْتَ عَلَى آلِ إِبْرَاهِيمَ ، وَبَارِكْ عَلَى مُحَمَّدٍ وَأَزْوَاجِهِ وَذُرِّيَّتِهِ كَمَا بَارَكْتَ عَلَى آلِ إِبْرَاهِيمَ ، إِنَّكَ حَمِيدٌ مَجِيدٌ .

متّفق عليه ، رواه الشيخان وأصحاب السنن وأحمد في المسند من طريق مالك رحمهم الله . وفي الأدب المفرد للبخاري عَنْ أَبِي هُرَيْرَةَ رضي الله عنه عن النبي ﷺ قَالَ : مَنْ قَالَ : **اللَّهُمَّ صَلِّ عَلَى مُحَمَّدٍ وَعَلَى آلِ مُحَمَّدٍ كَمَا صَلَّيْتَ عَلَى إِبْرَاهِيمَ وَآلِ إِبْرَاهِيمَ ، وَبَارِكْ عَلَى مُحَمَّدٍ وَعَلَى آلِ مُحَمَّدٍ كَمَا بَارَكْتَ عَلَى إِبْرَاهِيمَ وَآلِ إِبْرَاهِيمَ ، وَتَرَحَّمْ عَلَى مُحَمَّدٍ وَعَلَى آلِ مُحَمَّدٍ كَمَا تَرَحَّمْتَ عَلَى إِبْرَاهِيمَ وَآلِ إِبْرَاهِيمَ ، شَهِدْتُ لَهُ يَوْمَ الْقِيَامَةِ بِالشَّهَادَةِ وَشَفَعْتُ لَهُ** . حسّنه الحافظ السخاوي في القول البديع .

وعَنْ أَبِي هُرَيْرَةَ عَنْ النَّبِيِّ ﷺ قَالَ : **مَنْ سَرَّهُ أَنْ يَكْتَالَ بِالْمِكْيَالِ الأَوْفَى إِذَا صَلَّى عَلَيْنَا أَهْلَ الْبَيْتِ فَلْيَقُلْ : اللَّهُمَّ صَلِّ عَلَى مُحَمَّدٍ وَأَزْوَاجِهِ أُمَّهَاتِ الْمُؤْمِنِينَ وَذُرِّيَّتِهِ وَأَهْلِ بَيْتِهِ كَمَا صَلَّيْتَ عَلَى آلِ إِبْرَاهِيمَ إِنَّكَ حَمِيدٌ مَجِيدٌ** . أخرجه أبو داود والبخاري في التاريخ الكبير والبيهقي في الكبرى والاعتقاد والشعب ثم قال : فكأنه ﷺ أفرد أزواجه وذريته بالذكر على وجه التأكيد ثم رجع إلى التعميم ليدخل الأزواج والذرية من أهل بيته ﷺ وعليهم وعليهن أجمعين . اهـ . وألفاظه قريبة من حديث أبي حميد الساعدي . (فائدة) تسنّ الصلاة على الآل عند دخول المسجد وخروجه ، قال القاضي إسماعيل المالكي في فضل الصلاة على

النبي ﷺ : حدثنا يحيى بن عبد الحميد ، ثنا عبد العزيز بن محمد عن عبد الله بن الحسن ، عن أمه فاطمة بنت الحسين ، عن فاطمة بنت النبي ﷺ ، قالت : قال لي رسول الله ﷺ : **إِذَا دَخَلْتِ الْمَسْجِدَ فَقُولِي بِسْمِ اللهِ وَالسَّلَامُ عَلَى رَسُولِ اللهِ اللَّهُمَّ صَلِّ عَلَى مُحَمَّدٍ وَعَلَى آلِ مُحَمَّدٍ وَاغْفِرْ لَنَا وَسَهِّلْ لَنَا أَبْوَابَ رَحْمَتِكَ فَإِذَا فَرَغْتِ فَقُولِي مِثْلَ ذَلِكَ غَيْرَ أَنْ قُولِي وَسَهِّلْ لَنَا أَبْوَابَ فَضْلِكَ** . أورده ابن القيم في جلاء الخاطر من رواية أبي العباس الثقفي ، وروى مثله الترمذي وابن ماجه وأحمد وقال الترمذي : حديث فاطمة حديث حسن وليس إسناده بمتصل وفاطمة بنت الحسين لم تدرك فاطمة الكبرى ، إنما عاشت فاطمة بعد النبي ﷺ أشهُراً . اهـ . فهذا مرسل . وتتمته في باب البخاري . (ومن اللطائف والفوائد) ما ذكر الحافظ في المعجم المفهرس عن الوادي آشي قال : في إسناد ابن هارون مزيّتان : رجاله كلهم قرطبيون إلى يحيى بن يحيى ، والثاني أن ليس فيه إجازة . وقال أبو سالم العيَّاشي في فهرسه : روى الموطأ عن مالك اثنان ، كل منهما يسمى يحيى ، أحدهما صاحب الرواية المشهورة الآن ، وهو أبو محمد يحيى بن يحيى بن كثير بن وسلاس الليثي الأندلسي (ت ٢٣٤) ، ولا رواية له في شيء من الصحيحين ولا بقية الكتب الستة . والآخر أبو زكرياء يحيى بن يحيى بن بُكَير بن عبد الرحمن التميمي الحنظلي النيسابوري (ت ٢٢٦) ،

روى عنـه البخاري ومسـلم في صحيحيهما . (تنبيهـان) وقع خطأ في بعـض الأثبـات كإتحاف المسـتفيد بغُـرَر الأسـانيد للفـاداني والعقود اللؤلؤية لشيخنا المالكي عند قولهم : (أنا محمد بن جابر الوادي آشي ، أنـا عبد الله بن محمد الطائـي ، أنا القاضي أبو العبـاس أحمد بن يزيد) فانتقلـت كنية القـاضي ابن الغمّـاز إلى أحمد بن يزيـد ، والصحيح ما صوّبناه من فهرس الفهارس للكتاني وأسانيد الفقيه ابن حجر الهيتمي للفـاداني واقتفاء الأثر بعد ذهاب أهل الأثر لأبي سـالم العيَّاشي ، والله أعلم . ثم سـقط ذكر (محمد بن سِنَّة) شيخ الفُلاّني في إتحاف المستفيد بغُـرَر الأسـانيد للفـاداني وأثبتـه السـيد فالـح الظاهـري ـ من عرب الظواهـر وهـم قبيلـة ـ في حسـن الوفا لإخـوان الصفا المطبوع سـنة ١٣٢٣ في حياة الظاهري . وله ثبت كبير إسمه الشَّيْم البارق من ضَيم المَهـارِق . (تنبيـه مهم) قال الإمام الكوثـري في ثبته : في رواية صالح الفُلاّني عن غير الحجازيين نظر . وألّف الشيخ أحمد الغُماري رسالة في تضعيفه حتى جزم فيها أن شـيخه ابنَ سِـنَّة وشـيخَ الأخير الوَاوُلاتي (الصواب وُلاّتي كما مرّ) لا وجود لهما في الحقيقة . والله تعالى أعلم .

❑ ❑ ❑

٣

مسند أبي داود الطيالسي

(١٣٣-٢٠٤)

إِنِّي وَإِيَّاكِ وَهٰذَيْنِ ، وَأَحْسَبُهُ قَالَ : وَهٰذَا الرَّاقِدَ . يَعْنِي عَلِيّاً . يَوْمَ الْقِيَامَةِ فِي مَكَانٍ وَاحِدٍ .

أنبأنا السيد الفقيه المسند الأديب **الحبيب إبراهيم بن عمر بن عقيل بن عبد الله آل يحيى الحسيني** الشافعي (١٣٢٧- ١٤١٥) مفتي تَعِزّ باليمن ، عن الحبيب عبد الرحمن بن عبيد الله السقاف (١٣٠٠-١٣٧٥) مفتي الديار الحضرمية ، عن السيد أبي العباس أحمد بن زيني دحلان المكي الشافعي (١٢٣١-١٣٠٤) مفتي مكّة عالياً ، عن عثمان بن حسن الدمياطي (١١٩٧-١٢٦٥) ، عن محمد بن علي الشنواني العلامة أحد كبار علماء الأزهر (ت ١٢٣٥) ، عن السيد أبي الفيض محمد مرتضى الزبيدي (١١٤٥-١٢٠٥) ، ثنا محمد بن محمد القِرْمي المقدسي ، ثنا محمد بن أحمد الخليلي ، ثنا المسنِد القاضي برهان الدين إبراهيم بن أبي شريف المقدسي المصري ، ثنا محمد بن

عبد الهادي الحصَّاري ، ثنا الجلال عبد الرحمن بن أبي بكر السيوطي ، ثنا مسنِد الدنيا محمّد بن مقبِل الحلبي إجازةً ، ثنا محمد بن إبراهيم الصالحي ، ثنا أبو عبد الله الذهبي ، ثنا أحمد بن سلامة كتابةً ، أنبأنا مسعود الجمّال وأبو المكارم أحمد بن جعفر اللبَّان التَيمي ، قالا : ثنا أبو علي الحسن بن أحمد بن الحسن الحدّاد المقرئ ، ثنا أبو نعَيم الحافظ ، ثنا عبد الله بن جعفر بن أحمد بن فارس الأصبهاني ، ثنا يونس بن حبيب ابن عبد القاهر العِجلي ، قال : حدثنا **أبو داود سليمان بن داود بن الجارود الطيالسي** ، حدثنا عمرو بن ثابت ، عن أبيه ، عن أبي فاختة ، قال : قَالَ عَلِيٌّ : زَارَنَا رَسُولُ اللهِ ﷺ ، فَبَاتَ عِنْدَنَا ، وَالْحَسَنُ وَالْحُسَيْنُ نَائِمَانِ ، فَاسْتَسْقَى الْحَسَنُ فَقَامَ رَسُولُ اللهِ ﷺ إِلَى قِرْبَةٍ لَنَا ، فَجَعَلَ يَعْصِرُهَا فِي الْقَدَحِ ثُمَّ يَسْقِيهِ ، فَتَنَاوَلَهُ الْحُسَيْنُ لِيَشْرَبَ فَمَنَعَهُ ، وَبَدَأَ بِالْحَسَنِ ، **فَقَالَتْ فَاطِمَةُ : يَا رَسُولَ اللهِ ، كَأَنَّهُ أَحَبُّهُمَا إِلَيْكَ ؟ فَقَالَ : لَا ، وَلٰكِنَّهُ اسْتَسْقَى أَوَّلَ مَرَّةٍ . ثُمَّ قَالَ** رَسُولُ اللهِ ﷺ : **إِنِّي وَإِيَّاكِ وَهٰذَيْنِ ، وَأَحْسَبُهُ قَالَ : وَهٰذَا الرَّاقِدَ - يَعْنِي عَلِيّاً - يَوْمَ الْقِيَامَةِ فِي مَكَانٍ وَاحِدٍ .**

رواه من طريق الطيالسي الطبراني في الكبير وأبو نعيم في معرفة الصحابة ، وابن عساكر في التاريخ . ورواه من طرق أخرى : أحمد

في المسند والفضائل بلفظ **فَقَامَ النَّبِيُّ ﷺ إلى شَاةٍ لنا بِكْرٍ فَحَلَبَهَا فَدَرَّتْ** والبزّار بلفظ **فَقَامَ رَسُولُ اللهِ ﷺ إلى إِنَاءٍ لنا فَصَبَّ فِي الْقَدَحِ** وابن أبي عاصم وأبو يعلى كلاهما مختصراً . ورواه الحاكم عن أبي سعيد الخدري مختصراً وصححه . والحديث صحيح بمجموع طرقه . (القِرْبة) وِعاء مصنوع من الجلد لحفظ الماء واللبن .

أسنده الفاداني في الأربعين من أربعين كتاباً عن أربعين شيخاً وقال : فيه فضل آل البيت ومكانة العترة منه ﷺ يوم القيامة .

❑ ❑ ❑

٤

مسند الشافعي

(١٥٠-٢٠٤)

إِنَّمَا بَنُو هَاشِمٍ وَبَنُو الْمُطَّلِبِ شَيْءٌ وَاحِدٌ هٰكَذَا ، وَشَبَّكَ بَيْنَ أَصَابِعِهِ .

وهو عبارة عن الأحاديث التي وقعت في مسموع أبي العباس الأصم على الربيع بن سليمان من كتاب الأم والمبسوط التقطها بعض النيسابوريين من الأبواب

حدّثنا من لفظه في داره بميدان دمشق **العلّامة السيد عِصام عَرَار ابن العلامة السيد يوسف عرار الحسني الصوفي الدمشقي** ، عن السيد محمد المنتصر بن محمد الزمزمي الكتّاني وعن الزمزمي مباشرة ، كلاهما عن والد الأخير الحافظ محمّد بن جعفر الكتاني والشيخ عمر حمدان المحرسي ، (ح) وأنبأنا عالياً محدّث الدنيا **الحافظ أبو الفضل عبد الله بن السيد محمد بن الصدّيق الغُماري** المغربي الطانْجي الحسني (١٣٢٧-١٤١٣) ، عن ابن جعفر الكتاني والمَحرسي ، الأول عن والده

الشيخ جعفر بن إدريس بن الطائع الكتاني ، عن السيّد علي الوتري ، عن الشيخ منّة الله الأزهري ، عن الأمير الكبير وعن الكزبري بسنده المارّ إلى الحافظ ابن حجر ، والثاني عن السيد أحمد بن إسماعيل البرزنجي ، عن السيد أحمد بن زيني دحلان ، عن الشيخ عثمان الدمياطي ، عن الأمير الكبير ، عن أبي الحسن علي بن أحمد الصَّعِيدي ، عن الشمس محمد بن أحمد بن محمد بن سعيد ـ عُرف بابن عقيلة المكي . (ح) وأعلى منه بدرجتين : الغُماري ، عن مسند عصره أحمد بن محمد بن عبد العزيز بن رافع الحسيني الطهطاوي (١٢٧٥-١٣٥٥) ، عن العلّامة الشمس أبي عبد الوهاب محمد بن مصطفى الخضري الدمياطي الكبير الأزهري (ت ١٢٨٧) ، عن الأمير الكبير عالياً ـ وهذه رواية أثبتها الطهطاوي في المسعى الحميد في بيان وتحرير الأسانيد والكتّاني في فهرس الفهارس ـ عن الصعيدي ، عن ابن عقيلة ، عن أبي الأسرار حسن بن علي العُجَيمي ، عن الشمس محمد بن علاء الدين البابلي ، عن سالم السَّنهوري ، عن الشهاب الرملي ، عن الحافظ الشمس أبي الخير السخاوي عن الحافظ ابن حجر ؛ (ح) العجيمي ، عن القُشاشي ، عن الشمس الرملي ، عن شيخ الإسلام ، عن الحافظ ، أخبرنا أبو علي محمد بن محمد بن علي

الزفتاوي ثم الحيري وأبو الحسن علي بن محمد بن محمد بن أبي المجد الدمشقي ، بإجازة كل من الشيخين إن لم يكن سماعاً على ست الوزراء وزيرة بنت عمر بن أسعد بن المُنَجَّا التنوخية ولو لبعضه ، قالت : أنبأنا أبو عبد الله الحسين ابن أبي بكر المبارك بن محمد بن يحيى الزبيدي ، أنبأنا أبو زرعة طاهر بن محمد بن طاهر ، أنبأنا أبو الحسن مكي بن محمد بن منصور بن عِلَّان السَّلَّار ، أنبأنا القاضي أبو بكر أحمد بن الحسن الحِيْرِي ، حدثنا أبو العباس محمد بن يعقوب بن يوسف الأصمّ ، أنبأنا الربيع بن سليمان المُرادي ، أنبأنا **الإمام أبو عبد الله محمد بن إدريس الشافعي** ، قال : أخبرنا مطرِّف بن مازن ، عن مَعْمَر بن راشد ، عن ابن شهاب ، قال : أخبرني محمد بن جبير بن مطعم ، عن أبيه ، قال : لَمَّا قَسَمَ رَسُولُ اللهِ ﷺ سَهْمَ ذِي الْقُرْبَى بَيْنَ بَنِي هَاشِمٍ وَبَنِي الْمُطَّلِبِ ، أَتَيْتُهُ أَنَا وَعُثْمَانُ بْنُ عَفَّانَ ، فَقُلْنَا : يَا رَسُولَ اللهِ ، هٰؤُلاءِ إِخْوَانُنَا مِنْ بَنِي هَاشِمٍ ، لا نُنْكِرُ فَضْلَهُمْ لِمَكَانِكَ الَّذِي وَضَعَكَ اللهُ بِهِ مِنْهُمْ ؛ أَرَأَيْتَ إِخْوَانَنَا مِنْ بَنِي الْمُطَّلِبِ ؟ أَعْطَيْتَهُمْ وَتَرَكْتَنَا أَوْ مَنَعْتَنَا ، وَإِنَّمَا قَرَابَتُنَا وَقَرَابَتُهُمْ وَاحِدَةٌ . فَقَالَ رَسُولُ اللهِ ﷺ : **إِنَّمَا بَنُو هَاشِمٍ وَبَنُو الْمُطَّلِبِ شَيْءٌ وَاحِدٌ هٰكَذَا** ، وَشَبَّكَ بَيْنَ أَصَابِعِهِ . وبه إليه قال الشافعي : أخبرني عمّي محمد بن علي بن

شافع ، عن علي بن الحسين ، عن رسول الله ﷺ مثلَه ، وزاد : **لَعَنَ اللهُ مَنْ فَرَّقَ بَيْنَ بَنِي هَاشِمٍ وَبَنِي المُطَّلِبِ** .

رواه البخاري وأحمد وأصحاب السنن سوى الترمذي ، قال البخاري : حدثنا عبد الله بن يوسف حدثنا الليث عن عقيل عن ابن شهاب عن ابن المسيب عن جبير بن مطعم قال : مَشَيْتُ أَنَا وَعُثْمَانُ بْنُ عَفَّانَ إِلَى رَسُولِ اللهِ ﷺ فَقُلْنَا : يَا رَسُولَ اللهِ أَعْطَيْتَ بَنِي الْمُطَّلِبِ وَتَرَكْتَنَا وَنَحْنُ وَهُمْ مِنْكَ بِمَنْزِلَةٍ وَاحِدَةٍ فقال رسول الله ﷺ : **إِنَّمَا بَنُو الْمُطَّلِبِ وَبَنُو هَاشِمٍ شَيْءٌ وَاحِدٌ** . قال الليث : حدثني يونس وزاد قال جبير ولم يَقسِم النبي ﷺ لبني عبد شمس ولا لبني نوفل . وقال ابن إسحاق : عبد شمس وهاشم والمطلب إخوة لأم ، وأمّهم عاتكة بنت مُرّة ، وكان نوفل أخاهم لأبيهم . قال البيهقي في مناقب الشافعي : إنما قال ذلك ـ والله أعلم ـ لأنّ هاشم بنَ عبد مناف أبو جَد رسول الله ﷺ تزوّج امرأة من بني النّجّار بالمدينة ، فولدت له شَيْبَةَ الحمْد جدّ رسول الله ﷺ ، ثم توفّي هاشم وهو مع أمّه ، فلمّا ترَعْرَعَ خرج إليه عمّه المطلب بن عبد مناف ، فأخذه من أمّه وقَدِمَ به مكّة وهو مُرْدِفُهُ على راحلته ، فقيل : عبْدٌ مَلَكَه المُطَّلِبُ . فغلب عليه ذلك الاسم ، فقيل : عبد المطَّلِب . وحين بُعِثَ رسول الله ﷺ

بالرسالة آذاه قومه وهَمُّوا به ، فقامت بنو هاشم وبنو المطّلب مُسْلِمُهُم وكافرهم دُوْنَه ، فأَبَوْا أن يُسْلِمُوه . فلمّا عرفت سائر قريش أن لا سبيل إليه معهم ، اجتمعوا على أن يكتبوا فيما بينهم كتاباً على بني هاشم وبني المطلب : أن لا يُنَاكِحُوهُم ولا يبايعوهم . وعمد أبو طالب فأدخلهم الشِّعْبَ في ناحيةٍ من مكة ، وجَهِدُوا فيه جهداً كبيراً سنتين أو ثلاثاً ، حتى جاءهم الله ـ عز وجل ـ بالفرج بإرسال الأَرَضَةِ على صحيفتهم حتى أكلت ما فيها من [غير] أسماء الله تعالى . وأخبر بذلك رسولَ الله ﷺ ، وأخبر به رسوله أبا طالب ، واستنصر به أبو طالب على قومه حتى نقضوا أمْرَ الصحيفة . وفي تخصيص النبي ﷺ وآله بني هاشم وبني المطلب بإعطائهم سَهْمَ ذي القربى وقولِه : **إِنَّمَا بَنُو هَاشِمٍ وَبَنُو الْمُطَّلِبِ شَيْءٌ وَاحِدٌ** فضيلةٌ أخرى ، وهي أنّه حرّم الله عليهم الصدّقة وعوَّضهم منها هذا السَّهْم من الخُمُس ، وقال : **إِنَّ الصَّدَقَةَ لَا تَحِلُّ لِمُحَمَّدٍ وَلَا لِآلِ مُحَمَّدٍ** [الخطيب ، وأصله في السنن] ، فدلّ بذلك على أنّ آله الذين أَمَرَ بالصلاة عليهم معه ، هم الذين حرّم الله عليهم الصدقة وعَوَّضَهم منها هذا السهمَ من الخُمُسِ . فالمسلمون من بني هاشم وبني المطلب يكونون داخلين في صَلَواتِنَا على آل نبينا ﷺ في فَرَائِضنَا ونوافلنا ، والشافعي المِّطلبي من جُمْلَتِهم ، ومن جملة مَنْ أمَرَ المصطفى ﷺ بمحبّتهم من أهل بيته لِحُبِّه . اهـ .

وفي المعرفة والتاريخ للفسوي عن عبيد الله بن موهب : أول من فرّق بين بني هاشم والمطلب في الدعوة : عبد الملك . فمن أمثال المُطَّلِبيِّين المقرَّبين : عبد الله بن الزبير بن عبد المطَّلب ، هو ابن عم المصطفى ﷺ ، أمّه عاتكة بنت أبي وهب المخزومية ، أسلم وهاجر ومات شهيداً يوم أجنادَين في خلافة أبي بكر رضي الله عنهم أجمعين .

قال صاحب (ذخائر العقبى) دون ذكر سند : كان رسول الله ﷺ يقول له : **ابن عمِّي وحِبِّي** . وقال الحافظ في الإصابة : روى الزبير من طريق حسين بن علي قال كان ممن ثبت يوم حنين العباس وعلي وعبد الله بن الزبير بن عبدالمطلب وغيرهم وكذا قال الواقدي وابن عائذ وأبو حذيفة وحكى المُبَرِّد في الكامل أن عبد الله بن الزبير أتى رسول الله ﷺ فكساه حلة وأقعده إلى جنبه وقال إِنَّهُ ابْنُ أُمِّي وَكَانَ أَبُوهُ بِي بَرّاً ويقال إن الزبير بن عبد المطلب كان يرقّص النبي ﷺ وهو صغير ويقول :

مُحَمَّدُ بْنُ عَبْدَمْ   عِشْتَ بِعَيْشٍ أَنْعَمْ   فِي عِزِّ فَرْعٍ أَسْنَمْ

قال الواقدي وغيره : قُتل بأجنادَين سنة ثلاث عشرة . قال الواقدي : وكان أول قتيل من الروم المبارز لعبد الله بن الزبير فقتله عبد الله ، ثم برز آخر فقتله ، ثم وُجد في المعركة قتيلا وحوله عشرة

مـن الروم قتلى ، وكان له يوم توفي النبي ﷺ نحو ثلاثين سـنة . اهـ .
وقال الشيخ مساعد سالم العبد الجادر رحمه الله في كتابه معالي الرُتَب لمـن جمع بين شرفي الصحبة والنسـب : وفي صحيـح البخاري : عَنْ عُرْوَةَ بْـنِ الزُّبَيْرِ قَالَ : كَانَ عَبْدُ اللهِ بْنُ الزُّبَيْرِ أَحَبَّ الْبَشَرِ إِلَى عَائِشَـةَ بَعْـدَ النَّبِـيِّ ﷺ وَأَبِي بَكْرٍ وَكَانَ أَبَرَّ النَّاسِ بِهَا . وفيه عَنْهُ أيضاً : ذَهَبَ عَبْدُ اللهِ بْنُ الزُّبَيْرِ مَعَ أُنَاسٍ مِنْ بَنِي زُهْرَةَ إِلَى عَائِشَةَ وَكَانَتْ أَرَقَّ شَيْءٍ عَلَيْهِمْ لِقَرَابَتِهِمْ مِنْ رَسُولِ اللهِ ﷺ .

قال ابن عادل في تفسـيره اللباب في علوم الكتاب في قوله تعالى ﴿وَٱعْلَمُوٓاْ أَنَّمَا غَنِمْتُم مِّن شَىْءٍ فَأَنَّ لِلَّهِ خُمُسَهُۥ وَلِلرَّسُولِ وَلِذِى ٱلْقُرْبَىٰ﴾ الأنفال ٤١ : أي أنَّ سَهْماً من خُمُس الخُمُس لذوي القربى ، وهم أقارب النبي ﷺ ، واختلفوا فيهم ، فقال قومٌ هم جميع قريش ، وقـال قومٌ هـم الذين لا تحل لهم الصَّدقـة . وقال مجاهـدٌ وعلي ابنُ الحسـينِ : هم بنُو هاشـمٍ وبنو المطلب ، وليس لبني عبد شمس ولا لبنـي نوفل منـه شيء وإن كانوا إخوة ، لما روي عن جُبير بن مطعم ، ثم سـاق الحديث . ثم قال : واختلف العلماءُ في سهم ذوي القربى ، هـل هو ثابتٌ اليـوم ؟ فذهب أكثرهم إلى أنَّهُ ثابـت وهو قول مالك والشـافعي ، وذهب أصحابُ الرَّأي إلى أنَّهُ غير ثابت ، وقالوا سهم

رسـول الله ﷺ وسـهم ذوي القـرى مَـرْدُودان في الخُمس ، فيقسـم خمس الغنيمة لثلاثةِ أصناف : اليتامى والمساكين وابن السبيل . وقال بعضهـم : يعطـى للفقراء منهم دون الأغنيـاء ، أي : يعطى لفقره لا لقرابته . والكتاب والسـنة يدلاَّن على ثبوته وكذا الخلفاء بعد رسُول الله ﷺ كانـوا يعطونـه ، ولا يُفَضَّـل فقـير على غنـي ، لأنَّ النبي ﷺ والخلفـاء بعده كانوا يعطـون العباس بن عبد المطلب مع كثرة ماله ، وألحقه الشافعي بالميراث الذي يستحق باسم القرابة ، غير أنه يعطى القريـب والبعيد ، وقال : يفضَّـل الذكر على الأنثـى فيعطى الرجل سهمين والأنثى سهماً .

روى البيهقي في مناقبه بأسـانيده إلى الإمام الشـافعي رضي الله عنه أنه أنشد :

وأُشـهِدُ ربيّ أنَّ عثـمانَ فاضِـلٌ
وأنَّ عليّـاً فضلُـهُ متخصِّـصُ

وقال فيه :

آلُ النبـيِّ ذريعتـــي
وهُـمُ إليـه وسـيلتـي

أرجو بـأنْ أُعطَى غداً
بِيَدِي اليْمِينِ صَحِيفَتِي

وقال فيه :

إِنْ كَانَ رَفْضاً حُبُّ آلِ مُحُمَّدٍ
فَلْيَشْهَدِ الثَّقَلانِ أَنيِّ رَافِضِي

وقال فيه :

إذا نحن فضّلنا عَلِيًّا فإنَّنا
رَوَافضُ بالتفضيل عند ذوي الجهلِ
وفَضلُ أبي بكر إذا ما ذكرتُهُ
رُمِيتُ بِنَصْبٍ عند ذِكْرِي الفضلِ
فلا زِلْتُ ذا رفضٍ ونصبٍ كلاهما
بحُبِّيهما حتَّى أُوَسَّدَ في الرملِ

وقال في ديوانه :

يَا آلَ بَيْتِ رَسُولِ اللهِ حُبُّكُمُ
فَرْضٌ مِنَ اللهِ في القُرْآنِ أَنْزَلَهُ

يَكْفِيكُمُ مِنْ عَظِيمِ الفَخْرِ أَنَّكُمُ
مَنْ لَمْ يُصَلِّ عَلَيْكُمْ لاَ صَلاَةَ لَهُ

❑ ❑ ❑

٥

مصنَّف ابن أبي شيبة

(١٥٩-٢٣٥)

> أَلاَ إِنَّ عَيْبَتِي الَّتِي آوِي إِلَيْهَا أَهْلُ بَيْتِي ، وَإِنَّ كَرِشِي الأَنْصَارُ ، فَاعْفُوا عَنْ مُسِيئِهِمْ وَاقْبَلُوا مِنْ مُحْسِنِهِمْ .

أخبرني سيدي الحبيب عباس بن محمد بن علي السقاف السنغافوري (١٩٢٣-٢٠١٨ / ١٣٤٢-١٤٣٩) رحمه الله - بقراءتي عليه في داره بسنغافورة ، عن شيخه العلّامة الشيخ عبد القادر بن عبد المطلب المنديلي - نسبةً لمدينة منديلين في جزيرة سومطرة بإندونيسيا - ثم المكي الشافعي (١٣٢٢-١٣٨٥) ، عن السيد حسن بن سعيد بن محمّد يماني الحسني (١٣١٢-١٣٩١) وعن سيبويه زمانه العلامة محمد علي بن حسين بن إبراهيم المالكي المكي (١٢٨٧-١٣٦٨) ، الأوّل عن والده والسيد عبد الرحمن بن أحمد الدّهّان ، والثاني عن السيد زين العابدين بكري بن محمد شطا الدمياطي المكّي الحسيني (١٢٦٦-١٣١٠) صاحب (إعانة الطالبين) في فروع الشافعيّة ، ثلاثتهم عن مفتي مكّة السيد أحمد بن زيني دحلان ، عن عثمان بن حسن

الدمياطي ، عن الأمير الكبير ، عن شيخ الشيوخ البدر محمد بن سالم الحَفْناوي الشافعي الخلوتي المتوفَّى في مجلس قراءة الشمائل المحمّديّة ، عن البُدَيري ، عن الملا إبراهيم الكُوراني الكردي النقشبندي ، عن شيخه الصفي القُشاشي المدني ، عن الشمس الرَّملي ، عن شيخ الإسلام زكريا ، عن مسند الديار المصرية العز عبد الرحيم ابن محمد بن عبد الرحيم بن الفُرات الحنفي ، عن شيخ الإسلام التاج السُّبكي ، عن الحافظ الذهبي ، عن الحافظ ابن طرخان ، عن المسنِد ضياء الدين موسى بن عبد القادر الجيلاني (٥٣٩-٦١٨) نزيل دمشق ، عن مسند بغداد سعيد ابن أحمد بن الحسن الحنبلي ، عن الحافظ الثَّبْت العديم النظير **أبي بكر عبد الله بن محمّد ابن أبي شيبة العَبْسي مولاهم الكوفي** ، قال : حَدَّثَنَا أَبُو أُسَامَةَ ، عَنْ زَكَرِيَّا ، عَنْ عَطِيَّةَ ، عَنْ أَبِي سَعِيدٍ ، قَالَ : قَالَ رَسُولُ اللهِ ﷺ : **أَلاَ إِنَّ عَيْبَتِي الَّتِي آوِي إِلَيْهَا أَهْلُ بَيْتِي ، وَإِنَّ كَرِشِي الأَنْصَارُ ، فَاعْفُوا عَنْ مُسِيئِهِمْ وَاقْبَلُوا مِنْ مُحْسِنِهِمْ** .

رواه الترمذي وحسّنه . وأخرج أحمد في المسند وأبو يعلى وابن الجعد من طريق عطية الكوفي عن أبي سعيد مرفوعاً : **الأَنْصَارُ كَرِشي وَأَهْلُ بَيْتِي وَعَيْبَتِي الَّتِي آوِي إِلَيْهَا فَاعْفُوا عَنْ مُسِيئِهِمْ وَاقْبَلُوا مِنْ مُحْسِنِهِمْ** .

ورواه الشيخان عن أنس مرفوعاً بلفظ **الأَنْصَارُ كَرِشي وَعَيْبَتِي ، وَإِنّ النّاسَ سَيَكْثُرونَ وَيَقِلّونَ ، فَاقْبَلُوا مِنْ مُحْسِنِهِمْ وَتجَاوَزُوا عن**

مُسِيئِهِم . قال الخطابي : ضرَب مثلاً بالكرش لأنه مستقر غذاء الحيوان الذي يكون به بقاؤه . وقال التُّورَبَشْتِي : الكرش بمنزلة المَعِدة للإنسان ، والعرب تستعمل الكرش في كلامهم موضِعَ البطن ، والبطن مستودَع مكتوم السِّرِّ ، والعَيبة مستودع مكنون المتاع ، والأول أمر باطن والثاني أمر ظاهر . ويحتمل أنه ضرب المثل بهما إرادة اختصاصهم به في أموره الظاهرة والباطنة . وقال القاضي عياض في الإكمال : قال ابن الأنباري : يعنى (كَرِشي) أصحابي وجماعتي الذين أعتمد عليهم ، وأصل الكرِش فى اللغة : الجماعة ، وجعل الأنصار عيبته : خصوصيته إياهم ؛ لأنه يُطْلعهم على أسراره . (فائدة) أفادني الأستاذ الشيخ المؤرخ الأديب المحقِّق الدكتور ليث سُعُود جاسم العراقي حفظه الله ـ صاحب كتاب ابن عبد البر الأندلسى وجهوده فى التاريخ والرعاية و الخدمة الاجتماعية في عصر النبوة و دور المرأة ومحقّق مناقب المربِّيات وسِيرَ الصالحات للتقي الحِصني ـ : آل الكُوراني من أكراد العراق أصلاً ، فالكاف معقودة (گ) ، ويقال لها أيضاً كاف أعجمية ، وكاف فارسية .

❑ ❑ ❑

٦

مسند أحمد بن حنبل

(١٦٤-٢٤١)

اللَّهُمَّ هَؤُلَاءِ أَهْلُ بَيْتِي وَخَاصَّتِي ، فَأَذْهِبْ عَنْهُمُ الرِّجْسَ وَطَهِّرْهُمْ تَطْهِيرًا ! اللَّهُمَّ هَؤُلَاءِ أَهْلُ بَيْتِي وَخَاصَّتِي ، فَأَذْهِبْ عَنْهُمُ الرِّجْسَ وَطَهِّرْهُمْ تَطْهِيرًا

حدثني من لفظه الوزير الشريف الرحّالة الداعية إلى الله ، العالم النسيب الحسيب ، **السيد أبو يعقوب يوسف بن السيد هاشم الرفاعي الكويتي** (١٣٥١-١٤٣٩) - رحمه الله - في ديوانه بمزّة دمشق المحروسة ، قال : أخبرني شيخنا المجيز المعمَّر الشريف الشيخ عبد القادر بن أحمد بن عبد الرحمن بن عبيد الله السقّاف السَّيْؤوني الحجازي (١٣٣١-١٤٣١) ، عن والده ، عن مسند اليمن شيخه العلّامة المحدّث السيد عيدروس بن عمر بن عيدروس الحَبْشي ، عن والده (ت ١٢٥٠) ، عن السيدين عمر وعلوي ابني أحمد الحدّاد ، - علوي هو صاحب مصباح الأنام في رد شبهات المبتدع النجدي التي أضلّ بها العوامّ وشارح راتب الحدّاد - عن جدّهما حسن (ت ١١٨٨) ، عن أبيه القطب

عبد الله بن علوي بن محمّد الحداد (ت ١١٣٢)، قال: أخبرنا صفي الدين أحمد بن محمد بن يونس القُشاشي المدني، نا أبو المواهب أحمد بن علي بن عبد القُدّوس العباسي الخامي الشِّنَّاوي، نا علي بن حسام الدين المتَّقي الهندي، نا الإمام عبد الوهاب بن أحمد الشعراني، نا الحافظان شيخ الإسلام زكريا الأنصاري وعبد الرحمن بن أبي بكر السيوطي مؤلف عقود الزبرجد على مسند الإمام أحمد، قالا نا الحافظ أبو الفضل علي بن حجر العسقلاني مؤلف القول المسدد في الذب عن مسند الإمام أحمد، نا الحافظ علم القراء أبو الخير محمد بن محمد بن علي بن الجزري الدمشقي مؤلف المسند الأحمد فيما يتعلق بمسند الإمام أحمد، نا أبو حفص عمر بن أميلة المراغي، ثنا خاتمة المسندين الفخر أبو الحسن علي بن أحمد بن عبد الواحد ابن البخاري الأنصاري السعدي المقدسي الصالحي (٥٩٦-٦٩٠)، ثنا أبو علي حنبل بن عبد الله بن الفرح الرُصافي، نا أبو القاسم هبة الله بن محمد بن عبد الواحد بن الحُصين، نا أبو علي الحسن بن علي التميمي ابن المُذْهِب، ثنا أبو بكر أحمد بن جعفر القَطِيعي، ثنا **أبو محمّد عبد الله بن أحمد بن محمد بن حنبل، حدثني أبي**، قال: حَدَّثَنَا عَبْدُ الله بْنُ نُمَيْرٍ قَالَ حَدَّثَنَا عَبْدُ المَلِكِ يَعْنِي ابْنَ أَبِي سُلَيْمَانَ عَنْ

عَطَاءِ بْنِ أَبِي رَبَاحٍ قَالَ حَدَّثَنِي مَنْ سَمِعَ أُمَّ سَلَمَةَ تَذْكُرُ أَنَّ النَّبِيَّ ﷺ كَانَ فِي بَيْتِهَا ، فَأَتَتْهُ فَاطِمَةُ بِبُرْمَةٍ فِيهَا خَزِيرَةٌ ، فَدَخَلَتْ بِهَا عَلَيْهِ ، فَقَالَ لَهَا : **ادْعِي زَوْجَكِ وَابْنَيْكِ** . قَالَتْ : فَجَاءَ عَلِيٌّ وَالْحُسَيْنُ وَالْحَسَنُ ، فَدَخَلُوا عَلَيْهِ ، فَجَلَسُوا يَأْكُلُونَ مِنْ تِلْكَ الْخَزِيرَةِ وَهُوَ عَلَى مَنَامَةٍ لَهُ ، عَلَى دُكَّانٍ تَحْتَهُ كِسَاءٌ لَهُ خَيْبَرِيٌّ . قَالَتْ : وَأَنَا أُصَلِّي فِي الْحُجْرَةِ ، فَأَنْزَلَ اللهُ عَزَّ وَجَلَّ هَذِهِ الْآيَةَ : ﴿ إِنَّمَا يُرِيدُ ٱللَّهُ لِيُذْهِبَ عَنكُمُ ٱلرِّجْسَ أَهْلَ ٱلْبَيْتِ وَيُطَهِّرَكُمْ تَطْهِيرًا ﴾ [الأحزاب ٣٣] . قَالَتْ : فَأَخَذَ فَضْلَ الْكِسَاءِ فَغَشَّاهُمْ بِهِ ، ثُمَّ أَخْرَجَ يَدَهُ فَأَلْوَى بِهَا إِلَى السَّمَاءِ ، ثُمَّ قَالَ : **اللَّهُمَّ هَؤُلَاءِ أَهْلُ بَيْتِي وَخَاصَّتِي ، فَأَذْهِبْ عَنْهُمُ الرِّجْسَ وَطَهِّرْهُمْ تَطْهِيرًا ! اللَّهُمَّ هَؤُلَاءِ أَهْلُ بَيْتِي وَخَاصَّتِي ، فَأَذْهِبْ عَنْهُمُ الرِّجْسَ وَطَهِّرْهُمْ تَطْهِيرًا !** قَالَتْ : فَأَدْخَلْتُ رَأْسِي الْبَيْتَ ، **فَقُلْتُ : وَأَنَا مَعَكُمْ يَا رَسُولَ اللهِ ؟ قَالَ : إِنَّكِ إِلَى خَيْرٍ ، إِنَّكِ إِلَى خَيْرٍ .**

رواه الطبراني في الكبير . وفي المسند أيضاً عَنْ أُمِّ سَلَمَةَ : بَيْنَمَا رَسُولُ اللهِ ﷺ فِي بَيْتِي يَوْمًا ، إِذْ قَالَتْ الْخَادِمُ : إِنَّ عَلِيًّا وَفَاطِمَةَ بِالسُّدَّةِ . قَالَتْ : فَقَالَ لِي : قُومِي ، فَتَنَحَّيْ لِي عَنْ أَهْلِ بَيْتِي . قَالَتْ : فَقُمْتُ ، فَتَنَحَّيْتُ فِي الْبَيْتِ قَرِيبًا ، فَدَخَلَ عَلِيٌّ وَفَاطِمَةُ وَمَعَهُمَا الْحَسَنُ وَالْحُسَيْنُ وَهُمَا صَبِيَّانِ صَغِيرَانِ ، فَأَخَذَ الصَّبِيَّيْنِ فَوَضَعَهُمَا فِي حِجْرِهِ ، فَقَبَّلَهُمَا ،

قَالَ : وَاعْتَنَقَ عَلِيًّا بِإِحْدَى يَدَيْهِ وَفَاطِمَةَ بِالْيَدِ الأُخْرَى فَقَبَّلَ فَاطِمَةَ وَقَبَّلَ عَلِيًّا ، فَأَغْدَفَ عَلَيْهِمْ خَمِيصَةً سَوْدَاءَ ، فَقَالَ : **اللَّهُمَّ إِلَيْكَ لاَ إِلَى النَّارِ أَنَا وَأَهْلُ بَيْتِي . قَالَتْ : فَقُلْتُ : وَأَنَا يَا رَسُولَ اللهِ ؟ فَقَالَ : وَأَنْتِ !** رواه الدولابي في الكنى والأسماء ، والترمذي مختصراً من طريق سُفْيَانَ عَنْ زُبَيْدٍ عَنْ شَهْرٍ ، وقَالَ : هذا حَدِيثٌ حَسَنٌ صَحِيحٌ ، وَهُوَ أَحْسَنُ شيْءٍ رُوِيَ فِي هَذَا الْبَابِ ، وَفِي الْبَاب : عَنْ عُمَرَ بْنِ أَبِي سَلَمَةَ وَأَنَسِ بْنِ مَالِكٍ وَأَبِي الحَمْرَاءِ وَمَعْقِلِ بْنِ يَسَارٍ وَعَائِشَةَ رَضِيَ اللهُ عَنْهُمْ .

قال السيد يوسف : (البُرْمَة) وِعاءٌ من فخّار يوضع فيه الماء للتبريد أو العسل أو التمر وما يشبه ذلك . (الدُّكَّان) دكّة مرتفعة . (خَيْبَرِي) مصنوع في خيبَر . (أَلْوَى) أشار . (فَأَدْخَلْتُ رَأْسِي الْبَيْتَ) أي أدخلته الكِساءَ . (**إِنَّكِ إِلَى خَيْرٍ**) أي لم يأذن لها أن تدخل . (وَاعْتَنَقَ عَلِيًّا بِإِحْدَى يَدَيْهِ وَفَاطِمَةَ بِالْيَدِ الْأُخْرَى) أي وضع يديه الشريفتين على عنق كل منهما . (فَأَغْدَفَ عَلَيْهِمْ) رمى أو قذف . اهـ . وقوله لم يأذن لها : أي على بعض الروايات لا قطعاً ، والله أعلم .

ويوضّح ما هُم إليه من الخير ما رواه الحافظان الحارث بن أبي أسامة في مسنده وابن عساكر في الأربعين في مناقب أمّهات المؤمنين ،

كـما يأتي ذكره إن شـاء الله تعالى . (فائدة) قال الشـيخ محمد التَّاوُدِي ابن سَوْدة في فهرسته : معنى عَيْدَرُوس : سلطان الأولياء .

❑ ❑ ❑

٧

سنن الدارمي

(١٨١-٢٥٥)

يَا أَيُّهَا النَّاسُ ، إِنَّمَا أَنَا بَشَرٌ ، يُوشِكُ أَنْ يَأْتِيَنِي رَسُولُ رَبِّي فَأُجِيبَهُ ، وَإِنِّي تَارِكٌ فِيكُمُ الثَّقَلَيْنِ ، أَوَّلُهُمَا كِتَابُ اللهِ ، فِيهِ الهُدَى وَالنُّورُ ، فَتَمَسَّكُوا بِكِتَابِ اللهِ وَخُذُوا بِهِ ، وَأَهْلَ بَيْتِي أُذَكِّرُكُمُ اللهَ فِي أَهْلِ بَيْتِي

أنبأني شيخ الإسلام في البلد الحرام المسند المجاهد الداعية المربّي المصنّف الشيخ الدكتور **محمد حسن بن علوي بن عباس بن عبدالعزيز المالكي الحسني المكي** (١٣٦٧-١٤٢٥) رحمه الله في داره حي الرُّصَيفة بمكّة المكرّمة عام الحجّ الأكبر سنة ١٩٩٩م ، عن والده والشيخ حسن بن محمد المشاط ، كلاهما عن عمر حمدان المحرسي ، عن أحمد البرزنجي ، عن أحمد بن زيني دحلان ؛ (ح) المالكي عن حسن بن سعيد يماني (١٣١٢-١٣٩١) ، عن السيد عبد الرحمن بن أحمد الدهان ، عن دحلان ، عن عثمان بن حسن الدمياطي ؛ (ح) المالكي عن الحبيب سالم بن أحمد بن جِنداان ابن الشيخ أبو بكر بن سالم عالياً ، عن الحبيب عثمان بن عبد الله بن عقيل بن يحيى العلوي مفتي

بتـاوي ، عـن عثمان بن حسـن الدمياطـي ، عن الأمـير الكبير ، عن الحَفنـاوي ، عن البُديري ، عن الملا إبراهيـم الكوراني ، عن الصفي أحمـد القُشـاشي ، عـن الشـمس الرملي ، عن شيخ الإسـلام زكريا الأنصاري ، عن مسـند الدنيـا محمد بن مقبل الحلبـي ، عن جويرية بنت أحمد الكردي الهكاري ، قالت : أخبرنا أبو الحسن علي بن عمر الكردي ، قال أخبرنا مسند وقته أبو المُنَجَّا عبد الله بن عمر بن علي بن زيـد الحريمي القـزاز البغدادي المشـهور بابـن اللَّتِّـي (٥٤٥-٦٣٥) ، حضـوراً لجميعـه ، قال : أخبرنـا أبو الوقـت عبد الأول السـجزي الهـروي ، قـال : أخبرنا أبـو الحسـين عبد الرحمن الـداودي ، قال : أخبرنا عبد الله بن أحمد السرخسي ، قال : أخبرنا أبو عمران عيسى بن عمر السمرقندي ، قال : أخبرنا **أبو محمد عبد الله بن عبد الرحمن بن الفضـل التميمي الدارمي** ، قال : حدثنـا جعفر بن عون ، حدثنا أبو حيـان ، عـن يزيد بن حيان ، عن زيد بن أرقـم رضي الله عنه ، قال : قَامَ رَسُولُ اللهِ ﷺ يَوْمًا خَطِيبًا فَحَمِدَ اللهَ وَأَثْنَى عَلَيْهِ ، ثُمَّ قَالَ : **يَا أَيُّهَا النَّـاسُ ، إِنَّمَا أَنَـا بَـشَرٌ ، يُوشِـكُ أَنْ يَأْتِيَنِي رَسُـولُ رَبِّي فَأُجِيبَهُ ، وَإِنِّي تَـارِكٌ فِيكُمُ الثَّقَلَيْنِ ، أَوَّلُهُمَا كِتَابُ اللهِ ، فِيهِ الْهُدَى وَالنُّورُ ، فَتَمَسَّـكُوا بِكِتَـابِ اللهِ وَخُذُوا بِهِ** . فَحَثَّ عَلَيْهِ وَرَغَّبَ فِيهِ ، ثُمَّ قَالَ : **وَأَهْلَ بَيْتِي**

أُذَكِّرُكُمُ اللَّهَ فِي أَهْلِ بَيْتِي ثَلَاثَ مَرَّاتٍ .

أخرجه أحمد ومسلمٌ في صحيحه وزاد فيه : فَقَالَ لَهُ حُصَيْنٌ أي ابن سَبْرَةَ : وَمَنْ أَهْلُ بَيْتِهِ يَا زَيْدُ ؟ أَلَيْسَ نِسَاؤُهُ مِنْ أَهْلِ بَيْتِهِ ؟ قَالَ : نِسَاؤُهُ مِنْ أَهْلِ بَيْتِهِ ، وَلَكِنْ أَهْلُ بَيْتِهِ مَنْ حُرِمَ الصَّدَقَةَ بَعْدَهُ . قَالَ : وَمَنْ هُمْ ؟ قَالَ : هُمْ آلُ عَلِيٍّ ، وَآلُ عَقِيلٍ ، وَآلُ جَعْفَرٍ ، وَآلُ عَبَّاسٍ . قَالَ : كُلُّ هَؤُلَاءِ حُرِمَ الصَّدَقَةَ ؟ قَالَ : نَعَمْ . اه . قال الطيبي : أي أحذّركم الله في شأنهم ، فالتذكير بمعنى الوعظ .

وأخرج الترمذي وقال حسن غريب ، والحاكم في المستدرك ، عَنْ زَيْدٍ ، قَالَ رَسُولُ اللَّهِ ﷺ : إِنِّي تَارِكٌ فِيكُمْ مَا إِنْ تَمَسَّكْتُمْ بِهِ لَنْ تَضِلُّوا بَعْدِي ، أَحَدُهُمَا أَعْظَمُ مِنَ الآخَرِ : كِتَابُ اللَّهِ حَبْلٌ مَمْدُودٌ مِنَ السَّمَاءِ إِلَى الْأَرْضِ ، وَعِتْرَتِي أَهْلُ بَيْتِي ، وَلَنْ يَتَفَرَّقَا حَتَّى يَرِدَا عَلَيَّ الْحَوْضَ ، فَانْظُرُوا كَيْفَ تَخْلُفُونِي فِيهِمَا . وأخرجه أحمد وأبو يعلى عن أبي سعيد الخدري ، والترمذي والطبراني في الكبير عن جابر . وله رواية أخرى مشهورة ، تأتي في باب خصائص أمير المؤمنين علي للنسائي إن شاء الله . (فوائد وشروح) الأزواج كالذرّيّة من الآل كما مرّ في حديث الموطأ ، وقول عائشة رضي الله عنها في صحيح مسلم : مَا شَبِعَ آلُ مُحَمَّدٍ ﷺ مُنْذُ قَدِمَ الْمَدِينَةَ مِنْ طَعَامِ بُرٍّ ثَلَاثَ لَيَالٍ تِبَاعًا

حَتَّى قُبِضَ ، ومن الأهل كما في قول الله تعالى حكاية عن ضيف سيدنا إبراهيم الملائكة ـ على نبينا وعليهم الصلاة والسلام ـ : ﴿ قَالُوٓاْ أَتَعۡجَبِينَ مِنۡ أَمۡرِ ٱللَّهِۖ رَحۡمَتُ ٱللَّهِ وَبَرَكَٰتُهُۥ عَلَيۡكُمۡ أَهۡلَ ٱلۡبَيۡتِۚ إِنَّهُۥ حَمِيدٞ مَّجِيدٞ ﴾ [هود] . وأهل البيت محمول على الأزواج في آية التطهير عند جمهور أهل التفسير . بل في البخاري من قصة الإفك : عَنْ عَائِشَةَ رَضِيَ اللهُ عَنْهَا : قَالَ رَسُولَ اللهِ ﷺ : **مَنْ يَعْذِرُنَا فِي رَجُلٍ بَلَغَنِي أَذَاهُ فِي أَهْلِ بَيْتِي** ؟ وفي الصحيحين عن أنس رضي الله عنه : خَرَجَ النَّبِيُّ ﷺ فَانْطَلَقَ إِلَى حُجْرَةِ عَائِشَةَ فَقَالَ **السَّلَامُ عَلَيْكُمْ أَهْلَ الْبَيْتِ وَرَحْمَةُ اللهِ** ! فَقَالَتْ : وَعَلَيْكَ السَّلَامُ وَرَحْمَةُ اللهِ ، كَيْفَ وَجَدْتَ أَهْلَكَ ، بَارَكَ اللهُ لَكَ ! فَتَقَرَّى حُجَرَ نِسَائِهِ كُلِّهِنَّ يَقُولُ لَهُنَّ كَمَا يَقُولُ لِعَائِشَةَ وَيَقُلْنَ لَهُ كَمَا قَالَتْ عَائِشَةُ .

قال المُلّا علي القاري في مرقاة المفاتيح : **أُذَكِّرُكُمُ اللهَ** بكسر الكاف المشددة أي أحذِّرُكُمُوه في أهل بيتي ، وضَع الظاهر موضع المُضمَر اهتماماً بشأنهم وإشعاراً بالعلّة ، والمعنى : أنبّهكم حقَّ الله في محافظتهم ومراعاتهم واحترامهم وإكرامهم ومحبّتهم ومودّتهم . وقال الطيبي : أي أحذّركم الله في شأن أهل بيتي وأقول لكم : اتقوا الله ولا تؤذوهم واحفظوهم ، فالتذكير بمعنى الوعظ ، يدل عليه

قولـه : **وَوَعَـظَ وَذَكَّـرَ** عند مسـلم . قلـت ـ أي القاري : وقـد تقدّم التغاير بينهما ، والحمل على التأسيس أولى . **أُذَكِّرُكُمُ اللهَ فِي أَهْلِ بَيْتِي** كـرر الجملـة لإفـادة المبالغـة ، ولا يبعـد أن يكـون أراد بأحدهما آله وبالأخرى أزواجه لما سبق من أن أهل البيت يطلق عليهما . اهـ .

أمّا الزكاة فلا تُدفع لبني هاشـم إجماعـاً ، ولا لبني المطلب عند الشافعي ، ولا لمواليهم ، كثوبان مولى رسول الله ﷺ ـ يأتي حديثه في بـاب زوائـد القَطيعي على فضائل الصحابة إن شـاء الله ـ وكسلمان الفـارسي الّـذي أعتقـه رسـول الله ﷺ فصار مـولاه ـ ويـأتي حديثه المشـهور في باب تفسير البغوي إن شـاء الله ـ وأمّ أيمن بركة الحَبَشية مولاة رسـول الله ﷺ وحاضنته ، ورثها من أبيـه ثم أعتقها لمّا تزوّج بخديجـة وكانت من المهاجرات الأُول ، قال عنهـا ﷺ : **مَنْ سَرَّهُ أَنْ يَتَـزَوَّجَ امْـرَأَةً مِـنْ أَهْـلِ الجَنَّـةِ ، فَلْيَتَـزَوَّجْ أُمَّ أَيْمَنَ** ، رواه ابن سـعد مرسـلاً . فتزوجهـا زيـد فولـدت له أسـامة رضي الله تعـالى عنهم . وروى بإسـناد واه عن شيخ من بني سـعد بن بكر قال : كَانَ رَسُولُ اللهِ ﷺ يَقُـولُ لِأُمِّ أَيْمَـنَ : **يَا أُمَّهْ !** وَكَانَ إِذَا نَظَـرَ إِلَيْهَا قَالَ : **هَذِهِ بَقِيَّةُ أَهْـلِ بَيْتِي** . وحكى ابن عبد البر الإجماع بتحريم الزكاة على زوجاته ﷺ كما في (أنموذج اللبيب) للسيوطي .

قد أجاز بعض العلماء إعطاءهم من مال الزكاة عوضاً عن الخُمُس إذا ضاع حقّه، كما روى الطبري في اختلاف الفقهاء والطحاوي في شرح معاني الآثار عن الإمام أبي حنيفة إذا حُرِموا سهمَ ذوي القربى لأنه محل حاجة وضرورة. قال السخاوي في كتاب استجلاب ارتقاء الغُرَف: وهذا أيضا محكيٌّ عن الأبهري من المالكية، بل هو وجه لبعض الشافعية. قال محققه: فقد قال به أبو سعيد الإصطخري منهم كما في المجموع شرح المهذب. اهـ. وإلّا، فالنصوص صريحة بأن الزكاة لا تحل لأهل البيت وقد سماها الرسول ﷺ **(غُسالة الأيدي)** و **(أوساخ الناس)**. قال السيوطي في الخصائص الكبرى: قال العلماء: لمّا كانت الصدقة أوساخ الناس، نزّه منصبه الشريف عن ذلك وأنجز الى آله بسببه. وأيضاً فالصدقة تُعطَى على سبيل الترحُّم المبني على ذلّ الآخذ، فأُبدلوا عنها بالغنيمة، المأخوذة بطريق العز والشرف المنبئ عن عز الآخذ وذل المأخوذ منه. وقد اختلف علماء السلف هل شاركه في ذلك الأنبياء أم اختص به دونهم؟ فقال بالأول الحسن البصري، وبالثاني سفيان بن عيينة. ثم الزكاة وصدقة التطوع بالنسبة إليه ﷺ سواء، **وأما آله فمذهبنا أنه لا يحرم عليهم سوى الزكاة، وأما صدقة التطوع، فتحلّ لهم في الأصح**.

اهـ . من الخصائص الكبرى . وبجواز أخذهم صدقة التطوع قال الحنابلة كما في المغني والإنصاف ، وأكثر الحنفية كما في أحكام القرآن للجصّاص .

❑ ❑ ❑

٨

صحيح البخاري

(١٩٤-٢٥٦)

> النَّاسُ تَبَعٌ لِقُرَيْشٍ فِي هَذَا الشَّأْنِ . مُسْلِمُهُمْ تَبَعٌ لِمُسْلِمِهِمْ . وَكَافِرُهُمْ تَبَعٌ لِكَافِرِهِمْ . وَالنَّاسُ مَعَادِنُ ، خِيَارُهُمْ فِي الجَاهِلِيَّةِ خِيَارُهُمْ فِي الإِسْلَامِ إِذَا فَقُهُوا . تَجِدُونَ مِنْ خَيْرِ النَّاسِ أَشَدَّ النَّاسِ كَرَاهِيَةً لِهَذَا الشَّأْنِ حَتَّى يَقَعَ فِيهِ .

حدّثني الأستاذ المحقِّق **السيد بسّام الحمزاوي** بن عبد الكريم بن محمد حسين بن عبد الكريم بن محمد سليم بن محمد نسيب بن حمزة الحمزاوي الشافعي الحسيني في منزله بكَفَرسُوسَة وأخبرني صاحب المؤلفات في علوم الحديث الدكتور **محمد أبو الليث بن الحاج شمس الدين الخيرآبادي** بقراءتي عليه لبعض الكتاب وسماعاً منه لبعض ، الأول بسماعه على الشيخ عبد الرشيد النُعماني ، والثاني بسماعه على شيخ الحديث الشيخ السيد فخر الدين بن أحمد الحسيني الأجميري المرادآبادي (١٣٠٧-١٣٩٢) ، كلاهما بسماعهما على المحدث شيخ الهند محمود حسن الديوبندي العثماني (١٢٦٨-١٣٣٩) ، عن الشيخ المحدث

عبد الغني الدهلوي ، عن الشيخ محمد إسحاق الدهلوي ، عن شاه عبد العزيز بن أحمد بن عبد الرحيم الدهلوي ، أخبرنا والدي الشاه ولي الله الدهلوي ، أخبرنا أبو طاهر محمد عبد السميع بن إبراهيم الكوراني ، أخبرنا أبو الأسرار حسن بن علي العجيمي ، أخبرنا أبو مهدي عيسى بن محمد الثعالبي الجعفري (ت ١٠٨٠) ، أخبرنا أبو العزائم سلطان بن أحمد بن سلامة المَزَّاحِي ، أخبرنا أحمد بن خليل بن إبراهيم السبكي ، أخبرنا النجم محمد بن أحمد بن علي الغَيطي السكندري ، أخبرنا شيخ الإسلام القاضي زكريا بن محمد الأنصاري ، أخبرنا إبراهيم بن صدقة الحنبلي ، أخبرنا أبو النجم عبد الرحيم بن عبد الوهاب بن عبد الكريم بن رَزين الحَمَوي ، أخبرنا مسند الدنيا المعمَّر الشهير بابن الشِّحْنَة الشيخ أحمد بن أبي طالب الحجّار الدمشقي الحنفي ، أخبرنا سراج الدين أبو عبد الله الحسين بن المبارك الرَّبَعي الزَّبيدي البغدادي ، أخبرنا أبو الوقت عبد الأول بن عيسى السِّجْزي الهَرَوي ، أخبرنا شيخ الإسلام أبو الحسن عبد الرحمن بن محمد بن مظفر الداوُدي البُوشَنْجي ، أخبرنا شيخ الإسلام أبو محمد عبد الله بن أحمد بن حَمُّويَه السَّرخسي ، أخبرنا شيخ الإسلام أبو عبد الله محمد بن يوسف بن مطر الفَرِبْري ، أخبرنا

أمير المؤمنين في الحديث شيخ الإسلام **أبو عبد الله محمد بن إسماعيل البُخاري**، قال : حَدَّثَنا قُتَيْبَةُ بْنُ سَعِيدٍ ، حَدَّثَنا الْمُغِيرَةُ ، عَنْ أَبِي الزِّنَادِ ، عَنْ الأَعْرَجِ ، عن أبي هريرة ـ رضي الله عنه ـ أَنَّ النَّبِيَّ ﷺ قَالَ : **النَّاسُ تَبَعٌ لِقُرَيْشٍ فِي هَذَا الشَّأْنِ . مُسْلِمُهُمْ تَبَعٌ لِمُسْلِمِهِمْ . وَكَافِرُهُمْ تَبَعٌ لِكَافِرِهِمْ . وَالنَّاسُ مَعَادِنُ ، خِيَارُهُمْ فِي الْجَاهِلِيَّةِ خِيَارُهُمْ فِي الْإِسْلَامِ إِذَا فَقُهُوا . تَجِدُونَ مِنْ خَيْرِ النَّاسِ أَشَدَّ النَّاسِ كَرَاهِيَةً لِهَذَا الشَّأْنِ حَتَّى يَقَعَ فِيهِ .**

رواه الشيخان . قال السيد بسّام : قال الحافظ : بدأ البخاري صحيحه بالرواية عن الحميدي الهاشمي لحديث **قدِّموا قريشاً ولا تَقَدَّموها** الذي مرّ ذكره ، وهذا نحوه . قال ابن الملقن في التوضيح : قوله : **أَشَدَّهُمْ لَهُ كَرَاهِيَةً** يعني : الإمارة ، مَن نالها من غير مسألة أُعين عليها ، ومن نالها عن مسألة وُكِل إلى نفسه . والكراهة بسبب علمه بصعوبة العدل فيها والمطالبة في الأخرى . وقال الخطابي : معناه : إذا وقعوا فيها لم يجُز أن يكرهوها ؛ لأنهم إذا أقاموا فيها كارهين ضيّعوها . اهـ . وقال النووي : قال القاضي عياض : يحتمل أن المراد به : الإسلام ، كما كان من عمر بن الخطاب وخالد بن الوليد وعمرو بن العاص وعكرمة بن أبي جهل وسهيل بن عمرو وغيره

من مَسْلَمَةِ الفتح وغيرهم ممن كان يكره الإسلام كراهية شديدة ، فلمّا دخـل فيـه أخلـص وأحبّه وجاهد فيه حقّ جهاده . اه . (فوائد) قال السيد بسّام : أفضل صيغ الصلاة على النبي ﷺ صيغتان : الأولى الصـلاة الإبراهيمية المعروفة ، والثانيـة : **اللهُمَّ صَلِّ عَلَى مُحَمَّدٍ وَعَلَى أَزْوَاجِهِ وَذُرِّيَّتِهِ وَآلِهِ كَمَا صَلَّيْتَ عَلَى إِبْرَاهِيمَ فِي العَالَمِينَ ، إِنَّكَ حَمِيدٌ ، مَجِيدٌ ، وَبَارِكْ عَلَى مُحَمَّدٍ وَعَلَى أَزْوَاجِهِ وَذُرِّيَّتِهِ وَآلِهِ كَمَا بَارَكْتَ عَلَى إِبْرَاهِيمَ فِي العَالَمِينَ ، إِنَّكَ حَمِيدٌ ، مَجِيدٌ** . وقال أغلب شراح الحديث وشراح الصحيحين : كان ﷺ يواظب على الصيغة الثانية في صلاته . وجـاء في أذكار الإمـام النـووي رحمـه الله : الأفضـل أن يقـول : **اللَّهُمَّ صَلِّ على مُحَمَّدٍ عَبْدِكَ وَرَسُولِكَ النَّبِيِّ الأُمِّيِّ وَعَلَى آلِ مُحَمَّدٍ وَأَزْوَاجِهِ وَذُرِّيَّتِهِ ، كَمَا صَلَّيْتَ على إِبْرَاهِيمَ وَعلى آلِ إِبْرَاهِيمَ ، وَبَارِكْ على مُحَمَّدٍ النَّبِيِّ الأُمِّيِّ وَعَلَى آلِ مُحَمَّدٍ وَأَزْوَاجِهِ وَذُرِّيَّتِهِ ، كَمَا بَارَكْتَ على إِبْرَاهِيمَ وَعَلَى آلِ إِبْرَاهِيمَ فِي العَالَمِينَ إِنَّكَ حَمِيدٌ مَجِيدٌ** . لأنها أجمع الصيغ لما نقلته الروايـات . قـال : وروينا هـذه الكيفية في صحيح البخاري ومسـلم عن كعب بن عُجْرَة عـن رسول الله ﷺ إلا بعضها ، فهو صحيـح مـن روايـة غير كعب . اه . وبها ختم كتابه العظيم رياض الصالحين . وفي الشفا للقاضي عياض : كان الحسن البصري يقول :

مـن أراد أن يـشرب بالـكأس الأوفى من حوض المصطفـى فليقل : اللهـم صلِّ على محمد وعلى آله وأصحابـه وأولاده وأزواجه وذريته وأهـل بيته وأصهاره وأنصاره وأشـياعه ومحبيه وأمته ، وعلينا معهم أجمعين ، يا أرحم الراحمين .

❑ ❑ ❑

٩

صحيح مسلم

(٢٠٦-٢٦١)

رَأَيْتُ رَسُولَ اللهِ ﷺ وَاضِعًا الحَسَنَ بْنَ عَلِيٍّ عَلَى عَاتِقِهِ وَهُوَ يَقُولُ : اللَّهُمَّ إِنِّي أُحِبُّهُ فَأَحِبَّهُ

أخبرني الفقيه الجواد المصنّف الزاهد المحدث **الدكتور ساجد الرحمن بن إشفاق الرحمن البكري الصدّيقي** الكاندهلوي ثم السندي الحنفي (٧ ذو الحجة ١٣٦٢-٤ صفر ١٤٣٣) بقراءتي عليه لجميع صحيح مسلم في داره بسلطنة بروناي دار السلام جبرها الله ، وأنبأني **الحبيب أحمد مشهور بن طه الحداد الحسيني** (١٣٢٥-١٤١٦) عالياً - رحمهما الله - قال الأوّل : أخبرني المحدّث الفقيه الشيخ ظَفَر أحمد العثماني التهانوي والعلامة المحدّث الشيخ محمد يوسف البَنُوري قراءة عليهما ، الأول قراءة على الشيخ محمد شَبِّير العثماني التهانوي ، قراءة على العلامة الجهبذ أَنْوَر شاه بن معظَّم شاه الكشميري ، والثاني عن أَنْوَر شاه الكشميري بلا واسطة ، قال : قرأت على

المحدّث الشيخ محمد إسحاق الكشميري المدني ، عن خير الدين نعمان بن محمود الآلوسي (ت ١٣١٧) عن والده السيد أبي الثناء شهاب الدين محمود بن عبد الله الآلوسي الحسيني (ت ١٢٧٠) العراقي صاحب التفسير ، عن عبد اللطيف بن علي فتح الله البيروتي (ت ١٢٥٠ ؟ وأجاز لأهل عصره) ، عن مسند الشام شيخ الحديث وإمام الشافعية في جامع بني أميّة شهاب الدين أحمد بن عبيد الله بن عسكر العطار ، أنبأني الشيخ محمد بن سليمان الكردي المدني ، قال : عن الإمام فقيه العصر محمد سعيد الشافعي الشهير بسنبل ، عن محدث مكة الشهاب النخلي ، بسماعه لغالب صحيح مسلم على الشمس البابلي ، والإجازة لسائره ، عن أبي النَّجَا سالم بن محمد السنهوري ، بقراءته على النجم محمد الغَيْطي ، بسماعه لجميعه على شيخ الإسلام زكريا الأنصاري ، قال : أخبرني الحافظ المفيد الزين أبي النَّعِيم رضوان بن محمد العَقبي ثم القاهري (مستملي الحافظ ابن حجر) بقراءتي ، أخبرنا الشرف أبو طاهر محمد بن محمد بن عبد اللطيف الكويك الرَبَعي التكريتي الأصل ثم الاسكندري نزيل القاهرة سماعاً ، أنبأنا أبو محمد عبد الرحمن بن محمد بن عبد الحميد بن عبد الهادي المقدسي ثم الصالحي قدم القاهرة ، أنبأنا أبو العباس

أحمد بن عبد الدائم بن نِعْمَة النابلسي سماعاً عليه ، أنبأنا أبو عبد الله محمد بن علي بن صدقة الحرَّاني سماعاً عليه ، أنبأنا فقيه الحرم أبو عبد الله محمد بن الفضل بن أحمد الصاعدي الفُراوي ؛ (ح) وقال الحبيب أحمد مشهور : عن الحبيب أحمد بن حسن العطاس عالياً ، عن محمد عابد السندي ، عن مسند اليمن الحافظ الوجيه عبد الرحمن بن سليمان بن يحيى ، عن والده مفتي زبيد ، عن جدّه الإمام يحيى بن عمر مقبول الأهدل ، عن أبي بكر بن علي الأهدل ، عن عمّه يوسف بن محمد البطّاح الأهدل ، عن محدث اليمن السيد الطاهر بن حسين الأهدل ، عن حافظ اليمن ومؤرخها ومحيي علوم الأثر بها الإمام المحقق الفهامة أبي الضيا وجيه الدين عبد الرحمن بن علي بن محمد بن عمر المعروف بابن الدِّيْبَع ـ بكسر الدال المهملة ، ومعناه الأبيض بِلُغَة النُّوبة ـ الشيباني العبدري الزبيدي الشافعي الأثري (٨٦٦-٩٤٤) صاحب المولد الشهير ، عن محدث الديار اليمنية زين الدين أبي العباس أحمد بن أحمد بن عبد اللطيف الشَّرْجِي الزَّبِيدِي التَّعِزّي (ت ٨٩٣) صاحب التجريد الصريح ، عن شمس الدين محمد ابن محمد بن محمد الجزري الدمشقي ، قال : أنا أبو العباس أحمد بن عبد الكريم بن حسين الصوفي سماعاً ، قال : أنبأتنا

الشيخة الصالحة أم محمد زينب بنت عمر الكندي سماعاً ، قالت : أخبرني به مسند خراسان المعمّر أبو الحسن المؤيد بن محمد بن علي الطوسي ، عن الفُراوي ، أنبأنا أبو الحسين عبد الغافر بن محمد الفارسي ، أنبأنا أبو أحمد محمد بن عيسى بن عمرويه الجُلُودي ، أنبأنا إبراهيم بن محمد بن سفيان ، أنبأنا **مسلم بن الحجّاج بن مسلم القشيري النيسابوري** سماعاً عليه : حَدَّثَنَا مُحَمَّدُ بْنُ بَشَّارٍ وَأَبُو بَكْرِ بْنُ نَافِعٍ ، قَالَ ابْنُ نَافِعٍ : حَدَّثَنَا غُنْدَرٌ ، حَدَّثَنَا شُعْبَةُ ، عَنْ عَدِيٍّ - وَهُوَ ابْنُ ثَابِتٍ - عَنِ الْبَرَاءِ ، قَالَ : **رَأَيْتُ رَسُولَ اللهِ ﷺ وَاضِعًا الْحَسَنَ بْنَ عَلِيٍّ عَلَى عَاتِقِهِ وَهُوَ يَقُولُ : اللَّهُمَّ إِنِّي أُحِبُّهُ فَأَحِبَّهُ !**

رواه الترمذي وقال : حسن صحيح . والطبراني بزيادة **وَأَحِبَّ مَنْ أَحَبَّهُ** . ورواه مسلم وأحمد والحميدي عن أبي هريرة بلفظ **فَأَحِبَّهُ وَأَحْبِبْ مَنْ يُحِبُّهُ** . وفي الباب عن عائشة رواه الطبراني في الكبير وابن عساكر ، وعن سعيد بن زيد بن نفيل قال الهيثمي رواه الطبراني ورجاله رجال الصحيح غير يزيد بن يُحَنَّس وهو ثقة .

❑ ❑ ❑

١٠

سنن أبي داود

(٢٠٢-٢٧٥)

لَا تَذْهَبُ أَوْ لَا تَنْقَضِي الدُّنْيَا حَتَّى يَمْلِكَ الْعَرَبَ رَجُلٌ مِنْ أَهْلِ بَيْتِي يُوَاطِئُ اسْمُهُ اسْمِي

أنبأنا الشقيقان **الحبيب عمر والحبيب عطاس ابنا العلامة الشهيد الحبيب محمد بن سالم بن حفيظ** بن الشيخ أبي بكر ، عن والدهما ، عن شيخه العلامة المسند شمس الدين أبي عبد الله محمد بن سالم بن علوي السَّري با هارون جمل الليل الحسيني التريمي ، عن المسند الشمس محمد بن ناصر الحازمي الأثري عالياً ، عن مسند اليمن السيد الوجيه عبد الرحمن بن سليمان بن يحيى بن عمر مقبول الأهدل بسنده المارّ آنفاً إلى ابن الدِّيْبَع ـ وقد تعجّب السيد عبد الحي الكتاني لحسن هذا الإسناد في فهرسه ـ عن شيخه الحافظ شمس الدين أبي الخير محمد بن عبد الرحمن السخاوي ، عن شيخه الحافظ ابن حجر ، قال في المعجم المفهرس : أخبرني أبو علي محمد بن أحمد بن علي بن

عبد العزيز الفاضلي البزاز المَهْدَوِي المعروف بابن المُطَرِّز بقراءتي عليه لجميعه ، أنبأنا أبو المحاسن يوسف بن عمر بن حسين الخُتَني سماعاً عليه في سنة ٧٢٤ ، أنبأنا الحافظ زكي الدين أبو محمد عبد العظيم بن عبد القوي بن عبد الكريم المنذري وأبو الفضل محمد بن محمد بن محمد البكري ، قالا : أنبأنا أبو حفص عمر بن محمد بن معمر بن طبرزذ البغدادي سماعاً عليه بدمشق ، أنبأنا الشيخان أبو البدر إبراهيم بن محمد بن منصور الكرخي وأبو الفتح مفلح بن أحمد الدومي ، قالا : أنبأنا الحافظ أبو بكر أحمد بن علي بن ثابت الخطيب البغدادي ، أنبأنا أبو عمر القاسم بن جعفر بن عبد الواحد الهاشمي ، أنبأنا أبو علي محمد بن أحمد بن عمرو اللؤلؤي ، أنبأنا **أبو داود سليمان بن الأشعث بن إسحاق بن بشر بن شداد بن عمرو بن عامر الأزدي السجستاني** قال : حَدَّثَنَا مُسَدَّدٌ أَنَّ عُمَرَ بْنَ عُبَيْدٍ حَدَّثَهُمْ . (ح) وحَدَّثَنَا مُحَمَّدُ بْنُ الْعَلاَءِ ، حَدَّثَنَا أَبُو بَكْرٍ يَعْنِي ابْنَ عَيَّاشٍ . (ح) وحَدَّثَنَا مُسَدَّدٌ حَدَّثَنَا يَحْيَى عَنْ سُفْيَانَ . (ح) وحَدَّثَنَا أَحْمَدُ بْنُ إِبْرَاهِيمَ ، حَدَّثَنَا عُبَيْدُ اللهِ بْنُ مُوسَى ، أَخْبَرَنَا زَائِدَةُ . (ح) وحَدَّثَنَا أَحْمَدُ بْنُ إِبْرَاهِيمَ ، حَدَّثَنِي عُبَيْدُ اللهِ ابْنُ مُوسَى ، عَنْ فِطْرٍ - المَعْنَى وَاحِدٌ - كُلُّهُمْ عَنْ عَاصِمٍ ، عَنْ زِرٍّ ، عَنْ عَبْدِ اللهِ ، عَنْ

النَّبِيِّ ﷺ قَالَ: **لَوْ لَمْ يَبْقَ مِنَ الدُّنْيَا إِلَّا يَوْمٌ** - قَالَ زَائِدَةُ فِي حَدِيثِهِ: **لَطَوَّلَ اللهُ ذَلِكَ الْيَوْمَ**، ثُمَّ اتَّفَقُوا - **حَتَّى يَبْعَثَ فِيهِ رَجُلًا مِنِّي أَوْ مِنْ أَهْلِ بَيْتِي يُوَاطِئُ اسْمُهُ اسْمِي وَاسْمُ أَبِيهِ اسْمَ أَبِي**. زَادَ فِي حَدِيثِ فِطْرٍ: **يَمْلَأُ الْأَرْضَ قِسْطًا وَعَدْلًا كَمَا مُلِئَتْ ظُلْمًا وَجَوْرًا**. وَقَالَ فِي حَدِيثِ سُفْيَانَ: **لَا تَذْهَبُ أَوْ لَا تَنْقَضِي الدُّنْيَا حَتَّى يَمْلِكَ الْعَرَبَ رَجُلٌ مِنْ أَهْلِ بَيْتِي يُوَاطِئُ اسْمُهُ اسْمِي**.

رواه أحمد والترمذي وابن حبان والحاكم والطبراني وغيرهم بعضهم باختصار، قال الترمذي: وفي الباب عن علي وأبي سعيد وأم سلمة وأبي هريرة وهٰذا حديث حسن صحيح. وعدّه الحافظ محمد بن جعفر الكتاني من المتواتر في نظم المتناثر إذ بلغ عدد الرواة في خروج المهدي عشرين صحابياً. قال: قد نقل غير واحد عن الحافظ السخاوي أنها متواترة، والسخاوي ذكر ذلك في فتح المغيث ونقله عن الآبُرِّي (ت ٣٦٣) في مغاني الوفا بمعاني الإكتفا: قال الشيخ أبو الحسن الآبُرِّي: قد تواترت الأخبار واستفاضت بكثرة رواتها عن المصطفى ﷺ بمجيء المهدي وأنه سيملك سبع سنين وأنه يملأ الأرض عدلاً اهـ. قال الكتاني: وفي تأليف للحافظ أبي العلاء إدريس بن محمد بن إدريس الحسيني العراقي الفاسي (١١٢٠-١١٨٤)

في المهـدي أن أحاديثـه متواترة أو كادت ، قـال : وجزم بالأول غير واحد من الحفاظ النقاد . قلت : هذا التأليف محفوظ بمؤسسة الملك عبد العزيز بالدار البيضاء ؛ لكنه غير تام . ثم قال الكتاني : وفي شرح عقيدة الشيخ محمد بن أحمد السَّـفَّاريني الحنبلي مـا نصُّه : قد كثرت بخروجه الروايات حتى بلغت حد التواتر المعنوي وشـاع ذلك بين علـماء السـنة حتـى عُدّ مـن معتقداتهـم . وقـد رُوي عمّـن ذُكر مِن الصحابـة وغيرِ مَـن ذُكر منهم بروايـات متعددة وعـن التابعين مِن بعدهـم مما يفيـد مجموعُه العلـمَ القطعي ، فالإيمان بخـروج المهدي واجـب كـما هو مقـرر عند أهل العلـم ومدوَّن في عقائد أهل السـنة والجماعة . اهـ .

قلت : فيه أن اسم المهدي محمّد بن عبد الله وليس اسمه محمد بن الحسـن العسـكري كما زعمت فرقة الشـيعة . ثم العسكري حسيني والمهدي حَسَـني كما رواه أيضاً في سـننه أبو داود : قال عليّ رضي الله عنـه ونظر إلى ابنه الحسـن ، فقال : **إنّ ابْنِي هَذَا سَـيّدٌ كَمَا سَـمّاهُ النّبِيُّ ﷺ ، وَسَـيَخْرُجُ مِنْ صُلْبِهِ رَجُلٌ يُسَـمّى بِاسْـمِ نَبِيّكُم ﷺ يُشْـبِهُهُ فِي الخُلُـقِ وَلاَ يُشْـبِهُهُ فِي الخَلْقِ . ثُمّ ذَكَرَ قِصّةَ يَمْـلأُ الأَرْضَ عَدْلاً** . قال المـلا علي القاري في المرقاة : هذا الحديث دليل صريح على ما قدّمناه

من أنّ المهدي من أولاد الحسن ويكون له انتساب من جهة الأُم إلى الحسين ، جمعاً بين الأدلّة . وبه يبطل قول الشيعة : إن المهدي هو محمّد بن الحسن العسكري القائم المنتظر ، فإنّه حسيني بالإتّفاق . اهـ . وفي إثبات التواتر المعنوي عند أهل معرفة السنن والآثار رد على من زرع الشك في حقيقة المهدي وخروجه آخر الزمان ، كقولهم : صحيحه غير صريح وصريحه ضعيف ؛ فهذا غير صحيح ، لأن وجود التواتر يغني عن النظر في الأسانيد ما لم يكن موضوعاً . والله الموفّق .

❑ ❑ ❑

١١

سنن ابن ماجه

(٢٠٩-٢٧٣)

مَا بَالُ أَقْوَامٍ يَتَحَدَّثُونَ ، فَإِذَا رَأَوا الرَّجُلَ مِنْ أَهْلِ بَيْتِي قَطَعُوا حَدِيثَهُمْ ؟ وَاللهِ لاَ يَدْخُلُ قَلْبَ رَجُلٍ الإِيمَانُ حَتَّى يُحِبَّهُمْ لله وَلِقَرَابَتِهِمْ مِنِّي !

أخبرني إمام جامع با علوي بسنغافورة **الحبيب حسن بن محمد بن سالم بن أحمد بن حسن بن عبد الله العطاس** (ولد ١٣٧١/ ١٩٥١) بقراءتي عليه وأنبأني **الشيخ زكريا باغريب السنغافوري** ابن عبد الله بن أحمد بن عبد الله بن عمر بن آل الشيخ محمد النقيب باغريب الحضرمي التريمي (١٣٥٤-١٤٣٠/ ١٩٣٦-٢٠٠٩) رحمه الله ، الأوّل عن والده ، عن جدّه الحبيب سالم ، عن العارف النبراس الحبيب أحمد بن حسن العطاس ، والثاني عن العلّامة الفقيه المحدث الأديب الشيخ عمر بن عبد الله بن أحمد بن عبد الله بن أبي بكر بن سالم الخطيب الأنصاري الخزرجي الحضرمي التريمي ثم السنغافوري الشافعي (١٣٢٦- ١٤١٨) ـ سليل عبّاد بن بشر الأوسي الأنصاري

الحضرمي رضي الله عنه ـ عن عمّه العلامة الشيخ أبي بكر بن أحمد بن عبد الله الخطيب ، عن الحبيب أحمد بن حسن العطاس ، عن أبي بكر وصالح ابني عبد الله العطاس ، عن الوجيه عبد الرحمن الأهدل ، عن الحافظ محمد مرتضى الزبيدي ، عن محدث المدينة أبي الحسن السندي الصغير هو محمد بن صادق السندي (١١٢٥-١١٨٧) ، عن محدث الحجاز محمد حياة السندي وسالم بن عبد الله البصري ، كلاهما عن والد الأخير المسند عبد الله بن سالم البصري ، عن شيخه محمد بن علاء الدين البابلي ، عن البرهان إبراهيم بن إبراهيم بن حسن اللَّقَاني وعلي بن إبراهيم الحلبي ، كلاهما عن الشمس محمد بن أحمد الرملي ، عن شيخ الإسلام زكريا ، عن الحافظ ابن حجر ، قراءة على أبي العباس أحمد بن عمر بن علي بن عبد الصمد بن أبي البدر البغدادي اللؤلؤي نزيل القاهرة ، أنبأنا الحافظ أبو الحجاج يوسف بن الزكي عبد الرحمن المزي قراءة عليه وأنا أسمع لجميعه ، أنبأنا به شيخ الإسلام الشمس عبد الرحمن بن أبي عمر بن قدامة المقدسي سماعاً ، أنبأنا الإمام أبو محمد موفق الدين عبد الله بن أحمد ابن قدامة سماعاً ، أنبأنا أبو زرعة طاهر بن أبي الفضل المقدسي سماعا عليه لجميعه ، أنبأنا أبو منصور محمد بن الحسين بن أحمد بن الهيثم المُقَوِّمي القزويني

سماعاً لجميعه ، أنبأنا أبو طلحة القاسم بن أبي المنذر الخطيب ، أنبأنا أبو الحسن علي بن إبراهيم بن سلمة بن بحر القطان ، أنبأنا **أبو عبد الله محمد بن يزيد القزويني المعروف بابن ماجه** ، قال : حَدَّثَنَا مُحَمَّدُ بْنُ طَرِيفٍ ، حَدَّثَنَا مُحَمَّدُ بْنُ فُضَيْلٍ ، حَدَّثَنَا الْأَعْمَشُ ، عَنْ أَبِي سَبْرَةَ النَّخَعِيِّ ، عَنْ مُحَمَّدِ بْنِ كَعْبٍ الْقُرَظِيِّ ، عَنِ الْعَبَّاسِ بْنِ عَبْدِ الْمُطَّلِبِ ، قَالَ : كُنَّا نَلْقَى النَّفَرَ مِنْ قُرَيْشٍ وَهُمْ يَتَحَدَّثُونَ ، فَيَقْطَعُونَ حَدِيثَهُمْ ، فَذَكَرْنَا ذَلِكَ لِلنَّبِيِّ ﷺ فَقَالَ : **مَا بَالُ أَقْوَامٍ يَتَحَدَّثُونَ ، فَإِذَا رَأَوا الرَّجُلَ مِنْ أَهْلِ بَيْتِي قَطَعُوا حَدِيثَهُمْ ؟ وَاللهِ لَا يَدْخُلُ قَلْبَ رَجُلٍ الْإِيمَانُ حَتَّى يُحِبَّهُمْ للهِ وَلِقَرَابَتِهِمْ مِنِّي !**

حديث حسن ، روى مثله الترمذي وأحمد والنسائي في الكبرى والفضائل والبغوي في المصابيح وابن نصر المروزي في السنة كما بيّنه السخاوي في كتابه استجلاب ارتقاء الغُرَف بِحُبِّ أقرباء الرسول ﷺ وذوي الشرف . وفي الباب عن ابن عباس مرفوعاً : **أَيُّهَا النَّاسُ ، أَيُّ أَهْلِ الْأَرْضِ أَكْرَمُ عَلَى اللهِ ؟ قَالَ : قُلْنَا : أَنْتَ . قَالَ : فَإِنَّ الْعَبَّاسَ مِنِّي وَأَنَا مِنْهُ . لَا تُؤْذُوا الْعَبَّاسَ فَتُؤْذُونِي . وَقَالَ : مَنْ سَبَّ الْعَبَّاسَ فَقَدْ سَبَّنِي** . رواه عبد الله بن أحمد في زوائد فضائل الصحابة ورواه ابن عساكر عنه وعن ابن مسعود . (لطائف وفوائد) ولد الشيخ زكريا في

مسجد باغريب المعروف اليوم بمسجد خديجة في سنغافورة ، ووالده الشيخ عبد الله (١٣٠٠-١٣٨٨) كان ملقَّباً بالمعلِّم ، رتَّب دعاء إيصال الأجور لأهل القبور وهو مشهور في بلاد شرق جنوب آسيا . وأُخبرت أن الشيخ عمر الخطيب كان يتواضع للشيخ زكريّا ويقبّل يده تكريماً لوالده الذي كان أستاذ الشيخ عمر رحمهم الله تعالى . ويُروى عن جد الشيخ زكريا أنه حج مشياً خمس وثلاثين حِجّة ، وجَدُّه الرابع منعوت بصاحب الكَنْزيّة لغزارة علومه ، قُطِّب بالصدّيقية الكبرى وتخرّج عليه ألف حافظ للقرآن الكريم ، منهم القطب عبد الله الحداد رضي الله عنهم .

❑ ❑ ❑

١٢
أخبار مكة في قديم الدهر وحديثه للفاكهي
(٢١٧ ؟ - ٢٨٠ ؟)

> يَا بَنِي عَبْدِ المُطَّلِبِ! إنِّي سَأَلْتُ اللهَ عَزَّ وَجَلَّ لَكُمْ ثَلَاثاً : أَنْ يُثَبِّتَ قَائِمَكُمْ ، وَأَنْ يَهْدِيَ ضَالَّكُمْ ، وَأَنْ يُعَلِّمَ جَاهِلَكُمْ ، وَسَأَلْتُهُ أَنْ يَجْعَلَكُمْ جُوداً نُجُداً رُحَمَاءَ ، وَلَوْ أَنَّ رَجُلاً صَفَّنَ بَيْنَ الرُّكْنِ وَالمَقَامِ وَصَلَّى وَصَامَ ثُمَّ لَقِيَ اللهَ تَعَالَى وَهُوَ مُبْغِضٌ لِأَهْلِ بَيْتِ مُحَمَّدٍ ﷺ : دَخَلَ النَّارَ .

حدثني السيد الفاضل الطبيب عبد الله بن السيد محمد مكي الكتاني الصوفي في عيادته بدمشق المحروسة ، عن والده المسند محمد مكي بن محمد بن جعفر الكتاني الدمشقي (ت ١٣٩٣) ، عن محدّث الحجاز الشريف الشيخ فالح الظاهري (ت ١٣٢٨) ، عن الحافظ محمد بن علي السنوسي الخطابي (١٢٠٢-١٢٧٦) ، بالسند العالي المذكور في باب الموطأ إلى الحافظ ابن حجر ، قال : أخبرنا به أبو علي الفاضلي إذناً مشافهة ، عن علي بن عمر الخلّاطي ، عن عبد الرحمن بن مكي ، عن جده لأمه الحافظ أبي طاهر السِّلَفِي ، عن أبي ياسر محمد بن عبد العزيز البغدادي (ت ٤٩٥) ، عن مسند العراق المعمّر أبي القاسم

عبد الملك بـن محمد بن عبد الله بن بِشْران الأُمـوي مولاهم القَنْدي البغـدادي الواعـظ (٣٣٩-٤٣٠) ، عن مسـند مكـة ومحدّثها أبي محمد عبد الله بن محمد الفاكهي المكي (ت ٣٥٣) بها ، عن أبيه مؤلف الكتاب **أبي العبـاس محمد بـن إسـحاق بن العبـاس الفاكهي المكـي** ، قال : حدثنـا محمد بـن إسـماعيل البخاري ، ثنـا إسـماعيل بن أبي أويس ، حدثنـي أبي : هـو عبد الله بـن عبد الله بـن أويـس الأصبحـي ، عن حُميد بن قيس المكي مولى بني أسـد بن عبد العزى ، عن عطاء بن أبي رباح وغـيره مـن أصحاب ابـن عباس ، عـن ابن عبـاس رضي الله عنهـما ، عـن النبي ﷺ قال : **يَا بَنِي عَبْدِ المُطَّلِبِ ! إِنِّي سَـأَلْتُ اللهَ عَزَّ وَجَـلَّ لَكُمْ ثَلَاثاً : أَنْ يُثَبِّتَ قَائِمَكُـمْ ، وَأَنْ يَهْدِيَ ضَالَّكُمْ ، وَأَنْ يُعَلِّمَ جَاهِلَكُـمْ ، وَسَـأَلْتُهُ أَنْ يَجْعَلَكُـمْ جُوداً نُجُـداً رُحَمَاءَ ، وَلَـوْ أَنَّ رَجُلاً صَفِـنَ بَيْنَ الرُّكْنِ وَالمَقَامِ وَصَلَّى وَصَامَ ثُمَّ لَقِيَ اللهَ تَعَالَى وَهُوَ مُبْغِضٌ لِأَهْلِ بَيْتِ مُحَمَّدٍ** ﷺ : **دَخَلَ النَّارَ** . وقال الشاعر يذكر الصُّفُون :

لَـزِمَ الصُّفُـونَ فَـمَا يَـزَالُ كَأَنَّـهُ

مِمَّـا يَقُـومُ عَـلَى الثَّـلَاثِ كَسِـيرَا

رواه الطـبراني في معجمه الكبير والفسـوي في المعرفة والتاريخ وابـن أبي عاصم في السـنّة وابن بشران في أماليـــه والحاكم وقال :

صحيح على شرط مسلم ولم يخرّجاه ، لكنّه من أفراد إسماعيل بن أبي أويس ، فهو مع كونه احتجّ به الشيخان ، لا يحتمل هو ولا أبوه الانفراد بمثل هذا الحديث عن حميد بن قيس ـ شيخ مَعْمَر ابن راشد وأبي حنيفة ومالك والسُّفْيَانَين ـ فلعلّه السبب الذي من أجله عدّه أبو حاتم منكراً في كتاب العلل ، ولم يروه الإمام الشافعي مع كونه حريصاً على الروايات المرفوعة في مناقب بني المطلب ولو بسند مبهَم أو منقطع . ومع ذلك لم يجتنب الإمام البخاري روايته ؛ والواقع يؤيّد صحّة معناه وتحقيق دعائه ﷺ ، كما أن الوعيد ثابت فيمن يبغض فاطمة وعليّاً وابنيهما كما في الباب الّذي بعده وباب معرفة الصحابة ، وكذا العبّاس كما في بابي سنن ابن ماجه ودلائل النبوّة للبيهقي وقد ورد عن أبي سعيد مرفوعاً : **لَا يُبْغِضُنَا ـ أَهْلَ الْبَيْتِ ـ أَحَدٌ إِلَّا أَدْخَلَهُ اللهُ النَّارَ** . رواه الحاكم وصحّحه . (الغريب) صَفِنٌ أي وَقَفَ صافّاً قدميه ، والقول الثاني أَن الصَّافِنَ من الخيل الذي قد قَلَب أَحدَ حوافره وقام على ثلاث قوائم ، يقال خيلٌ صُفُونٌ كقاعدٍ وقُعُودٍ . لسان . والكسيرة من الدوابّ : المنكسرة الرجل التي لا تقدر على المشي . نهاية . (الشرح) قال الدكتور عبد الله الكتاني حفظه الله : **قَائِمَكُمْ** أي رايتُهم عالية وبيوتهم معمورة ؛ **يُعَلِّمَ جَاهِلَكُمْ** أي

يعلّمهم من العلم اللَّدُنِّي ؛ **وَأَنْ يَهْدِيَ ضَالَّكُمْ** آية أهل البيت ؛ **جُوداً** كرماء ، والكَرَم عندهم فِطْري ؛ **نُجُداً** من النجدة وهي الشجاعة ، وهي الخدمة ، وكان السيّد الوالد دائماً في خدمة الناس . فهم كرماء ، شُجعان ، علماء ، وهي ثلاثة لا تفارق سليل أهل البيت ولو كان أمّيّاً ، كالسيد عبد العزيز الدّبّاغ ـ وهو أعلى نسب ـ مع الكتّانيّين ـ في بني إدريس ؛ **رُحَمَاءَ** من رحمة جدّهم الذي هو الرّحمة المُهداة ﷺ ، فرحمتهم وراثة ، ومن أمثالها تلبيسه عبد الله بن أبيّ قميصه ﷺ ، ولأن الرحمة الإلهية سبقت كل شيء . قال : وأوّل علامة الولي : احترامه لأهل البيت وأبناء النبي ﷺ ، وحبّهم وتقديسهم ، وإن كان منهم ، قال الشيخ عبد القادر السقّاف : الصلاة على الآل فرض على الآل . وقالوا عن السيّد مكّي : كان يحترمنا دون أن نشعر . قال : قال لي أحدهم : حاول أن تجلس خلف أبيك في المجلس . ففعلت ، فرأيته حاز كرسيّه بكرسيّي شيئاً فشيئاً . فعلمت احترام أبي لأهل البيت وإن كانوا من دمه . **مُبْغِضٌ لِأَهْلِ بَيْتِ مُحَمَّدٍ** ﷺ : **دَخَلَ النَّارَ** لأنّ بُغْض أهل البيت بغضٌ لسيّدنا محمّد ﷺ ، وهو كفر إجماعاً . ثم استمرار حبّ أهل البيت على مدى الأجيال : استمرارٌ لحبّه ﷺ . وهي معجزةٌ ظاهرة خالدة ملموسة له ﷺ ، خلافاً لحُبِّنا

لسائر الأنبياء عليهم السّلام . قال : وأهل البيت فتنةٌ لأهل الأرض الآن ، والعقوق لا يُلغِي الحقوق ـ كانوا صالحين أم لا ـ وهذه هي الفتنة . اهـ . (قلت) أنشدني الحافظ المقرئ المنشد النبيل الشيخ عبد الرحمن الحمّامي الميداني ـ حفظه الله ـ عن السيد الرَّوَّاس قال :

فَانْظُرْ تَرَ الطُّهْرَ الْمُكَرَّمَ جَدَّنَـــا
وَالْمُرْتَـضَى أَسَـدَ الرِّجَـالِ أَبَانَـا
هَلْ ثَمَّ مِنْ أَجْزَاءِ طَــهَ فِي الْوَرَى
شَيْءٌ يُـرَى نَاسُـوتُهُ لَوْلَانَــا

وسيأتي في الخاتمة من كلام الشيخ محيي الدين ابن عربي ما يؤيّد مغزاه إن شاء الله تعالى .

❑ ❑ ❑

١٣

جامع الترمذي « السُّنَن »

(٢٠٩-٢٧٩)

مَنْ أَحَبَّنِي وَأَحَبَّ هٰذَيْنِ وَأَبَاهُمَا وَأُمَّهُمَا كَانَ مَعِي فِي دَرَجَتِي يَوْمَ الْقِيَامَةِ

أخبرني سيدي الشيخ **محمد تاج الدين بن محمد مكّي بن محمّد بن جعفر الكتّاني** (١٣٤٥-١٤٣٣) ـ رحمه الله ـ بقراءتي عليه في جامع الدَّلاميّة بدمشق الثلاثاء ٧ ربيع الأنور ١٤٢٥ الموافق ٢٧ نيسان ٢٠٠٤ بعد الحضرة المباركة وقُبيل المغرب ، بإجازته الخطّيّة عن المحدّث الأكبر العلامة الشيخ بدر الدين الحسني ، عن شيخه العمدة إبراهيم بن علي السقا الأزهري ، عن الشيخ الولي ثعليب بن سالم الفَشْنِي ، عن أحمد بن عبد الفتّاح المَلَّوِي ، عن المسند عبد الله بن سالم البصري ، عن البابلي ، بالسند المار في باب صحيح مسلم إلى شيخ الإسلام ، (ح) كما حدّثنا من لفظه لجميعه المقرئ الفقيه المحدّث الداعية الطبيب **الشيخ سامر بن ممدوح بن شريف النص**

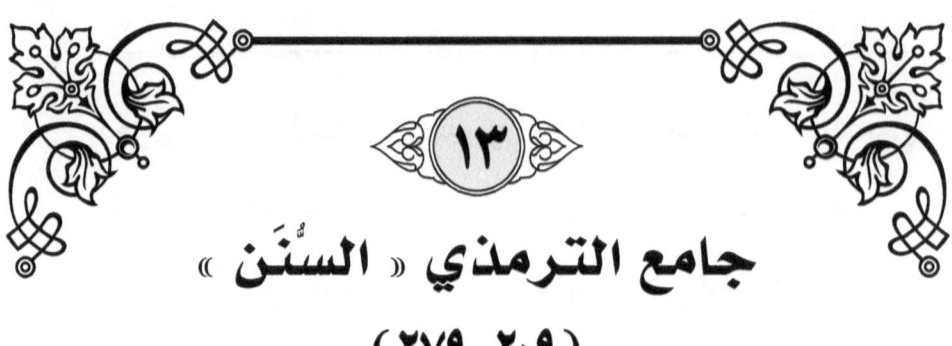

الحنفي ، عن المسنِد علم الدين أبي الفيض محمد ياسين الفاداني (١٣٣٥-١٤١٢) ، عن عبد القادر شَلَبي الطرابلسي ، عن المسند محمد أبي النّصْر الخطيب ، عن الوجيه عبد الرحمن الكزبري الصغير ، عن مصطفى بن محمّد الرَّحمتي ، عن عبد الكريم بن أحمد الشَّراباتي ، عن الشمس محمّد ابن عقيلة المكّي ، قال : أرويه مسلسلاً بالصوفية ، عن الشيخ حسن العُجيمي الصوفي ، عن الشيخ أحمد بن محمد القُشاشي الصوفي ، عن شيخه الشيخ أحمد بن علي الشَّنَّاوِي الصوفي ، عن والده الشيخ علي بن عبد القدوس الشَّنَّاوِي الصوفي ، عن الشيخ عبد الوهَّاب الشَّعراني الصوفي ، عن الشيخ زكريا بن محمد الفقيه الصوفي شيخ الإسلام ، عن العارف بالله تعالى محمّد بن زين الدين المَرَاغي العثماني الصوفي ، عن أستاذ الصوفية شرف الدين إسماعيل بن إبراهيم الجَبَرْتي العَقيلي الصوفي ، عن المسند أبي الحسن علي بن عمر الواني الصوفي ، عن أستاذ أهل التحقيق الشيخ محيي الدين محمد بن علي ابن عربي الطَّائي الحاتِمي الصوفي ، عن شيخ الشيوخ عبد الوهاب بن علي بن سُكَينة البغدادي الصوفي ، عن أبي الفتح عبد الملك بن عبد الله الكَرُوخي الصوفي ، عن شيخه المحقق الحافظ أبي إسماعيل عبد الله بن محمد الأنصاري الهروي شيخ الاسلام

الصوفي ، عن عبد الجبار الجرّاحي ، عن أبي العباس محمد بن أحمد بن محبوب المحبوبي ، عن مؤلِّفه **الترمذي أبي عيسى محمد بن عِيسَى بن سَوْرَة الضّحّاك السُّلَمي الضرير البُوغي** ـ نسبةً إلى بوغ ، قرية من قرى تِرمِذ ، وترمذ مدينة قديمة على طرف نهر بلخ المسمَّى جَيْحُون ، وهذا من أنهار الجنّة الأربعة المذكورين في الحديث ـ قال : حَدَّثَنَا نَصْرُ بْنُ عَلِيٍّ الْجَهْضَمِيُّ ، حَدَّثَنَا عَلِيُّ بْنُ جَعْفَرِ بْنِ مُحَمَّدِ بْنِ عَلِيٍّ ، قَالَ : أَخْبَرَنِي أَخِي مُوسَى بْنُ جَعْفَرِ بْنِ مُحَمَّدٍ ، عَنْ أَبِيهِ جَعْفَرِ بْنِ مُحَمَّدٍ ، عَنْ أَبِيهِ مُحَمَّدِ بْنِ عَلِيٍّ ، عَنْ أَبِيهِ عَلِيِّ بْنِ الْحُسَيْنِ ، عَنْ أَبِيهِ ، عَنْ جَدِّهِ عَلِيِّ بْنِ أَبِي طَالِبٍ ، أَنَّ النَّبِيَّ ﷺ أَخَذَ بِيَدِ حَسَنٍ وَحُسَيْنٍ ، فَقَالَ : **مَنْ أَحَبَّنِي وَأَحَبَّ هٰذَيْنِ وَأَبَاهُمَا وَأُمَّهُمَا كَانَ مَعِي فِي دَرَجَتِي يَوْمَ الْقِيَامَةِ** . قال أبو عيسى : هذا حديث حسن غريب ، لا نعرفه من حديث جعفر بن محمد إلّا من هذا الوجه .

رواه عبد الله بن أحمد في زيادات المسند وابن الجزري في أسنى المطالب في مناقب أسد الله الغالب علي بن أبي طالب من طريق الْقَطِيعِي ، حَدَّثَنَا عَبْدُ اللهِ بْنُ أَحْمَدَ ، حَدَّثَنِي نَصْرُ بْنُ عَلِيٍّ ، به . حكى أبو نعيم في تاريخ أصبهان : قال أحمد بن حنبل : لو قرأتَ هذا الإسناد ـ أي السُّلالة ـ على مجنون لبرئ من جِنّته . قال الذهبي في

السِّيَر : هذا حديث منكر جداً ، قال عبد الله بن أحمد : لمّاَ حدّث نصر بهذا ، أمر المتوكِّل بضربه ألف سوط ، فكلّمه جعفر بن عبد الواحد ، وجعل يقول له : الرجل من أهل السنة ، ولم يزل به حتى تركه . قال الخطيب عُقيبه : إنما أمر المتوكل بضربه لانه ظنّه رافضيّاً . قلت : والمتوكل سنّي ، لكن فيه نصب . وما في رواة الخبر إلا ثقة ما خلا علي بن جعفر ، فلعلّه لم يضبط لفظ الحديث ـ وما كان النبي ﷺ مِنْ حُبِّه وبثّ فضيلة الحسنين ليجعل كل من أحبّهما في درجته في الجنة ! فلعلّه قال : فهو معي في الجنة . وقد تواتر قوله عليه السلام **الْمَرْءُ مَعَ مَنْ أَحَبَّ** . اهـ . وأنكر في الميزان أن يكون الترمذي حسّنه أو صحّحه ، فالتحسين من اختلاف بعض النسخ . ثم قال : إنّ علي بن جعفر لم يليّنه أحد ، وكأنّه يردّ على نفسه ، وفي استنكاره وتعليله تحكيم الظنّ وضرب تنقيص لشأن العترة .

وقد رفع الترمذي في هذا الباب ـ سوى ما أسندناه في هذا المصنَّف ـ أحاديث أخرى ، منها عن حذيفة : **إِنَّ هَـذَا مَلَكٌ لَمْ يَنْزِلِ الْأَرْضَ قَطُّ قَبْلَ هَذِهِ اللَّيْلَةِ ، اسْتَأْذَنَ رَبَّهُ أَنْ يُسَلِّمَ عَلَيَّ وَيُبَشِّرَنِي بِأَنَّ فَاطِمَةَ سَيِّدَةُ نِسَاءِ أَهْلِ الْجَنَّةِ وَأَنَّ الْحَسَنَ وَالْحُسَيْنَ سَيِّدَا شَبَابِ أَهْلِ الْجَنَّةِ** . وعن ابن عباس : **أَحِبُّوا اللهَ لِمَا يَغْذُوكُمْ بِهِ مِنْ نِعَمِهِ ، وَأَحِبُّونِي**

لِحُبِّ اللهِ، وَأَحِبُّوا أَهْلَ بَيْتِي لِحُبِّي. يأتي في باب البلدانية لابن عساكر إن شاء الله. وعَنْ زَيْدِ بْنِ أَرْقَمَ ﷺ قَالَ لِعَلِيٍّ وَفَاطِمَةَ وَالْحَسَنِ وَالْحُسَيْنِ: أَنَا حَرْبٌ لِمَنْ حَارَبْتُمْ وَسِلْمٌ لِمَنْ سَالَمْتُمْ. استغربه، ورواه ابن ماجه والبزار وابن أبي شيبة وابن حبان والحاكم والطبراني في معاجمه الثلاثة والآجرّي في الشريعة. وله شواهد: في مسند أحمد وفضائل الصحابة له والحاكم والطبراني في الكبير والآجرّي عن أبي هريرة، وفي فضائل سيدة النساء لابن شاهين عن أبي سعيد، وفي معجم الشيوخ لابن جُمَيع وتاريخ ابن عساكر عن أم سلمة. وعن يَعْلَى بْنِ مُرَّةَ العامِري: حُسَيْنٌ مِنِّي وَأَنَا مِنْ حُسَيْنٍ، أَحَبَّ اللهُ مَنْ أَحَبَّ حُسَيْنًا، حُسَيْنٌ سِبْطٌ مِنَ الْأَسْبَاطِ حسّنه. وغيرها. والأخير هو لفظ الترمذي وأحمد وابن أبي شيبة والبخاري في الأدب المفرد والطبراني وابن حبان وأبو نعيم في المعرفة. وجاء بلفظ حُسَيْنٌ مِنِّي وأنا مِنْهُ، أَحَبَّ اللهُ مَنْ أَحَبَّ حُسَيْنًا، الْحَسَنُ وَالْحُسَيْنُ سِبْطَانِ مِنَ الْأَسْبَاطِ عند البخاري في التاريخ والطبراني في الكبير والمسند وأبي نعيم في المعرفة. أي: أمّةٌ من الأمم في الخير، والأسباط في أولاد إبراهيم عليه السلام بمنزلة القبائل في ولد إسماعيل، واحدهم سِبْط. نهاية. وورد عن المقدام ابن مَعْدِيكَرْبٍ، قال: قال رسول الله ﷺ حَسَنٌ مِنِّي وَالْحُسَيْنُ مِنْ عَلِيٍّ. رواه الطبراني وابن عساكر

وحسّن إسناده الذهبي والعراقي والمناوي مع عنعنة بقية ابن الوليد . أي : الحسن يَشْبَهني والحسين يشبه علياً ، وكان الغالب على الحسن الحلم والأناة كالنبي ﷺ وعلى الحسين الشدّة كعلي ؛ قاله المناوي في التيسير بشرح الجامع الصغير . وقال القاري في المرقاة : لأنه أراد قسمة الولدين للأبوين فالكبير للجد والصغير للأب كما هو معروف في العرف . اهـ . وقد ثبت في صحيح البخاري والمسند والسنن عن أبي بكرة قال : **بَيْنَا النَّبِيُّ ﷺ يَخْطُبُ جَاءَ الحَسَنُ فَقَالَ النَّبِيُّ ﷺ : ابْنِي هَذَا سَيِّدٌ وَلَعَلَّ اللهَ أَنْ يُصْلِحَ بِهِ بَيْنَ فِئَتَيْنِ مِنْ المُسْلِمِينَ** . (لطائف) قال لي السيّد تاج إنه رأى سيدنا جبريل عليه السلام . أقول : نعم ، ورد أنه يسلّم على كلّ مؤمن ليلة القدر ، رزقنا الله تحيّةً وسلاماً !

قُلُوبُ الْعَارِفِينَ لَهَا عُيُونٌ
تَرَى مَا لَا يَرَاهُ النَّاظِرُونَا

سألني عند عودتي من فرض الحج والعمرة هل دعوتَ للأمّة ؟ وأعرته نسخة نادرة من (الأربعين في فضل أهل البيت) لجدّه الحافظ محمد بن جعفر ثم فُقدت .

❑ ❑ ❑

١٤

المنتقى من مسند الحارث بن أبي أسامة

(١٨٦-٢٨٢)

سَأَلْتُ رَبِّي أَنْ لَا أَتَزَوَّجَ إِلَى أَحَدٍ مِنْ أُمَّتِي وَلَا يَتَزَوَّجَ إِلَيَّ أَحَدٌ مِنْ أُمَّتِي إِلَّا كَانَ مَعِي فِي الْجَنَّةِ ، فَأَعْطَانِي ذٰلِكَ .

أنبأنا الشيخ المعمّر المقرئ المبجَّل الولي الصالح سيّدي الشيخ **محمّد سليم الحمّامي الميداني الشافعي** (١٣٢٦-١٤٣٤) رحمه الله في داره بميدان دمشق المحروسة وأستاذ الحديث بكليّة الشريعة بجامعة بيروت الإسلامية المؤرّخ المسنِد **الشيخ يوسف بن عبد الرحمن بن فؤاد المَرْعَشْلي الحسيني** (ولد ١٩٥٢م) صاحب المشيخات والتحقيقات والفهارس ، قال الأوّل : أنبأنا المحدّث الأكبر السيد بدر الدين الحسني ، عن العلّامة السيّد عبد القادر بن صالح الخطيب (١٢٢١-١٢٨٨) ، عن الكزبري الحفيد ، عن مصطفى بن محمّد الرحمتي (١١٣٥-١٢٠٥) ، عن العارف الشيخ عبد الغني النابلسي ؛ وقال الثاني : أنبأنا محمّد بن عبد الرزّاق بن محمّد الخطيب الحسني ، عن أبي

النصـــر نَصْر الله بن عبد القادر بن صالح الخطيب (١٢٥٣-١٣٢٥) ، عن عبد الله بن محمّد التَّلِّي الشـامي (١١١٥ ؟ -١٢٦٥) ، عن النابلسـي (١٠٥٠-١١٤٣) إن صحّ ، بالسـند المارّ في باب جامع مَعْمَر إلى الحافظ ابـن حجر ، بقراءته على المسـندة فاطمـة بنت محمّد بـن عبد الهادي المقدسيّة ثمّ الصالحيّة ، بإجازتها من إبراهيم بن صالح بن العَجْمي ، بسماعه من يوسف بن خليل الحافظ ، قال : أنا خليل بن بدر الرّارَاني ، قال : أنا أبو علي الحدّاد ، قال : أنا أبو نعيم ، قثتنا أبو بكر بن خلّاد ، عن **أبي محمّد الحارث بن محمّد بن أبي أسامة** ، قال : حَدَّثَنَا إِسْحَاقُ بْنُ بِشْرٍ ، حَدَّثَنَـا عَمَّارُ بْنُ يُوسُـفَ الضَّبِّيُّ وَصِيُّ سُـفْيَانَ الثَّـوْرِيِّ ، عَنْ هِشَامِ بْنِ عُرْوَةَ ، عَنْ أَبِيهِ ، عَنْ عَبْدِ اللهِ بْنِ عُمَرَ أَوْ عَبْدِ اللهِ بْنِ عَمْرٍو -رَضِيَ اللهُ عَنْهُمْ- أَنَّ النَّبِيَّ ﷺ قال : **سَأَلْتُ رَبِّي أَنْ لَا أَتَزَوَّجَ إِلَى أَحَدٍ مِنْ أُمَّتِي وَلَا يَتَزَوَّجَ إِلَيَّ أَحَدٌ مِنْ أُمَّتِي إِلَّا كَانَ مَعِي فِي الجَنَّةِ ، فَأَعْطَانِي ذٰلِكَ** .

رواه الطـبراني والحاكـم عـن عبد الله بـن أبي أوفى . وأخـرج الشـيرازي في الألقاب عن ابن عباس رضي الله عنهما أن رسـول الله ﷺ قال : **سَأَلْتُ رَبِّي أَنْ لَا أُزَوِّجَ إِلَّا مِنْ أَهْلِ الجَـنَّةِ وَلَا أَتَزَوَّجَ إِلَّا مِنْ أَهْلِ الجَنَّةِ** . وأخرج أحمد والحاكم عن المِسْوَر رضي الله عنه أن النبي

ﷺ قال : **فَاطِمَةُ بَضْعَةٌ مِنِّي ، يَقْبِضُنِي مَا يَقْبِضُهَا وَيَبْسُطُنِي مَا يَبْسُطُهَا ، وَإِنَّ الْأَنْسَابَ تَنْقَطِعُ يَوْمَ الْقِيَامَةِ غَيْرَ نَسَبِي وَسَبَبِي وَصِهْرِي** . يأتي بألفاظه في باب مسند أبي يعلى . قال في فيض القدير : الظاهر أن ذلك شامل لمن تَزَوَّجَ أو زَوَّجَ من ذريته فتكون بشرى عظيمة لمن صاهر شريفا أو شريفة . اهـ .

ويوضّح ما هم إليه من الخير ما رواه الحافظ ابن عساكر رحمه الله في الأربعين في مناقب أمهات المؤمنين حيث قال : الحديث السابع والثلاثون : بإسناده إلى سيدنا علي رضي الله عنه ، قال : قال رسول الله ﷺ : **لَا يَدْخُلُ النَّارَ مَنْ تَزَوَّجَ إِلَيَّ أَوْ تَزَوَّجْتُ إِلَيْهِ** . قال : هذا حديث حسن من حديث أمير المؤمنين أبي الحسن علي ابن أبي طالب كرّم الله وجهه ، وفي هذا الحديث دليل على فضل أصهاره وأختانه ، وهذه شهادة لهم بالجنة إذ كانوا مؤمنين ، والله أعلم اهـ .

وروى الحارث عن محمّد ابن الحنفيّة مرسلاً وأبو يعلى وابن أبي الدنيا وابن عساكر عن أبي هريرة : اصْطَرَعَ الْحَسَنُ وَالْحُسَيْنُ عند رَسُولِ اللهِ ﷺ فَجَعَلَ رَسُولُ اللهِ ﷺ يَقُولُ : **هَيَّ حَسَنُ** ! فَقَالَتْ لَهُ فَاطِمَةُ رَضِيَ اللهُ عَنْهَا : يَا رَسُولَ اللهِ ، كَأَنَّهُ - يَعْنِي الْحَسَنَ - أَحَبُّ إِلَيْكَ مِنَ الْحُسَيْنِ ؟ قَالَ ﷺ : **إِنَّ جِبْرِيلَ يُعِينُ الْحُسَيْنَ وَأَنَا أُحِبُّ أَنْ**

أُعِينَ الحَسَـنَ . (فوائد) قال السـيّد محمّد أبو الهدى اليعقوبي : كنّا لا نشكّ أنّ الشيخ سليم الحمامي من الأبدال . قال : زرته رحمه الله مرة في داره ، فدخل إلى بيت له ثم خرج ومعه مبلغ كبير من المال أهداني إيـاه وقال لي أريد منك أن تقول : سـليم منا أهـل البيت . قال العبد الضعيـف : مِـن آل الحمامـي أشراف ، مـن فروع السـادة الموسـوية الحسـينية العراقيين ، من ذرّية السيد هاشم بن إبراهيم بن جعفر بن موسـى بن أحمد المدني ، كان صاحـب حمّام في محلّة المشراق في نجف العراق ؛ ومنهم عُمَريّون ينتهي نسبهم إلى الفاروق عمر بن الخطاب رضي الله تعـالى عنه ، لا سـيّما في فلسـطين والأردن . وصلّى الله على سيّدنا محمّدٍ وآله وسلّم تسليماً .

❑ ❑ ❑

١٥

السُنَّة لابن أبي عاصم

(٢٠٦-٢٨٧)

> قالَ لِي جِبْرِيلُ عَلَيْهِ السَّلَامُ : قَلَّبْتُ الأَرْضَ ، مَشَارِقَهَا وَمَغَارِبَهَا ، فَلَمْ أَجِدْ رَجُلاً أَفْضَلَ مِنْ مُحَمَّدٍ عَلَيْهِ الصَّلَاةُ وَالسَّلَامُ ؛ وَقَلَّبْتُ الأَرْضَ ، مَشَارِقَهَا وَمَغَارِبَهَا ، فَلَمْ أَجِدْ بَنِي أَبٍ أَفْضَلَ مِنْ بَنِي هَاشِمٍ .

أنبأنا بحلب الفَرَضي المعمّر فوق المئة السيد **محمد بن درويش بن محمد الخطيب بن مصطفى بن محمد عرب الحسيني الشافعي** (١٣٢٢-١٤٣٢/ ١٩٠٤-٢٠١١) رحمه الله ، عن أستاذه مؤرّخ حلب الشيخ محمد راغب الطبّاخ الحنفي (١٢٩٣-١٣٧٠) ، عن السيد خالد بن محمد بن عبد الستار الأتاسي الحمصي (١٢٥٣-١٣٢٦) ، عن والده وعمه سعيد والشيخ محمد بن سليمان الجُوخَدار ، الأولان عن عبد الستار الأتاسي ، والأخير عن السيد سعيد الحبال الحلبي ، الأتاسي عن الشمس محمد بن عبد الرحمن الكزبري (١١٤٠-١٢٢١) الشهير بالأوسط ، عن والده عبد الرحمن الكزبري الكبير ، عن أبي المواهب الحنبلي ، عن والده الشيخ عبد الباقي ، عن أبي حفص عمر

القاري ، عن البدر محمّد الغزّي ، عن شيخ الإسلام القاضي زكريّا ، عن الحافظ ابن حجر ، أخبرنا أبو العباس أحمد بن أبي بكر المقدسي وأبو محمد إبراهيم بن محمد بن صديق ، قالا أنبأنا إسحاق بن يحيى الآمدي ، عن يوسف بن خليل الحافظ ، أنبأنا المسنِد المعمَّر أبو جعفر محمد بن أحمد بن نصر الصيدلاني (ليلة عيد الأضحى ٥٠٩-٦٠٣) قراءة عليه ، أنبأنا محمود بن إسماعيل الصيرفي ، أنبأنا أبو بكر محمد بن عبد الله بن شاذان ، أنبأنا أبو بكر عبد الله بن محمد القباب ، أنبأنا **أبو بكر أحمد بن عمرو بن الضحاك ابن أبي عاصم النبيل الشيباني** : ثنا محمد بن المثنى بن عبيد ، ثنا بُهلول بن المورِّق الشامي ، حدثنا موسى بن عُبَيدة ، حدثني عمرو بن عبد الله بن نوفل ـ من بني عَدِيِّ بن كعب ـ ، عن محمد بن مسلم الزهري ، عن أبي سلمة بن عبد الرحمن ، عن عائشة رضي الله عنها ، **قالت : قال رسول الله ﷺ** :

قالَ لي جِبْرِيلُ عَلَيْهِ السَّلامُ : قَلَّبْتُ الأَرْضَ ، مَشَارِقَها وَمَغَارِبَها ، فَلَمْ أَجِدْ رَجُلاً أَفْضَلَ مِنْ مُحَمَّدٍ عَلَيْهِ الصَّلاَةُ وَالسَّلَامُ ؛ وَقَلَّبْتُ الأَرْضَ ، مَشَارِقَهَا وَمَغَارِبَها ، فَلَمْ أَجِدْ بَنِي أَبٍ أَفْضَلَ مِنْ بَنِي هَاشِمٍ .

رواه الطبراني في الأوسط وأبو نعيم في الدلائل وحديث الكُدَيمي والدولابي في الذرّيّة الطاهرة والقطيعي في زوائد الفضائل

ومن طريقه الشجري في أماليه الخميسية ورواه الحاكم في الكنى والبيهقي في الدلائل وابن عساكر في التاريخ . قال الحافظ ابن حجر في الأمالي المطلقة : هذا حديث غريب ، تفرد به موسى بن عُبيدة ، وموسى وإن كان ضعيفاً وشيخه وإن كان مجهولاً ، لكن لوائح الصدق لائحةٌ على صفحات هذا المتن ، والله اعلم . قلت : فيه مزيد كلام في باب نوادر الأصول . وقال البيهقي : هذه الأحاديث ، وإن كان في رواتها من لا تصح به ، فبعضها يؤكد بعضاً ، ومعنى جميعها يرجع لما روينا عن واثلة بن الأسقع وأبي هريرة ، والله أعلم . يريد بالأوّل : حديث **بُعِثْتُ مِنْ خَيْرِ قُرُونِ بَنِي آدَمَ قَرْنًا فَقَرْنًا حَتَّى كُنْتُ مِنْ الْقَرْنِ الَّذِي كُنْتُ فِيهِ** - رواه البخاري - وبالثاني : **إنّ اللهَ تعالى اصْطَفَى كِنانَةَ مِنْ وَلَدِ إسْماعِيلَ واصْطَفَى قُرَيْشاً مِنْ كِنانَةَ واصْطَفَى مِنْ قُرَيْشٍ بَنِي هاشِمٍ واصْطفانِي منْ بَنِي هاشِمٍ** رواه مسلم . وأخرجه بسنده القاضي أبو الفرج المعافى بن زكرياء في الجليس الصالح ثم قال : فالحمد لله الذي فضّل نبيَّنا محمداً ﷺ على سائر الأنبياء ، وفضّل بني أبيه على سائر بني الآباء ، وجعلَنا من أمّته التي هي خير أمةٍ أخرجت للناس وهدانا لتصديقه والإيمان به ، ووفّقنا لاتِّباعه ، وأَبانَنا ممّن عانده وجَحَدَه وبغى عليه وحسده ، وعَصَمَنا من أن

نُنْفِسَ على رهطه وأسرته وأقْرَبيه وعترته بما آتاهم الله من فضله وكرامته، وحَبَاهم به من شريف نعمته، وذلك بحسن توفيقه وجميل عصمته، وفضَّلَنا به على كثيرٍ مِنْ أنْسِبَائه الرَّاصدين لمحاربته والجادِّين في مخالفته، فقد هلك كثير منهم بِمُشَاقَّتِه؛ ألا تسمعون إلى ما أنزل الله في أبي لهب وإن كان أحد الهاشميين، وإلى قول الرسول ﷺ في سلمان الفارسي رضي الله عنه وهو من العَجَم الأجنبيين؟ وقال الله تعالى: ﴿إِنَّ أَوْلَى ٱلنَّاسِ بِإِبْرَٰهِيمَ لَلَّذِينَ ٱتَّبَعُوهُ وَهَٰذَا ٱلنَّبِيُّ وَٱلَّذِينَ ءَامَنُوا۟ۗ وَٱللَّهُ وَلِيُّ ٱلْمُؤْمِنِينَ ۶۸﴾ [آل عمران]. (فائدة) قال الماوردي في الحاوي الكبير: مذهب البغداديين من أصحابنا أنَّ قريشاً يتفاضلون بقربهم من رسول الله ﷺ ولا يتكافؤون، لرواية عائشة هذه، ولأن قريشاً لما شَرُفت برسول الله ﷺ على سائر العرب، كان أقربهم برسول الله ﷺ أشرفَ من سائر قريش، ولأنهم لما ترتّبوا في الديوان بالقرب حتى صاروا فيه على عشر مراتب، دلَّ على تمييزهم بذلك في الكفاءة؛ وإذا كان كذلك فجميع بني هاشم وبني المطلب أكْفاء، ثم يليهم سائر بني عبد مناف وبني زُهرة، ولا يُفضَّل بني عبدِ شمسٍ في كفاءة النكاح على بني نوفل، ولا بني عبد العزى على بني عبد الدار، ولا بني عبد مناف على بني زهرة؛ ثم جمعنا بين

بني عبد مناف وبني زهرة في كفاءة النكاح ـ وإن لم يكونا بطناً واحدة ـ لرواية الأوزاعي أن النبي ﷺ قال: **صَرِيحُ قُرَيْشٍ اِبْنَا كِلَابٍ** [أخرجه ابن عساكر] يعني بني قُصَيٍّ وبني زُهرة، ولأن النبي ﷺ يرجع إلى قصي بأبيه، وإلى زهرة بأمه، فتقاربا في الكفاءة بأبويه ﷺ، ثم يلي عبدَ مناف وبني زهرة سائرُ قريش، فيكونوا جميعاً أكْفاءً. فأما سائر العرب سوى قريش: فهُم على اختلاف أصحابنا في قريش، فعلى قياس قول البصريين: أنّ جميعهم أكْفاء من عدنان وقحطان، لأن في عدنان سابقة المهاجرين، وفي قحطان سابقة الأنصار؛ وعلى قياس قول البغداديين: أنهم يتفاضلون ولا يتكافئون، فتُفَضَّلُ مُضَرُ في الكفاءة على رَبيعة، ويُفَضَّلُ عدنان على قحطان، اعتباراً بالقُرْب من رسول الله ﷺ.

❑ ❑ ❑

١٦

الآحاد والمثاني لابن أبي عاصم

(٢٠٦-٢٨٧)

يَا أَيُّهَا النَّاسُ ! مَا لِي أُوذَى فِي أَهْلِي ؟ فَوَاللهِ إِنَّ شَفَاعَتِي لَتَنَالُ بِقَرَابَتِي . حَتَّى حَا ، وَحَكَمَ ، وَصَدَاءَ ، وَسَلْهَبَ يَوْمَ الْقِيَامَةِ !

أخبرني العالم الرَّحَّالة الدَّاعية الخطيب **الحبيب علي زين العابدين بن عبد الرحمن الجِفْري** اليمني التَّريمي الصوفي (ولد ١٩٧١م) حفظه الله تعالى بقراءتي عليه في منزل والده في بلدة كَيْفُون بالمَتْن الجنوبي من جبل لبنان ، أخبرني سيدي الحبيب الشيخ عبد القادر بن أحمد السقاف رحمه الله ، عن والده ، بإسناده المارّ في باب مسند الإمام أحمد إلى الحافظ ابن حجر ، عن أبي هريرة ابن الذهبي عبد الرحمن بن محمد بن أحمد (٧١٥-٧٩٩) ، عن أبيه الحافظ محمد بن أحمد بن عثمان بن قايْماز التركماني الذهبي (٦٧٣-٧٤٨) ، عن شيخه الحافظ شرف الدين الدمياطي (٦١٣-٧٠٥) ، عن أبي محمد عبد الله بن بركات بن إبراهيم ابن الخشوعي الدمشقي (٥٧٣-٦٥٨) ، عن شيخه المجيز الحافظ الناقد

تقي الدين شيخ الإسلام سيد الحفاظ أبو موسى محمد بن أبي بكر عمر بن أبي عيسى أحمد المديني (٥٠١-٥٨١) ، قال : أنا أبو علي الحسن بن أحمد بن الحسن المقرىء الحداد ، ثنا أبو القاسم عبد الرحمن بن محمد بن عبد الرحمن ، ثنا أبو بكر عبد الله بن محمد بن محمد بن فورك القبَّاب ، عن مؤلفه **الإمام أبي بكر أحمد بن عمرو بن أبي عاصم الضحّاك بن مخلّد النبيل القاضي الشيباني البصري الظاهري** مؤلف كتاب السنّة وفضل الصلاة على النبي ﷺ والمولد وفضائل العباس بن عبد المطلب وفضائل معاوية بن أبي سفيان والحُلَماء ، قال في كتاب الآحاد والمَثَاني له : حدثنا أبو سعيد عبد الرحمن بن إبراهيم ، نا عبد الرحمن بن بشير ، عن محمد بن إسحاق ، حدثني نافع مولى ابن عمر وزيد بن أسلم : (١) عن ابن عمر ؛ و (٢) عن سعيد بن أبي سعيد المقبري ، عن أبي هريرة ؛ و (٣) عن محمد بن المنكدر ، عن أبي هريرة ؛ و (٤) عن عمّار بن ياسر ـ رضي الله عنهم ـ قالوا : قَدِمَتْ دُرَّةُ بِنْتُ أَبِي لَهَبٍ المَدِينَةَ مُهَاجِرَةً فَنَزَلَتْ دَارَ رَافِعِ بْنِ المُعَلَّى الزُرَقِيِّ ، فَقَالَ لَهَا نِسْوَةٌ جَلَسْنَ إِلَيْهَا مِنْ بَنِي زُرَيْقٍ : أَنْتِ ابْنَةُ أَبِي لَهَبٍ الَّذِي قَالَ اللهُ عَزَّ وَجَلَّ ﴿ تَبَّتْ يَدَآ أَبِي لَهَبٍ وَتَبَّ ﴿١﴾ مَآ أَغْنَىٰ عَنْهُ مَالُهُۥ وَمَا كَسَبَ ﴿٢﴾ ﴾ مَا يُغْنِي عَنْكِ مُهَاجَرُكِ !

فَأَتَتْ دُرَّةُ رَضِيَ اللهُ عَنْهَا النَّبِيَّ ﷺ ، فَشَكَتْ إِلَيْهِ مَا قُلْنَ لَهَا ، فَسَكَّنَهَا ، وَقَالَ : **اِجْلِسِي** . ثُمَّ صَلَّى بِالنَّاسِ الظُّهْرَ وَجَلَسَ عَلَى الْمِنْبَرِ سَاعَةً ، ثُمَّ قَالَ : **يَا أَيُّهَا النَّاسُ ! مَا لِي أُوْذَى فِي أَهْلِي ؟ فَوَاللهِ إِنَّ شَفَاعَتِي لَتَنَالُ ـ بِقَرَابَتِي ـ حَتَّى حَا ، وَحَكَمَ ، وَصَدَاءَ ، وَسَلْهَبَ يَوْمَ الْقِيَامَةِ !**

رواه الطحاوي في بيان مشكل الآثار بلفظ **فَوَاللهِ إِنَّ شَفَاعَتِي لَتُنَالُ بِقَرَابَتِي ، حَتَّى أَنَّ حَكَمًا ، وَحَا ، وَصَدَاءَ ، وَسَلْهَبَ لَتَنَالُهَا يَوْمَ الْقِيَامَةِ بِقَرَابَتِي** ، والطبراني في الكبير بلفظ **لَتَنَالُ حَيَّ حَا ، وَحَكَمَ** الحديث ، وأبو نعيم في معرفة الصحابة ، الأخير بلفظ : **حَتَّى أَرْحَاءَ ، وَحَكَمًا ، وَصَدَاءَ ، وَسَلْهَبَ بِهَا لَهَا يَوْمَ الْقِيَامَةِ لِقَرَابَتِي !** جميعهم من طريق عبد الرحمن بن بشير الدمشقي ، قال عنه أبو حاتم : منكر الحديث ، ففي علل ابن أبي حاتم : سألت أبي عن حديث رواه عبد الرحمن بن بشير ، وذكر الحديث وقول ابن اسحاق : سلهبٌ في نسب اليمن من دوس ، قال ابن اسحاق : وهذا الحديث مما يُصَدِّقُ نُسَّابَ مُضَرَ أنَّ هذه القبائل من مَعَدّ . قال أبي : هذا حديث ليس بصحيح عندي . اهـ . وضعّفه الحافظ في الإصابة . قلت : ابن بشير وثّقه دحيم وابن حبان وذكره محمّد بن عائذ بخير كما في اللسان ؛ ويتقوّى بحديث أم هانئ برجال ثقات في معناه ، سيأتي مسنداً في باب

المعجم الكبير إن شاء الله . وصحّ في المرفوع : **خَيْرُ الرِّجَالِ رِجَالُ أَهْلِ الْيَمَنِ ، وَالإِيمَانُ يَمَانٍ ، وَأَنَا يَمَانٍ** . رواه الإمام أحمد في مسنده عن عمرو بن عَبَسَة . قال الحبيب الجفري في معنى قوله ﷺ **وَأَنَا يَمَانٍ** : كانت بيوت بني هاشم من جهة الركن اليماني من الكعبة . وفي مناقب الشافعي للبيهقي من طريق يزيد بن عبد الملك النوفلي المدني وهو ضعيف ، عن سعيد بن أبي سعيد ، عن أبي هريرة ، أَنَّ سُبَيْعَةَ بِنْتَ أَبِي لَهَبٍ جَاءَتِ النَّبِيَّ ﷺ فَقَالَتْ : يَا رَسُولَ اللهِ ، إِنَّ النَّاسَ يَصِيحُونَ بِي ، يَقُولُونَ : إِنِّي ابْنَةُ حَطَبِ النَّارِ . **فَقَامَ رَسُولُ اللهِ ﷺ وَهُوَ مُغْضَبٌ شَدِيدَ الْغَضَبِ ، فَقَالَ : مَا بَالُ أَقْوَامٍ يُؤْذُونَنِي فِي قَرَابَتِي ؟ أَلَا وَمَنْ آذَى قَرَابَتِي فَقَدْ آذَانِي ، وَمَنْ آذَانِي فَقَدْ آذَى اللهَ عَزَّ وَجَلَّ !** ذكره في الميزان بلفظ **مَا بَالُ أَقْوَامٍ يُؤْذُونَ نَسَبِي وَذِي رَحِمِي ؟ أَلَا وَمَنْ آذَى نَسَبِي وَذَوِي رَحِمِي** . قال الحافظ في الإصابة : أخرجه ابن منده من طريق يزيد بن عبد الملك النوفلي ـ وهو واه ـ عن سعيد المقبري عن أبي هريرة ثم قال : رواه محمد بن إسحاق وغيره عن المقبري فقالوا : قدمت درة بنت أبي لهب ، فذكر نحوه . قال أبو نعيم : الصواب درة . قلت ـ أي الحافظ ابن حجر ـ يحتمل أن يكون لها اسمان ، أو أحدهما لقب ، أو تعدّدت القصة لامرأتين .

❑ ❑ ❑

١٧

نوادر الأصول للحكيم الترمذي

(؟ - ؟)

النُّجُومُ أَمَانٌ لأَهْلِ السَّمَاءِ ، وَأَهْلُ بَيْتِي أَمَانٌ لأُمَّتِي .

أنبأنا سيدي الحبيب سالم بن عبد الله بن عمر الشاطري (١٣٥٩-١٤٣٩) رحمه الله ، أنبأنا العلامة الحبيب سالم بن حفيظ بن الشيخ أبي بكر والفقيه النحوي الحبيب محمد بن هادي بن حسن السقاف السيؤوني (١٢٩١-١٣٨٢) ، كلاهما عن المسند عيدروس بن عمر الحبشي والعلامة المعمّر الشيخ عوض بن محمّد العفري الزَّبيدي (١٢٣١-١٣٤٤) والأخير عن والده هادي بن حسن السقاف (ت ١٣٣٦) وهو أجلّ مشايخه ؛ قال الحبشي في مِنحة الفتّاح : عن سيدي عبد الله بن عمر بن أبي بكر بن يحيى ، عن الشيخ يوسف بن محمد بن علاء الدين المِزْجاجي ، عن السيد أحمد بن محمد شريف مقبول الأهدل ، عن المسنِد عبد الله بن سالم البصري عالياً ؛ وقال العفري والسقاف : عن السيد إسماعيل بن زين العابدين البرزنجي ، عن

الشيخ صالح الفُلّاني ، عن محمد بن عبد الله المغربي ، عن مسند الحجاز جمال الدين عبد الله بن سالم البصري عالياً ، قال : أخذتها عن شيخنا شمس الدين وشهاب الدين أبي عبد الله محمّد بن علاء الدين البابلي الشافعي القاهري ، عن الزين عبد الله بن محمّد النّحْرِيري ، عن الجمال يوسف بن زكريا ، عن أبيه ، عن أبي الفضل أحمد بن حجر ، أخبرنا أبو الحسن علي بن محمد بن أبي المجد إذناً مشافهة ، عن سليمان بن حمزة الطيالسي ، عن عيسى بن عبد العزيز وهو آخر من حدّث عنه ، عن الحافظ النسّابة أبي سعد عبد الكريم بن محمد السَّمْعاني وهو آخر من حدّث عنه ، أنبأنا أبو الفضل محمد بن علي بن سعيد بن المُطَهَّر إجازة ، أنبأنا إسحاق بن إبراهيم بن محمد البُوْقي الخطيب نسبة إلى بوق من قرى أنطاكية ، أنبأنا أبو بكر محمد بن عبد الرحمن المقرئ أو المَقْبُري ، أنبأنا أبو نصر أحمد بن أَحِيد ابن حمدان البِيكَنْدي ، أنبأنا **الحكيم محمد بن علي الترمذي في الأصل** الثالث والعشرين والمائتين : حدثنا أبي رحمه الله ، ثنا الحِمّاني ، ثنا ابن نُمير ، عن موسى بن عُبَيدة ، عن إياس بن سلمة بن الأكوع ، عن أبيه رضي الله عنه قال : قال رسول الله : **النُّجُومُ أَمَانٌ لِأَهْلِ السَّماءِ ، وَأَهْلُ بَيْتِي أَمَانٌ لِأُمَّتِي** .

رواه مُسَدَّد وأَبُو بكر بن أبي شَيْبَة وعنه أبو يَعْلَى والطبراني في

الكبير والروياني في مسنده وابن الأعرابي في معجمه والفسوي في المعرفة والتاريخ والخطيب في الموَضِّح وابن عساكر في التاريخ، ومدار إسناده على موسى بن عُبَيدة الرَّبَذي، قال الترمذي: موسى بن عُبَيدة يُضَعَّف في الحديث من قِبَلِ حِفْظِهِ وهو صدوق. أي لتشاغله بالعبادة وهو من خيار الناس كما قال البزّار. وقد مشّاه الحافظ كما مرّ في باب السنّة لابن أبي عاصم. ثم لفظ **أَهْلُ بَيْتِي أَمَانٌ لِأُمَّتِي** رواه الحاكم عن ابن عباس وجابر والمنكدر بن عبد الله بن الهدير التميمي، والقَطِيعيُّ في زيادات الفضائل عن سيدنا علي ومن وجه آخر الشجري في أماليه، بلفظ **أَهْلُ بَيْتِي أَمَانٌ لِأَهْلِ الْأَرْضِ** من وجوه ضعيفة جداً، وكذا الديلمي. والمحفوظ: اقتصار اللفظ على الصحابة رضي الله عنهم كما جاء في صحيح مسلم، والله تعالى أعلم.

ثم قال الحكيم الترمذي: وأمّا قوله **أَهْلُ بَيْتِي أَمَانٌ لِأُمَّتِي** فأهل بيته مَن خَلَفَهُ مِن بعده على منهاجه وهم الصّدّيقون والأبدال الذين روى علي كرم الله وجهه، قال: سمعت رسول الله ﷺ يقول: **إِنَّ الْأَبْدَالَ يَكُونُونَ بِالشَّامِ وَهُمْ أَرْبَعُونَ رَجُلاً، كُلَّمَا مَاتَ مِنْهُمْ رَجُلٌ، أَبْدَلَ اللهُ مَكَانَهُ رَجُلاً. بِهِمْ يُسْقَى الْغَيْثُ، وَيُنْتَصَرُ بِهِمْ عَلَى الْأَعْدَاءِ، وَيُصْرَفُ عَنْ أَهْلِ الْأَرْضِ بِهِمُ الْبَلَاءُ** [أحمد بلفظ **وَيُصْرَفُ عَنْ أَهْلِ**

الشَّـامِ بِهِمُ الْعَذَابُ والراجح وقْفه وهو صحيح] . فهؤلاء أهل بيت رسول الله ﷺ وأمان هذه الأمّة ، فإذا ماتوا فسدت الأرض وخرِبت الدنيا ؛ قال الله تعالى : ﴿ وَلَوْلَا دَفْعُ ٱللَّهِ ٱلنَّاسَ بَعْضَهُم بِبَعْضٍ لَّفَسَدَتِ ٱلْأَرْضُ ﴾ [البقرة ٢٥١] .

❑ ❑ ❑

١٨

مسند البَزَّار المسمى بـ (البحر الزَخَّار)

(٢١٠-٢٩٢)

مَثَلُ أَهْلِ بَيْتِي مَثَلُ سَفِينَةِ نُوحٍ : مَنْ رَكِبَهَا نَجَا ، وَمَنْ تَرَكَهَا غَرِقَ .

حدثني مولانا الشيخ أبو سعيد محمد عدنان المجد الحسني (١٣٦٣-١٤٢٣) رحمه الله تعالى إمام ومدرّس جامع الشيخ رُسْلان في باب تُومَى أحد أبواب دمشق السبعة ، حدثني سيدي الشيخ إبراهيم اليعقوبي ، عن عمّه العلامة الشيخ السيد محمد الشريف اليعقوبي إمام المالكية في جامع بني أُمَيّة في دمشق ، عن الشريف المجاهد الأمير عبد القادر الجزائري والشريفين الشيخ بكري بن حامد العطّار والشيخ سليم بن ياسين العطّار (١٢٣٣-١٣٠٧) ، الأخيران عن جدّ الأخير حامد بن أحمد بن عبيد الله (١١٨٦-١٢٦٣) ، عن والده المجاهد المحدث الفقيه المفسر إمام الشافعية في الجامع الأموي الشيخ شهاب الدين أحمد العطّار (١١٣٨-١٢١٨) ، عن شيخه الشريف الشمس محمد بن

عبد الرحمن ابن زين العابدين الغزي (١٠٩٦-١١٦٧)، عن عمّه عبد الكريم الغزي والشريف البرهان إبراهيم بن محمد بن كمال الدين محمد بن حمزة النقيب الدمشقي والشيخ أبي المواهب محمد بن تقي الدين عبد الباقي بن عبد الباقي الحنبلي، الأخير عن والده، عن الشريف نجم الدين محمد الغزي، عن والده أبي البركات بدر الدين محمد بن رضي الدين محمد الغزي (٩٠٤-٩٨٤)، عن شيخ الإسلام التقي أبي الصدق أبو بكر بن عبد الله بن عبد الرحمن المعروف بابن قاضي عجلون (٨٤١- ٩٢٨)، عن أخيه الإمام شيخ الاسلام نجم الدين محمد بن عبد الله بن عبد الرحمن المعروف أيضا بابن قاضي عجلون (٨٣١- ٨٧٦)، عن الحافظ الشمس ابن ناصر الدين (٧٧٧-٨٤٢)، عن سارة بنت شيخ الإسلام التقي السبكي (٧٣٤-٨٠٥)، عن والدها (٦٨٣-٧٥٦)، عن شيخه حافظ عصره الشّرف الدمياطي (٦١٣-٧٠٥)، عن شيخه حافظ عصره الزّكي المنذري (٥٨١-٦٥٦)، عن شيخه الحافظ علي بن المفضَّل، عن شيخه الحافظ المعمَّر أبي طاهر السِّلَفي (٤٧٥-٥٧٦)، أنبأنا أبو الفتح أحمد بن محمد بن أحمد الحداد، أنا عبد الغفار بن إبراهيم المؤدِّب، أنا الحافظ أبو الشيخ عبد الله بن محمد بن جعفر بن حيَّان (ت ٣٦٩)، أنا الإمام

أبو بكر أحمد بن عمرو بن عبد الخالق العَتكي البزّار (بعد ٢١٠-٢٩٢) : حَدَّثَنَا يَحْيَى بْنُ مُعَلَّى بْنِ مَنْصُورٍ ، حَدَّثَنَا ابْنُ أَبِي مَرْيَمَ ، حَدَّثَنَا ابْنُ لَهِيعَةَ ، عَنِ ابْنِ الأَسْوَدِ ، عَنْ عَامِرِ بْنِ عَبْدِ اللهِ بْنِ الزُّبَيْرِ بْنِ العَوَّامِ ، عَنْ أَبِيهِ ، أَنَّ النَّبِيَّ ﷺ قَالَ : **مَثَلُ أَهْلِ بَيْتِي مَثَلُ سَفِينَةِ نُوحٍ : مَنْ رَكِبَهَا نَجَا ، وَمَنْ تَرَكَهَا غَرِقَ .**

هذا إسناد منوَّر ، شطره مسلسل بالأشراف الدمشقيين وفيه الأبناء عن الآباء والأقرباء والمتخرِّجين عن شيوخهم وحُذّاق أئمة الحديث رحمهم الله . ورمز السيوطي لحسنه في الجامع الصغير وإن كان ليّناً ، فالحديث يتقوّى بما رواه مرفوعاً : (١) القضاعي في مسند الشهاب وأبو نعيم في الحلية والبزار والطبراني ـ تلميذ البزّار ـ في الكبير عن ابن عباس ؛ (٢) وأبو يعلى ومن طريقه ابن عدي في الكامل والقطيعي في فضائل الصحابة والحاكم والقضاعي والطبراني في الثلاثة والبزّار والفسوي في المعرفة وأبو الشيخ في الأمثال وأبو نعيم والآجُرّي عن أبي ذرّ من طُرُقٍ ، بعضهم بزيادة : **وَمَنْ قَاتَلَنَا** ـ وفي لفظ **وَمَنْ قَاتَلَهُمْ** ـ **فِي آخِرِ الزَّمَانِ كَانَ كَمَنْ قَاتَلَ مَعَ الدَّجَّالِ** ؛ (٣) والطبراني في الثلاثة عن أبي سعيد ؛ (٤) والدولابي في الأسماء والكنى عن أبي الطفيل عامر بن واثلة ؛ (٥) والخطيب وابن عساكر عن أنس بلفظ **إِنَّمَا مَثَلِي وَمَثَلُ أَهْلِ بَيْتِي كَسَفِينَةِ نُوحٍ ، مَنْ رَكِبَهَا نَجَا**

وَمَنْ تَخَلَّفَ عَنْهَا غَرِقَ ؛ (٦) وابن أبي شيبة موقوفاً على سيدنا علي كرّم الله وجهه ورضي عنهم أجمعين بلفظ **إِنَّمَا مَثَلُنَا فِي هَذِهِ الأُمَّةِ كَسَفِينَةِ نُوحٍ وَكِتَابِ حِطَّةٍ فِي بَنِي إِسْرَائِيلَ** ورجاله رجال مسلم إلا المنهال بن عمرو ، روى عنه البخاري . (فوائد) ذكر الإمام السيوطي موجزاً نفيساً لخصائص أهل البيت عند ذكره هذا الحديث في خصائصه الصغرى المسمّى أنموذج اللبيب في خصائص الحبيب ﷺ ، قال فيه : وفي أثر أن آله ﷺ في أعلى ذروة في الجنة ، وفي الحديث : **مَثَلُ أَهْلِ بَيْتِي مَثَلُ سَفِينَةِ نُوحٍ : مَنْ رَكِبَهَا نَجَا ، وَمَنْ تَخَلَّفَ عَنْهَا غَرِقَ** ، وأن من تمسّك بهم وبالقرآن لن يضلَّ ، وأنهم أمانٌ للأمة من الاختلاف ، وأنهم سادة الجنة ، وأن الله وعد أن لا يعذّبهم ، وأن من أبغضهم أدخله الله النار ، ولا يدخل قلب أحدٍ الإيمان حتى يحبَّهم لله ولقرابتهم منه ﷺ ، وأن من قاتلهم كان كمن قاتل مع الدجال ، وأن من صنع إلى أحدهم يداً كافأه ﷺ يوم القيامة ، وأنهم ما من أحد منهم إلا وله شفاعة يوم القيامة ، وأن الرجل يقوم لأخيه من مجلسه إلا بني هاشم لا يقومون لأحد . اهـ .

❑ ❑ ❑

١٩

سنن النسائي «المُجتَبى»

(٢١٤-٣٠٣)

إِنَّهُ لَعَهْدُ النَّبِيِّ الأُمِّيِّ ﷺ إِلَيَّ :
أَنَّهُ لاَ يُحِبُّكَ إِلاَّ مُؤْمِنٌ وَلاَ يُبْغِضُكَ إِلاَّ مُنَافِقٌ .

أنبأنا رائد جمعية العشيرة المحمدية بمصر ـ وهي إحدى الجمعيّات الصوفية الشاذلية ـ الفقيه المحدث الشاعر **الشيخ زكي الدين أبو البركات محمد زكي إبراهيم الحسيني الأزهري** (١٣٣٤-١٤١٩) رحمه الله ، عن العلّامة المتبحِّر النِّحْرِير أبي المواهب محمد حبيب الله بن عبد الله بن أحمد مايأبى بن عبد الله بن محمد الطالب الشنقيطي الجَكَني المالكي (١٢٩٥-١٣٦٣) عن العلامة الشيخ عمر بن بركات بن أحمد الشامي البقاعي الأزهري ثم المكي (١٢٤٥-١٣١٣) ، عن شيخ الإسلام الباجوري (١١٩٨-١٢٧٧) (ح) وأعلى بدرجة : الشيخ محمد زكي عن الشيخ المعمّر محمد العربي بن عبد الله بن إبراهيم العَقوري الليبي (١٢٤٠ كما رواه عنه المشاط-١٤ ربيع الثاني ١٣٩٠ عن ١٥٠ سنة) عن الباجوري ، عن الأمير الصغير ، عن

والـده الأمـير الكبـير محمد بـن محمد بـن أحمد بـن عبد القادر بـن عبد العزيـز السـنباوي الازهـري (١١٥٤-١٢٣٢)، عـن الشـهاب المَلَّوي، عن الملا إلياس الكُوْرَاني الدمشـقي، عن عمر ابن البَلَوي الشـامي، عن المعمَّر مئة سـنة عمر الزفتاوي، عن شـيخ الإسـلام زكريا الأنصاري (ح) وحدثنا **الدكتور سامر النص** من لفظه، أنبأنا الشـيخ الفاداني، عن مسـند الدنيا العلامة محمد عـلي المالكي المكي سماعاً لكثير منه وإجازةً لباقيه، عن الشيخ العلامة أبي بكر بن محمد شـطا المكـي المعروف بالسـيد البكـري، عن السـيد أحمد بـن زيني دحـلان المكـي، عـن عثمان الدمياطـي، عـن العلامـة عبد الله بن حجـازى الشرقاوى، عن الشـمس محمد بن سـالم الحَفْنَاوي، (ح) الفاداني عن الشيخ عمر بن حمدان المَحْرَسِيّ سماعاً لكثير منه وإجازةً لباقيه، عن شيخه فالح بن محمد الظاهري، عن محمد بن علي الخطابي السـنوسي، عن السـيد محمد مرتضى الزبيدي، عن الحَفْنَاوي، عن عبد العزيـز الزيـاديّ، عـن الشـمس محمد بـن العـلاء البابلي، عن الشيخ سالم بن محمد السنهوري، عن النجم محمد بن أحمد الغَيطي، عـن القـاضي زكريا الأنصاري، عن الحافـظ أحمد بن علي ابن حجر العسقلاني، عن أبي إسحاق إبراهيم بن أحمد التَّنوخي، بسماعه على أيوب بـن نعمة الله النابلسي، أنبأنا إسـماعيل بن أحمد العراقي، عن

عبد الرزاق بن إسماعيل القوْمِسي ، أنا أبو محمد عبد الرحمن بن أحمد الدُّوني سماعاً ، أخبرنا القاضي أبو نصر أحمد بن الحسين الدِّينَوَري المعروف بالكسَّار ، أخبرنا الحافظ القاضي أبو بكر أحمد بن محمد بن إسحاق الدِّينَوَرِي المعروف بابن السُّنِّي ، قال أخبرنا **الحافظ أبو عبد الرحمن أحمد بن شُعيب النَّسائي** ، قال : أخبرنا يوسف بن عيسى ، قال : أنبأنا الفضل بن موسى ، قال : أنبأنا الأعمش ، عن عدي ، عن زِرٍّ ، قال : قَالَ عَلِيٌّ رضي الله عنه : **إِنَّهُ لَعَهْدُ النَّبِيِّ الْأُمِّيِّ ﷺ إِلَيَّ : أَنَّهُ لَا يُحِبُّكَ إِلَّا مُؤْمِنٌ وَلَا يُبْغِضُكَ إِلَّا مُنَافِقٌ** .

رواه مسلم والترمذي وابن ماجه وأحمد . وفي الترمذي عَنْ أَبِي سَعِيدٍ الْخُدْرِيِّ : قَالَ : إِنَّا كُنَّا لَنَعْرِفُ الْمُنَافِقِينَ نَحْنُ مَعْشَرَ الْأَنْصَارِ بِبُغْضِهِمْ عَلِيَّ بْنَ أَبِي طَالِبٍ . وفي استيعاب ابن عبد البر عَنْ جَابِرٍ : قَالَ : مَا كُنَّا نَعْرِفُ الْمُنَافِقِينَ إِلَّا بِبُغْضِ عَلِيِّ ابْنِ أَبِى طَالِبٍ رَضِىَ اللهُ عَنْهُ . وجاء في زوائد القطيعي على فضائل الصحابة للإمام أحمد ، عن أبي سعيد الخدري مرفوعاً : **مَنْ أَبْغَضَنَا أَهْلَ الْبَيْتِ ، فَهُوَ مُنَافِقٌ** .

❑ ❑ ❑

٢٠

خصائص أمير المؤمنين علي للنسائي

(٢١٤-٣٠٣)

اللَّهُمَّ ! مَنْ كُنْتُ مَوْلاهُ ، فَعَلِيٌّ مَوْلاهُ . اللَّهُمَّ ! وَالِ مَنْ وَالاهُ ، وَعَادِ مَنْ عَادَاهُ .

أنبأني رئيس الجامعة الإنسانية في سلطنة قدح دار الأمان بمليزيا السيد الدكتور **محمد عقيل بن السيد علي بن السيد علوي بن السيد حسن المَهْدَلي الأهدل الحسيني العلوي الهاشمي الإندونيسي الأزهري** صاحب المؤلّفات ، عن العلامة المصلح الأديب القاضي الداعية السيد أبي المواهب محمد بن عبد الهادي بن عبد الرحمن العُجَيل الحسني اليماني (١٣٤٤-١٤١٩) صاحب المؤلفات ، منها (الصارم البتار في الرد على خصوم آل النبي المختار) ، عن العلّامة الشاعر مفخرة اليمن محمد بن سالم بن حسين الكدادي البيحاني الأزهري (١٣٢٦-١٣٩٢) ، عن أستاذ المرشدين الحبيب عبد الله بن عمر الشاطري (١٢٩٠-١٣٦١) ، عن عيدروس الحبشي ، عن والده

عمر ابن عيدروس بن عبد الرحمن وعمّه محمد بن عيدروس بن عبد الرحمن الحبشي، كلاهما عن الإمام عمر بن عبد الكريم بن عبد الرسول العطّار، عن أبي الفيض محمد بن محمد مرتضى الزبيدي، عن الشمس محمد بن سالم الحفني ـ الحَفْنَاوي ـ بالسند المارّ آنفاً إلى **الحافظ أحمد بن شُعيب النَّسائي**، قال: أخبرنا محمد بن المثنى، حدثني يحيى بن حماد، حدثنا أبو عوانة، عن سليمان، قال: حدثنا حبيب بن أبي ثابت، عن أبي الطفيل، عن زيد بن أرقم، قال: لَمَّا رَجَعَ رَسُولُ اللهِ ﷺ عَنْ حَجَّةِ الْوَدَاعِ وَنَزَلَ غَدِيرَ خُمٍّ أَمَرَ بِدَوْحَاتٍ ـ في لسان العرب: الدَّوْحةُ: الشجرة العظيمة المتسعة من أيّ الشجر كانت ـ فَقُمِّمْنَ ثُمَّ قَالَ: **كَأَنِّي قَدْ دُعِيتُ فَأَجَبْتُ، وَإِنِّي قَدْ تَرَكْتُ فِيكُمُ الثَّقَلَيْنِ، أَحَدُهُمَا أَكْبَرُ مِنَ الْآخَرِ: كِتَابَ اللهِ وَعِتْرَتِي أَهْلَ بَيْتِي. فَانْظُرُوا كَيْفَ تَخْلُفُونِي فِيهِما فَإِنَّهُمَا لَنْ يَتَفَرَّقَا حَتَّى يَرِدَا عَلَيَّ الْحَوْضَ. ثُمَّ قَالَ: إِنَّ اللهَ مَوْلَايَ، وَأَنَا وَلِيُّ كُلِّ مُؤْمِنٍ. ثُمَّ أَخَذَ بِيَدِ عَلِيٍّ فَقَالَ: مَنْ كُنْتُ وَلِيَّهُ، فَهَذَا وَلِيُّهُ. اللَّهُمَّ، وَالِ مَنْ وَالَاهُ، وَعَادِ مَنْ عَادَاهُ!** فَقُلْتُ لِزَيْدٍ: سَمِعْتَهُ مِنْ رَسُولِ اللهِ ﷺ؟ فَقَالَ: مَا كَانَ فِي الدَّوْحَاتِ أَحَدٌ إِلَّا رَآهُ بِعَيْنَيْهِ وَسَمِعَهُ بِأُذُنَيْهِ.

ورواه الطحاوي في شرح مشكل الآثار بلفظ قَامَ مِنْ قِبَلِ سَعِيدٍ

سِتَّةٌ وَمِنْ قِبَلِ زَيْدٍ سِتَّةٌ فَشَهِدُوا أَنَّهُمْ سَمِعُوا رَسُولَ اللهِ ﷺ يَقُولُ لِعَلِيٍّ رَضِيَ اللهُ عَنْهُ يَوْمَ غَدِيرِ خُمٍّ : **أَلَيْسَ اللهُ أَوْلَى بِالْمُؤْمِنِينَ ؟ قَالُوا : بَلَى . قَالَ : اللَّهُمَّ ! مَنْ كُنْتُ مَوْلاهُ ، فَعَلِيٌّ مَوْلاهُ . اللَّهُمَّ ! وَالِ مَنْ وَالاهُ ، وَعَادِ مَنْ عَادَاهُ** . ورواه أحمد والحاكم والطبراني في الكبير والنسائي في الخصائص ، وله شاهد عن بريدة الأسلمي ، رووه جميعاً وابن أبي شيبة وابن حبان وأبو يعلى والبزار والدارمي ، بعضهم باختصار . ويروى أيضا عَنْ أَبِي سَرِيحَةَ أَوْ زَيْدِ بْنِ أَرْقَمَ رضي الله عنهما ـ شَكَّ شُعْبَةُ ـ عَنِ النَّبِيِّ ﷺ قَالَ : **مَنْ كُنْتُ مَوْلاهُ فَعَلِيٌّ مَوْلاهُ** . رواه الترمذي وقال : هذا حديث حسن غريب ، وأحمد . وجاء أيضاً هكذا دون زيادة عن سعد بن أبي وقاص ، رواه ابن ماجه والنسائي في الخصائص ؛ وعن ابن عباس ، رواه الحاكم ؛ وعن علي والبراء رضي الله عنهم أجمعين . وهو متواتر ، قاله الحافظان السيوطي والكتاني . وشَرَحَ الإمامان الشافعي والنووي الموالاة بموالاة الإسلام والنُّصرة والمحبّة : ﴿**ذَٰلِكَ بِأَنَّ ٱللَّهَ مَوْلَى ٱلَّذِينَ ءَامَنُوا۟ وَأَنَّ ٱلْكَٰفِرِينَ لَا مَوْلَىٰ لَهُمْ** ﴿١١﴾﴾ [سورة سيّدنا محمد ﷺ] . وفي الدارمي موقوفاً على ابن مسعود رضي الله عنه : **الْوَلَاءُ لُحْمَةٌ كَلُحْمَةِ النَّسَبِ لَا يُبَاعُ وَلَا يُوهَبُ** . رفعه السيوطي في الفانيد في حلاوة الأسانيد بإسناده

إلى الربيع ابن سليمان عن شيخه الشافعي عن شيخه محمد بن الحسن عن شيخه أبي يوسف عن عبد الله بن دينار عن ابن عمر رضي الله عنهما بلفظ **لَا تُبَاعُ وَلَا تُوهَبُ** .

وفي قولـه ﷺ **فَإِنَّهُمَا لَـنْ يَتَفَرَّقَا حَتَّى يَرِدَا عَلَيَّ الحَوْضَ** : دليل أن أهـل البيت محفوظون إلى يوم القيامة بحفظ الله كحفظه تعالى كتابَه ، وأنهم حرّاس السّنة وحاملو لوائها للمسلمين . ففي مصنَّف ابن أبي شـيبة عَنْ أَبِي مِجْلَزٍ : رَمَيْتُ الجِمَارَ فَلَمْ أَدْرِ بِكَمْ رَمَيْتُ ؟ فَسَـأَلْتُ ابْنَ عُمَـرَ ، فَلَـمْ يُجِبْنِي ، فَمَرَّ بِي ابْنُ الْحَنَفِيَّةِ فَسَـأَلْتُهُ ، فَقَـالَ : يَا عَبْدَ اللهِ ، لَيْسَ شَيْءٌ أَعْظَمَ عَلَيْنَا مِنَ الصَّلَاةِ ، وَإِذَا نَسِيَ أَحَدُنَا أَعَادَ . فَأَخْبَرْتُ ابْـنَ عُمَـرَ فَقَالَ إِنَّهُمْ أَهْـلُ بَيْتٍ مُفْهَمُونَ . وفحـواه موافق للحديث الصحيح الذي ذكره مالك في الموطأ ورواه الحاكم والبيهقي وغيرهما عن أبي هريرة وابن عباس وأنس وعمرو بن عوف رضي الله عنهم : **تَرَكْتُ فِيكُمْ شَيْئَيْنِ لَنْ تَضِلُّوا بَعْدَهُمَا : كِتَابَ اللهِ وَسُنَّتِي ، وَلَنْ يَتَفَرَّقَا حَتَّـى يَرِدَا عَـلَيَّ الحَوْضَ** . وهو محفوظ معروف مشـهور عنه ﷺ كما قـال ابن عبد البر وابـن حزم والغماريون وغيرهـم . وقال الهيتمي : الحاصل أن الحث وقع على التمسـك بالكتاب وبالسنة وبالعلماء بهما من أهل البيت ويسـتفاد من مجموع ذلك بقاء الأمور الثلاثة إلى قيام

الساعة . اه . وفيه أيضاً أن السنّة محفوظة بحفظ كتاب الله كما هو مفهوم السلف الصالح للقرآن العظيم ، فلما قيل لابن المبارك : هذه الأحاديث الموضوعة ؟ قال تعيش لها الجهابذة ، ثم تلا ﴿ نَحْنُ نَزَّلْنَا ٱلذِّكْرَ وَإِنَّا لَهُۥ لَحَٰفِظُونَ ٩ ﴾ [الحجر] . قال في الشفا : طوبى لأمّة الإسلام بحفظ ربّ الأرباب لدستورها القرآن ، وسنّة نبيّها ﷺ الطاهرة المطهّرة ، وآله الطاهرين الطيّبين رضوان الله تعالى عليهم أجمعين . وقال : اختلف المفسرون في معنى قوله تعالى في أم الكتاب ﴿ ٱهْدِنَا ٱلصِّرَٰطَ ٱلْمُسْتَقِيمَ ٦ ﴾ فقال أبو العالية والحسن : الصراط المستقيم هو رسول الله ﷺ وخيار أهل بيته وأصحابه ، حكاه عنهما الماوردي ، وحكى مَكّي عنهما نحوه وقال هو رسول الله ﷺ وصاحباه أبو بكر وعمر ، وحكاه أبو الليث السمرقندي عن أبى العالية في قوله تعالى ﴿ صِرَٰطَ ٱلَّذِينَ أَنْعَمْتَ عَلَيْهِمْ ﴾ قال فبلغ ذلك الحسن فقال صدق والله ونصح . وحكى الماوردي ذلك في تفسير ﴿ صِرَٰطَ ٱلَّذِينَ أَنْعَمْتَ عَلَيْهِمْ ﴾ عن عبد الرحمن بن زيد .

❑ ❑ ❑

٢١

السنن الكبرى للنسائي

(٢١٤-٣٠٣)

هٰذَانِ ابْنَايَ وَابْنَا ابْنَتِي . اللَّهُمَّ إِنَّكَ تَعْلَمُ أَنِّي أُحِبُّهُمَا ، فَأَحِبَّهُمَا !
اللَّهُمَّ إِنَّكَ تَعْلَمُ أَنِّي أُحِبُّهُمَا ، فَأَحِبَّهُمَا !

أنبأني فقيه آل باعلوي زين الشمائل ومعدن الفضائل السيد السند حافظ المذهب وفقيه الإجماع والخلاف قامع البدع ورافع راية أهل السنة العلّامة الزاهد المربي **الحبيب أبو محمد زين بن إبراهيم بن سُمَيط الشافعي** (ولد عام ١٣٥٧/ ١٩٣٨م) الإندونيسي مولداً المدني إقامة ، أنبأني العلامة المحدث الفقيه الداعية الحبيب عمر بن أحمد بن أبي بكر بن سُمَيط باعلوي (ت ١٣٨٧) صاحب النفحة الشذية من الديار الحضرمية قاضي زنجبار ومدرّس الحديث بجامعها ، أنبأني الحبيب شيخ بن محمد بن حسين الحبشي ، عن أبيه المسند العارف مفتي مكة الحبيب الشمس محمد بن حسين بن عبد الله بن شيخ الحبشي الذي بلغت مشايخه نحو المائة ، أنبأني الوجيه عبد الرحمن بن سليمان بن يحيى بن عمر مقبول الأهدل ، بالسند المار في باب سنن

ابن ماجه إلى البابلي ، عن السنهوري ، عن الشهاب أحمد ابن حجر الهيتمي المكي ، عن الشرف عبد الحق السنباطي ، عن الحافظ ابن حجر ، قراءة على أبي طاهر محمد بن أبي اليمن الربعي ، أنبأتنا زينب بنت الكمال أحمد بن عبد الرحيم إجازة ، عن أبي القاسم عبد الرحمن بن مكي سبط السِّلَفي ، عن أبي القاسم خَلَف بن عبد الملك بن بَشْكُوَال إجازة مكاتبة ، أنبأنا أبو محمد عبد الرحمن بن محمد بن عتاب ، أنبأنا أبي سماعاً ، أنبأنا عبد الله بن ربيع ، أنبأنا محمد بن معاوية بن الأحمر ، **أنبأنا أبو عبد الرحمن أحمد بن شُعيب النَّسائي** ، قال : حَدَّثَنِي خَالِدُ بْنُ مَخْلَدٍ ، قَالَ : حَدَّثَنِي مُوسَى ـ وَهُوَ بْنُ يَعْقُوبَ الزَّمْعِيُّ ـ ، عَنْ عَبْدِ اللهِ بْنِ أَبِي بَكْرِ بْنِ زَيْدِ بْنِ الْمُهَاجِرِ ، قَالَ : أَخْبَرَنِي مُسْلِمُ بْنُ أَبِي سَهْلٍ النَّبَّالُ ، قَالَ : أَخْبَرَنِي الْحَسَنُ بْنُ أُسَامَةَ بْنِ زَيْدِ بْنِ حَارِثَةَ ، قَالَ : أَخْبَرَنِي أَبِي ـ أُسَامَةُ ابْنُ زَيْدٍ ـ قَالَ : **طَرَقْتُ رَسُولَ اللهِ ﷺ لَيْلَةً لِبَعْضِ الْحَاجَةِ فَخَرَجَ وَهُوَ مُشْتَمِلٌ عَلَى شَيْءٍ لَا أَدْرِي مَا هُوَ ، فَلَمَّا فَرَغْتُ مِنْ حَاجَتِي قُلْتُ : مَا هٰذَا الَّذِي أَنْتَ مُشْتَمِلٌ عَلَيْهِ ؟ فَكَشَفَهُ ، فَإِذَا هُوَ الْحَسَنُ وَالْحُسَيْنُ عَلَى وَرِكَيْهِ . فَقَالَ : هٰذَانِ ابْنَايَ وَابْنَا ابْنَتِي . اللَّهُمَّ إِنَّكَ تَعْلَمُ أَنِّي أُحِبُّهُمَا ، فَأَحِبَّهُمَا ! اللَّهُمَّ إِنَّكَ تَعْلَمُ أَنِّي أُحِبُّهُمَا ، فَأَحِبَّهُمَا !**

رواه الترمذي وحسّنه ، وابن حبان ، والبخاري مختصراً ، وزاد

الترمذي : **وَأَحِبَّ مَنْ يُحِبُّهُما** ! فليُتنبَّه إلى عظمة هذا الدعاء وخطورته . وفي الباب عن أبي هريرة ، رواه ابن أبي شيبة ؛ وعن البراء ، رواه الترمذي . وفي جامع معمر عن عبد الله بن عثمان بن خُثَيم مرسلاً : أَخَذَ رَسُولُ اللهِ ﷺ يَوْمًا حَسَناً وَحُسَيْناً ، فَجَعَلَ هَذَا عَلَى هَذَا الْفَخِذِ وَهَذَا عَلَى هَذَا الْفَخِذِ ، ثُمَّ أَقْبَلَ عَلَى الْحَسَنِ فَقَبَّلَهُ ، ثُمَّ أَقْبَلَ عَلَى الْحُسَيْنِ فَقَبَّلَهُ ، ثُمَّ قَالَ : **اللَّهُمَّ إِنِّي أُحِبُّهُما ، فَأَحِبَّهُما** ! ثُمَّ قَالَ : **إِنَّ الْوَلَدَ مَجْبَنَةٌ مَبْخَلَةٌ مَجْهَلَةٌ** . (الغريب) الوَرِك بالفتح ثم الكسر : ما فَوْقَ الفَخِذِ كالكَتِفِ فوقَ العَضُدِ . تاج .

❑ ❑ ❑

٢٢

فضائل الصحابة للنسائي

(٢١٤-٣٠٣)

هُوَ مَلَكٌ مِنَ الْمَلَائِكَةِ لَمْ يَهْبِطْ إِلَى الأَرْضِ قَطّ قَبْلَ هٰذِهِ اللَّيْلَةِ ، اسْتَأْذَنَ رَبَّهُ أَنْ يُسَلِّمَ عَلَيَّ ، وَبَشَّرَنِي أَنَّ الحَسَنَ وَالحُسَيْنَ سَيِّدَا شَبَابِ أَهْلِ الجَنَّةِ ، وَأَنَّ فَاطِمَةَ سَيِّدَةُ نِسَاءِ أَهْلِ الجَنَّةِ .

أخبرني الشريف الجليل المعمَّر **الحبيب عبد الله بن هارون بن حسن الجنيد جمل الليل** السنغافوري بقراءتي عليه في داره ، عن والده ، عن الحبيب عبد الله بن عمر الشاطري ، عن مسنِد اليمن الحبيب عيدروس بن عمر ، بسنده المارّ في باب خصائص سيّدنا علي - رضي الله عنه - إلى **الحافظ أحمد بن شُعيب النَّسائي** ، أخبرنا الْحُسَيْن بن مَنْصُور ، قَالَ أَنا الْحُسَيْن بن مُحَمَّد أَبُو أَحْمد ، قَالَ أَنا إِسْرَائِيل بن يُونُس ، عَن مَيسرَة بن حبيب ، عَن الْمنْهَال بْنِ عَمْرٍو ، عَن زِرّ بْنِ حُبَيْشٍ ، عَن حُذَيْفَة بن الْيَمَان ، قَالَ : سَأَلَتْنِي أُمِّي : مُنْذُ مَتَى عَهْدُكَ بِالنَّبِيِّ ﷺ ؟ فَقُلْتُ : مُنْذُ كَذَا وَكَذَا . فَنَالَتْ مِنِّي وَسَبَّتْنِي ، فَقُلْتُ لَهَا : دَعِينِي ، فَإِنِّي آتِي النَّبِيَّ ﷺ فَأُصَلِّي مَعَهُ الْمَغْرِبَ ، وَلَا أَدَعُهُ

حَتَّى يَسْتَغْفِرَ لِي وَلَكِ . فَصَلَّيْتُ مَعَهُ المَغْرِبَ ، فَصَلَّى إِلَى الْعِشَاءِ ثُمَّ انْفَتَلَ ، وَتَبِعْتُهُ فَعَرَضَ لَهُ عَارِضٌ وَأَخَذَهُ وَذَهَبَ فَاتَّبَعْتُهُ ، فَسَمِعَ صَوْتِي فَقَالَ : مَنْ هٰذَا ؟ فَقُلْتُ : حُذَيْفَة . فَقَالَ : مَا لَكَ ؟ فَحَدَّثْتُهُ بِالْأَمْرِ . فَقَالَ : غَفَرَ اللهُ لَكَ وَلِأُمِّكَ . أَمَا رَأَيْتَ الْعَارِضَ الَّذِي عَرَضَ لِي قَبْلُ ؟ قُلْتُ : بَلَى . قَالَ : هُوَ مَلَكٌ مِنَ المَلَائِكَةِ لَمْ يَهْبِطْ إِلَى الْأَرْضِ قَطُّ قَبْلَ هٰذِهِ اللَّيْلَةِ ، اسْتَأْذَنَ رَبَّهُ أَنْ يُسَلِّمَ عَلَيَّ ، وَبَشَّرَنِي أَنَّ الحَسَنَ وَالحُسَيْنَ سَيِّدَا شَبَابِ أَهْلِ الجَنَّةِ ، وَأَنَّ فَاطِمَةَ سَيِّدَةُ نِسَاءِ أَهْلِ الجَنَّةِ .

رواه أحمد والترمذي ـ قال حديث حسن غريب ـ وابن أبي شيبة وأبو يعلى والنسائي في الكبرى والطبراني في الكبير والأوسط وابن حبان وأبو نعيم في الحلية والمعرفة والبيهقي في الدلائل وابن عساكر من طرق ، وعند بعضهم زيادة : **إِلَّا مَا كَانَ مِنْ مَرْيَمَ بِنْتِ عِمْرَانَ** وسيأتي في باب كتاب الشريعة للآجُرّي .

❑ ❑ ❑

٢٣

مسند فاطمة بنت رسول الله صلّى الله عليهما

من مسند أبي يعلى المَوْصِلي

(٢١٠-٣٠٧)

لِكُلِّ بَنِي أُمٍّ عَصَبَةٌ يَنْتَمُونَ إِلَيْهِ ، إِلَّا وَلَدَ فَاطِمَةَ : فَأَنَا وَلِيُّهُمْ ، وَأَنَا عَصَبَتُهُمْ .

أخبرني سيّدي الشيخ أبو سعيد محمود بن عثمان قُوَيْدِر (١٣٤٩-١٤٣١) رحمه الله ـ كان كثير الابتهال وقيل إنه كان من الأبدال ، وأمّه حسينية من آل الزُعْبِي ـ بقراءتي عليه في جامع عمر بن عبد العزيز بمزّة دمشق ، عن شيخه السيّد مكّي الكتاني ـ وكان هو وأخوه أبو الطيّب من أشدّ الناس ملازمةً له ـ عن محدّث الحجاز الشيخ فالح الظاهري بسنده الخُماسي المارّ في باب الموطأ إلى الحافظ ابن حجر ، (ح) وأنبأني شقيقه الشيخ أبو الطيب محمد قُوَيْدِر (ت ١٤٢٧) في داره بمَيدان دمشق ، عن الشيخ محمد أمين بن محمد سُوَيْد (١٢٧٣-١٣٥٥) ، عن المسند أبي المحاسن محمد بن خليل

القاوقجي (١٢٢٤-١٣٠٥) ، عن الأمير الكبير بسنده السُّداسي المارّ في باب مسند الشافعي إلى الحافظ ابن حجر ، عن مسنِد الدنيا الصلاح محمد بن أحمد بن إبراهيم بن أبي عمر المقدسي الصالحي ، عن الفخر ابن البخاري ، عن أبي رَوح عبد المُعِزّ بن محمّد الهَرَوي ، حدثنا تميم بن أبي سعيد الجُرجاني ، ثنا أبو سعد محمّد بن عبد الرحمن الكَنْجَرُوذي ، ثنا محمّد بن أحمد بن حَمْدان ، حدّثنا **الإمام أبو يعلى أحمد بن علي بن المثنَّى الموصلي** بموصل ، حَدَّثَنَا عُثْمَانُ بْنُ أَبِي شَيْبَةَ ، حَدَّثَنَا جَرِيرٌ ، عَنْ شَيْبَةَ بْنِ نَعَامَةَ ، عَنْ فَاطِمَةَ بِنْتِ الْحُسَيْنِ ، عَنْ فَاطِمَةَ الْكُبْرَى ، قَالَتْ : قَالَ رَسُولُ اللهِ ﷺ وآله : **لِكُلِّ بَنِي أُمٍّ عَصَبَةٌ يَنْتَمُونَ إِلَيْهِ ، إِلَّا وَلَدَ فَاطِمَةَ : فَأَنَا وَلِيُّهُمْ ، وَأَنَا عَصَبَتُهُمْ** .

رواه ابن عساكر من طريق أبي يعلى . ورواه الطبراني في الكبير والخطيب في التاريخ ، الأول بلفظ **كُلُّ بَنِي أُمٍّ يَنْتَمُونَ إِلَى عَصَبَةٍ** ، والثاني بلفظي **كُلُّ بَنِي آدَمَ يَنْتَمُونَ إِلَى عَصَبَةٍ** أو **إِلَى عَصَبَتِهِمْ** . وله شاهد من حديث جابر ، رواه الطبراني والحاكم . قال السخاوي في ارتقاء الغُرَف : يُروى أيضاً عن ابن عباس ، أخرجه أبو الخير الحاكمي - هو أحمد بن إسماعيل بن يوسف الطالْقاني (٥١٢-٥٩٠) - عن ابن عباس رضي الله عنهما قال : كنت أنا والعباس جالسين عند

رسـول الله ﷺ إذا دخل عليٌّ فسلّم فردّ عليه النبيّ ﷺ السلام وقام إليه وعانقه وقبّل بين عينيه وأجلسه عن يمينه . فقال العباس : يا رسول الله ! أتحبُّه ؟ فقال : **يا عَمُّ ! وَالله ، لَلهُ أَشَدُّ حُبّاً لَهُ مِنِّي ؛ إِنَّ اللهَ جَعَلَ ذُرِّيَّةَ كُلِّ نَبِيٍّ فِي صُلْبِهِ ، وَجَعَلَ ذُرِّيَّتِي فِي صُلْبِ هَذَا** . وبعضها يقـوّي بعضاً . وقـول ابن الجوزي في العلـل المتناهية : إنه لا يصح ، ليس بجيّد . وفيه دليل لاختصاصه ﷺ بانتساب أولاد ابنته إليه ، ولـذا قال (أي النووي) في الروضة تبعـاً لأصلها (أي شرح الوجيز للرافعي الذي اختصره في روضة الطالبين) في الخصائص : وأولاد بناته يُنسَبون إليه ﷺ ، وأولاد بنات غيره لا ينسبون إلى جدهم في الكفاءة وغيرها . اهـ . قلت : وبمثله قال ابن الملقِّن في غاية السُّول في خصائص الرسول ﷺ والسيوطي في الخصائص الكبرى والصغرى والخيضري الشافعي في اللفظ المكرَّم بخصائص النبي المعظَّم ﷺ والحافظ الصالحي في سيرته الكبرى سبل الهدى والرشاد والقاضي عياض في الشفا . وقال السخاوي في الأجوبة المرضية : قد كنت سئلت عن هذا الحديث وبسطت الكلام فيه ، ونبّهت أنه صالح للحُجَّة ، وبالله التوفيق . وقال الشيخ أحمد الغماري في المداوي : من شواهده : ما قد روى عبد الله بن أحمد بن حنبل في فضائل الصحابة

عن المستظل : إِنَّ عُمَرَ بْنَ الْخَطَّابِ خَطَبَ إِلَى عَلِيِّ بْنِ أَبِي طَالِبٍ أُمَّ كُلْثُومٍ ، فَاعْتَلَّ عَلَيْهِ بِصِغَرِهَا ، فَقَالَ : إِنِّي لَمْ أُرِدِ الْبَاهَ ، وَلٰكِنِّي سَمِعْتُ رَسُولَ اللهِ ﷺ يَقُولُ : **كُلُّ سَبَبٍ وَنَسَبٍ مُنْقَطِعٌ يَوْمَ الْقِيَامَةِ مَا خَلَا سَبَبِي وَنَسَبِي ، كُلُّ وَلَدِ أَبٍ فَإِنَّ عَصَبَتَهُمْ لِأَبِيهِمْ ، مَا خَلَا وَلَدُ فَاطِمَةَ ، فَإِنِّي أَنَا أَبُوهُمْ وَعَصَبَتُهُمْ** . قلت وما رواه الطبراني من طريق سفيان بن عيينة ، عن جعفر بن محمد ، عن ابيه ، عن جابر ، قال : سمعتُ عمر بن الخطاب يقول للناس حين تزوج بنتَ علي : ألا تُهَنِّئُوني ! سَمِعْتُ رَسُولَ اللهِ ﷺ يقول : **يَنْقَطِعُ يَوْمَ الْقِيَامَةِ كُلُّ سَبَبٍ وَنَسَبٍ إِلَّا سَبَبِي وَنَسَبِي** . قال الهيثمي رواه الطبراني في الأوسط والكبير ورجالهما رجال الصحيح غير الحسن بن سهل وهو ثقة . ورواه الطبراني في الكبير عن ابن عباس أيضاً بهذا اللفظ ، قال : ورجاله ثقات . ورواه البيهقي في مناقب الشافعي مرسلاً عن محمّد بن علي أنّ عمر خطب أم كلثوم إلى علي ، إلى أن قال : سمعتُ رسول الله ﷺ يقول : **إِنَّ كُلَّ سَبَبٍ وَنَسَبٍ يَنْقَطِعُ يَوْمَ الْقِيَامَةِ إِلَّا مَا كَانَ مِنْ سَبَبِي وَنَسَبِي** . حكى النسّابة ابن فندق عن بعضهم في قوله ﷺ **كُلُّ حَسَبٍ وَنَسَبٍ يَنْقَطِعُ إِلَّا حَسَبِي وَنَسَبِي** الحسب الشريعة والنسب الذرّيّة والعِتْرَة . (نكتة) في سبل الهدى والرشاد : روى ابن

أبي حاتم عن أبي الأسود الديلي وأبو الشيخ وروى الحاكم [والبيهقي في الكبرى وابن عساكر في التاريخ] عن عبد الملك بن عمير وعاصم بن بَهْدَلَةَ ، قالوا : اجتمعوا ثَمَّ الحجَّاج فذُكِر الحُسَيْنُ بْنُ عَلِيٍّ فَقَالَ الحَجَّاجُ : لَمْ يَكُنْ مِنْ ذُرِّيَّةِ النَّبِيِّ ﷺ ، وَعِنْدَهُ يَحْيَى بْنُ يَعْمَرٍ ، فقال له : كَذَبْتَ أيّها الأمير ! فقال : لَتَأْتِيَنِّي عَلَى مَا قُلْتَ بِبَيِّنَةٍ وَمِصْدَاقٍ مِنْ كِتَابِ اللهِ عَزَّ وَجَلَّ أَوْ لَأَقْتُلَنَّكَ قَتْلاً ! فقال : ﴿ **وَمِن ذُرِّيَّتِهِۦ دَاوُۥدَ وَسُلَيۡمَٰنَ وَأَيُّوبَ وَيُوسُفَ وَمُوسَىٰ وَهَٰرُونَۚ وَكَذَٰلِكَ نَجۡزِي ٱلۡمُحۡسِنِينَ ﴿٨٤﴾ وَزَكَرِيَّا وَيَحۡيَىٰ وَعِيسَىٰ** ﴾ [الأنعام] . أَلَيْسَ عِيسَى مِنْ ذُرِّيَّةِ إِبْرَاهِيمَ وَلَيْسَ لَهُ أَبٌ ؟ وَفِي لَفْظٍ : فَأَخْبَرَ اللهُ عَزَّ وَجَلَّ أَنَّ عِيسَى مِنْ ذُرِّيَّةِ آدمَ بِأُمِّهِ ، وَالْحُسَيْنُ بْنُ عَلِيٍّ مِنْ ذُرِّيَّةِ مُحَمَّدٍ ﷺ بِأُمِّهِ . اهـ . (فقه الشرف من قِبَل الأم) قال السيوطي في العَجاجة الزَّرْنَبية في السُّلالة الزينبية : ذكر الفقهاء من خصائصه ﷺ أنه يُنسب إليه أولادُ بناته ، ولم يذكروا مثل ذلك في أولاد بنات بناته ؛ فالخصوصية للطبقة العليا فقط . **فأولاد فاطمة الأربعة** ينسبون إليه ﷺ ، وأولاد الحسن والحسين ينسبون إليهما ، فينسبون إليه ﷺ ، وأولاد زينب وأم كلثوم ينسبون إلى أبيهم عمر وعبد الله ، لا إلى الأم ولا إلى أبيها ﷺ ، لأنهم أولاد بنت بنته لا أولاد بنته . فجرى الأمر فيهم على

قاعـدة الـشرع في أن الولد يَتْبع أباه في النسـب ، لا أمَّـه . وإنّما خرج أولاد فاطمـة وحدَهـا للخصوصيّـة التـي ورد الحديـث بهـا ، وهو مقْصـورٌ عـلى ذرّيّـة الحسـن والحسـين . وقـال الهيتمـي في الفتاوى الحديثيـة : فـأولاد فاطمة الأربع ـ (١) أم كلثوم زوجة عمر ولدتْ منـه زيداً ورقية ، ثم تزوّجتْ بعده وَلَدَ عمِّها ابنَ جعفر ، فولدت له ثلاثـة : عـون فمحمد فعبـد الله ، ولم يلد لأحد منهـم ، (٢) وزينب (٣) والحسـن (٤) والحسـين ـ فهـؤلاءِ الأربعـةُ يُنسبون إليه ﷺ ، وأولاد الحسـن والحسـين ينسـبون إليهما ، فينسـبون إليـه ، بخلاف أولاد زينب وأم كلثوم ، فإنهم إنّما ينسبون إلى أبويهما عمر وعبد الله ، لا إلى الأمّ ولا إلى جدّهمـا ﷺ ، عمـلاً بقاعدة الشرع : إنّ الولدَ يتْبع أبـاه في النسـب لا أمَّه . وإنّما خرج أولاد فاطمـةَ وحدَها خصوصيّةً لهم ، وذلك مقصور على ذرّيّة الحسـن والحسـين كـما يدل له حديث **لِكُلِّ بَنِي أُمٍّ عَصَبَةٌ** ، فخصّ الانتساب والتعصيب بهما دون أختَيهما . ولهذا جرى الخلف كالسـلف على أن ابـن الشريفة من غير شريف : غير شريف . ولو عمَّتْ الخصوصية أن ابن كل شريفة شريف : تَحْرُمُ عليه الصدقة ؛ وليس كذلك . ولا يختصّ ذلك بالحسن والحسين إلّا لانحصار الأمر فيهـا ، وإلّا لو فُرض إدخالُ زينب وأَعقبتْ ذَكَراً ،

كان مثلَها وإن لم يكن أبوه شريفاً هاشمياً ، لأنّ الشرف لم يأت إليهما إلا من جهته ﷺ لا غيره . واعلم أن اسم الشريف كان يُطلق في الصدر الأول على من كان من أهل البيت ولو عبّاسِيّاً أو عَقِيلِيّاً ، ومنه قول المؤرخين : الشريف العباسي ، الشريف الزينبي ؛ فلمّا وَلّى الفاطميّون بمصر ، قَصَرُوا الشَّرَفَ على ذرّيّة الحسن والحسين فقط ، واستمرّ ذٰلك إلى الآن . اهـ .

ثم جاء في الصحيحين عن أنس رضي الله عنه مرفوعاً : **إِنَّ ابنَ أُخْتِ الْقَوْمِ مِنْهُم** . قال النووي استدل به من يورِّث ذوي الأرحام ، وأجاب الجمهور بأنه ليس في هذا اللفظ ما يقتضي توريثه وإنما معناه أن بينه وبينهم ارتباطا وقرابة ولم يتعرض للإرث ، وسياق الحديث يقتضي أن المراد أنه كالواحد منهم في إفشاء سِرِّهم بحضرته ونحو ذلك . اهـ . (الشافعي هاشمي من جهة الأم) قال البيهقي في المناقب : الشافعي ـ رحمه الله ـ من صَلِيبة بني عبد المُطلب ابن عبد مناف من قِبَلِ آبائه ، وهو من بني هاشم بن عبد مناف من جهة جدّاته اللّاتي كنّ لآبائه . فقد ذكرنا في نسبه أن أم عبد يزيد جدّ الشافعي : الشَّفَّاءُ بنت هاشم بن عبد مناف ؛ وأم السائب بن عبيد جدّ الشافعي : الشَّفَّاء بنت الأرقم بن هاشم بن عبد مناف ؛ وأمّ الشَّفَّاء : خَلْدَةُ بنت

أسد ابن هاشم بن عبد مناف ، أخت فاطمة بنت أسد بن هاشم أم علي بن أبي طالب . فهو هاشميّ من هذه الوجوه التي ذكرناها ، وعلي بن أبي طالب ابن خالة جدّه . وهو داخل في الاصطفاء الذي أخبر عنه رسول الله ﷺ وأبَانَ به شرفَهم وفضلَهم على غيرهم من وجهين ، رحمة الله ورضوانه عليه . اهـ . (لطيفة) قال أبو العبّاس الوَنْشَرِيسي في المِعيار المُعْرِب ج ١٢ ص ٣٨٥ : سُئِلَ الشيخ الإمام ناصر الدين أبو علي منصور بن أحمد المشدالي نزيل بجاية رحمه الله عن مسألة الشرف من قِبَل الأم فأجاب : من كانت أمّه شريفة فقط يجوز أن ينتسب إليه ﷺ ، من أمّه ، ويدل على ذلك وجوه ، فذكرها . والله أعلم وأحكم .

❑ ❑ ❑

٢٤

تفسير ابن جرير الطَّبَري

(٢٢٤- ٣١٠)

خَيْرُ نِسَاءِ الجَنَّةِ مَرْيَمُ بِنْتُ عِمْرَانَ ، وَخَيْرُ نِسَاءِ الجَنَّةِ خَدِيجَةُ بِنْتُ خُوَيْلِدٍ .

أنبأني حافظ طنجة ومجتهدها السيد **أبو الفتوح عبد الله بن عبد القادر التليدي الإدريسي** الحسني (١٣٤٧-١٤٣٨) رحمه الله ، عن أبي الهدى محمد الباقر بن محمّد بن عبد الكبير الكتّاني ، عن جدّه جبل السّنّة والدين وربّاني عصره أبي المكارم عبد الكبير بن محمّد ، عن والده أبي عبد الله وأبي المَفَاخر محمّد بن عبد الواحد الكبير بن أحمد بن عبد الواحد (ت ١٢٨٩) ، عن الأخوين عمر وأبي عيسى المهدي ابني الطالب ابن سودة ، كلاهما عن أبي محمد عبد السلام الأزمي ، عن الشيخ أبي عبد الله محمد التَّاوُدِي ابن سودَة (١١١١-١٢٠٩) بفتح السين وضمّها نسبةً لأحد آبائهم أو أمّهاتهم ، عن المعمّر الشمس أبي عبد الله محمد بن عبد السلام بَنَّاني (١٠٨٣ ؟ -١١٦٣) ، عن المسند أبي

سـالم عبد الله بـن محمد بن أبي بكر العَيَّـاشي (١٠٣٧-١٠٩٠) ، عن أبي العباس أحمد بن محمد الأَبّار الفاسي (١٠٠١-١٠٧١) ، عن الخَفَاجي ، عـن العلقمـي ، عن السـيوطي ، عن الشـهاب أبو الطيّـب أحمد بن محمّد بـن علي الحجـازي (٧٩١-٨٧٥) ، عن إبراهيم بـن عبد الواحد التّنُوخـي ، عـن أحمد بـن أبي طالـب الحجّـار ، عـن جعفر بـن علي الهَمَذَاني ، عن الحافظ أبي طاهر السِّـلَفي ، أنبأنا أبو عبد الله محمد بن أحمد بـن إبراهيم بن الحطّاب الرازي ، عن أبي الفضل محمد بن أحمد السـعدي ، عـن الخَصِيب بـن عبد الله بن الخَصِيب سـماعاً ، عن أبي محمـد عبد الله بن محمـد الفرغاني ، أنبأنـا **أبو جعفـر محمّد بن جرير الطـبري** : حدثنـي يونس ، قـال : أخبرنا ابن وهب ، قـال : حدثني المنذر بـن عبـد الله الحزامي ، عن هشـام بن عـروة ، عـن أبيه ، عن عبد الله بن جعفر بن أبي طالب ، أنّ رسـول الله ﷺ قال : **خَيْرُ نِسَاءِ الجَنَّةِ مَرْيَمُ بِنْتُ عِمْرَانَ ، وَخَيْرُ نِسَاءِ الجَنَّةِ خَدِيجَةُ بِنْتُ خُوَيْلِدٍ** .

إسـناد الطـبري صحيـح وأصلـه في المسـند والصحيحـين والترمـذي ، عـن عبد الله بـن جعفـر ، عـن علـي رضي الله عنهـم ، مرفوعاً . وفي الصحيحين عنه : **خَيْرُ نِسَائِهَا مَرْيَمُ بِنْتُ عِمْرَانَ وَخَيْرُ نِسَـائِهَا خَدِيجَةُ بِنْتُ خُوَيْلِدٍ** . يعني نساء أهل الجنة . (فائدة) كان أبو

المكارم يقرئ تفسير الطبري في الزاوية الكتّانية بفاس .

(فائدة) أخبرني السيد محمد أبو الهدى مكاتبة: بيت البَنَّاني أسرة مشهورة في المغرب، وهي من أعرق بيوتات فاس، وما زال لهذه الأسرة جاه عريض ومكانة اجتماعية وتبريز في العلم والسياسة والتجارة. ولهم محبة عظيمة في آل البيت النبوي الشريف ويقال في المغرب : شريف أو بناني، إشادةً بهذا البيت لأن أحد أجدادهم فدى شريفًا من الشرفاء كان مطلوبًا لسلطان زمانه بأحد أبنائه، فرضي أن يسلّم ابنه ولم يسلّم الشريف.

❑ ❑ ❑

٢٥

الذُّرِّيَّة الطاهرة للدُّولَابِي

(٢٢٤- ٣١٠)

اللَّهُمَّ ! إِنَّكَ تَعْلَمُ أَنَّهُ كَانَ فِي حَاجَتِكَ وَحَاجَةِ رَسُولِكَ ، فَرُدَّ عَلَيْهِ الشَّمْسَ . فَرَدَّهَا عَلَيْهِ ، فَصَلَّى ، وَغَابَتِ الشَّمْسُ .

أخبرنا القاضي المعمّر محمد مرشد عابدين الحسيني الدمشقي الصالحي (١٣٣٢-١٤٢٨) والدكتور محمد مطيع الحافظ في داريهما شارع بَرْنِيَّة وحيّ الدَّحداح بدمشق ، الأول قراءةً عليه وأنا أسمع والثاني بقراءتي عليه ، قال الأول : أنبأنا والدي السيد محمد أبو الخير عابدين (١٢٦٩-١٣٤٣) ، عن والده السيد أحمد بن عبد الغني بن عمر عابدين النقشبندي (١٢٤٤-١٣٠٧) ، عن الوجيه عبد الرحمن الكزبري ، عن مرتضى الزبيدي ، وقال الثاني : أخبرنا قاضي الشام المسند السيد عبد المحسن الإسطواني ، عن السيد سليم بن ياسين بن حامد العطار ، عن جدّه السيد حامد العطار ، عن مرتضى الزبيدي ، بالسند السُّداسي المارّ في باب المجتبى إلى الحافظ ابن حجر ، قال :

أخبرنـا به أبو العباس أحمد بن أبي بكر المقدسي في كتابه ، قال : أنبأنا القاضي تقي الدين سليمان بن حمزة بن أبي عمر ، قال : أنبأنا الحسن بن علي بن السيد الهاشمي إجازة مكاتبة ، أنبأنا أبو الفضل محمد بن ناصر بن علي سماعا عليه ، أنبأنا أبو الطاهر محمد بن أحمد بن أبي الصقر ، أنبأنا أبو البركات أحمد بن عبد الواحد بن نظيف ، أنبأنا الحسن بن رشيق العسكري ، أنبأنا **أبو بشر محمد بن أحمد الدُّوْلَابي** ، حدثني إسحاق بن يونس ، حدثنا سويد بن سعيد ، عن المطلب بن زياد ، عن إبراهيم بن حيان ، عن عبد الله بن حسن ، عن فاطمة الصغرى ابنة الحسين ، عن الحسين بن علي ـ رضي الله عنهم ـ قال : **كَانَ رَأْسُ رَسُولِ اللهِ ﷺ فِي حِجْرِ عَلِيٍّ وَكَانَ يُوحَى إِلَيْهِ ، فَلَمَّا سُرِّيَ عَنْهُ قَالَ : يَا عَلِّي صَلَّيْتَ الْعَصْرَ ؟ قَالَ : لَا . قَالَ : اللَّهُمَّ ! إِنَّكَ تَعْلَمُ أَنَّهُ كَانَ فِي حَاجَتِكَ وَحَاجَةِ رَسُولِكَ ، فَرُدَّ عَلَيْهِ الشَّمْسَ . فَرَدَّهَا عَلَيْهِ ، فَصَلَّى ، وَغَابَتِ الشَّمْسُ .**

أخرجه الخطيب في (تلخيص المتشابه) من طريق سويد بن سعيد ، به . ورواه الطبراني في الكبير والطحاوي في شرح مشكل الآثار وابن أبي عاصم في السنة وابن عساكر من طرق ، عن أسماء بنت عميس . قال السيوطي في اللآلئ : وقفت على جزء مستقل في

جمع طرق هذا الحديث تخريج أبي الحسن شاذان الفضلي ، ثم ساقه . وقد صحّح هذا الحديث من كبار حفّاظ السلف : الفريابي في دلائل النبوة والطحاوي وأحمد بن صالح . وردّه طائفة من المتأخرين كأبي الفرج ابن الجوزي والحافظ المِزّي والشيخ أحمد بن تيمية وتلاميذه الذهبي وابن القيم وابن كثير . قال القاضي عياض في الشفا : أخرج الطحاوي في مشكل الحديث عن أسماء بنت عميس من طريقين أن النبي كان يوحى إليه ورأسه في حِجْر علي ، فذكر هذا الحديث . قال الطحاوي : وهذان الحديثان ثابتان ورواتهما ثقات . وحكى الطحاوي أن أحمد بن صالح كان يقول : لا ينبغي لمن سبيله العلم التخلّف عن حفظ حديث أسماء ، لأنه من علامات النبوة اهـ . من كتاب الشفا . وكذا صححه الولي العراقي في طرح التثريب والسيوطي في رسالته (كشف اللَّبْس في حديث رد الشمس) . وجاء نحوه عن جابر بسند حسن كما في مجمع الزوائد والفتح . قال ابن الجوزي : وقد رواه ابن مردويه من حديث داود بن فراهيج عن أبى هريرة ، وداود ضعيف ضعفه شعبة ؛ وردّه السيوطي في التعقُّبات ، قال : داود مختلَف فيه ، ولم يُتَّهم بكذب ، قال فيه ابن معين : لا بأس به ، وقال يحيى القطان : ثقة ، وروى عنه شعبة وقال : كان قد كبر ،

وقال أبـو حاتم : تغيّر حين كبر ، وهو ثقة صدوق . وأنشـد الحافظ ابن حجر في ديوانه :

وَعَيْنُ الشَّمْسِ رُدَّتْ بَعْدَ حَجْبٍ
لِـذِي الْحُسَـنَيْنِ مِنْـهُ بِالدُّعَـاءِ

❑ ❑ ❑

٢٦

مسنَد الحِبّ ابن الحِبّ لأبي القاسم البغوي (٢١٣-٣١٧)

أَحَبُّ أَهْلِي إِلَيَّ فَاطِمَةُ بِنْتُ مُحَمَّدٍ

أنبأني السيد نور الدين الخطيب في دكّانه حيّ ركن الدين بدمشق، عن والده المسنِد محمد صالح الخطيب بن أحمد بن عبد الرحمن الجيلي الحسني الدمشقي (١٣١٣-١٤٠١) (ح) وأنبأني المسنِد محمد صالح الخطيب عالياً، عن الشيخ محمد جمال الدين القاوقجي، عن والده المسند أبي المحاسن محمد بن خليل القاوقجي، عن محيي السنّة محمد عابد السندي (١١٩٠-١٢٥٧)، عن شيخه الوجيه عبد الرحمن بن سليمان الأهدل، عن والده، عن مسند الشام ومحرِّر المذهب الحنبلي الإمام الشمس أبي العون محمد بن أحمد بن سالم السَّفَّاريني النابلسي الدمشقي الأثري (١١٠٠-١١٨٨)، عن مفتي الحنابلة بدمشق أبي المواهب محمد بن عبد الباقي البَعْلي

(١٠٤٤-١١٢٦) ، عن والده المحدّث المقرئ تقي الدين عبد الباقي بن عبد الباقي البَعْلي الأثري (١٠٠٥-١٠٧٢) والإمام المحدّث الفقيه على المذاهب الأربعة محمد بن بدر الدين بن عبد القادر بن بَلْبان الخزرجي الصالحي (١٠٠٦-١٠٨٣) إمام الجامع المُظَفَّري ، كلاهما عن مفتي الحنابلة القاضي المحدث المعمَّر الشهاب أحمد بن أبي الوفاء علي بن مفلح الوفائي (٩٣٦-١٠٣٥) ، أخبرنا شيخ الإسلام مسنِد دمشق الإمام خاتمة الحفاظ أبو الفضل شمس الدين محمد بن علي بن أحمد بن طولون الصالحي (٨٨٠-٩٥٣) ، أخبرنا الحافظ المحقِّق يوسف بن حسن بن عبد الهادي الحنبلي الدمشقي الصالحي الشهير بابن المِبْرَد (٨٤١-٩٠٩) ، عن شهاب الدين أحمد بن الشريفة (٧٩٦-بعد ٨٧١) ، أخبركَ المشايخُ الثلاثةُ ابن الحرستانيِّ ، وابن البالِسِيِّ ، والمرْداويُّ إجازةً ، أنا الحافظ المِزّيُّ كذلك ، أنا خاتمة المسندين الفخر ابن البخاري ، أنا الإمام موفّق الدين ابن قدامة ، عن أبي القاسم عبيد الله بن علي بن محمّد بن محمّد بن الحسين بن الفرّاء (٥٢٧-٥٨٠) ، بسماعه من الحافظ أبي الفضل محمد بن ناصر بن محمّد السّلامي البغدادي (٤٦٧-٥٥٠) ، روايةً عن شيخ الحنابلة الإمام أبي الوفاء علي بن عقيل بن محمّد البغدادي الظَّفَري

(٤٣١-٥١٣) ، روايـةً عـن القاضي أبي يعلى ابن الفـرّاء الحنبلي ، روايةً عن أبي الحسـن علي بـن معروف بن محمّد البـزّاز الحنبلي ، روايةً عن المؤلِّـف المسـند الحجّـة المعمّـر **أبي القاسـم عبد الله بـن محمّد بـن عبد العزيز بـن المَرْزُبَان بن سـابور بن شاهنشـاه البغـوي البغدادي** قال : حدثنا ابن منيع ، قال : حدثنا هارون بن عبد الله ، قال : حدثنا أبو داود الطيالسي ، قال : حدثنا أبو عوانة [الوضّاح بن عبد الله مولى يزيد بن عطاء اليشكري] ، قال : حدثنا عمر بن أبي سلمة ، عن أبيه عبد الرحمن بـن عـوف ، قـال : حدثني أسـامة بن زيد ، قـال : قال العبـاس وعلي ـ عليهما السـلام ـ : **يَا رَسُـولَ اللهِ ، مَنْ أَحَـبُّ أَهْلِكَ إِلَيْكَ ؟ قَالَ : أَحَبُّ أَهْلِي إِلَيَّ فَاطِمَةُ بِنْتُ مُحَمَّدٍ** . فَقَالَا : يَا رَسُولَ اللهِ ، لَسْنَا نَسْأَلُكَ عَنْ فَاطِمَةَ . قَالَ : **وَأُسَامَةُ بْنُ زَيْدٍ ، الَّذِي ﴿أَنْعَمَ ٱللَّهُ عَلَيْهِ وَأَنْعَمْتَ عَلَيْهِ﴾** [الأحزاب ٣٧] .

رواه الترمـذي وقـال حسـن صحيـح ، والطيالـسي والطبراني والحاكـم . وإسـناده حسـن ، أخرجه الضيـاء في المختـارة ، وراويه عمر بن أبي سـلمة استشـهد به البخاري . وجـاء بعضه في البخاري عـن ابن عمـر بلفظ **قَدْ بَلَغَنِي أَنَّكُمْ قُلْتُمْ فِي أُسَـامَةَ وَإِنَّهُ أَحَبُّ النَّاسِ إِلَيَّ** وأحمـد والطبراني والحاكم بلفظ **أَحَبُّ النَّاسِ إِلَيَّ : أُسَـامَةُ** . وهو

عند البخاري بلفظ **إنَّ هٰذَا لَمِنْ أَحَبِّ النَّاسِ إِلَيَّ** . وفي الترمذي عن أنس : **سُئِلَ رَسُولُ اللهِ ﷺ أَيُّ أَهْلِ بَيْتِكَ أَحَبُّ إِلَيْكَ ؟ قَالَ : الحَسَنُ وَالحُسَيْنُ ، وَكَانَ يَقُولُ لِفَاطِمَةَ : ادْعِى لِي ابْنَيَّ فَيَشُمُّهُمَا وَيَضُمُّهُمَا إِلَيْهِ** ، قال حسن غريب (تحفة) . وروى عبد الرزاق عن فاطمة رضي الله عنها أنّ النبي ﷺ قال لها : **أَنْكَحْتُكِ أَحَبَّ أَهْلِي إِلَيَّ** . ولفظه في الذرية الطاهرة للدولابي : **أَنْكَحْتُكِ أَحَبَّ أَهْلِ بَيْتِي إِلَيَّ** . ومن المتّفق عليه ، (١) عن عبد الله بن عمرو بن العاص : **قُلْتُ أَيُّ النَّاسِ أَحَبُّ إِلَيْكَ ؟ قَالَ : عَائِشَةُ . فَقُلْتُ : مِنْ الرِّجَالِ ؟ فَقَالَ : أَبُوهَا . قُلْتُ : ثُمَّ مَنْ ؟ قَالَ : ثُمَّ عُمَرُ بْنُ الخَطَّابِ . فَعَدَّ رِجَالًا** . وفي الباب عن أنس وأبي سعيد . (٢) وعن أنس قوله ﷺ للأنصار : **أَنْتُمْ أَحَبُّ النَّاسِ إِلَيَّ** . وجاء أيضاً عندهما بلفظ **أَنْتُمْ مِنْ أَحَبِّ النَّاسِ إِلَيَّ** . يجوز أن تكون (مِن) التأكيد لا التبعيض . وأخرج الحافظ أبو سعد بن السّمّان في الموافقة بين أهل البيت والصحابة عن جعفر بن محمّد عن أبيه مرسلاً : كان آلُ أبي بكر يُدعَون في عهد رسول الله ﷺ آلَ محمّد ﷺ . ذكره الطبري في الرياض . وفي صحيح مسلم عن أبي موسى : قَدِمْتُ أَنَا وَأَخِى مِنَ الْيَمَنِ فَكُنَّا حِينًا وَمَا نُرَى ابْنَ مَسْعُودٍ وَأُمَّهُ إِلاَّ مِنْ أَهْلِ بَيْتِ رَسُولِ اللهِ ﷺ مِنْ كَثْرَةِ دُخُولِهِمْ وَلُزُومِهِمْ لَهُ . قال

العزيزي في شرح الجامع : ثبت أن أحبَّ أهله إليه ﷺ فاطمة في عدّة أحاديث أفاد مجموعها التواتر المعنوي . وقال في التيسير في شرح حديث **أحبُّ أهْل بَيْتِي إليَّ الحَسَنُ والحُسَيْنُ** : الحقّ أن فاطمة لها الأحبّية المطلقة ، ثبت ذلك في عدة أحاديث أفاد مجموعها التواتر المعنوي ، وما عداها : فَعَلى معنى مِنْ [التبعيضية] ، أو اختلاف الجهة اهـ .

❑ ❑ ❑

٢٧

شرح مشكل الآثار للطحاوي

(٢٢٩-٣٢١)

رَبِّ هَؤُلَاءِ أَهْلِي . قَالَتْ أُمُّ سَلَمَةَ فَقُلْتُ : يَا رَسُولَ اللهِ فَتُدْخِلُنِي مَعَهُمْ ؟ قَالَ : أَنْتِ مِنْ أَهْلِي .

أنبأنا **الحبيب علي بن جعفر العيدروس** (ت ١٤٣١/ ٢٠١٠) في باتو باهات بمليزيا على حدود سنغافورة ، وأخبرنا **العلّامة الشيخ محمد سعيد بن هانئ الكحيل الحسيني الحِمصي** (١٣٥٣-١٤٣٣) بقراءتي عليه في داره بحمص المَحْمِيّة ـ لعلّه من أبناء كَحِيلات المغرب الأشراف الذين استوطنوا الشام ـ رحمهما الله ، الأوّل عن والده العلّامة الحبيب جعفر بن أحمد بن عبد القادر بن سالم العيدروس (١٣٠٨-١٣٩٦) ، عن الحبيب عبد الله الشاطري ـ وكان من خواصّ تلاميذه ـ عن الحبيب عيدروس بن عمر الحبشي ، عن عمّه محمد بن عيدروس الحبشي ووالده عمر بن عيدروس بن عبد الرحمن الحبشي ، كلاهما عن الشيخ عمر بن عبد الكريم العطّار ، عن مرتضى الزبيدى ،

عن الشمس الحَفْنَاوي بالسند المارّ في باب المجتبى إلى شيخ الإسلام ، (ح) وقال الكحيل : أنبأني الشيخ محمد إبراهيم الخُتَني المدني ، أنبأني الشيخ محمد زاهد الكوثري ، أنبأني الشيخ الحسن بن عبد الله القَسْطَموني ، أنبأني مسند طرابلس الشام صاحب التصانيف وشيخ الطريقة النقشبندية - وهو مِن أكبر خلفاء مولانا خالد - السيد أحمد بن سليمان النقشبندي الخالدي الأروادي الطرابلسي (ت ١٢٧٥) دفين دمشق ، عن السيد الفقيه محمد أمين ابن عابدين الحنفي ، عن العلّامة أبي زيد عبد الرحمن بن محمّد بن زين الدين الكُزْبَري الكبير (١١٠٠ ؟-١١٨٥) ، عن العارف الشيخ عبد الغني النابلسي ، عن النجم الغزّي ، عن والده البدر الغزّي العامري ، عن شيخ الإسلام زكريا الأنصاري ، عن الإمام مسند الدنيا عز الدين أبي محمد عبد الرحيم بن علي بن الحسين بن الفرات الحنفي (٧٥٩-٨٥٠) ، عن المحدّث أبي الثناء شمس الدين محمود بن خليفة بن محمد المَنبِجي ثم الدمشقي الحنفي (٦٨٧-٧٦٧) ، عن الحافظ شرف الدين عبد المؤمن بن خلف بن أبي الحسن الدمياطي الشافعي (٦١٣-٧٠٥) ، عن الحافظ الفقيه أبي المظفَّر منصور بن سليم الهَمْدَاني الإسكندراني الشافعي المشهور بابن العِمادية (٦٠٧-٦٧٣) صاحب تحفة أهل

الحديث في إيصال إجازة القديم بالحديث، عن مسند العراق الحافظ المعمّر أبي الحسن محمد بن أحمد بن عمر البغدادي المعروف بابن القَطِيعي (٥٤٦-٦٤٣)، عن عبد الله بن جرير الكاتب، كذا في الأثبات ـ وهو أبو محمد عبد الله بن محمد بن جرير القرشي الأموي البغدادي المالكي الناسخ (٥١٠-٥٨٢) من ولد سعيد بن العاص بن أميّة ـ، عن الحافظ المؤرّخ أبي سعد تاج الإسلام عبد الكريم بن محمد بن منصور السَّمعاني المروزي (٥٠٦-٥٦٢) صاحب الأنساب وحفيد المفسّر، عن الإمام نجم الدين أبي حفص عمر بن محمد بن أحمد النسفي (٤٦١-٥٣٧)، عن القاضي أبي منصور أحمد بن محمد الحارِثي السرخسي الرئيس (٤٣٧-٥١٢)، إجازة عن القاضي أبي نصر محمد بن علي بن الحسين السرخسي الحنفي، عن القاضي أبي محمد عبد الله بن محمد الأكفاني ـ كذا في الجواهر المضيئة، وأما عند الكوراني فعبد الله بن عمر الأكفاني ـ عن الفقيه أبي بكر أحمد بن محمد بن منصور الدامَغاني الأنصاري الحنفي، عن **الإمام أبي جعفر أحمد بن محمد بن سلامة بن سلمة الأزدي المصري الطحاوي** في كتابه شرح مشكل الآثار: «باب بيان مشكل ما روي عنه ـ عليه الصلاة والسلام ـ في المراد بقول الله تعالى ﴿ إِنَّمَا يُرِيدُ ٱللَّهُ لِيُذْهِبَ عَنكُمُ

ٱلرِّجْسَ أَهْلَ ٱلْبَيْتِ وَيُطَهِّرَكُمْ تَطْهِيرًا ﴾ [الأحزاب ٣٣] مَنْ هُمْ ؟ » قال : حَدَّثَنَا أَبُو أُمَيَّةَ ، ثنا خَالِدُ بْنُ مَخْلَدٍ الْقَطَوَانِيُّ ، ثنا مُوسَى بْنُ يَعْقُوبَ الزَّمْعِيُّ ، أَخْبَرَنِي ابْنُ هَاشِمِ بْنِ عُتْبَةَ ، عَنْ عَبْدِ اللهِ بْنِ وَهْبٍ ، عَنْ أُمِّ سَلَمَةَ - رَضِيَ اللهُ عَنْهَا - **أَنَّ رَسُولَ اللهِ ﷺ جَمَعَ فَاطِمَةَ وَالحَسَنَ وَالحُسَيْنَ ثُمَّ أَدْخَلَهُمْ تَحتَ ثَوْبِهِ ، ثُمَّ جَأَرَ إِلَى اللهِ تَعَالَى : رَبِّ هَؤُلَاءِ أَهْلِي . قَالَتْ أُمُّ سَلَمَةَ فَقُلْتُ : يَا رَسُولَ اللهِ فَتُدْخِلُنِي مَعَهُمْ ؟ قَالَ : أَنْتِ مِنْ أَهْلِي .**

رواه الطبري في التفسير . وضعّف إسناده محقق مشكل الآثار بما نصُّه : خالد بن مخلد القَطَواني قال عنه أبو حاتم يُكتَب حديثه ولا يُحتجّ به ، وموسى بن يعقوب الزَّمْعِي سيء الحفظ . قلت : لم يزد أبو حاتم على القول بأنه (يكتب حديثه) . ثمّ القَطَواني من رجال الشيخين ، وثّقه العجلي وصالح جَزَرَة وقال يحيى بن معين وعثمان الدارمي وابن عدي لا بأس به ، وقال أبو داود (صدوق ولكنّه يتشيّع) ، وهذا خلاصة القول وأدقّ من مجرَّد حكم أبي حاتم فيه ، لذا ترى الحافظ اعتمده في التقريب ؛ وحديث الباب لا يؤيّد التشيّع ؛ وأمّا الزمعي فهو أيضاً من رجال البخارى والأربعة ، قال في التقريب : صدوق سيء الحفظ . فقوله إنه سيء الحفظ فحسب غير

دقيق . والحديث قوي بما مرّ في باب المسند وما يأتي من شواهد .

فقد ورد عنها رضي الله عنها عند الطبراني في الكبير : **فَقُلْتُ - أَيْ أُمُّ سَلَمَةَ - يَا رَسُولَ اللهِ أَنَا مِنْ أَهْلِ الْبَيْتِ ؟ قَالَ : إِنْ شَاءَ اللهُ** . وفي شرح السُّنَّة للبغوي : قالت : **فَقُلْتُ : يَا رَسُولَ اللهِ ، أَمَا أَنَا مِنْ أَهْلِ الْبَيْتِ ؟ قَالَ : بَلَى إِنْ شَاءَ اللهُ** . ثم قال عقبه : هذا حديث صحيح الإسناد . وفي شرح مشكل الآثار أيضاً من طريق شهر بن حوشب ، عنها : **قُلْتُ : يَا رَسُولَ اللهِ ، أَلَسْتُ مِنْ أَهْلِكَ ؟ قَالَ : بَلَى ، قَالَ : فَادْخُلِي فِي الْكِسَاءِ . قَالَتْ : فَدَخَلْتُ بَعْدَمَا قَضَى دُعَاءَهُ لِابْنِ عَمِّهِ عَلِيٍّ ، وَابْنَيْهِ ، وَابْنَتِهِ فَاطِمَةَ عَلَيْهِمُ السَّلامُ** . وفيه من طريق ابن لهيعة بالسند إلى عمرة الهمْدانيّة : سألَتْ عن عليٍّ بعد مقتله فسألَتْها أم سلمة : أتُحبّينه أم تُبغضينه ؟ قالت : ما أُحبّه ولا أُبغضه . فقالت : أنزل الله هذه الآية : ﴿إِنَّمَا يُرِيدُ ٱللَّهُ﴾ إلى آخرها ، وما في البيت إلا جبريلُ ورسولُ الله ﷺ وعليٌّ وفاطمةُ وحسنٌ وحسينٌ عليهم السلام ، **فَقُلْتُ : يَا رَسُولَ اللهِ ، أَنَا مِنْ أَهْلِ الْبَيْتِ ؟ فَقَالَ : إِنَّ لَكِ عِنْدَ اللهِ خَيْراً . فَوَدِدْتُ أَنَّهُ قَالَ : نَعَمْ ، فَكَانَ أَحَبَّ إِلَيَّ مِمَّا تَطْلُعُ عَلَيْهِ الشَّمْسُ وَتَغْرُبُ** .

قال الطحاوي رحمه الله : فَدَلَّ مَا رَوَيْنَا فِي هَذِهِ الْآثَارِ مِمَّا كَانَ مِنْ

رَسُولِ اللهِ ﷺ إِلَى أُمِّ سَلَمَةَ مِمَّا ذَكَرَ فِيهَا ، [أنه ﷺ] لَمْ يُرِدْ بِهِ أَنَّهَا كَانَتْ مِمَّـنْ أُرِيـدَ بِهِ مِمَّا فِي الْآيَةِ الْمَتْلُوَّةِ فِي هَذَا الْبَـابِ ، وَأَنَّ الْمُرَادِينَ بِمَا فِيهَا : هُمْ رَسُـولُ اللهِ ﷺ وَعَلِيٌّ وَفَاطِمَةُ وَحَسَنٌ وَحُسَيْنٌ ـ عَلَيْهِمُ السَّلَامُ ـ دُونَ مَنْ سِوَاهُمْ . وَمِمَّا يَدُلُّ عَلَى مُرَادِ رَسُولِ اللهِ ﷺ بِقَوْلِهِ لِأُمِّ سَلَمَةَ فِيمَا رُوِيَ فِي هَذِهِ الْآثَارِ مِنْ قَوْلِهِ لَهَا : **أَنْتِ مِنْ أَهْلِي** : حديث واثلة بن الأسـقع : ثُمَّ لَفَّ عَلَيْهِـمْ ثَوْبًا وَأَنَا مُنْتَبِذٌ ، ثُـمَّ قَالَ ﴿إِنَّمَا يُرِيدُ ٱللَّهُ﴾ الْآيَةَ ، ثُمَّ قَالَ : **اللَّهُمَّ هَؤُلَاءِ أَهْلِي إِنَّهُمْ أَهْلُ حَقٍّ ! فَقُلْتُ : يَا رَسُـولَ اللهِ وَأَنَـا مِـنْ أَهْلِكَ ؟ قَـالَ : وَأَنْتَ مِنْ أَهْـلِي** . قَالَ وَاثِلَـةُ : فَإِنَّهَا مِنْ أَرْجَـى مَـا أَرْجُـو . قال في مجمـع الزوائد عـن حديث واثلـة : رواه الطبراني بإسنادين رجال أحدهما رجال الصحيح غير كلثوم بن زياد ووثقه ابن حبان وفيه ضعف . وسـيأتي مسنَداً في باب زوائد فضائل الصحابـة إن شـاء الله . ثم قال الطحـاوي : وَوَاثِلَةُ أَبْعَدُ مِنْـهُ ـ عَلَيْهِ السَّلَامُ ـ مِنْ أُمِّ سَلَمَةَ مِنْهُ ، لِأَنَّهُ إِنَّمَا هُوَ رَجُلٌ مِنْ بَنِي لَيْثٍ ، لَيْسَ مِنْ قُرَيْشٍ ، وَأُمُّ سَـلَمَةَ مَوْضِعُهَا مِنْ قُرَيْـشٍ مَوْضِعُهَا الَّذِي هِيَ بِهِ مِنْهُ ؛ فَكَانَ قَوْلُهُ لِوَاثِلَةَ : **أَنْتَ مِنْ أَهْلِي** عَلَى مَعْنَى : لِاتِّبَاعِك إِيَّايَ وَإِيمَانِكَ بِي ، فَدَخَلْـتَ بِذَلِكَ فِي جُمْلَتِي . وَقَدْ وَجَدْنَا اللهَ تَعَالَى قَدْ ذَكَرَ فِي كِتَابِهِ مَـا يَدُلُّ عَلَى هَـذَا الْمَعْنَى بِقَوْلِـهِ ﴿وَنَادَىٰ نُوحٌ رَّبَّهُۥ فَقَالَ رَبِّ إِنَّ ٱبْنِي

مِنْ أَهْلِي﴾ فَأَجَابَهُ فِي ذَلِكَ بِأَنْ قَالَ لَهُ: ﴿قَالَ يَٰنُوحُ إِنَّهُۥ لَيْسَ مِنْ أَهْلِكَ إِنَّهُۥ عَمَلٌ غَيْرُ صَٰلِحٍ﴾، فَكَمَا جَازَ أَنْ يُخْرِجَهُ مِنْ أَهْلِهِ وَإِنْ كَانَ ابْنَهُ لِخِلَافِهِ إِيَّاهُ فِي دِينِهِ، جَازَ أَنْ يَدْخُلَ فِي أَهْلِهِ مَنْ يُوَافِقُهُ عَلَى دِينِهِ وَإِنْ لَمْ يَكُنْ مِنْ ذَوِي نَسَبِهِ. فَمِثْلُ ذَلِكَ أَيْضًا: مَا كَانَ مِنْ رَسُولِ اللهِ ﷺ جَوَابًا لِأُمِّ سَلَمَةَ أَنْتِ مِنْ أَهْلِي يَحْتَمِلُ أَنْ يَكُونَ عَلَى هَذَا المَعْنَى أَيْضًا، وَأَنْ يَكُونَ قَوْلُهُ لَهَا ذَلِكَ كَقَوْلِهِ مِثْلَهُ لِوَاثِلَةَ. اهـ. والله أعلم بالصّواب.

❑ ❑ ❑

٢٨

صحيح ابن حبان «التقاسيم والأنواع»

(٢٧٢ ؟ - ٣٥٤)

وَالَّذِي نَفْسِي بِيَدِهِ لاَ يُبْغِضُنَا أَهْلَ الْبَيْتِ رَجُلٌ إِلاَّ أَدْخَلَهُ اللهُ النَّارَ.

حدّثني بلفظه ثم بقراءتي عليه **الأستاذ محمّد عجاج الخطيب** بن محمد تميم بن محمد صالح آل الشيخ عبد القادر الخطيب الحسني (١٩٣٢_٢٠٢١) رحمه الله في داره بمزّة دمشق، عن الشيخ المسنِد محمد صالح الخطيب بن أحمد بن عبد الرحمن الجيلي الحسني الدمشقي (١٣١٣-١٤٠١) (ح) وأنبأني **المسنِد محمد صالح الخطيب** عالياً، بالسند المارّ إلى السندي في باب مسنِد البغوي، عن المحدث الفقيه مفتي الشافعية في زمانه بمكة المكرّمة محمد سعيد بن محمد سُنبُل المكّي (ت ١١٧٥)، عن الإمام المعمَّر أحمد بن محمد النَّخْلي الصوفي (١٠٤٠-١١٣٠) أحد مجددي علم الإسناد السبعة في الحجاز، عن سيوطي زمانه مسند الحرمين الإمام النحْوي المفسّر المحدث عالم الحجاز في القرن الحادي عشر ومقرئ

البخاري من أوله إلى آخره في جوف الكعبة : الشمس محمد علي بن محمد علّان الصّدّيقي العلوي سبط آل الحسن الشافعي المكّي (٩٩٦-١٠٥٧) صاحب المُبْرِد المُبْكِي في ردّ الصَّارم المُنْكِي وإعلام الإخوان بتحريم الدخان وغيرهما ، عن شمس الدين محمد حجازي بن محمد الشعراني الواعظ القلقشندي صاحب فتح المولى النصير بشرح الجامع الصغير ، عن المسنِد أحمد بن سَنَد ، عن الحافظ المسند الإمام شيخ الإسلام محيي السنّة أبي عمرو فخر الدين عثمان بن شمس الدين محمد بن فخر الدين عثمان بن ناصر الدين الدِّيَّمي - بكسر الدال المشدّدة وفتح الياء المشدّدة نسبةً إلى قرية من قرى مصر - الشافعي المصري ، عن سيد الحفاظ ابن حجر ، وهو من كبار المتخرِّجين به ، أنا شيخ القراء أبو إسحاق إبراهيم بن أحمد التَّنوخي ، عن محمد بن أحمد بن أبي الهيجاء بن الزَراد ، أنا الحافظ أبو علي الحسن بن محمد بن محمد البكري ، أنا أبو رَوح عبد العزيز بن محمد الهروي ، أنا تميم بن أبي سعيد الجرجاني ، أنا به أبو الحسن علي بن محمد البَحَّاثي ، أنا بن أبو الحسن محمد بن أحمد بن هارون الزَّوْزَني ، أنا **الحافظ أبو حاتم محمد بن حِبّان بن أحمد بن حبان التميمي البُستي** ، قال : أَخْبَرَنَا الْحُسَيْنُ ابْنُ عَبْدِ اللهِ بْنِ يَزِيدَ الْقَطَّانِ بِالرَّقَّةِ ، قَالَ : حَدَّثَنَا

هِشَـامُ بْنُ عَمَّارٍ ، قَالَ : حَدَّثَنَا أَسَدُ بْنُ مُوسَى ، قَالَ : حَدَّثَنَا سَلِيمُ بْنُ حَيَّانَ ، عَنْ أَبِي الْمُتَوَكِّلِ النَّاجِي ، عَنْ أَبِي سَـعِيدٍ الْخُدْرِيِّ ، قَالَ : قَالَ رَسُـولُ اللهِ ﷺ : **وَالَّـذِي نَفْسِي بِيَدِهِ لَا يُبْغِضُنَا أَهْـلَ الْبَيْتِ رَجُلٌ إِلَّا أَدْخَلَهُ اللهُ النَّارَ** .

رواه الحاكـم وصححه على شرط مسـلم . (تنبيه) هذا الحديث مترّتب على حديث مبغض سيّدنا عليٍّ ـ كرّم الله وجهه ـ الذي رويناه في باب المُجتَبى ، وحديث **مَنْ أَبْغَضَنَا أَهْلَ الْبَيْتِ ، فَهُوَ مُنَافِقٌ** المذكور فيه أيضاً ، إذ مآل المنافق إلى النار ، أعاذنا الله وإيّاكم من عذاب النّار ومن الفتن جميعاً .

❑ ❑ ❑

٢٩

المعجم الكبير للطبراني

(٢٦٠ـ ٣٦٠)

مَا بَالُ أَقْوَامٍ يَزْعُمُونَ أَنَّ شَفَاعَتِي لا تَنَالُ أَهْلَ بَيْتِي ؟ وَإِنَّ شَفَاعَتِي تَنَالُ حَا وَحُكْمَ !

أنبأني الحبيب علي بن محمد الحداد التريمي ثم الإندونيسي في جاكرتا ، عن الحبيب هود بن مِحضار الحبشي المعمَّر ١١٤ سنة عالياً ، عن مسند اليمن عيدروس بن عمر بن عيدروس الحبشي (١٢٣٧-١٣١٤) صاحب الأثبات ـ عقد اليواقيت وسمط العين الذهبية في أسانيد السادة العلوية ، وعقود اللآل في أسانيد الرجال ومنحة الفتّاح الفاطر بذكر أسانيد السادة الأكابر ، جميعها مطبوعة ـ عن عمّه محمد بن عيدروس بن عبد الرحمن الحبشي ووالده عمر بن عيدروس بن عبد الرحمن الحبشي ، كلاهما عن الشيخ الجامع عمر بن عبد الكريم بن عبد الرّسول العطّار (ت ١٢٤٩) ، عن الحافظ محمد بن محمد بن محمد مرتضى الزبيدي (١١٤٥-١٢٠٥) ، عن الشهاب أحمد بن

علي بن عمر المَنيني ، عن أبي المواهب محمد بن عبد الباقي الحنبلي ، عن أيوب الخلوتي العِذْوي ، عن المحدث المعمّر إبراهيم الأحدب ، عن الشهاب ابن حجر الهيتمي ، عن السيوطي ، أنبأني عالياً الشمس محمّد بن مقبل الحلبي الصيرفي ، عن الصلاح محمّد بن إبراهيم بن أبي عمر المقدسي الصالحي الحنبلي آخر أصحاب الفخر ابن البخاري في الدنيا ، عن الفخر ابن البخاري ، عن أبي جعفر الصيدلاني ، أنبأتنا فاطمة بنت عبد الله الجوزدانية ، أنا أبو بكر محمّد بن عبد الله بن رِيْدَةَ الضَّبِّي الأصفهاني ، أخبرنا **الحافظ أبو القاسم سُلَيْمان بن أحمد بن أيوب الطبراني** ، حَدَّثَنَا زَكَرِيَّا بن يَحْيَى السَّاجِيُّ ، ثنا هُدْبَةُ بن خَالِدٍ ، ثنا حَمَّادُ بن سَلَمَةَ ، عَنْ عَبْدِ الرَّحْمَنِ بن أَبِي رَافِعٍ ، أَنَّ أُمَّ هَانِئٍ بنت أَبِي طَالِبٍ خَرَجَتْ مُتَبَرِّجَةً قَدْ بَدَا قُرْطَاهَا ، فَقَالَ لَهَا عُمَرُ بن الْخَطَّابِ : اعْلَمِي فَإِنَّ مُحَمَّداً لا يُغْنِي عَنْكِ شَيْئًا . فَجَاءَتْ إِلَى النَّبِيِّ ﷺ فَأَخْبَرَتْهُ ، فَقَالَ رَسُولُ اللهِ ﷺ : **مَا بَالُ أَقْوَامٍ يَزْعُمُونَ أَنَّ شَفَاعَتِي لا تَنَالُ أَهْلَ بَيْتِي ؟ وَإِنَّ شَفَاعَتِي تَنَالُ حَا وَحُكْمَ !** حَا وَحُكْمَ قَبِيلَتَانِ .

مرسل ، ورواه عبد الرزاق ، عن معمر ، عن خلّاد بن عبد الرحمن ، عن أبيه مرسلاً . قال الهيثمي : هو مرسل ورجاله ثقات . ورواه عبد الرزاق عن قتادة مرسلاً ، وعنه عبد الله بن أحمد

في فضائل الصحابة ، وابن عدي والسمعاني في الأنساب والبيهقي في البعث والنشور عن أبي هريرة مسنداً ، جميعهم بلفظ : **وَالَّذِي نَفْسِي بِيَدِهِ إِنَّهُ لَتَرْجُو شَفَاعَتِي صَدَاءُ وَسَلْهَبُ** . ورواه الطبراني في الكبير عن ابن عمر وأبي هريرة وعمّار بن ياسر في قصّة دُرّة بنت أبي لهب وقد مرّ مسنَداً في باب الآحاد والمثاني . (الغريب) القُرْط نوع من حُلِيِّ الأُذُن معروف ، وحَا وَحُكْمَ قبيلتان جافيتان من وراء رمل يَبْرِين . نهاية . قال السمعاني : من أقصى اليمن . وقال ياقوت : يَبْرِين قرية كثيرة النخل والعيون العذبة بحذاء الأحساء من بني سعد بالبحرين . وقال أبو عبيد : صدى وسلهب حيّان من اليمن . (بُشرى أهل البيت بالشفاعة) يؤيد حديث الباب ما ورد في المعجم الكبير أيضاً عن ابن عباس ، قال : قال رسول الله ﷺ لفاطمة رضي الله عنها : **إِنَّ اللهَ تَعَالَى غَيْرُ مُعَذِّبِكِ وَلَا وَلَدَكِ** . قال في مجمع الزوائد رجاله ثقات . ثم أخرج الحاكم عن أنس رضي الله عنه أن النبي ﷺ قال : **وَعَدَنِي رَبِّي فِي أَهْلِ بَيْتِي ، مَنْ أَقَرَّ مِنْهُمْ للهِ بِالتَّوْحِيدِ وَلِي بِالْبَلَاغِ ، أَنْ لَا يُعَذِّبَهُمْ** . وأخرج أبو القاسم بن بشران في أماليه عن عمران بن حصين أن رسول الله ﷺ قال : **سَأَلْتُ رَبِّي أَنْ لَا يُدْخِلَ أَحَداً مِنْ أَهْلِ بَيْتِي النَّارَ فَأَعْطَانِي** . وهذا المعنى الشريف أثبته ابن عبّاس في تفسير ﴿ وَلَسَوْفَ يُعْطِيكَ رَبُّكَ فَتَرْضَىٰٓ ﴾ قال : رضا محمّد ﷺ أن لا يدخل

أحـد من أهل بيته النـار . رواه الطبري ، ومن طريقه الثعلبي . وقيل هي الشـفاعة في جميع المؤمنـين . وروى الثعلبي بسـنده إلى محمّد بن عـلي ـ الباقر ـ أنّه قال : إنّكم معـشر أهل العراق تقولون : إنّ أرْجَى آيةٍ في القـرآن ﴿ قُلْ يَـٰعِبَادِيَ ٱلَّذِينَ أَسْرَفُواْ عَلَىٰٓ أَنفُسِهِمْ لَا تَقْنَطُواْ مِن رَّحْمَةِ ٱللَّهِ ﴾ [الزمر ٥٣] . قالوا إنّا لنقـول ذلك ، قال : ولكنّا ـ أهلَ البيـت ـ نقول إنّ أرجى آية في كتاب الله تعالى ﴿ وَلَسَوْفَ يُعْطِيكَ رَبُّكَ فَتَرْضَىٰٓ ﴾ ، وهـي الشـفاعة . وفي المعجم الكبـير أيضاً : عن أبي جميلة أن الحسـن بن عـلي رضي الله عنهما حين قُتل علي رضي الله عنه استـخلف ، فبينـما هـو يصلي بالنـاس إذ وثـب عليه رجـل ، فطعنه بخنجـر في وَرِكِهِ ، فتمرّض منها أشـهراً ، ثم قـام على المنبر يخطب ، فقـال : **يَا أَهْلَ الْعِـرَاقِ ، اِتَّقُوا اللهَ فِينَـا ! فَإِنَّا أُمَرَاؤُكُـمْ وَضِيفَانُكُمْ ، وَنَحْـنُ أَهْلُ الْبَيْتِ ، الَّذِي قَالَ اللهُ عَزَّ وَجَلَّ** : ﴿ إِنَّمَا يُرِيدُ ٱللَّهُ لِيُذْهِبَ عَنكُمُ ٱلرِّجْسَ أَهْلَ ٱلْبَيْتِ وَيُطَهِّرَكُمْ تَطْهِيرًا ﴾ [الأحزاب] . فـما زال يومئـذ يتكلـم حتى ما يـرى في المسـجد إلا باكيا . قـال في المجمع : رجالـه ثقـات . ورواه وابـن أبي حاتـم في التفسـير وابن عسـاكر في التاريخ .

❑ ❑ ❑

٣٠

المعجم الأوسط للطبراني

(٢٦٠- ٣٦٠)

فَضَّلَ اللهُ قُرَيْشاً بِسَبْعِ خِصَالٍ : فَضَّلَهُمْ بِأَنَّهُمْ عَبَدُوا اللهَ عَشْرَ سِنِينَ لاَيَعْبُدُهُ إِلَّا قُرَيْشٌ ، وَفَضَّلَهُمْ بِأَنَّهُ نَصَرَهُمْ يَوْمَ الْفِيلِ وَهُمْ مُشْرِكُونَ ، وَفَضَّلَهُمْ بِأَنَّهُ نَزَلَتْ فِيهِمْ سُورَةٌ مِنَ الْقُرْآنِ لَمْ يَدْخُلْ فِيهَا غَيْرُهُمْ مِنَ الْعَالَمِينَ وَهِيَ ﴿لِإِيلَـٰفِ قُـرَيْشٍ﴾ وَفَضَّلَهُمْ بِأَنَّ فِيهِم النُّبُوَّةَ وَالخِلاَفَةَ والْحِجَابَةَ والسِّقَايَةَ .

أنبأني العلّامة المربّي **الحبيب عبد القادر بن محمد بن أحمد الحداد الإندونيسي** (ت ١٤٣٤/ ٢٠١٢) رحمه الله ، مدير معهد دار الحاوي في جاكرتا ، عن الحبيب عبد القادر بن أحمد بلفقيه عالم جاوة الشرقية ، عن الحبيب عبد الله بن عمر الشاطري وأحمد بن حسن بن علي العطاس وعلي بن محمد بن حسين الحبشي (١٢٥٩-١٣٣٣) صاحب (سمط الدرر) ، جميعهم عن المسند عيدروس بن عمر ، بالسند المارّ آنفاً إلى أبي جعفر الصيدلاني ، أنا أبو علي الحدّاد ، أنا الحافظ أبو نعيم الأصبهاني ، أنا **أبو القاسم سُلَيْمان بن أحمد الطبراني** ، حدثنا مصعب ،

حدثني أبي ، نا عبد الله بن مصعب بن ثابت بن عبد الله بن الزبير ، عن هشام بن عروة ، عن أبيه ، عن الزبير بن العوّام ، قَالَ رَسُولُ اللهِ ﷺ : **فَضَّلَ اللهُ قُرَيْشاً بِسَبْعِ خِصَالٍ : فَضَّلَهُمْ بِأَنَّهُمْ عَبَدُوا اللهَ عَشْرَ سِنِينَ لاَيَعْبُدُهُ إِلَّا قُرَيْشٌ ، وَفَضَّلَهُمْ بِأَنَّهُ نَصَرَهُمْ يَوْمَ الْفِيلِ وَهُمْ مُشْرِكُونَ ، وَفَضَّلَهُمْ بِأَنَّهُ نَزَلَتْ فِيهِمْ سُورَةٌ مِنَ الْقُرْآنِ لَمْ يَدْخُلْ فِيهَا غَيْرُهُمْ مِنَ الْعَالَمِينَ وَهِيَ ﴿لِإِيلَٰفِ قُرَيْشٍ﴾ وَفَضَّلَهُمْ بِأَنَّ فِيهِم النُّبُوَّةَ وَالخِلاَفَةَ والْحِجَابَةَ والسِّقَايَةَ** . لم يروِ هذا الحديث عن هشام بن عروة إلا عبد الله بن مصعب ، ولا يُروى عن الزبير إلا بهذا الإسناد .

رواه والبيهقي في مناقب الشافعي وابن عساكر في التاريخ وحسّنه الحافظ العراقي في (مَحَجَّة القُرَب في محبّة العَرَب) . ورواه البخاري في التاريخ الكبير والطبراني في الكبير والحاكم والبيهقي في الخلافيات عن أم هانىء بنت أبي طالب رضي الله عنها مرفوعاً ، مسلسل المَخْرَج بأهل البيت لكن رجّح البخاري إرساله من طريق ابن شهاب الزهري .

❑ ❑ ❑

٣١

الشريعة للآجُرِّي

(٢٨٠ - ٣٦٠)

فَاطِمَةُ سَيِّدَةُ نِسَاءِ عَالَمِـهَا إِلَّا مَا جَعَلَ اللهُ عَزَّ وَجَلَّ لِمَرْيَمَ بِنْتِ عِمْرَانَ .

أنبأني السيد أبو محمّد مالك بن العربي بن أحمد الشريف بن محمد الشريف بـن الحافظ محمد بن علي السنوسي الخطّـابي (١٣٥١-١٤٣٤) رحمه الله ، عن السيد أحمد بن محمد عابد والمَلِك إدريس والسيد أحمد حَمِيدة بـن محمد بـن أحمد بـن عبد القـادر الريفي ، ثلاثتهـم عن جد الأخير السـيد أحمد الرِّيفي ، عن الحافظ محمد بن علي بن السنوسي ، عن المَازُوني ، عن أبي إسـحاق إبراهيم بن حسن الكُوراني الكردي الشـافعي ، عن العـارف بالله تعالى صفي الديـن أحمد بن محمد المدني الأنصاري القُشاشي ، عن الشمس الرملي ، عن شيخ الإسلام القاضي زكريا الأنصاري ، عن ابن الفُرات ، عن ابن جماعة ، عن المسـنِد ابن الزبير الغرناطي ، عن أبي الحسـن ابن محمد السَّرَّاج ، عن خاله المسنِد أبي بكر محمد بن خير بن عمر بن خليفة الإشـبيلي الأَموي (ت ٥٧٥) ،

قال في فهرسته : كتاب الشريعة لأبي بكر محمد بن الحسين الآجري رحمه الله حدثني به الشيخ الإمام أبو بكر محمد بن أحمد بن طاهر ، عن أبي علي الغَسّاني ، عن أبي العاصي حَكَم بن محمد الجُذَامي ، عن أبي عبد الله محمد بن خليفة البَلَوي وأبي القاسم عبيد الله بن محمد السَقَطي وأبي الفرج عبْدُوس بن محمد الطليلي ، قالو كلهم : أنا شيخ الحرم الشريف الأخباري المحدث الحافظ الثقة القدوة الزاهد الدَّيِّن الورع **الإمام أبو بكر محمد بن الحسين بن عبد الله البغدادي الآجُرِّي** ثم المكّي (٢٨٠-٣٦٠) : حدثنا أبو حفص عمر بن أيوب السقطي قال : حدثنا الحسن بن عرفة قال : حدثنا عمر بن عبد الرحمن ، عن يزيد بن أبي زياد ، عن عبد الرحمن بن أبي نُعْم ، عن أبي سعيد الخدري رضي الله عنه قال : قال رسول الله ﷺ : **فَاطِمَةُ سَيِّدَةُ نِسَاءِ عَالَمِهَا إِلَّا مَا جَعَلَ اللهُ عَزَّ وَجَلَّ لِمَرْيَمَ بِنْتِ عِمْرَانَ .**

حديث حسن ، إسناده جيد ، وله متابعة عند الحاكم بلفظ **فَاطِمَةُ سَيِّدَةُ نِسَاءِ أَهْلِ الْجَنَّةِ إِلَّا مَا كَانَ مِنْ مَرْيَمَ بِنْتِ عِمْرَانَ** . وروي نحوه مما أوردناه في باب فضائل الصحابة للنسائي .

❑ ❑ ❑

٣٢

زوائد القَطيعي
على فضائل الصحابةَ للإمام أحمد
(٢٧٣-٣٦٨)

أَنَّ النَّبِيَّ ﷺ دَعَا لِأَهْلِ بَيْتِهِ ، فَذَكَرَ عَلِيّاً وَفَاطِمَةَ وَغَيْرَهُمَا ، فَقُلْتُ : يَا رَسُولَ الله ، أَمِنْ أَهْلِ الْبَيْتِ أَنَا ؟ قَالَ : فَسَكَتَ . ثُمَّ قُلْتُ : أَمِنْ أَهْلِ الْبَيْتِ أَنَا ؟ قَالَ : فَسَكَتَ . ثُمَّ قَالَ فِي الثَّالِثَةِ : نَعَمْ ، مَا لَمْ تَقُمْ عَلَى سُدَّةٍ أَوْ تَأْتِ أَمِيراً تَسْأَلُهُ .

أنبأني مفتي جمهورية سنغافورة سابقاً ، العالم الشريف النبيل الحبيب **عيسى بن محمد بن سُمَيط الأزهري** (ولد ١٣٥٧) فيها ، عن العلّامة المشارك مفتي جُوهُور الحبيب علوي بن طاهر الحداد (١٣٠١-١٣٨٢) دفين مقبرة المحمودية بولاية جوهور جنوب ماليزيا ، (ح) وأنبأني الحبيب **علوي بن طاهر الحداد** عالياً ، عن عمّه الإمام السيد صالح بن عبد الله بن طه الحداد والمسنِد المعمَّر عمر بن عثمان ابن محمّد باعثمان العَمودي ـ نسبةً للشيخ سعيد بن عيسى بن أحمد الملقب بعَمود الدين ـ كلاهما عن السيّد الوجيه مفتي اليمن ومسندها

عبد الرحمن بن سليمان بن يحيى الأهدل عالياً ، عن والده ، عن الإمام عبد الرحمن بن أحمد باعلوي الحسيني ، عن الملا إبراهيم الكُوراني ، عن القُشاشي ، عن الشمس محمّد الرملي ، عن شيخ الإسلام زكريا ، عن ابن حجر والتقي ابن فهد والكمال محمد بن محمد بن الزين ، الأوّل عن عمر بن محمد بن أحمد بن سلمان البالسي ، والثلاثة عن مسندة الشام أم عبد الله عائشة بنت محمّد بن عبد الهادي المقدسيّة الصالحيّة ، كلاهما عن مسنِدة الشام المعمَّرة المحدّثة العذراء أم عبد الله زينب بنت الكمال أحمد بن عبد الرحيم بن عبد الواحد المقدسيّة (٦٤٦-٧٤٠) ، بإجازتها من الحافظ شمس الدين أبي المُظفَّر يوسف بن قِزُغْلِي بن عبد الله سِبْط ابن الجوزي (٥٨١-٦٥٤) ، عن جدّه الحافظ أبي الفرج عبد الرحمن بن علي بن محمّد بن الجوزي ، عن شيخه الحافظ أبو الفضل محمّد بن ناصر بن محمّد بن علي البغدادي السّلامي ، قرأت على الشيخ الصالح أبي الحسين المبارك بن عبد الجبار بن أحمد بن القاسم الصيرفي الطيوري ، أنا أبو طاهر محمد بن علي بن محمّد بن يوسف المُقْرِيُّ المعروف بان العَلَّاف قراءةً عليه ، أنا **أبو بكر أحمد بن جعفر بن حمدان بن مالك القَطِيعي** قراءة عليه ، قال : حدثنا أبو مسلم إبراهيم بن عبد الله بن مسلم الكُجِّي

البصري قال نا عبد الله بن عبد الوهاب الحَجَبِي قثنا خالد بن الحارث قال حدثني طَرِيف بن عيسى العنبري ، قال : حدثني يوسف بن عبد الحميد ، قال : لَقِيتُ ثَوْبَانَ ، فَرَأَى عَلَيَّ ثِيَاباً ، فَقَالَ : مَا تَصْنَعُ بِهٰذِهِ الثِّيَابِ ؟ وَرَأَى فِي يَدِي خَاتِماً ، فَقَالَ : مَا تَصْنَعُ بِهٰذَا الْخَاتِمِ ؟ إِنَّمَا الْخَوَاتِيمُ لِلْمُلُوكِ . قَالَ : فَمَا اتَّخَذْتُ بَعْدَهُ خَاتِماً . قَالَ : فَحَدَّثَنَا ثَوْبَانُ **أَنَّ النَّبِيَّ ﷺ دَعَا لِأَهْلِ بَيْتِهِ ، فَذَكَرَ عَلِيّاً وَفَاطِمَةَ وَغَيْرَهُمَا ، فَقُلْتُ : يَا رَسُولَ اللهِ ، أَمِنْ أَهْلِ الْبَيْتِ أَنَا ؟ قَالَ : فَسَكَتَ . ثُمَّ قُلْتُ : أَمِنْ أَهْلِ الْبَيْتِ أَنَا ؟ قَالَ : فَسَكَتَ . ثُمَّ قَالَ فِي الثَّالِثَةِ : نَعَمْ ، مَا لَمْ تَقُمْ عَلَى سُدَّةٍ أَوْ تَأْتِ أَمِيراً تَسْأَلُهُ .**

رواه الطبراني في الأوسط ، ورواه أبو نعيم في باب ثوبان من حلية الأولياء والبيهقي في السنن والاعتقاد وابن عساكر في التاريخ والشجري في أماليه ، جميعهم من طريق خالد بن الحارث ، به . قال الذهبي كان أبو بكر القطيعي أَسْنَدَ أهلِ زمانِه . ووصفه الدارقطني بالثقة الزاهد ، وقال عنه الحاكم ثقة مأمون . أمّا رجال سنده فأثبات ثقات إلا طَرِيف بن عيسى العنبري وشيخه يوسف بن عبد الحميد ، ذكرهما البخاري في التاريخ وابن أبي حاتم في الجرح والتعديل وسكتوا عنهما ، وذكر ابن حبان طريفاً في الثقات والدارقطنيُّ في

الضعفاء . وقال المنذري في الترغيب والهيثمي في المجمع والسيوطي في جزء ما رواه الأساطين في عدم المجيء إلى السلاطين والهيثمي في الزواجر : رواته ثقات . وذكر الحافظان ابن حجر في الإصابة والسيوطي في حسن المحاضرة أنّ ابن السَّكَن رواه من طريق يوسف بن عبد الحميد ، وابن السكن ثالث الصحيحين عند ابن حزم ، حكاه الذهبي في تذكرة الحفّاظ . (الغريب) قال الحافظ المنذري في الترغيب والترهيب : المراد بالسُّدَّة هنا : باب السلطان ونحوه . (لطيفة) قوله (مَا تَصْنَعُ بِهٰذَا الْخَاتِمِ ؟ إِنَّمَا الْخَوَاتِيمُ لِلْمُلُوكِ) أُخبرت أن الشيخ بدر الدين الحسني ـ رحمه الله ـ كان ينهى الرّجال عن لبس الخواتيم . وهو سنّة عند الشافعيّة والحنابلة كما في كتاب التختّم للبيهقي ولابن رجب . والله أعلم .

❑ ❑ ❑

٣٣

المستدرك على الصحيحين للحاكم

(٣٢١-٤٠٥)

مَا بَالُ أَقْوَامٍ يَقُولُونَ : إِنَّ رَحِمِي لَا يَنْفَعُ ؟ بَلَى وَاللهِ إِنَّ رَحِمِي مَوْصُولَةٌ فِي الدُّنْيَا وَالْآخِرَةِ ! وَإِنِّي . أَيُّهَا النَّاسُ . فَرَطُكُمْ عَلَى الْحَوْضِ ! فَإِذَا جِئْتُ ، قَامَ رِجَالٌ ، فَقَالَ هٰذَا : يَا رَسُولَ اللهِ أَنَا فُلَانٌ ، وَقَالَ هٰذَا : يَا رَسُولَ اللهِ أَنَا فُلَانٌ ، وَقَالَ هٰذَا : يَا رَسُولَ اللهِ أَنَا فُلَانٌ ، فَأَقُولُ : قَدْ عَرَفْتُكُمْ ، وَلٰكِنَّكُمْ أَحْدَثْتُمْ بَعْدِي ، وَرَجَعْتُمُ الْقَهْقَرَى .

أنبأني السيّد **محمد فاتح الكتّاني** (ولد ١٣٣٨) (ت ١٤٤٢ رحمه الله) ابن السيد محمد مكي ابن محمد بن جعفر الكتّاني في دار سيدي الشيخ محمّد أبي الهدى اليعقوبي بالصَّبُّورة بريف دمشق ، عن السيد أحمد الشريف السَّنوسي (١٢٩٠-١٣٥١) ، عن عمّه السيد محمد المهدي السنوسي والسيد أحمد الرِّيفي ، كلاهما عن السيد محمد بن علي السنوسي ، عن أبي طالب محمد بن علي بن الشارف المازوني ، عن المسندة قريش بنت عبد القادر الطبرية ، عن المسند عبد الواحد بن إبراهيم الحصَّاري ، عن شيخ الإسلام زكريا الأنصاري ، عن الحافظ ابن حجر ، قال : أنبأنا أبو

هريـرة ابن الذهبي إجازة ، عن القاسـم بن مظفَّر ابن عسـاكر ، عن المسند أبي الحسن ابن المُقَيَّر ، عن أبي الفضل الميهني ، عن أبي بكر أحمد ابن علي بـن خلف ، عن **الحاكم** ، قال : أخبرنا أبو الحسـين أحمد بن عثمان بن يحيى المقـري ببغداد ، حدثنا أبو قلابة الرقاشي ، حدثنا أبو حذيفة ، حدثنا زهير بن محمد ، عن عبد الله بن محمد بن عقيل ، عن حمزة بن أبي سـعيد الخدري ، عن أبيه رضي الله عنه ، قال : سـمعت رسـول الله ﷺ يقول على المنبر : **مَـا بَالُ أَقْوَامٍ يَقُولُـونَ : إِنَّ رَحِمِي لَا يَنْفَـعُ ؟ بَـلَى وَاللهِ إِنَّ رَحِمِـي مَوْصُولَـةٌ فِي الدُّنْيَا وَالْآخِـرَةِ ! وَإِنِّي - أَيُّهَا النَّاسُ - فَرَطُكُمْ عَلَى الْحَوْضِ ! فَإِذَا جِئْتُ ، قَامَ رِجَالٌ ، فَقَالَ هٰذَا : يَا رَسُولَ اللهِ أَنَا فُلَانٌ ، وَقَالَ هٰذَا : يَا رَسُولَ اللهِ أَنَا فُلَانٌ ، وَقَالَ هٰذَا : يَا رَسُـولَ اللهِ أَنَا فُلَانٌ ، فَأَقُولُ : قَدْ عَرَفْتُكُمْ ، وَلٰكِنَّكُمْ أَحْدَثْتُمْ بَعْدِي ، وَرَجَعْتُمُ الْقَهْقَرَى .**

قال الحاكم : هذا حديث صحيح الإسناد ، ولم يخرجاه . ورواه بألفاظ مختلفة أبو داود الطيالسي وابن أبي شيبة وعبد بن حُميد وأحمد وأبـو يعلى ، قـال الهيثمي : ورجاله رجـال الصحيح غير عبد الله بن محمد بن عقيل وقد وثق . والبيهقي في مناقب الشـافعي بإسناد نازل بدرجة ، قال : حدثنا أبو محمد عبد الله بن يوسف الأصبهاني ، أنبأنا

أبـو بكـر محمد بـن الحسـين القطـان ، حدثنـا إبراهيم بـن الحـارث البغدادي ، حدثنا يحيى بن أبي بكير ، حدثنا زهير بن محمد ، به ، دون الشطر الثاني أي دون عبارة **فَإِذَا جِئْتُ** . قال ابن عبد البر في التمهيد : قيـل لشريك : يا أبا عبد الله ، علامَ حملتـم هذا الحديث ؟ قال : على أهل الردة . رواه الطبري .

❑ ❑ ❑

٣٤

معرفة علوم الحديث للحاكم

(٣٢١-٤٠٥)

إِنَّ اللهَ اصْطَفَى كِنَانَةَ مِنْ وَلَدِ إِسْمَعِيلَ وَاصْطَفَى قُرَيْشًا مِنْ كِنَانَةَ وَاصْطَفَى مِنْ قُرَيْشٍ بَنِي هَاشِمٍ وَاصْطَفَانِي مِنْ بَنِي هَاشِمٍ .

أخبرني الأستاذ المبجَّل ، مرشد الأئمة ومخرّج العلماء ، مؤلف إعلام الأنام شرح بلوغ المرام بأدلة الأحكام ، المفسّر الحافظ الفقيه الأصولي اللغوي الأستاذ الفريد ، رئيس قسم علوم القرآن والسنّة في كلّيّة الشريعة بجامعتي دمشق وحلب وأستاذ الحديث وعلومه في عدد من الجامعات والكليات ، شيخنا **الدكتور نور الدين بن محمد بن حسن بن محمد عِتر** الحلبي الدمشقي الحنفي الحسيني أباً وأمّاً (ولد ١٣٥٦/ ١٩٣٧) (ت ١٤٤٢ رحمه الله) بقراءتي عليه في مسجد ظَبْيَان بجنب منزله في حي المهاجرين بسفح جبل قاسيون بعد صلاة المغرب ليلة السبت ١٧ ربيع الآخر ١٤٢٥ الموافق ٤ حزيران ٢٠٠٤ ، عن شيخه المربّي وخاله ووالد زوجه شيخ الإسلام الحافظ

الشريف الشيخ أبي النجيب عبد الله بن العارف العلّامة محمد نجيب بن الحاج محمد سراج الدين الحسيني الحلبي الرفاعي ، عن والده ، عن شيخه بل عمدته في الرواية مفتي الديار الحلبية ، العلامة الشيخ بكري بن أحمد الزَبْري الأزهري ، عن شيخه الشيخ برهان الدين إبراهيم بن محمد الباجوري المصري ، عن شيخه الأمير الصغير ، عن والده وشيخه أبي عبد الله محمد بن محمد الأمير الكبير المصري المالكي ، عن شيخيه العلامتين الشافعيين : الشهاب أحمد بن عبد الفتاح المَلَّوي ، والشهاب أحمد بن الحسن الجَوهري ، كلاهما عن شيخهما الإمام الحافظ أبي سالم جمال الدين عبد الله بن سالم البصري المكي ، عن الشيخ المعمّر عبد العزيز بن محمد بن عبد العزيز الزمزمي المكي ، عن والده ، عن جدّه لأمه شهاب الدين والدنيا الشيخ أحمد بن محمد بن حجر الهيتمي المكي ، عن شيخه شيخ الإسلام زكرياء الأنصاري ، عن شيخه الحافظ ابن حجر ، قال في المعجم المفهرس له : إنه كَمُل له الكتاب على شيخين قرأ جزأً منه على كل منهما : التقي أبو محمد عبد الله بن محمد بن أحمد بن عبيد الله والعماد أبي بكر بن إبراهيم الفَرَضي ، بإجازتهما إن لم يكن سماعاً من أبي عبد الله محمد بن أحمد بن أبي الهَيْجاء بن الزَّرَّاد ، بسماعه له على

الحافظ أبي علي الحسن بن محمد بن محمد البَكري ، بسماعه له على أبي محمد القاسم بن أبي سعد عبد الله بن عمر الصَّفَّار ، أنبأنا أبو بكر وجيه بن خلف الشيرازي : أنبأنا **الحافظ أبو عبد الله محمد بن عبد الله الضَّبِّي النَّيسابوري الحاكم** ، حدثنا أبو العباس محمد بن يعقوب ، قال : حدثنا محمد بن إسحاق الصغاني ، قال : حدثنا عبد الله بن بكر السهمي ، قال : حدثنا يزيد بن عوانة ، عن محمد بن ذكوان خال ولد حماد بن زيد ، عن عمرو بن دينار ، عن ابن عمر رضي الله عنهما ، قال : **إِنَّا لَقُعُودٌ بِفِنَاءِ رَسُولِ اللهِ ﷺ ، إِذْ مَرَّتِ امْرَأَةٌ ، فَقَالَ بَعْضُ الْقَوْمِ : هٰذِهِ بِنْتُ رَسُولِ اللهِ ﷺ ، فَقَالَ أَبُو سُفْيَانَ : مَثَلُ مُحَمَّدٍ فِي بَنِي هَاشِمٍ مَثَلُ الرَّيْحَانَةِ فِي وَسَطِ النَّتْنِ ، فَانْطَلَقَتِ الْمَرْأَةُ فَأَخْبَرَتِ النَّبِيَّ ﷺ ، فَجَاءَ النَّبِيُّ ﷺ وَيُعْرَفُ فِي وَجْهِهِ الْغَضَبُ ، فَقَالَ : مَا بَالُ أَقْوَالٍ تَبْلُغُنِي عَنْ أَقْوَامٍ ؟ إِنَّ اللهَ عَزَّ وَجَلَّ خَلَقَ السَّمَاوَاتِ سَبْعًا ، فَاخْتَارَ الْعُلَى مِنْهَا فَأَسْكَنَهَا مَنْ شَاءَ مِنْ خَلْقِهِ ، ثُمَّ خَلَقَ الْخَلْقَ فَاخْتَارَ مِنَ الْخَلْقِ بَنِي آدَمَ ، وَاخْتَارَ مِنْ بَنِي آدَمَ الْعَرَبَ ، وَاخْتَارَ مِنَ الْعَرَبِ مُضَرَ ، وَاخْتَارَ مِنْ مُضَرَ قُرَيْشًا ، وَاخْتَارَ مِنْ قُرَيْشٍ بَنِي هَاشِمٍ ، وَاخْتَارَنِي مِنْ بَنِي هَاشِمٍ ، فَأَنَا مِنْ خِيَارٍ إِلَى خِيَارٍ ، فَمَنْ أَحَبَّ الْعَرَبَ فَبِحُبِّي أَحَبَّهُمْ ، وَمَنْ أَبْغَضَ الْعَرَبَ فَبِبُغْضِي أَبْغَضَهُمْ .**

رواه الطبراني في الكبير والأوسط بلفظ **فَاخْتَارَ الْعُلْيَا مِنْهَا فَسَكَنَهَا ، وَأَسْكَنَ سَمَاوَاتِهِ مَنْ شَاءَ مِنْ خَلْقِهِ** ، قال الهيثمي : فيه حماد بن واقد وهو ضعيف يعتبر به ، وبقية رجاله وثقوا . ورواه الحاكم والبيهقي في الدلائل وذكر ابن أبي حاتم عن أبيه أنه قال : حديث منكر . أي من جهة الإسناد ، ففي الميزان : محمد بن ذكوان قال البخاري منكر الحديث وقال النسائي ليس بثقة وقال الدارقطني ضعيف ، وقوّاه ابن حبان . وأمّا من جهة المتن فقد حسّنه الحافظ في الأمالي المُطلقة . وأصله في صحيح مسلم : عن وَاثِلَةَ بْنِ الْأَسْقَعِ : سَمِعْتُ رَسُولَ اللهِ ﷺ يَقُولُ : **إِنَّ اللهَ اصْطَفَى كِنَانَةَ مِنْ وَلَدِ إِسْمَعِيلَ وَاصْطَفَى قُرَيْشًا مِنْ كِنَانَةَ وَاصْطَفَى مِنْ قُرَيْشٍ بَنِي هَاشِمٍ وَاصْطَفَانِي مِنْ بَنِي هَاشِمٍ** . قال البيهقي في مناقب الشافعي : معناهما واحد . وروى أحمد بسند قوي والترمذي ـ حسّنه ـ عَنْ سَلْمَانَ ، قَالَ : قَالَ لِي رَسُولُ اللهِ ﷺ : **يَا سَلْمَانُ لَا تُبْغِضْنِي فَتُفَارِقَ دِينَكَ ! قَالَ : قُلْتُ : يَا رَسُولَ اللهِ وَكَيْفَ أُبْغِضُكَ وَبِكَ هَدَانَا اللهُ ؟ ! قَالَ تُبْغِضُ الْعَرَبَ فَتُبْغِضُنِي** . ومن أحسنها في الباب : حديث المسند عن جابر مرفوعاً **إِذَا ذَلَّتُ الْعَرَبُ ذَلَّ الْإِسْلَامُ** . (تنبيه) قال الأستاذ نور الدين : لعلّه كان قبل إسلام أبي سفيان .

ثـم قال الحاكم إثْـرَه : فَلْيَعْلَمْ طَالِبُ هٰذَا الْعِلْـمِ أَنَّ كُلَّ مُضَرِيٍّ عَـرَبِيٌّ ، فَإِنَّ مُضَرَ شُـعْبَةٌ مِنَ الْعَـرَبِ ، وَأَنَّ كُلَّ قُـرَشِيٍّ مُضَرِيٌّ ، فَإِنَّ قُرَيْشاً شُعْبَةٌ مِنْ مُضَرَ ، وَأَنَّ كُلَّ هَاشِمِيٍّ قُرَشِيٌّ ، فَإِنَّ هَاشِماً شُعْبَةٌ مِنْ قُرَيْشٍ ، وَأَنَّ كُلَّ عَلَوِيٍّ هَاشِـمِيٌّ ، وَقَدِ اخْتَلَفُوا فِي الْعَلَوِيَّةِ : لِمَ سُمُّوا عَلَوِيَّةً ؟ فَقِيلَ : إِنَّهُ انْتِمَاءٌ إِلَى عَلِيٍّ ، وَقِيلَ : إِنَّهُ انْتِمَاءٌ إِلَى أَعْلَى الرُّتَبِ مِنْ رَسُـولِ اللهِ ﷺ ، فَمَنْ عَرَفَ مَـا أَشَرْتُ إِلَيْهِ مِنْ قَبِيلَةِ الْمُصْطَفَى ﷺ ، جَعَلَهُ مِثَالاً لِسَـائِرِ الْقَبَائِلِ ، فَيَعْلَمُ أَنَّ الْمُطَّلِبِيَّ قُرَشِيٌّ ، وَأَنَّ الْعَبْشَمِيَّ قُـرَشِيٌّ ـ قال الأستاذ نور الدين : عَبْشَـمِيٌّ مِن (عَبْدِ شَـمْسٍ) وهو تركيب مَزْجِيّ ـ وَأَنَّ التَّيْمِـيَّ قُـرَشِيٌّ ، وَأَنَّ الْعَـدَوِيَّ قُـرَشِيٌّ ، وَأَنَّ الْأُمَوِيَّ قُرَشِيٌّ ، فَالْأَصْلُ قُرَيْشٌ وَهٰذِهِ شُـعَبٌ ، وَكَذٰلِكَ النَّهْشَلِيُّونَ تَمِيمِيُّونَ ، وَالدَّارِمِيُّونَ تَمِيمِيُّونَ ، وَالسَّعْدِيُّونَ تَمِيمِيُّونَ ، وَالسَّلِيطِيُّونَ تَمِيمِيُّـونَ ، وَالْقَيْسِـيُّونَ تَمِيمِيُّـونَ ، وَالْأَهْتَمِيُّـونَ تَمِيمِيُّـونَ ، وَكَذٰلِكَ الْخَزْرَجِيُّـونَ أَنْصَارِيُّـونَ ، وَالنَّجَّارِيُّـونَ أَنْصَارِيُّـونَ ، وَالْحَارِثِيُّـونَ أَنْصَارِيُّـونَ ، وَالسَّـاعِدِيُّونَ أَنْصَارِيُّـونَ ، وَالسَّـلِمِيُّونَ أَنْصَارِيُّـونَ ، وَالْأَوْسِـيُّونَ أَنْصَارِيُّـونَ . قَالَ رَسُـولُ اللهِ ﷺ : **فِي كُلِّ دُوْرِ الْأَنْصَارِ خَيْرٌ** . [رواه مسلم وأحمد] فَهٰذَا مِثَالٌ لِمَعْرِفَةِ الشُّعَبِ مِنَ الْقَبَائِلِ .

❑ ❑ ❑

٣٥

معرفة الصحابة لأبي نعيم

(٣٣٦- ٤٣٠)

يَا عَمْرُو وَاللهِ لَقَدْ آذَيْتَنِي . قُلْتُ : أَعُوذُ بِاللهِ أَنْ أُوذِيَكَ يَا رَسُولَ اللهِ !
قَالَ : بَلَى ؛ مَنْ آذَى عَلِيًّا فَقَدْ آذَانِي .

أنبأنا السيد **عبد العزيز الغُماري الطانجي** (١٣٣٨-١٤١٨) ، عن والده السيد محمّد بن الصدِّيق بن أحمد بن عبد المؤمن الغُماري الحسني (ت ١٣٥٤) ، عن خال والدته الفقيه المعمَّر عبد القادر بن أحمد بن عجيبة (ت ١٣١٣) ، عن والده الولي المشهور صاحب التفسير وشرح الحكم أحمد بن عجيبة (ت ١٢٢٥) ، عن شيخ الجماعة التاوُدِي ابن سودة ، عن الشمس البَنَّاني ، عن أبي سالم العَيَّاشي ، عن الشهاب القليوبي ، عن الشمس الرَّمْلي ، عن شيخ الإسلام زكرياء ، عن الحافظ ابن حجر ، عن الزين أبي الفضل العراقي ، عن أبي الفضل العلائي ، عن المزّي ، عن الدمياطي ، عن المنذري ، عن أبي الفضل المقدسي ، عن الحافظ عبد الغني بن عبد الواحد بن علي بن

سرور المقدسي ، قراءة له على أبي موسى محمّد بن أبي بكر بن أبي عيسى المديني والضياء محمد بن أحمد بن أبي بكر الجُوزَداني وأبي علي حمزة بن أبي الفتح بن عبد الله عتيق مسافر الطبري ، بروايتهم عن أبي علي الحداد ، عن الحافظ **أبي نُعَيم أحمد بن عبد الله بن إسحاق الأصبهاني** ، ثنا عبد الله بن جعفر ، ثنا إسماعيل بن عبد الله ، ثنا مالك بن إسماعيل وإسماعيل بن أبان ، قالا : ثنا مسعود بن سعد الجعفي ، ثنا محمد بن إسحاق ، (ح) وحدثنا أبو أحمد محمد بن أحمد بن إسحاق الأنماطي ، ثنا عبدان بن أحمد ، ثنا زيد بن الحريش ، ثنا محمد بن الصلت ، ثنا مندل بن علي ، عن محمد بن إسحاق ، (ح) وحدثنا القاضي أبو أحمد محمد بن أحمد بن إبراهيم ، ثنا الحسين بن علي بن الحسن السلولي ، ثنا محمد بن الحسن السلولي ، ثنا صالح بن أبي الأسود ، عن محمد بن إسحاق ، (ح) وحدثنا أبو بكر بن مالك ، ثنا عبد الله بن أحمد بن حنبل ، حدثني يعقوب بن إبراهيم بن سعد ، حدثني أبي ، عن محمد بن إسحاق ، واللفظ لإبراهيم بن سعد ، عن أبان بن صالح ، عن الفضل بن معقِل بن سنان ، عن عبد الله بن نِيَار الأسلمي ، عن عمرو بن شأس الأسلمي ـ وكان من أصحاب الحديبية ـ قال : خَرَجْتُ مَعَ عَلِيٍّ رَضِيَ اللهُ عَنْهُ إِلَى الْيَمَنِ فَجَفَانِي فِي

سَفَرِي ذَلِكَ حَتَّى وَجَدْتُ فِي نَفْسِي عَلَيْهِ ، فَلَمَّا قَدِمْتُ أَظْهَرْتُ شِكَايَتَهُ فِي المَسْجِدِ حَتَّى بَلَغَ ذَلِكَ رَسُولَ اللهِ ﷺ ، فَدَخَلْتُ المَسْجِدَ ذَاتَ غَدَاةٍ ، وَرَسُولُ اللهِ ﷺ فِي نَاسٍ مِنْ أَصْحَابِهِ ، **فَلَمَّا رَآنِي أَمَدَّنِي عَيْنَيْهِ ـ يَقُولُ : حَدَّدَ إِلَيَّ النَّظَرَ ـ حَتَّى إِذَا جَلَسْتُ ، قَالَ : يَا عَمْرُو وَاللهِ لَقَدْ آذَيْتَنِي . قُلْتُ : أَعُوذُ بِاللهِ أَنْ أُوذِيَكَ يَا رَسُولَ اللهِ ! قَالَ : بَلَى ؛ مَنْ آذَى عَلِيًّا فَقَدْ آذَانِي** . ورواه المُحارِبي ويونس بن بكير وأبو زهير عن محمد ابن إسحاق نحوَه .

صحيح ، رواه أحمد في المسند والفضائل والبزّار وابن أبي شيبة والرُّوياني كلاهما مختصراً وابن حبان والحاكم والبيهقي في الدلائل . وفي الخصائص للنسائي والحاكم وابن أبي شيبة عن أم سلمة وأحمد عن سعد مرفوعاً : **مَنْ سَبَّ عَلِيّاً فَقَد سَبَّنِي** . وفيه وغيره عن عبد المطلب بن ربيعة مرفوعاً **مَنْ آذَى الْعَبَّاسَ فَقَد آذَانِي** . (لطيفة) روى البيهقي في المناقب : ذُكِر عليّ بن أبي طالب عند الشافعي ، فقال رجل من القوم : ما نَفَرَ الناسَ من علي بن أبي طالب إلّا أنّه كان لا يبالي بأحد . فقال الشافعي : مهلاً ؛ لِأَنَّه كان فيه أربع خصال لا تكون خِصلة واحدة منها في أحد إلا حقَّ له أن لا يبالي بأحد : إن علي بن أبي طالب كان زاهداً ، والزاهد لا يبالي بالدنيا ولا بأهلها .

وكان عالماً ، والعالم لا يبالي بأحد . وكان شجاعاً ، والشجاع لا يبالي بأحد . وكان شريفاً ، والشريف لا يبالي بأحد .

❑ ❑ ❑

٣٦

منتخب دلائل النبوّة لأبي نعيم

(٣٣٦- ٤٣٠)

> اللّٰهُمَّ هٰذَا الْعَبَّاسُ عَمِّي ، وَهٰؤُلَاءِ أَهْلُ بَيْتِي ، فَاسْتُرْهُمْ مِنَ النَّارِ كَسَتْرِي إِيَّاهُمْ بِمُلَاءَتِي هٰذِهِ . فَأَمَّنَتْ أُسْكُفَّةُ الْبَابِ وَحَوَائِطُ الْبَيْتِ : آمِينَ ! آمِينَ ! آمِينَ !

أنبأني شيخ الطريقة الإدريسية الأحمدية الشاذلية الحسيب النسيب الزاهد العلامة صاحب المؤلفات العارف بالله الداعية الرحالة الشيخ **السيد أحمد بن إدريس السوداني الأُمُّدُرْماني الأزهري** (ت ١٤٣٩ رحمه الله) (ولد ١٣٥٠/ ١٩٣٢) ابن محمد الشريف بن عبد العال بن الإمام العارف السيد أحمد بن إدريس الإدريسي الحسني ، عن والده السيّد إدريس، عن والده السيد محمد الشريف ، عن والده السيد عبد العالي ، عن والده الإمام العارف السيد أحمد بن إدريس الفاسي مؤسس الطريقة الأحمديّة ، عن أبي المواهب التازي ، عن العُجَيمي ، بسنده الثلاثي المار في باب مسند الشافعي إلى الحافظ ابن حجر ، بسنده المار آنفاً إلى المنذري (٥٨١-٦٥٦) ، عن أبي الحسن زين الدين علي بن ابراهيم بن نجا

الدمشقي ثم المصري الحنبلي الواعظ الانصاري (٥٠٨-٥٩٩)، أخبرنا الشيخ الإمام الثقة الحافظ سعد الخير محمد بن سهل الأنصاري (ت ٥٤١) ـ رحمه الله تعالى ـ قراءةً عليه ونحن نسمع، وذلك في سنة تسع وثلاثين وخمسمائة في منزله بدار الخلافة ـ عمَّرها الله ـ قال: أنا الشيخ الفقيه أبو سعد محمد بن محمد بن محمّد المطرِّز رحمه الله تعالى قراءة عليه في داره بأصبهان وأنا أسمع، قال: أنا **الإمام أبو نعيم أحمد بن عبد الله بن أحمد بن إسحاق** قراءة عليه، قال: حدثنا القاضي أبو أحمد، قال: ثنا الحسن بن علي بن زياد، قال: ثنا عبد الرحمن بن يحيى الهاشمي المدني، قال: ثنا عبد الله بن عثمان، عن جدّه ـ أبي أمّه، واسمه مالك بن حمزة بن أبي أُسَيد الساعدي، قال: شَهِدْت جدّي يحدّث، قال: قال رسول الله ﷺ للعباس: **لَا تَبْرَحْ أَنْتَ وَبَنُوكَ غداً، فَإِنَّ لِي فِيكُمْ حَاجَةً. قَالَ: فَجَمَعَهُمُ الْعَبَّاسُ فِي بَيْتٍ، فَأَتَاهُمْ رَسُولُ اللهِ ﷺ فَقَالَ: السَّلَامُ عَلَيْكُمْ كَيْفَ أَصْبَحْتُمْ؟ قَالُوا: بِخَيْرٍ، نَحْمَدُ اللهَ، بِأَبِينَا أَنْتَ وَأُمِّنَا يَا رَسُولَ اللهِ. قَالَ: تَقَارَبُوا، تَقَارَبُوا. فَزَحَفَ بَعْضُهُمْ إِلَى بَعْضٍ. قَالَ: فَلَمَّا أَمْكَنُوهُ، اشْتَمَلَ عَلَيْهِمْ بِمُلَاءَتِهِ ثُمَّ قَالَ ـ صَلَّى اللهُ عَلَيْهِ وَسَلَّمَ ـ: اللَّهُمَّ هٰذَا الْعَبَّاسُ عَمِّي، وَهٰؤُلَاءِ أَهْلُ بَيْتِي، فَاسْتُرْهُمْ مِنَ النَّارِ كَسَتْرِي إِيَّاهُمْ بِمُلَاءَتِي**

هٰذِهِ . فَأَمَّنَتْ أُسْكُفَّةُ الْبَابِ وَحَوَائِطُ الْبَيْتِ : آمِينَ ! آمِينَ ! آمِينَ ! ثَلَاثاً .

رواه الطبراني في الكبير والأوسط وحسّن اسناده الهيثمي في مجمع الزوائد ورواه التيمي الأصفهاني والبيهقي كلاهما في الدلائل ورواه ابن ماجة في سننه ، الأخير دون ذكر الستر والدعاء والتأمين بأسانيد مدارها عبد الله بن عثمان بن إسحاق بن سعد بن أبي وقاص ، وأورده ابن كثير في البداية في باب تسبيح الحصى في فصل دلائل النبوة من كتاب الشمائل . الغريب : لا تَبْرَحْ : لا تغادر . اشتَمَل عليهم بمُلاءته : لَفَّها عليهم . الأُسْكُفَّة : عَتَبَة تكون تحت الباب . وهذا الحديث من أدلّة السّنة للدعاء الجماعي ، إذ فيه تأمين السامع على دعاء الداعي . (لطيفة) أبو الحسن علي بن ابراهيم بن نجا الدمشقي تزوّج أم عبد الكريم فاطمة بنت الحافظ سعد الخير الانصاري المغربي لمّا قدمت بغداد مع أبيها من أصبهان وحضرت السماع ونقلها معه وسكن بها مصراً . قاله الدُبَيْثي في تاريخه . وفي السيرة الزنكية أنه صحب الشيخ عبد القادر الجيلاني ببغداد وقال : اشتغلت عليه بالعلم ففتح الله عز وجل علي في سنة بما لم يفتح على غيري في عشرين سنة . وكان من مستشاري صلاح الدين . قال ابن

رجب في ذيل طبقات الحنابلة : لمّاً فتح صلاح الدين القدس كان معه ، وتكلم أول جمعة أقيمت فيه على كرسي الوعظ . وكان يوماً مشهوداً . وفي توضيح المشتبه لابن ناصر الدين : كان واعظاً فصيحاً ذا قبول عند الملوك وغيرهم ، ذا ثروة ومال ، من جملته كان له عشرون جارية للفراش تساوي كل جارية ألف دينار .

❑ ❑ ❑

٣٧

شعب الإيمان للبيهقي «الجامع»

(٣٨٤-٤٥٨)

لَا يُؤْمِنُ عَبْدٌ حَتَّى أَكُونَ أَحَبَّ إِلَيْهِ مِنْ نَفْسِهِ ، وَتَكُونَ عِتْرَتِي أَحَبَّ إِلَيْهِ مِنْ عِتْرَتِهِ ، وَتكونَ ذَاتِي أَحَبَّ إِلَيْهِ مِنْ ذَاتِهِ ، وَيَكُونَ أَهْلِي أَحَبَّ إِلَيْهِ مِنْ أَهْلِهِ .

أنبأني الشيخ المعمَّر الحبيب عمر بن سالم المِحضار (١٣٤١- ١٢ ربيع الأول ١٤٣٥) رحمه الله نزيل باتو پاهات في سلطنة جوهور الماليزية فيها ، عن شيخ الوادي الإمام المربي العارف الحبيب علوي بن عبد الله بن عيدروس بن شهاب الدين (١٣٠٣-١٣٨٦) ، عن مفتي الديار الحضرمية الإمام الحبيب عبدالرحمن بن محمد بن حسين المشهور (١٢٥٠-١٣٢٠) صاحب (بغية المسترشدين) عالياً ، عن العلامة الحبيب محمد بن إبراهيم بن عيدروس بن عبد الرحمن بلفقيه ، عن أبيه إبراهيم وعمه أحمد ، عن والدهما عيدروس بن عبد الرحمن ، عن أبيه ، عن السيد عبد الله بن أحمد بلفقيه (ت ١١١٢) ، عن الصفي القُشاشي ، بإسناده إلى الحافظ شمس الدين الذهبي المارّ

في باب مصنّف ابن أبي شيبة ، أخبرنا أحمد بن سلامة الحداد ، أَخْبَرَنَا الْإِمَامُ الْحَافِظُ بَهَاءُ الدِّينِ أَبُو مُحَمَّدٍ الْقَاسِمُ بْنُ الْحَافِظِ أَبِي الْقَاسِمِ عَلِيِّ بْنِ الْحُسَيْنِ بْنِ هِبَةِ اللهِ بْنِ عَبْدِ اللهِ الشَّافِعِيُّ - ابن عساكر - (٥٢٧-٦٠٠) قِرَاءَةً عَلَيْهِ قَالَ : أَخْبَرَنَا الْفَقِيهُ أَبُو عَبْدِ اللهِ مُحَمَّدُ بْنُ الْفَضْلِ الصَّاعِدِيُّ الْفُرَاوِيُّ (ت ٥٣٠) وَأَبُو الْقَاسِمِ زَاهِرُ بْنُ طَاهِرِ بْنِ مُحَمَّدٍ الشَّحَّامِيُّ (٤٤٦-٥٣٣) ، وَحَدَّثَنِي أَبِي (٤٩٩-٥٧١) - صاحب تاريخ دمشق - وَأَبُو الْحَسَنِ عَلِيُّ بْنُ سُلَيْمَانَ بْنِ أَحْمَدَ الْمُرَادِيُّ الشَّقُورِيُّ (ت ٥٤٤) ، [كِلاهما] عَنْ زَاهِرٍ ، قَالَ : أَخْبَرَنَا الشَّيْخُ الْإِمَامُ الْحَافِظُ شَيْخُ السُّنَّةِ **أَبُو بَكْرٍ أَحْمَدُ بْنُ الْحُسَيْنِ بْنِ عَلِيِّ بْنِ مُوسَى الْبَيْهَقِيُّ** رَحِمَهُ اللهُ ، قَالَ : أَخْبَرَنَا أَبُو عَبْدِ اللهِ الْحَافِظُ ، أخبرنا أَبُو الْعَبَّاسِ مُحَمَّدُ بْنُ يَعْقُوبَ ، حدثنا الْعَبَّاسُ بْنُ مُحَمَّدٍ الدُّورِيُّ (ح) وَأَخْبَرَنَا أَحْمَدُ بْنُ أَبِي الْعَبَّاسِ الزَّوْزَنِيُّ ، حدثنا أَبُو بَكْرِ بْنُ خَنَبٍ ، حدثنا أَبُو بَكْرٍ مُحَمَّدُ بْنُ سُلَيْمَانَ الْبَاغَنْدِيُّ ، قَالَا : حدثنا مُحَمَّدُ بْنُ عِمْرَانَ بْنِ أَبِي لَيْلَى ، حدثنا سَعِيدُ بْنُ عَمْرٍو السَّكُونِيُّ ، عَنِ [محمد بن عبد الرحمن] ابْنِ أَبِي لَيْلَى ، عَنِ الْحَكَمِ ، عَنْ عَبْدِ الرَّحْمَنِ ابْنِ أَبِي لَيْلَى ، عَنْ أَبِي لَيْلَى ، قَالَ : قَالَ رَسُولُ اللهِ ﷺ : **لَا يُؤْمِنُ عَبْدٌ حَتَّى أَكُونَ أَحَبَّ إِلَيْهِ مِنْ نَفْسِهِ ، وَتَكُونَ عِتْرَتِي أَحَبَّ إِلَيْهِ مِنْ عِتْرَتِهِ ، وَتكونَ ذَاتِي أَحَبَّ إِلَيْهِ مِنْ ذَاتِهِ ، وَيَكُونَ أَهْلِي أَحَبَّ إِلَيْهِ مِنْ أَهْلِهِ .**

رواه الطبراني وأبو الشيخ في الثواب والشَّجَري في أماليه، جميعهم من طريق محمّد بن عبد الرحمن بن أبي ليلى قاضي الكوفة، وهو ـ مع سوء حفظه في الحديث ـ من رجال السنن، وهذا الحديث صحيح بمجموع شواهده، والله أعلم.

قال البيهقي إثْرَه: وَيَدْخُلُ فِي جُمْلَةِ حُبِّ النَّبِيِّ ﷺ حُبُّ أَصْحَابِهِ، لأَنَّ اللهَ عَزَّ وَجَلَّ أَثْنَى عَلَيْهِمْ وَمَدَحَهُمْ فَقَالَ: ﴿مُّحَمَّدٌ رَّسُولُ ٱللَّهِۚ وَٱلَّذِينَ مَعَهُۥٓ أَشِدَّآءُ عَلَى ٱلْكُفَّارِ رُحَمَآءُ بَيْنَهُمْ﴾ [الفتح ٢٩] وَقَالَ: ﴿لَّقَدْ رَضِىَ ٱللَّهُ عَنِ ٱلْمُؤْمِنِينَ إِذْ يُبَايِعُونَكَ تَحْتَ ٱلشَّجَرَةِ فَعَلِمَ مَا فِى قُلُوبِهِمْ فَأَنزَلَ ٱلسَّكِينَةَ عَلَيْهِمْ وَأَثَٰبَهُمْ فَتْحًا قَرِيبًا ﴿١٨﴾﴾ [الفتح] وَقَالَ: ﴿وَٱلسَّٰبِقُونَ ٱلْأَوَّلُونَ مِنَ ٱلْمُهَٰجِرِينَ وَٱلْأَنصَارِ وَٱلَّذِينَ ٱتَّبَعُوهُم بِإِحْسَٰنٍ رَّضِىَ ٱللَّهُ عَنْهُمْ وَرَضُوا۟ عَنْهُ﴾ [التوبة ١٠٠] الْآيَةَ، وَقَالَ ﴿وَٱلَّذِينَ ءَامَنُوا۟ وَهَاجَرُوا۟ وَجَٰهَدُوا۟ فِى سَبِيلِ ٱللَّهِ وَٱلَّذِينَ ءَاوَوا۟ وَّنَصَرُوٓا۟ أُو۟لَٰٓئِكَ هُمُ ٱلْمُؤْمِنُونَ حَقًّاۚ لَّهُم مَّغْفِرَةٌ وَرِزْقٌ كَرِيمٌ ﴿٧٤﴾﴾ [الأنفال]. فَإِذَا نَزَلُوا هٰذِهِ الْمَنْزِلَةَ اسْتَحَقُّوا عَلَى جَمَاعَةِ الْمُسْلِمِينَ أَنْ يُحِبُّوهُمْ وَيَتَقَرَّبُوا إِلَى اللهِ عَزَّ وَجَلَّ بِمَحَبَّتِهِمْ، لأَنَّ اللهَ تَعَالَى إِذَا رَضِيَ عَنْ أَحَدٍ أَحَبَّهُ، وَوَاجِبٌ عَلَى الْعَبْدِ أَنْ يُحِبَّ مَنْ يُحِبُّهُ مَوْلَاهُ. وَرُوِّينَا عَنْ عُمَرَ بْنِ الْخَطَّابِ عَنِ النَّبِيِّ ﷺ أَنَّهُ قَالَ: **أَكْرِمُوا أَصْحَابِي** [عبد

الـرزاق والطيالسي والطحاوي في معاني الآثار والطبراني في الصغير والخطيب والحميدي والبغوي في شرح السنة والشافعي في الرسالة] ، وَفِي رِوَايَةٍ أُخْرَى : **اِحْفَظُونِي فِي أَصْحَابِي** [ابن ماجه والحاكم وله شواهد منها **أُوْصِيكُمْ بِأَصْحَابِي** الترمذي والحاكم عن عمر ومنها **اِسْتَوْصُوا بِأَصْحَابِي خَيْراً** أحمد والحاكم عن ابن عمر ومنها **أَحْسِنُوا إِلَى أَصْحَابِي** أحمد وابن أبي عاصم وأبو يعلى والطحاوي وابن حبان عن جابر وابن أبي شيبة وابن أبي عاصم عن عمر] . وَفِي حَدِيثِ أَبِي سَعِيدٍ الْخُدْرِيِّ ، عَنِ النَّبِيِّ ﷺ : **لَا تَسُبُّوا أَصْحَابِي ، فَلَوْ أَنَّ أَحَدَكُمْ أَنْفَقَ مِثْلَ أُحُدٍ ذَهَبًا مَا بَلَغَ مُدَّ أَحَدِهِمْ وَلَا نَصِيفَهُ ، وَلَا يُبْغِضُ الْأَنْصَارَ رَجُلٌ يُؤْمِنُ بِاللهِ وَالْيَوْمِ الْآخِرِ** [رواه الجماعة ، وعن ابن مسعود عند الحارث والطبراني **إِذَا ذُكِرَ أَصْحَابِي فَأَمْسِكُوا** قال الهيثمي : فيه مسهر بن عبد الملك وثقه ابن حبان وغيره وفيه خلاف وبقية رجاله رجال الصحيح] .

ومن أحسن المصنَّفات في الباب سوى ما سبق أن ذكرناه : فضائل الصحابة للدارقطني ، وفضائل الخلفاء وغيرهم لأبي نعيم ، والفتح المبين في فضائل الخلفاء الراشدين وأهل البيت الطاهرين لدحلان ، وفضائل الصحابة والدفاع عن كرامتهم للتليدي ، وتحقيق

منيف الرتبة لمن ثبت له شريف الصحبة للعلائي ، والحسام المسلول على منتقصي أصحاب الرسول ﷺ لبَحْرَق ، وصبّ العذاب على من سبّ الأصحاب لمحمود شكري الآلوسي ، والنهي عن سبّ الأصحاب للضياء المقدسي ؛ جميعه مطبوع .

❑ ❑ ❑

٣٨

دلائل النبوة للبيهقي

(٣٨٤-٤٥٨)

أَنَا مُحَمَّدُ بْنُ عَبْدِ اللهِ بْنِ عَبْدِ الْمُطَّلِبِ . إِنَّ اللهَ خَلَقَ الخلْقَ فَجَعَلَنِي فِي خَيْرِ خَلْقِهِ ، وَجَعَلَهُمْ فِرْقَتَيْنِ ، فَجَعَلَنِي فِي خَيْرِ فِرْقَةٍ ، وَجَعَلَهُمْ قَبَائِلَ ، فَجَعَلَنِي فِي خَيْرِهِمْ قَبِيلَةً ، وَجَعَلَهُمْ بُيُوتاً فَجَعَلَنِي فِي خَيْرِهِمْ بَيْتاً . فَأَنَا خَيْرُكُمْ بَيْتاً ، وَخَيْرُكُمْ نَفْساً .

أنبأني وليُّ نِعمتي ومرشدي القطب المتصرِّف مَدَدُ الحقّ شيخ الطريقة النقشبنديّة الناظِميّة مولانا الشيخ **محمّد هشام بن الحاج محمد سليم القبّاني الحسيني الشافعي** (ولد ١٣٦٤/ ١٩٤٥) والشيخ **حسين بن أحمد عُسيران** (١٣٢٩-١٤٢٦/ ١٩١١-٢٠٠٥) رحمه الله - أصله من بني أسد بن خزيمة المُضَرِيِّين المُوالين لآل البيت - البيروتِيّان الشافعيان النقشبنديان ، كلاهما عن أمين فتوى لبنان الشريف محمد العربي العَزُّوزي الزَّرْهُوني الفاسي ثم البيروتي (١٣٠٨-١٣٨٢) ، عن والده أبي عيسى محمد المهدي ، عن والده العلّامة محمد العربي بن محمد الهاشمي ، عن أبي حامد العربي بن المعطي الشرقاوي التادلي ،

عن شيخه أبي العباس أحمد بن أبي القاسم التادلي الرباطي ، عن أبي العباس محمد بن عبد العزيز الهلالي السِّجِلْمَاسي ، عن أبي العباس أحمد الحبيب الصديقي السجلماسي ، عن أبي عبد الله محمد بن عبد الجبار العَيَّاشي ، عن رحّالة المغرب أبي سالم عبد الله بن محمّد بن أبي بكر العيّاشي ، عن المعمّر الشهاب أحمد بن أحمد بن سلامة القليوبي الشافعي ، عن شيخه الشمس محمد بن أحمد بن حمزة الرملي ، عن شيخ الإسلام زكرياء ، أخبرني عالياً أبو ذر الزركشي ، عن أبي عبد الله البَيَاني ، أخبرنا أبو حفص ابن غَدِير القوّاس ، سماعاً وإجازةً عن قاضي القضاة الجمال أبي القاسم الحرستاني ، عن أبي عبد الله محمد بن الفضل الفُراوي وعبد الجبّار بن أحمد الخُواري ، قالا : أخبرنا مؤلّفها **الحافظ أبو بكر أحمد بن الحسين البيهقي** رحمه الله ، قال : أخبرنا أبو منصور محمد بن محمد بن عبد الله بن نوح من أولاد إبراهيم النخعي بالكوفة ، قال : أخبرنا أبو جعفر محمد بن علي بن دحيم ، قال : حدثنا أحمد بن حازم بن أبي عَزْرة ، قال : حدثنا الفَضل بن دُكَيْن ، قال : حدثنا سفيان ، عن يزيد بن أبي زياد ، عن عبد الله بن الحارث بن نوفل ، عن المطّلب بن أبي وَداعة ، قال : قال العبّاس ـ وبلغه بعضُ ما يقول الناس له ـ (ح) قال **البيهقي** : وأخبرنا

أبو الحسين بن الفضل ، أخبرنا عبد الله بن جعفر ، حدثنا يعقوب بن سفيان ، حدثنا أبو نعيم وهو الفضل بن دكين ، به إلى المطلب بن أبي وداعة ، قال : **قَالَ رَسُولُ اللهِ ﷺ ـ وَبَلَغَهُ بَعْضُ مَا يَقُولُ النَّاسُ** [أي في العبّاس] ـ **فَصَعِدَ المِنْبَرَ فَحَمِدَ اللهَ تَعَالَى وَأَثْنَى عَلَيْهِ وَقَالَ مَنْ أَنَا ؟ قَالُوا : أَنْتَ رَسُولُ اللهِ . قَالَ : أَنَا مُحَمَّدُ بْنُ عَبْدِ اللهِ بْنِ عَبْدِ المُطَّلِبِ . إِنَّ اللهَ خَلَقَ الخَلْقَ فَجَعَلَنِي فِي خَيْرِ خَلْقِهِ ، وَجَعَلَهُمْ فِرْقَتَيْنِ ، فَجَعَلَنِي فِي خَيْرِ فِرْقَةٍ ، وَجَعَلَهُمْ قَبَائِلَ ، فَجَعَلَنِي فِي خَيْرِهِمْ قَبِيلَةً ، وَجَعَلَهُمْ بُيُوتاً فَجَعَلَنِي فِي خَيْرِهِمْ بَيْتاً . فَأَنَا خَيْرُكُمْ بَيْتاً ، وَخَيْرُكُمْ نَفْساً .**

رواه أحمد والترمذي ـ حسّنه ، وكذا الحافظ في الأمالي المطلقة ؛ والطبراني في الأوسط والحاكم عن جابر نحوه . تحقّق به أن أهل بيته ﷺ خيرُ بيوتات بني آدم .

وهذا الحديث الشريف مثلٌ لشيخنا المُرشد الشيخ محمّد هشام القبّاني ـ حفظه الله ـ فقد أوذي في الله كثيراً بعد خروج مولانا الشيخ ناظم ـ رحمه الله ـ من الدنيا وزُوحِم على السجّادة النقشبنديّة مع كونه خَلِيفَتَهُ المحقَّق بل الخليفةَ الثاني لشيخ الشيخ قولاً واحداً ـ زِدْ كونَه سليلَ النبيّ ﷺ ومحلَّ عناية سلطان الأولياء الشيخ عبد الله فائز الداغستاني (١٢٩٤-١٣٩٣) الخاصّةِ ومولانا الشيخ ناظم منذ بلوغه ،

ونشْأَتَه في بيت علم مشهور ، فيه خالاه الحسنيّان : الشيخ مختار العلايلي (١٨٩٩-١٩٨٤م) أمين الفتوى في الجمهورية اللبنانية ورئيس مجلس العلماء ببيروت ، الّذي وصفه العَزُّوزي بثَبَته المسمّى إتحاف ذَوي العِناية ببعض ما لي من المَشْيَخَة بالصلاح والتقوى وسلامة الطَوِيّة والسخاء والجود وبالعلّامة المشارِك ثم قال عنه : هو رفيقي بل شقيق روحي بل مؤانِسي في غُربتي ؛ وأخوه الصغير العلّامة الأديب الجِهْبِذ ، مجدّدُ العربية على رأس المئة الرابعة عَشَر الشيخ عبدُ الله العلايلي (١ محرّم ١٣٣٣-١٤١٧/ ١٩١٤-١٩٩٦) ، وصفه العزّوزي بأعلاهم وأنبَهُهم وأذكاهم وأعلمهم بجميع الفنون ولا سيما اللغة والأدب ، وقال فيه : ما فاوَضْتُه في علم إلا وجدته بحراً زاخرا ، يعرف الحديث والتفسير والأصول معرفةً ما رأيتُ من يُجاريه فيها أو يُدانيه ؛ كما يعتبره بلغ النهاية في الأدب واللغة والنحو ، وأما حِفْظه للتاريخ وأيام العرب ووقائعهم فحَدِّثْ عن البحر ولا حرج ! ثم قال إنه أعجوبة الدهر ، بل مفخرة هذا العصر على العصور الماضية .

❑ ❑ ❑

٣٩

تفسير أبي محمّد البغَوي «معالم التنزيل»

(٤٣٣-٥١٦)

سَلْمَانُ مِنَّا ، أهلَ الْبَيْتِ !

حدثني شيخي المربّي ، محي السّنّة المحمّديّة ، سلطان الأولياء ، مولانا **الشيخ الرّبّاني محمّد ناظم عادل بن أحمد بن حسن القبرصي الدمشقي الصالحي النقشبندي الحَقَّاني الحنفي** (١٣٤١-١٤٣٥/ ١٩٢٢-٢٠١٤) الجيلاني أباً ، المولوي البكري أُمّاً ، عن شيخ القرّاء العلّامة الشيخ عبد العزيز بن محمد علي عيون السود الحِمصي (١٣٣٥-١٣٩٩) المتوفَّى ساجداً ، عن مسند الحرمين الشيخ أبي حفص عمر بن حمدان المَحْرَسي التونسي المالكي ثم المكي ، عن الشيخ محمد بن سليمان حسب الله المكي ، عن الشيخ عبد الغني الدمياطي وأحمد الدَّمْهوجي ومصطفى المبلِّط ، ثلاثتهم عن الشيخ عبد الله بن حجازي الشرقاوي ، عن الشيخ محمد بن سالم الحِفْني ، عن الشيخ محمد بن

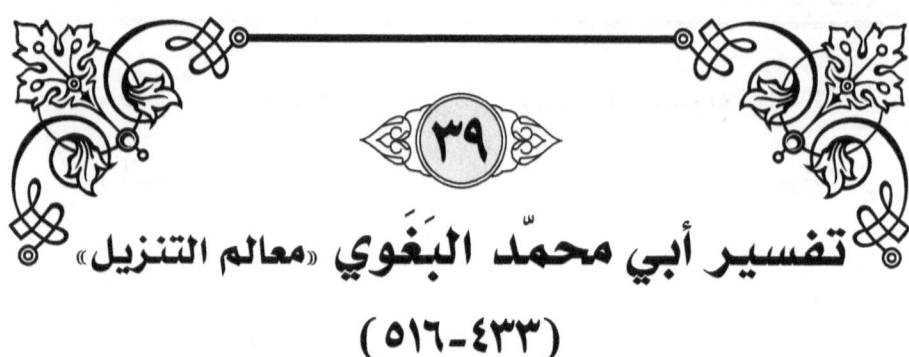

محمد البُدَيْري الدمياطي الشهير بابن الميّت ، عن سيبويه زمانه الشيخ نور الدين أبي الضياء علي الشَّبْرَامَلِّسي ، عن البرهان إبراهيم اللَّقَاني المالكي ، عن أبي النَّجا سالم السَّنْهوري ، عن النجـم الغَيْطي ، عن شيخ الإسلام زكريا الأنصاري ، عن العز عبد الرحيم بن الفُرَات ، عن الصلاح ابن أبي عمر ، عن الفخر ابن البخاري ، عن فضل الله بن سعد النَوقَاني ، **عن محيي السّنّة الإمام الفقيه الحافظ الحسين بن مسعود البغوي الشافعي** ، قال في تفسير سورة الأحزاب الآيات 7-9 من قوله تعالى ﴿ وَإِذْ أَخَذْنَا مِنَ ٱلنَّبِيِّـۧنَ مِيثَـٰقَهُمْ ﴾ إلى قوله ﴿ وَكَانَ ٱللَّهُ بِمَا تَعْمَلُونَ بَصِيرًا ﴾ : أخبرنا أبو سعيد الشُرَيحي ، أنا أبو إسحاق الثعلبي ، أنا عبد الله بن حامد الأصبهاني ، أنا محمد بن جعفر الطبري ، ثنا حماد بن الحسن ، ثنا محمد بن خالد بن عَثْمَةَ ، ثنا كثير بن عبد الله بن عمرو بن عوف ، حدثني أبي ، عن أبيه رضي الله عنه ، قال : خَطَّ رَسُولُ اللهِ ﷺ الْخَنْدَقَ عَامَ الْأَحْزَابِ ، ثُمَّ قَطَعَ لِكُلِّ عَشَرَةٍ أَرْبَعِينَ ذِرَاعاً . قَالَ : فَاحْتَجَّ الْمُهَاجِرُونَ وَالْأَنْصَارُ فِي سَلْمَانَ الْفَارِسِيِّ ـ وَكَـانَ رَجُلاً قَوِيّاً ـ فَقَالَ الْمُهَاجِرُونَ : سَلْمَانُ مِنَّا . وَقَالَ الْأَنْصَارُ : سَلْمَانُ مِنَّا . فَقَالَ النَّبِيُّ ﷺ : سَلْمَانُ مِنَّا ، أَهْلَ الْبَيْتِ !

حديث مشهور ، أخرجه موسى بن عقبة عن الزهري مرسلاً

في المغازي وابن سعد في طبقاته والطبري في التفسير والتاريخ والطبراني في المعجم الكبير وأبو الشيخ في طبقات المحدثين بأصبهان والحاكم في المستدرك والبيهقي في الدلائل وأبو نعيم في معرفة الصحابة وأخبار أصبهان ، وأصحاب السِيَر ، جميعهم عن ابن أبي فُدَيك ، عن كثير بن عبد الله بن عمرو بن عوف المُزَني ، عن أبيه ، عن جدّه . استغربه ابن كثير في البداية وقال الهيثمي عن كثير بن عبد الله : قد ضعّفه الجمهور وحسّن الترمذي حديثه ، وبقية رجاله ثقات . ومن أجل هذا التحسين قال الذهبي قوله الذي قال فيه (فلذا لا يعتمد العلماء على تحسين الترمذي) ، وانظر رد هذا القول بما يشفي الصدر في كتاب أستاذنا المبجَّل الشيخ نور الدين عِتر الحلبي الإمام الترمذي والموازنة بين جامعه وبين الصحيحين ، جزاه الله خير الجزاء . وله شاهد في طبقات المحدِّثين بأصبهان وأبي يعلى والبزّار - كما في إتحاف المهرة - من طريق النضر بن حميد ، عن سعد الإسكاف عن أبي جعفر محمد بن علي بن الحسين بن علي بن أبي طالب عن أبيه عن أبيه عن جدّه رضي الله عنهم . فقيل : الصحيح وقفه على سيدنا علي رضي الله عنه وأرضاه . ورواه الواقدي في المغازي عن ابن أبي سبرة - هو أبو بكر بن عبد الله بن محمد بن أبي سبرة القرشي المدني ،

متروك ـ عن مروان بن أبي سعيد بن المُعَلَّى المدني مرسلاً . والله تعالى أعلم . (لطائف) سمعت مولانا الشيخ ناظم قدس الله سرّه سنة ١٩٩٦ في رحلته الثانية إلى أمريكا تكلّم بالتركيّة لحَرَمِه الحاجة آمنة رحمهما الله وكنت معهما في حُجرة الفندق في مدينة نيو يورك ، فقال لها ما معناه : جِبْرِيلُ مِنَّا . وبعد ما خرّجت خبر **سَلْمَانُ مِنَّا** بصرت في منامي صباح يوم الجمعة ٢ ربيع الأول ١٤٢٥ الموافق ٢١ نيسان ٢٠٠٤ كأني أنا الفقير ابن مولانا الشيخ ناظم الحِسّي ، وكأنّ ابني عبدَ الغني حفيدُه ـ وهو الّذي سمّاه ، كما أنّه سمّى أخَوَيه طاهراً وعلاء الدين ، أحسن الله إليهم جميعاً ـ ، وكنّا في بيت مولانا وأنا أسأله عن ضبط كلمة سمعتها منه ، فأتى عبد الغني يلعب وعمره ثلاث سنين فقال مولانا دعه لا يرانا ، وجعل يديه أمام وجهه المنير ضاحكاً ليتوارى منه ، ولم ألبث حتى دعوته إلينا ، ثم رأيتُني حملت مولانا على ظهري فنام وأنا أنقله من غرفة إلى غرفة ، فلما استنختُ أفاق وقال لي : كنت مسافراً كعادتي عند النوم ، أرحل هنا وهناك ، فقلت له : أتأتي تلك الأماكن حقيقةً مولانا ؟ قال نعم ، فقلت : كالأنبياء ؟ يعني : رؤياك حقّ . قال نعم . وبصرته في المنام مرة أخرى بعد وفاته بأشهر ، ليلة آخر جمعة من رمضان سنة ١٤٣٥/ ٢٠١٤

يأتيني صاعداً وهو في عنفوان عمره ضاحكاً فقال لي فُكَّ لَفَّتي ففككتها كَوْراً كَوراً مع الذِّكْر والحُضور على الأصول وهي خضراءُ ثقيلةٌ ، فشممتها وضممتها إليّ وتضلّعت منها باكياً ، ثم نظرت إليه وقد ربط على رأسه عمامة أخرى بيضاء وبُنِّيّة وانصرف . ورأيت أيّام تحرير هذا السِّفر ليلة جمعة عاشوراء عام ١٤٣٧/ ٢٠١٥ قبل الفجر كأني مسافر بصحبة خليفته الأكبر سيّدي الشيخ هشام القبّاني ثَمِير الحقّ وجبل الحِلْم قُدِّس سرُّه ، لا ثالث لنا سوى الله ، وكأنّا في بادية جبال وَعِرة وأودية وغابات ، فرأيت قصرَين عظيمين متلاصقين بعضاً ببعض لكنهما مغمورَان في قعر البحر وكأن الوادي بحرٌ مظلِم ، والنظر إليهما مخيف ، فقلت ـ وكأني دليل سِياحي ـ : هذان قصران لمِلكين لم يتقبّلِ الله منهما . ثم قصدنا قصراً آخَر ظاهراً ، فيه مقام ضريح مولانا الشيخ ناظم قدّس الله روحه ، فسلّمنا ، ورفع الشيخ هشام يديه داعياً ، وإذ بمولانا الشيخ ناظم قد خرج واتّجه إلى الشيخ هشام واحتضنه وقبّل وجهه ، وقال له كلمة خفيّة ، ثم مسح بساعدي وانصرف . فأوّلته على ما مرّ في الباب السابق .

❑ ❑ ❑

٤٠

الأَنْوَار في شمائل النَّبِيِّ المُخْتَار ﷺ للبغوي (٤٣٣-٥١٦)

اللَّهُمَّ اجْعَلْ رِزْقَ آلِ مُحَمَّدٍ قُوتًا .

حدّثني المُشْرف العام لمدرسة الجنيد الإسلامية في سنغافورة ، العالم الزاهد المربي الأزهر الأديب الأصولي الشيخ **السيد عبد المقصود وعبد المصوّر بن السيد فارس بن السيد أحمد بن السيد إسماعيل الحسني القاهري ثم السنغافوري** (١٣٥٢ ؟ -١٥ ربيع الأول ١٤٣٢) من علماء الأزهر الشريف رحمه الله ، حدّثنا الشيخ عمر الخطيب الأنصاري ، عن أعمامه : العلّامة الفقيه النحرير أبي بكر الخزرجي التريمي (ت ١٣٥٦) وعبد الله ومحمد بني أحمد بن أحمد بن عبد الله بن أبي بكر بن سالم الخطيب ، عن أبيهم ، عن السيد دحلان ، بسنده الثُّماني إلى ابن حجر المارّ في باب مسند الشافعي ، عن الصلاح ابن أبي عمر ، عن الفخر ابن البخاري ، عن أبي المكارم فضل الله بن

محمّد بن أحمد النُّوْقاتي الشافعي (٥١٤-٦٠٠) ، باستجازة والده له عن الإمام الأجلّ السيد الزاهد شيخ الإسلام **محيي السنة أبو محمد الحسين بن مسعود الفَرَّاء** ـ نسبة لعمل الفِراء جمع فَرْوٍ أي جلود تُدبَغ وتُخاط وتُلبس ، وكان أبوه يصنع ذلك ـ **البَغَوِي** ـ نسبةً على غير قياس إلى بَغْ ويقال لها أيضاً بَغْشُور بخُراسان ـ ، قال : أخبرنا إسماعيل بن عبد القاهر ، أنا عبد الغافر بن محمد ، أنا محمد بن عيسى ، أنا إبراهيم بن محمد بن سفيان ، نا مسلم بن الحجاج ، حدثني زهير بن حرب ، نا محمد بن فضيل ، عن أبيه ، عن عمارة بن القعقاع ، عن أبي زرعة ، عن أبي هريرة ـ رضي الله تعالى عنه ـ قال : قال رسول الله ﷺ : **اللَّهُمَّ اجْعَلْ رِزْقَ آلِ مُحَمَّدٍ قُوتًا** .

في الصحيحين والسنن . قال صاحب (النهاية) : قوله : (قوتاً) أي بقدر ما يُمسك الرَّمَقَ من المَطْعَم . وقال القرطبي : أي اكْفِهِمْ من القوت بما لا يُرهقهم إلى ذلّ المسألة ، ولا يكون فيه فُضول يبعث على التَّرَفُّه والتبَسُّط في الدنيا . قال : ومعنى الحديث أنه طلب الكفاف ، فإن القوت ما يقوت البدن ويكفّ عن الحاجة ، وفي هذه الحالة سلامة من حالات الغنى والفقر جميعاً ، انتهى . وقال ابن بطّال : فيه دليل على فضل الكفاف وأخذ البُلْغة من الدنيا والزهد

فيما فوق ذلك رغبة في توفير نعيم الآخرة ، وإيثاراً لما يبقى على ما يفنى ، فينبغي أن تقتدي به أمته في ذلك ، انتهى . قال العبد الضعيف : قال لي السيد عبد المقصود فارس الحسني : معناه اللهم اجعل رزق آل محمد كَفافاً . أي ما كَفَّ عن الناسِ وأغْنَى ، كما في القاموس . ثم قال : قال الحبيب علي بن عطاس الإندونيسي : يا ولدي لا تَخَفْ أبداً ، والمَعونةُ على قَدْر المَؤُونَة . قال العبد الضعيف : فعلى هذا يومئ الحديث إلى حقيقة التوكّل عند أهل البيت وصبرهم على البلاء وكرامة أنفسهم الطاهرة وعلى ادّخار واستيداع جدّهم المصطفى ﷺ أعلى المقامات والمنازل لهم في الآخرة . (فائدة) قال السيد عبد المقصود فارس : كان الشيخ عمر الخطيب رحمه الله يحفظ ديوان المتنبِّي ويعرّبه كلّه ، سمعنا عليه (المنهاج) للنووي وغيره . (لطيفة) أفادني السيّد أنه رأى النبي ﷺ في المنام يقول له : **أَنْتَ عَبْدُ المُصَوِّرِ** .

❑ ❑ ❑

٤١

الأربعين الأبدال العوالي المسموعة بالجامع الأُمَوي لابن عساكر

(٤٩٩-٥٧١)

هَذَا الْعَبَّاسُ ، عَمُّ نَبِيِّكُمْ ، أَجْوَدُ قُرَيْشٍ كَفّاً وَأَوْصَلُهَا !

أخبرني العلامة الفقيه المعمّر شيخ الجامع الأموي والمدرّس فيه **الشيخ عبد الرزاق الحلبي الحنفي** (١٣٤٣-١٤٣٣/ ١٩٢٥- ٢٠١٢) رحمه الله ، بقراءتي عليه في مكتبه بالجامع الأموي يوم الثلاثاء ٨ رمضان المبارك ١٤٢٦ : أنبأني المفتي العلامة السيد محمد أبو اليسر عابدين ، عن جده السيد أحمد بن عبد الغني عابدين ، عن عمّه الإمام محمد أمين عابدين صاحب (الحاشية) ، عن هبة الله بن محمد البَعلي ، عن أحمد بن عبد الفتّاح المُلَّوي ، عن المسند عبد الله بن سالم البصري ، عن محمد بن علاء الدين البابلي ، عن نور الدين سالم بن محمد السنهوري ، عن النجم الغيطي والهيتمي ، كلاهما عن شيخ الإسلام

زكريا الأنصاري ، عن الحافظ ابن حجر ، سماعاً عن شيخه المسند المُكثر علي بن محمد بن أبي المجد الدمشقي المعروف بابن الصائغ ، عن القاسم بن مظفر بن عساكر ، أخبرنا محمد بن نصر بن محمد ، عن **الحافظ ابن عساكر** سماعاً ، أخبرنا أبو القاسم هبة الله بن محمد بن عبد الواحد بن الحصين ، أنا أبو طالب محمد بن محمد البزّاز ، نا الشافعي ، نا معاذ بن المثنى ، نا إبراهيم بن حمزة وعلي بن المديني ، قالا : نا محمد بن طلحة ، عن أبي سهيل بن مالك ، عن سعيد بن المسيِّب ، عن سعد بن أبي وقّاص ، قال : **خَرَجَ رَسُولُ اللهِ ﷺ يُجَهِّزُ بَعْثاً بِسُوقِ الخَيْلِ** ـ وهو اليومَ موضع النَّخَّاسين ـ **فَطَلَعَ الْعَبَّاسُ بْنُ عَبْدِ الْمُطَّلِبِ عَلَى رَسُولِ اللهِ ، فَقَالَ رَسُولُ اللهِ ﷺ : هَذَا الْعَبَّاسُ ، عَمُّ نَبِيِّكُمْ ، أَجْوَدُ قُرَيْشٍ كَفّاً وَأَوْصَلُهَا !** قال الحافظ ابن عساكر : أخرجه النَّسائي ، عن حُميد بن مَخلد النسائي ، عن علي بن عبد الله بن جعفر بن المديني ، فوقع لي موافَقَةً في شيخ شيخه ، وهو معدود في أفراد محمد بن طلحة التَّيمي المدني ، عن أبي سهيل نافع بن مالك بن أبي عامر الأصبحي . اهـ .

رواه الإمام أحمد في المسند وفضائل الصحابة والنسائي في الكبرى والدَّورقي في مسند سعد بن أبي وقاص والحاكم صححه

وابن حبان في الصحيح والحافظ أبو القاسم السهمي في الأربعين في فضائل العباس والطبراني في الأوسط وابن عساكر في التاريخ والشاموخي في أحاديثه والمِزّي في تهذيب الكمال . وقوّى إسناده الحافظ الهيثمي في مجمع الزوائد وذكر أنه عند أحمد وأبي يعلى والبزار والطبراني بألفاظ متقاربة .

❑ ❑ ❑

٤٢

الأربعين البلدانية لابن عساكر

(٤٩٩-٥٧١)

أَحِبُّوا اللهَ لِمَا يَغْذُوكُمْ مِنْ نِعَمِهِ ، وَأَحِبُّونِي بِحُبِّ اللهِ ، وَأَحِبُّوا أَهْلَ بَيْتِي لِحُبِّي

أنبأنا **السيد عبد الرحمن ابن مسند الدنيا عبد الحي بن عبد الكبير الكتاني الفاسي** (ولد ١٣٣٨) وأخبرني **الدكتور محمد مطيع الحافظ** ابن السيد محمد واصل الحنفي النقشبندي (ولد ١٣٥٩) حفظهما الله ، الأول عن والده (١٣٠٢-١٣٨٢) ، عن الشيخ عبد الله بن درويش السُّكَّري (١٢٢٧-١٣٢٩) والثاني بقراءتي عليه في داره حي الدحداح بدمشق غُرّة رجب ١٤٢٧ الموافق ٢٨ تمّوز ٢٠٠٦ ، عن شيخه العمدة العلامة المحدّث الشيخ محمد أبي الخير المَيداني النقشبندي (١٢٩٣-١٣٨٠) رئيس رابطة علماء الشام ، عن السُّكَّري ، عن فقيه الشام سعيد بن حسن بن أحمد الحلبي الدمشقي (١١٨٨-١٢٥٤) ، عن إسماعيل بن محمّد المَواهبي ، عن أبيه ، عن جدّه صالح ، عن أحمد بن

محمّد النخلي ، عن المسند الفَلَكي محمّد بن محمد بن سليمان الرُّودَاني المغـربي (ت ١٠٩٤) ؛ (ح) الحلبـي أيضاً عن عبد الرحـن ومحمّد ابني عثمان الحلبي ، عـن أبيهـما أبي الفضل عثـمان العقيـلي الحلبي ، عن طه بـن مُهَنّا الجبرتي ، عن عبد الله بن سـالم البصري ، عن الرُّوداني ، عن شـيخه أبي عثمان سـعيد بن إبراهيم التونسي ثم الجزائري عرف بقدُّورة (ت ١٠٦٦) مفتي الجزائر ، عن شيخه أبي عثمان سعيد بن أحمد المَقَّـري التلمسـاني (ت ١٠١٠) ، عن أبي زيـد عبد الرحمن بن علي ابن أحمد العاصمي السُّفياني الشهير بسُقَّين (ت ٩٥٦) ، عن شيخ الإسلام زكريّا الأنصاري والبرهان القلقشندي ، كلاهما عن إمام الحُفّاظ أبي الفضـل أحمد بن علي ابن حجر ، قال : قرأته على أبي الحسـن علي بن محمد بـن أبي المجـد بإجازتـه ـ إن لم يكـن سـماعاً ـ مـن القاسـم بن المظفَّر بـن عسـاكر ، وأخبرنا أبـو هريرة ابـن الذهبي إجـازةً ، أنبأنا القاسـم بن مظفر سـماعاً ، أنبأنا عمُّ أبي : عز الدين محمد بن أحمد بن الحسـن النسـابة وتاج الدين عبد الله بن عمر بن حمويه ونصر الدين أبو الفتح نصر الله بن مكارم الأنصاري والعز أبو محمد عبد العزيز بن محمد بن علي بن أبيه الصالحي قراءة عليهم وأنا حاضرٌ أسـمع ، قال الأربعة : أخبرنا الشيخ الإمام الحافظ شيخ الإسلام **أبو القاسم علي**

ابن الحسن بن هبة الله بن عبد الله بن الحسين الشافعي الشهير بابن عساكر قراءةً عليه ونحن نسمع ، قال : البلد التاسع : مَرْوُ الشَاهِجَانِ . قَصْبَة خُراسان ، وهي من بناء ذي القرنين . أخبرنا أبو يعقوب يوسف بن أيوب بن الحسين بن وَهْرَة الهَمَذاني الصوفي الواعظ بقراءتي عليه بمرو في شهر ربيع الاول سنة إحدى وثلاثين وخمسِ مئة ، أنبأ القاضي الشريف أبو الحسين محمد بن علي بن محمد بن عبيد الله بن عبد الصمد بن المهتدي بالله من لفظه ببغداد ، ثنا أبو الحسن علي بن عمر بن محمد بن الحسن بن شاذان بن إسحاق بن إبراهيم بن علي بن إسحاق الحربي السُّكَّري إملاءً وكنت أنا المستملي عليه في يوم الجمعه لثلاثٍ خَلَوْن من جمادى الآخرة سنةَ خمسٍ وثمانين وثلاثِ مئة ـ وقال لي قُلْ : لأُلْحِقَنَّ الصِّغارَ بالكبار ـ ، ثنا أبو عبد الله أحمد بن الحسن بن عبد الجبار ، ثنا أبو زكريا يحي بن معين ، ثنا هشام بن يوسف ، عن عبد الله بن سليمان النَّوفلي ، عن محمد بن علي ، عن أبيه ، عَنِ ابْنِ عَبَّاسٍ ، قَالَ : قَالَ رَسُولُ الله ﷺ : **أَحِبُّوا اللهَ لِمَا يَغْذُوكُمْ مِنْ نِعَمِهِ ، وَأَحِبُّونِي بِحُبِّ الله ، وَأَحِبُّوا أَهْلَ بَيْتِي لِحُبِّي** . قال الحافظ ابن عساكر هذا حديث حسن من حديث أبي العباس عبد الله بن العباس بن عبد المطلب القرشي الهاشمي ـ

رضي الله عنهما - ابن عم رسول الله ﷺ وترجُمان القرآن وحَبْر هذه الأمة ، وعزيز من حديث ابنه أبي محمد - ويقال أبو الحسن - علي بن عبد الله ، تفرّد به عنه ابنه أبو عبد الله محمد بن علي أبو الخلائف ، ولم نكتبه الا من حديث عبد الله بن سليمان النوفلي ، عنه .

رواه الترمذي بلفظ **بِحُبِّي** وقال : حسن غريب ، ورواه عبد الله بن أحمد في زوائد فضائل الصحابة والفسوي في المعرفة والتاريخ والطبراني في الكبير والآجُرِّي في الشريعة وأبو نعيم في الحلية والحاكم وقال صحيح الإسناد والبيهقي في الشُعَب والاعتقاد والمناقب والآداب وغيرهم . وقوله **لِحُبِّ اللهِ** أي لحبّ الله لي . وأخرجه الحافظ الذهبي في سِيَر أعلام النبلاء بسنده ، قال : قرأت على أبي المعالي أحمد بن إسحاق بن محمد بن المؤيد القرافي بمصر ، أخبرنا أبو العباس أحمد بن أبي الفتح والفرج بن عبد الله الكاتب ببغداد ، قالا : أخبرنا محمد بن عمر القاضي ، أخبرنا أبو الحسين أحمد بن محمد بن النَّقُّور ، أخبرنا علي بن عمر الحربي في سنة خمس وثمانين وثلاث مئة ، حدثنا أحمد بن الحسن بن عبد الجبار الصوفي ، حدثنا أبو زكريا يحيى بن معين سنة سبع وعشرين ومئتين ، به . قال الذهبي : هذا حديث غريب فرد ، ما رواه عن ابن عباس إلا ولده

علي ، ولا عن علي إلا ابنه محمّد أبو الخلفاء ، تفرّد به عنه قاضي صنعاء عبد الله بن سليمان ، ولم يروه عنه إلا هشام . وقد رواه يعقوب الفَسَوي في تاريخه عن زياد بن أيوب عن ابن معين ، والناس فيه عيال على يحيى ، وليس النوفلي بمعروف . اهـ . (فوائد) مَرْو الشاهِجان قال ياقوت هي مرو العظمى ، أشهر مدن خراسان وقصبتها . وأما الشاهِجان فهي فارسية معناها نَفَس السلطان لأن الجان هي النَفَس أو الروح ، والشاه هو السلطان ، سُمِّيَت بذلك لجلالتها عندهم . اهـ . والقصبة : المدينة العظمى . وقال الأستاذ محمّد مطيع : يقال هَمْدان بتسكين الميم بعدها دال مهمَلة للقبيلة ، وهَمَذان بفتح الميم بعدها ذال معجَمة للبلد . وأمّا قول الراوي : قُلْ : لأُلْحِقَنَّ الصِّغارَ بالكبار ، فإشارة إلى العلوّ في السند . (تنبيه) قال الأستاذ محمد شريف الصوّاف في معجم الأُسَر الدمشقية : آل الحافظ (دبس وزيت) من الأسر القديمة في حي العُقيبة ، قيل : إنهم ينتسبون إلى القطب السيد عبد القادر الجيلاني الحسني الحسيني رضي الله عنه .

❑ ❑ ❑

٤٣

الأحاديث المختارة للضياء المقدسي

(٥٦٩-٦٤٣)

مَنْ صَنَعَ إِلَى أَحَدٍ مِنْ وَلَدِ عَبْدِ المُطَّلِبِ يَدًا ، فَلَمْ يُكَافِئْهُ بِهَا فِي الدُّنْيَا ، فَعَلَيَّ مُكَافَأَتُهُ غَدًا إِذَا لَقِيَنِي .

أنبأني الحبيب علي بن عبد الرحمن بن أحمد بن عبد القادر بن (ت يوم الجمعة ١ جمادى الآخرة ١٤٤٢ رحمه الله) علي بن عمر بن سقاف السقاف آل صافي الإندونيسي ، عن والده ، عن المعمّر الحبيب علي بن عبد الرحمن بن عبد الله الحبشي البَتَاوي الملقَّب بِكْوِيتَا (١٢٨٧-١٣٨٨) ، عن العارف المسنِد الحبيب أحمد بن حسن العطاس ، عن أبي بكر وصالح ابني عبد الله العطاس ، عن الوجيه عبد الرحمن الأهدل ، عن الحافظ محمد مرتضى الزبيدي ، بالسند السُّداسي المارّ في باب المجتبى إلى الحافظ ابن حجر ، قراءةً على أمّ الحسن فاطمة بنت محمد بن أحمد بن أحمد بن محمد بن عثمان بن المُنَجَّا التَّنُوخِيَّة بدمشق ، بإجازتها لجميعها من أبي الفضل سليمان بن حمزة بن أحمد بن عمر بن أبي عمر المقدسي ، بسماعه من الحافظ

محمد بن عبد الواحد المقدسي الضياء، وبإجازتها أيضاً من عيسى بن عبد الرحمن بن مَعالي بسماعه من الضياء، أخبرنا محمد بن أحمد بن نصر بن أبي الفتح ـ الصيدلاني ـ قراءةً عليه بأصبهان، أَنَّ أَبَا علي الحداد المقرئ أخبرهم قراءة عليه وهو حاضر، أنا أحمد بن عبد الله ـ الحافظ أبو نعيم ـ، أنا سليمان بن أحمد الطبراني، ثنا أحمد بن محمد بن صدقة، ثنا محمد بن المُؤَمَّل بن الصَّبَّاح، ثنا يوسف بن نافع بن عبد الله بن أَشْرَسَ المدني، ثنا عبدالرحمن بن أبي الزِّنَاد، عن أبيه، عن أَبَانَ بن عثمان، قال سمعت عثمان يقول: قال رسول الله ﷺ: **مَنْ صَنَعَ إِلَى أَحَدٍ مِنْ وَلَدِ عَبْدِ المُطَّلِبِ يَدًا، فَلَمْ يُكَافِئْهُ بِهَا فِي الدُّنْيَا، فَعَلَيَّ مُكَافَأَتُهُ غَدًا إِذَا لَقِيَنِي**.

أخرجه عبد الله بن أحمد في زوائده على فضائل الصحابة والطبراني في الأوسط والخطيب جميعهم من طريق عبد الرحمن بن أبي الزناد، عن أبيه، عن أبان بن عثمان، سمعت عثمان بن عفان يقول: قال رسول الله ﷺ: **مَنْ صَنَعَ صَنِيعَةً إِلَى أَحَدٍ مِنْ خَلَفِ عَبْدِ المُطَّلِبِ فِي الدُّنْيَا، فَعَلَيَّ مُكَافَأَتُهُ إِذَا لَقِيَنِي**. هذا لفظ الخطيب. قال الهيثمي: فيه عبد الرحمن المذكور وهو ضعيف. اهـ. وأفرط ابن الجوزي إذ أدخله في الواهيات وقال: هذا حديث لا يصح وقد

ضَعَّف أحمدُ عبدَ الرحمن بنَ أبي الزناد وقال : لا يُحتجّ به . اهـ . بل في التقريب أنّه صدوق ، تغيّر حفظه لما دخل بغداد ، وروى له الأربعة والبخاري تعليقاً ومسلم في المقدّمة ، ووثّقه مالك والترمذي والعجلي ، وقال الذهبي إنه حسن الحال في الرواية ، وقال الحافظ في الفتح : غاية أمره أنه مختلَفٌ فيه ، فلا يتّجه الحكم بصحة ما ينفرد به ، بل غايته أن يكون حسناً اهـ . لذا عدّه الحافظ الضياء من الحسن بإخراجه له في المختارة . وقول الطبراني بانفراد يوسف بن نافع عنه وَهَمٌ ، إذ تابعه يوسف بن يعقوب المديني ـ ابن أبي سلمة الماجشون ـ في فضائل الصحابة والنضر بن طاهر في المجلس الأول من المجالس الخمسة لأبي الحسن الأزدي . وقول المناوي : أبان بن عثمان متكلَّم فيه ، أيضاً مردود ، إذ المتكلَّم فيه أبان آخر ، أما ابن عثمان بن عفان فهو تابعي ثقة من رجال مسلم ، قال عمرو بن شعيب : ما رأيت أعلم بحديث ولا أفقه منه . وأخرجه ابن عساكر في التاريخ من طريق محمد بن يحيى بن ضُرَيس ، حدثني عيسى بن عبد الله بن محمد بن عمر بن علي بن أبي طالب ، حدثني أبي [هو عبد الله] ، عن أبيه [محمّد] ، عن جدّه [عمر] ، عن عليٍّ ، قال : قال رسول الله ﷺ : **مَنْ صَنَعَ إِلَى أَحَدٍ مِنْ أَهْلِ بَيْتِي يَداً ، كَافَأْتُهُ يَوْمَ الْقِيَامَةِ** . (فوائد) عن

أنس قال : يقولون : لا يجتمع حبُّ علي وعثمان في قلب مؤمن ، وقد جمع الله حبَّهما في قلوبنا . وكان الأوزاعي يقول : لا يجتمع حبُّ علي وعثمان إلا في قلب مؤمن . وعن سفيان نحوه ، ذكر الجميع الذهبي في السِيَر . والحديث حاوٍ على قاعدة غرّاء في اصطناع المعروف لإرضاء الله بإقامة حقّ رسوله ﷺ والعمل ببراهين محبّته في مواساة ولده وقرابته بالنفس والمال لا نقاش فيها ، وفيه أيضاً التنبيه على قصر الأمل بالحياة الدنيا والاطمئنان إلى سريع الثواب في الآخرة بقوله غَداً ، والخصوصيّة بالقرب منه ﷺ لمن استحقّه . والله تعالى أعلم وأحكم وأكرم . وصلى الله على سيّدنا محمد وآله وسلّم والحمد لله رب العالمين .

❑ ❑ ❑

تتمّة الخطبة
وخاتمة في معنى الآل

وذكر بعض ما أُلِّف أو قيل في خصائصهم فقهاً وحكمةً

لـمّا بيّن رسـول الله ﷺ معـاني العـدل الإلهـي في تفضيل بعض الناس على بعضٍ ، جعل الإيمان هو الفارق بين الصالح والطالح لا النسـب ، فقال **أَلَا إِنَّ آلَ أَبِي ـ يَعْنِي فُلَانًا ـ لَيْسُـوا لِي بِأَوْلِيَاءَ إِنَّمَا وَلِيِّيَ اللهُ وَصَالِـحُ الْمُؤْمِنِـينَ** ، وقـال : **إِنَّ أَوْلَى النَّـاسِ بِي الْمُتَّقُونَ مَـنْ كَانُوا وَحَيْثُ كَانُوا** ، وأَنْذَرَ عشـيرته المقرّبين ، وهم قريشٌ ـ قال أبو هريرة رضي الله عنه : لما نزلت ﴿ وَأَنذِرۡ عَشِيرَتَكَ ٱلۡأَقۡرَبِينَ ﴾ [الشعراء] ، قال النبـي ﷺ : **يَا مَعْـشَرَ قُرَيْشٍ** ـ ثم بنو عبد المطلب ، ثم العباس عمُّه ، ثم صفيّة عمّته ، ثم فاطمةُ ابنته ، فقال لهم : **اِشْتَرُوا أَنْفُسَكُمْ مِنَ اللهِ ! لَا أُغْنِي عَنْكُمْ مِنَ اللهِ شَـيْئًا !** وقال : **لَوْ أَنَّ فَاطِمَةَ بِنْتَ مُحَمَّدٍ سَرَقَتْ لَقَطَعْتُ يَدَهَا** . وقال : **مَنْ بَطَّأَ بِهِ عَمَلُـــهُ لَمْ يُسْرِعْ بِهِ نَسَبُهُ** . قـــال بعض الشرّاح : أي لم يقدِّمْه نسـبه ، يعني لم يَجْبُر نقيصتَه لكونه نسيباً في قومـه ، إذ لا يَحصُـل التقـرّب إلى الله تعالى بالنسـب بـل بالأعمال الصالحه . قال تعالى : ﴿ إِنَّ أَكۡرَمَكُمۡ عِندَ ٱللَّهِ أَتۡقَىٰكُمۡ ﴾ [الحجرات ١٣] ، وشـاهِد ذلك : أن أكثر علماء السلف والخلف لا أنسابَ لهم يُتفاخر

بها ، بل كثيرٌ من علماء السلف مَوالٍ ، ومع ذلك : هم سادات الأمة وينابيع الرحمة ؛ وذوُو الأنساب العليّة الّذين ليسوا كذلك : في مواطن جهلهم نَسْياً منسيّاً . ولذلك قال ﷺ : **إِنَّ اللهَ يَرْفَعُ بِهَذَا الدِّينِ أَقْوَاماً وَيَضَعُ بِهِ آخَرِينَ** . اهـ . وفي سنن الترمذي ـ حسّنه ـ عن ابن عمر رضي الله عنهما مرفوعاً : **يَا أَيُّهَا النَّاسُ إِنَّ اللهَ قَدْ أَذْهَبَ عَنْكُمْ عُبِّيَّةَ الجَاهِلِيَّةِ وَتَعَاظُمَهَا بِآبَائِهَا ، فَالنَّاسُ رَجُلَانِ : بَرٌّ تَقِيٌّ كَرِيمٌ عَلَى اللهِ ، وَفَاجِرٌ شَقِيٌّ هَيِّنٌ عَلَى اللهِ . وَالنَّاسُ بَنُو آدَمَ ، وَخَلَقَ اللهُ آدَمَ مِنْ تُرَابٍ** . قَالَ اللهُ تعالى : ﴿ يَٰٓأَيُّهَا ٱلنَّاسُ إِنَّا خَلَقْنَٰكُم مِّن ذَكَرٍ وَأُنثَىٰ وَجَعَلْنَٰكُمْ شُعُوبًا وَقَبَآئِلَ لِتَعَارَفُوٓا۟ ۚ إِنَّ أَكْرَمَكُمْ عِندَ ٱللَّهِ أَتْقَىٰكُمْ ۚ إِنَّ ٱللَّهَ عَلِيمٌ خَبِيرٌ ﴿١٣﴾ ﴾ [الحجرات] . وقال ﷺ : **أَوْلِيَائِي يَوْمَ الْقِيَامَةِ : الْمُتَّقُونَ ، فَلَا يَأْتِينِي النَّاسُ بِالْأَعْمَالِ وَتَأْتُونِي بِالدُّنْيَا ، تَحْمِلُونَهَا عَلَى رِقَابِكُمْ فَأَقُولُ هٰكَذَا وَهٰكَذَا : أَلَا** ، وَأَعْرَضَ فِي كُلِّ عِطْفَيْهِ . جميعه في الصحيح إلا الأخير ففي الأدب المفرد والسنة لابن أبي عاصم ومراسيل أبي داود . وأخرج في سننه عن ابن عمر مرفوعاً : **فِتْنَةُ السَّرَّاءِ دَخَنُهَا مِنْ تَحْتِ قَدَمَيْ رَجُلٍ مِنْ أَهْلِ بَيْتِي يَزْعُمُ أَنَّهُ مِنِّي ، وَلَيْسَ مِنِّي ؛ وَإِنَّمَا أَوْلِيَائِي : الْمُتَّقُونَ** . وأخرج الطبراني في الأوسط والصغير ، وعنه ابن مردويه في التفسير والبيهقي في سننه وابن عدى في الكامل من طريق نعيم بن حماد ، حدثنا نوح بن أبي مريم ، عن يحيى بن سعيد الأنصاري ، عن أنس ، قال : **سُئِلَ رَسُولُ اللهِ ﷺ مَنْ آلُكَ ؟ فَقَالَ :**

كُلُّ تَقِيٍّ ، وَتَلَا : ﴿إِنْ أَوْلِيَآؤُهُۥٓ إِلَّا ٱلْمُتَّقُونَ وَلَٰكِنَّ أَكْثَرَهُمْ لَا يَعْلَمُونَ﴾ [الأنفال ٣٤] . قال الحافظ في الفتح : أخرجه الطبراني لكن سنده واهٍ جداً ، وأخرج البيهقي عن جابر نحوَه من قوله بسند ضعيف اهـ . قلت : لفظ جابر : **آلُ مُحَمَّدٍ** ﷺ **أُمَّتُهُ** . قال الحافظ : وأخرجه تمّامٌ الرّازي من طريق شيبانَ بن فَرّوخ ـ قلت : والبيهقي في السنن من طريق أحمد بن يونس اليَربوعي ـ ثنا نافعٌ أبو هُرْمُزٍ وهو ضعيف أيضاً ، لكن قال في الميزان : تابعه مسلم بن إبراهيم . اهـ . وقال السخاوي في المقاصد : له شواهدُ كثيرة . اهـ . قال صاحب كشف الخفا : منها ما في الصحيحين من قوله ﷺ **إِنَّ آلَ أَبِي فُلَانٍ لَيْسُوا لِي بِأَوْلِيَاء إِنَّمَا وَلِيِّيَ اللهُ وَصَالِحُ الْمُؤْمِنِينَ** وتتمته **وَلَكِنْ لَهُمْ رَحِمٌ أَبُلُّهَا بِبَلَاهَا يَعْنِي أَصِلُهَا بِصِلَتِهَا** . ولفظ **وَصَالِحُ الْمُؤْمِنِينَ** في رواية البُرْقاني . وقال الحافظ الزرقاني في مختصر المقاصد الحسنة هو حسنٌ لغيره . وأما : **أنا جَدُّ كلِّ تقِّي** فلم يَرِدْ . وقال ﷺ : **أَلَا لَا فَضْلَ لِعَرَبِيٍّ عَلَى أَعْجَمِيٍّ وَلَا لِعَجَمِيٍّ عَلَى عَرَبِيٍّ** ، رواه أحمد والحارث وابن أبي حاتم ، حتى لا يتركَ الناسُ العملَ ولا يتّكلوا ولا يفتخروا .

ثم أَعْلَمَ الأنامَ ـ عليه الصلاة والسلام ـ أنّ فضل الله على قرابته أمرٌ قطعيٌّ وتخصيصٌ مؤبّدٌ ، فقال : **هُنَاكَ نَسَبٌ أَقْرَبُ مِنْ نَسَبٍ** ، وقال : **كُلُّهُ يَنْقَطِعُ يَوْمَ الْقِيَامَةِ إِلَّا سَبَبُهُ وَنَسَبُهُ** ، وقال : **أَنَا مُحَمَّدُ بْنُ**

عَبْدِ اللهِ بْنِ عَبْدِ الْمُطَّلِبِ ، أَنَا خَيْرُكُمْ بَيْتاً وَخَيْرُكُمْ نَفْساً ، وقال : اخْتَارَ [اللهُ] مِنْ بَنِي آدَمَ الْعَرَبَ ، وقال : وَاصْطَفَى قُرَيْشًا مِنْ كِنَانَةَ وَاصْطَفَى مِنْ قُرَيْشٍ بَنِي هَاشِمٍ ، وقال : لَوْ أَنِّي أَخَذْتُ بِحَلْقَةِ بَابِ الجَنَّةِ مَا بَدَأْتُ إِلَّا بِكُمْ يَا بَنِي هَاشِمٍ ، وقال : فَوَاللهِ إِنَّ شَفَاعَتِي لَتَنَالُ قَرَابَتِي ، وقال : كِتَابُ اللهِ مَمْدُودٌ بَيْنَ السَّمَاءِ وَالْأَرْضِ ، وَعِتْرَتِي أَهْلُ بَيْتِي ، أَلَا إِنَّهُمَا لَنْ يَفْتَرِقَا حَتَّى يَرِدَا عَلَيَّ الحَوْضَ فدخلت العترةُ بمعاني الحِفظ الإلهي للقرآن المجيد ، وقال ﷺ في الحسن والحسين وأبويهما مَنْ أَحَبَّنِي وَأَحَبَّ هٰذَيْنِ وَأَبَاهُمَا وَأُمَّهُمَا كَانَ مَعِي فِي دَرَجَتِي يَوْمَ الْقِيَامَةِ . فإذا كان المُحِبُّ لآل النبيِّ ﷺ مع المحبوب في تلك الدرجة العالية ، فعلوُّ درجة المحبوب من آله ﷺ من باب أولى ، وهو محتَّمٌ لا نقاش فيه ، بالشرط الذي أشار إليه ﷺ إذ قال : وَعَدَنِي رَبِّي فِي أَهْلِ بَيْتِي - مَنْ أَقَرَّ مِنْهُمْ بِالتَّوْحِيدِ وَلِي بِالْبَلَاغِ - أَنْ لَا يُعَذِّبَهُمْ . رواه الحاكم وصححه واستنكره الذهبي فأثبت السيوطي تصحيحَه .

ومذهب أهل السنة والجماعة : محبّة وتوقير أهل البيت الكرام والصحابة أجمعين بلا استثناء ، ابتداءً بالعترة وأمهات المؤمنين والذرّية الطاهرة إلى يوم الدين . فعن الشعبي - رحمه الله - قال : رَكِب زيد بن ثابت ، فأخذ ابنُ عباس بِرِكَابِه فقال : لا تفعل يا ابنَ

عمّ رسول الله ! فقال : هكذا أمرنا أن نفعل بعلمائنا . فقبَّل زيد بن ثابت يده وقال : هكذا أمرنا أن نفعل بأهل بيت نبينا . رواه يعقوب بن سفيان الفَسَوي في المعرفة والتاريخ وصححه الحافظ في الإصابة ورواه الخطيب في الفقيه والمتفقِّه وابن سعد في الطبقات والطبراني في الكبير والحاكم ـ صححه ـ والبيهقي في المدخل وأورده القاضي عياض في الشِّفا وقال فيه أيضاً : اِعلَمْ أن حرمة النبي ﷺ بعد موته و توقيرَه و تعظيمه لازمٌ كما كان حالَ حياته ، وذلك عند ذكره ﷺ وذكر حديثه وسنّته ، وسماع اسمه وسيرته ، ومعاملة آله وعترته ، وتعظيم أهل بيته وصحابته . وفي مرآة الجنان لليافعي نقلاً عن تاريخ بغداد : دخل يحيى بن معاذٍ الرازيُّ على علويٍّ بِبَلْخٍ زائراً له ومسلِّماً عليه ، فقال له العلوي : أَيَّدَ اللهُ الأستاذ ! ما تقول فينا أهلِ البيت ؟ قال : ما أقول في طينٍ عُجِنَ بماء الوحي ، وغُرِست فيه شجرةُ النبوَّة ، وسُقِي بماء الرسالة ؟ فهل يفوح منهما إلا مِسْك الهُدى وعَنبرُ التُّقى ؟ فحشا العلويُّ فَاهُ بالدُّرّ .

قرأت على شيخنا السيّد العلامة النحرير محمد أبي الهدى اليعقوبيِّ حفظه الله : قال القاضي عبدُ النبيِّ بنُ عبدِ الرسول الأحمدنَگْرِي ـ من علماء القرن الثاني عشر ـ في جامع العلوم في

اصطلاحات الفنون الشهير بدُسْتُور العلماء ـ بأربعة أجزاءٍ وقد طبع سنة ١٣٢٩ في دائرة المعارف النظامية بحيدَر آباد ـ في مادة (الآل) من أول كتابه ما نصُّه : (الآل) أصله : أهل ، بدليل أُهيل ، لأن التصغير مَحَكُّ الألفاظ ، يُعرف به جواهرُ حروفها وأعراضُها أي أصولُها وزوائدُها ، سَواءٌ كانت مُبْدَلَةً من الحروف الأصلية أو لا ؛ فأُبْدِل الهاءُ بالهمزة لقُرْب المَخْرَج ، ثم أُبدلت الهمزةُ الثانية بالألف على قانونِ (آمَنَ) . لكن الآلَ يُستعمَل في الأَشْراف ، والأهل فيه وفي الأرْذال أيضاً ، فيقال : أهل الحَجَّام ولا آلُه ، وآلُ النبي ﷺ ولا أهلُه . وأيضاً يضاف الأهلُ إلى المكان والزمان دونَ الآل ، فيقال : أهلُ مِصْرَ وأهل الزمان ، لا آلُ مصر وآل الزمان . وأيضاً يضاف الأهلُ إلى الله تعالى بخلاف الآل ، فيقال : أهلُ الله ولا يقال : آل الله . واختُلِف في آل النبي ﷺ ، فقال بعضهم : آلُ هاشمٍ والمُطَّلِب [عند الشافعي ؛ قال ابن حجر : لكن بالنسبة إلى الزكوٰة والفَيْء ، أمّا في مقام الدعاء فكلّ مؤمن تقي] ، وعند البعض : أولاد سيدة النساء فاطمةَ الزهراءِ رضي الله تعالى عنها كما رواه النووي رحمه الله تعالى . وروى الطبراني بسند ضعيف : **إِنَّ آلَ مُحَمَّدٍ كُلُّ مُؤْمِنٍ تَقِيّ** ، واختاره جلال العلماء [يعني جلال الدين الدوّاني] في شرح هياكل النور

[للشهاب يحيى السهروردي المقتول] . وفي مناقب آل النبي ﷺ وهم بنو فاطمة رضي الله عنها كتبٌ ودفاترُ . واعلم أن فضيلة الخلفاء الأربعة مخصوصةٌ بما عدا بني فاطمةَ رضي الله تعالى عنها ، كما في تكميل الإيمان [للمحدث عبد الحق الدهلوي] . وقال الإمام جلال الدين السيوطي رحمه الله في الخصائص الكبرى : أخرج ابن عساكر (١٣/ ٢٢٦) عن أنس رضي الله تعالى عنه ، قال : قال رسول الله ﷺ وآله : **لَا يَقُومَنَّ أَحَدٌ مِنْ مَجْلِسِهِ إِلَّا لِلْحَسَنِ وَالْحُسَيْنِ أَوْ ذُرِّيَّتِهِمَا** . وفي شِرعة الإسلام [لركن الإسلام محمد بن أبي بكر المعروف بإمام زاده الحنفي] : يُقدِّم أولادَ الرسول ﷺ وآله بالمَشْيِ والجُلوس . وفي التشريح للإمام فخر الدين الرازي : لا يجوز للرجل العالِمِ أن يَجلِسَ فوق العلوي الأُمِّيّ ، لأنه إساءةٌ في الدّين . وفي جامع الفتاوى [إما لقرق أمير الحميدي الرومي (ت ٨٨٠) وإما لأبي الوجاهة عبد الرحمن بن عيسى المرشدي (ت ١٠٣٧) وإما هو الجامع الكبير في الفتاوى لناصر الدين أبي القاسم محمد بن يوسف السمرقندي (ت ٥٥٦) جميعهم من السادة الأحناف] : وَلَد الأَمَة من مولاه حُرٌّ لأنه مخلوق من مائه ، وكذا ولد العلوي من جارية الغير لا يدخل في مِلك مولاها ولا يجوز بيعُه ، كرامةً وشرفاً لجده رسول الله ﷺ ؛

ولا يشارِك في هذا الحكم أحدٌ من أُمّته . وكذا في الفتاوى الغِياثية [لداود بن يوسف الخطيب الحنفي] . وقال الإمام علم الدين العراقي [عبد الكريم بن علي ت ٧٠٤ ، له مصنفات] رحمه الله : إن فاطمة وأخاها إبراهيم أفضل من الخلفاء الأربعة بالاتفاق . وقال الإمام مالك رضي الله عنه : ما أُفضِّل على بَضْعَةِ النبي ﷺ أحداً . وقال الشيخ ابن حجر العسقلاني رحمه الله : فاطمة أفضل من خديجة وعائشة بالإجماع ، ثم خديجة ، ثم عائشة . واستدل السهيلي بالأحاديث الدالّة على أن فاطمة رضي الله عنها بِضعة رسول الله ﷺ وآله وعلى أن شَتْمَها رضي الله عنها يوجب الكفر ، وكما أن لِنَسَب النبي ﷺ شرافةً على غيرهم ، كذلك لسببه ﷺ كرامةٌ على من سِوَاهم لما جاء في الروايات الصحيحة عن عمر بن الخطاب - رضي الله عنه - أنه خطب أمّ كلثوم من علي ، فاعتَلَّ بصغرها وبأنه أعدّها لابن أخيه جعفر ، فقال : ما أردتُ الْبَاهَ ، ولكن سمعت رسول الله ﷺ وآله يقول **كُلُّ سَبَبٍ وَنَسَبٍ يَنْقَطِعُ يَوْمَ الْقِيَامَةِ مَا خَلَا سَبَبِي وَنَسَبِي ، وَكُلُّ بَنِي أُنْثَى عَصَبَتُهُمْ لِأَبِيهِمْ مَا خَلَا وَلَدُ فَاطِمَةَ ، فَإِنِّي أَنَا أَبُوهُمْ وَعَصَبَتُهُمْ** اهـ . من كتاب (دُستور العلماء) .

وفي صِحّة بعض نقوله نظر ، قال الحافظ في الفتح : قال السبكي

الكبير : الذي نَدِينُ اللهَ به : أن فاطمة أفضلُ ثم خديجةُ ثم عائشة ، والخلاف شهير ولكن الحقَّ أحقُّ أن يُتَّبَعَ به . وقال ابن تيمية : جهات الفضل بين خديجة وعائشة متقاربة ـ وكأنه رأى التوقّف ـ وقال ابن القيّم : إنْ أُريد بالتفضيل كثرةُ الثواب عند الله ، فذاك أمرٌ لا يُطَّلَعُ عليه ، فإنَّ عمل القلوب أفضل من عمل الجوارح ؛ وإن أريد كثرة العلم فعائشة لا مَحَالَةَ ؛ وإن أريد شرف الأصل ففاطمة لا محالة ، وهي فضيلة لا يشاركها فيها غير إخوتها ؛ وإن أريد شرف السيادة فقد ثبت النص لفاطمةَ وحدها . قال الحافظ : امتازت فاطمة عن أخواتها بأنهن مُتْنَ في حياة النبي ﷺ وأما ما امتازت به عائشة من فضل العلم فإن لخديجة ما يقابله ، وهي أنها أولُ من أجاب إلى الإسلام ودعا إليه وأعان على ثبوته بالنفس والمال والتوجّه التّامّ . فلها مثل أجر من جاء بعدها ، ولا يُقدِّر قدر ذلك إلا الله . وقيل : انعقد الإجماع على أفضلية فاطمة ، وبقي الخلاف بين عائشة وخديجة ، انتهى . وقال القاري في المرقاة : قال السيوطي في النُقاية : نعتقد أن أفضل النساء مريم وفاطمة ، وأفضل أمهات المؤمنين خديجة وعائشة ؛ وفي التفضيل بينهما أقوال ، ثالثها التوقف . أقول ـ أي القاري ـ التوقّف في حق الكل أولى ، إذ ليس في المسألة دليل

قطعي ، والظنّيّات متعارضة غير مفيدة للعقائد المبنيّة على اليقينيّات ، انتهى . ثمّ قرأت في (عقد الدرر البهية في شرح الرسالة السمرقندية) المعروف بالشرح الكبير للمَلَّوي (ت ١١٨١) في شرح قول صاحب المتن وهو أبو القاسم الليثي السمرقندي (ت ٨٨٨) **(والصلاة على خير البرية وآله)** : أي أتباعِه ، والمراد : أتباعُه بالعمل الصالح على ما يشير إليه قوله تعالى : ﴿ قَالَ يَٰنُوحُ إِنَّهُۥ لَيۡسَ مِنۡ أَهۡلِكَۖ إِنَّهُۥ عَمَلٌ غَيۡرُ صَٰلِحٖۖ فَلَا تَسۡـَٔلۡنِ مَا لَيۡسَ لَكَ بِهِۦ عِلۡمٌۖ إِنِّيٓ أَعِظُكَ أَن تَكُونَ مِنَ ٱلۡجَٰهِلِينَ ﴿٤٦﴾ ﴾ [هود] . والصحابة أشدّ الناس اتّباعاً له ﷺ فهم داخلون في الآل ، فلا يَرِد على المصنِّف إهمال . وقول الشارح ـ أي عصام الدين الإسفراييني (ت ٩٤٥) ـ : فيه إيهام ، أراد الإيهام البديعي كما حمله عليه حفيده أي علي بن إسماعيل بن عصام الدين الشافعي المكي المعروف بالعصامي (ت ١٠٠٧) ، وهو أن يُطلَقَ لفظٌ ذو مَعنيَين : قريبٍ وبعيد ، ويراد البعيدُ مع قرينته خفيَّةً . وهو قد فسّر الآل بالأَتْباع وهو معنى بعيد ، لأن (الآل) إذا أطلق : انصرف الفهم إلى مؤمني بني هاشم والمطَّلب ، وبهذا يندفع الاعتراض على الشارح بأنه : إنْ أراد أنَّ الأَتْباع معنى بعيدٌ في مقام الدعاء فممنوع ، لما سيأتي أنّ المرادَ ليس مطلقُ الأتباع بل الأتباعُ الذين لهم عمل صالح ، فلا

نسلّم أنّ هذا معنىً بعيد ، لأنه اشتهر حُسنُ أن يراد بالآل الأتباع في العمل الصالح ، وهو معنى قولهم : آل النبي ﷺ في مقام الدعاء لكل مؤمن تقي . اهـ .

وقال الإمام السيوطي في العَجاجة الزرنبية في السُّلالة الزينبية رحمه الله : إن اسم الشريف كان يطلق في الصدر الأول على كل مَن كان من أهل البيت ، سواءٌ كان حسنياً أم حسينياً أم علوياً من ذرية محمد بن الحنفية وغيره من أولاد علي بن أبي طالب ، أم جعفرياً أم عَقِيلياً أم عبّاسياً . ولهذا تجد تاريخ الحافظ الذهبي مشحوناً في التراجم بذلك ، يقول : الشريف العباسي ، الشريف العَقيلي ، الشريف الجعفري ، الشريف الزينبي . فلما وُلي الخلفاء الفاطميون بمصر ، قصَّروا اسم الشريف على ذرّيّة الحسن والحسين فقط ، فاستمرّ ذلك بمصر إلى الآن . وقال الحافظ ابن حجر في كتاب الألقاب : الشريف ببغداد لقبٌ لكل عباسي وبمصر لقب لكل علوي ، انتهى . ولا شك أن المصطلَح القديم أولى ، وهو إطلاقه على كل علوي وجعفري وعقيلي وعباسي كما صنعه الذهبي وكما أشار إليه الماوردي من أصحابنا والقاضي أبو يعلى ابن الفراء من الحنابلة كلاهما في الأحكام السلطانية . ونحوُه قول ابن مالك في الألفية (وآلِه المستكمِلين

الشُرَفا) ، فلا ريب في أنه يطلق على ذرية زينب المذكورين أشرافٌ ، وكَمْ أَطلق الذهبي في تاريخه في كثير من التراجم قولَه الشريف الزينبي . وقد يقال : يُطلق على مصطلح أهل مصر الشرف أنواعٌ : عامٌ لجميع أهل البيت وخاصٌ بالذرية ؛ فيدخل فيه الزينبية ، وأخص منه شرف النسبة ، وهو مختص بذرية الحسن والحسين . اهـ .

أخبرنا الشيخ محمد مرشد بن السيد أبي الخير بن السيد أحمد بن عبد الغني بن محمد أمين عابدين رحمهم الله قراءةً عليه وأنا أسمع ، قال الإمام محمد أمين عابدين في باب الكفاءة من كتاب النكاح من حاشيته المشهورة على الدر المختار ـ من أمهات المراجع عند السادة الحنفية ـ : (الْعَجَمِيُّ لَا يَكُونُ كُفْأً لِلْعَرَبِيَّةِ وَلَوْ) كَانَ الْعَجَمِيُّ (عَالِمًا) أَوْ سُلْطَانًا (وَهُوَ الْأَصَحُّ) فَتْحٌ عَنْ الْيَنَابِيعِ وَادَّعَى فِي الْبَحْرِ أَنَّهُ ظَاهِرُ الرِّوَايَةِ وَأَقَرَّهُ الْمُصَنِّفُ لَكِنْ فِي النَّهْرِ فَسَّرَ الْحَسِيبَ بِذِي الْمَنْصِبِ وَالْجَاهِ فَغَيْرُ كُفْءٍ لِلْعَلَوِيَّةِ كَمَا فِي الْيَنَابِيعِ وَإِنْ بِالْعَالِمِ فَكُفْءٌ لِأَنَّ شَرَفَ الْعِلْمِ فَوْقَ شَرَفِ النَّسَبِ وَالْمَالِ كَمَا جَزَمَ بِهِ الْبَزَّازِيُّ وَارْتَضَاهُ الْكَمَالُ وَغَيْرُهُ وَالْوَجْهُ فِيهِ ظَاهِرٌ وَلِذَا قِيلَ : إنَّ عَائِشَةَ أَفْضَلُ مِنْ فَاطِمَةَ رَضِيَ اللهُ عَنْهُمَا ذَكَرَهُ الْقُهُسْتَانِيُّ . **الشَّرْحُ** : (قَوْلُهُ لَكِنْ فِي النَّهْرِ إلَخْ) حَيْثُ قَالَ وَدَلَّ كَلَامُهُ عَلَى أَنَّ غَيْرَ الْعَرَبِيِّ لَا يُكَافِئُ الْعَرَبِيَّ ، وَإِنْ

كَانَ حَسِيبًا لَكِنْ فِي جَامِعِ قَاضِي خَانْ قَالُوا الْحَسِيبُ يَكُونُ كُفْأً لِلنَّسِيبِ ، فَالْعَالِمُ الْعَجَمِيُّ يَكُونُ كُفْأً لِلْجَاهِلِ الْعَرَبِيِّ وَالْعَلَوِيَّةِ لِأَنَّ شَرَفَ الْعِلْمِ فَوْقَ شَرَفِ النَّسَبِ وَارْتَضَاهُ فِي فَتْحِ الْقَدِيرِ وَجَزَمَ بِهِ الْبَزَّازِيُّ وَزَادَ وَالْعَالِمُ الْفَقِيرُ يَكُونُ كُفْأً لِلْغَنِيِّ الْجَاهِلِ وَالْوَجْهُ فِيهِ ظَاهِرٌ لِأَنَّ شَرَفَ الْعِلْمِ فَوْقَ شَرَفِ النَّسَبِ فَشَرَفُ الْمَالِ أَوْلَى . نَعَمْ الْحَسَبُ قَدْ يُرَادُ بِهِ الْمَنْصِبُ وَالْجَاهُ كَمَا فَسَّرَهُ بِهِ فِي الْمُحِيطِ عَنْ صَدْرِ الْإِسْلَامِ وهَذَا لَيْسَ كُفْأً لِلْعَرَبِيَّةِ كَمَا فِي الْيَنَابِيعِ . اهـ . كَلَامُ النَّهْرِ مُلَخَّصًا . أَقُولُ : حَيْثُ كَانَ مَا فِي الْيَنَابِيعِ مِنْ تَصْحِيحِ عَدَمِ كَفَاءَةِ الْحَسِيبِ لِلْعَرَبِيَّةِ مَبْنِيًّا عَلَى تَفْسِيرِ الْحَسِيبِ بِذِي الْمَنْصِبِ وَالْجَاهِ لَمْ يَصِحَّ مَا ذَكَرَهُ الْمُصَنِّفُ مِنْ تَصْحِيحِ عَدَمِ الْكَفَاءَةِ فِي الْعَالِمِ ، وَعَزْوِهِ فِي شَرْحِهِ إِلَى الْيَنَابِيعِ ، وَذَكَرَ الْخَيْرُ الرَّمْلِيُّ عَنْ مَجْمَعِ الْفَتَاوَى : الْعَالِمُ يَكُونُ كُفْأً لِلْعَلَوِيَّةِ لِأَنَّ شَرَفَ الْحَسَبِ أَقْوَى مِنْ شَرَفِ النَّسَبِ وَعَنْ هَذَا قِيلَ إِنَّ عَائِشَةَ أَفْضَلُ مِنْ فَاطِمَةَ لِأَنَّ لِعَائِشَةَ شَرَفُ الْعِلْمِ كَذَا فِي الْمُحِيطِ ، وَذَكَرَ أَيْضًا أَنَّهُ جَزَمَ بِهِ فِي الْمُحِيطِ وَالْبَزَّازِيَّةِ وَالْفَيْضِ وَجَامِعِ الْفَتَاوَى وَصَاحِبِ الدُّرَرِ الخ . ثم قال صاحب الحاشية : قَوْلُ الشَّارِحِ وَادَّعَى فِي الْبَحْرِ إِلَخْ يُفِيدُ أَنَّ كَوْنَهُ ظَاهِرَ الرِّوَايَةِ مُجَرَّدُ دَعْوَى لَا دَلِيلَ عَلَيْهَا سِوَى قَوْلِهِمْ فِي الْمُتُونِ وَغَيْرِهَا وَالْعَرَبُ أَكْفَاءٌ أَيْ فَلَا

يُكَافِئُهُمْ غَيْرُهُمْ وَلَا يَخْفَى أَنَّ هَذَا وَإِنْ كَانَ ظَاهِرُهُ الْإِطْلَاق ، وَلَكِنْ قَيَّدَهُ الْمَشَايِخُ بِغَيْرِ الْعَالِمِ وَكَمْ لَهُ مِنْ نَظِيرٍ فَإِنَّ شَأْنَ مَشَايِخِ الْمَذْهَبِ إِفَادَةُ قُيُودٍ وَشَرَائِطَ لِعِبَارَاتٍ مُطْلَقَةٍ اسْتِنْبَاطًا مِنْ قَوَاعِدَ كُلِّيَّةٍ أَوْ مَسَائِلَ فَرْعِيَّةٍ أَوْ أَدِلَّةٍ نَقْلِيَّةٍ وَهُنَا كَذَلِكَ ، فَقَدْ ذُكِرَ فِي آخِرِ الْفَتَاوَى الْخَيْرِيَّةِ فِي قُرَشِيٍّ جَاهِلٍ تَقَدَّمَ فِي الْمَجْلِسِ عَلَى عَالِمٍ أَنَّهُ يَحْرُمُ عَلَيْهِ إِذْ كُتُبُ الْعُلَمَاءِ طَافِحَةٌ بِتَقَدُّمِ الْعَالِمِ عَلَى الْقُرَشِيِّ ، وَلَمْ يُفَرِّقْ سُبْحَانَهُ بَيْنَ الْقُرَشِيِّ وَغَيْرِهِ فِي قَوْلِهِ ﴿ أَمَّنْ هُوَ قَٰنِتٌ ءَانَآءَ ٱلَّيْلِ سَاجِدًا وَقَآئِمًا يَحْذَرُ ٱلْءَاخِرَةَ وَيَرْجُواْ رَحْمَةَ رَبِّهِۦۗ قُلْ هَلْ يَسْتَوِى ٱلَّذِينَ يَعْلَمُونَ وَٱلَّذِينَ لَا يَعْلَمُونَۗ إِنَّمَا يَتَذَكَّرُ أُوْلُواْ ٱلْأَلْبَٰبِ ﴿٩﴾ ﴾ [الزمر] إِلَى آخِرِ مَا أَطَالَ بِهِ فَرَاجِعْهُ فَحَيْثُ كَانَ شَرَفُ الْعِلْمِ أَقْوَى مِنْ شَرَفِ النَّسَبِ بِدَلَالَةِ الْآيَةِ وَتَصْرِيحُهُمْ بِذَلِكَ اقْتَضَى تَقْيِيدَ مَا أَطْلَقُوهُ هُنَا اعْتِمَادًا عَلَى فَهْمِهِ مِنْ مَحَلٍّ آخَرَ ، فَلَمْ يَكُنْ مَا ذَكَرَهُ الْمَشَايِخُ مُخَالِفًا لِظَاهِرِ الرِّوَايَةِ ، وَكَيْفَ يَصِحُّ لِأَحَدٍ أَنْ يَقُولَ إِنَّ مِثْلَ أَبِي حَنِيفَةَ أَوْ الْحَسَنِ الْبَصْرِيِّ وَغَيْرِهِمَا مِمَّنْ لَيْسَ بِعَرَبِيٍّ أَنَّهُ لَا يَكُونُ كُفْأً لِبِنْتِ قُرَشِيٍّ جَاهِلٍ ، أَوْ لِبِنْتِ عَرَبِيٍّ بَوَّالٍ عَلَى عَقِبَيْهِ ، فَلَا جَرَمَ إِنَّهُ جَزَمَ بِمَا قَالَهُ الْمَشَايِخُ صَاحِبُ الْمُحِيطِ وَغَيْرُهُ كَمَا عَلِمْتَ وَارْتَضَاهُ الْمُحَقِّقُ ابْنُ الْهُمَامِ ، وَصَاحِبُ النَّهْرِ وَتَبِعَهُمْ الشَّارِحُ فَافْهَمْ وَاللهُ سُبْحَانَهُ أَعْلَمُ .

وأنبأني الحبيب حامد المهدلي مناولةً عن الحبيب سقّاف بن علي الكاف السّقاف المدني ، قال في كتابه دراسة في نسب السادة بني علوي ذرّيّة الإمام المهاجر أحمد بن عيسى : الفَرع السابع من المبحث التاسع (شرط الكفاءة في النكاح) : اختَصّ نساءُ العرب واختصّ منهم نساءُ آل البيت بمراعاة شرط النسب في نكاحهن بحيث لا يَنكِح الهاشميةَ إلا هاشمي ، قال بذلك الجمهور ومنهم أبو حنيفة وأحمد والشافعي رضي الله عنهم ، ومستندهم في ذلك : الحديث : عن أمير المؤمنين سيدنا عمر بن الخطاب رضي الله عنه ، قال : لأمنعنّ تزوّج ذوات الأحساب إلا من الأكفاء ، رواه الدارقطني ، وقول الإمام أحمد إن غير قريش من العرب لا يكافئها وغير بني هاشم لا يكافئهم ، وهذا قول الشافعية ، واستندوا لقولهم هذا لما روى واثلة بن الأسقع أنّه قال سمعت رسول الله ﷺ وآله يقول **إِنَّ اللهَ اصْطَفَى كِنَانَةَ مِنْ وَلَدِ إِسْمَعِيلَ وَاصْطَفَى مِنْ كِنَانَةَ قُرَيْشًا وَاصْطَفَى مِنْ قُرَيْشٍ بَنِي هَاشِمٍ وَاصْطَفَانِي مِنْ بَنِي هَاشِمٍ** . رواه مسلم وأحمد والترمذي والسمعاني . أنظر المغني لابن قدامة والمجموع شرح المهذّب ونيل الأوطار وكتاب الأحوال الشخصيّة في التشريع الإسلامي للدكتور أحمد الغندور . اهـ .

قال الحافظ في فتح الباري : (باب الأَكْفاء في الدين) وقوله ﴿ وَهُوَ ٱلَّذِى خَلَقَ مِنَ ٱلْمَآءِ بَشَرًا فَجَعَلَهُۥ نَسَبًا وَصِهْرًا ﴾ [الفرقان ٥٤] .

قوله (باب الأكفاء في الدين) جمع كُفْءٍ بضم أوّله وسكون الفاء بعدها همزة : المثل والنظير . واعتبار الكفاءة في الدين متفق عليه ، فلا تحل المسلمة لكافر أصلاً . قوله (وهو الذي خلق من الماء بشرا فجعله نسبا وصهرا الآية) قال الفراء النسب من لا يحل نكاحُه ، والصهر من يحل نكاحه . فكأن المصنف لما رأى الحصر وقع بالقسمين صلح التمسك بالعموم لوجود الصلاحية إلا ما دل الدليل على اعتباره وهو استثناء الكافر ، وقد جزم بأن اعتبار الكفاءة مختص بالدين مالك ، ونقل عن ابن عمر وابن مسعود ، ومن التابعين عن محمد بن سيرين وعمر بن عبد العزيز . واعتبر الكفاءة في النسب الجمهور . وقال أبو حنيفة : قريش أكفاء بعضهم بعضاً ، والعرب كذلك ، وليس أحد من العرب كُفْأً لقريش كما ليس أحد من غير العرب كُفْأً للعرب ، وهو وجه للشافعية والصحيح تقديم بني هاشم والمطلب على غيرهم ، ومن عدا هؤلاء أكفاء بعضهم لبعض وقال الثوري : إذا نكح المولى العربية بفسخ النكاح ، وبه قال أحمد في رواية . وتوسَّط الشافعي فقال ليس نكاحُ غير الأَكْفاء حراماً فأَرُدَّ به

النكاح، وإنما هو تقصير بالمرأة والأولياء، فإذا رَضُوا صحَّ، ويكون حقّاً لهم تَرَكوه، فلو رضُوا إلا واحداً، فله فَسْخُه. وذَكَرَ أن المَعنى في اشتراط الوِلاية في النكاح كَيْلَا تُضِيعَ المرأة نفسها في غير كُفْءٍ، انتهى. ولم يَثبت في اعتبار الكفاءة بالنسب حديثٌ، وأما ما أخرجه البزار من حديث معاذ رفعه: **اَلْعَرَبُ بَعْضُهُمْ أَكْفَاءُ بَعْضٍ، وَالْمَوَالِي بَعْضُهُمْ أَكْفَاءُ بَعْضٍ**، فإسناده ضعيف. واحتج البيهقي بحديث واثلة مرفوعاً **إنَّ اللهَ اصْطَفَى بَنِي كِنَانَةَ مِنْ بَنِي إِسْمَعِيلَ** الحديث، وهو صحيح أخرجه مسلم، لكن في الاحتجاج به لذلك نظر، لكن ضمّ بعضهم إليه حديث **قَدِّمُوا قُرَيْشاً وَلَا تَقَدَّمُوهَا**. ونقل ابن المنذر عن البويطي أن الشافعي قال: الكفاءة في الدين. وهو كذلك في مختصر البويطي قال الرافعي: وهو خلاف مشهور. ونقل الأَبْرِي عن الربيع أن رجلاً سأل الشافعي عنه فقال: أنا عربي لا تسألني عن هذا. اهـ. من فتح الباري.

وقال الشيخ محيي الدين ابن عربي الطائي رضي الله عنه في الباب التاسع والعشرين من الفتوحات المكية الذي عنوانه: (في معرفة سر سلمان الذي أَلْحَقَهُ بأهل البيت والأقطاب الَّذين وَرَثَهُ منهم ومعرفة أسرارهم) وهو من أنفع ما رأيته في الباب، أَقْرَأَنِيه الشيخ محمد أبو

الهدى ثم قرأته مرة أخرى على الشيخ عبد المقصود السيد فارس رحمه الله ضمن قراءتي كتاب المقريزي في فضل أهل البيت عليه ؛ قال :

اِعلم ـ أيّدك الله ـ أنّا رُوِّينا من حديث جعفر بن محمد الصادق ، عن أبيه محمد بن علي ، عن أبيه علي بن الحسين ، عن أبيه الحسين بن علي ، عن أبيه علي بن أبي طالب رضي الله عنه عن رسول الله ﷺ أنه قال : **مَوْلَى الْقَوْمِ مِنْهُمْ** [الترمذي والنسائي والحاكم عن أبي رافع والدارمي عن عمرو بن عوف المزني وأبو يعلى والطبراني عن ابن عباس وابن أبي شيبة عن فارسي مولى بني معاوية وأحمد عن رفاعة وأبي موسى والشيخان عن أنس بلفظ **مِنْ أَنْفُسِهِمْ**] وخرّج الترمذي عن رسول الله ﷺ أنه قال : **أَهْلُ الْقُرْآنِ هُمْ أَهْلُ اللهِ وَخَاصَّتُهُ** وقال تعالى في حق المختصّين من عباده ﴿ **إِنَّ عِبَادِى لَيْسَ لَكَ عَلَيْهِمْ سُلْطَـٰنٌ إِلَّا مَنِ ٱتَّبَعَكَ مِنَ ٱلْغَاوِينَ** ﴿٤٢﴾ ﴾ [الحجر] . فكل عبدٍ إلهي توجّه لأحد عليه حق من المخلوقين : فقد نَقَصَ من عبوديته لله بِقَدَرِ ذلك الحقّ .

ولمّا كان رسول الله ﷺ عبداً محضاً قد طهّره الله وأهل بيته تطهيراً وأذهب عنهم الرِّجْس ، وهو كلُّ ما يَشِينُهم ـ فإنّ الرجس هو القَذَر عند العرب ، هكذا حكى الفرّاء ـ قال تعالى : ﴿ **إِنَّمَا يُرِيدُ**

اَللَّهُ لِيُذْهِبَ عَنكُمُ ٱلرِّجْسَ أَهْلَ ٱلْبَيْتِ وَيُطَهِّرَكُمْ تَطْهِيرًا ﴾ [الأحزاب ٣٣]، فلا يُضاف إليهم إلا مُطَهَّرٌ، ولا بُدَّ، فإنَّ المضاف إليهم هو الذي يُشْبِهُهُم فما يُضيفون لأنفسهم إلا من له حكمُ الطهارة والتقديس. فهذه شهادةٌ من النبيّ ﷺ لسلمان الفارسيّ بالطهارة والحفظ الإلهي والعِصمة، حيث قال فيه رسول الله ﷺ: سَلْمَانُ مِنَّا أَهْلَ الْبَيْتِ. وشهد الله لهم بالتطهير وذهاب الرجس عنهم. وإذا كان لا يَنضاف إليهم إلّا مطهَّر مقدَّسٌ، وحصَلت له العناية الإلهية بمجرَّد الإضافة، فما ظنّك بأهل البيت في نفوسهم؟ فهُم المطهَّرون، بل هم عينُ الطَّهارة!

فهذه الآية تدل على أنّ الله قد شرَّك أهلَ البيت مع رسول الله ﷺ في قوله تعالى ﴿ لِيَغْفِرَ لَكَ ٱللَّهُ مَا تَقَدَّمَ مِن ذَنبِكَ وَمَا تَأَخَّرَ ﴾ [الفتح ٢]. وأيُّ وسَخٍ وقذرٍ أقذر من الذنوب وأوسخ؟ فطهَّر الله سبحانه نبيَّه ﷺ بالمغفرة، فما هو ذنبٌ بالنسبة إلينا، لو وقع منه ﷺ لكان ذنباً في الصورة لا في المعنى، لأنَّ الذمَّ لا يَلحق به على ذلك من الله ولا مِنَّا شرعاً. فلو كان حُكْمُهُ حُكْمَ الذَّنْبِ، لَصَحِبَه ما يَصحب الذنبَ من المَذَمَّة ولم يَصدُق قوله ﴿ إِنَّمَا يُرِيدُ ٱللَّهُ لِيُذْهِبَ عَنكُمُ ٱلرِّجْسَ أَهْلَ ٱلْبَيْتِ وَيُطَهِّرَكُمْ تَطْهِيرًا ﴾ [الأحزاب ٣٣].

فدخل الشرفاءُ ـ أولاد فاطمة ـ كلُّهم ، ومن هو من أهل البيت مثل سلمان الفارسي ، إلى يوم القيامة في حكم هذه الآية من الغفران . فهم المطهَّرون اختصاصاً من الله وعنايةً بهم لشرف محمد ﷺ وعنايةِ الله به . ولا يَظهر حكمُ هذا الشرف لأهل البيت إلا في الدار الآخرة ، فإنهم يُحشَرون مغفوراً لهم ؛ وأمّا في الدنيا : فمَنْ أتى منهم حدّاً أُقيم عليه ، كالتّائب إذا بَلغ الحاكمَ أمرُه وقد زَنى أو سرق أو شرب ، أُقيم عليه الحدّ مع تحقُّق المغفرة كماعِزٍ وأمثاله ؛ ولا يجوز ذمُّه .

وينبغي لكل مسلم مؤمن بالله وبما أنزله أن يصدِّقَ اللهَ تعالى في قوله ﴿لِيُذْهِبَ عَنكُمُ ٱلرِّجْسَ أَهْلَ ٱلْبَيْتِ وَيُطَهِّرَكُمْ تَطْهِيرًا﴾ [الأحزاب ٣٣] ، فيعتقد في جميع ما يصدر من أهل البيت : أن الله قد عفا عنهم فيه ، فلا ينبغي لمسلمٍ أن يُلحِق المَذمَّةَ بهم ، ولا ما يَشْنَأُ أعراضَ مَنْ قد شَهِد الله بتطهيره وذهاب الرجس عنه ، لا بعملٍ عمِلوه ، ولا بخيرٍ قدَّموه ، بل سابقِ عِنايةٍ من الله بهم . ﴿ذَٰلِكَ فَضْلُ ٱللَّهِ يُؤْتِيهِ مَن يَشَآءُ ۚ وَٱللَّهُ ذُو ٱلْفَضْلِ ٱلْعَظِيمِ ﴿٤﴾﴾ [الجمعة] .

وإذا صحّ الخبر الوارد في سلمان الفارسي ، فله هذه الدرجة ؛ فإنّه لو كان سلمان على أمر يَشنَؤُه ظاهر الشرع وتَلْحق المذمّة بعامله ، لكان مضافاً الى أهل البيت مَن لم يُذهَبْ عنه الرجسُ ، فيكون لأهل

البيت من ذلك بقدْر ما أضيف إليهم ، وهم المطهَّرون بالنصّ . فسلمانُ منهم بلا شك ، فأرجو أن يكون عَقِبُ عليٍّ وسلمانَ تَلحَقُهم هذه العناية كما لَحِقت أولادَ الحسن والحسين وعَقِبَهم وموالي أهلِ البيت ، فإن رحمة الله واسعة يا وليُّ !

وإذا كانت منزلة مخلوقٍ عند الله بهذه المثابة ، أنْ يَشْرُف المضافُ إليهم بشَرَفِهم ـ وشرفُهم ليس لأنفسهم ، وإنما الله تعالى هو الذي اجتباهم وكساهم حِلّة الشرف ـ كيف ـ يا وَليُّ ! ـ بمن أُضيف إلى من له الحمدُ والمجد والشرف لنفسه وذاته ؟ فهو المجيد ـ سبحانه وتعالى ـ فالمضاف إليه من عباده : الّذين هم عباده ؛ وهُم الّذين لا سلطانَ لمخلوقٍ عليهم في الآخرة . قال تعالى لابليس : ﴿ إِنَّ عِبَادِى ﴾ فأضافهم إليه ﴿لَيْسَ لَكَ عَلَيْهِمْ سُلْطَـٰنٌ ﴾ [الإسراء ٦٥] . وما تجد في القرآن عباداً مضافين إليه سبحانه الا السُّعَداء خاصة ؛ وجاء اللفظ في غيرهم بالعباد ـ فما ظنّك بالمعصومين المحفوظين منهم ، القائمين بحدود سيّدهم ، الواقفين عند مَراسِمه ؟ فَشَرَفُهُم أعلى وأتمّ ! وهؤلاء هم أقطاب هذا المقام .

ومِن هؤلاء الاقطاب وَرِثَ سلمانُ شرفَ مقام أهل البيت ، فكان ـ رضى الله عنه ـ مِن أعلم الناس بما لله على عباده من الحقوق ،

الفوق

وما لأنفسهم والخلق عليهم من الحقوق ، وأَقْواهُم على أدائها . وفيه قال رسـول الله ﷺ : **لَـوْ كَانَ الْإِيمَانُ بِالثُّرَيَّا لَنَالَـهُ رِجَالٌ مِنْ فَارِسٍ** - وأشار الى سلمان الفارسى [متفق عليه عن أبي هريرة] . وفى تخصيص النبـيّ ﷺ ذكرَ الثُرَيَّا دون غيرها من الكواكب : إشـارةٌ بديعة لمُثبتي الصفات السبعة [يعني الأشاعرة] لأنّها سبعة كواكب ، فافهَمْ ! فسِرُّ سـلمان الذي ألحقه بأهل البيت : ما أعطاه النبيُّ ﷺ من أداء كتابته . وفي هـذا فقه عجيب : فهـو عتيقه ﷺ - **وَمَوْلَى الْقَـوْمِ مِنْهُمْ** - وَالكلُّ مَوالي الحقّ ، ورحمته وسعت كل شئ ، وكل شئ عبده ومولاه .

وبعْـدَ أن تبـيّن لك منزلـةُ أهل البيـت عند الله ، وأنّـه لا ينبغي لمسـلم أن يذمَّهم بما يقع منهم أصلاً - فإنّ الله طهّرهم - فلْيَعلَمِ الذامُّ لهم أنّ ذلك راجع إليه ولو ظلموه . فذلك الظلم هو في زعمه ظلم ، لا في نفـس الأمـر ، وإن حَكَمَ عليـه ظاهرُ الشرع بأدائـه . بل حُكْمُ ظُلمهم إيّانا ، في نفس الأمر ، يُشـبه جَرْيَ المقادير على العبد في ماله ونفسه بغَرْقٍ أو بحَرْقٍ وغيرِ ذلك من الأمور المُهلِكة ؛ فيحترق ، أو يمـوت له أحدُ أحبابه ، أو يصاب في نفسـه ، وهـذا كلّه مما لا يوافق غرضَه .

ولا يجـوز له أن يذُمَّ قَـدَرَ الله ولا قضاءَه . بل ينبغى له أن يقابل

ذلك كلّه بالتسليم والرِّضا ؛ وإنْ نزل عن هذه المرتبة فبالصبر ؛ وإن ارتفع عن تلك المرتبة فبالشّكر . فإنّ في طيّ ذلك نِعَماً من الله لهذا المصاب . وليس وراءَ ما ذكرناه خيرٌ . فإنّه ما وراءَه ليس إلّا الضَّجَرُ والسَّخَط وعدَمُ الرِّضا وسوء الأدب مع الله . فكذا ينبغي أن يقابِل المسلمُ جميع ما يطرأُ عليه من أهل البيت في ماله ونفسه وعِرْضه وأهله وذويه . فيقابل ذلك كلّه بالرضا والتسليم والصبر ، ولا يُلحق المَذمَّة بهم أصلاً . وإن تَوَجَّهت عليهم الأحكام المقرَّرَةُ شرعاً : فذلك لا يقدح في هذا ، بل يُجْرِيه مُجْرَى المَقادير . وإنّما مَنَعْنَا تعليقَ الذَّمِّ بهم إذ ميَّزَهُم اللهُ عنا بما ليس لنا معهم فيه قَدَمٌ .

وأمّا أداء الحقوق المشروعة ، فهذا رسول الله ﷺ كان يقترض من اليهود ، وإذا طالبوه بحقوقهم أدّاها على أحسن ما يمكن ، وإن تطاول اليهوديُّ عليه بالقول ، يقول : **دَعُوهُ ! إِنَّ لِصَاحِبِ الحَقِّ مَقَالاً** [متفق عليه عن أبي هريرة] . وقال ﷺ في قصّةٍ : **لَوْ أَنَّ فَاطِمَةَ بِنْتَ مُحَمَّدٍ سَرَقَتْ قَطَعْتُ يَدَهَا** . فوضْعُ الأحكام لله : يضَعُها كيف يشاء وعلى أيّ حال يشاء . فهذه حقوق الله ، ومع هذا لم يذُمَّهم الله .

وإنّما كلامنا في حقوقنا وما لنا أن نطالبَهم به . فنحن مخيَّرون : إن شئنا أخذنا وان شئنا تركنا ، والترك أفضل عموماً ، فكيف في

أهـل البيت ؟ وليس لنـا ذمّ أحد ، فكيف بأهل البيت ؟ فإنّا إذا نزلنا عن طلب حقوقنا وعفَونا عنهم في ذلك ـ أى فيما أصابوه منا ـ كانت لنا بذلك عند الله اليدُ العظمى والمكانة الزُّلفى .

فـإنّ النبى ﷺ ما طلب منا عن أمـر الله ﴿ إِلَّا ٱلْمَوَدَّةَ فِي ٱلْقُرْبَىٰ ﴾ [الشورى ٢٣] ، وفيـه سرّ صلة الأرحـام . ومن لم يَقبَل سـؤال نبيه فيما سـأله فيه مِمّا هو قـادر عليه ، بأيّ وجهٍ يلْقاه غداً أو يرجو شـفاعته ، وهـو ما أسـعف نبيَّه ﷺ فيما طلب منه من المـودّة في قرابته ؟ فكيف بأهل بيته ، فهم أخصّ القرابة ؟

ثم إنّه جاء بلفظ المودّة ، وهو الثبوت على المحبة . فإنه من ثبت وُدُّهُ في أمر ، اسـتصحبه في كل حال ؛ وإذا اسـتصحبته المودّة في كل حـال ، لم يؤاخِـذ أهل البيت بما يَطْرَأُ منهم في حقّـه مما له أن يطالبَهم به . فيتركه تركَ محبّةٍ ، وإيثاراً لِنفسه ، لا عليها . قال المحبّ الصادق :

وَكُلُّ مَا يَفْعَلُ المَحْبُوبُ مَحْبُوبُ

وجاء بإسـم الحب ، فكيـف حال المودّة ؟ ومِـن البُشرى ورود اسم الودود لله تعالى .

ولا معنى لثبوتها إلّا حصول أثَرها بالفعل في الدار الآخرة وفي

النار : لكل طائفة بما تقتضيه حكمةُ الله فيهم . وقال الآخَر في المعنى :

أُحِبُّ لِحُبِّهَا السُّودَانَ حَتَّى
أُحِبُّ لِحُبِّهَا سُودَ الْكِلَابِ

ولنا في هذا المعنى :

أُحِبُّ لِحُبِّكِ الْحُبْشَانَ طُرًّا
وَأَعْشَقُ لِاسْمِكِ الْبَدْرَ الْمُنِيرَا

قيل : كانت الكلاب السود تناوشه وهو يتحبب إليها . فهذا فعل المُحِبّ في حب من لا تُسْعِدُه محبّتُه عند الله ولا تُورِثه القربة من الله . فهل هذا إلّا من صِدْق الحبّ وثبوت الوُدّ في النفس ؟

فلو صحَّت محبّتك لله ولرسوله ، أحببتَ أهل بيت رسول الله ﷺ ورأيتَ كلَّ ما يصدُر منهم في حقّك ممّا لا يوافق طَبْعَك ولا غَرَضَك ، أنه جَمالٌ تَتَنَعَّم بوقوعه منهم ، فتَعلَمَ عند ذلك : أنّ لك عنايةً عند الله الّذي أحببتَهم من أجله ، حيث ذَكَرَكَ من يُحِبُّه وخَطَرْتَ على باله : وهُمْ أهلُ بيت رسوله ﷺ . فتَشكرَ اللهَ تعالى على هذه النعمة ؛ فانّهم ذكروك بألسنةٍ طاهرة بتطهير الله ، طهارةً لم يَبلُغْها عِلمُك .

وإذا رأيناك على ضدّ هذه الحالة مع أهل البيت ، الّذي أنت محتاج إليهم ولرسول الله ﷺ حيث هداك الله به ، فكيف أثق أنا بِوُدِّك الذي تزعُم به أنّك شديد الحبّ فيَّ ، والرعايةِ لحقوقي أو لِجانبي ، وأنت في حقّ أهل نبيّك بهذه المثابة من الوقوع فيهم ؟ واللهِ ما ذاك إلّا من نَقْص إيمانك ، ومِن مَكْر الله بك واستدراجِه إياك من حيث لا تعلم !

وصورة المكر : أن تقول وتعتقد أنّك في ذلك تذبّ عن دين الله وشرعه ، وتقول في طلب حقّك : إنك ما طلبت إلا ما أباح الله لك طلبه . ويندرج الذمّ في ذلك الطلب المشروع ، والبُغض والمقت ، وإيثارك نفسك على أهل البيت وأنت لا تشعر بذلك . والدواء الشافي من هذا الداء العُضال : أن لا ترى لنفسك معهم حقّاً ، وتَنزِلَ عن حقّك لئلا يندرج في طلبه ما ذكرته لك . وما أنت من حكّام المسلمين حتى يتعيّن عليك إقامةُ حدٍّ أو إنصافُ مظلوم أو رَدُّ حق إلى أهله . فإن كنت حاكماً ولا بُدَّ ، فاسْعَ فِي استنزال صاحبَ الحقّ عن حقّه إذا كان المحكومُ عليه من أهل البيت . فإن أبى ، حينئذٍ يتعيّن عليك إمضاء حكم الشرع فيه . فلو كشف الله لك ـ يا وليُّ ! ـ عن منازلهم عند الله في الآخرة ، لَوَدَدْتَ أن تكون مولىً من مواليهم . فاللهُ يُلهِمُنا رُشْد أنفسنا ! فانظر ما أشرفَ منزلةَ سلمانَ ـ رضى الله عن جميعهم .

ولما بيّنتُ لك أقطاب هذا المقام وأنهم عَبيدُ الله المصطَفَونَ الأخيار، فاعلم أنّ أسرارهم الّتي أطلَعَنا الله عليها تجهلُها العامّةُ، بل أكثر الخاصّة الّتى ليس لها هذا المقام. والخَضِرُ منهم - رضى الله عنه - وهو من أكبرهم، وقد شهد الله له أنّه آتاه رحمة من عنده، وعلّمه من لَدُنْه علماً اتّبعه فيه كليمُ الله موسى - عليه السلام - الّذي قال فيه ﷺ: **لَوْ كَانَ مُوسَى حَيّاً مَا وَسِعَهُ إِلَّا أَنْ يَتَّبِعَنِي** [رواه أحمد عن جابر وعبد الله بن ثابت والدارمي عن جابر].

فمن أسرارهم ما قد ذكرناه من العلم بمنزلة أهل البيت وما قد نبّه الله على علوّ رتبتهم في ذلك. ومن أسرارهم علم المكر الّذي مَكَر الله بعباده في بُغضهم - مع دعواهم حبَّ رسول الله ﷺ - وسؤاله ﴿ٱلْمَوَدَّةَ فِى ٱلْقُرْبَىٰ﴾ وهو ﷺ من جملة أهل البيت: فما فعل أكثر الناس ما سألهم فيه رسول الله ﷺ عن أمر الله؛ فعصَوا الله ورسولَه وما أحبُّوا من قرابته إلا مَن رأَوْا مِنه الإحسانَ. فأغراضهم أَحَبُّوا، وبنفوسهم تَعَشَّقُوا. اهـ. من الفتوحات المكّية الباب التاسع والعشرين.

وخلاصة الكلام أنّ عامّة آل بيت خاتم النبوّة ﷺ المؤمنين شُرِّفوا فوق عامّة المؤمنين غير المنسوبين، فكيف إذا كانوا من العلماء

الأتقياء ؟ لذا جُعل بِرُّهم والتقرُّبُ إليهم ومودّتهم من أسباب السعادة والنجاة من النار بل من الدرجات العُليا ورجاء مَعِيَّةِ سيّد الأبرار ﷺ . فوجب التعريف بهم وبفضائلهم ورُتَبِهم وحقوقهم ، وإظهار الشكر على نعمة وجودهم في الأمّة ، والانشغال بنوال ما يترتّب على هذا الفضل من أعمال الصِلة والفضيلة ، دون إفراطٍ ولا تفريط ولا تزكية لأحد على الله ، ولكن طاعةً للأمر المقدَّر في قوله تعالى ﴿إِلَّا ٱلْمَوَدَّةَ فِى ٱلْقُرْبَىٰ﴾ [الشورى ٢٣] وعملاً بأبواب عُصْمٍ من أرجى أبواب سنّة المصطفى ﷺ ، ﴿إِلَّا ٱبْتِغَآءَ وَجْهِ رَبِّهِ ٱلْأَعْلَىٰ ﴿٢٠﴾﴾ [الليل] . وعلى أداء هذا الحقّ جرى علماء السلف الصالح من المصنّفين المذكّرين للأمّة في فضائل أهل البيت ، فمن أشهر مؤلّفاتهم : الذرّية الطاهرة النبوية للحافظ أبي بِشر محمد ابن أحمد بن حمّاد الدُولَابي ؛ وإحياء المَيْت بفضائل آل البيت للإمام السيوطي جمع فيه ستين حديثاً ؛ وقد أفرد الإمام الهيتمي في كتابه الصواعق المحرقة في الرد على أهل البدع والزندقة فصلاً في سرد أربعين حديثاً واردة في أهل البيت ، وكذا الحافظ محمّد بن جعفر الكتّاني في أربعينه في فضل أهل البيت ، ثلاثتهم دون تحرّي الصحيح منها مع التكرار ؛ وجواهر العِقْدين بفضل الشرفَين العلم الجلي والنسب النبوي للمحدّث الشريف نور الدين أبي الحسن علي بن عبد الله السَّمْهُودي المدني

الشافعي تلميذ المناوي وهو كتاب جليل القدر بثلاثة مجلدات ، طبع حديثاً بمجلد ، رتّبه على قسمين ، الأول في فضل العلم والعلماء وفيه ثلاثة أبواب ، والثاني في فضل أهل البيت النبوي وشرفهم ؛ وذخائر العُقبى في فضائل ذوي القُربى للمحدث الشريف محب الدين الطبري جد كبار مسنِدي الحجاز ، انتُقِد لإيراده الضِعاف والموضوعات دون الأسانيد ولا بيان رتبة الحديث ؛ وكذلك ولتشيّعه الشيخ سليمان بن إبراهيم القُندوزي الحنفي (ت ١٢٩٤) مؤلف ينابيع المودّة لذوي القربى ؛ ومن أحسنها استجلاب ارتقاء الغُرَف بِحُبِّ أقرباء الرسول ﷺ وذوي الشرف للحافظ المتقن الشمس السخاوي ؛ وكتاب حسّان أحمد ﷺ الشيخ يوسف النبهاني الشرف المؤبَّد لآل محمّد ﷺ ؛ وكتاب رشفة الصادي من بحر فضائل بني النبي الهادي ﷺ للحبيب أبي بكر بن عبد الرحمن بن محمد بن علي بن عبد الله بن عيدروس آل شهاب الدين وهو كتاب قيّم جداً ؛ وكتاب نور الأبصار في مناقب آل بيت النبي المختار للشبلنجي ؛ وكتاب الإتحاف بحبّ الأشراف للشَّبَراوي ـ رحمهم الله ـ جميعها محذوفة الأسانيد إلا الأول وكلّها مطبوعة . ومن كتب المعاصرين : علِّموا أولادكم حب آل النبي ﷺ للوزير محمد عبده يماني رحمه الله . وهذا العنوان أصله حديث ضعيف لفظه **أَدِّبُوا أَوْلَادَكُمْ عَلَى ثَلَاثِ**

خِصَـالٍ : حُـبِّ نَبِيِّكُمْ ، وَحُبِّ أَهْـلِ بَيْتِهِ ، وَعَلَى قِـرَاءَةِ الْقُرْآنِ ، فَإِنَّ حَمَلَـةَ الْقُرْآنِ فِي ظِـلِّ اللهِ يَوْمَ لَا ظِـلَّ إِلَّا ظِلُّهُ ، مَعَ أَنْبِيَائِـهِ وَأَصْفِيَائِهِ .

رواه ابـن النَّجَّـار في تواريخـه و أبـو النـصر عبد الكريم بـن محمـد الشيرازي في فوائده . والدرّ الثمين في نسب السادة الطاهرين لشيخنا القاضي محمد مرشـد عابدين رحمه الله ؛ ومن أوسعها وأتقنها كتاب بديع للشـيخ مساعد سـالم العبد الجادر رحمه الله ، سمّاه معالي الرُتَب لمـن جمـع بـين شرفي الصحبة والنسـب ، مطبوع بسـبعمئة وسـبعين صفحة بالكويت . ومما لم أقف عليه : مسند علي بن موسى الرضا في فضـل أهل البيـت وجـزء فضائل أهـل البيت لأبي الحسـن علي بن معروف البزاز (ت بعد ٣٨٥) ومعالم العترة النبوية ومعارف أهل البيت الفاطمية للحافظ أبي محمد عبد العزيز بن الأخضر الجُنَابِذي ـ جنابذ ناحيـة بنيسـابور ـ الحنبـلي (ت ٦١١) وفتـح الوهـاب في فضائل الآل والأصحـاب للشـعراني ، ذكـر الجميع في كشـف الظنـون إلا جزء البـزاز ، ففي بسـتان المحدّثـين للدهلوي ، وكتاب نـشر قلب الميْت بفضل أهل البيت للسُّرَّمَرِّي (ت ٧٧٦) . وَاللهُ الموَفِّق

□ □ □

وإنّما المَرءُ حديثٌ بعدَه
فكُنْ حديثاً حسناً لِمَن وَعَى

تمّ الكتاب وكان فراغه ليلة الثلاثاء ٦ جمادى الأول ١٤٣٩

الموافق ٢٢ كانون الثاني ٢٠١٨ على يد مؤلّفه الفاني

جبريل بن فؤاد بن نَصرِيْ حدّاد الصالحي

وصلى الله على سيّدنا محمّد وآله

وصحبه وسلّم تسليماً

والحمد لله ربّ

العالمين

م م م

م م

م

الكتاب	الشيخ	البلد	الصحابي
١ جامع معمر بن راشد	صلاح فخري	بيروت	مرسل ابن أبي حثمة
٢ موطأ مالك بن أنس	محمد اليعقوبي	دمشق	أبو حميد الساعدي
٣ مسند الطيالسي	إبراهيم بن عقيل	تعزّ	علي بن أبي طالب
٤ مسند الشافعي	عصام عرار عبد الله الغماري	الميدان طنجة	جبير بن مطعم
٥ مصنف ابن أبي شيبة	عباس السقاف	سنغافورة	أبو سعيد الخدري
٦ مسند أحمد	يوسف الرفاعي	المزّة	أم سلمة
٧ سنن الدارمي	محمد بن علوي	مكة	زيد بن أرقم
٨ صحيح البخاري	بسام الحمزاوي أبو الليث الخيرآبادي	كفرسوسة كوالا لمفور	أبو هريرة
٩ صحيح مسلم	أحمد مشهور الحداد ساجد الرحمن الصديقي	جدة بروني	البراء بن عازب
١٠ سنن أبي داود	عمر وعطاس ابنا حفيظ	تريم	ابن مسعود
١١ سنن ابن ماجه	حسن العطاس زكريا باغريب	سنغافورة	العباس بن عبد المطلب
١٢ أخبار مكة للفاكهي	عبد الله الكتاني	دمشق	ابن عباس
١٣ جامع الترمذي	تاج الكتاني سامر النص	دمشق تامبين ماليزيا	علي بن أبي طالب

الكتاب	الشيخ	البلد	الصحابي
١٤ مسند الحارث	سليم الحمامي يوسف المرعشلي	الميدان بيروت	ابن عمرو أو ابن عمر
١٥ السنة لابن أبي عاصم	درويش الخطيب	حلب	عائشة
١٦ الآحاد والمثاني له	علي الجفري	كيفون	عمار بن ياسر وغيره
١٧ نوادر الأصول للحكيم	سالم الشاطري	بروني	سلمة بن الأكوع
١٨ مسند البزار	عدنان المجد	باب توما	عبد الله بن الزبير
١٩ سنن النسائي	محمد زكي إبراهيم سامر النص	القاهرة تامبين ماليزيا	علي بن أبي طالب
٢٠ خصائص علي للنسائي	عقيل المهدلي	بروني	زيد بن أرقم
٢١ السنن الكبرى له	زين بن سميط	جاكرتا	أسامة بن زيد
٢٢ فضائل الصحابة له	عبد الله الجنيد	سنغافورة	حذيفة بن اليمان
٢٣ مسند أبي يعلى	أبو سعيد قويدر أبو الطيب قويدر	المزة الميدان	فاطمة بنت رسول الله ﷺ
٢٤ تفسير الطبري	عبد الله التليدي	طانجة	عبد الله بن جعفر
٢٥ الذرية الطاهرة للدولابي	مرشد عابدين والحافظ	دمشق	الحسين بن علي
٢٦ مسند أسامة للبغوي	نور وصالح الخطيب	دمشق	أسامة بن زيد

الكتاب	الشيخ	البلد	الصحابي
٢٧ مشكل الآثار للطحاوي	علي العيدروس سعيد الكحيل	باتو باهات حمص	أم سلمة
٢٨ صحيح ابن حبان	عجاج وصالح الخطيب	دمشق	أبو سعيد الخدري
٢٩ معجم الطبراني الكبير	علي الحداد	جاكرتا	مرسل ابن أبي رافع
٣٠ المعجم الأوسط له	عبد القادر الحداد	جاكرتا	الزبير بن العوام
٣١ الشريعة للآجري	مالك السنوسي	المدينة	أبو سعيد الخدري
٣٢ زوائد فضائل الصحابة للقطيعي	عيسى بن سميط علوي بن طاهر الحداد	سنغافورة	ثوبان
٣٣ مستدرك الحاكم	فاتح الكتاني	الصبورة	أبو سعيد الخدري
٣٤ معرفة علوم الحديث له	نور الدين عتر	قاسيون	ابن عمر
٣٥ معرفة الصحابة لأبي نعيم	عبد العزيز الغماري	طانجة	عمرو بن شأس
٣٦ دلائل النبوة له	أحمد بن إدريس أمدرماني	كوالا لمفور	ابن أبي أُسيد
٣٧ شعب الإيمان للبيهقي	عمر بن سالم المحضار	باتو باهات	أبو ليلى الأنصاري
٣٨ دلائل النبوة له	الشيخ هشام القباني حسين عسيران	كوالا لمفور بيروت	المطلب بن أبي وداعة
٣٩ تفسير البغوي	الشيخ محمد ناظم عادل	قبرص	عمرو بن عوف
٤٠ أنوار الشمائل له	عبد المقصود فارس	سنغافورة	أبو هريرة

الكتاب	الشيخ	البلد	الصحابي
٤١ أربعين العوالي لابن عساكر	عبد الرزاق الحلبي	دمشق	سعد بن أبي وقاص
٤٢ الأربعين البلدانية له	عبد الرحمن الكتاني محمد مطيع الحافظ	فاس دمشق	ابن عباس
٤٣ الأحاديث المختارة للضياء	علي السقاف آل صافي	جاكرتا	عثمان بن عفان

«وصْفُهم للحديث بأنّه مُسْنَدٌ ، يريدون أن إسناده متّصلٌ بين راوِيْه وبين من أَسند عنه ؛ إلاّ أن أكثر استعمالهم هذه العبارةَ هو فيما أُسند عن النّبي ﷺ خاصَّةً .» الخطيب البغدادي

❑ ❑ ❑

فهرس الأحاديث المسندة

أَحَبُّ أَهْلِي إِلَيَّ فَاطِمَةُ بِنْتُ مُحَمَّدٍ . : وَأُسَامَةُ بْنُ زَيْدٍ ١٣٧

أَحِبُّوا اللهَ لِمَا يَغْذُوكُمْ مِنْ نِعَمِهِ ، وَأَحِبُّونِي بِحُبِّ اللهِ ، وَأَحِبُّوا
أَهْلَ بَيْتِي لِحُبِّي ٢٠٩

أُذَكِّرُكُمُ اللهَ فِي أَهْلِ بَيْتِي ثَلَاثَ مَرَّاتٍ ٤٣

أَلَا إِنَّ عَيْبَتِي الَّتِي آوِي إِلَيْهَا أَهْلُ بَيْتِي ، وَإِنَّ كَرِشِي الأَنْصَارُ ٣٣

اللَّهُمَّ اجْعَلْ رِزْقَ آلِ مُحَمَّدٍ قُوتًا ٢٠١

اللَّهُمَّ إِنَّكَ تَعْلَمُ أَنِّي أُحِبُّهُمَا ، فَأَحِبَّهُمَا ١١٥

اللَّهُمَّ إِنِّي أُحِبُّهُ فَأَحِبَّهُ ٥٧

اللَّهُمَّ هَذَا الْعَبَّاسُ عَمِّي ، وَهَؤُلَاءِ أَهْلُ بَيْتِي ، فَاسْتُرْهُمْ مِنَ
النَّارِ كَسَتْرِي إِيَّاهُمْ بِمُلَاءَتِي هَذِهِ ١٨١

اللَّهُمَّ هَؤُلَاءِ أَهْلُ بَيْتِي وَخَاصَّتِي ، فَأَذْهِبْ عَنْهُمُ الرِّجْسَ
وَطَهِّرْهُمْ تَطْهِيرًا ٣٧

اللَّهُمَّ ! إِنَّكَ تَعْلَمُ أَنَّهُ كَانَ فِي حَاجَتِكَ وَحَاجَةِ رَسُولِكَ ، فَرُدَّ

عَلَيْهِ الشَّمْسَ ١٣٣

أَمِنْ أَهْلِ الْبَيْتِ أَنَا ؟ فَسَكَتَ . ثُمَّ قَالَ فِي الثَّالِثَةِ : نَعَمْ ، مَا لَمْ تَقُمْ عَلَى سُدَّةٍ أَوْ تَأْتِ أَمِيراً تَسْأَلُهُ ١٦٣

أَنَا خَيْرُكُمْ بَيْتاً ، وَخَيْرُكُمْ نَفْساً ١٩١

إِنَّ اللهَ خَلَقَ الخَلْقَ فَجَعَلَنِي فِي خَيْرِ خَلْقِهِ ، وَجَعَلَهُمْ فِرْقَتَيْنِ ، فَجَعَلَنِي فِي خَيْرِ فِرْقَةٍ ١٩١

إِنَّ اللهَ مَوْلَايَ ، وَأَنَا وَلِيُّ كُلِّ مُؤْمِنٍ . ثُمَّ أَخَذَ بِيَدِ عَلِيٍّ ١١٠

إِنَّ شَفَاعَتِي لَتَنَالُ - بِقَرَابَتِي - حَتَّى حَا ، وَحَكَمَ ، وَصَدَاءَ ، وَسَلْهَبَ يَوْمَ الْقِيَامَةِ ٩٣

إِنَّا مِنْ خِيَارٍ إِلَى خِيَارٍ فَمَنْ أَحَبَّ الْعَرَبَ فَبِحُبِّي أَحَبَّهُمْ ، وَمَنْ أَبْغَضَ الْعَرَبَ فَبِبُغْضِي أَبْغَضَهُمْ ١٧٣

إِنَّمَا بَنُو هَاشِمٍ وَبَنُو الْمُطَّلِبِ شَيْءٌ وَاحِدٌ هَكَذَا ٢٣

إِنِّي - أَيُّهَا النَّاسُ - فَرَطُكُمْ عَلَى الحَوْضِ ! فَإِذَا جِئْتُ قَامَ رِجَالٌ فَقَالَ هٰذَا : يَا رَسُولَ اللهِ أَنَا فُلَانٌ ١٦٧

إِنِّي تَارِكٌ فِيكُمُ الثَّقَلَيْنِ ٤٣

إِنِّي وَإِيَّاكِ وَهٰذَيْنِ وَعَلِيّاً يَوْمَ الْقِيَامَةِ فِي مَكَانٍ وَاحِدٍ ١٩
بَشَّرَنِي أَنَّ الحَسَنَ وَالحُسَيْنَ سَيِّدَا شَبَابِ أَهْلِ الجَنَّةِ ، وَأَنَّ فَاطِمَةَ سَيِّدَةُ نِسَاءِ أَهْلِ الجَنَّةِ ١١٩
تَجِدُونَ مِنْ خَيْرِ النَّاسِ أَشَدَّ النَّاسِ كَرَاهِيَةً لِهَذَا الشَّأْنِ حَتَّى يَقَعَ فِيهِ ٥١
جَمَعَ فَاطِمَةَ وَالحَسَنَ وَالحُسَيْنَ ثُمَّ أَدْخَلَهُمْ تَحْتَ ثَوْبِهِ ، ثُمَّ جَأَرَ إِلَى اللهِ تَعَالَى ١٤٦
خَيْرُ نِسَاءِ الجَنَّةِ مَرْيَمُ بِنْتُ عِمْرَانَ ، وَخَيْرُ نِسَاءِ الجَنَّةِ خَدِيجَةُ بِنْتُ خُوَيْلِدٍ ١٢٩
دَعَا لِأَهْلِ بَيْتِهِ ، فَذَكَرَ عَلِيّاً وَفَاطِمَةَ وَغَيْرَهُمَا ، فَقُلْتُ : يَا رَسُولَ اللهِ ، أَمِنْ أَهْلِ الْبَيْتِ أَنَا ١٦٣
رَأَيْتُ رَسُولَ اللهِ ﷺ وَاضِعًا الحَسَنَ بْنَ عَلِيٍّ عَلَى عَاتِقِهِ ٥٧
رَبِّ هَؤُلَاءِ أَهْلِي . قَالَتْ أُمُّ سَلَمَةَ فَقُلْتُ : يَا رَسُولَ اللهِ فَتُدْخِلُنِي مَعَهُمْ ؟ قَالَ : أَنْتِ مِنْ أَهْلِي ١٤٣
سَأَلْتُ رَبِّي أَنْ لَا أَتَزَوَّجَ إِلَى أَحَدٍ مِنْ أُمَّتِي وَلَا يَتَزَوَّجَ إِلَيَّ أَحَدٌ مِنْ أُمَّتِي إِلَّا كَانَ مَعِي فِي الجَنَّةِ ٨٣

السَّلَامُ عَلَيْكُمْ كَيْفَ أَصْبَحْتُمْ ؟ تَقَارَبُوا ، تَقَارَبُوا ١٨٢

سَلْمَانُ مِنَّا ، أَهْلَ الْبَيْتِ ١٩٥

فَاطِمَةُ سَيِّدَةُ نِسَاءِ عَالَمِهَا إِلَّا مَا جَعَلَ اللهُ عَزَّ وَجَلَّ لِمَرْيَمَ بِنْتِ عِمْرَانَ ١٦١

فَضَّلَ اللهُ قُرَيْشاً بِسَبْعِ خِصَالٍ ١٥٩

قُولُوا : اللَّهُمَّ صَلِّ عَلَى مُحَمَّدٍ وَأَزْوَاجِهِ وَذُرِّيَّتِهِ ١١

كَأَنِّي قَدْ دُعِيتُ فَأَجَبْتُ ، وَإِنِّي قَدْ تَرَكْتُ فِيكُمُ الثَّقَلَيْنِ ١١٠

كِتَابَ اللهِ وَعِتْرَتِي أَهْلَ بَيْتِي . فَانْظُرُوا كَيْفَ تَخْلُفُونِي فِيهِمَا ١١٠

لَا تَبْرَحْ أَنْتَ وَبَنُوكَ غَداً ، فَإِنَّ لِي فِيكُمْ حَاجَةً . قَالَ : فَجَمَعَهُمُ الْعَبَّاسُ ١٨٢

لَا تُعَلِّمُوا قُرَيْشًا ، وَتَعَلَّمُوا مِنْهَا ٧

لَا تَنْقَضِي الدُّنْيَا حَتَّى يَمْلِكَ الْعَرَبَ رَجُلٌ مِنْ أَهْلِ بَيْتِي يُوَاطِئُ اسْمُهُ اسْمِي ٦١

لَا يُبْغِضُنَا أَهْلَ الْبَيْتِ رَجُلٌ إِلَّا أَدْخَلَهُ اللهُ النَّارَ ١٥١

لَا يُحِبُّكَ إِلَّا مُؤْمِنٌ وَلَا يُبْغِضُكَ إِلَّا مُنَافِقٌ ١٠٥

لَا يَدْخُلُ قَلْبَ رَجُلٍ الْإِيمَانُ حَتَّى يُحِبَّهُمْ لله وَلِقَرَابَتِهِمْ مِنِّي ٦٧
لَا يُؤْمِنُ عَبْدٌ حَتَّى أَكُونَ أَحَبَّ إِلَيْهِ مِنْ نَفْسِهِ ، وَتَكُونَ عِتْرَتِي أَحَبَّ إِلَيْهِ مِنْ عِتْرَتِهِ ١٨٥
لَا ، وَلٰكِنَّهُ اسْتَسْقَى أَوَّلَ مَرَّةٍ ٢٠
لَعَنَ اللهُ مَنْ فَرَّقَ بَيْنَ بَنِي هَاشِمٍ وَبَنِي الْمُطَّلِبِ ٢٦
لِكُلِّ بَنِي أُمٍّ عَصَبَةٌ يَنْتَمُونَ إِلَيْهِ ، إِلَّا وَلَدَ فَاطِمَةَ : فَأَنَا وَلِيُّهُمْ ، وَأَنَا عَصَبَتُهُمْ ١٢١
لَمْ أَجِدْ رَجُلاً أَفْضَلَ مِنْ مُحَمَّدٍ وَلَمْ أَجِدْ بَنِي أَبٍ أَفْضَلَ مِنْ بَنِي هَاشِمٍ ٨٨
لَوْ أَنَّ رَجُلاً لَقِيَ اللهَ وَهُوَ مُبْغِضٌ لِأَهْلِ بَيْتِ مُحَمَّدٍ ﷺ : دَخَلَ النَّارَ ٧١
لَوْ لَمْ يَبْقَ مِنَ الدُّنْيَا إِلَّا يَوْمٌ ٦٣
مَا بَالُ أَقْوَالٍ تَبْلُغُنِي عَنْ أَقْوَامٍ ؟ إِنَّ اللهَ عَزَّ وَجَلَّ خَلَقَ السَّمَاوَاتِ سَبْعًا ١٧٣
مَا بَالُ أَقْوَامٍ يَتَحَدَّثُونَ ، فَإِذَا رَأَوا الرَّجُلَ مِنْ أَهْلِ بَيْتِي قَطَعُوا حَدِيثَهُمْ ٦٧

مَـا بَـالُ أَقْوَامٍ يَزْعُمُـونَ أَنَّ شَـفَاعَتِي لا تَنَالُ أَهْـلَ بَيْتِي ؟ وَإِنَّ شَفَاعَتِي تَنَالُ حَا وَحُكْمَ ١٥٥

مَـا بَالُ أَقْوَامٍ يَقُولُـونَ : إِنَّ رَحِمِي لَا يَنْفَعُ ؟ بَـلَى وَاللهِ إِنَّ رَحِمِي مَوْصُولَةٌ فِي الدُّنْيَا وَالْآخِرَةِ ١٦٧

مَثَلُ أَهْلِ بَيْتِي مَثَلُ سَـفِينَةِ نُوحٍ : مَنْ رَكِبَهَـا نَجَا ، وَمَنْ تَرَكَهَا غَرِقَ ١٠١

مَـنْ أَحَبَّنِي وَأَحَبَّ هٰذَيْنِ وَأَبَاهُمَا وَأُمَّهُـمَا كَانَ مَعِي فِي دَرَجَتِي يَوْمَ الْقِيَامَةِ ٧٧

مَنْ آذَى عَلِيًّا فَقَدْ آذَانِي ١٧٧

مَنْ أَنَا ؟ قَالُوا : أَنْتَ رَسُولُ اللهِ . قَالَ : أَنَا مُحَمَّدُ بْنُ عَبْدِ اللهِ بْنِ عَبْدِ الْمُطَّلِبِ ١٩١

مَـنْ صَنَعَ إِلَى أَحَدٍ مِنْ وَلَدِ عَبْـدِ الْمُطَّلِبِ يَدًا ، فَلَمْ يُكَافِئْهُ بِهَا فِي الدُّنْيَا فَعَلَيَّ مُكَافَأَتُهُ غَدًا إِذَا لَقِيَنِي ٢١٥

مَـنْ كُنْتُ وَلِيَّهُ ، فَهَذَا وَلِيُّـهُ . اللَّهُمَّ ، وَالِ مَنْ وَالَاهُ ، وَعَادِ مَنْ عَادَاهُ ١١٠

النَّاسُ تَبَعٌ لِقُرَيْشٍ فِي هَذَا الشَّأْنِ ٥١

النَّـاسُ مَعَـادِنُ ، خِيَارُهُمْ فِي الجَاهِلِيَّةِ خِيَارُهُمْ فِي الْإِسْـلَامِ إِذَا فَقِهُوا ٥١

النُّجُومُ أَمَانٌ لِأَهْلِ السَّمَاءِ ، وَأَهْلُ بَيْتِي أَمَانٌ لِأُمَّتِي ٩٧

هَذَا الْعَبَّاسُ ، عَمُّ نَبِيِّكُمْ ، اَجْوَدُ قُرَيْشٍ كَفّاً وَأَوْصَلُهَا ٢٠٦

هٰذَانِ ابْنَايَ وَابْنَا ابْنَتِي . اللَّهُمَّ إِنَّكَ تَعْلَمُ أَنِّي أُحِبُّهُمَا ، فَأَحِبَّهُمَا ١١٥

هُوَ مَلَكٌ مِنَ الْمَلَائِكَةِ لَمْ يَهْبِطْ إِلَى الْأَرْضِ قَطُّ قَبْلَ هٰذِهِ اللَّيْلَةِ ١١٩

وَالَّـذِي نَفْسِي بِيَدِهِ لَا يُبْغِضُنَا أَهْلَ الْبَيْـتِ رَجُلٌ إِلَّا أَدْخَلَهُ اللهُ النَّارَ ١٥١

يَا أَيُّهَا النَّاسُ ! مَا لِي أُوْذَى فِي أَهْلِي ٩٣

يَـا أَيُّهَا النَّـاسُ ، إِنَّمَا أَنَـا بَشَرٌ ، يُوشِـكُ أَنْ يَأْتِيَنِي رَسُـولُ رَبِّي فَأُجِيبَهُ ٤٣

يَا بَنِي عَبْدِ الْمُطَّلِبِ ! إِنِّي سَأَلْتُ اللهَ عَزَّ وَجَلَّ لَكُمْ ثَلَاثاً ٧١

يَا عَلِيُّ صَلَّيْتَ الْعَصْرَ ؟ ١٣٤

يَـا عَمْـرُو وَاللهِ لَقَـدْ آذَيْتَنِـي . قُلْتُ : أَعُـوذُ بِـاللهِ أَنْ أُوذِيَكَ يَا رَسُولَ اللهِ ١٧٧

❑ ❑ ❑

المؤلِّف في سطور

ولد في بيروت عام ١٩٦٠ وأسلم في أمريكا لما جاوز الثلاثين من العمر ثم انتقل إلى دمشق حيث أقام تسع سنين وقرأ العلم على المشايخ ، من أبرزهم الدكتور نور الدين عِتر . وأخذ علم الإسناد عن العلّامة محمّد أبي الهدى اليعقوبي . ثم تحوّل إلى شرق جنوب آسيا حيث عُيِّن أستاذاً مساعداً بارزاً في مركز السلطان عمر علي سيف الدين للدراسات الإسلاميّة في جامعة برونَي دار السلام . وقد نشر ما يزيد على أربعين كتاباً جُلُّها باللغة الإنجليزية في تاريخ السّنة والعقيدة والحديث ، منها سِيَر الأئمة الأربعة وموسوعة الأحاديث الموضوعة والموسوعة المتكاملة للقرآن الكريم والحزب الأوّل من تفسير القاضي البيضاوي تحقيقاً وشرحاً وترجمة ، أخرجه على ثلاثين أصلاً ونال جائزة الشيخ حمد للترجمة سنة ٢٠١٧ ، والنّور المحمّدي في القرآن والحديث وآثار الصحابة رضي الله عنهم . وسلك الطريقة النقشبنديّة على الشيخ محمّد ناظم القبرصي وخليفته الشيخ محمّد هشام القبّاني وهو ممثّلها في إندونيسيا وغيرها من دول القطر .